Service Design Practices for Healthcare Innovation

Mario A. Pfannstiel • Nataliia Brehmer •
Christoph Rasche
Editors

Service Design Practices for Healthcare Innovation

Paradigms, Principles, Prospects

Springer

Editors
Mario A. Pfannstiel
Department of Healthcare Management
Neu-Ulm University of Applied Sciences
Neu-Ulm, Germany

Nataliia Brehmer
Management, Professional Services
and Sport Economics
University of Potsdam
Potsdam, Germany

Christoph Rasche
Management, Professional Services
and Sport Economics
University of Potsdam
Postdam, Germany

ISBN 978-3-030-87275-5   ISBN 978-3-030-87273-1   (eBook)
https://doi.org/10.1007/978-3-030-87273-1

Preface

Introductory Remarks

This anthology provides an overview of diverse service design practices. It covers important core topics pertaining to service design in health care which we would like to make accessible to a wide audience. The articles demonstrate that research and development is moving in an environment that strives for success and is subject to social change, changes in values, technologies and business models. The compact cross section of the topics shows that it is worthwhile to look beyond the obvious for new ideas. Four dimensions describe the spectrum of the articles in this book: service design, practice types, healthcare market, and healthcare innovation, which are addressed in more depth in the following (see Fig. 1).

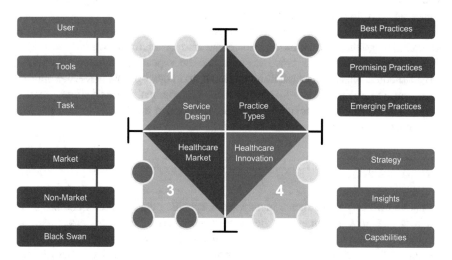

Fig. 1 Service design practices for healthcare innovation. *Source* Author's own illustration (2021)

Service Design

The term "service design" describes the process of designing services. Often it is not just the services themselves that are changed, but also the related products, processes, systems and technologies. Innovations result from repeated and sometimes disruptive improvement processes stemming from the needs and desires of customers and the creativity of stakeholders. In addition to target groups and market-driven design mechanisms, the multidimensionality of service design also entails non-target groups and market-based components, such as the influence of the media on the public, the influencing of politicians by special interest groups with demands for quid pro quo or the justification of de facto rules under false pretenses for their own agendas.

When applying service design, users must see that the subject matter, the requirements, the expectations and the specific details are precisely defined. This is necessary because although the actions are being carried out in the present, it is only in the future that they lead to measurable outcomes and show their effects. Users must assign roles for the design process; they must create room for agency and plan for the use of resources. Resorting to the strategy guru, Ansoff healthcare providers must master the present and preempt the future in a balanced fashion.

Tools assist designers in improving or optimizing something or systematically designing or developing value creating problem solutions on behalf of many stakeholders, being omnipresent in complex healthcare systems. They can be used in health care to respond to new conditions, react to current changes or to make adjustments. Tools consist of a series of methods, instruments and materials that can generate innovative success. In the course of this, users can bring in and realize ideas, alone or together with other stakeholders.

The added value of service design is created through work tasks that lead to the reaching of goals. Innovations do not come into being from nothing, but rather follow clear patterns and processes that can be repeatedly applied. Technical, organizational, business-oriented, institutional and social problem-solving approaches are the main focus of research and development. Observations, market impetus, inspiration and scientific concepts are applied to projects to find the best solution to a problem.

Practice Types

In health care and in healthcare management, specific practices are often missing to address and take advantage of the existing potential of new services, products, processes and technologies and to focus them on the patients who stand at the center of the supply chain. New and promising practices must be tried, tested, analyzed and evaluated. The application of practices is equivalent to a maturity model of emerging practices, promising practices and best practices.

Through the use of service design, it is possible to develop new approaches, possible implementations and solutions that can be referred to as emerging practices. These represent the starting point for innovative changes and can evolve into convincing results. It is important to note that everything that is new must be subjected to critical scrutiny, robust testing, as well as proven and documented research in order to avoid unknown risks. For example, emerging practices exist in the area of personalized medicine, digital assistants in the form of chatbots and in the development of medications using artificial intelligence.

Promising practices are present if there is sufficient evidence of their efficacy. Such evidence can refer to safety, reliability, quality, effectiveness, etc. This available and established evidence can be applied to new areas of application. However, sufficient evidence is not available to identify these as best practices.

The goal in health care is to follow apply and push best practices for the sake of establishing a new, better and smarter norma. A characteristic of best practices is that they have proven themselves to be effective in practice. Best practices are based on a systematic research design and are scientifically proven, e.g., through repeated testing. Best practices can frequently be transferred to and applied in other fields, whereby it is possible to achieve better outcomes than with conventional approaches.

Healthcare Market

The healthcare market faces many challenges that must be met in the coming years, among which is the lack of skilled labor, the financing of medical services, digitalization and the increasing use of artificial intelligence with all of the questions about data protection and data security that arise as a result. Alongside these challenges are threats.

Businesses are often not prepared for immediate threats and are thus challenged to accumulate a set of dynamic capabilities to be prepared for often cited VUCA constellations. Business models are vulnerable to natural catastrophes, legislative changes, increased competition, disruptions in the supply chain, fluctuations in personnel, data theft, financial risks such as high market prices or outstanding debts and internal risks such as a predominating management style, corporate culture or the presence or absence of effective communication in the workplace. These threats influence customers, suppliers and the relationships with other stakeholders.

Threats also exist in nonmarket-driven settings for institutions, nonprofit organizations and associations. These include rising real estate costs, donation and subsidy risks, risks related to earnings from financial investments or operating risks in development, manufacturing, procurement, sales, logistics and environmental management.

Unforeseen outcomes (black swans) are rare and can occur in the market or apart from it and exercise an extreme effect on the healthcare market. For this reason, agile service designs must excel in anti-fragility, responsiveness and change readiness. Market anomalies, such as the Great Depression, the Iraq war, the oil crash, the global financial crisis, SARS and COVID-19 are outliers that affect peoples' lives. These events are unforeseeable and cannot be prevented; however, principles and reaction strategies can be identified with the help of service design to be better prepared for unexpected events.

Service design can represent an opportunity to create stability for businesses and organizations to get themselves out of a precarious situation. It is important to analyze existing problems, the affected stakeholders, the diverse interests of the stakeholders, possible solutions and scenarios, the feasibility of implementation and identified actions and their effects.

Healthcare Innovation

There are many hurdles on the rocky path to innovation in health care: government restrictions, inaccessible technologies, limited funding and the lack of personnel with the required expertise and competence to generate innovation. Innovation begins with customers, employees, business partners, scientists, creative thinkers, start-ups and innovation hubs.

Cutting-edge innovations come from strategic approaches involving innovators, visionaries, makers, networkers, analysts, team players in the process of reaching goals in order to use the full potential of their expertise. The participating actors must be supervised, trained, motivated and inspired. The activities to reach the goal encompass structured and systematic definition of goals, focus on goals, the monitoring of success and communication of successes to motivate the participants.

Innovations require an exchange of information between the participating actors. Corroborating and differing experiences must be discussed. A goal-oriented relationship is to be established to avoid disappointments, misinterpretations and lowered performance. Existing knowledge and skills must be used to mobilize performance reserves for development and design and to maintain a sustainable innovation process.

Success in service design is dependent on the right approach and the right combination of available resources and their professional deployment according to value generating objectives. The required resources determine the value, rarity, imitability and the resilience of innovations. Alongside the resources, the ideas about the goal, purpose and use held by providers and customers must align with each other in regard to the expected services. Only in this way, the innovative process can be accelerated and maintain stable in relation to external influences and lead to the desired outcome. In broader meaning, bundles of managed resources may evolve into knowledge-intensive capabilities underpinning competitive advantages in health care, which are anything but purely hardware- and software-driven. Sustainable advantages in health care are predominately epitomized by invisible assets such as advanced brainware and peopleware—strategic assets that are endemically hard to copy, to replace, to displace or to source, since they have be crafted, created and co-aligned.

The contributions of the authors in this anthology are structured in the following fashion: contribution title, summary, introduction, main part, conclusion, bibliography and biography. Furthermore, each author sums up his or her explanations and insights in the article for a summary at the end of the article.

We would like to thank the numerous authors of this anthology who brought a wide array of fascinating issues from practical experience and engrossing science topics into our anthology. Finally, we want to extend our warmest gratitude to Springer Publishing AG at this point who contributed our ideas to support us in compiling the layout of this anthology and put the whole book with the chapter together.

Neu-Ulm, Germany
2021

Mario A. Pfannstiel
Nataliia Brehmer
Christoph Rasche

Contents

Editors and Contributors

About the Editors

Mario A. Pfannstiel is a researcher and lecturer in the field of hospital and healthcare management at the University of Applied Sciences Neu-Ulm. He holds a diploma from the University of Applied Sciences Nordhausen in the field of social management with the major subject finance management, an MSc degree from the Dresden International University in patient management and an MA degree from the Technical University of Kaiserslautern and the University of Witten/Herdecke in healthcare and social facilities management. He worked as an executive assistant to the medical director in the Heart Centre Leipzig in Germany. At the University of Bayreuth, he worked as a research assistant in the Department of Strategic Management and Organization. He received his doctorate from the Faculty of Social Sciences and Economics and the Chair of Management, Professional Services and Sport Economics at the University of Potsdam. His research includes numerous articles, journals and books on management in the healthcare and hospital industry. Prof. Pfannstiel holds lectures in Germany and abroad at regular intervals. His current research interests focus on service management, digitalization of services, service business model innovation, service design, service thinking and innovative services. e-mail: mario.pfannstiel@hnu.de

Nataliia Brehmer is Research Associate at the Chair of Management, Professional Services and Sports Economics. She is teaching healthcare management and economics at the University of Potsdam and is a supervisor for a number of bachelor and master theses at the field of strategic management, consulting, sports and healthcare management on the Faculties of Human Sciences and Economics and Social Studies at the University of Potsdam. She was engaged in the project DIGILOG and assisted the research efforts toward creating the innovative business models in health and elderly care. Practically, she is supervising the internships of sports management students and provides career consulting for young professionals. After finishing her master studies in the field of International Business and Negotiations, she is working on her PhD thesis with the topic Non-Market Strategies that provide business with non-economic means in the social and political arenas to tackle the hypercompetition and sustain the competitive advantage. She is multilingual and is fluent in Polish, Ukrainian, English, German and Russian languages. e-mail: nbrehmer@uni-potsdam.de

Christoph Rasche heads the chair of professional and corporate services at the University of Potsdam. He adopted visiting professorships at the Universities of Innsbruck, Alcalá de Henares as well as the Hochschule Osnabrück. He teaches strategic and general management in national and international MBA programs with special respect to subjects connected with the healthcare and hospital industry. Formerly, he consulted with Droege International AG and was co-founder of Stratvanguard and the General Management Institute Potsdam. His research subjects circle around the field of strategic and general management in the healthcare and hospital sector, which witnesses an era of professional value creation by means of a strong management and leadership focus. Practically, he consults with healthcare players and is actively involved in executive trainings—ranging from corporate universities to MBA and PhD programs for healthcare professionals. e-mail: chrasche@uni-potsdam.de

Contributors

Outi Ahonen Laurea University of Applied Sciences, Espoo, Finland

Patrick O. Akomolafe Lecturer, Computer Science Department, University of Ibadan, Ibadan, Oyo, Nigeria

Çağdaş Erkan Akyürek Department of Healthcare Management, Ankara University, Keçiören/Ankara, Turkey

Patricia E. Alafaireet University of Missouri, Columbia, MO, USA

Mira Alhonsuo Faculty of Art and Design, University of Lapland, Rovaniemi, Finland

Gianluca Antonucci DEA—Department of Business Administration, "G. d'Annunzio" University of Chieti—Pescara, Pescara, Italy

Massimo Bianchini Department of Design, Politecnico di Milano, Milano, Italy

Nataliia Brehmer Humanwissenschaftliche Fakultät, Wirtschafts- und Sozialwissenschaftliche Fakultät Department für Sport-und Gesundheitswissenschaften, Lehrstuhl für Management, Sportökonomie and Professional Services, Universität Potsdam, Potsdam, Germany

Martina Čaić Department of Design, School of Arts, Design and Architecture, Aalto University, Espoo, Finland

Fernando Carvalho School of Design, San Francisco State University, San Francisco, USA

Antonio Chirico Department of Management and Law, University Tor Vergata, Rome, Italy

Lesley Collier Faculty of Health and Well-Being, School of Llied Health Professions, University of Winchester, Winchester, England

Alessandra Sara Cutroneo Customer Experience Design e Canali Digitali, Generali Italia S.P.A, Milano, Italy

Chintan Desai Ascension, All Saints, Racine, WI, USA

Gareth Durrant DSIL Global, Republic of Singapore, Singapore

Philip Ely The State of Design Research Network, School of Design and Built Environment, Curtin University, Kent St, Western Australia, Australia

Joshua O. Eniwumide Senior Research Fellow, Department für Sport- und Gesundheitswissenschaften, Lehrstuhl für Management, Sportökonomie & Professional Services, Universität Potsdam, Humanwissenschaftliche Fakultät, Wirtschafts- und Sozialwissenschaftliche Fakultät, Potsdam, Germany

Elif Erbay Department of Healthcare Management, Ankara University, Keçiören/Ankara, Turkey

Ragnhild Halvorsrud SINTEF Digital, Oslo, Norway

Charlotte J. Haug SINTEF Digital, Oslo, Norway

Stefan Holmlid Department of Computer and Information Science, Linköping University, Linköping, Sweden

Howard L. Houghton University of Missouri, Columbia, MO, USA

Javier Jasso Graduate School of Accounting and Management, National Autonomous University of Mexico (UNAM), Mexico City, México

Nanna Dam Johansen København, Denmark

Margrit Kärp University of Tartu Pärnu College, Pärnu, Estonia

Christopher Kueh School of Arts and Humanities, Edith Cowan University, Perth, Western Australia, Australia

Bertil Lindenfalk Jönköping, Sweden

Fabio Lucchi Centro Di Salute Mentale Rovereto, APSS Trento, Provincia Autonoma di Trento, Italy

Colin Macduff Aberdeen, Scotland, UK

Stefano Maffei Department of Design, Politecnico di Milano, Milano, Italy

Birgit Mager University of Applied Sciences Cologne, Köln, Germany

Dominik Mahr Department of Marketing and Supply Chain Management, Maastricht University, Maastricht, Netherlands

Satu Miettinen Faculty of Art and Design, University of Lapland, Rovaniemi, Finland

Wilian Molinari Köln, Deutschland

Andrew Morrison Centre for Design Research, Institute of Design, The Oslo School of Architecture and Design, Oslo, Norway

Rike Neuhoff København, Denmark

Felicia Nilsson The Oslo School of Architecture and Design, Oslo, Norway

Gaby Odekerken-Schröder Department of Marketing and Supply Chain Management, Maastricht University, Maastricht, Netherlands

Anna-Sophie Oertzen Düsseldorf, Germany

Gabriele Palozzi Department Management and Law, University Tor Vergata, Rome, Italy

Fanke Peng UniSA Creative, University of South Australia, Adelaide, SA, Australia

Marit Piirman University of Tartu Pärnu College, Pärnu, Estonia

Päivi Pöyry-Lassila Unit Information and Analysis, Finnish National Agency for Education, Helsinki, Finland

Shivani Prakash The Oslo School of Architecture and Design, Oslo, Norway

Alison Prendiville Elephant and Castle, LCC, University of the Arts London (UAL), London, England

Francesco Ranalli Department Management and Law, University Tor Vergata, Rome, Italy

Pavani Rangachari Department of Interdisciplinary Health Sciences (CAHS), Department of Family Medicine (MCG), The Graduate School, Augusta University, Augusta, GA, USA

Christoph Rasche Humanwissenschaftliche Fakultät, Wirtschafts- und Sozialwissenschaftliche Fakultät Department für Sport-und Gesundheitswissenschaften, Lehrstuhl für Management, Sportökonomie and Professional Services, Universität Potsdam, Potsdam, Germany

Andrea Resmini Jönköping, Sweden

Raphael Roth Vetterli Roth & Partners AG, Zug, Switzerland

Karianne Rygh Institute of Design, The Oslo School of Architecture and Design, Oslo, Norway

Anna Salmi Laurea University of Applied Sciences, Vantaa, Finland

Daniela Sangiorgi Dipartimento Di Design, Politecnico Di Milano, Milano, Italy

Melanie Sarantou Faculty of Art and Design, University of Lapland, Rovaniemi, Finland

Irene Schettini Department of Management and Law, University Tor Vergata, Rome, Italy

Luca Simeone København, Denmark

Heli Tooman University of Tartu Pärnu College, Pärnu, Estonia

Arturo Torres Department of Economics, Metropolitan Autonomous University-Xochimilco (UAM-X), Coapa Coyoacán, México

Şükrü Anıl Toygar Department of Healthcare Management, Tarsus University, Tarsus/Mersin, Turkey

Michelina Venditti DEA—Department of Business Administration, "G. d'Annunzio" University of Chieti—Pescara, Pescara, Italy

Christophe Vetterli Vetterli Roth & Partners AG, Zug, Switzerland

Beatrice Villari Department of Design, Politecnico di Milano, Milano, Italy

Josina Vink The Oslo School of Architecture and Design, Oslo, Norway

Craig M. Vogel DAAP School of Design, Aronoff Center, University of Cincinnati, Cincinnati, OH, USA

Shaun A. Wahab Department of Radiology, University of Cincinnati, Cincinnati, OH, USA

Cecilia Xi Wang University of Minnesota, St. Paul, MN, USA

Konstantin Weiss Köln, Deutschland

Yuanyuan Yin Winchester School of Art, Faculty of Arts and Humanities, University of Southampton, Winchester, England

Service Design Within a Multiplicity Logics in Health Care

1

Felicia Nilsson, Shivani Prakash, and Josina Vink

Abstract

Within health care, there are a plurality of varying, sometimes conflicting, logics at play that unconsciously shape people's actions and decisions. When doing service design in health care, there is a need for a greater understanding of the often taken for granted logics that enable and constrain value cocreation. Without this understanding, there is a risk that service design inappropriately perpetuates the dominance of particular logics over others. This paper unpacks the logics in particular service situations with empirical examples from designing decentralized care in Norway. We show how an acknowledgment of the existing and possible future dynamics between logics can support a more critical approach to innovation through service design in complex healthcare systems.

1.1 Introduction

"Practices designed to foster 'patient choice' erode existing practices that were established to ensure 'good care'" (Mol, 2008). In her book, The Logic of Care: Health and the Problem of Patient Choice, Mol investigates the clash between two different logics guiding healthcare practices, the logic of choice and the logic of care. She highlights and challenges the appropriateness of one logic dominating

F. Nilsson (✉) · S. Prakash · J. Vink
The Oslo School of Architecture and Design, Maridalsveien 29, 0175 Oslo, Norway
e-mail: felicia.nilsson@aho.no

S. Prakash
e-mail: shivani.prakash@aho.no

J. Vink
e-mail: josina.vink@aho.no

© The Author(s), under exclusive license to Springer Nature Switzerland AG 2022
M. A. Pfannstiel et al. (eds.), *Service Design Practices for Healthcare Innovation*,
https://doi.org/10.1007/978-3-030-87273-1_1

healthcare practices and undermining another logic that she shows at times might be more appropriate. She highlights that these logics reflect modes of ordering within the healthcare context that invites "a comparison of different ways of thinking and acting that coexist in a single time and place." This plurality of logics is well documented within institutional theory in discussions about different social domains being associated with often taken for granted rationales that guide people's behavior (Thornton et al., 2012). This literature points out that health care is a particular domain that must actively grapple with the coexistence of multiple, sometimes conflicting logics (Goodrick & Reay, 2011).

While service design is increasingly acknowledged to be a way to intentionally shape institutional logics (Kurtmollaiev et al., 2018; Vink et al., 2021), there has been little attention to how service design can grapple appropriately with multiple competing logics. As service design's presence in health care is rapidly expanding (Mager, 2017), there is a need for a greater understanding of how service design can recognize the multiplicity of logics at play and help actors to thoughtfully determine the logics guiding their innovation efforts. Without this understanding, service design risks inappropriately perpetuating certain dominant logics over others and doing potential harm in the process. Therefore, the purpose of this chapter is to build an understanding of the multiplicity of logics in health care and explore how service design can mindfully work with these competing logics when innovating. To do so, we draw from institutional theory to delineate six different logics of care with illustrative examples. Furthermore, based on our research through design work within the context of health care in Norway, we share practical approaches used to unpack the logics of care in particular care situations, ways of reflecting on the dynamics between different logics and attempts to do service design in ways that are mindful of these dynamics. By doing so, this book chapter offers a framework for service designers and healthcare practitioners to think with and some practical strategies they might employ as they navigate the complexity of logics when doing service design work.

1.2 Institutional Logics

Institutional logics are established, widespread organizing principles that provide a rationale for people to make decisions and interpretations within a particular social context (Friedland & Alford, 1991). Institutional logics are often defined as "the socially constructed, historical patterns of material practices, assumptions, values, beliefs, and rules by which individuals produce and reproduce their material subsistence, organize time and space, and provide meaning to their social reality" (Thornton & Ocasio, 1999; 804). There is widespread acknowledgement that different social domains have different institutional logics, including divergent systems of rationale associated with markets, corporations, professions, states, families, religions, and communities (Thornton et al., 2012). These logics guide people's expectations in their relationships and behavior based on this context.

However, it is critical to recognize that within Western societies these logics coexist and present contradictory prescriptions for different practices and beliefs (Alford & Friedland, 1985). The health care field has long been recognized as a site of multiple logics, including influences from the market, the state, and the professional logics (Scott et al., 2000). People in the healthcare context may be influenced by different logics to varying degrees. For example, a physician might be strongly guided by the logic of profession emphasizing expertise and association, whereas a next of kin may be guided by unconditional loyalty within a family logic, and a health technology company may be working within the constraints of a profit-driven market logic. However, to complicate things further, many times individual people or healthcare organizations face competing logics simultaneously (Goodrick & Reay, 2011).

Research suggests that there are different ways in which these coexisting logics play out, for example, sometimes one logic dominates and guides behavior, sometimes logics battle with each other, and sometimes logics more directly influence specific people or specific contexts (ibid). It is highlighted that competing logics can actually become a toolkit for people as they intentionally innovate within service systems (Siltaloppi et al., 2016). These logics can become intentional building blocks for carefully crafting service interactions and professional identities (Reay et al., 2017). It is acknowledged that service design can support a transformation of logics in organizations (Kurtmollaiev et al., 2018). Recent research recognizes that service design can aid people in building awareness of these hidden logics and intentionally shaping them toward preferred value cocreation forms (Vink et al., 2021). However, in order to appropriately contend with the multiplicity of logics in service design within healthcare, there is a need for a better understanding of how these logics might manifest and practical approaches for building an awareness of them.

1.3 Logics of Care

To make the institutional logics more applicable in the healthcare context, we contextualize them in care by framing them as different logics of care (see Fig. 1.1). To do this, we integrate the institutional logics (Thornton et al., 2012) with Mol's insight around how different logics entail different approaches and practices of care (Mol, 2008). Figure 1.1 shows how each logic of care is informed by an institutional logic associated with different domains and offers alternative rationales. It should be noted that these logics of care are intended to show ideal types of different logics, but this list is in no way definitive, complete, and these logics are not mutually exclusive. Below we briefly elaborate on each of these logics of care and practices that might exemplify their enactment.

The market logic signifies transactions and is driven by profit and self-interest. For people to care for themselves, there are several choices available based on what one desires. Caring through a market logic could mean caring by providing ample

Institutional logic	Logic of Care	Example
1. Market Transactional, profit-driven and self-interest	**Care as Choice** Individuals can choose what option is best for them, based on their own needs or desires.	Buying a facemask or a scented candle. 
2. Professional Expertise, education and association	**Care as Expertise** Deep knowledge and tracking inform the best ways to care.	A doctor's prescription or a surgery. 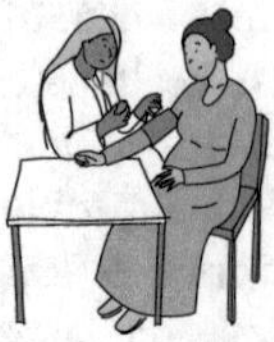
3. State Democratic participation and bureaucratic processes	**Care as Control** Boundaries and regulations provide conditions for population health and equal care.	Covid19 regulations or high taxes on alcohol. 
4. Community Reciprocity and emotional connection	**Care as Social Connection** Emotional connection and reciprocity form the backbone of caring in communities.	Helping someone with their groceries or volunteering. 
5. Family Unconditional loyalty and non-negotiable membership	**Care as Unconditional Involvement** Some relationships have a non-negotiable bond creating a responsibility to care.	Giving a hug or cooking food. 
6. Religion Faith, symbolism and greater purpose	**Care as a Way of Life** Caring involves connecting with a greater purpose, enacting rituals or beliefs.	Going on a mountain trip, practising yoga or attending mass at church. 

Fig. 1.1 Contextualizing logics—from institutional logics to logics of care. *Source* Author's own illustration (2021)

choice. Therefore, we call this logic of care, Care as Choice (aligned with Mol, 2008). Care as Choice values satisfying wants in multiple aspects of life and places a focus on self-interest and the individual's wants. Notions of self-care and caring through consumption could manifest, for example, in buying a facemask or a scented candle. However, with the freedom of choice comes, responsibility and choices are not equally available to everyone in society.

The professional logic is connected with values of expertise, education, and association. If one falls sick, the disease of the body will be the point of departure for a diagnosis. In the diagnosis, certain aspects of the body will be measured, tested, and tracked. To care through a professional logic could mean to care using medical standards which exist to provide precise care to one or multiple parts of the body. We call this logic of caring, Care as Expertise. Professional norms and procedures determine the boundaries of care based on how sick the body is. This logic values medical knowledge and to care in this way requires strenuous education. An example of enacting the logic of care as expertise could be seen in a doctor's prescription or performing a surgery.

The state logic, which is connected with democratic participation and bureaucratic processes, is contextualized in care as Care as Control. This logic works toward ensuring access to care for all citizens at scale. This access is enabled through taxes which are divided among different health regions. The state decides what is the best way to provide healthcare services for populations across class, cultures, and backgrounds. Regulations maintain boundaries to keep people healthy and to ensure they receive adequate care. This logic values scalable regulations. Examples of enacting care as control could be seen in Covid-19 regulations or high taxes on alcohol.

The community logic upholds reciprocity and emotional connection as a central part of its rationale. Communities thrive on people coming together and sharing with each other. Caring through a community logic is manifested in Care as Social Connection. Emotional connection and reciprocity form the backbone of caring in communities and this logic values reciprocal relationships. To care for a community means to see people beyond their illness and looking at them as a part of a living network. In this logic, one may need to share without expectations and learn together with everyone. An enactment of this logic might be seen by an individual helping a neighbor with their groceries or volunteering.

The family logic supports unconditional loyalty and non-negotiable membership. To care through a family logic can be viewed as Care as Unconditional Involvement. Individuals in families and some other long-term relationships are bound together. This bond can be through love, familial or social expectations. This logic values reliability in kinship. When someone falls ill in a family, the responsibility of care falls onto family members. The dynamic in the family is influenced by how serious the illness is, how resilient the family is, and how long it lasts. An enactment of this logic could be as simple as giving a hug, or helping a family member bathe.

The last logic of care, Care as a Way of Life, stems from the religion logic which is connected to faith, symbolism, and greater purpose. Within this logic, people are influenced by a greater purpose or by something they believe in and this logic values alignment of purpose. The ideas of belief can be measurable or immeasurable, and are often situated. One could believe in the healing effects of hiking in nature, practicing yoga, or running as an activity. On the other hand, one may believe in a universal force which guides life. Care as a way of life could also include rituals and morals. An enactment of caring as a way of life could be going on a mountain trip or attending mass at church.

1.4 Research Through Design

To explore how service design can mindfully work within a plurality of logics when innovating in health care, we conducted a research through design study over the course of two years as part of the Center for Connected Care in Norway. The Center for Connected Care is currently focused on supporting a systemic shift from centralized care in hospitals and clinics toward decentralized care in homes and communities. In the context of what is called the "Perspectives in Transition" project, our research through design work has experimented with alternative service design approaches to grapple with the multiplicity of logics at play in this ongoing transition. This study has been a partnership with two hospitals, one municipality, three health technology companies, two universities, as well as patients and family members.

Over the course of this study, partners have participated in five workshops that have explored the logics at play within various service contexts connected with the decentralization of care, such as remote care provided by municipalities and home hospitals, where inpatients receive care from hospital staff in their own home. These workshops have also been informed by over 40 semi-structured interviews and over 45 informal conversations with patients, family members, nurses, doctors, researchers, politicians, healthcare leaders, community service providers, and other allied health professionals. In the sections that follow, we present some of the experimental approaches that we have been working with in an attempt to respectfully understand and shape the plurality of logics at play within the shift toward digital, decentralized care.

1.5 Conflicting Logics in the Decentralization of Care

To explore how multiple logics in care settings emerge and influence each other, a series of "hotspots" were created. Here, hotspots are service moments where multiple stakeholders need to collaborate to deliver a healthcare service. They capture a snapshot of a possible dialog among the different stakeholders along with the context in which this conversation transpires. The dialog attempts to capture the different perspectives of care from the position of each stakeholder. The hotspots presented below are based on experiences shared in semi-structured interviews and conversations with healthcare professionals, innovation managers at hospitals, and health technology providers.

These hotspots were used in a workshop setting where the service moments were unpacked using the framework of the logics of care together with participants from different healthcare institutions and organizations. This process became a way for the partners to enter the framework of institutional logics and the logics of care, and start exploring how they might manifest in their own practices. Figure 1.2 shows an example of the template used to explore the logics of care in the workshop.

1. Meeting to create a self-management plan

The first hotspot was focused on a meeting to create a self-management plan. In Fig. 1.3, we see that a general practitioner, patient, and municipality nurse meet online to create a self-management plan for a patient who has chronic obstructive pulmonary disease (COPD). They use the self-management planning application to create the plan. The design of the application opens the conversation with a question for the patient, "What is important to you?". The following vignette shows how a situation like this could play out. This vignette was constructed from interviews with a remote-care nurse in a Norwegian municipality and a healthtech provider who works on the creation of the self-management planning application in Norway.

Jens clicks on the link emailed to him by Ida from Agder municipality a few days ago. Ida has been following Jens for a week since he moved back home from the hospital. She is engaged and enjoys making small talk with him. Ida and the general practitioner, Mizan arrive some minutes late to the video call. Mizan is nice, but a bit impatient. She begins to share her screen where all three participants can see an application screen for setting up a self-management plan for supporting Jens to manage his COPD. Mizan begins to speak, "Okay, let's start. So, the first question, what's important to you in this recovery process? What would you like to focus on?". Jens responds, "I don't know, maybe not to be short of breath often. On second thought, I really miss my cigarettes. I want to smoke again." Ida, who knows Jens' way of talking pipes in, "Heh, you are good at contradicting yourself Jens. Let us work towards those goals. Maybe you can try some nicotine gum?" Mizan brushes off Ida's comment and says, "The self-management plan could help you stay healthier. Should we look into your green, yellow and red status?".

If we look at this care context through the logics of care, Care as Expertise makes the healthcare provider ask the patient "What is important to you?" as this is becoming a professional norm in Norway. But this logic of care stands in conflict with Care as Control, which works to regulate the consumption of cigarettes and restricts the amount of time the general practitioner has to fully engage and understand what is important for the patient. The professional logic of Care as Expertise might not fully align with what is important for the patient (e.g., a COPD patient wanting to continue smoking).

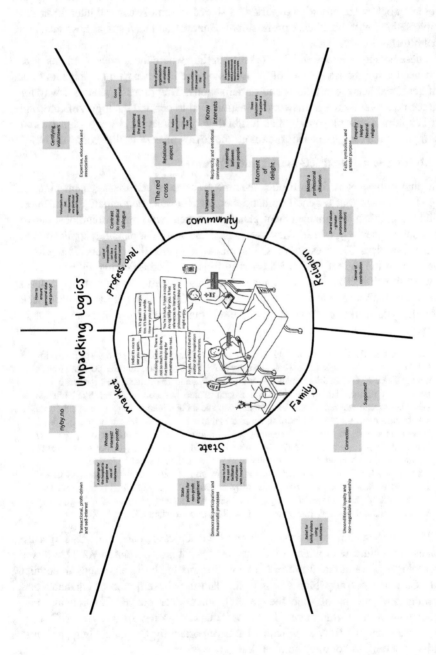

Fig. 1.2 Workshop template to support participants to unpack the logics of care in the hotspots. *Source* Author's own illustration (2021)

Fig. 1.3 Hotspot showing a meeting to create a self-management plan. *Source* Author's own illustration (2021)

2. Meeting to create a self-management plan to support remote-care services

The second hotspot was focused on a general practitioner, home-care nurse, specialized doctor, along with the patient and their next of kin to set up a self-management plan to support remote care for the patient. The specialist is attending the meeting over a phone call, while the rest are present in-person. The vignette below describes how a situation plays out and is depicted in Fig. 1.4. This vignette was constructed from a case which transpired in a Norwegian municipality, and it was gathered through an interview with a remote-care nurse who worked on the case.

It had been a month since Hanna, the home-care nurse, had been trying to connect with the hospital specialist. The specialist was handling Henrik's COPD at the hospital before he was discharged. Henrik's general practitioner, Sigurd didn't have much information about Henrik's symptoms and therefore needed the specialist to help set up a remote-care plan for him. After some attempts Hanna finally got in-touch with the specialist and he agreed to spend ten minutes sharing what he knew about the patient over a phone call. The meeting started, and the specialist was dialled in. The specialist describes the symptoms, "... and lastly, a mild sore throat is often a sign of an upcoming infection. This is important for Henrik to identify by himself." After hearing the symptoms, Sigurd didn't sound optimistic, "I think that the patient's condition is too challenging for remote care." The specialist responded, "Well, the patient needs to apply to service control to start remote care. Can we wrap this up now? I have to move to my next appointment." While the meeting was dominated by the doctors, Hanna was thinking about getting the technology installed at the patients home soon after the meeting.

Fig. 1.4 Hotspot showing a meeting to create a self-management plan to support a remote-care service for a patient. *Source* Author's own illustration (2021)

Setting up remote-care plans requires multiple healthcare professionals to come together. It is often challenging to find time for everyone to connect as the professionals belong to different institutions which care in different ways. When unpacking this service situation using the logics of care, the participants observed that Care as Control is dominant over Care as Expertise. Care of Expertise needs the different actors to meet and plan together, but Care as Control straps the specialist short of time, causes the general practitioner to be skeptical, and stresses out the home-care nurse who oversees the implementation of the technology supporting the service.

3. A volunteer spends time with a patient

The third hotspot was focused on a volunteer from the Red Cross who has come to visit the same patient again. They have had a few meaningful conversations together. Based on those conversations, the volunteer has brought a book which the patient might enjoy reading. The following vignette shows how a meeting like this could look like and is depicted in Fig. 1.5. This vignette was constructed from a description about a volunteer service facilitated by the Red Cross in Norway. The description was found on their Web site.

Lene started volunteering for the Red Cross six months ago and enjoys spending an occasional evening talking to patients. Dounia has been appreciative of Lene coming to visit her as her family does not live in Oslo. Lene is visiting Dounia for the third time. Dounia is pleased to see her again and greets Lene, "Hello! It's nice to see you again.". Lene replies, "Yes, it's great to see you too. It's been a while. How are you doing?". Dounia says that she has been doing well and has been longing to read something new.

Fig. 1.5 Hotspot showing a conversation between a volunteer and a patient in a hospital. *Source* Author's own illustration (2021)

Lene responds positively, "You're in luck, I have a copy of Arv og Miljø for you. It has references to literature and philosophy which I think you might enjoy." Dounia is excited, "Ah yes, I've heard that the author draws inspiration from Freuds's theories".

Residents who volunteer to spend time with patients who do not have family, might do it out of good will, guided by Care as Social Connection. But for the state to care through control, there is a need to bring in volunteers who can ensure patient privacy, and not harm the patient by doing or saying something "wrong". Participants in the workshop revealed some conflicts between those logics. They raised questions about who is responsible for organizing and training the volunteers. This makes the volunteers seem like a burden as the state will have to fund the cost of facilitating for them within healthcare institutions.

4. A home-care visit from the hospital

The fourth Hotspot focuses on a nurse visiting a patient at their home, which is represented in Fig. 1.6. She is on a tight schedule but tries to be considerate about the caregivers' situation. The following vignette captures the dialog which takes place in the care setting. The dialog was constructed from an interview with a home-care nurse working with a home hospital service in Norway.

Patricia lays on the sofa at home. She came back home to recover after her stem cell transplant which took place two weeks ago. The 'Hospital at Home' service has been great. Her partner, Maria, is waiting for Tove, the nurse, to come by and do the routine checks

Fig. 1.6 Hotspot showing a dialog between a home-care nurse and next of kin at the patients' house. *Source* Author's own illustration (2021)

needed. A medical kit lays on the table in anticipation for Tove. Maria hears the main door open. She sees Tove walk up the stairs and greets her, "Welcome back. Would you like some coffee? I made a pot a few minutes back." Tove gladly accepts, "Thanks, I'll help myself to some from the kitchen." She doesn't want to put more work on Maria who looks tired. Maria hesitatingly says, "Also, I haven't stepped out since a day, can I go for a walk while you are here?" Tove replies, "Yeah, don't worry about that. I hope that it is all going okay. Let me know if you need more support." Maria, still sounding hesitant, says, "I just need a break. See you soon."

Professional time dictates how much care the nurse can extend to the patient, and to their next of kin. Care as Control dictates how much time a nurse can spend with one patient and therefore stands in conflict with Care as Expertise. The next of kin is reaching out for help, but the nurse has to negotiate with the time allocations she has for each patient during their work day.

These hotspots and the reflections on the multiplicity of interacting logics at play show the conflicting prescriptions for action that different logics create within specific healthcare situations. By reflecting these service moments with our partners, we were able to better understand the patterns in the dynamics of these logics in this systemic transition.

1.6 Dynamics Between the Logics of Care

In our work around logics, it became evident that some logics of care seem more dominant than others. Through unpacking the hotspots, we learnt that there is a risk imposing the traditionally more formal logics, including the market, state, and professional logics, onto informal care settings. This is especially important to note when repositioning care into people's homes and when working toward distributed care. In an attempt to reflect on the hierarchies of the logics of care, the mapping

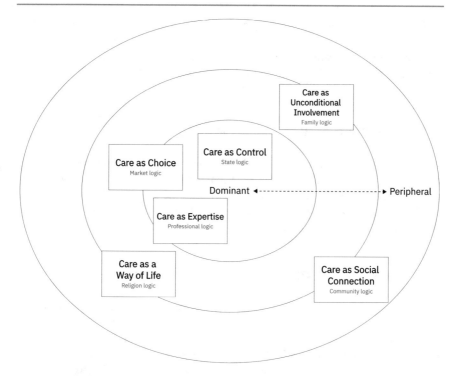

Fig. 1.7 Compiled map of the relational maps created on the workshop with stakeholders. *Source* Author's own illustration (2021)

template below (see Fig. 1.7) was used to explore the relation between the logics with our partners. Together we were guided by the question: Which logics of care are more dominant, and which are more peripheral, in care situations? By dominant, we referred to where this rationale or prescription took precedence over others.

We explored this in a workshop with our partners, where we had first unpacked the logics in four different care situations, or hotspots, as mentioned in the section above. Through the mapping template, we asked the participants to map the relations between the different logics of care as they observed in the previous exercise.

From this relational mapping activity, it became clear that Care as Control (state), Care as Choice (market), and Care as Expertise (profession) are the most dominant in the explored care situations. An important insight which arose is how this relationship between the logics is not static, but rather it is dynamic and shifting. As well as how the logics are intertwined and often build on each other, for example, many of the morals and values of the Care as Control (state logic) stems from Care as a Way of Life (religion logic).

Together we recognized that there is a need to be mindful of which logics dominate our care situations and better balance some of the different logics when working within the care context, and especially when working toward shifting health care to become distributed into people's homes and lives.

1.7 Positioning Service Design in Practice

In this section, we present intentional strategies to do work in relation to the logics of care and explore the dynamics between the logics. Below are examples of practical approaches to work with a multiplicity of logic in healthcare service design. The strategies consist of reflecting on the institutional logics, materializing tensions to spark reflection, and attempts at strengthening peripheral logics.

1.7.1 Reflecting on the Influence of Institutional Logics

The Web of Logics is a reflection exercise designed to unpack the influence of the six institutional logics on you as an individual and the organization you belong to. In a template (see Fig. 1.8), the first step is to fill in the point where you position yourself as an individual in relation to the various institutional logics. The further away from the center, the more influence this logic has on you. The next step is to do the same procedure for the organization you are associated with or employed/served by, in a different color. The result creates a map resembling a spider web, where the differences and similarities between the logics influencing individuals and their organization become clear.

In Fig. 1.8, you see an example of a filled out template of the Web of Logics which charts a participant's reflections on the influencing logics on them as an individual and within their organization. What stands out the most in this collection of webs is how much more the organizations are influenced by state, market, and professional logic and much less by family, religion, and community logics. This is in contrast to the individual where the opposite situation is occurring. This was a pattern in our workshop. It raised questions around the tension between the formal and informal logics and if there is a risk of imposing the more formal logics (state, market, and profession) in informal settings, for example, when care is repositioned into patient's homes.

The logics are subliminally incorporated into our decision making and reflecting on this helps create an awareness of how they influence the design of healthcare services. This exercise is a simplified way of examining the institutional logics at play. Some of the participants reflected on how in their work the logics are more nuanced and depend on the situation. It became one way to reflect on the relation between the individual and the organization within a multiplicity of logics. As well as a way to spot similarities and differences, and through this explore where the tensions or conflicts appear most strongly.

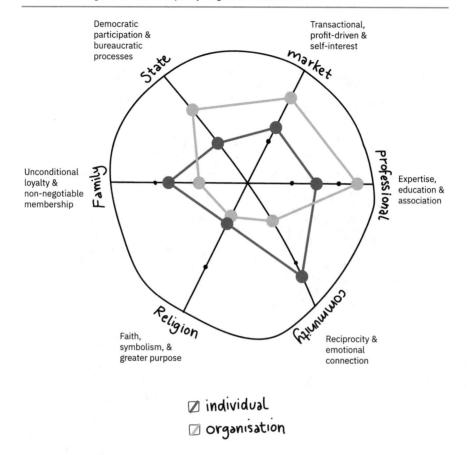

Democratic
participation &
bureaucratic
processes

Transactional,
profit-driven &
self-interest

Unconditional
loyalty &
non-negotiable
membership

Expertise,
education &
association

Faith,
symbolism, &
greater purpose

Reciprocity &
emotional
connection

☑ individual
☑ organisation

Fig. 1.8 Example of a filled out template created to facilitate the Web of Logics reflection. *Source* Author's own illustration (2021)

1.7.2 Materializing Tensions in Logics to Spark Reflection

In order to cultivate the reflections around the dominance of some logics, and the centering of the peripheral ones, it is of importance how we frame the projects and questions that lead our service design work forward. This framing in relation to the multiplicity of logics has a great impact on our designs and concepts. When working with partners, mostly situated in formal healthcare settings that are highly influenced by the professional, state, and market logics, centering the more peripheral logics can seem "illogical" and even un-useful. We believe service design can be an approach to grapple with illogical ideas and concepts that play with the in-betweenness among logics and elevate logics thought to be less legitimate in certain spaces. Critically reflecting in designerly ways becomes a means to explore the illogical ideas and flesh out the potential implications of the futures we

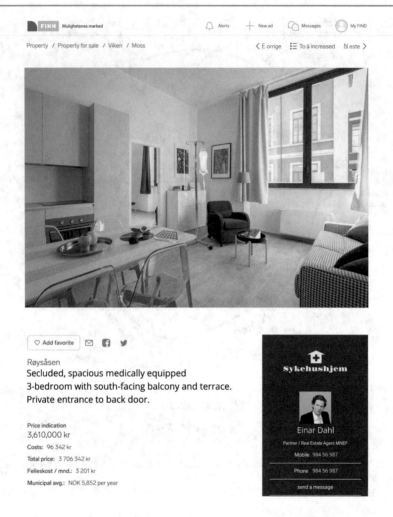

Fig. 1.9 Finn advertisement adaptation. *Source* Illustration by Shivani Prakash & Felicia Nilsson, photos by Deborah Cortelazzi (2018) & Icons8 Team (2018)

are enacting through the designs of our current solutions. Figure 1.9 is an altered Finn advertisement that serves as an example of materializing tensions with an aim to spark reflection through (critical) service design.

Finn.no is a commonly used online Norwegian marketplace, which can be used to find homes, either for rent or for sale online. It relies heavily on a market logic, and the apartments on the Web site are regularly staged to portray an idyllic life, mostly stripped of the mundane routines or messes. To materialize tensions in logics to spark reflection, an existing advertisement for a house on sale from finn.no was adapted. The adaption uses an already existing format combined with unfamiliar elements in an attempt to spark reflection on which logics are undermining other logics, and what happens in the tension between them. For example, it plays with what is highlighted in the marketing image and description of the apartment. In Fig. 1.9, some of the measuring devices used in distributed care for chronic patients are placed in the home advertisement. The descriptive text emphasizes the apartment being medically equipped, having the latest accessibility and safety standards, closeness to pharmacies and parking space for ambulances, to mention a few. The visualization works with logics through aiming at portraying the tensions between the market logic (through the advertisement and the real estate market) and the professional logic (through medical equipment).

This altered advertisement helped to reflect on questions such as: In a future where health care is increasingly distributed, how will our homes be affected? How does biomedical care fit into the image of the idyllic home? What purposes will the home have in the future? Are we in the process of hospitalizing the home? Will this in the future be something attractive for potential buyers? Does it disrupt the homeliness of the home? Is this a future we want to work toward?

1.7.3 Strengthen Peripheral Logics Through Service Design

Acknowledging a multiplicity of logics or ways of caring demands a multiplicity of articulations and framings of projects as points of inquiry into the healthcare system. We attempted to do this through crafting projects, together with our partners, that placed a particular focus on the peripheral logics of care: Care as Social Connection, Care as Unconditional Involvement, and Care as a Way of life. This turned into six different service projects in which both service providers and service design students were involved. We will share two examples which attempt to help explore how service design can boost peripheral logics in healthcare service settings:

1. My pocket coordinator: There is recognition that the family caregiver is not well supported in the healthcare system; this was addressed through a student project called "My Pocket Coordinator - A service design approach to challenge the power dynamics of communication in the inter-institutional care planning" (see Fig. 1.10). The project aimed at putting focus on the family caregiver and creating an add-on service to support them in the healthcare services. In this way, the project attempted to bolster Care as Unconditional Involvement or the family logic, in healthcare services, one that has not been as much in focus in the decentralization of care.

2. The Culture Program: There is recognition that patients and families from minority cultural backgrounds risk not receiving similar offers of care as the patients from the dominant cultural background in Norway. Within this context, a student project focused on attempting to foster cultural humility within healthcare staff at a ward in a Norwegian hospital. The project is called "The Culture Program: Where Bubbles Meet," and it proposed a course (see Fig. 1.11) which would support healthcare staff to reflect on their experiences of working with patients and

Background - **user journey**

Acute ward   Arrival at Sunnaas   Next of kin seminar   Test visit   Moving home

Fig. 1.10 Folder and timeline proposed by the 'My Pocket Coordinator' project. *Source* Work by Lisa Siegel, Francesca Masnaghetti, Silvia Lesoil and Åse Lilly Salamonsen (2021)

families from a cultural background different from their own, and attempt to understand how they can better support those patients. This works at protecting Care as a Way of Life and Care as Social Connection, and other ways of caring not captured by the Western institutional logics, within the delivering of care in the home.

The two examples illustrate strategies that attempt to protect the peripheral logics in healthcare settings through service design. The projects helped frame the discussion by placing a focus on family caregivers and the need for equal healthcare services across cultures. The proposed service redesign helped service providers think about how they could better acknowledge peripheral logics in their services. However, while attempting to boost peripheral logics, we noticed the focus often radiating back toward the dominant logics. For example, when discussing what

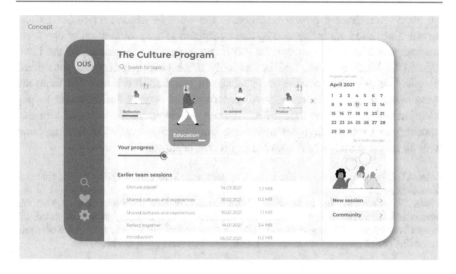

Fig. 1.11 Proposed digital platform called The Culture Program. *Source* Work by Elizabeth Bjelke Stein, Eila Regine Evensen Rishvod, Kjersti Karoline Fretland (2021)

support is required to implement a course to build cultural humility, the involved partners from the hospital reflected that it might be difficult to receive funding for the course as it is not a top priority for the hospital management right now. What is considered logical in a situation is often dictated by the dominant logics, and therefore, the logical solutions will be in favor of the dominant logics. This is due to the fact that peripheral logics and the design proposals boosting them when viewed from the perspective of dominant logics makes them seem illogical or less valuable. Traditionally, service design has been brought into contexts to deliver "solutions," but it could contribute differently by recognizing dominant logics and exploring what is being rendered illogical by them.

1.7.4   Mindful Service Design Amid Multiplicity

In this chapter, we have worked to illuminate and contextualize the multiplicity of logics at play within the healthcare context. Our hope is that by paying attention to the different logics of care when doing service design in health care, we can aid in building a more mindful practice and preventing the harm that might come from unknowingly perpetuating dominant logics, while eroding others. Through our research through design work, we have shown strategies that we have used when doing service design in health care to help unpack and reflect on the different logics at play and their conflicts. We have also shared attempts at designing in a way that remains critical of existing dynamics between logics and works to protect more peripheral logics in health care through the service design process. In sharing these attempts at grappling with plurality in this domain through the framework of logics, we hope to cultivate a greater attention to the ways in which service design and service innovation are influenced by and contribute to the proliferation of divergent institutionalized logics. However, we also recognized the limitations of the institutional logics framework, and in that only those guiding principles considered "rational" in Western societies are depicted in this framework and that there are many other modes of ordering, or disordering, that service design needs to pay attention to depending on the context. We see working with the logics of care as a starting place for building this awareness but certainly insufficient for grappling with all of the plurality that coexists in diverse healthcare domains.

Acknowledgements We would like to express our gratitude to Thiago Freitas for his contributions to the research through design work and thinking that informed the development of this article. We would also like to thank all of our partners for their collaboration throughout this process and the service design students who were involved in conducting projects as part of the Perspectives Project. We would like to acknowledge our funding support from the Norwegain Research Council through the Center for Connected Care (C3), grant #237766/O30.

References

Alford, R. R., & Friedland, R. (1985). *Powers of theory: Capitalism, the state, and democracy.* Cambridge University Press.

Cortelazzi, D. (2018). *Room* [digital]. Available at https://unsplash.com/photos/gREquCUXQLI.

Friedland, R., & Alford, R.R. (1991). Bringing society back in: Symbols, practices, and institutional contradictions. In W. W. P. & Paul J. DiMaggio (Eds.), *The New Institutionalism in Organizational Analysis* (pp. 232–263). University of Chicago Press.

Fretland, K.K.F., Rishvod, E.R.E., & Stein, B.E. (2021). *The Culture Program* [digital].

Goodrick, E., & Reay, T. (2011). Constellations of institutional logics: Changes in the professional work of pharmacists. *Work and Occupations, 38*(3), 372–416. https://doi.org/10.1177/0730888411406824.

Icons8 Team. (2018) Untitled [digital]. Available at https://unsplash.com/photos/m0oSTE_MjsI.

Kurtmollaiev, S., Fjuk, A., Pedersen, P. E., Clatworthy, S., & Kvale, K. (2018). Organizational transformation through service design: The institutional logics perspective. *Journal of Service Research, 21*(1), 59–74. https://doi.org/10.1177/1094670517738371.

Lesoil, S., Masnaghetti, F., Salamonsen, A.L., & Siegel, L. (2021). *My pocket coordinator* [digital].

Mager, B. (2017). Service design impact report: Health sector. Service Design Network. Retrieved February 22, 2018, from https://www.service-design-network.org/books-and-reports/impact-report-health-sector.

Mol, A. (2008). *The logic of care: Health and the problem of patient choice.* Routledge.

Reay, T., Goodrick, E., Waldorff, S. B., & Casebeer, A. (2017). Getting leopards to change their spots: Co-creating a new professional role identity. *Academy of Management Journal, 60*(3), 1043–1070. https://doi.org/10.5465/amj.2014.0802.

Scott, W. R., Ruef, M., Mendel, P. J., & Caronna, C. A. (2000). *Institutional change and health care organizations: From professional dominance to managed care.* University of Chicago Press.

Siltaloppi, J., Koskela-Huotari, K., & Vargo, S. L. (2016). Institutional complexity as a driver for innovation in service ecosystems. *Service Science, 8*(3), 333–343. https://doi.org/10.1287/serv.2016.0151.

Thornton, P., & Ocasio, W. (1999). Institutional logics and the historical contingency of power in organizations: executive succession in the higher education publishing industry, 1958–1990. *American Journal of Sociology, 105*(3), 801–843. https://doi.org/10.1086/210361.

Thornton, P. H., Ocasio, W., & Lounsbury, M. (2012). *The institutional logics perspective: A new approach to culture, structure & process*. Oxford University Press.

Vink, J., Koskela-Huotari, K., Tronvoll, B., Edvardsson, B., & Wetter-Edman, K. (2021). Service ecosystem design: Propositions, process model, and future research agenda. *Journal of Service Research, 24*(2), 168–186. https://doi.org/10.1177/1094670520952537.

Felicia Nilsson is an Assistant Professor and Design Researcher at the Oslo School of Architecture and Design (AHO) and within the Center for Connected Care (C3) in Norway. Felicia's research explores norm-critical approaches to design in diverse care contexts. Previously Felicia worked as a Design Researcher at Karolinska Institute in Stockholm within the Division of Innovative Care Research and as a Service Designer at Experio Lab in Karlstad, Sweden.

Shivani Prakash is a Designer and Researcher at the Oslo School of Architecture and Design (AHO) and within the Center for Connected Care (C3) in Norway. Shivani's research interests lie in challenging the design practice to embrace a culturally humble lens, exploring how service design practices can respond to complex and diverse perspectives, and bringing design academia and practice closer to each other.

Josina Vink is an Associate Professor of Service Design at the Oslo School of Architecture and Design (AHO) and Design Lead within the Center for Connected Care (C3) in Norway. Josina has over 10 years of experience as a service designer working in international healthcare contexts, including in Canada, the United States, and Sweden. Josina has developed new services, supported policy change, facilitated shifts in practices across sectors, and led social lab processes. Josina's research aims to contribute to building more systemic service design theories and approaches, as well as understanding health systems transformation.

Service Design for Hybrid Market Constellations in Healthcare—From VUCA 2 VUCAR

2

Christoph Rasche and Nataliia Brehmer

Abstract

The service design in healthcare is anything but trivial, because of the co-alignment of corporate commercial activities (CCAs) and corporate political activities (CPAs). Healthcare systems are highly regulated due to trust-based services that are generated on behalf of multiple stakeholders. Occasionally, patients adopt the role of customers of free choice. However, they adopt the role of needy cases in other constellations such as emergency rooms and acute areas. In a nutshell, the healthcare industry resembles a pattern of heterogeneous services and business models ranging from commercial target group capitaliza tion to social welfare services on behalf of patients, public institutions, and vested political interests. The service design for non-market constellations hinges on hybrid capabilities and corresponding strategies. The latter represents far more than the sum of CCAs and CPAs but incorporate a logical self-propelling stamina. In a similar vein, supra-additivity reflects a logic of synergistic and exponential benefit when taking advantage of complementary assets. Contrarily, textbook economics service design in healthcare is a rather "septic" issue because of strong non-market forces influencing and driving the market forces. This is especially valid for up-and-coming healthcare platforms and health-tech firms entering the arena of artificial intelligence (AI)-based services that may get in conflict with political, societal, and moral issues.

C. Rasche (✉) · N. Brehmer
Lehrstuhl für Management, Sportökonomie & Professional Services, Department für Sport- und Gesundheitswissenschaften, Humanwissenschaftliche Fakultät, Wirtschafts- und Sozialwissenschaftliche Fakultät, Universität Potsdam, Karl-Liebknecht-Straße 24-25, Haus 24, Raum 126, 14476 Potsdam, Germany
e-mail: chrasche@uni-potsdam.de

N. Brehmer
e-mail: nbrehmer@uni-potsdam.de

2.1 Pitfalls of Aseptic Service Design in Healthcare

Service design in healthcare resembles an aseptic process of linear decision-making aiming at creating maximum patient value as well shareholder value. The entrenched market system logic is all-pervading incorporating a value-generating cascade of managerial resource utilization according to pre-defined objectives. While economic service design intends to get the maximum value out of resource mobilization, commercial service design meets stockholder objectives. Value generation in healthcare is multi-dimensional since financial value, patient value, employee value, and stakeholder value must be co-aligned in a balanced fashion. Moreover, health services show no classic signs of products but display features of trust-based goods having information asymmetries and principal-agent problem in its track (Major, 2019). Parenthetically, they go beyond market mechanisms because of regulated demand- and supply-side constellations stemming from political interventions and legislation. Service designs in healthcare are often septic because they are outcomes of political power play and selfish interest groups. Thus, this paper addresses the aseptic nature of healthcare designs unfolding their value under hybrid strategy regimes. Market activities and political activities rather go for a complex mix than being isolated (Baron, 1995). Hence, service design in healthcare must be braced for political and social issues management, including power play and hidden agenda setting.

2.1.1 Non-Market Forces in Healthcare

On the one hand, non-market forces in healthcare are prevalent since patient-centered services are trust-based, risky, and often invasive. On the other hand, they are ethically and economically relevant because of a low-price elasticity, leading to the effect, that needy patients are willing to pay any price as an equivalent for healing and relief. Without regulation, clinics could command high prices and/or produce low-cost health services at the price of poor quality. The latter is endemically difficult to assess causing principal-agent problems. Apart from, dabbling in politics is all-pervading in the healthcare sector, because many stakeholders are eager to push their vested interests to gain non-market advantages paying-off later on. Non-market advantages in the shape of strong bargaining positions materialize in strategic and financial benefits (Hillman et al., 2004). Non-market forces and market forces cannot be separated but go for a hybrid market system. The following issues display classic signs of non-market forces in healthcare:

Political forces: The healthcare industry represents the bedrock of modern welfare states that must assure affordable, accessible, and safe services to avoid societal injustice or unrest. If healthcare systems fail, vast parts of the population might be underserved with medical treatment impacting employment rates or economic growth. Many politicians make it a point of their honor to promise healthcare and insurance services utilizing market regulation. Curtailing free-wheeling market forces is seen as a necessity to prevent market failure, which is characteristic for healthcare services that should be available for everyone, irrespective of market forces (Ghosh, 2008). Justness, fairness, and quality are moral dimensions outside a capitalistic market order, politicians must consider. Healthcare services are social services that lie at the heart of welfare states that are challenged to offer public services under conditions of regulated market regimes. Political forces curtail rude market forces for the purpose of non-discrimination and availability.

Legal forces: Political forces often have legal forces in their track, because parliamentary debates on healthcare issues often result in legislation. The latter displays the framework and governance system incorporating, provisions, stipulations, and codes of conduct to strike a balance between the interests of different stakeholders. The legislation is anything but sacrosanct because healthcare institutions may have an indirect bearing on the lawmaking process due to corporate political activities such as lobbying, hearings, or campaigning. Legal forces can be molded and crafted when being involved in the early-stage legislation process though diplomatic power play and appropriate corporate political activities.

Moral forces: Market, moral, medicine, and money are the cornerstones of healthcare systems that must address moral issues. The public pressures often generate the impression of money-making medicine regimes that do not care for patients but profits. Regarding corona pandemic, it becomes visible that triage systems of prioritization and rationing may lead to moral and ethical issues. Who is eligible for scarce healthcare services, who is placed first on the transplantation waiting list, and should costly high-tech medicine be applied to patients that are doomed to die within a few days? Moral issues often drive political as well as legal forces because they represent the over-arching normative gestalt of societal values. The vaccine and corona debate was inspired by moral trains of thought to trigger legislation incorporating a non-market logic of procedural and distributive justice.

Medical forces: Medical forces may foster or thwart market forces because medical services can be seen as a source of profit as well as a source of public value creation outside a capitalistic doctrine. Medical forces often spur innovation since scientists are eager to push the envelope toward hitherto unachieved dimensions of outcome and performance. However, medical high-end innovations hinge on political support to be rolled-out and adopted by means of public funding. Promising healthcare start-ups are still in their infancy facing an embryonic state of commercialization. Nevertheless, they represent the future of medicine deserving political dedication to make them flow as well as digital health is thought to become a transforming force of current health systems (Rinsche, 2017). The design and development of corona vaccines firstly is a race of outcome value irrespective of cost, profit, or market issues that have secondly entered the political arena to assure reimbursement. Political and legislation forces must show up with adequate financial incentives to assure and channel medical progress. So, why investing in vaccines if the business is not profitable?

Societal forces: The public and society are driving forces of change moments, because normative value migrations toward paramedic care, alternative healthcare or high-tech medicine, such as precision medicine or genetic engineering, have a strong bearing on politics and legislation. The same is valid for genetic cloning, embryonic stem cell research, abortion, or enforced life termination erupting into controversial debates representing non-market forces at first sight. At second sight, economic and financial issues arise because they adopt the role of curtailing forces according to management tool-set that can be applied to healthcare constellations. Societal forces bolster market forces because patients, citizens, and professionals call for a high-scalable vaccine mass market. Everyone should not only have access to vaccines, but should be enforced to endure vaccination for the reason of public health. So, vaccination is a public duty to be accepted. Opposite this line of argumentation, the vaccination market may be dampened through the intervention of critical stakeholders resisting any kind of vaccination.

Ecological forces: Pharmaceutical mass production may contaminate the environment in the case of antibiotics causing not bacteria resistance and severe infections that are difficult to handle with conventional medication (Larsson, 2014). The ecological footprint of healthcare goes far beyond this issue with respect to energy-efficient hospitals (Gatea et al., 2020) and telemedical services that may help to reduce traveling costs. All too often medication is over-dosed, not necessary or pills, and ampullas are stockpiled and destroyed after reaching expiring date.

Non-market forces complement the five market forces of the well-known Porter's framework that only unfolds its usefulness when being co-aligned with the aforementioned non-market forces. The political impact management especially highlights political and legislation forces to achieve bargaining advantages under non-market constellations (Rasche et al., 2019).

2.1.2 Political Impact Management in Healthcare

Strategic management is driven by the notion of market forces while often neglecting non-market forces, displaying septic features power, politics, and pervasive interventions (Doh et al., 2012). Political impact management acknowledges the fact that political power play in healthcare is an integral part of the business as can be seen in the race of masks, vaccines, and respiratory devices. The market of pandemic devices is so attractive that many players do not shy away from illegal malpractices of corruption and unfair advantages when capitalizing on political mandates or exerting massive power on decision-makers. The pandemic evidences that fair-play among governments, companies, and patients evolve into a political process of power play for the sake of sourcing advantages to safeguard the population within national borders. Political impact management is a matter of first choice when the marketing mix loses traction because of regulation. Political impact management incorporates the set of tools and techniques that exert direct or indirect influence on legislation and political decision-making. The spectrum of "interventions" ranges from weak to strong and from legal to illegal. Most of the weak interventions such as campaigning, lobbying, and hearings are legal, while strong measures are often not law-abiding when it comes to corruption, bribery, or intimidation. Defining a PIM-compliance test should resemble the following topics:

Economic Compliance (effectiveness and efficiency): PIM can be very resource-consuming challenging the management to conduct a cost-at-value-analysis. "Doing the right things right" is the silver bullet to reach political aims in resource protecting way. Sustainable PIM capitalizes on leverage effects when pulling a tiny trigger that unfolds a huge effect. Think of the multiple options of social media and digital platform communication for social activists or viral political impact management spreading over the Internet while not investing in information dissemination anymore (Hadani et al., 2019).

Legal Compliance (law-abiding): Rubbing elbows with politicians and the official body can be a risky high-stakes game because of corruption allegations. Enforced compliance rules all over the world should motivate healthcare managers to place a great bearing on law-abiding non-market strategies. Salient negative cases show that corruption does not payoff in the long run because of irreversible reputation damage-end ensuing lawsuits. Aside, promising AI solutions contribute to the detection of criminal minds in healthcare because of digital tracing, tracking, and profiling.

Moral Compliance (conformance to value and norms): This category falls in line with the ethical bedrock of a society and its unwritten rules, morale, and codes of conduct. Ingrained values and norms contribute to a culture of fairness, transparency, and justice-driving social institutions, individuals, and managers, alike. Employing PIM as a means of strategic positioning implies a zest for the achievement of fair competitive advantages. Sustainability management evidenced a creating shared value doctrine (CSV) makes both ends meet because "money and morale" can become self-enforcing dimensions.

Corporate Compliance: Political impact management must fit with the standards and codes of conduct of a healthcare corporation. Adjustment is needed for the purpose of customized PIM solutions reflecting the context of a single firm. Corporate compliance can be a source of advantage if it is unique in the meaning of a core competence. PIM standard recipes are generic assets that must be transformed into special-purpose tools to achieve lasting political advantages.

Political impact management in healthcare resembles a system non-market-strategies that should be co-aligned with market strategies. So-called hybrid strategies arise a self-enforcing system of market and non-market strategies. Hybrid strategies reflect managerial competence and do not exist on their own. They must be actively sketched out and implemented.

2.1.3   Asymmetric Knowledge, Impacted Information, and Trust-Based Services

What makes healthcare services unique, special, and sophisticated? First, they ground on asymmetric knowledge, because healthcare professionals are in better bargaining positions than patients or relatives (Muehlbacher et al., 2018). Second, information about diseases is often anything but clear and unequivocal, because of ambiguity and fuzziness issues accruing from complex information pattern following the logic of a mosaic. Sometimes, diagnosis is akin to pattern recognition in terms of big data leading to AI solutions machine learning, and the like. Impacted information is often of septic nature because it carries opportunistic dimensions of power play since the amount, access, and quality of information contribute to bargaining power. Professionals derive their status of power from their ability to take advantage of impacted information. Third, healthcare services are trust-based because they often defy assessment, evaluation, and quality measurement. For this reason, they are prone to political issues and opportunistic behavior. Healthcare services are anything but aseptic, because they are outcomes of highly political organizations. The latter reflects the institutional context as represented by political bodies, NGOs, and a flurry of interest groups. Service design in healthcare must incorporate commercial as well as political activities within an era of full-swing digitalization. Political activities in healthcare resemble dimensions of power play, bargaining prowess, and sinister opportunism akin to world Machiavellian selfishness. But, non-market activities go beyond political and CSR activities because they may also include contingencies of altruism, moral compliance, and idealism (Bruyaka et al., 2013). Hence, non-market activities range from selfish political power play to fair dealmaking and ultimate altruism. The variety of non-market activities—although contributing to institutional success and failure—is often neglected in service design because they tarnish the septic logic of business modeling.

2.2   Service Design Under Septic VUCA Constellations

The VUCA paradigm is all-pervading entering the management and healthcare arena. VUCA resembles a rather aseptic state of environmental turbulence as reflected by volatility, uncertainty, complexity, and ambiguity (Bennett & Lemoine, 2014). The following discussion extends the VUCA logic to 4 VUCAR constellations to come up with a holistic framework for service design in healthcare.

2.2.1   Toward a Holistic VUCAR Framework for Service Design

Service design in healthcare should be confronted with VUCA constellations that are held responsible for volatile, uncertain, complex, and ambiguous states of management and leadership. This paper will be differentiated between external

VUCA challenges and internal coping strategies since service design in healthcare must be braced for an era of the 4-D (discontinuity, disorder, disruption, and destruction). External VUCA challenges call for internal VUCA responses such as vision, understanding, clarity, and agility. Here, VUCAR will replace conventional VUCA, because 2 "Rs" should be added. On the internal side, "radical" should be added, while on the external side, "resilience" is a precondition for business model stamina and robustness. In a nutshell, the logic of VUCAR-1 and VUCAR-2 is introduced when it comes to service design. VUCAR-1 stands for the exogenous 4-D calling for a hyperdynamic view on service design. VUCAR-2 represents the antagonistic counterpart of a healthcare service organization to reduce vulnerability to the 4-D implications. Additionally, VUCAR-3 erupts into a political issue reflecting the crucial aspects of the non-market system. Violence, unethicality, crime, aggressiveness, and recklessness as well as their moral counterparts in the shape of altruistic behavior must be incorporated into service design. Finally, VUCAR-4 epitomizes the digitalization imperative in healthcare. Volume, usability, computation, ambient IT, and reframing are reflection points of digitalized service design. So, how to define and design a VUCAR-1234 framework for healthcare service design?

2.2.2 VUCAR-1—Volatility, Uncertainty, Complexity, Ambiguity, Radicality

VUCAR-1 represents the prevalent textbook situation of service design strategy in healthcare. Service models in healthcare witness a high degree of volatility because of digital disruption (Mk, 2017). The best examples are telemedicine, artificial intelligence, or big data applications as well as of globalization of healthcare because of professional service outsourcing to India ICT giants entering digital healthcare markets. It is endemically difficult to arrive at safe bets in healthcare because of huge uncertainties. Service model design in healthcare must embrace uncertainty as well as complexities due to increasing specialization, compartmentalization, and inter-disciplinarily topics. The flurry of information in healthcare causes a high degree of ambiguity as big data issues vividly demonstrate. It is safe to say that healthcare is challenged by radical and path-breaking innovations such as precision medicine, robotics, telemedicine, and the like. ICT giants as well as start-ups aim at destroying prevalent healthcare orders instead of preserving them. Amazon, Facebook, Apple, or IBM have one strategic intent in common: They employ radical service design as means of destruction to progress with path-breaking healthcare solutions—transcending legacy models of service design.

2.2.3   VUCAR-2—Vision, Understanding, Clarity, Agility, Resilience

Healthcare service design requires visions, common understanding, clarity, agility, and resilience to be braced for aforementioned VUCAR-1 constellations. Adopting a competence-based perspective VUCAR-2 resembles a set of competences that must be accumulated to respond to the external VUCAR-1 setting in a professional fashion. The performance and quality of service designs are a function of competence and asset endowment. Vision stands for the strategic intent of a service design, while the dimension of understanding incorporates the corps d'esprit of involved persons. Clarity ensures determination, commitment, and resource focus in unequivocal manner. Agility is the outcome dynamic capabilities that are employed as means to foster environmental responsiveness. Modular service designs, in-built flexibilities and compatible interfaces, and open innovation may contribute agile service strategies. Resilience reflects a state of immunization and robustness when it comes to disruptive shocks to be buffered by anti-fragile service designs. Service design can be agile, but fragile opening the debate on anti-fragility as the desired state of service design in healthcare. For safety and security issues, the latter should never collapse and must withstand to be endangered by the 4-D (discontinuity, disorder, disruption, destruction).

2.2.4   VUCAR-3—Violence, Unethicality, Crime, Aggressiveness, and Recklessness

VUCAR-3 stands for the political dimension of service design, reflecting the behavioral view of healthcare services. Malpractices and unfair dealmaking often accompany the process of service design development. Violent and vicious behavior cannot be tolerated but is omnipresent as can be seen in terms of unethical, criminal, aggressive, and reckless non-market strategies aiming to achieve unfair advantages. Aggressive digital giants as well as digital start-ups may employ non-compliant behavior push aside entrenched healthcare incumbents. Thus, the VUCAR-3 setting also corresponds with altruistic and benevolent non-market behavior. The VUCAR-3 setting resonates with Donald Trump world of deal-making that is also valid for many service designs in healthcare. The war for vaccines is driven by the notion that power play and devious behavior should be employed as means to push economic interests. It should be differentiated between the process and outcome dimension of service design. How to implement service designs in VUCAR-3 settings and what are the outcomes and intentions of service designs. The latter may oscillate between aggressiveness and altruism.

2.2.5 VUCAR-4—Volume, Usability, Computation, Ambient IT, Reframing

VUCAR-4 epitomizes the digitalization imperative in healthcare having a strong bearing on service designs. Service designs excel in high data volumes and user-driven designs. Computation emerges as a hardware and software issue of service design architectures. Service designs should be ambient in so far as they must not reflect the perspective of nerds but of users as reflected by patients, doctors, nurses, etc. All too often entrenched service designs all too often show classic signs of legacy systems that should be reframed for the purpose of gaining and sustaining competitiveness. VUCA-4 settings jumped into prominence because digitalization is deemed the driving force of service design in healthcare.

To turn full circle, a VUCAR-1234 framework that co-aligns the stand-alone VUCAR models is sketched out (Fig. 2.1).

The VUCAR-1234 framework fulfills can be regarded as role model for service design in healthcare because extends the dominant VUCA logic to meet the contemporary requirements in business model design when being confronted with states 4-D turbulence such as discontinuity, disorder, disruption, and destruction. Path-breaking service design innovators in healthcare such as health-techs or med-techs go in line with platform economics that underlie the most flourishing business models of the world as epitomized by Amazon. Digital healthcare platforms—irrespective of regulative constraints—inaugurate a new era of scalable service designs in healthcare taking full advantage of artificial intelligence, big data,

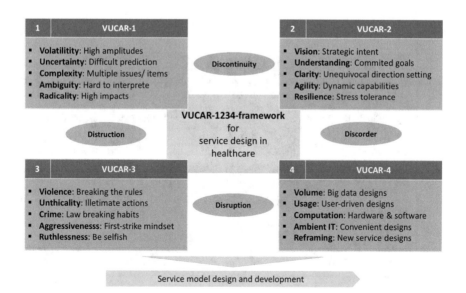

Fig. 2.1 VUCAR-1234 framework. *Source* Author's own illustration (2021)

machine learning, and associated issues of advanced digitalization. We should like to coin the term of advanced digitalization as opposed to legacy digitalization, resembling "old school" applications such as waterfall software and service designs. User-driven service designs are often platform-based, support ease of access, and foster user migration to achieve a huge installed base for the purpose of capitalizing on critical mass efficiencies. Healthcare platforms endorse knowledge sharing and co-value creation by means of complementary assets as well as tipping point management. This is one of the reasons why many IT and Internet giants are fully committed platform races in healthcare. Thus, we assume that individualized, localized, and personalized healthcare data correspond with TTTPPP approach standing for tracing, tracking, tapping, profiling, prediction, and profit (Knape et al., 2020). While this approach formerly served commercial ambitions, it can also be applied non-commercial value creation in healthcare, when profits are replaced by non-financial value categories such patient benefit, medical outcome, or smarter treatments.

2.3 Service Design Under Hybrid Market Conditions

Hybrid service design corresponds with hybrid strategies oscillating between market and non-market conditions. For this reason, we developed an illustrating strategy matrix to shed light on hybrid service designs. Figure 2.2 underpins the logic of hybridization in healthcare.

Fig. 2.2 Hybrid strategies. *Source* Author's own illustration (2021)

Although the model is rather plain and simple, it contributes to a clear-cut understanding of hybrid strategies that are outcomes of managerial voluntarism and actively crafted. The model arrives at four main categories having a strong bearing on service design strategy.

2.3.1 Service Designs Without Strategies

Missing strategy: Service design in healthcare sometimes misses on strategy if business models are developed and implemented without an underlying strategy. Adopting a conventional management stance service model design and strategy design should go hand in hand for the purpose of strategic fit. Conventional wisdom evidences that strategy design should be a precondition for service model design. This cascading strategy process is valid for stable environmental settings, but not necessarily for VUCAR-1234 settings resembling states of discontinuity, disorder, disruption, and destruction. But, how to define and design a service design strategy if environmental surroundings a so opaque and erratic that linear strategies are doomed to fail. For this reason, some firms employ a muddling-through approach to stay flexible and adaptive. But, muddling-through service designs compromise on analytic acumen and strategic foresight because they neither incorporate market and non-market issues in a pre-defined manner. They happen accidently without managerial commitment. Service designs without strategies sometimes make sense; strategy is regarded as a process of "guided evolution" in face of endemically unstable futures resisting conventional strategic planning. By and large missing strategies often lead to disadvantages, value destruction, and non-commitment due to a rather passive service design approach.

2.3.2 Market-Driven Service Designs

Market strategies: Market-driven service designs reflect conventional management wisdom aiming at commercial advantages and superior competitive value positions. Market-driven service designs compete on economic key success factors such as cost, quality, time, smartness, innovation. Market-driven service designs incorporate the viewpoint of classic strategic management assuming free markets and unregulated competition in a rather neo-classic sense. Service design strategy is dominated by the analytic tool-set of consulting, providing management with aseptic theories and techniques for an ensuing cascade of waterfall planning. But, we must beware of the fact that aseptic market strategies neglect crucial non-market issues that accompany service model design. Nevertheless, market-driven service design can be very helpful due to the employment of analytic acumen. Market-driven service designs hinge on top-down and bottom-up planning and should follow the logic of a balanced strategy when striking a compromise between user and technology priorities. In a nutshell, top-down-/bottom-up planning of market-driven service design should be complemented by an inside-out as well as an outside-in approach to go for a balanced market strategy also incorporating a competence-based train of thought.

2.3.3   Non-Market-Driven Service Designs

Non-market strategies: Many healthcare segments face a high degree of regulation devaluating market strategies, because the classic marketing mix stands to fail. Corporate political activities as well as corporate social responsibility issues call for a political impact management, including a full range of activities extending a septic market logic (Mellahi et al., 2016). Non-market-driven designs not only include corporate political activities but also include a portfolio of stakeholder strategies to interfere with relevant institutions in a direct or indirect manner. Non-market-driven service designs ground the premise that economic success is a function of accompanying political activities that must be actively planned for. We should acknowledge the septic nature of non-market settings ranging for reckless selfishness and dealmaking to truly altruistic behavior. Opposite market strategies strategic management did little research on septic strategies and service designs unfolding their usefulness in impacted settings of opportunism, bounded rationality, and hidden agenda setting. Non-market strategies capitalize on diplomacy, bargaining, and ambassadorship rather than economic agenda setting. Thus, we should like to come up with the idea of non-market capabilities complementing market capabilities being the main targets of resource-based theory (Voinea & Emaus, 2017).

2.3.4   Hybrid Service Designs

Hybrid strategies: This category does not represent "chaotic" mesh-up strategies, but stands for holistic service designs that are crafted on purpose from the onset. Although strategic realities are often emergent in nature, but for didactic reasons, define hybrid service designs as outcomes of entrepreneurial voluntarism. Corporate political activities and corporate commercial activities are co-aligned in a truly professional manner to benefit from synergies and supra-additivity. Money, moral, and management not only go for a mesh-up mix, but resemble a system of intertwined market and non-market capabilities. Hybrid capabilities are the underlying assets of ensuing service designs and service strategies in healthcare. Hybrid service designs call for a specific leadership style "making both ends meet" under septic and aseptic conditions. Being a service design ambassador as well as service design manager is paramount to success in healthcare settings that are anything but linear, aseptic, and predictable.

It goes without saying that the model is coarse and cryptic but serves an analytic framework for service design in healthcare alongside four categories.

2.4   Concluding Remarks: From Proposal 2 Profit

Service design innovation in healthcare is a rather non-linear and recursive process of unleashing creativity, competence deployment, capital mobilization, customer focus, competitive positioning, and capitalization. For didactic reasons, we condensed the service design logic in a sequential way—commencing with service design proposals that finally materialize in profits or equivalent outcomes such as patient benefit. It is worth mentioning that the eight steps resemble a process value transformation since embryonic service design proposals must be translated into concrete value dimensions, such as profits, patient benefit, or return on healthcare. The model at hand is anything but a conclusive paradigm and cannot command rigor theoretic evidence. Nevertheless, it serves as a heuristic framework for value transformation in healthcare. Service designs can be regarded as a means to the end of value capture that can be commercial or non-commercial, if you think of non-profit organizations in healthcare. The model incorporates the idea of non-market strategy/management accompanying each stage of the model. To make things even more complex, we should like to pay special heed to digital data and knowledge flows arising from each of the eight steps. These data flows can be of commercial and political nature generating a conclusive picture of service design leadership in healthcare. Corporate digital activities are the third force of service design strategy.

We prefer service design leadership or entrepreneurship to management for the purpose of stressing the septic nature hybrid healthcare strategies incorporating corporate political activities, corporate commercial activities, and corporate digital activities (Fig. 2.3).

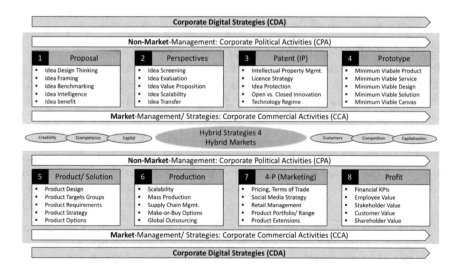

Fig. 2.3 From proposal 2 profit. *Source* Author's own illustration (2021)

The p2p model is a service design blueprint meeting the demands of a masterplan for innovation management and business modeling in healthcare. The framework is conceptual in nature still in its infancy. Right now, it is case study-induced deserving rigor empirical evidence paving the way for promising empirical research that should be done on this issue in the future.

We should like to conclude with ten tenets concerning the future of service design in healthcare.

Tenet 1—Preponderance of digitalization: The digitalization of service designs in healthcare is an all-pervading issue commanding out attention to avoid competence devaluation by means of radical innovations obliterating legacy regimes patient care.

Tenet 2—Preponderance of hybrid strategies: Commercial activities, political activities, and digital activities for a hybrid triangle of value creation in healthcare. According to the p2p framework, value creation not only incorporates financial value creation but also value creation for patients, employees, and society.

Tenet 3—Preponderance of user-driven service design: Opposite legacy models and waterfall planning agile service design architectures hinge on user-driven bottom-up designs resembling the logic of gross-root and open innovation.

Tenet 4—Preponderance healthcare ambassadorship: While many managers assume a rather aseptic stance when resorting to the toolbox of strategic management, healthcare ambassadors take full advantage of the vivid option of non-market systems, when co-aligning them with market strategies.

Tenet 5—Preponderance disruptive healthcare designs: The 4-D standing for discontinuity, disorder, disruption, and destruction may pave the way for business development and blue ocean strategies because of path dependencies and legacies of age that have to be shunted aside. Disparaging the old while creating the new reflects the motto of many start-ups.

Tenet 6—Preponderance of digital giants: Sooner or later, the digital giants will enter the market arena of healthcare and command huge stakes in digital service design. One the one hand, they have full access to deep pockets to launch brownfield investments by means of acquisitions, while they could also engineer a flurry of greenfield project to get a close grip on digital service designs.

Tenet 7—Preponderance of patient-centered service designs: Patient-centeredness is anything but a buzzword, but the new market reality as patients emerge as healthcare customers with concrete benefits and value expectations they are willing to pay for.

Tenet 8—Preponderance networked healthcare solutions: Platform economics foreshadow an era of networking, sharing, and co-value creation to take full advantage of complementary assets and competence pooling. The fastest growing business models of the world are entirely platform-driven inaugurating a new era of networked and digital value creation.

Tenet 9—Preponderance of blue ocean strategies and business development: Why always sticking to the knitting when the knitting is increasingly devaluated and dismantled through disruptive service designs? So, please adopt a refurbished stance toward innovation and business development to compete for the future!

Tenet 10—Preponderance of value-based healthcare: Value in healthcare is not only a matter of financial value creation, but of multi-dimensional value categories, such as patient value, customer value, employee value of society value. So, how to strike the right and fair balance between these value categories that can be optimized to a certain amount.

References

Baron, D. (1995). Integrated Strategy—Market and Nonmarket Components. *California Management Review, 37*(2), 47–65. https://doi.org/10.2307/41165788

Bennett, N., & Lemoine, G. J. (2014). What a difference a word makes: Understanding threats to performance in a VUCA world. *Business Horizons, 57*(3), 311–317. https://doi.org/10.1016/j.bushor.2014.01.001

Bruyaka, O., Zeitzmann, H. K., Chalamon, I., Wokutch, R. E., & Thakur, P. (2013). Strategic corporate social responsibility and orphan drug development: Insights from the US and the EU biopharmaceutical industry. *Journal of Business Ethics, 117*(1), 45–65. https://doi.org/10.1007/s10551-012-1496-y

Doh, J. P., Lawton, T. C., & Rajwani, T. (2012). Advancing nonmarket strategy research: institutional perspectives in a changing world. *Academy of Management Perspectives, 26*(3), 22–39. https://doi.org/10.5465/amp.2012.0041

Gatea, A. A., Batcha, M. F. M., & Taweekun, J. (2020). Energy efficiency and thermal comfort in hospital buildings: A review. *International Journal of Integrated Engineering, 12*(3), 33–41. https://doi.org/10.30880/ijie.2020.12.03.005.

Ghosh, B. N. (2008). Rich doctors and poor patients: Market failure and health care systems in developing countries. *Journal of Contemporary Asia, 38*(2), 259–276. https://doi.org/10.1080/00472330701546525

Hadani, M., Doh, J. P., & Schneider, M. (2019). Social movements and corporate political activity: Managerial responses to socially oriented shareholder activism. *Journal of Business Research, 95*(Issue C), 156–170. https://doi.org/10.1016/j.jbusres.2018.10.031.

Hillman, A. J., Keim, G. D., & Schuler, D. (2004). Corporate political activity: A review and research agenda. *Journal of Management, 30*(6), 837–857. https://doi.org/10.1016/j.jm.2004.06.003

Knape, T., Hufnagl, P., & Rasche, C. (2020). Innovationsmanagement unter VUKA-Bedingungen: Gesundheit im Fokus von Digitalisierung, Datenanalytik, Diskontinuität und Disruption. In: M. A. Pfannstiel, K. Kassel & C. Rasche (Hrsg.), *Innovationen und Innovationsmanagement im Gesundheitswesen: Technologien, Produkte und Dienstleistungen voranbringen* (pp. 1–24). Springer Fachmedien. https://doi.org/10.1007/978-3-658-28643-9_1.

Larsson, D. G. J. (2014). Antibiotics in the environment. *Upsala Journal of Medical Sciences, 119* (2), 108–112. https://doi.org/10.3109/03009734.2014.896438

Major, I. (2019). Two-sided information asymmetry in the healthcare industry. *International Advances in Economic Research, 25*(2), 177–193. https://doi.org/10.1007/s11294-019-09732-9

Mellahi, K., Frynas, J. G., Sun, P., & Siegel, D. (2016). A review of the nonmarket strategy literature: Toward a multi-theoretical integration. *Journal of Management, 42*(1), 143–173. https://doi.org/10.1177/0149206315617241

Mk, U. (2017). Eminence or evidence? The volatility, uncertainty, complexity, and ambiguity in healthcare. *Journal of Pharmacology & Pharmacotherapeutics, 8*(1), 1–2. https://doi.org/10.4103/jpp.jpp_12_17

Muehlbacher, A. C., Amelung, V. E., & Juhnke, C. (2018). Contract design: The problem of information asymmetry. *International Journal of Integrated Care, 18*(1), 1. https://doi.org/10.5334/ijic.3614

Rasche, C., Fink, D., Knoblach, B., & Brehmer, N. (2019). Political impact management. wisu. Jg. 48. Heft 1. https://pub.h-brs.de/frontdoor/index/index/docId/4464.

Rinsche, F. (2017). The role of digital health care startups. In: A. Schmid & S. Singh (Hrsg.), *Crossing borders-Innovation in the U.S. Health Care System*. Schriften zur Gesundheitsökonomie. P.C.O. Verlag. Bayreuth. Vol. 84. S. 185–195.

Voinea, C., & Emaus, M. (2017). The effect of nonmarket capabilities on firm performance: How knowledge and capabilities accumulated from nonmarket arenas contribute to firm performance. *International Business Research., 11*(1), 1. https://doi.org/10.5539/ibr.v11n1p1

Christoph Rasche heads the chair of professional and corporate services at the University of Potsdam. He adopted visiting professorships at the Universities of Innsbruck, Alcalá de Henares as well as the Hochschule Osnabrück. He teaches strategic and general management in national and international MBA programs with special respect to subjects connected with the healthcare and hospital industry. Formerly, he consulted with Droege International AG and was co-founder of Stratvanguard and the General Management Institute Potsdam. Prof. Rasche's research subjects circle around the field of strategic and general management in the healthcare and hospital sector, which witnesses an era of professional value creation by means of a strong management and leadership focus. Practically, he consults with healthcare players and is actively involved in executive trainings—ranging from corporate universities to MBA and PhD programs for healthcare professionals.

Nataliia Brehmer is a research associate at the Chair of Management, Professional Services and Sports Economics. She is teaching healthcare management and economics at the University of Potsdam and is a supervisor for a number of bachelor and master theses at the field of strategic management, consulting, sports- and healthcare management on the Faculties of Human Sciences and Economics and Social Studies at the University of Potsdam. Natalia Brehmer was engaged in the project DIGILOG and assisted the research efforts toward creating the innovative business models in health and elderly care. Practically, she is supervising the internships of sports management students and provides career consulting for young professionals. After finishing her master studies in the field of International Business and Negotiations she is working on her PhD Thesis with the topic Non-Market-Strategies that provide business with non-economic means in the social and political arenas to tackle the hypercompetition and sustain the competitive advantage. Mrs. Brehmer is multilingual and is fluent in Polish, Ukrainian, English, German and Russian languages.

Toward a Conceptual Framework of Hybrid Strategies in Healthcare: Co-Alignment of Market and Non-Market Activities

3

Christoph Rasche and Nataliia Brehmer

Abstract

The healthcare industry is anything but a free-market forces system due to a high degree of regulation and governmental interference. Healthcare organizations are unable to take full advantage of free-wheeling market strategies, while resisting implementation under rigorous regulatory conditions. For this reason, so called non-market strategies are necessary to gain and sustain corporate advantages. All too often, market strategies (ms) and non-market strategies (nms) are seen as juxtaposing postures, lacking co-alignment. In practice, however, many corporations employ hybrid strategies that are driven by corporate commercial activities and corporate political activities in an integrated fashion. In addition to complementing each other, these adhere to the reasoning of hybrid actions, resulting from hybrid strategies. This paper is a rather conceptual contribution to healthcare management, aiming at developing a holistic framework for hybrid strategies. We describe a complex of management concepts corresponding with hybrid market constellations and hybrid capabilities.

C. Rasche (✉) · N. Brehmer
Humanwissenschaftliche Fakultät, Wirtschafts- und Sozialwissenschaftliche Fakultät Department für Sport-und Gesundheitswissenschaften, Lehrstuhl für Management, Sportökonomie and Professional Services, Universität Potsdam, Karl-Liebknecht-Straße 24–25, Haus 24, Raum 126, 14476 Potsdam, Germany
e-mail: chrasche@uni-potsdam.de

N. Brehmer
e-mail: nbrehmer@uni-potsdam.de

© The Author(s), under exclusive license to Springer Nature Switzerland AG 2022
M. A. Pfannstiel et al. (eds.), *Service Design Practices for Healthcare Innovation*,
https://doi.org/10.1007/978-3-030-87273-1_3

3.1 In Search of a Holistic View on Healthcare

The inherent idiosyncrasies of the healthcare sector require dedicated holistic approaches. The following six frameworks offer substantial values to the healthcare sector and help to gain a deep insight into an industry that displays classic signs of market and non-market systems (Doh et al., 2012; Rasche, 2020). Firstly, the rationalization, rationing and prioritization paradigm, RRP will be described. Secondly, the RRP logic will be complemented by the EID formula resembling entrepreneurship, innovation, and digitalization in healthcare (Rasche et al., 2020). Thirdly, the 5-D concept services as an approach for ensuring decision-makers' awareness of the states of discontinuity, disorder, disruption, destruction, and development needs. Fourthly, 3-M, which represents the co-alignment of management, medicine, and moral, will be discussed. This is particularly important, since shareholder value and stakeholder value must go hand in hand. Following this, the successful service design in healthcare depends on the dynamic positioning when being cheaper, better, different, faster, or smarter. Finally, attention will be given to the AMLE approach, namely: the administration, management, leadership, and entrepreneurship, which are anything but closed categories. Moreover, they can be combined and may complement each other. This paper is conceptual one deserving empirical evidence on the one hand. But on the other hand, a holistic view of healthcare and service design (innovation) calls for a conceptual groundwork turn full circle in the healthcare sector that resembles a mosaic of pieces, patterns, principles, and paradigms deserving holistic integration with respect to market and non-market decisions (Baron, 1995; Mellahi et al., 2016). The paper develops the idea of hybrid strategies and represents far more than the gray zones between market strategies and non-market strategies (Rasche, 2020; Rasche et al., 2019). Moreover, hybrid strategies display the features of a strategy category of its own because the professional co-alignment of non-market and market elements of corporate strategies may contribute to the supra-additivity of value creation. For this reason, healthcare providers should harness the power of political impact management (Hillman et al., 2004).

3.2 5-D Framework as Starting Point for Healthcare Analysis

The healthcare industry faces increasing levels of risk, uncertainty, and complexities as reflected by the VUCA logic, which stands for volatility, uncertainty, complexity, and ambiguity (Bennett & Lemoine, 2014; Mk, 2017; Knape et al., 2020). From the viewpoint of business disruption, it is safe to say that the only constant is change. Predominantly, the changes are driven by entrepreneurship, innovation, and digitalization (EID). EID strategies are employed by many med-tech and health-tech firms as path-breaking means to side-attack incumbent players. It is worth noting that EID strategies incorporate many non-market aspects due to market regulation and political interference. Unlike EID strategies, rationalization, rationing, and prioritization (RRP) resembles the old school of healthcare management, when focusing on system optimization under stable and often regulated market conditions. RRP strategies and non-market strategies often go hand in hand because legislators put rationalization, rationing, and prioritization on the agenda of healthcare management. EID strategies as well as RRP strategies will be discussed after having discussed the 5-D framework with respect to market and non-market issues.

3.2.1 Managing the 5-D: Change Readiness as a Core Competence

The 5-D framework displays the cascading features of business transformation. Beginning with the states of discontinuity and disorder, which may culminate in disruption and destruction. To some extent, business developments depend on path-breaking trigger points to replace the old for the new. Business transformation in healthcare is not only a matter of sober market strategies but of clear-cut non-market leadership. In contrast to management leadership insinuates a state of political mindfulness and strategic ambassadorship (see also Rasche, 2020, Rasche, Schultz & Brehmer, 2021a, b).

Discontinuity: Moderate changes can be often anticipated such that healthcare providers are braced for transformation processes. They occur in a rather non disruptive fashion, involving no path-breaking shocks. Moreover, slight discontinuities may contribute to path progression, owing to improvements to entrenched routines and best practices. If the discontinuities do not comply with the established order, the new normal is established incrementally by means of path shifting.

Disorder: Faced with a rising state of order, management must be prepared to some extent, for the unthinkable, as new norms may either result in rapid path progression or result in path-breaking incidents, challenging the agility, anti-fragility, and resilience of entrenched systems. States of disorder are challenging, but may not necessarily result in a complete destruction of the old order. Nevertheless, dynamic capabilities are required to prevent system collapse. For example, telemedicine endangers the classic patient-to-doc relations, just as digital healthcare platforms endorse multi-channel, multi-stakeholder, and many-to-many communication processes. These examples raise the question of whether conventional doc-to-patient formats will outlive their usefulness in the face of the current global pandemic?

Disruption: Disruptive forces are mostly path-breaking, which devaluate the current best practices, core competencies and entrenched wisdoms, abruptly. Opposite to disorder (described above), core elements of established systems are dismantled or replaced by the new normal. Nevertheless, the strategic architecture of a system can be preserved although its core elements run the risk of anhelation. For instance, neither AI-supported health-bots, autonomous systems, nor path-breaking precision medicine, which despite all being disruptive, are destructive. This is owing to the essential principles of the healthcare system being sustained. Namely, healing and helping and healing patients to recover in a professional pre-defined manner.

Destruction: The state of turmoil resembles far more than "paradigm lifting and shifting," because the new order is at odds with the old. This is represented by a portfolio of path-dependent systems, process, designs, technologies, and best practices. The new mantra of platform economics may lead to rapid business model and service design destruction with respect to the technology tycoons such as Facebook, Amazon, Google, Apple, or SAP. These game changers are defining and designing healthcare in a digital and disruptive manner. Patients, diseases, and diagnoses reflect big data applications, on which artificial intelligence, deep learning, autonomous expert solutions, and precision medicine incorporate their seeds of destruction. The convergence of medicine, management, digitalization, and genetic analytics of the new norm contribute to the destruction of the old norm. The demise of the traditional retail sector foreshadows an era of connected healthcare going far beyond electronic data interchange and system-based knowledge sharing.

Development: An economic, medical, technological, and societal progress often hinges on path-breaking developments to establish its new norm. The aforementioned 4-D's may be regarded as harmful, pain-points, and triggers to leave comfort zones for the sake of entrepreneurship, innovation, and digitalization. In contrast to EID strategies, rationalization, rationing, and prioritization (RRP) resemble the old normal of efficiency seeking, resource budgeting, and operative excellence, while not challenging the gestalt and governance of healthcare. The pandemic may usher in an era of digital development in healthcare because the power of data is a source of true value creation with respect to handling the crisis efficiently and effectively.

In a nutshell, the 5-D framework calls for change readiness, in order to fully benefit from the new norm and its underlying digitalization imperatives. Change readiness derives from the VUCA concepts (volatility, uncertainty, complexity, ambiguity) requiring healthcare providers to accumulate corresponding capabilities such as vision engineering, understanding, clarity, and agility. The 5-D framework is strongly influenced by non-market forces because ever-changing legislation, regulation, and stakeholder interference have a strong bearing on service design in healthcare. For this reason, corporate political activities and corporate commercial activities must go hand in hand. Figure 3.1 is a visual aid, resembling the 5-D hockey stick logic, starting with the 4-D that culminates in the destruction of the "old normal." Non-market strategies may accompany and support this process of institutional change in healthcare and thus should be explicitly included in a hybrid leadership and management framework. In face of VUCA conditions and digitalization imperatives, healthcare providers must master the present and preempt the future in a balanced manner. Fortunately, most of the changes can be anticipated by means of strategic forecasting, weak signal analysis, or future studies, so that healthcare providers can anticipate the future to some extent. But, they should also be braced for "environmental tsunamis," happening in an ad hoc, radical, and non-predictable fashion. Agility, responsiveness, resilience, and anti-fragility are

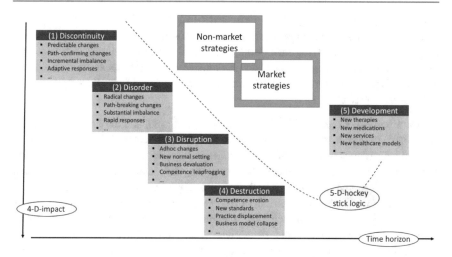

Fig. 3.1 5-D framework—managing the transition to the new normal in healthcare. *Source* Author's own illustration (2021)

not only management buzzwords. They denote an era of disturbance in healthcare causing high amplitudes and frequencies of change. The following ideas and concepts challenge entrenched wisdoms to pave the way for the proclaimed transition from the old to the new normal (Rasche, Schultz & Brehmer, 2021a).

3.2.2 From RRP 2 EID: Competing for the Future in Healthcare

The so called RRP framework is very prevalent in the healthcare sector, standing for a philosophy of relentless resource management and efficiency seeking. Rationalization, rationing, and prioritization reflect a resource-based constraint logic, which culminates in triage decisions when critical healthcare resources are in short supply, while the demand side is shooting up. According to Larry Bossidy, the former Allied Signal CEO, companies cannot shrink to greatness, but the record of past legislations, stipulations, and regulations focused on cost dampening, resource curtailing, and budget constraints rather than entrepreneurship, innovation, and digitalization. But, things begin to change, since progressive politicians call for an era of connected healthcare and full-swing digitalization. It is our aim not only to coalesce the conservative RRP framework with the progressive EID framework, but also to reflect the discussion against non-market constellations intruding on healthcare.

3.2.2.1   Hybrid Strategies and the RRP logic

The RRP logic can be also applied to hybrid economic systems oscillating between market and non-market regimes. Here, we discuss rationalization, rationing, and prioritization from the viewpoint of corporate political and corporate commercial activities, because they represent different sides of the same coin (Rasche, Brehmer & Schultz, 2021b).

Rationalization: Connected healthcare, digital platforms, and integrated workflows contribute to better resource utilization and value creation. The core aim of rationalization goes beyond limiting resource supply, because management is eager to mobilize stocks for the sake of better, faster, and smarter outcomes. Seamless workflows, bridged interfaces, and connected professionals are paramount to rationalization, because internal and external transaction costs hamper patient-centered resource allocations. Resource mis-management refers to hardware, software, brainware, and peopleware that should have been handled systematically to take full advantage of time, quality, and cost advantages. Adopting a non-market perspective, legislators calls for rationalization in healthcare for the sake of better, faster, and leaner asset utilization. For this reason, the industrial flow principle and the cornerstones of mass manufacturing are transferred to hospital management. Toyota production principles of lean management, platform designs, Kanban or global supply chain management have been adopted by the healthcare sector in order to transform hospitals into high-tech assembly line institutions. In a similar vein, clinics can be regarded as inter-connected, inter-professional, and inter-disciplinary high-serve expert organizations, benefitting not only from the digitalization imperative, but from the paradigm networked production architectures as displayed by hub-and-spoke systems, which extend enterprise and virtual remote solutions. Due to the masterpiece of full-swing, digitalization rationalization efforts can be so far reaching that manpower is replaced by machine power resulting in labor force problems. For instance, healthcare experts running the danger of falling prey to rationalization endeavors such as artificial intelligence, deep learning, or sophisticated big data applications. On the one hand, legislators pushed for a rationalization by means of digitalization, evolving as the new mantra in healthcare, while on the other hand, critical stakeholders oppose a fully industrialized healthcare system. On the face of job losses, an unhuman bot- and app-based labor conditions. The dawning era of platform economics implies that the next step of digitalization in healthcare due to efficient many-to-many omni-channel communication taking place among multiple agents sharing data, information, and competence (Major., 2019, Rasche, 2020). Left-wing politics came up with the idea of raising rationalization taxes to compensate for the manpower replaced by the advancing of AI production systems. These correspond with high degrees of automation, standardization and economies of scale, and a scope for digitalized platform designs. The question at hand: defining the prospective role of manpower in healthcare systems. As such, the 5.0 product system brings into question, the role of manpower within the healthcare system. Rationalization is not only about cheaper, leaner, and meaner! It is also about a better, faster, and smarter asset utilization and disposition. This is demonstrated by inter-connected healthcare. But, we should bear in mind that radical rationalization regimes in healthcare call for a political agenda to be implemented from the viewpoint of the providers. Since legacy systems, path dependencies and entrenched wisdoms of operation are all-pervading in the healthcare sector, non-market strategies should complement and bolster technology strategies and innovation policy because of expected multi-stakeholder resistance watching out for reasons and arguments to fight the new digital normal.

Rationing: When resources scarcely satisfy inflating market demands, service gaps are sure to ensue. Triage decisions incorporate the logic of rationalization because critical healthcare resources are allocated to pre-defined principles and standards to achieve the highest possible value in healthcare. For ethical and/or strategic reasons, resource allocation does not follow a market system order, but is the outcome of non-market decisions reflecting a political rather than an economic doctrine. Since market regimes may cause unethical and medically as well as politically unfavorable outcomes, legislators and health authorities administer resource allocation strategies, when shunting aside free-wheeling market forces. Administrations, authorities, and provisions epitomizing non-market regimes are deemed more useful than market outcomes contributing to social injustice and societal upheaval if, for example, access to corona vaccines was to become subjected to market forces. Non-market decisions lie at the heart of rationing, thus resembling an authority-induced process of resource allocation for medical reasons, differing from a pure commercial market logic.

Prioritization: Bearing the ABC analysis in mind, healthcare providers often cannot afford to focus on orphan phenomenon, but have to take full advantage of the "big points" when accentuating blockbuster therapies, medications, or technologies. Resource leverage, asset mobilization, and value in healthcare hinge on clear-cut asset utilization to avoid waste of scarce resources with respect to orphan arenas of healthcare being discriminated de-prioritized. On the one hand, prioritization is necessary for every healthcare system to keep right on track, since scarce resource must unfold their medical and economic values. No hospital, no healthcare regime, no medical provider can afford to spend its energy on fruitless efforts, low-value operations, or high-care and resource-absorbing patients, in direct competition with high-value alternatives. Adopting an ethical standpoint, the issue at dispute is the definition of value in healthcare, as healing, life preservation, and patient-centeredness often defy an economic discounted cashflow interpretation. Nevertheless, value calculations such quality-adjusted life years foreshadow the direction toward an economized healthcare that cannot ignore prioritization decisions. Scarce resources are always competing against high-value alternatives. Placing the bets on low-value options displaces a set of high-value alternatives that should not be neglected for economic, medical, and ethical reasons. Prioritization display classic features of market segmentation, making marketers focusing on target groups while discriminating non-targets at the same time. Non-targets in a healthcare sense are low-value bets with respect to resource consumptions, expected outcomes or the resource/outcome ratio. Non-market decisions may lead to prioritization, because of healthcare roadmaps representing the enforced will of the political authorities. Politicians put healthcare issues on the agenda by means of legislation while not always calculating for the market and technology consequences (Hadani, Doh & Schneider, 2019). Currently, electric mobility and connected traffic systems are sacrosanct, reflecting top-priorities being immune to any criticism (Köhler, Schultz & Rasche, 2020). Likewise, inter-connected healthcare, precision medicine, and digitalization are tech-driven top-priorities, while the nurses shall be given a stronger say to stress their substantial importance for healthcare systems.

To summarize, the RRP logic represents the old norm in healthcare, namely: a system of efficient and effective resource management. Resource leadership goes far beyond professional budgeting and resource controlling to be braced for prospective challenges. On the one hand, mastering the present by means of RRP is important, on the other hand, preparing for the future through entrepreneurship, innovation, and digitalization is a sign for the prevalence of the VUCA principles within the healthcare sector.

3.2.2.2 Hybrid Strategies and the EID Logic

RRP and EID complement each other and should co-align to master the present and preempt the future. Entrepreneurship, innovation, and digitalization increasingly enter healthcare arenas when it comes platform-based healthcare architectures, on which, to establish a flurry of health-tech and med-tech businesses. Technology tycoons such as Amazon, Google, Facebook, Apple, or SAP are eager to establish a new EID norm in healthcare, transcending, either enhancing the EID logic or complementing it by means of entrepreneurship, innovation, and digitalization.

Entrepreneurship: How to bring the Silicon Valley culture into healthcare to trigger innovation end boost entrepreneurial zest? This is a question to be answered by the technology tycoons when investing in med-tech and health-tech ventures, or taking a full advantage of artificial intelligence, deep learning, and advanced big data applications. Instead of accepting the rules of the old norm, they set the rules for the new. On the one hand, healthcare entrepreneurship aims to optimize the old RRP norm. On the other hand, it is about pushing the envelope toward a "new norm." The new norm represents an era of connected, platform-based, and data-sharing world of value generation by means of precision decision-making (PDM). PDM is driven by the notion of data currencies, because data access, data transformation, and data capitalization reflect VUCA core competencies, on which to launch new healthcare business models. To some extent, they may be adjuvant, supportive, and complementary. On the other hand, they may be disturbing, disruptive, or destructive. Entrepreneurship in healthcare benefits from hybrid strategies because regulation, legislation, and societal constraints are entrance barriers for entrepreneurs having to adopt a political ambassador logic to push their vested interests.

Innovation: New products, services, process, technologies, and problem solutions can be both path dependent, as well as path breaking when establishing a new norm incrementally or radically. All too often, innovations are reduced to product, service of therapies, while neglecting the power of business model innovations within healthcare sector. This is demonstrated by platform solutions and new regimes of integrated healthcare solutions that are akin to architectural innovations, such as telemedicine. The latter is far more than a technology set, because it amounts to an advanced ecosystem of heterogenous agents, eager to benefit from platform-based supra-additivities. Innovations may refer to the old as well to the new norm, because they can deepen and improve entrenched paths of best practices and dynamic routines as exemplified by RRP. Path-breaking innovations go beyond this train of thought because they disrupt, destroy, and displace common wisdoms and regimes of balance. Due to their aggressive and ruthless intent, they will have to go many extra miles owing to stakeholder resistance and non-market strategies employed by incumbents to defend their turf (Rasche, 2020).

Digitalization: The "new" norm in the seventies was electronics, while the contemporary new norm is digitalization in the face of the telecommunications, information, media, and entertainment (TIME). Even healthcare solutions can be entertaining, with respect to gamification options that foster preventive activities and therapy compliance. Lifestyles emerge as health styles with respect to the quantified self-movement and shared fitness data. Digitalization in healthcare resembles a full range of cross-over options, brought about by scalable, transferrable, and lightweight business solutions that can be applied to first, second, and third healthcare market. The bedrock of digitalization can be seen in the TTTPPP framework that capitalizes on data tracing, tracking, and tapping in a first step and data profiling, prediction, and profit in the second. These benefit from the value of a cascading process of data transformation. While digitalized and connected healthcare in China is no problem, data privacy and data protection issues hamper digitalization in healthcare. Digital solution providers in healthcare are challenged to side-step toward hybrid strategies and a non-market management, to overcome the obstacles resulting from data regulation.

To sum it up, the new norm of EID is driven by the notion of a paradigm shift instead paradigm confirmation. EID strategies, though often induced by commercial interests, such as IPOs, royalty revenues, or fast market and value capture, will lose momentum and outlive their effectiveness without explicit employment of non-market elements. EID strategies are more about leadership than management, as establishing the new norm calls for a set of navigating capabilities.

3.2.2.3 Co-Alignment of RRP and EID

As previously mentioned, both the RRP and the EID logics call for an integrative framework to master the present and preempt the future. Figure 3.1 proposes a return on healthcare (RoH) focus, which can be achieved by means of nominator and denominator managements. If healthcare providers wish to boost returns, they should take full advantage of the EID logic and business development strategies. If they intend to increase investment efficiency, they are challenged to employ the necessary RRP steps. Nominator as well as denominator managements may be short-, mid-, or long-term focused, depending in the planning horizon. In many instances, healthcare management are forced to resort to a balanced approach, striking a balance between short- and long-term goals on the one hand, while on the other hand, they must harmonize RRP with EID imperatives. Field experiences suggest that many firms employ a hybrid of both strategies. Hybrid strategy concepts also have to acknowledged that RRP–EID strategies are designed and implemented under hybrid market constellations, incorporating the genes of market and non-market systems (Hadani, Doh, Schneider, 2019). Figure 3.2 delineates in a rather coarse manner, the options of increasing the return on healthcare (RoH) by means of either EID or RRP strategies. Both strategies resort to market and non-market activities. Furthermore, we propose alternative planning horizons and degrees of hardness in accordance with either EID or RRP strategies.

Figure 3.3 continues with the logic of Fig. 3.2, when placing special emphasis on dedicated RRP and EID topics. Nominator and denominator activities should be planned together under the umbrella of market and non-market imperatives. A multi-focal leadership in healthcare implies that the multiple vectors of decision-making go for cockpit system of balanced management, as displayed by balanced score cards, which are widely used within for profit and non-profit contexts.

3.2.3   3-M framework Four Healthcare: Co-Alignment of Medicine, management, and Moral

Service designs in the healthcare sector follow the logic of a leadership triangle, which consists of medicine, management, and moral. All three elements underlie political restrictions and societal influences exposing them to non-market forces.

Medicine: Medicine represents the core discipline of the healthcare sector, irrespective of other substantial disciplines such as nursing, clinic admission, or patient-centered convenience services. Medical innovations call for hybrid strategies, as they are driven by market and non-market elements that complement each other.

Management: Healthcare and hospital management should not be reduced to proper consulting tool-box employment. Moreover, it resembles political impact strategies and a full array of non-market activities to position clinics and healthcare institutions in complex stakeholder networks. Diplomatic bargaining, ambassador-like shrewdness, and political power play are pillars of non-market leadership to gain and sustain corporate advantages.

Moral: Fair-play, legitimacy, ethics are driving forces of healthcare service designs reflecting the ingrained values that come to play when the zest for money making, market segmentation, and target group orientation conflicts with philanthropic

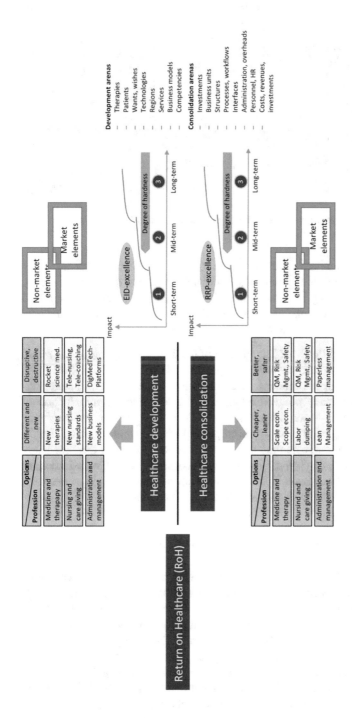

Fig. 3.2 Return on healthcare (RoH). *Source* Author's own illustration (2021)

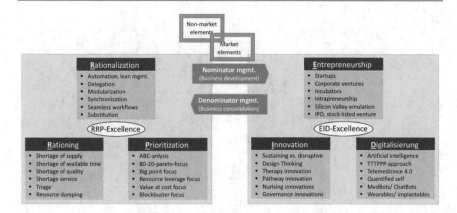

Fig. 3.3 Toward an integrative view on RRP and EID. *Source* Author's own illustration (2021)

healing ambitions. Similarly, patients are not seen as customers but as needy humans that should not be exposed to an economic logic, based on profit-making. An ethical health economy is about waste reduction, better resource allocation, and asset mobilization for the sake of better, faster, and safer outcomes to achieve an excellent patient value at cost ratio.

Hybrid strategies and the 3-M: The triangle of medicine, management, and moral in healthcare defines a clear-cut market logic because dabbling in politics is an endemic issue for regulated markets. Even medicine, often deemed a natural science, interferes with many political issues when it comes to the introduction of disruptive innovations. Moral issues itself are non-market-driven because they channel market strategies toward philanthropic and non-commercial aims. Healthcare management, although stemming from an economic bedrock, displays many non-market features as displayed by multi-agent constellations of vested interests and power play. For this reason, hybrid strategies should be employed as means to take full advantage of the professional 3-M triangle handling.

3.2.4 Hybrid Strategies and the AMLE Framework

Service designs in healthcare should be discussed with respect to the implications of the AMLE framework. AMLE stands for administration, management, leadership, and entrepreneurship in healthcare. These four styles of running a healthcare institution are not mutually exclusive, but go for a corporate navigation system. To some extent, they follow a cascading order, reaching the management, leadership, or entrepreneurship level often and depending on an administrative foundation. In reality, many healthcare start-ups lack professional administration and management, while emphasizing leadership orientation or entrepreneurship. While healthcare incumbents run path dependence by means of administration and management, new entrants prefer leadership and entrepreneurship style, in order to break the entrenched paths and to adopt a first mover position as an innovator. This is exemplified by the digital healthcare platform providers that have their origin in the ICT sector.

Administration: Bureaucracies are all-pervading in the healthcare sector often lacking management, leadership, and entrepreneurship focus. Static routines, provisions and thigh command, and order regimes may contribute to scale economies, operational effectiveness and pre-defined rules of conduct. Under VUCA conditions, the administration style alone is not enough to survive, as nobody is competing for the future. Moreover, past best practices are translated into a future, that is, anything but safe and easy to anticipate. Certainly, sure administration is of substantial value in the face of lean principles and enforced digitalization, but often resembles an old school style of top-down and inside-out coordination and communication. Highly regulated and pre-defined market rules offer huge space for administration and little space for management, leadership, and entrepreneurship since the latter cannot unleash energy due to a system of constraints and straightjackets.

Management: Planning, decision-making, implementation, and controlling embody a logic of short-, mid-, and long-term forecasting to help prepare for the unthinkable. Management is closely related to a toolset of analytic frameworks, consulting heuristics and MBA methodologies to arrive at better, faster, and smarter decisions. This is evidenced by artificial intelligence, deep learning, and advanced decision support systems. Business analytics, big data, and best practices are outcomes of rather aseptic management philosophies, hailing numbers and systems, while displacing the people. The introduction of balanced scorecards, dashboard management systems, and medicine controlling epitomizes an era of evidence-based management style akin to the natural sciences. On the one hand, facts and figures sharpen managerial sensemaking, while on the other hand, they cannot embody the soft and political issues healthcare organizations. Non-market or political management acknowledges the aseptic features of decision-making. The concept of balanced healthcare management stands for (1) top-down and bottom-up-planning, (2) outside-in and inside-out planning, and (3) the dedicated employment of market and non-market strategies.

Leadership: Running the ship is not enough in the face of stormy waters, which challenges the upper echelons of the healthcare sector. Navigating is about people, power, pride, perspectives, and prowess, reflecting the emotional state of an organization. The most valuable companies in the world not only resort to administration and management; they employ leadership style as a means to change, push, and convince people. Leadership, more than management, is about connecting people, not systems, data or interfaces. An excellent leadership in healthcare excels in stretched goals, strategic intent, and committed people. Servant leadership goes beyond transactional and transformational leaderships, as these leaders create a setting for unleashing creativity, personal development, and executives that are willing to serve their organization instead of dominating it. On the other hand, leadership may also display the relentless features, when distressed hospitals and healthcare providers must be restructured to avoid bankruptcy. Navigation always includes the employment of market and non-market strategies, since leadership make deciders to adopt the role of diplomats, ambassadors, and politicians instead of sober managers of admins.

Entrepreneurship: Emulating Silicon Valley implies the adoption of a start-up and new venture philosophy not that much internalized by the incumbents. Porsche consulting differentiates between (1) current traditional health incumbents, (2) current traditional health challengers, and (3) new non-traditional insurgents. The first group stands for administration and management, while the second group places emphasis on management and leadership. The third group as represented by tech-giants, cloud services providers and or med-robotics. These define themselves as game changers or rule breakers, and they enter the healthcare markets by means of disruptive service designs, business models, and problem solutions. To make elephants dance, the incumbents must change their strategic DNA and evolve into intrapreneurs, respectively entrepreneurs through a process of corporate venturing, design thinking, or radical business development. Legacies of age, path dependencies, and core rigidities may hamper this process of institutional transformation that challenges the not-invented here mindsets. Healthcare entrepreneurs are very often idea-driven and fascinated by innovations while paying little attention to the legal , political, or societal constraints, which cause bounded rationality or a dominant logic of doing business. Empirical evidence shows that successful entrepreneurial activities are often accompanied by corporate political activities, to push the envelope through non-market engagements.

Holistic AMLE framework for Healthcare: The AMLE framework is valid for all organizations and thus can be applied to them in an adapted manner (see Fig. 3.4). Approaching AMLE means balancing its four dimensions in a contingent way to turn a full circle. Entrepreneurial start-ups often lack administrative and managerial skills, while incumbents should invest on leadership and entrepreneurship issues. Each of the four dimensions may incorporate market and non-market elements as figure four depicts.

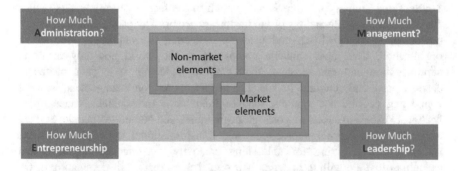

Fig. 3.4 AMLE framework. *Source* Author's own illustration (2021)

3.3   Toward a Holistic Framework

There is a need to integrate the 5-D, 3-M, RRP, EID, and AMLE into a holistic framework with respect to market and non-market strategies. They are not mutually exclusive, but represent a framework system that can be applied to healthcare providers.

The hybrid strategy pentagon (HSP, see Fig. 3.5) co-aligns substantial strands of a balanced healthcare management. Taken together, the five frameworks tend toward a meta-framework for healthcare management, which incorporates both market and non-market elements. Platform, service, and product strategies reflect a means end constellation of problem solution. While hybrid strategies can be narrowed to an integrated mix of market and non-market elements; the view on them can be widened toward a flurry of other strategy categories, such as (1) top-down versus bottom-up focus, (2) outside-in versus inside-out focus, and (3) path breaking versus path confirming or consolidation versus expansion focus.

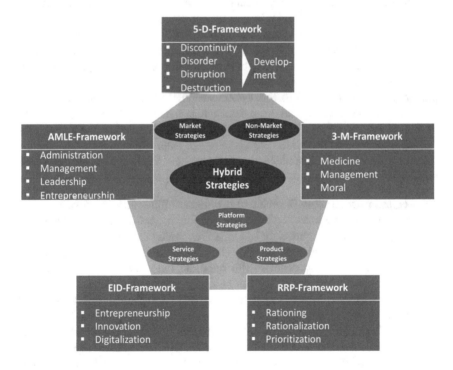

Fig. 3.5 Hybrid strategy pentagon (HSP). *Source* Author's own illustration (2021)

3.4 Conclusion: Hybrid Capabilities for Healthcare

According to the resource-based view, gaining and sustaining substantial advantages are a matter of strategic asset management, which incorporate the access, transformation, utilization, and capitalization of resources. Knowledge-based resources represent invisible assets that meet the requirements of capabilities. The latter represents bundles of knowledge, enabling organizations to apply stocks of (1) hardware, (2) software, (3) brainware, and (4) peopleware to tasks, challenges, and jobs that are performed in a value generating way. Core capabilities are difficult to trade, to imitate, to replace, or to outsource, as they are in short supply and sometimes cannot be procured, due to insufficient factor markets. Core capabilities may directly or indirectly contribute to multi-dimensional value creation. For instance, patient, shareholder, employee, and public values. Value creation within the healthcare sector is not only a matter of shareholder value, rather also, of stakeholder values, as observed with respect to corporate social responsibility issues (Bruyaka et al., 2013). The creating shared value paradigm (CSV) represents a hybrid strategy logic that strikes a balance between shareholder and stakeholder values (Porter & Kramer, 2011). Moreover, enhancing stakeholder value and following the aim of corporate social responsibility contribute to shareholder value in parallel. Hybrid strategies call for a corresponding set of capabilities. Hybrid capabilities, unlike commercial capabilities, enable companies to perform excellently under multi-dimensional market conditions (Voinea & Emaus, 2017). The latter represents a complex PESTEL system standing for political, economic, social, technological, ecological, and legal issues that reflect a portfolio of risks and opportunities, alike. PESTEL compliance is the ability not only to comply with the PESTEL challenges but also to take advantage of them (Rasche, 2014). Defining a manifesto for hybrid capabilities incorporates the following six tenets to be considered.

(1) **Access or ownership**: The value of hybrid capabilities does not always depend on ownership regimes, because the sharing economy paints a picture of co-value creation. Lightweight and virtual capability regimes follow a sourcing logic, since strategic assets may be rented or accessed by means of hub-and-spoke supply systems. This questions the value of accumulating and owning capabilities, when they can be easily accessed or rented.

(2) **Hard to imitate**: Hybrid capabilities are often institutionally engrained and socially complex and are, therefore, endemically difficult to rebuild or benchmark. In contrast to technological capabilities, hybrid capabilities cannot be blueprinted and redesigned in a linear fashion. Hybrid capabilities epitomize the full range of PESTEL requirements and are thus multi-dimensional by nature. They are deeply ingrained in socio-political systems and cannot be isolated and copied easily.

(3) **Hard to replace**: Although the danger of substitution is omni-present under VUCA conditions, hybrid capabilities are often hard to replace, as they represent a system of sub-capabilities. While single micro-capabilities can be replaced, they are not that easy to substitute for an idiosyncratic capability architecture. If capabilities, skills, and competencies could be replaced easily, they will be devalued by disruptive discontinuities.

(4) **Hard to accumulate**: Hybrid core capabilities must often be crafted and created, internally, if they cannot be sourced. Thus, hybrid capabilities are internalized for the reason of market failure. Unlike commodity assets, hybrid capabilities display the features of agility, resilience, and dynamism making them idiosyncratic assets. The latter falls prey to market failures and must, therefore, be built by means of complex learning within a hierarchical instead of a market order.

(5) **Hard to source**: If markets for hybrid capabilities fail, they must be internalized by means of hierarchy of hybrid arrangements and as such co-value creation together with partners. Corporate political capabilities are hard to source because they are anything but commodities. The more complex a capability is, the more difficult it is to replicate, procure, or imitate. This is true of hybrid capabilities, thus qualifying them as value-generating assets.

(6) **Contribution to shared value creation**: Hybrid capabilities comfortably fit with the creating shared value logic. In contrast to corporate social responsibilities, it denotes that both shareholder and stakeholder values are not juxtaposing objectives (Porter & Kramer, 2011). Moreover, they can be co-aligned and be part of a self-enhancing value system. Corporate political and corporate social responsibilities denote the end to commercial value creation instead of diminishing it. Hybrid capabilities are designed for performing corporate, commercial, and political activities in order to achieve multiple objectives (Voinea & Emaus, 2017). This is relevant for healthcare organizations serving multiple value aims such as patient value, customer value, employee value, and shareholder value.

We conclude with a plea for hybrid leadership, which incorporates hybrid strategies as well as hybrid capabilities. Strategic management is driven by the rather aseptic notion of commercial value creation and value capture by means of sound tool-box employment. Non-market strategies are outcomes of politically imposed activities, having a great impact on highly regulated healthcare institutions. The present paper not only integrated market and non-market activities into a holistic system of hybrid management. It also resorted to the resource-based view, culminating in the challenge to underpin hybrid strategies with the corresponding (hybrid) capabilities (Voinea & Emaus, 2017). The latter represents value-creating assets that transform resources into value streams and desired healthcare outcomes.

References

Baron, D. (1995). Integrated strategy—Market and nonmarket components. *California Management Review, 37*(2), 47–65. https://doi.org/10.2307/41165788

Bennett, N., & Lemoine, G. J. (2014). What a difference a word makes: Understanding threats to performance in a VUCA world. *Business Horizons, 57*(3), 311–317. https://doi.org/10.1016/j.bushor.2014.01.001

Bruyaka, O., Zeitzmann, H. K., Chalamon, I., Wokutch, R. E., & Thakur, P. (2013). Strategic corporate social responsibility and orphan drug development: Insights from the US and the EU biopharmaceutical industry. *Journal of Business Ethics, 117*(1), 45–65. https://doi.org/10.1007/s10551-012-1496-y

Doh, J. P., Lawton, T. C., & Rajwani, T. (2012). Advancing nonmarket strategy research: Institutional perspectives in a changing world. *Academy of Management Perspectives, 26*(3), 22–39. https://doi.org/10.5465/amp.2012.004

Hadani, M., Doh, J. P., & Schneider, M. (2019). Social movements and corporate political activity: Managerial responses to socially oriented shareholder activism. *Journal of Business Research, 95*(C), 156–170. https://doi.org/10.1016/j.jbusres.2018.10.031.

Hillman, A. J., Keim, G. D., & Schuler, D. (2004). Corporate political activity: A review and research agenda. *Journal of Management, 30*(6), 837–857. https://doi.org/10.1016/j.jm.2004.06.003

Knape, T., Hufnagl, P., & Rasche, C. (2020). Innovationsmanagement unter VUKA-Bedingungen: Gesundheit im Fokus von Digitalisierung, Datenanalytik, Diskontinuität und Disruption. In M. A. Pfannstiel, K. Kassel, & C. Rasche (Eds.), *Innovationen und Innovationsmanagement im Gesundheitswesen – Technologien* (pp. 1–24). Produkte und Dienstleistungen voranbringen, Springer Gabler Verlag.

Köhler, W., Schultz, C., & Rasche, C. (2020). When handing out presents is not enough!— Influencing factors on the user´s willingness to share data for connected car services, 25. G-Forum Konferenz 2020, Karlsruhe (Conference Paper).

Major, I. (2019). Two-sided information asymmetry in the healthcare industry. *International Advances in Economic Research, 25*(2), 177–193. https://doi.org/10.1007/s11294-019-09732-9

Mellahi, K., Frynas, J. G., Sun, P., & Siegel, D. (2016). A review of the nonmarket strategy literature: Toward a multi-theoretical integration. *Journal of Management, 42*(1), 143–173. https://doi.org/10.1177/0149206315617241

Mk, U. (2017). Eminence or evidence? The volatility, uncertainty, complexity, and ambiguity in healthcare. *Journal of Pharmacology & Pharmacotherapeutics, 8*(1), 1–2. https://doi.org/10.4103/jpp.jpp_12_17

Porter, M. E., & Kramer, M. (2011). Creating shared value. *Harvard Business Review, 89*(1/2), 62–77.

Rasche, C. (2020). Nicht-Markt-Strategien im Gesundheitswesen—Wettbewerbsvorteile durch indirektes Management. *For-MED, Zeitschrift Für Das Management Im Gesundheitswesen, Ausgabe, 04*(2020), 9–19.

Rasche, C., Schultz, C., & Braun von Reinersdorff, A. (2020). EID-Leadership im gesundheitswesen—Entrepreneurship. *Innovation, Digitalisierung FOR-MED, Zeitschrift Für Das Management Im Gesundheitswesen, Ausgabe, 01*(2020), 1–11.

Rasche, C., Schultz, C., & Brehmer, N. (2021). Innovationstransfer im regulierten Gesundheitswesen: Technologiestrategien für Hybrid-Marktsysteme. *For-MED, Zeitschrift Für Das Management Im Gesundheitswesen, Ausgabe, 01*(2021), 13–21.

Rasche, C., Brehmer, N., & Schultz, C. (2021). Hybridstrategien für die Pharmaindustrie als machtpolitische Arena des Gesundheitswesens. *For-MED, Zeitschrift Für Das Management Im Gesundheitswesen, Ausgabe, 01*(2021), 1–11.

Rasche, C., Brehmer, N., Fink, D., & Knoblach, B. (2019). Political impact management, in wisu, 48(1), S. 78–87.

Rasche, C. (2014). PESTEL-Compliance, in wisu, 43(8–9), 1008–1014.

Voinea, C., & Emaus, M. (2017). The effect of nonmarket capabilities on firm performance: How knowledge and capabilities accumulated from nonmarket arenas contribute to firm performance. *International Business Research, 11*(1), 1–18. https://doi.org/10.5539/ibr.v11n1p1

Christoph Rasche heads the chair of professional and corporate services at the University of Potsdam. He adopted visiting professorships at the Universities of Innsbruck, Alcala de Henares as well as the Hochschule Osnabruck. He teaches strategic and general management in national and international MBA programs with special respect to subjects connected with the healthcare and hospital industry. Formerly, he consulted with Droege International AG and was co-founder of Stratvanguard and the General Management Institute Potsdam. Prof. Rasche's research subjects circle around the field of strategic and general management in the healthcare and hospital sector, which witnesses an era of professional value creation by means of a strong management and leadership focus. Practically, he consults with healthcare players and is actively involved in executive trainings—ranging from corporate universities to MBA and PhD programs for healthcare professionals.

Nataliia Brehmer is a research associate at the Chair of Management, Professional Services and Sports Economics. She is teaching healthcare management and economics at the University of Potsdam and is a supervisor for a number of bachelor and master theses at the field of strategic management, consulting, sports- and healthcare management on the Faculties of Human Sciences and Economics and Social Studies at the University of Potsdam. Natalia Brehmer was engaged in the project DIGILOG and assisted the research efforts toward creating the innovative business models in health and elderly care. Practically, she is supervising the internships of sports management students and provides career consulting for young professionals. After finishing her master studies in the field of International Business and Negotiation she is working on her PhD Thesis with the topic Non-Market Strategies that provide business with non-economic means in the social and political arenas to tackle the hypercompetition and sustain the competitive advantage. Mrs. Brehmer is multilingual and is fluent in Polish, Ukrainian, English, German and Russian languages.

When the Patient Innovates. Emerging Practices in Service Ecosystems

4

Stefano Maffei, Massimo Bianchini, and Beatrice Villari

Abstract

Exploring the patient innovation culture is essential to design future solutions regarding service innovation in healthcare. A new family of collaborative, participatory and social, informal, independent, and experimental practices and experiences is emerging from below. Patients and their caregiving system create an emerging and pervasive phenomenon that can be identified as patient innovation. When we talk about it, we refer to a set of product, service, process, or system innovations generated by end-users. In a broader perspective, patient innovation represents the final step, perhaps the most radical or revolutionary, of a process of action and organization of individuals. The study of these bottom-up and independent innovations and innovators has been considered more concerning the research and political sphere than the strictly productive and service ones. Cure and care services are changing, incorporating inclusion, and the processes' enhancement guaranteed by the idea of an open and distributed (access to) augmentative technology. The healthcare system needs, thus, to question its more traditional techno-scientific and organizational models. Furthermore, it includes the patient perspective into service design processes.

S. Maffei (✉) · M. Bianchini · B. Villari
Department of Design, Politecnico di Milano, via Durando, 7, 20158 Milano, Italy
e-mail: stefano.maffei@polimi.it

M. Bianchini
e-mail: massimo.bianchini@polimi.it

B. Villari
e-mail: beatrice.villari@polimi.it

© The Author(s), under exclusive license to Springer Nature Switzerland AG 2022
M. A. Pfannstiel et al. (eds.), *Service Design Practices for Healthcare Innovation*,
https://doi.org/10.1007/978-3-030-87273-1_4

4.1 Toward a Patient-Driven Innovation Culture

Nowadays, exploring the patient innovation culture is essential to design future solutions regarding service innovation in healthcare. The first step is to understand what patient innovation is and how this form of user and bottom-up innovation fits into a broad framework of transformations in the healthcare ecosystem. The second step is to understand the evolution of the role and design agency of the patient in innovation processes for care to frame patient-driven innovation from a service perspective.

4.1.1 What is Patient Innovation?

Suppose that, we try to explore the world of innovation for care from a systemic and inclusive perspective, looking at the current processes of innovation in healthcare.

If so, we will immediately notice that a new family of collaborative, participatory and social, informal, independent, and experimental practices and experiences is emerging from below. In particular, we will immediately notice that patients and their caregiving system create an emerging and pervasive phenomenon—made of product-service solutions—that can be identified as patient innovation, patient-driven innovation, patient-led innovation, patient-driven healthcare, people-powered health, participatory healthcare, user-centered healthcare, open-source healthcare.

All these terms describe a particular form of user-driven innovation (Bogers et al., 2010; Trott et al., 2013; Von Hippel, 2009), a close relative of Von Hippel's free innovation (Von Hippel, 2016). It arises from the often unmet needs of user-patients and develops thanks to the activation of co-design processes with designers, makers, or specialists in the healthcare sector and/or the creation of alliances and coalitions between and with economic and institutional actors.

Patient innovation (Demonaco et al., 2019) is rapidly catching the attention of organizations and institutions operating in the healthcare sector and is climbing policymakers' agendas. Because it is the bearer of a powerful message of the future: an individual can act autonomously and personally on his/her condition of illness or disability to improve it. Acting as a designer, he/she projects and plans himself/herself into a better solution.

When we talk about patient innovation, we refer to a set of product, service, process, or system innovations generated by end-users (patients or caregivers). More generally, we talk about solutions for the treatment and fight against disabilities developed by individuals, groups, and communities as independent innovators.

In a broader perspective, patient innovation represents the final step, perhaps the most radical or revolutionary, of a forty-year process of reaction and organization of individuals (users) concerning the availability of mass-produced goods and services made by industry and endorsed by policies of economic-industrial states. From an operational perspective, approaches and practices such as user-driven innovation and participatory design (Von Hippel, 2005, 2016; Oliveira et al., 2015) allow people to collaborate in defining needs to propose new solutions. It also asks political and productive organizations to be more effective in integrating this perspective into existing solutions.

It concerns the progressive expansion of the agency of individuals through the digital transformation and democratization of information technologies, design, and (more recently) materialization of artifacts. This enabling of a dense and pervasive technological landscape contributes to expanding users' independence and possibilities in defining their forms of innovation in various sectors, including that of health.

For example, we speak of hackers, makers, and citizen science as people with a socially and technologically increased agency that focuses on the open, participatory and distributed design, and production of goods and services characterized by antagonistic or alternative positions toward the consumer society. They act in various fields of economic activity to acquire more power than the modification of available goods and services and progressive operational independence in the development of new solutions. Its enabling of a dense and pervasive technological landscape contributes to expanding users' independence and possibilities in defining their forms of innovation in various sectors, including that of health.

Thus, the study of bottom-up and independent innovators (Delfanti, 2013; Rosa et al., 2018), especially the one related to the theme of healthcare, has been considered more concerning the political sphere than the strictly productive and service ones.

Our research hypothesis is then to understand how this important change is progressively extending to the healthcare service field beyond the major drivers of socio-technical transformation (digitization, automation,...), and why and how it might have a specific impact on the transformation of the healthcare service sector.

Cure and care services are changing, incorporating inclusion and the processes' enhancement guaranteed by the idea of an open and distributed (access to) augmentative technology. The healthcare system needs to (partially) question its more traditional techno-scientific and organizational models and to be contaminated by more open, collective, circular, bottom-up, and user-driven forms of innovation that affect the world of patients.

What is the nexus between the world of healthcare services and patient innovation?

What is it about? What does it look like? How should it be observed and interpreted? To answer those questions, we need to understand what to observe and decide how to observe it.

What to observe concerns which are the factors that generate patient innovation within the world of services. The second thing to look at is the impact and effects that patient innovation has on the transformation of services in healthcare: welfare models linked to services, ways of (co)design of services, ecosystems of actors involved, models of services' development and adoption, the definition of new roles and competences.

Further, we can consider three different perspectives to analyze the relationship between service and patient innovation: the service provider's point of view, the service designer's point of view, and the patient innovator's point of view.

These three standpoints allow us to define: (i) the role of the patient innovator in the processes of ideation, design, management, and delivery of healthcare services; (ii) the dynamics of integration, adoption, and generation of patient innovation within the healthcare services, with a focus on the role of (service) design and technology; (iii) the role of legislative and regulatory systems that enable, hinder, and/or regulate the development of patient innovation within the healthcare services.

The lens we will adopt is that of the service design to better investigate the role of patients when they act as designers or makers. Indeed, design is a discipline that plays a mediating role between patient innovation and the healthcare service ecosystems (Maffei et al., 2019). Within the relationship between patient and service innovation, service design can work specifically on knowledge transfer processes from patient innovators to service providers, on the organization of co-creation/co-production processes of patient-centered and patient-driven services, on the scalability of patient innovator solutions in the market, and on the institutionalization of patient innovation (Trisher et al., 2020).

4.1.2 Current Challenges and Drivers in the Healthcare Ecosystem

The demand for healthcare services is proliferating. The resources available to national welfare states are increasingly limited, and the system and organizations are faced with a delicate process of cutting costs and improving the service quality.

Healthcare is predominantly a cost to society. In many European countries, the expenditure exceeds 10% of GDP (OECD/European Union, 2020) and will increase in the future due to current social and economic changes. This is why, reducing healthcare spending has become one of the crucial issues on the political agenda. However, healthcare is, in fact, a structural element of society and individuals, and today, it is a sector undergoing significant transformation. As mentioned, one of the main drivers that have a significant impact on healthcare transformation is the demographic one (World Health Organization, 2016) related to the aging of the population (European Commission, 2021). Another influential factor is the constant growth of public expenditure due to both the increase in administrative processes and the increase in professional services (Bauchner & Fontanarosa, 2018). In terms of change, the technology significantly influences the sector's transformation by fostering the delivery of new products services and more effective, personalized and patient-centered solutions (Hermes et al., 2020). Examples are the use of artificial intelligence, e-health, and applied robotics that has led to unthinkable solutions a few decades ago. However, the use of technology also involves taking into account risks and new challenges, such as the possibility of replicating human tissues or organs synthetically, or, on a different level, the issues related to production, use, and management of patients' data.

Last but not least, patients' expectations about the quality of services are influencing the demand for new services and benefits. Patients are more informed, more aware of treatments and cures, and more generally interested in an extended concept of well-being (Francis, 2010). Further, they have acquired greater purchasing power over time (Røtnes & Staalesen, 2009).

Care is, therefore, only one element of the patient experience, so much so that the current paradigm is one of "from cure to care" in which issues such as autonomy, prevention, constant education, and even attention to sustainability become central elements.

On this basis, there is an urgent need for transformation in healthcare (Berry, 2019) at various levels: from the world of policy and organizations to services.

One of the mechanisms for innovation in this area is to adopt people-centered solutions (World Health Organization, 2007) that consider the needs of the individual and their cognitive, emotional, and contextual aspects. Despite the growing interest in people-centered approaches and solutions, (Sinaiko et al., 2019) identify some barriers to their diffusion. In particular, they refer to the lack of available data, a low level of trust in exchanging data and information between actors in the system, the difficulty of introducing new processes and practices in organizational contexts, as well as the lack of incentives and the need for greater collaboration between different competencies and between organizations, institutions, and end-users (Patricio et al., 2020).

Collaboration between different actors is crucial to propose and implement changes in the healthcare system. The landscape involves a large number of actors with different roles and competencies: policymakers and government institutions, providers (hospitals, doctors, caregivers…), financing institutions (e.g., insurance companies), suppliers (e.g., pharmaceutical companies and pharmacies), and finally, the large patient population, whose number far exceeds the other categories.

This is a huge tank of collective and individual intelligence (Mulgan, 2018) derived from everyday practice and experience, which represents, and its involvement can, in practice, accelerate the grounding of certain specific solutions, the simplification of processes, and the modification of certain operational practices. Therefore, it is a question of adopting management and coordination models that favor collaboration between the actors in the network (Kodama, 2018) by balancing the needs of the individual and the system itself.

Participatory approaches, co-creation, and co-design themes are thus a way to foster innovation in healthcare (OECD, 2017; World Health Organization, 2016), favoring open and bottom-up processes that consider the complexity of the ecosystem.

4.1.3 From Co-Design to Co-Production: The Shift in User's Involvement

The relationship between design and healthcare has a long tradition, starting in the 1960s with the redefinition of hospital spaces and continuing to the present day with an increased focus on service (Cousin, 1965). Today, service design—understood both as a professional practice and a design research process—is one of the crucial players in healthcare innovation.

The focus on user experience by healthcare providers has strengthened the need to rethink the products' and services' offer and their delivery in the marketplace to respond to new socio-economic needs and the increased awareness of citizens on healthcare and well-being issues. It has contributed to the development of healthcare services and patients' role evolution as active participants in innovation processes.

In design, the collaboration between experts and non-experts is outlined through three main strategies that revolve around the concept of inclusion and participation. In healthcare, we talk about co-design when there is a collaboration between patients, professionals, and the community to develop a new solution. We call it co-production when the participation of people is focused on service delivery and co-creation when users are involved in all phases of development, from conception to development and implementation (Freire and Sangiorgi, 2010). Thus, co-creation processes imply empowerment and emancipation of end-users as active participants in change (Sangiorgi, 2011).

Freire and Sangiorgi (Freire and Sangiorgi, 2010, see Table 4.1) describe a healthcare innovation ladder, which outlines a shift from mass production to mass collaboration, underlining how, in a "mass collaboration" model, the design focuses on behavioral change and new services models adopting co-creation processes.

Design intervention considers the whole journey of the patient and its community, with an approach that goes beyond the care itself: therefore, it evaluates the whole experience (i.e., before, during, and after the interaction with the cure/care process). In this evolution, co-creation and co-design of solutions assume a significant value since they feed the design paths of a system of needs, skills, and perspectives that revolve around daily life.

Table 4.1 Healthcare service innovation ladder

Production and value model	Service philosophy	Design focus	Design model	Examples
Mass production	Disease-centered	Service efficiency	Process analysis	The productives
Mass customization	Patient-centered	Interaction and service relationship	Co-design and experience-based methods	Agenda cards enable
Mass collaboration	Patient-led	Behavioral change and new service models	Co-creation	Open-door actimobs

Source Freire and Sangiorgi (2010), p. 46.

Service design helps this scenario by focusing on the human-centered perspective, activating collaborative practices, and supporting a systemic change that considers social, economic, technological, and environmental factors. It is indeed an interdisciplinary approach, focusing on the user experience and the interaction between different actors in an ecosystem.

Examples are the American Mayo Clinic Center for Innovation, which was the first to include a service design team in the organization, the Helix Center (UK), an innovation laboratory launched as a joint venture between Imperial College London and the Royal College and then based in St. Mary's Hospital; Kaiser Permanente Design Consultancy which provides design solutions for complex internal healthcare challenges. Alternatively, The Point of Care Foundation (UK), which bases its activities on the experience-based co-design (EBCD) and patient and family-centered care (PFCC) methodologies, and ExperioLab in Sweden, which focuses its activities on the patient-oriented service innovation and co-creation principles.

Another interesting example is represented by some living laboratories of the ENOLL network specialized in healthcare—such as the living laboratory Thessa, Hall of Thessaloniki University—that are creating a network of infrastructures able to provide services to support patient innovation in the healthcare system.

Considering service design also as a research practice, several initiatives in the healthcare field can be recognized. In general, they combine co-creation and service design theory and practice dealing with specific areas, such as mental health (Sangiorgi et al., 2019), cognitive deficiencies (Carr, 2018), or communities of the elderly (Kälviäinen & Morelli, 2013).

All these experiences are characterized by the collaboration between service designers, researchers, patients, and caregivers, supporting communities with a solid connection to their territory. However, such processes require resources in terms of time and money (both in the organizational and implementation phases), empathy from all stakeholders (Bate & Robert, 2007), and a high level of commitment. Moreover, the initiatives often remain in the exploratory and ideational phase, with difficulties in bringing solutions to the market.

However, the crucial aspect is that service design in healthcare does not apply exclusively to service performance but extends to the whole system precisely because of its transformative capacity on processes and organizations (Anderson et al., 2018; Cottam & Leadbeater, 2004; Sangiorgi, 2011). Furthermore, it implies a stronger connection between service design and system thinking and a stronger focus on value co-creation between patient communities and providers (Wetter-Edman et al., 2014).

Service design can, therefore, offer a "(…) full spectrum of action-oriented research approaches, from design science focused on supporting expert decision-making and problem-solving, to participatory service design focused on sensemaking to collectively build innovative health futures" (Patricio et al., 2019, p. 117). It implies co-creating solutions capable of responding to the needs of individuals, organizations, and society itself. It means moving from the micro-level of touchpoints and interactions (Sangiorgi, 2009) to the definition of new service concepts capable of creating value for the ecosystem (Patrício et al., 2018), up to institutional change (Vink et al., 2019).

4.1.4 Patient-Driven Innovation: A Service Perspective

The healthcare industry has long recognized the importance of re-establishing the relationship with patients and their families, considering the different experiences, needs, and ways of relating between providers and users. As early as 2001, the IOM outlined a more efficient, safe, equitable, and patient-centered healthcare model (IOM, 2001).

On the one hand, it implies the transformation of the role of the patient from a passive element to an active and integral element of the innovation process; on the other hand, the transformation of the healthcare model to go beyond the strictly medical one integrating the social dimension.

In a model where the patient is at the center, hierarchies change as well as the decision-making processes, and the difference between experts and non-experts thins out. It implies a stronger collaboration between different actors and competencies so that end-users become co-creators (co-developers and co-innovators) (Schiavone, 2020), again underlining the value of the social dimension and of experience-based learning.

Recent innovations are open, interactive, collaborative, multi-dimensional, and systemic processes that incorporate external stimuli to contribute to the growth of organizations. In this perspective, innovation is produced by opening up processes to the outside world that traditionally preserve organizations. Traditional forms of research and development have evolved to include processes that involve actors outside the organization to change as part of a broader ecosystem.

In these models, therefore, the exchange of knowledge, even tacit (Collins, 1974; Polany, 1967), is essential, as well as the role of lead users and citizens in innovation processes (von Hippel, 2005).

In this perspective, NESTA outlines an approach described as people-powered health which proposes a model of healthcare in which prevention and treatment are not relegated to hospitals and physicians alone, but are supported by communities, are accessible at home or in the workplace, and supported by infrastructure, and other services (Horne et al., 2013). This model also redefines the relationship with technology that is available to professionals and centers of expertise and is a technology distributed in communities and used by patients through personalized solutions.

This contribution poses some reflections on the processes and services that patient-driven innovation generates, investigating collaborative, distributed and networked product-service models in which the patient is a critical factor in the innovation process as a bearer of knowledge and skills and an active part of a broader social community.

For decades, the healthcare industry has relied on traditional models of innovation and development where solutions were built in the laboratory, distributed, and administered to patients. This model has evolved through a concept that includes care as one of the phases of the patient experience and considers patient communities, families, caregivers as knowledge and value bearers. In this perspective, communities (and individuals) assume an active role in developing and improving health solutions contributing to the conception and even implementation (Maffei et al., 2017). It can be possible thanks to the advantages brought by digital and new technologies and the possibility of sharing knowledge directly among peers through digital networks.

Therefore, reasoning in terms of patient-driven innovation involves redefining the relationship with the individual patient, with the social and territorial community of reference, with technology and digital, and with the healthcare ecosystem. In terms of solutions, new products/services emerge. Patients can manage their care journey more independently. They can control, monitor, and share data autonomously (patient-generated content), compare themselves with peers, and participate in co-creation and co-design processes with different communities of stakeholders. The role of the patient shifts "(…) from being a minimally informed advice recipient to an active participant, instigating collaborator, information sharer, peer leader, and self-tracker engaged in participative medicine; a transition is underway from paternalistic health care to partnership models (…)." (Swan et al., 2009; p. 513).

These are, therefore, processes in which change is not just about the product/service but involves systemic innovation, where the aim is to redefine relationships, governance models, hierarchies, and responsibilities (Mulgan & Leadbeater, 2013).

From a service design perspective, it is possible to create different kinds of innovative solutions on-demand and on-site, co-created within a large community and shared across a network, and that takes into account the whole patient journey, not just the treatment phase.

This is especially evident in the area of community-based services, in which solutions arise thanks to the involvement of communities of practice (often active on the territory) in co-design and co-creation processes.

In this service type, the patient is an integral part of a social network that supports or enables his or her relationship with the healthcare system. Moreover, as it has already been pointed out, the community of patients is a vast community of practice, which—through experiential learning—can provide specific solutions to even very complex problems. In this framework, the relationship between the individual and the social communities (e.g., other patients, caregivers, family members) becomes crucial for innovation. Therefore, the communities and the territory in which they operate are the fertile ground where mutual help and collaboration are central values and generators of innovation. In social innovation, ideas are generated collectively to improve community well-being (Dawson & Daniels, 2010). In healthcare services, initiatives in this area are linked to co-design and co-creation processes developed with and for people belonging to specific groups. Therefore, the patient is the one who creates and designs the solutions by collaborating both with physicians, external experts, and social communities involved in the health pathway. Peer-support services beyond the specific care pathways (e.g., educational activities, sports, entertainment, time banks,…) are also created by training new figures, such as health trainers and well-being coaching services (Horne et al., 2013). These figures are simultaneously members of the territorial community (e.g., pharmacists, carers, volunteers…) and elements of support to the community itself.

In the development of solutions, patients are, therefore, considered experts by experience (NESTA, 2013) who contribute to the design of new services or improve existing ones through direct participation.

In the area of personality disorders or emotional and behavioral problems, an example is the service user network (SUN) project supported by Mind Croydon in the UK. It has led to the creation of several support centers for people with mental health problems and involved the communities themselves in promoting co-created services together with professionals. Similarly, the Recovery Net project (https://www.recovery.net) on mental health services was developed in which patient communities and expert communities were involved in co-design and co-production. It has led to the formation of three Recovery Co-Labs in Brescia (Italy) (Sangiorgi et al., 2020), creating new services based on the needs and characteristics of local communities. Another example is the work carried out by the British organization Groundswell (http://www.groundswell.org.uk), which supports homeless people and their access to care by providing a training course of peers dedicated to homeless people and aimed at improving access to health services also in the prevention phase, such as a visit to the dentist or optician. It has made it possible to improve the relationship between the service provider and the community, starting from people's direct experiences, strengthening both the social values and the relationship with the public service and the network of local associations. In these cases, therefore, innovation has a collaborative and social nature. The patient is not the recipient of the process or solution but also assumes a decision-making role in both designing and implementing solutions.

Only in the last few years, we have seen an institutional recognition of patient innovation, mainly through experiments and pilot projects that try to connect and formalize these processes and the places that enable them—such as makerspaces and FabLabs within the healthcare system. Through its Agency VINNOVA, Sweden has stimulated the development of makerspaces connected to hospitals explicitly working in the field of patient innovation. Svensson and Hartmann (2018) point out that laboratories such as hospital makerspaces can play a crucial role in developing patient innovation and that these innovations generate an economic return. More specifically, hospital makerspaces can operate as centers that select and support the ideas of patient innovators to support the development of solutions. Finally, these models can be used as a policy incubator to support service innovation in healthcare.

4.2 Enhanced Patient Role in Service Care: A New Interplay

The current traditional ecosystem of healthcare services has not yet transitioned toward participatory forms where the role of the main actor, the patient, is significant in orienting the exploration and choice of the production of public and private service offerings. Despite this resistance, many areas of experimentation are progressively emerging which challenge this status quo.

The area of platforms/social networks where communities exchange practices and knowledge is an interesting arena where patients can be better informed, more attentive to care, demand transparency and have a more mature perception of the products and services available. Online platforms and social networks play an essential role in facilitating connections between people, exchanging information, and collaboration among peers. In addition, the use of platforms enables patients to build a dialog, support bottom-up initiatives, raise funds, and share solutions on very specific problems. Platforms are divided into those dealing with generic issues, those dealing with specific causes and those involving physicians.

Perhaps the best-known example for platforms dealing with generic content is Patient-Innovation (http://www.patient-innovation.com), the platform founded by Pedro Oliveira. It is a platform that collects solutions created by patients and caregivers on any topic and in any geographical area to share and create solutions to improve the quality of life, not only concerning care. Another example is the platform Healthtalk (http://www.healthtalk.org), which collects video experiences from patients to support people with similar problems. The same concept is developed—even earlier—by PatientsLikeMe (http://www.patientslikeme.com), which allows creating connections between people with similar problems through a question and answer mechanism. The well-known platform was created in 1998 by Stephen Heywood, who was diagnosed with ALS. Since then, the family has been working to find a way to slow down the progress of the disease, and one of the significant needs that emerged was to understand how other people were reacting to the disease and what knowledge they had about treatments and therapies. Today, PatientsLikeMe is the largest online community for sharing experiences in healthcare.

One particular community is the e-NABLE platform (http://www.enablingthefuture.org), a global community of volunteers who use 3D printing to design and make low-cost prostheses for children and adults. The Web site says the community is made up of around 20,000 volunteers who have created open-source solutions (for arms and legs) adopted in more than 100 countries worldwide. On a different scale is Mirrorable™ (http://www.fightthestroke.org), a platform offering home-based rehabilitation therapy for children who have suffered brain damage at a very early stage in their lives. The platform, linked to the Fightthestroke Foundation, was created by two parents whose son suffered a stroke with infantile cerebral palsy. From this initiative, activities and services—such as opening a Neonatal and Pediatric Stroke Center in collaboration with the Gaslini Pediatric Hospital in Genoa (Italy) —have sprung up. These examples arise from patients' or caregivers' direct experience and their relationship with peers, and then develop, grow, and spread thanks to technology.

From the direct and unmediated interaction with the expression of the personal needs and visions, which do not find an offering in the healthcare service solutions' market, we find the emergent area of the self-developed technological devices (artifacts, product-services, apps). In this area, patients participate as experts or even as designers and developers of solutions.

The benefits of involving patients in the design, supply, and distribution of healthcare solutions derive, in fact, from the diffusion and adoption of new technologies by citizens and non-experts. The possibility of prototyping solutions even in unconventional spaces (think of the spread of 3D printing, open software, and the role of FabLabs) has enabled new areas of innovation. They have facilitated the emergence of new solutions tailored around the final user, customizable, wearable, allowing the patient to use the services even from home. These are, therefore, products services that represent alternatives to mass-produced solutions and are tailored to the specific patients' and communities' needs.

The development of technology has also enabled advanced solutions, in line with the so-called 4Ps model, which requires healthcare to be predictive, preventive, personalized, and participative. An example is the adoption of digital twins, which allow decentralizing some monitoring and data collection processes through AI. In this context, technological devices and wearable devices are data collection centers supporting the patient and enabled by a complex system of touchpoints (thanks to IoT).

Polifactory (the Makerspace of the Politecnico di Milano, http://www.polifactory. it) has carried out the mapping of patient-driven solutions through the platform Design Healthcare Innovation (http://www.designhealthcareinnovation.it). It describes the ecosystem of widespread innovation of products and services in healthcare and collects significant cases on different patient-driven and patient-centered solutions. One example is DHEART (http://www.d-heartcare.com), a device that can convert any smartphone into a portable electrocardiograph, which can be managed by the patient himself, who can share his ultrasound scan directly with his doctor through an app. The collection and sharing of data allow daily monitoring of heart patients or rapid diagnosis in an emergency, communicating the patient's health status to medical staff for rescue. This solution was developed by a cardiac patient who later founded the start-up. The same process was followed in the case of Amiko (http://www.amiko.io). This electronic device is attached to the drug (blister, inhaler, or insulin pen) to track its use in detail and transfer the data to a platform that allows family members and the doctor or pharmacist to verify the correct intake of the drug, improving the process of patient care and monitoring. In this case, a caregiver (who was caring for his father) conceived the product and came up with the solution that became a start-up. In these examples, therefore, the direct experience of the patient, the explanation of particular needs, and the adoption of technology led to identifying particular solutions that could dialog with the components of the healthcare system (hospitals, doctors, carers,...) but managed directly by the end-user. Moreover, the patient and caregivers change their role within the system, from the one who receives the care to the one who proposes a new solution, experiments with it, and puts it into practice. What emerges then—for the patient and their communities—is the paradigmatic shift from service user to service provider.

Finally, we may identify some recurrent elements that correlate patient and service innovation from the literature analysis and the best practices.

The relationship between patient innovation and service culture builds an experimentation space that stimulates the interaction between a prototyping-based culture, typical of maker culture, with a trial-based culture that belongs to the medical, scientific approach. In this space, there is the possibility to think of more radical solutions by experimenting with out-of-the-box models of innovation. A close relationship exists between solving situated care challenges and the development of large-scale service solutions: they are props of possible future directions where the patient-driven processes of (co)design-prototyping experimentation originate a plurality of experimented design solutions which constitute an open innovation landscape.

These solutions might enter the market through a social adoption and test (e.g., mediated by Patients Associations) that might use the digital platforms for disseminating and distributing this innovative approach. It might enable a patient innovation systemic accessibility—from spaces to technologies, from data and information flows to the solutions themselves—which defines a more open and inclusive model of healthcare service innovation.

It may become a new service for all perspectives, which empowers diversity in product-service systems offerings with an interplay between customization and standardization, i.e., economies of scope and scale. The personalization of solutions generates an area that overlaps economies of scale and scope. Finally, it enhances the accountability of this transformative space, making these processes traceable, measurable, and assessable.

4.3 Conclusions: Enabling Solutions for a Co-Creating Space in the Healthcare Ecosystem

What are the possible evolutionary trajectories of patient innovation, and how can this phenomenon contribute to defining future scenarios for the healthcare (eco) system?

To answer this question, we have to understand the evolution of the patient's role and his design agency.

Thanks to an unprecedented socio-technical development, a lot of innovative fields and processes, usually guided by large-scale institutions and companies, within a mission-oriented innovation perspective (Mazzuccato, 2018) might be now enabled starting from an individual need.

It means that a patient innovator, through his/her action, might be imagined in a future (service) designer role. According to the evolution of the role of the patient in society, this future trajectory depends on the socio-technical enabling of augmented individuals or individuals-organizations and from the constitution of forms of free and independent innovation spaces dedicated to the healthcare field (e.g., open innovation environment). All these conditions will be able to configure new care product-service solutions in a collaborative and entrepreneurial dimension, influencing the way in which we might design or procure public services related to healthcare.

The recent pandemic has revealed much about the capabilities and limitations of both the organizational models of the health system and the open and bottom-up innovation processes applied to healthcare. The COVID-19 crisis has redefined health and safety care standards, expanded digital access to health services, restored the centrality of local health organization models in terms of geographical distribution, widespread coverage, and proximity medicine and gave strong social recognition to health workers. The pandemic has also accelerated the debate on the potential of distributed production, from more professional and industrial forms to do-it-yourself. During the initial phases of the health emergency, an extraordinary global mobilization of designers, makers, FabLabs—engaged in the manufacture of protective devices, valves, and components for respirators (The story of the hacked Decathlon diving mask is emblematic, Decathlon (2021))—however, clashed with their limits in the confrontation with the healthcare system, the demand for certification, and quality control. If observed as a whole, these two phenomena outline precisely the need for an open and patient innovation ecosystem based on a more integrated relationship between healthcare service, open design, distributed production, industrial production, and legislative/regulatory system.

Empowered patients are thus individuals who can take greater control over decision-making and treatment processes. Thanks to more accessible access to information, peer-to-peer exchange of knowledge between patients, caregivers, and physicians, the use of mobile apps and smart healthcare devices, they might act as innovation enablers. Using a combination of health literacy, digital literacy, self-efficacy, some empowered patients become expert patients. They consciously manage to extract from their health experience a knowledge value useful for the orientation of decision-making and organizational choices in care, research, and social responsibility (Iorno, 2019). The final step from patient expert to patient innovator occurs when there are the technical-scientific, mutual respect, trust, and safety conditions between patient and service provider to move from a process of shared decision-making to one of shared solution making. This transition needs to be supported by special innovation spaces (labs, makerspaces, FabLabs). It requires tools that can increase the speed, quality, and synchronization between the decision-making and design processes dedicated to caring and, therefore, the effectiveness of the solutions. Technologies such as collaborative platforms (e.g.,. collaborative design platforms, AR/VR collaborative platforms) with simultaneous access to data generated by patient innovation ecosystems and service healthcare ecosystems could allow patients and service providers to collaborate in an evolved way on decision-making and design choices. They are shaping care processes almost in real time. This transition needs the co-design of a new generation of services that shift the learning models applied in medical education to those of patient literacy and try to shift the use of enabling technologies from primarily rehabilitative environments (e.g., stroke and orthopedic rehabilitation) to design-driven healthcare innovative environments.

Some cases like Lookoflife, Tommi, and Rehability (see http://www.lookoflife.it, http://www.tommigame.com), http://www.rehability.it tell us that this transition is not only possible but already started. In Tommi and Lookoflife, the use of enabling technologies translates into solutions based on patients' augmented participation through a processes' gamification supporting care or rehabilitation.

In Rehability, the user-patient involvement occurs directly in the co-design phase of the product-service solution based on the use of enabling technologies. This approach also outlines a possible digital twin model applicable to all phases of the patient innovation process. The digital twin is a digital replica that allows the modeling of the state of a physical asset or system. In the healthcare field, serious steps have been taken in creating digital twins of patients and medical devices (Tolga et al., 2020). The digital twin of a patient innovation process would connect the innovation environments for care: patient innovators and service providers are always in contact to co-design and co-produce PSS solutions.

In conclusion, the relationship between patient and service innovation in healthcare can be seen as a progressive path of convergence, interaction, and hybridization between individuals (patient innovators) and organizations (service providers). It is a path that began a few decades ago and is inevitably intertwined with the development of the digitalization of our society.

The first phase, coinciding with the first digitization of the society, allowed patients and their caregivers to connect to organize themselves more and better to start exercising patient advocacy in the care process and society.

The second phase, coinciding with the distributed digitalization of the society, already allows patients and their associations to develop the first patient innovation processes by collaborating in peer-to-peer mode with specialists, designers, makers, and FabLabs and proposing care solutions to service providers.

The third phase, coinciding with the digital transformation of the society, will allow patient innovators to operate in an evolved, organic way in the healthcare system, participating in the transformation of care services. In two words: a patient revolution.

References

Anderson, S., Nasr, L., & Rayburn, S. W. (2018). Transformative service research and service design: Synergistic effects in healthcare. *Service Industries Journal, 38*(1–2), 99–113. https://doi.org/10.1080/02642069.2017.1404579

Bate, P., & Robert, G. (2007). Bringing user experience to healthcare improvement: the concepts. Methods and practices of experience-based design. Abingdon: Radcliffe.

Bauchner, H., & Fontanarosa, P. B. (2018). Health care spending in the United States compared with 10 other high-income countries. *JAMA, 319*(10), 990. PMID: 29536083. https://doi.org/10.1001/jama.2018.1879.

Berry, L. L. (2019). Service innovation is urgent in healthcare. *AMS Review, 9*(1–2), 78–92. https://doi.org/10.1007/s13162-019-00135-x

Bogers, M., Afuah, A., & Bastian, B. (2010). Users as innovators: A review, critique, and future research directions. *Journal of Management, 36*(4), 857–875. https://doi.org/10.1177/0149206309353944

Carr, V. (2018). *Adapting the design process for different learning styles and abilities, ServDes2018—Service design proof of concept* (pp. 266–280). Linkoping University Electronic Press.

Collins, H. (1974). The TEA set: Tacit knowledge and scientific networks. *Science Studies, 4*(2), 165–186. https://doi.org/10.1177/030631277400400203CorpusID:26917303

European Commission. (2021). The 2021 Ageing ReportEconomic & Budgetary Projections for the EU Member States (2019–2070). https://ec.europa.eu/info/sites/default/files/economy-finance/ip148_en_0.pdf. Accessed 15 June 2021.

Cottam, H., & Leadbeater, C. (2004). *Open Welfare designs on the public good*. Design Council.

Cousins, J. (1965). A general purpose bedstead for hospitals. *Design, 195*(March), 52–57.

Dawson, P., & Daniels, L. (2010). Understanding social innovation: A provisional framework. *International Journal of Technology Management, 51*(1), 9–21. https://doi.org/10.1504/IJTM.2010.033125

Decathlon (n. d.) Decathlon easybreath mask: COVID-19 update. https://www.decathlon.com/blogs/inside-decathlon/decathlon-easybreath-mask-covid-19-update. Accessed 29 July 2021.

Delfanti, A. (2013). *Biohackers*. Pluto Press, London.

DeMonaco, H., Oliveira, P., Torrance, A., Von Hippel, C. & Von Hippel, E. (2019). When patients become innovators. MIT Sloan Management Review, Magazine Spring 2019, Issue Research Future. https://sloanreview.mit.edu/article/when-patients-become-innovators/. Accessed 24 June 2021.

Francis, R. (2010). Independent Inquiry into care provided by Mid Staffordshire NHS Foundation Trust January 2005—March 2009, Vol. I. https://assets.publishing.service.gov.uk/government/uploads/system/uploads/attachment_data/file/279109/0375_i.pdf. Accessed 15 June 2021.

Freire, K., & Sangiorgi, D. (2010). Service design and healthcare innovation: From consumption to co-production and co-creation. In *Paper presented at the 2010 Nordic Conference on Service Design and Service Innovation, Linkoping, Sweden, December 1–3*. https://ep.liu.se/konferensartikel.aspx?series=ecp&issue=60&Article_No=4. Accessed 15 June 2021.

Hermes, S., Riasanow, T., Clemons, E. K., Böhm, M., & Krcmar, H. (2020). The digital transformation of the healthcare industry: Exploring the rise of emerging platform ecosystems and their influence on the role of patients. *Business Research, 13*(3), 1033–1069. https://doi.org/10.1007/s40685-020-00125-x

Horne, M., Khan, H., & Corrigan, P. (2013). *People powered health: Health for people, by people and with people*. London: NESTA. https://media.nesta.org.uk/documents/health_for_people_by_people_and_with_people.pdf. Accessed 29 June 2021.

Institute of Medicine. (2001). *Crossing the quality chasm: A new health system for the 21st century*. Washington (DC): National Academies Press (US).

Iorno, T. (2019). Associazioni di pazeinti e innovazione sanitaria contemporanea. In S. Maffei, M. Bianchini, B. Parini, L. Cipriani (Eds.) MakeToCare[2]. *La patient innovation in Italia tra progetto e mercato* (Lapland University Press). Monza: Libraccio Editore.

Kälviäinen, M., & Morelli, N. (2013). Developing services to support elderly everyday interaction. In S. Miettinen (Ed.) *Service Design with Theory: Discussions on Change, Value and Methods* (1st edn, vol. 1). Rovaniemi: Lapland University Press.

Kodama, M. (2018). *Collaborative dynamic capabilities for service innovation*. Palgrave Macmillan.

Maffei, S., Bianchini, M., Parini, B., & Delli Zotti, E. (2017). *MakeToCare. An ecosystem of actors and user-centred solutions for innovation in the healthcare sector*. Monza: Libraccio Editore.

Maffei, S., Bianchini, M., Parini, B., & Cipriani, L. (2019). MakeToCare[2]. *La patient innovation in Italia tra progetto e mercato*. Monza: Libraccio Editore.

Mazzuccato, M. (2018). Mission-oriented innovation policies: Challenges and opportunities. *Industrial and Corporate Change, 27*(5), 803–815. https://doi.org/10.1093/icc/dty034

Mulgan, G. (2018). *Big mind: How collective intelligence can change our world*. Princeton University Press.

Mulgan, G., & Leadbeater, C. (2013). *Systems Innovation Discussion Paper*. NESTA, London. https://media.nesta.org.uk/documents/systems_innovation_discussion_paper.pdf. Accessed 29 June 2021.

NESTA. (2013). More than medicine: New services for people powered health. NESTA. https://media.nesta.org.uk/documents/more_than_medicine.pdf. Accessed29 June 2021.

OECD. (2017). The next generation of health reforms. https://www.oecd.org/health/ministerial/ministerial-statement-2017.pdf. Accessed 15 June 2021.

OECD, European Union,. (2020). *Health at a Glance: Europe 2020: State of Health in the EU Cycle*. OECD Publishing. https://doi.org/10.1787/82129230-en

Oliveira, P., Zejnilovic, L., Canhão, H., & Von Hippel, E. (2015). Innovation by patients with rare diseases and chronic needs. *Orphanet Journal of Rare Diseases, 10*(1), 1–9. PMID: 25887544 PMCID: PMC4404234. https://doi.org/10.1186/s13023-015-0257-2.

Patrício, L., Pinho, N., Teixeira, J., & Fisk, R. P. (2018). Service design for value networks: Enabling value co-creation interactions in healthcare. *Service Science, 10*(1), 76–97. https://doi.org/10.1287/serv.2017.0201

Patrício, L., Teixeira, J. G., & Vink, J. (2019). A service design approach to healthcare innovation: From decision-making to sense-making and institutional change. *Academy of Marketing Science Review, 9*(1/2), 115–120. https://doi.org/10.1007/s13162-019-00138-8

Patrício, L., Sangiorgi, D., Mahr, D., Čaić, M., Kalantari, S., & Sundar, S. (2020). Leveraging service design for healthcare transformation: Toward people-centered, integrated, and technology-enabled healthcare systems. *Journal of Service Management, 31*(5), 889–909. https://doi.org/10.1108/JOSM-11-2019-0332

Polanyi, M. (1967). *The tacit dimension*. Routledge & Kegan Paul.

Rosa, P., Guimarães Pereira, A., & Ferretti, F. (2018). *Futures of work: Perspectives from the maker movement*. Publications Office of the European Union. https://publications.jrc.ec.europa.eu/repository/bitstream/JRC110999/kjna29296enn.pdf. Accessed 29 June 2021.

Røtnes, R., & Staalesen, P. D. (2009). New methods for user driven innovation in the health care sector Report, Nordic Innovation Centre project. https://www.diva-portal.org/smash/get/diva2:707163/FULLTEXT01.pdf. Accessed 15 June 2009.

Sangiorgi, D. (2011). Transformative services and transformation design. *International Journal of Design, 5*(1), 29–40.

Sangiorgi, D., Farr, M., McAllister, S., Mulvale, G., Sneyd, M., Vink, J., & Warwick, L. (2019). Designing in highly contentious areas: perspectives on a way forward for mental healthcare transformation. *The Design Journal, 22*(Sup. 1), 309–330. https://doi.org/10.1080/14606925.2019.1595422.

Sangiorgi D., Lucchi F., & Carrera M. (2020). Recovery-net: A multilevel and collaborative approach to mental healthcare transformation. In A. Battisti, M. Marceca, S. Iorio (Eds.) *Urban Health. AIMETA 2019. Green Energy and Technology* (pp. 189–200). Cham, Switzerland: Springer International Publishing.

Sangiorgi, D. (2009). Building up a framework for service design research. In *8th European Academy of Design Conference, The Robert Gordon University* (Ed.) (pp. 415–420). Scotland: Aberdeen.

Schiavone, F. (2020). *User innovation in healthcare how patients and caregivers react creatively to illness*. Switzerland: Springer International Publishing.

Sinaiko, A. D., Szumigalski, K., Eastman, D. Alyna, T., & Chien. (2019). Delivery of patient centered care in the US healthcare system: What is standing in its way? Robert Wood Johnson Foundation Optimizing Value in Health Care Program: Academy Health. https://www.academyhealth.org/sites/default/files/deliverypatientcenteredcare_august2019.pdf. Accessed 29 June 2021.

Svensson, P. O., & Hartmann., R. K. (2018). Policies to promote user innovation: Makerspaces and clinician innovation in Swedish hospitals. *Research Policy, 47*(1), 277–288. https://doi.org/10.1016/j.respol.2017.11.006

Swan, M. (2009). Emerging patient-driven health care models: An examination of health social networks, consumer personalized medicine and quantified self-tracking. *International Journal of Environmental Research and Public Health, 6*(2), 492–525. https://doi.org/10.3390/ijerph6020492

Tolga, E., Arif Furkan, M., & Dilara, D. (2020). The digital twin revolution in healthcare. In *4th International Symposium on Multidisciplinary Studies and Innovative Technologies (ISMSIT)*. University of Turku, Aalborg University Hospital, BioCon Valley (Eds.). https://doi.org/10.1109/ISMSIT50672.2020.9255249.

Trischler, J., Johnson, M., & Kristensson, P. (2020). A service ecosystem perspective on the diffusion of sustainability-oriented user innovations. *Journal of Business Research, 116* (August 2020), 552–560. https://doi.org/10.1016/j.jbusres.2020.01.011.

Trott, P., Van der Duin, P., & Hartmann, D. (2013). Users as innovators? Exploring the limitations of user-driven innovation. *Prometheus, 31*(2), 125–138. https://doi.org/10.1080/08109028.2013.818790

Vink, J., Edvardsson, B., Wetter-Edman, K., & Tronvoll, B. (2019). Reshaping mental models enabling innovation through service design. *Journal of Service Management, 30*(1), 75–104. https://doi.org/10.1108/JOSM-08-2017-0186

von Hippel, E. (2005). *Democratizing innovation*. MIT Press.

von Hippel, E. (2009). Democratizing innovation: The evolving phenomenon of user innovation. *International Journal of Innovation Science, 1*(1), 29–40. https://doi.org/10.1260/175722209787951224

von Hippel, E. (2016). *Free innovation*. MIT Press.

Wetter-Edman, K., Sangiorgi, D., Edvardsson, B., Holmlid, S., Gronroos, C., & Mattelmaki, T. (2014). Design for value co-creation: Exploring synergies between design for service and service logic. *Service Science, 6*(2), 106–121. https://doi.org/10.1287/serv.2014.0068.

World Health Organization. (2007). People-centred Health Care. A Policy Framework. https://www.who.int/publications/i/item/9789290613176. Accessed 15 June 2021.

World Health Organization. (2016). Framework on Integrated, People-Centred Health Services. https://apps.who.int/gb/ebwha/pdf_files/WHA69/A69_39-en.pdf?ua=1&ua=1. Accessed 15 June 2021.

Stefano Maffei Architect and PhD in Design. Full Professor at the Design Department, Politecnico di Milano, where he teaches Advanced Product-Service System at the School of Design. He's the Director of Polifactory, the FabLab/Makerspace of Politecnico di Milano. He's also the Director of the Specializing Master in Service Design, POLI.design, Politecnico di Milano. His research interests are focused on service design innovation, on new models of production and distribution of goods and systems of advanced and distributed micro-production.

Massimo Bianchini Designer and PhD in Design. Assistant professor at the Design Department, Politecnico di Milano where he teaches Integrated Product Design at the School of Design. He's the Lab Manager at Polifactory, the FabLab/Makerspace of Politecnico di Milano. His research interests are focused on open and distributed design and production, small urban manufacturing, user-driven innovation, indie innovation, and circular innovation.

Beatrice Villari PhD in Design. Associate Professor at the Design Department, Politecnico di Milano. She teaches Service Design and Design methods at the School of Design, Politecnico di Milano. She is also the Co-Director of the Specializing Master in Service Design, POLI.design, Politecnico di Milano. Her main research interests are focused on service innovation, service design, design for social innovation, and design for policy and governments.

Negotiating Care Through Tangible Tools and Tangible Service Designing in Emergent Public Health Service Ecosystems

5

Karianne Rygh and Andrew Morrison

Abstract

In shaping relations between service design and public health, one key challenge is how to meaningfully and systemically negotiate prospective services and long-term design-informed care support. In this chapter, we address this through a heuristic and exploratory 'case' centred in design-ethnographic and research through design qualitative inquiry by way of co-design with an inter-professional team in a non-dualist view of building care in PH. The focus is on the development and use of tangible tools in the early phase of service design to support processes of negotiation in this team concerned with building shared understanding and related strategies for allocating and connecting care in the context of establishing a new oncology ward at a leading Nordic hospital. The chapter assembled a transdisciplinary review of related research, drawing on developments in human–computer interaction on tangibility and tangible and embodied interaction. Tangible tools are three-dimensional, mediating artefacts designed to facilitate multimodal communication and interaction via situated actions afforded by an artefact's designed physical attributes, representational and social semiotic properties. In discussion of transdisciplinary framings and actual use, we discuss the role of such tools in service design in PH and connect them to a wider approach to service ecosystems design, closing a positioning of the design-research in what we term 'Tangible Service Design'.

K. Rygh (✉)
Institute of Design, The Oslo School of Architecture and Design, St. Olavs Plass, PO Box 6768, 0130 Oslo, Norway
e-mail: Karianne.Rygh@aho.no

A. Morrison
Centre for Design Research, Institute of Design, The Oslo School of Architecture and Design, St. Olavs Plass, PO Box 6768, 0130 Oslo, Norway
e-mail: Andrew.Morrison@aho.no

5.1 Introduction

Shaping relations between service design and public health calls for a systematic negotiation of prospective services and long-term design-informed care support. In developing and integrating tangible tools in supporting processes of negotiation in early phase service development of new healthcare services, we first give an introduction to public health, service design and service ecosystems Design and the accompanying research questions we address in this chapter.

5.1.1 Public Health, Service Design and Service Ecosystems Design

Care within public health (PH) is becoming an increasingly important policy issue in most societies (Kröger, 2009). The significant demographic changes taking place in Europe, such as an aging population, changing family patterns, growing participation of women in the labour market, increased workforce mobility and expected increases in retirement age is leading to a shortage in available carers (OECD, 2018). As care demands grow in complexity (Tinetti et al., 2012), several shifts are taking place within primary healthcare (PHC): from health to well-being, from health delivery to services and from treatment to care. Healthcare is, therefore, in many respects, becoming one of the fastest growing areas of focus within service design (SD) with increasing attention to public health systems (Jones, 2013), patient centricity in SD (Helse- og omsorgsdepartementet, 2013, 2014; Ringard, Sagan, Sperre Suanes & Lindahl, 2013; Sundby & Hansen, 2017), development and its implementation (Martins, 2016; Overkamp & Holmlid, 2017; Yu & Sangiorgi, 2014).

With the arrival of the COVID-19 pandemic, the already developing care deficit (Tronto, 2013) has been amplified and catalysed, putting more pressure on primary care teams who are already facing overwhelming workloads. The risk of healthcare workforce burnout threatens an overall quality of care (Haynes, 2021). Addressing care challenges within PH therefore becomes a complex task leading policy makers, healthcare professionals, private companies and public organizations to have to think creatively and responsibly about how to anticipate future health contexts. This development calls for new strategies of shifting workloads and resources while still providing quality of care in healthcare services.

In the Nordic countries in particular, innovative partnerships are being set up between and across public, non-profit and for-profit sectors in order to achieve goals that would otherwise not be possible by the same actors working independently (Becker & Smith, 2018). Societal expectations of the impact that inter-professional collaborations (Paradis & Reeves, 2013) should have on quality of care are high (Schot et al., 2020) despite the challenges that exist within PH. Strong disciplinary boundaries, siloed expertise, separate IT systems and differences in working cultures and practices greatly influence, and often create barriers to collaborative practices within cross-sector, healthcare partnerships. The task of creating and facilitating the right conditions for inter-professional collaboration has traditionally fallen on healthcare managers; however, scholars have argued that developing collaborative practices requires a more active contribution from healthcare professionals themselves (Schot et al., 2020).

Service design (SD) and co-design practices are being increasingly called upon to support complex, collaborative processes, especially in the early phases of service development, in order to drive service innovation (Rygh & Clatworthy, 2019). The early phases of such collaborative processes are often characterized by contested topics, disputes and resistance to engaging in new change processes where an alignment of diverse actors is needed. This makes up an area of service designing that requires negotiation in order to create a common point of departure for later engaging in processes of co-designing new service concepts. Although SD has been mainly understood in relation to the design and development stages of new service development (e.g. Fitzsimmons & Fitzsimmons, 2000), what kind of service offerings can be developed to support multidisciplinary service development teams in this early phase, in activities of collective planning, alignment and strategy development, is less known.

Given the prevalence of the tangible and embodied interaction in human–computer interaction (HCI) and digital culture, it is surprising that tangibility and tangible tools (TTs) have not been adopted and adapted more widely in SD (Rygh & Clatworthy, 2019). TTs encompass multimodal representations, embedded affordances, mixed materialities and mediating artefacts (Morrison, 2010) realized, for example, through touch, gesture, proximity and movement (see Fig. 5.1).

In the context of PH and 'connected care', this chapter takes up co-design in early phase SD in establishing a new oncology (cancer) ward in a large university

Fig. 5.1 Example of a service design engagement using the tangible tool 'Allocator' for negotiating the reallocation of hospital beds, patients and connected care professionals in establishing a new hospital ward. *Source* Design of tool a image, K. Rygh = Author's own illustration (2021)

hospital in Norway. The design and research is conducted as part of a national research centre for connecting service innovation to health within a public health system centred on fulfilling wider democratic and well-being principles. The SD focus is on the development and application of TTs to support given and emerging needs and negotiations of inter-professional teams, including medical and design professionals and researchers. As Jones (2013: 302) observes:

The medical and institutional care traditions do not offer a ready berth for design, and our traditional positions have little systemic impact if employed without strategic intent. Until we prove to be valuable contributing members of the care team, we risk being seen as specialists and even marginal players in the story of care.

In a holistic view of care and design, we situate the tools and their uses within a wider service design ecosystems view (Vink et al., 2021: 172). This entails the ways in which actor collectives seek to facilitate co-creation forms, embedded with desired values, so as to intentionally shape institutional arrangements and their physical enactment, supported by way of reflexive and reformative critical design-research activity.

5.1.2 Focus and Methods

Accordingly, the following interlinked questions are addressed:

(1) In what ways might a relational view of 'connected care' be included in a tangible approach to early phase service design for PH?
(2) What role may TTs play in SD that connects inter-professional relations, needs and negotiations in 'careful' resource allocations and long-term strategies in PH?
(3) How might TTs and interaction contribute to 'A Service Design Ecosystem of Connected Care' and a framing of 'Tangible Service Design'?

Drawing on a transdisciplinary relational framing—on care, SD, tangibility and TTs and service ecosystems design—the chapter presents an exploratory heuristic 'case' located in qualitative inquiry (Denzin & Lincoln, 1994). This case is a reflexive, and critically recursive designerly and ethnographically located, textured and voiced outcome (Cross, 2007; Crabtree. et al., 2012; Murphy & Marcus, 2013) of processes of embodied co-design with health and design professionals. It draws on multiple and mixed methods (Lury et al., 2018), including participant observation, embodied interaction (touch, gestural, proxemic, kinetic, spatial and verbal) and designer enacted photography (Raijmakers and Miller, 2016), in an action research pragmatist frame (Green-wood & Levin, 2007). The research is positioned within a practice-based research through design methodology (Frayling, 1993; Zimmerman et al., 2010; Stappers & Giaccardi, 2017), linking research methodologies, design techniques, research methods and design tools (Morrison, Rygh & Mainsah, 2019).

The primary design work was carried out by the first author as part of a wider consultative, iterative and situated process of shaping the TTs and reflecting on their use in an actual context of exploring prospective provisions of care in the complex conditions of PH. The chapter has also been co-authored with a transdisciplinary design researcher with wide experience in service design research and practice-based inquiry spanning the human and technical sciences.

5.2 Related Research

With a transdisciplinary, relational framing in approaching the above-mentioned research questions; in this section, we next present a literature review bridging care, design and tangibility in a context of service designing in PH.

5.2.1 Health, Care and Design

In light of the growing deficit in care, innovations within PH policy are increasingly centred on reducing workload for primary care physicians (MacDonnel & Darzi, 2013). Some examples of innovations reducing workload have been task shifting, (shifting care tasks from physicians to non-physician health professionals through the establishing care teams) and the development of connected care services (empowering patients to take more active responsibility for their own health). The goal of expanding primary health care teams through task shifting is to include efficient utilization of all providers and improving quality in care (Freund et al., 2015). Similarly, building upon the notion of connected health (Frist, 2014), including more digital touchpoints and online networks within connected care services, enables care to be offered to a larger population of patients using less human resources. These examples give insights into how healthcare professionals are increasingly being encouraged to work together with experts in fields other than their own in the delivery of care to patients.

The need for multidisciplinary teams within PH has contributed to growing research on inter-professional collaboration in the medical sector (Paradis & Reeves, 2013). The authors describe inter-professional collaboration as taking form through: (1) Bridging professional's social, physical and task-related gaps, (2) In negotiating overlaps in roles and tasks and (3) In creating spaces to bridge and negotiate these aspects. Schot et al. (2020) argue that fostering such collaboration is not only the task of managers and policy makers, but also requires an active contribution of healthcare professionals themselves. Designing for quality in care to come through new health care service concepts therefore also becomes a question of tending to the conditions and resources needed by such teams to operate and collaborate most effectively and establishing ways of engaging healthcare professionals in contributing to this effort.

Providing and receiving care are aspects that follow us throughout our life course (Barnes, 2012) and are central components of the design of new health care services. For Fisher and Tronto (1991, cit, in Tronto, 1993:103), care connects to continued repair of our world that '… includes our bodies, ourselves, and our environment all of which we seek to interweave in a complex, life sustaining web'. Care is thereby a social construct, taking place in and through relationships, involving our physical, emotional, mental and spiritual selves (Weicht, 2016). It also relates to conceptualisations of 'care as body work' (Twigg, 2000) that values that which is often unacknowledged, gendered or 'dirty work' involving close, considered embodied and what we term 'tangible care'.

Design, as a practice of care, can, in this view, be understood as a relational practice, situated in an ecology of care (Vaughan, 2018), where all elements need to be considered and designed for as things and living beings matter (Light & Akama, 2014) and because 'mattering' is relationally 'always inside connections' (Haraway, 2008: 70). For us, a wider view of care does not merely entail 'matters of concern' (Latour, 2004) but 'matters of care' as Puig de la Bellacasa (2017) distinguishes this as to do with assemblies of people and neglected things (Puig de la Bellacasa, 2011) and, from an STS view, extending 'mattering' to care in practice (Mol et al., 2010). Attention to design and care has grown in recent years (e.g. Coxon & Bremner, 2019). Building on the work of Hamington (2010: 676), Vaughan describes actions or performances of care as resulting from the work of a 'moral imagination that both empathizes and favourably anticipates making a difference' (2018: Kindle Locations 509–510). Conceiving of design as a practice of relational care can in this way be understood as a conscious means of articulating a sustainable and sustaining approach to design.

5.2.2 Service Design and the Front End of New Service Development

Service design as a field has been understood in relation to the development and design stages of NSD where this understanding has later expanded to also include the improvement of existing services (Zeithaml & Bitner, 1996). In light of the societal challenges facing PH, the need for establishing multidisciplinary care teams is only continuing to grow. A developing trend within SD practice is that service designers are being called upon to offer their designerly methods also in the early phases of service development (Rygh & Clatworthy, 2019), known as the 'Fuzzy Front End' of service innovation processes (Koen et al., 2001).

Much of the reason for this is that aligning the day-to-day practices, working cultures and profession-oriented views, beliefs and assumptions of healthcare professionals while forging new, interconnected relations of care that make up new healthcare services, requires negotiation of the more intangible aspects influencing service development. The wide array and often conflicting values of involved healthcare professionals are not explicitly expressed due to hierarchical power dynamics and political disputes over the distribution of available resources, as organizational culture within medical contexts are often characterized by rivalry and competition between groups (Davies et al., 2000), where healthcare has been referred to as almost 'tribal' (Harrison, Hunter & Marnoch, et al., 1992; Harrison & Nutley, 1996).

Holopainen (2010) has proposed that SD should be understood in relation to the entire service development process, yet little attention has been given to understanding what service designing and service support could entail within early phases of service innovation processes. Supporting diverse professionals within this early phase calls for SD approaches to consider and design for matters of care along a continuum stretching from the individual patient to aspects of policy making, influenced by societal, economic and environmental factors. Furthermore, developing a notion of how tangible service support in early phase formation of innovative partnerships could be conceptualized involves a multi-level shift in perspectives within SD: First, shifting views of what constitutes service designing, second, shifting a co-design view in regards to how and in which ways relevant experts are supported in taking an active part in service designing in this phase and lastly, shifting the view on external representations used in co-design tools and methods, from solely visual, to visual and tangible.

As the early phases of service development are characteristically different than the later phases of designing and developing service concepts, arriving at how we can support healthcare professionals and other related experts in navigating complex, multidisciplinary collaborations therefore becomes a matter of tending to (1) the alignment and negotiation of professional working practices, cultures and views to enable diverse professionals in thinking and working together (2) the relational conditions necessary for teams to establish inter-professional collaboration (as bridging professional gaps in care and negotiating overlaps in roles and tasks are essential foundations of caring relationships healthcare services) and (3) the politics influencing resource reallocation/reconfiguration that can prove to create tension and disputes rather than forging new healthcare relationships.

5.2.3 Recent Developments Within Service Design

Service design practice makes use of tools and methods in supporting the shaping of new service solutions (Blomkvist et al., 2010; Wetter-Edman et al., 2014). Co-design is understood as a central approach within SD, focussing on the development of tools and methods where most SD tools build upon a human-centred approach (Manzini, 2011), design thinking (Clatworthy, 2013) and a 'Double Diamond' design process (Drew, 2019). As such, most tools have been developed for the design and development of new service concepts, where tools for early phase service development engagement supporting alignment and negotiation are currently lacking.

Service design has been understood as an interdisciplinary approach and design discipline (Stickdorn & Schneider, 2010) intersecting with other design domains such as interaction and product design. As service design has grown as a design discipline, emerging from design management, marketing and services, it has also broadened its relations to other domains and specialisations. The ServDes 2020 Conference turned its focus to discussion, reflection and critique of SD across cultural, organizational and institutional borders, creating a response on topics such as the interrelations of culture and institutional logic and the role of indigenous knowledge. 'Articulatory, Respectful Service Design' was introduced (Sheenan, 2021), contributing to enabling theory through plurality in voices, views and values set in motion by the process of designing, questioning power distributions, politics and ethics within service designing.

Focus has also grown on the experiential in SD (Clatworthy, 2019) and inter-sections with cultural theories and studies, encompassing cultural intermediaries, trends and popular/consumer culture (Dennington, 2021) and symbolic and 'ritual' aspects in an experiential model of SD (Mathews, 2021). Recently, Vargo and Lush (2017: 58–59) opened out the much-used service-dominant logic (SDL) via trans-disciplinary vectors of SDL diffusion. In connecting TTs and care in PH, we see potential for extending the focus in SDL on services marketing to that of mediated experiential action and SD, via (HCI) and related notions of tangible, embodied and mediated interaction. This connection alters the positioning of 'cognitive mediators/assistants' (in the context of cognitive computing and big data) as heuristic tools in complex service ecosystems (Vargo & Lusch, 2017: 61–62) to designerly ways of knowing through mediated tools and activities (Morrison, 2010).

5.2.4 Tangibility, Design and Service Design

In service design, the notion of tangibility is often understood as the physical touchpoints of a service journey (the physical products that make up a particular service), the physical components of product service systems (PSS), and tangibility as external representations in relation to SD and co-design methods—making abstract and intangible aspects of service development visible and understandable so that they can be used as a design material. Related methods range from service prototyping (Blomkvist & Holmlid, 2010), mapping and modelling (Morelli, 2002; Patricio et al., 2008), Giga-mapping (Sevaldson, 2011), Service Blue-printing (Bitner, et al., 2008) and role-playing (Vaajakallio et al., 2010) where different SD techniques are used in different aspects of services.

In HCI and interaction design, the term 'tangible' has been developed in terms of tangible interaction (TI) but has seldom been translated into SD. Building upon principles from product and industrial design, arts and architecture, tangible interaction is understood as being an interdisciplinary area specializing in physi-cally embodied interfaces and systems, from physical artefacts to physical envi-ronments (Ishii & Ullmer, 1997; Wellner et al., 1993). TI was initially conceived in terms of 'Tangible User Interfaces' (TUI's) to 'allow users to grasp data with their hands and to unify representation and control' (Hornecker, 2017). TUIs link verbal and screen and information systems-based communication and mediation with contexts of bodily use drawing on a multitude of senses (visual, auditory, tactical, olfactory, kinetic, spatial etc.).

Hoven and Mazalek (2009) positioned 'Tangible Gesture Interaction' at the intersection between TI and the gestural, incorporating the affordance of manipulating digital data through physical objects from TI and communicative intent from gestures. Nordby and Morrison (2010) took up the material of short-range RFID in the design of tangible interaction and a touch-based gestural 'vocabulary' that has since infiltrated many mobile payment and service applications. Korper et al. (2020) recently argued, in regard to sound, that service experience can be co-created while a service is being performed, as the interplay of different stimuli influences interactions within servicescapes.

5.2.5   On Tangible Tools

In exploring the role TTs may play in SD and how TTs and interaction may contribute to a SD ecosystem of connected care, we next present how TTs have been taken up in other related domains and also present work that is currently being undertaken on developing tangible approaches in SD.

5.2.5.1   Domains and Components

Tangible Tools, central to HCI (Djajadiningrat et al., 2004, 2007; Hornecker & Buur, 2006; Kaptelinin, 2014) have been taken up within co-design (Sanders & Stappers, 2014), participatory design (Binder et al., 2015; Sanders et al., 2010) and SD (Rygh & Clatworthy, 2019). Overall, these developments concern ways in which the physical materiality of objects and artefacts and contexts of their enactment may be connected through embodied use and human skills (Angelini et al., 2015).

A TT is a three-dimensional, mediating artefact (Wartofsky, 1979) designed to facilitate multimodality in communication and interaction through situated actions afforded by the artefact's designed physical attributes, representational and social semiotic properties. TTs are designed to establish, support and nurture relations between diverse individuals in contexts where communication, understanding and willingness to contribute or collaborate have broken down or are influenced by differences in working practices, world views, power relations, hierarchical dynamics or political tensions (Morrison, 2010). This view on TTs positions design as a means to orchestrate, direct and calibrate participation, engagement and communication from individuals interacting with the tools.

This is achieved through a process of embedding context-appropriate, facilitative qualities within the form, aesthetics, functions, materials and sensorial qualities within the physical attributes of a tool. These affordances and connotative and denotative aspects of TTs are designed with intent and materialized through a rigorous and iterative co-design process with experts based on research drawing upon contextual data and design principles from multiple design disciplines and practices. A TT is implemented as a designed boundary object, where the design choices resulting in its final form are based on the contextual research conducted within each field, organization, specialization or sociocultural practice that make up the boundaries the tool aims to support in overcoming. TTs embed multimodal and multisensory qualities and characteristics for the purpose of conveying content and communication (Morrison, 2010). It is through their materialities, tag-token relations (Ishi & Ullmer, 1997), associations and metaphors, affordances and significations that TTs sconvey, communicate and project both values and potential for mediated action (e.g. Eikenes & Morrison, 2010).

5.2.5.2 On Affordances, Mediated Action and Service Design

Following the work of Gibson (1977) on affordances and animals in ecological psychology, affordances have been taken up in HCI (Norman, 1988) as actual and perceived in a determinist sense of possible use via clues for operationalization. Kaptelinin (2014) categorizes affordances in HCI as concerned with (1) direct perception, (2) purposeful user action and 3) meaning making. For Gaver (1991: 82) affordances may be realized as (a) sequential (acting on an embedded affordance leads to yet another being revealed) and (b) nested (where one affordance functions as the context for another being manifested). Affordances are further elaborated as complex objects being revealed through active exploration, guided through metaphors, and not only visually but also multi- and trans-modally mediated making for perceptible and actionable meaning making (Gaver, 1991). In graphic user interfaces, Norman (1988) talks about affordances as clues to operation, such as an item being clickable.

In work on emergent technologies and potential embedded in processes and prototypes, Nordby and Morrison (2010) include 'design affordances' and need-based affordances. Kaptelinin (2014) points to affordances as relational between the designed artefact and the environment and user and connected to mediated action (Kaptelinin, 2014; Kaptelinin & Nardi, 2012) with way interaction between persons or groups, mediational means and environments. For Morrison (2010), affordances contribute to mediating artefacts in signifying meaning potential (see also Norman, 2013) and appeal (Withagen et al., 2012) and through performative use. Mediated action is changed in and by experience in cultural settings (Dohn, 2009).

Affordances have begun to be taken up in SD. Kim et al. (2012) looked at a PSS design method that integrated both design and service elements through the use of affordances and where affordances offer means for the design of product elements from service elements applied to an example of urban umbrella rental in a service-dominant logic approach and the enabling of the activities of various stakeholders. Recently, Tomej and Xiang (2020) see the involvement of tourists in relation to affordances designed as part of a wider 'servicescape', with focus on the experiential co-creation of value in a wider affordance-based framework. Tomej and Xiang (2020: 8) accentuate that '... each design choice creates not only affordances intended by the designer but also a multitude of others which may or may not be anticipated by the designer'.

5.2.5.3 Tangible Tools and Service Design

Few studies exist on how TTs may be conceptualized and designed to support service interactions. TTs are increasingly being taken up in service design engagements due their characteristics of enabling the co-creation of shared understandings through offering multimodality in communication. In meeting challenges of managing multidisciplinary collaborative processes in relation to service innovation, Rygh and Clatworthy (2019) have described TTs as three-dimensional cognitive scaffolds, affording bodily interaction as a means of accelerating and enabling collective sense-making. They argue that product, interaction and graphic designers are well-positioned to design tools to be context-specific and thereby of more adequate benefit, building upon design principles from co-design and participatory design. Furthermore, the first author as part of her doctoral research at the Oslo School of Architecture and Design (AHO) has conducted workshops with SD master-level students, exploring how to develop design processes of materialising TTs (see Fig. 5.2), studying students' iterative processes and design choices. Through the workshops, students developed TTs for engaging architects and medical professionals in dialogue about care in the context of a design lab, in a SD project supporting the establishment of a new hospital wing at a rehabilitation hospital (see Romm, Agudelo, Freitas, 2020).

In this view, TTs are seen as a means to establish common ground through a shared understanding of stakeholder networks and enable strategic insights as well as aligning expectations and goals among stakeholders in design and conceptualization across industries. These may further be seen in a service ecosystems design view.

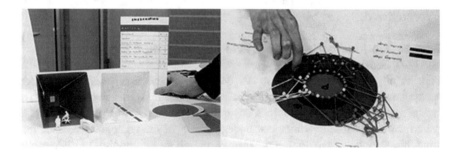

Fig. 5.2 'Excursion into Materiality' workshop with examples of TTs created by students at AHO. The TT on the left (by Pippich, M.) invites exploration of how patients with cognitive impairments experience the architecture/interior of a rehabilitation facility. The TT on the right (by Hozhabri, M.) explores shifting care relations between healthcare professionals and patients through having to move into a new facility. *Source* Photos, K. Rygh = Author's own illustration (2021)

5.2.6 Service Ecosystem Design

In leveraging the reconceptualization of SD practice in a wider view on tangibility and its related potential embodied engagement in service encounters, we see the potential to further develop a service ecosystems design perspective. In the following section, we present this approach, drawing upon a multi-level process model for service ecosystems design.

5.2.6.1 On a Service Ecosystem Design Perspective

Drawing on the framework of service-dominant logic (Vargo & Lush, 2017) and recent related work in the domain of service design, Vink et al., (2021: 172) propose an approach for the extension of the conceptual building blocks of SD by focussing on the perspective of service ecosystem design. 'Service ecosystem design' is defined as '…the intentional shaping of institutional arrangements and their physical enactments by actor collectives through reflexivity and reformation to facilitate the emergence of desired value co-creation forms'. (Vink, et al.:172).

Vink et al., (2021: 173) outline four core propositions for service ecosystem design. These are patterned around two axes: (1) a set of conceptual building blocks (purpose, design material, processes and actor involvement) and (2) design of services, design for service and service ecosystem design. The conceptual and tabular mapping offered indicates a shift and increasing alignment with service-dominant logic. Consequently, in a service ecosystems design view, purpose is concerned to 'facilitate the emergence of desired forms of value co-creation'. Design material is concerned with 'institutional arrangements and their physical enactments'. On processes, attention is given to the 'embedded feedback loop of reflexivity and reformation'. Actor involvement is realized by way of 'collective designing by actors'.

5.2.6.2 Working with a Multi-Level Process Model for Service Ecosystem Design

Vink et al., (2021: 176) develop 'A Multi-Level Process Model for Service Ecosystem Design'. This is based on the conceptual aspects mentioned above together with four core propositions advanced. As a whole, this process model is geared towards offering 'a nuanced understanding of the complex processes that bring life to intentional, long-term change in service ecosystems' (Vink et al., 2021:176). In our view, this work offers considerable leverage for reconceptualising service design practice and analysis and is pertinent to working with the development and instantiation of TTs in PH. Here, the additional move to demarcating micro, meso and macro levels of aggregation of dynamic processes provides a means to linking elements and processes in a wider view on the tangibility and its related potential embodied engagement in service encounters.

This model provides a useful framing for situating TTs and SD in a wider systems view. However, the underlying SDL base is located epistemologically within the domain of marketing and service/s marketing (Vargo & Lush, 2017).

SDL is open to cross-pollinations from a diversity of disciplines as this recent text offers. However, a number of potential elements are missing in our view.

First, there may be added attention to notions and practices of care, less marketing, of SD and also SD-infused notions of care. Second, the emergence of the experiential in SD (e.g. Dennington, 2021; Mathews, 2021) that is located in regard to culture and cultures (popular, work, identities etc.) has the potential to contribute to a service ecosystem approach and work as a complement to the multi-level process model offered by Vink et al. (2021). Third, we see there is ample room for the inclusion in SDL of concepts and situated practices of mediating artefacts, encompassing TTs, and related mediated action that allows us to shifts from tools and signs, contexts and mediations, to action and agency in which meaning and 'careful' SD for PH may be articulated. Here, we refer to emerging articulations (Morrison, 2010) as 'matters of care' in the sense of linking and voicing or materialising, and mediated and process means of making material and actualising TTs for mediated careful professional communication in PH.

In support of these claims and aspirations, next we attend to the contexts and methods of the heuristic and exploratory research and the ethnographic case that follows.

5.3 An Exploratory Case: Context, Care, and Tangible Tools in Service Design and Public Health

5.3.1 Contextualising the Design Space of Tangible Tools

In the following section, we examine ways in which context and needs influence the design of TTs through an exploratory case undertaken in a hospital setting and outline relevant characteristics of a careful SD approach to engaging healthcare professionals within service development in PH.

5.3.1.1 Contexts of Development and Collaboration

As part of a doctoral study at the Oslo School of Architecture and Design, the first author has conducted an exploratory study on the role of tangibility in tools for negotiation for a hospital setting in the early phases of service development. The research was conducted in collaboration with Centre for Connected Care (C3), a national research initiative aiming to accelerate the adoption and diffusion of patient centric service innovations within healthcare. C3 is an eight-year initiative started in 2015 by the Centre for Research-based Innovation (SFI), funded by the Norwegian Research Council. A project partner of C3, Akershus University Hospital (AHUS), expressed a need for a SD approach in relation to the planning of a new cancer centre, in connection to the planned establishment of a new specialist radiation unit at the hospital (Utviklingsplan for AHUS 2017). AHUS is a leading emergency hospital in Norway, serving a population of approximately 500 000 people, the equivalent of 10% of Norway's population. As the development of the new radiation unit was projected to take several years, there was a short-term need to improve services for existing patients. Focus was therefore placed on first establishing an oncology inpatient unit.

Service Design and Needs

Although cancer treatment has been one of AHUS' leading priorities since 2012, the hospital did not have dedicated oncology beds at the time of this study. What that meant in practice was that cancer patients requiring oncology treatment were admitted to the corresponding speciality ward. For example, if a patient operated for stomach cancer subsequently required admission for non-surgical complications related to chemo- or immunotherapy, they were admitted to the upper gastrointestinal surgery ward. Ideally, through establishing an inpatient oncology unit, cancer patients would benefit from being admitted to an oncology ward where nursing staff would consist of skilled oncology nurses who are used to dealing with these type of patients. Furthermore, oncology doctors would not have to traipse around the hospital to do consults on patients, scattered far and wide.

As new cancer treatments are rapidly being developed, new side-effects of such treatments are emerging, requiring increased coordination of care and sharing of expertise between healthcare professionals. Access to resources and expertise needed for treating complications associated with cancer disorders, may vary from ward to ward, potentially creating differences in the quality of care patients receive. The aim of the new cancer centre was therefore to centralize available resources and create a more holistic service offering where each cancer patient, regardless of cancer type, would have equal access to care, resources and expertise. This in turn aimed to improve quality in care and reduce number of days spent in hospital.

As the establishment of the cancer centre is expected to take several years (expected completion by 2027), the case presented is indirectly linked to this centre through an intermin measure. This measure consisted of negotiating how to dedicate and reallocate existing hospital beds to cancer patients, from one department to another, in order to create a new oncology ward within the hospital. This phase preceded the phase of establishing a new building for the new cancer centre, where additional beds would be provided. In approaching where repurposed beds could come from, historical data was used to estimate how many beds on average were filled by oncology patients on a given ward. Furthermore, oncology patients were defined as those meeting the inclusion criteria for admission to an oncology ward, had it existed. However, relocating beds from one department to another meant that some wards would 'lose' a certain number of existing hospital beds.

Reconfiguring and shifting resources in this way is a common pain point for hospital reorganization. Here, the challenge lies in how well new configurations of resources and other factors influencing collaborative care relations can be explored, addressed and negotiated with healthcare professionals themselves in order to make them workable and sustainable. Currently, such specific tools and methods are lacking from SD practice despite service designers already intervening in such phases of planning.

Shifting where and how healthcare professionals need to work together in the coordination of a patients' care brings with it a disruption in day-to-day collaborative care practices, something which can potentially jeopardize the care capacity in each ward. This calls for methods and processes that facilitate surfacing, exploring and addressing underlying issues and tensions that can potentially negatively affect inter-professional collaboration and negotiating strategies for shifting resources and workloads in the ways in which healthcare professionals offer care to patients.

5.3.1.2 Characteristics and Offerings of 'Careful' Service Support

In the planning of the new oncology ward, a working group within AHUS was established consisting of hospital managers, oncologists, surgeons and other doctors and nurses from other specialities to collectively evaluate and determine the number of beds to be reallocated and which wards were best suited to 'offer' beds. The working group was tasked with developing proposals for how this could best be done and map potential consequences of new changes. In anticipating potential negative consequences in regards to patient capacity in each ward, healthcare professionals could become more concerned with 'holding on to' hospital beds than exploring how many beds they could contribute to the new oncology ward, leading to tensions potentially blocking discussion on the topic. It was therefore important to accommodate discussion, exploration and suggestions according to different proposals and to negotiate different understandings and interpretations of various suggestions.

Being a project partner of C3, some members of the AHUS working group had an awareness of the potential SD methods and tools can have in addressing the more relational and intangible aspects of service planning and development. The team wished to have a more sustainable approach of meeting top-down changes with bottom up proposals of how changes could be best accommodated, from the point of view of the healthcare professionals themselves. To achieve this, a smaller SD team was created consisting of a designer-researcher (first author), a designer-facilitator, the oncology ward project lead and the cancer centre project director. Collectively, the team determined that an interventionist SD approach of pre-defined workshops would work less well within this hospital setting due to the limited time frame, the relational nature of topics to be discussed and because healthcare professionals needed to be given the room and opportunity to voice their opinions. It was requested by the oncology ward project lead and hospital manager that a SD engagement and accompanying tools ought to be co-conceptualized by several experts, not only from SD and facilitation design but also from hospital management and clinical care.

Moving away from imposing a pre-designed engagement, towards a more careful SD approach, the SD team collaborated in co-conceptualising a context-specific SD engagement in the form of a working session using TTs, termed: 'Tangible Service Design Engagement using Tangible Tools'. The tool 'Allocator' (See Fig. 5.1) was materialized by the designer-researcher through an iterative co-design process with the SD team, consisting of physical bed tokens that could be used to discuss and negotiate hospital bed reallocation within the frame of the participatory engagement.

5.3.2 Designing

The design process of TTs developed within a SD context is often underreported in literature, giving little indication to the design choices that have led to a final tool or prototype. In this section, we therefore examine various aspects of designing TTs, exemplifying not only the complexity involved in their materialisation but also the possibilities and potential within their design.

5.3.2.1 Design Tools and Processes

The materialisation of the tool 'Allocator' followed a design process of TTs production in a wider view of developing SD methods and tools (Alves & Nunes, 2013; Miettinen, 2009). Design specifications for the tool derived from contextual research conducted by the designer-researcher in a series of meetings with the cancer centre project director, the oncology ward project lead and a facilitation expert. Here, discussions resulted in an outline of aspects, themes and underlying assumptions to be surfaced and addressed, types of activities to best support this and types of actions that were desired from participants in expressing underlying issues. These aspects were then applied to the design of the physical tools by the designer–researcher, examining which tool attributes could be best suited to afford certain actions based on bodily interactions through the senses in response to the form of the tool and the texture of incorporated materials. The aim was to enable healthcare professionals to explore and negotiate the number of hospital beds to be reallocated (number of bed tokens), from which wards beds should be moved (arrangements of tokens) and the potential impact this could have on individual wards and individual healthcare professionals (relations between healthcare professionals, location of wards and availability of resources).

Through incorporating physical mock-ups of tools in each meeting with the SD team, it was possible for the designer-researcher to make design suggestions towards the team and receive immediate feedback. This led to adjustments being made so that the final tool could be as context appropriate as possible. This participatory, iterative and collaborative process was understood as a 'codification of Tangible Tools' where desired action possibilities were mapped onto physical tools through discussion and incorporated into their design. Building upon the notion of perceptible affordances offering a direct link between perception and action (Gaver, 1991), the design and materialisation process of the 'Allocator' tool became an intricate sequence of critical design choices. The tool consisted of coloured, rectangular, wooden tokens, representing hospital beds with cancer patients, circular signs indicating name and colour of ward and plastic and coloured markers indicating patient health status. The design choices incorporated to arrive at the design of the 'Allocator' tool are presented below.

5.3.2.2 Appearance, Appeal and Metaphorical Representation

Materials and form determine TT's appearance and appeal to participants, in turn affecting participants' willingness to engage with them. With medical professionals' environments consisting of top-notch medical equipment and rooms designed for optimal efficiency, the 'Allocator' tool was designed to come across as being finalized and 'polished' for the purpose of establishing trust. The aim was for the tool to be perceived as being well-designed and well thought-out, making it more desirable and more likely to be adopted. Appeal is closely linked with metaphorical representations, making certain topics more relatable through seeing one thing in terms of another (Lakoff & Johnson, 1980). Translating healthcare professionals' situated experience into commonly relatable metaphors was done to lower the potential for confrontation and the threshold for both sharing and discussing difficult matters. The metaphor of a token was chosen according to what was thought to be the best support for participants in enacting appropriate 'input actions' in relation to mediated 'output' responses (building upon HCI). In the context of needing to negotiate resources in relation to beds and their allocation, the tokens were chosen to represent identifiable beds (see Fig. 5.3). These bed tokens could be collected, arranged, placed, offered or negotiated.

5.3.2.3 Size and Form

The size and form of TTs were determined by parameters of the designed engagement: the number of representations necessary to make abstract topics graspable and the size of the surface the tools would be placed onto. In this case, tools would be placed onto a table, where the table dimensions determined the proximity available between tools and participants for moving objects, gesturing or making visual arrangements. The form language of the tools was decided upon through iterative dialogue sessions with the SD team using physical representations/suggestions of form. This resulted in the size and shaping of the token hospital bed, in relation to the overall number of items to be placed in front of participants. Each token was roughly the size of a domino piece so that tokens

Fig. 5.3 Rectangular, wooden tokens were chosen to represent hospital beds, as these could be easily placed in the hand, negotiated, moved and placed. The left image shows the determined size of tokens, the middle image possible arrangements of tokens, and the right image shows the materialization of the ward sign posts. *Source* Tool production & photos, K. Rygh = Author's own illustration (2021)

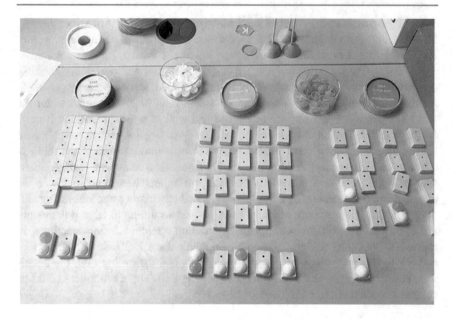

Fig. 5.4 Tests of tool enactments and layouts representing the various wards, exploring spatial factors and how bed tokens could be marked, grouped, categorized and combined through enactments. *Source* Tool design and photo, K. Rygh = Author's own illustration (2021)

could fit well into the human hand, and a participant could, for example, pick up a handful of bed tokens in negotiation (see Figs. 5.3 and 5.4).

5.3.2.4 Texture and Materials

The appearance of TTs evokes emotions and associations through the materials that shape them, creating a need to carefully consider which materials and aesthetics are most appropriate for a given context and connected participants. Here, material choice is determined through an extension of what has been referred to as 'a dialogue with materials' (Schön, 1992) towards a more anticipatory dialogue through embedded affordances. In this way, the expressive-sensorial dimension of materials (Ragnoli & Levi, 2004) determines perception and interpretation tools, and the associations that tools will evoke. Similar to designing digital interfaces, object attributes are mapped to intangible feelings, abilities and values, represented through materials.

In establishing a material interface (Ragnoli & Levi, 2004) in tools for the AHUS context and making tools communicative and facilitative by their design, wood was chosen for its natural feel in the hand and its weight in relation to lightness and ease in moving tokens while still being 'weighty' enough to indicate value, being taken seriously as representative artefacts. Discussions were had within the SD team that it was important to ensure that tools did not come across as being too playful or trivial in nature to avoid alienating health personnel or trivialising the

Fig. 5.5 'Allocator' tangible tool. Hospital beds are represented by the metaphor of negotiative, rectangular tokens in wood. Blue, plastic markers are placed onto the tokens to indicate cancer patients. Tokens are painted in two colours representing two different medical specialties sharing one ward. Ward is represented by a round, wooden sign post with ward name. *Source* Tool design and photo, K. Rygh = Author's own illustration (2021)

serious nature of the topic for discussion. For the same reasons, it was determined that there was a need for judicious use of colour.

Tokens were painted indicating the corresponding ward. Holes were made in tokens to accommodate plastic markers being placed, indicating cancer patients (blue) and in particular, which patients could be moved to the new oncology ward (orange). Round, circular, wooden pieces, slightly larger than the bed tokens, were designed to represent each ward. A slanted surface accommodated improved legibility of the names of wards (to be viewed by participants either sitting or standing) and enabled discussion on the level of wards as a whole, through affording the physical act of grouping or arranging not only bed tokens but also ward sign posts (see Fig. 5.5).

5.3.3 Settings of Use

Next, we present phases of co-conceptualising TTs. This consists of framing a SD engagement, determining tangible interactions and designing appropriate TTs. We take up the ways and formats in which this can be achieved and exemplify it through the exploratory case undertaken within a hospital setting.

5.3.3.1 Three Related Phases

The co-conceptualisation process of the tangible SD engagement using TTs took the form of three related phases: (1) defining the frame for the tangible SD engagement (defining healthcare actors' needs, clarifying questions for SD engagement and ideation on supportive activities), (2) determining the desired tangible interactions (defining which tasks within the activities would be asked of participants and codifying these in relation to potential attributes in tools that could afford potential actions) and (3) designing the TTs in use (designing tools to incorporate affordances to motivate and enable participants to carry out those tasks and actual uses).

5.3.3.2 Healthcare Actor's Needs

Defining the frame for the tangible SD engagement involved developing an understanding of healthcare actors' needs within this medical context and defining topics and questions for the engagement. In the first phase, meetings were held between the oncology ward project lead from the working group and the service designer-researcher (first author). The meetings consisted of unpacking the complexity of how various hospital wards operate and how they are structured, both in regards to responsibility and accountability for patients in connection to how different hospital wards are organized and distributed throughout the hospital, and in relation to other facilities outside the hospital that wards are also connected to. This could not be easily summarized or shown quantitatively through spreadsheets and needed to be communicated through explanations and examples. Discussions revealed that the coordinated efforts and inter-professional, collaborative relations of bridging different medical specialisations in accommodating overlaps and covering gaps in patient care, are very complex. Developing an understanding of this complexity made the roots of resistance to change more apparent as the implications of changes to the collaborative practices of care are far reaching into the multiple levels of a healthcare ecosystem.

5.3.3.3 Working Sessions

Three meetings were held between the designer-researcher and the oncology ward project lead in planning the tangible SD engagement, followed by an ideation session on potential participatory activities together with an invited facilitation design expert. The facilitation expert supported the development of best approaches and best questioning styles for a context that was characterized by political tensions. A draft of a program for a potential engagement was made, including an overview of suggested activities and indications to which aspects of activities TTs could support, and presented to the hospital manager as a proposal for a tangible SD engagement.

The response to the proposal was that in the next, second phase, an engagement should be organized with the AHUS cancer centre working group, in the form of a working session meeting, with the main aim being determining which cancer patients could be moved to a new oncology ward and which should remain. Each participant, on behalf of their ward, would then be able to respond to this question, describe the status quo in their particular ward and discuss the implications that potential changes could have. The challenge presented to participants would be the question of whether or not they agreed with the proposed number of beds to be moved that had been determined by simulation modelling. This created an opportunity for those offering care first-hand to have a voice in top-down decision-making processes, and hospital managers to have the opportunity to gain insights on potential blockages in arriving at the desired numbers. It was also decided that TTs would be used to represent hospital beds in each ward, externalising the ward's situation and challenges through potential movements and placements of the bed tokens. It was also determined that activities and questions should be as open ended as possible to create a working session environment where tools would facilitate discussions to be directed on the initiative of participating actors.

5.3.3.4 Spatial Relations of Care

Building upon the program presented to the cancer centre project director, each topic and question on the agenda were matched with a corresponding activity as a motivator for participants to make use of the tools in front of them. A visualization of a conceptual tool was created, designed on the basis of anticipating the actions the activity could trigger. Combined, this proposal was incorporated into the already planned meetings of the working group. By presenting a proposal of what such a SD event could look like, the cancer centre project director could more easily see the potential of the approach, leading to an agreement to proceed with tangible SD methods (See Fig. 5.6).

Fig. 5.6 Cancer centre project director, facilitation expert, oncology ward project lead and design researcher discussing agenda and activities for the working session, using TTs as points of reference. *Source* Photo, K. Rygh = Author's own illustration (2021)

Based on further feedback, the working session agenda was iterated and activities were tweaked on the basis of what the hospital manager anticipated would be most likely to work well and be of most interest to explore within the working group. The third phase of co-conceptualising the TT did not take place after the second phase, but was instead an active phase throughout phase 1 and 2, as sketch models of TTs were iterated along the way. Each meeting with the oncology ward project lead, facilitation designer and hospital manager had TT mock-ups present so that feedback could be given on these as well as supporting ideation on determining activities for the working session (Fig. 5.7). Here, it was possible to discuss ways in which participants could be expected to interact with tools through holding them in our hands and enacting certain scenarios as a test. Integrating physical mock-ups of TTs in these working sessions enabled tangible explorations of how grouping, categorizing and clustering hospital beds could be done in physical form and what the added value of these actions could be.

The designer-researcher codified each question and task with affordances the TTs could have in supporting specific actions in each task. She questioned which moments the tools should be used to represent and visualise the status quo of hospital wards and when the wooden tokens (beds) could be used in acts of negotiation. The design and form of the hospital beds therefore needed to accommodate several actions and possibilities. Tangible hospital bed representations were iterated in scale and form to accommodate multi-level discussions. On a meta-level,

Fig. 5.7 Facilitation expert and oncology ward project lead discussing how to lower the threshold for participants to make use of the TTs in discussion. *Source* Photo, K. Rygh = Author's own illustration (2021)

Fig. 5.8 Tool mock-ups representing macro-level hospital bed (larger rectangular wooden piece) and medical experts connected to a particular type of patient. It was later decided to omit macro-level tools as the time for the planned engagement was too limited. *Source* Photo, K. Rygh = Author's own illustration (2021)

discussion and negotiation (smaller bed tokens, see Fig. 5.7) concerned how beds could re-allocated and by being arranged in larger numbers and have markers placed on them to indicate type of patients. On a macro-level (larger wooden hospital bed representation, see Fig. 5.8) discussions could take place in regards to which networks of medical experts were connected to each hospital bed and according to type of patient. After iterating the colour coding of the wards and adjusting the numbers of hospital beds to be represented, the tool mock-ups was finalized as the 'Allocator tool' where the choice was made to focus on meta-level discussion and use of tools.

5.3.3.5 Changing Beds

Seven representatives from various wards managing oncology patients at AHUS were invited to a working session as part of their monthly meetings. The set agenda was to firstly gain a common understanding of the number and flow of cancer patients in each ward, secondly to acquire a broader understanding of the need for oncology beds and thirdly, to discuss the possibility of re-allocating a certain number of beds from different wards towards a new oncology ward. Lastly, the aim was to discuss the different factors that would affect these possible changes.

A working session agenda was prepared and facilitated by an external SD facilitator (the facilitation design expert). The external facilitator was supported by the SD team and the director of the cancer centre project. The designer-researcher (first author) observed the session, collecting data through participant observation and photography of the interactions between workshop participants and between participants and the physical tools provided.

5.3.3.6 'Touching the Beds'

The working session started with the participants (oncologists, consultants and nurses from other medical and surgical specialities who all dealt with oncology patients), some seated and some walking around the room, gathering around the boardroom table. This moment offered the opportunity to familiarize themselves with the tools by observing the table and touching the various physical pieces, picking them up, turning them upside down, feeling their texture and carefully placing them back again in their original position. Additionally, it enabled them to see their own ward in comparison to others.

On the table were TTs representing hospital beds in each ward, which had been placed in a particular arrangement in front of each participant (see Fig. 5.9). These visual arrangements had been set up by the designer-researcher and the oncology ward project lead prior to the working session, based on the data that the team had accumulated for each ward. Colour-coded markers had been placed onto the tools in advance, indicating the status of each patient occupying the beds and suggesting which patients could potentially be moved to a new ward.

Fig. 5.9 Participants seated around a boardroom table with their corresponding ward visualized in front of them by TTs. *Source* Photo, K. Rygh = Author's own illustration (2021)

5.3.3.7   Folding Away One's Own Assets

Engagement and enthusiasm was low upon arrival and tensions could be sensed towards the facilitators and objects on the table. As participants took their seats at the table, faces turned serious and arms were crossed. Some participants lent their bodies backwards in their seats as though to distance themselves as much as they could from the topic at hand. The phenomenon, or topic, that had just been dropped onto the table in physical form was unavoidable. It could not be made to disappear through conversation, neither through long arguments, distractions nor any change of subject. Through the tools' physical form, the topic and its challenges were materialized and were as present at the table as the participants themselves. This moment of participants being confronted with the topic in physical form was a good opportunity for both the cancer centre project director and the facilitators to 'read the room', so to speak. It became quite clear that an approach of avoiding discussion on the topic was also a means to protect one's own assets (maintain current number of hospital beds respective wards).

5.3.3.8   Beyond the Status Quo of 'Hospital Corners'

After presenting the agenda for the meeting, the first question from one participant was a request to clarify what specifically the objects on the table represented. When given the answer, the participant scoffed and replied that this was definitely not the current situation of the ward, to which the facilitator could easily follow up by answering 'Please *show* us what you mean'. And without delay, spoken word or explanation, the participant re-organized the wooden pieces and coloured markers and made the status quo of that particular ward immediately visible and known to all participants at the table (Fig. 5.10), much like the act of tidily making 'hospital

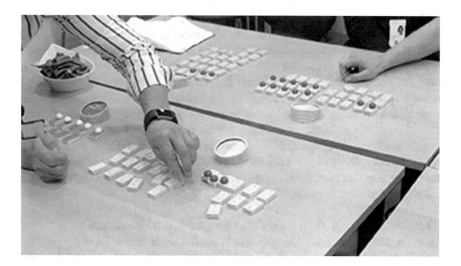

Fig. 5.10 A Participant moves hospital bed tokens to visualize the status quo of the ward in which she works. *Source* Photo, K. Rygh = Author's own illustration (2021)

corners' on beds. In this moment, additional questions or directions weren't needed, instead the tools were facilitative by their design, by their placement and through the action possibilities they afforded. The participant had just carried out one of the planned exercises on the agenda while also simultaneously expressing her opinion on the matter.

The speed, confidence and force with which the participant moved the pieces, made it possible to get a sense of the mood and emotions of the individual, how they were feeling, how they carried themselves according to the power dynamics and hierarchy in the room and their willingness to show their lived experience of a given situation. Furthermore, it was possible to read other participants' reactions to this gesture and visualization, whether it was already known to them or if they were gaining new insights. The visualizations made the contextual information visible and accessible to other participants, triggering them to also alter their own bed representation to make needed corrections.

5.3.3.9 Touch, Tokens and Futures

Throughout the meeting, a gesture from one participant, reaching over and moving another participant's tokens clearly showed a disagreement with what the participant had proposed. By moving hospital bed tokens in another ward, she entered into an act of negotiating possible future scenarios according to her interpretation of the other ward's needs and according to suggestions from the participant sitting opposite her, not beside her, as her arm movement and visual contact indicates (see Fig. 5.11). This raises questions of whether or not this participant would have spoken up in a meeting without the tools. The tools in this setting contributed the value of clearly concretizing elements of a proposal so that the participant could easily engage in a specific aspect of the proposal.

When researching the role that design plays in TTs, it is perhaps of equal interest to study what didn't happen in this situation: the TTs on the table were not rejected. There was no confusion about whether or not a participant could touch or move the tools. There was no misunderstanding about the association between representation of hospital beds and the actual, real-life context of the hospital ward. Participants were not confused about what purpose the wooden pieces were meant to serve, although a confirmation was needed on the assumption of its visualization, as mentioned previously (which in this case was interpreted not so much as a misunderstanding but rather a challenge on the participant's side towards the proposed visualization). The participant did not make fun of the tools as not taking the topic seriously and did not criticize the design of tools. The observation was therefore made that participants respected the physical objects as tools they could make use of at their disposal.

5.3.3.10 Crossing Thresholds and Embedded Affordances

For every action that did not happen within the SD event, an aspect of the physical object's design could be considered a success, in regards to being context appropriate. The tool's embedded affordances within its designed form, accommodated and facilitated the actions the tool designer had anticipated. Furthermore the quality,

Fig. 5.11 The reaching gesture, moving tokens representing hospital beds in another participant's ward, indicates a disagreement with the visualized proposal. *Source* Photo, K. Rygh = Author's own illustration (2021)

considerations and refinement of the design prevented anticipated, possible negative, undesired or unproductive reactions. The actions taken by participants in the SD event thereby exemplifies some of the complexity that is involved in designing TTs, especially in regards to hospital use. Furthermore, these interactions also illustrate how such tools are not neutral facilitation tools. Their design and affordances accommodate and direct desired actions and prevent, to some extent, other undesirable actions from taking place.

However, the threshold for participants to continuously use the tools throughout the meeting was a challenge and required 'all hands on deck' with the cancer centre project director, facilitation expert and oncology ward project lead all facilitating discussion (see Fig. 5.12).

Reaching for Future Ideations

When there was a strong disagreement with a visualization, there was a low threshold for engagement, but when discussion moved onwards and there was less disagreement, it was more difficult to engage participants in ideating future scenarios. The focus, for some, was still on keeping the status quo and not offering anything towards the new service concept. In total, the working session indicated

Fig. 5.12 Cancer centre project director, facilitation designer and oncology ward project lead facilitating engagement later in the working session. *Source* Photo, K. Rygh = Author's own illustration (2021)

that certain aspects of resource reallocation and negotiation can benefit from support with TTs and more research and exploration is needed to further investigate how this engagement can be prolonged to extend discussion and exploration of the topic.

5.4 Discussion

Through exemplifying a process of co-conceptualising a tangible service design engagement and designing accompanying TTs questions arise in regards to shifting perspectives within SD practice and how healthcare professionals can take a more active part in designing for complex relations of care. Here, we discuss the potentials of a careful SD approach and tangible service design in furthering research and exploration on emergent SD practice within PH.

5.4.1 Shifting Perspectives on SD and TTs

Supporting diverse professionals within early phase development calls for SD approaches to consider and design for matters of care stretching from the individual patient to aspects of policy making, influenced by societal, economic and environmental factors. Furthermore, developing a notion of how tangible service support in early phase formation of innovative partnerships can be conceptualized involves a multi-level shift in perspectives within SD: First is shifting a SD view of what constitutes service designing. Second, is shifting a co-design view in regards to how and in which ways relevant experts are supported in taking an active part in service designing in this phase and last, shifting the view on external representations used in co-design tools and methods, from solely visual, to visual and tangible.

In this multi-level shift, we view service support in what we call an 'Alignment in Early Phase SD Development'. Davis et al. (2000) have described organizational culture as emerging from that which is shared between individuals within an organization—beliefs, attitudes, values, norms of behaviour—and characterized organizational culture as a common way of making sense of an organisation. Within complex, cross-sector healthcare collaborations, there are limited possibilities for developing such a cultural alignment between diverse professionals. We therefore see 'Alignment in Early Phase SD Development' as a surrogate and intermediary support in addressing and negotiating underlying aspects relevant to creating a common point of departure for later phases of designing new service concepts.

In this alignment, the human centred approach of SD within a healthcare context is shifted from patient centric to what we term 'Patient and Health Care Professional Centric' in order to support healthcare professionals in taking an active part in fostering inter-professional collaboration. Here, service support is not imposed on experts and attempts are not made at directing them. Instead, focus is on fostering the conditions necessary for healthcare professionals themselves to forge new relations of care, collectively. This might be followed through in terms of intervention/disruption, although such approaches should be carried out with care within a healthcare context as relations are easier to break than to forge.

How design can support healthcare professionals in the anticipatory practice of collaboratively developing strategies for future healthcare contexts, calls for seeing co-design as a '... reflexive, embodied process of discovery and actualization' where tools and methods support 'being and becoming'. (Akama & Prendiville, 2016: 30). In regards to developing co-design tools within SD and to using tools as a mode of inquiry for design research, designing also becomes an act of 'attuning' as a means of making the understandings of various actors more concrete and thereby making it possible to carefully develop modes of approaching them (Akama & Prendiville, 2016). In this way, 'attuning' can also be seen as shifting focus from pre-designed proposals and methods, towards establishing an awareness of the participation of materials and formatting co-designing '... in the situation and network where people and materials meet, align and make each other act' (Eriksen, 2012: 24). In this way, designers are forced to 'entangle themselves' into a given space and while they are crafting this space, they are also being 'crafted by it' (Akama & Prendiville, 2016: 32). This form of designing supports service designing with care.

5.4.2 The Service Ecosystems Model, Tangible Tools and Tangible Service Design

Alignment and attuning may also be connected to the service ecosystems model (Vink et al., 2021) with its focus on purpose, material, processes and actor involvement. First, attending to purpose and emergence is crucial in early phase development where co-design and the co-creation and potential for its continued, iterative and recursive realization may be intentionally and embedded. This may be done explicitly in physical artefacts and within the embedding of communicative affordances in anticipation of prospective and engagement entailing tangible interaction.

On design material, developing TTs requires attention to the selection of physical materials and their properties and relations to contributing to human scale interplay via enactments of embodied artefacts. These are linked with and within tactile, gestural and embodied interaction and constitute contributions to material communicative and professional and organizational affordances in use in service-centred, institutionally located and care-based negotiative events.

In relation to the third element processes, the development of TTs may be rendered through iterative, recursive and critical reflection in and through making and use. Such a dynamic view on developing tools attends to embodied and spatial aspects of tangible service interactions and engagement. As the tools are developed via co-creative and co-design activities, they may be looped, cataphorically and anaphorically, within the processes of phases of service development. Further, they may be viewed and reviewed in design, development, trialling and use via active, open and critical reflexive reviews, shifts and even reformations via processes of redesign to better suit contexts of need and purpose, in an interplay between the intended, emergent, projected and enacted.

In the context of designing TTs for the 'careful' clarification and negotiation of needs and medical and patient-centred outcomes and nurturing practices, actor involvement may be realized by way of shared design in teams. These teams may be reconstituted or even recombined across the processes of designing with and through the tangible for situated negotiations on resources uses, dynamic interactions between diverse stakeholders and longer-term collective involvement in shaping public health via the design and uses of TTs and related experiential service interactions.

These brief orientations to TTs that have been co-created and range from design to use and reflexive review within and through a view on service ecosystem design are located within '... the intentional shaping of institutional arrangements and their physical enactments by actor collectives' (Vink, et al., 2021: 172). However, they are also indicative of aspects of what we term Tangible Service Design (TSD) in a wider service-systems set and relational interplays at a level of articulation, mediation and design-centred multimodal communication (Morrison, 2010). By this, we mean that such a dimensional and connected mapping may be read and understood by way of attention to its realization in contexts of exploratory design and use.

In addition to earlier conceptualizations, these propositions contribute to 'The Multi-level Process Model of Service Ecosystem Design' and its micro, meso and macro levels and dynamics (Vink et al., 2021). At a micro level, feedback loops are central. At a meso level, focus on a desired form of co-creation may align or conflict with their aims. When working at a macro level, focus is on the dynamic between the designer actors and others and the weighting given to them in affecting aligned and promoted or deflected and resisted institutional change processes. Overall, this connects with the argument by Puig de la Bellacasa (2011: 100) that 'The notion of "matters of care" is a proposition to think with'.

5.5 Conclusion

The case presented in this chapter is an instance of exploring the situated development and use of TTs in early phase development in support of intra-professional team negotiation of the understanding and allocation of multi-purpose uses of specific and shared resources within a specialist PH care facility. The focus on TTs is situated within a service design ecosystems perspective. In this view, attention has been extended to both the designing of tools and to mediated action conceptualized as articulations, that is, connected activities and amplifying notions of care through shaping relations between physical tools, touch, gesture and spatially enacted embodied negotiations. SD-supported TTs contributed to the co-creation of long-term care-based decisions in which multiple interests needed to be considered and reconfigured in rethinking disciplinary/domain boundaries, tensions and potential intersections and overlaps of needs, wants, visions and preferred and potential futures in PH.

This indicates the potential for attending to change paradigmatically through what we call 'Tangible Service Design' (TSD). It points to the need to explore emergent praxis and related principles through exploratory heuristic methods and participative activities by diverse stakeholders and through intersecting expertise between SD and PH. Crucial too are the prospects for TSD in offering detailed theoretical and elaborated practice accounts of interplays between materialities and interactions in realising potential and prospective change in PH care. How to engage within this context then becomes a matter of developing alternative early phase approaches to both the traditional interventionist and emergent disruptive approaches within SD shown to work less favourably in early phase service development in healthcare contexts.

We envisage that possible and potential links and application between tangibility and services in SD need to be considered as a whole In TSD. We propose that this may be achieved through the focus on the following connected categories (1) values and artefacts, (2) the choice of materials, (3) form and appeal, (4) relations between sensory modes and mediation, (5) design and representation, (6) embedded and tangible affordances and (7) metaphors in support of enactments. While attention is needed to each of these aspects in developing TTs and service design interactions and enactment, it is critical that their design and dynamics of purposive use also centre on their intersections and holistic relations, and thereby their alignment and potential as service centred components and offerings to a wider SD ecosystem.

Following Vink et al. (2021), one of the main challenges in design that supports the connection of services in the provision of public health is for such design to be positioned and enacted within what we term 'A Service Design Ecosystem of Connected Care'. This may be enabled through the embodiment of TTs used in co-design negotiations realized via situated, shared framing and embodied enactment of meaningful, effective and connected services for PH also situated in an ecosystems view. Such an ecology may be realized through the multimodal and multisensory through their embodied, performative and affective affordances and uses by multiple actors to purposive health care encounters and their interplays.

This requires that we pay attention on how to conceptualise, realise and review the design of such services as innovations, as Lury (2018) reminds us, in and through service designing. Here, underlying psychological aspects that create hesitation and resistance to service development processes are in need of further research in continuing to build SD contributions to connected care in PH through embodied perception, mediated action and dynamic interaction by participants and stakeholders to durative support and change.

References

Akama, Y., & Prendiville, A. (2016). Embodying, enacting and entangling design: A phenomenological view to co-designing services. *Swedish Design Research Journal, 9*(1), 29–40. https://doi.org/10.3384/svid.2000-964X.13129

Alves, R., & Nunes, N. (2013). Towards a taxonomy of service design methods and tools. In J. Cunha, M. Snene, & M. Eusébio Sampaio da Nóvoa (Eds.), *IESS'2013, Proceedings of the 4th International Conference on Exploring Service Science*, Porto, 7–8 February 2013 (pp. 215–229). Berlin: Springer.

Angelini, L., Lalanne, D., Van den Hoven, E., & Mugellini, E. (2015). Move, hold and touch: A frame work for Tangible Gesture Interactive Systems. *Machines, 3*(3), 173–207. https://doi.org/10.3390/machines3030173

Becker, J., & Smith, D. (2018). The need for cross-sector collaboration. In *Stanford Social Innovation Review*. https://ssir.org/articles/entry/the_need_for_cross_sector_collaboration. Accessed 3 July 2021.

Binder, T., Brandt, E., Ehn, P., & Halse, J. (2015). Democratic design experiments: Between parliament and laboratory. *CoDesign Journal, 11*(3–4), 152–165. https://doi.org/10.1080/15710882.2015.1081248

Bitner, M., Ostrom, A., & Morgan, F. (2008). Service blueprinting: A practical technique for service innovation. *California Management Review, 50*(3), 66–94. https://doi.org/10.2307/41166446

Blomkvist, J., & Holmlid, S. (2010). Service prototyping according to service design practitioners. In S. Holmlid, J. Nisula, & S. Clatworthy (Eds.) *ServDes'10, Proceedings of the 2nd Service Design and Service Innovation conference, Exchanging Knowledge, Linköping*, 1–3 December 2010 (pp. 1–13). Linköping: Linköping University Electronic Press. https://ep.liu.se/ecp/060/001/ecp10060001.pdf.

Barnes, M. (2012). *Care in everyday Life - An ethic of care in practice, University of Bristol*. The Policy Press.

Clatworthy, S. (2013). Design support at the front end of the new service development (NSD) process: The role of touch-points and service personality in supporting team work and innovation processes (Doctoral dissertation). Oslo: Oslo School of Architecture and Design.

Clatworthy, S. (2019). *The Experience Centric Organization - How to win through customer experience*. O'Reilly Media.

Coxon, I., & Bremner, C. (2019). Who cares? ...but first, what is the who, and what is care? In T. Mattelmäki, R. Mazé, S. Miettinen (Eds.) *NORDES'19: Proceedings of the 8th Bi-Annual Nordic Design Research Society Conference—Who Cares?* Helsinki, 2–4 June 2019 (Vol. 8, pp. 1–8). Helsinki: Aalto University School of Arts, Design and Architecture, Nordic Design Research.

Crabtree, A., Rouncefield, M., & Tolmie, P. (2012). *Doing Design ethnography*. Springer.

Cross, N. (2007). *Designerly ways of knowing*. Birkhauser.

Davies, H., Nutley, S., & Mannion, R. (2000). Organisational culture and quality of health care. *Quality & Safety in Health Care, 9*(2), 111–119. https://doi.org/10.1136/qhc.9.2.111PMCID: PMC1743521 PMID: 11067249.

Dennington, C. (2021). Refashioning service design: designing for popular cultural service experience. Ph.D. thesis. Oslo: Oslo School of Architecture and Design. https://aho.brage.unit. no/aho-xmlui/handle/11250/2739283. Accessed 27 June 2021.

Denzin, N., & Lincoln, Y. (1994). (Eds.) *Handbook of Qualitative Research*. Thousand Oaks: SAGE.

Djajadiningrat, T., Wensween, S., Frens, J., & Overbeeke, K. (2004). Tangible products: Redressing the balance between appearance and action. *Personal and Ubiquitous Computing, 8* (5), 294–309. https://doi.org/10.1007/s00779-004-0293-8

Djajadiningrat, T., Matthews, B., & Stienstra, M. (2007). Easy doesn't do it: Skill and expression in tangible aesthetics. *Personal and Ubiquitous Computing, 11*(8), 657–676. https://doi.org/10. 1007/s00779-006-0137-9

Dohn, N. (2009). Affordances revisited: Articulating a Merleau-Pontian view. *International Journal of Computer-Supported Collaborative Learning, 4*(2), 151–170. https://doi.org/10. 1007/s11412-009-9062-z

Drew, C. (2019). *The Double Diamond, 15 years on ... Medium*. https://medium.com/design-council/the-double-diamond-15-years-on-8c7bc594610e. Accessed 29 June 2021.

Eikenes, J. O., & Morrison, A. (2010). Navimation: Exploring time, space & motion in the design of screen-based interfaces. *International Journal of Design, 4*(1), 1–16.

Eriksen, M. (2012). Material Matters in co-designing. PhD thesis. Malmö University, Faculty of Culture and Society: Malmö. Dissertation series in New Media, Public Spheres and Forms of Expression, 3. https://www.diva-portal.org/smash/get/diva2:1404319/FULLTEXT01.pdf. Accessed 27 June 2021.

Fitzsimmons, J., & Fitzsimmons, M. (2000). *New service development: Creating memorable experiences*. Thousand Oaks: SAGE.

Frayling, C. (1993). *Research in art and design* (Vol. 1(1), pp. 1–5). London: Royal College of Art Research Papers. https://researchonline.rca.ac.uk/384/3/frayling_research_in_art_and_design_ 1993.pdf. Assessed 8 July 2021.

Freund, T., Everett, C., Griffiths, P., Hudon, C., Naccarella, L., & Laurant, M. (2015). Skill mix, roles and remuneration in the primary care workforce: Who are the healthcare professionals in the primary care teams across the world? *International Journal of Nursing Studies, 52*(3), 727–743. PMID: 25577306. https://doi.org/10.1016/j.ijnurstu.2014.11.014.

Frist, W. H. (2014). Connected health and the rise of the patient-consumer. *Health Aff: Intersection of Health Care Policy, 33*(2), 191–193. PMID: 24493759. https://doi.org/10.1377/hlthaff.2013. 1464.

Gaver, W. (1991). Technology affordances. In P. Robertson, G. Olson, & J. Olson (Eds) *CHI'91, Proceedings of the SIGCHI conference on Human Factors in Computing Systems*, New Orleans, 27 April–2 May 1991 (pp. 79–84). New York: ACM Press.

Gibson, J. (1977). The theory of affordances. In R. Shaw & J. Bransford (Eds.), *Perceiving, acting, and knowing: Toward an ecological psychology* (pp. 67–82). Lawrence Erlbaum Associates.

Greenwood, D. J., & Levin, M. (2007). *Introduction to action research* (2nd ed). Thousand Oaks: SAGE. https://doi.org/10.4135/9781412984614.

Hamington, M. (2010). The will to care: Performance, expectation and imagination. Hypatia. *Journal of Feminist Philosophy, 25*(3), 675–695. https://doi.org/10.1111/j.1527-2001.2010.01110.

Haraway, D. (2008). *When species meet*. University of Minnesota Press.

Harrison, S., Hunter, D., Marnoch, G., & Politt, C. (1992). *Just managing: Power and culture in the national health service*. Macmillan.

Harrison, J., & Nutley S. (1996). Professions and management in the public sector: The experience of local government and the NHS in Britain. In J. Leopold, I. Glover, & M. Hughes (Eds.) *Beyond reason?* The National Health Service and the limits of management (pp. 227–248). Avebury: Alderschot.

Haynes, L. (2021). Primary care teams need support to manage spiraling workload, warns PCN network. GPOnline. https://www.gponline.com/primary-care-teams-need-support-manage-spiralling-workload-warns-pcn-network/article/1714484. Accessed 27 June 2021.

Helse-og omsorgsdepartementet (Ministry of Health and Care Services). (2013). Morgendagens omsorg 29 (Tomorrow's care) (2013–2014). Helse og omsorgsdepartementet, (Ministry of Health and Care Services), Oslo.

Helse- og omsorgsdepartementet (Ministry of Health and Care Services). (2014). HelseOmsorg21, et kunnskapssystem for bedre folkehelse: Nasjonal forsknings- og innovasjonsstrategi for helse og omsorg. (Health and care 21, a knowledgesystem for improved public health: National insurance and innovation strategy for health and care services), Helse- og omsorgsdepartementet (Ministry of Health and Care Services), Oslo.

Holopainen, M. (2010). Exploring service design in the context of architecture. *The Service Industries Journal, 30*(4), 597–608.

Hornecker, E., & Buur, J. (2006). Getting a grip on trangible interaction: A framework on physical space and social interaction. In: R. Grinter, T. Rodden, P. Aoki, E. Cutrell, R. Jeffries, G. Olson (Eds.) *CHI'6, Proceedings of the 2006 Conference on Human Factors in Computing Systems*, Montreal, 22–27 April 2006 (pp. 437–446). New York: Association for Computing Machinery.

Hornecker, E. (2017). Tangible Interaction, HCI and computing: Tangible user interfaces. In M. Soegaard, & R. Friis-Dam (Eds.) *The encyclopaedia of human-computer interaction* (2nd ed.). The Interaction Design Foundation. https://www.interaction-design.org/literature/book/the-glossary-of-human-computer-interaction/tangible-interaction. Accessed 27 June 2021.

Ishii, H., & Ullmer, B. (1997). Tangible bits: Towards seamless interfaces between people, bits and atoms. In *CHI'97, Proceedings of the SIGCHI conference on Human factors in computing systems*, Atlanta, 22–27 March 1997 (pp. 234–241). New York: ACM Press.

Jones, P. (2013). *Design for care: Innovating healthcare experience*. Rosenfeld Media.

Kaptelinin, V., & Nardi, B. (2012), Affordances in HCI: Toward a mediated action perspective. In *CHI'12 Proceedings of the SIGCHI Conference on Human Factors in Computing Systems*, 5–10 May 2012, New York (pp. 967–976). https://doi.org/10.1145/2207676.2208541. Accessed 27 June 2021.

Kaptelinin, V. (2014). Affordances. In M. Soegaard, & R. Dam (Eds.) *The encyclopaedia of human-computer interaction* (2nd Ed.). Interaction Design Foundation. https://www.interaction-design.org/literature/book/the-encyclopedia-of-human-computer-interaction-2nd-ed/affordances. Accessed 27 June 2021.

Kim, Y. S., Lee, S. W., Kim, S. R., Jeong, H., & Kim, J. H. (2012). A product-service Systems design method with integration of product elements and service elements using affordances. In P. Tossavainen, & M. Harjula (Eds.) *ServDes'12, Proceedings of the 3rd Service Design and Service Innovation Conference*, Espoo, 8–10 February 2012 (pp. 111–119). Linköping: Linköping Electronic Conference Proceedings. https://ep.liu.se/ecp/067/013/ecp1267013.pdf.

Koen, P., Ajamian, G., Burkart, R., Clamen, A., Davidson, J., D'Amore, R., Elkins, C., Herald, K., Incorvia, M., Johnson, A., Karol, R., Seibert, R., Slavejkov, A., & Wagner, K. (2001). Providing clarity and a common language to the "Fuzzy Front End." *Research-Technology Management, 44*(2), 46–55. https://doi.org/10.1080/08956308.2001.11671418

Korper, A., Blomkvist, J., Rodrigues, V., & Holmlid, S. (2020), Hear hear! Why sound in service design should matter. In Y. Akama (Ed.) *ServDes'20, Proceedings of the 7th Service Design and Service Innovation Conference*, RMIT University, Melbourne, 6–9 July 2020 (pp. 384–396). Linköping: Linköping Electronic Conference Proceedings. https://ep.liu.se/ecp/173/036/ecp20173036.pdf.

Kröger, T. (2009). Care research and disability studies: Nothing in common? *Critical Social Policy, 29*(3), 398–420. https://doi.org/10.1177/0261018309105177

Lakoff, G., & Johnson, M. (1980). *Metaphors we live by.* Chicago University Press.

Latour, B. (2004). Why has critique run out of steam? From matters of fact to matters of concern. *Critical Inquiry, 30*(2), 225–248. https://doi.org/10.1086/421123

Light, A., & Akama, Y. (2014). Structuring future social relations: The politics of care in participatory practice. In H. Winschiers-Theophilus, A. Vincenzo & O. Iversen (Eds.) *PDC'14, Proceedings of the 13th Participatory Design Conference, Reflecting Connectedness*, Windhoek, 6–10 October 2014 (Vol. 1, pp. 151–160). New York: ACM Press.

Lury, C. (2018). Introduction—Activating the present of interdisciplinary methods. In C. Lury, R. Fenshan, A. Heller-Nicholas, S. Lammes, A. Last, M. Michael, & E. Uprichard (Eds.), *Routledge handbook of interdisciplinary research methods* (pp. 1–25). Routledge.

Macdonnel, A., & Darzi, A. (2013). A key to slower health spending growth worldwide will be unlocking innovation to reduce the labor-intensity of care. *Health Aff (Milwood), 32*(4), 653–660. PMID: 23569044. https://doi.org/10.1377/hlthaff.2012.1330.

Manzini, E. (2011). Small, local, open and connected: Design research topics in the age of networks and sustainability. *The Journal of Design Strategies, 4*(1), 8–11.

Martins, R. (2016). Increasing the success of service design implementation: Bridging the gap between design and change management. *Touchpoint, 8*(2), 12–14.

Mathews, T. (2021). Exploring sacred service design. Ph.D. Thesis. Oslo: Oslo School of Architecture and Design. https://aho.brage.unit.no/aho-xmlui/handle/11250/2758408. Accessed 29 June 2021.

Miettinen, S. (2009). Service designers' methods. In S. Miettinen & M. Koivisto (Eds.), *Designing services with innovative methods* (pp. 60–77). University of Art and Design Helsinki.

Mol, A., Moser, I., & Pols, J. (2010). *Care in practice: On tinkering in clinics, homes and farms.* Transcript Publishing.

Morelli, N. (2002). Designing product/service systems: A methodological exploration. *Design Issues, 18*(3), 3–17. https://doi.org/10.1162/074793602320223253

Morrison, A. (2010). *Inside multimodal composition.* Hampton Press.

Morrison, A., Mainsah, H., & Rygh K. (2019). Sharp edges, blunt objects, clean slices. Exploring design research methods. *The Design Journal, 22*(1), 2267–2273. https://doi.org/10.1080/14606925.2019.1595025.

Murphy, K., & Marcus, G. (2013). Epilogue: Ethnography and design, ethnography in design, ethnography by design. In W. Gunn, T. Otto, & R. Charlotte-Smith (Eds.), *Design anthropology: Theory and practice* (pp. 251–268). Bloomsbury.

Nordby, K., & Morrison, A. (2010). Designing tangible interaction using short-range RFID. *FORMakademisk, 3*(2). http://www.formakademisk.org/index.php/formakademisk/article/view/78/106. Accessed 29 June 2021.

Norman, D. (1988). *The psychology of everyday things.* Basic Books.

Norman, D. (2013). *The design of everyday things: Revised and expanded.* Basic Books.

OECD. (2018). *Challenges in long-term care in Europe - A study of national policies 2018.* European Commission - Employment, social affairs and inclusion, KE-01-18-637-EN-N.

Overkamp, T., & Holmlid, S. (2017). Implementation during design: Developing understanding about service realization before implementation. *The Design Journal, 20*(1), 4409–4421.

Paradis, E., & Reeves, S. (2013). Key trends in interprofessional research: A macrosociological analysis from 1970 to 2010. *Journal of Interprofessional Care, 27*(2), 113–122.

Patricio, L., Fisk, R. P., Cunha, E., & Falcao, J. (2008). Designing multi-interface service experiences: The service experience blueprint. *Journal of Service Research, 10*(4), 318–334. https://doi.org/10.1177/1094670508314264

Puig, M. (2011). Matters of care in technoscience: Assembling neglected things. *Social Studies of Science, 41*(1), 85–106. https://doi.org/10.1177/0306312710380301

Puig, M. (2017). *Matters of care: Speculative ethics in more than human worlds*. University of Minnesota Press.

Ragnoli, V., & Levi, M. (2004). Emotions in design through materials: An expressive-sensorial atlas as a project tool for design of materials. In A. Kurtgözü (Ed.) *D&E'4, Proceedings of the 4th International Design and Emotion conference*, Middle East Technical University, Ankara, 12–14 July 2004 (pp. 1–13). https://doi.org/10.5281/zenodo.2619752.

Raijmakers, B., & Miller, S. (2016). *Viewfinders—Thoughts on visual design research*. STBY Ltd.

Ringard, Å., Sagan, A., Saunes, I. S., & Lindahl, A. K. (2013). Norway: Health system review. *Health Systems in Transition, 15*(8), 1–162. https://www.euro.who.int/__data/assets/pdf_file/0018/237204/HiTNorway.pdf.

Romm, J., Agudelo, N., & Freitas, T. (2020). Shaping physical, social and imaginary spaces in healthcare design labs. Spaces for health and care. *Artifact Journal of Design Practice, 7*(1–2), 13.1–13.29. https://doi.org/10.1386/art_00013_1.

Rygh, K., & Clatworthy, S. (2019). The use of tangible tools as a means to support co-design during service design innovation projects in healthcare. In M. Pfannstiel & C. Rasche (Eds.) *Service design and service thinking in healthcare and hospital management. Theory, concepts, practice* (pp. 93–115). Cham: Springer.

Sanders, E., Brandt, E., & Binder, T. (2010), A framework for organizing the tools and techniques of participatory design. In *PDC'10, Proceedings of the 11th Participatory Design Conference*, Sydney, 29 November–3 December 2010 (pp. 195–198). New York: ACM Press.

Sanders, E., & Stappers, P. J. (2014). Probes, toolkits and prototypes: Three approaches to making in codesigning. *CoDesign Journal, 10*(1), 5–14. https://doi.org/10.1080/15710882.2014.888183,CorpusID:108955372

Schneider, J., & Stickdorn, M. (2010). *This is service design thinking*. BIS Publishers.

Schön, D. (1992). Designing as reflective conversation with the materials of a design situation. *Research in Engineering Design, 3*(3), 131–147. https://doi.org/10.1007/BF01580516

Schot, E., Tummers, L. & Noordegraaf, M. (2020). Working on working together. A systematic review on how healthcare professionals contribute to interprofessional collaboration. *Journal of Interprofessional Care, 34*(3), 332–342. PMID: 31329469. https://doi.org/10.1080/13561820.2019.1636007.

Sevaldson, B. (2011). Giga-Mapping: Visualisation for complexity and systems thining in design. In I. Koskinen, T. Härkäsalmi, R. Mazé, B. Matthews & J. Lee (Eds.) *NORDES'11, Proceedings of the 4th Nordic Design Research Conference*, The School of Art & Design, Aalto Unviersity, Helsinki, 29–31 May, pp. 137–156. https://archive.nordes.org/index.php/n13/article/view/104.

Sheenan, N. (2021). Articulatory, respectful service design. Keynote. In *ServDes '20, Proceedings of the 7th Service Design and Service Innovation Conference—Tensions, Paradoxes, Plurality*, RMIT University, Melbourne, 2–5 February 2021 (p. 2). Linköping: Linköping Electronic Conference Proceedings. https://servdes2020.s3-ap-southeast-2.amazonaws.com/uploads/assets/ServDes2020_FullProceedings.pdf.

Stappers, J., & Giaccardi, E. (2017). Research through Design. *The encyclopaedia of human-computer interaction* (pp. 1–94). Hershey: Idea Group Reference.

Sundby, I. J., & Hansen, L. U. (2017). *Brukerne i sentrum: En kartlegging av staten's fellesføring om brukerretting (Users in the centre: A study of the state's common venture on user centricity)*. The Digitization Council (Digdir). https://www.digdir.no/media/512/download

Tinetti, M., Fried, T., & Boyd, C. (2012), Designing health care for the most common chronic condition—multimorbidity. *American Medical Association, 307*(23), 2493–2494. PMID: 22797447; PMCID: PMC4083627. https://doi.org/10.1001/jama.2012.5265.

Tomej, K., & Xiang, Z. (2020). Affordances for tourism service design. Annals of Tourism Research, 85 November 2020. PMID: 32863477; PMCID: PMC7441883. https://doi.org/10.1016/j.annals.2020.103029.

Tronto, J. (1993). *Moral boundaries – A political argument for an ethic of care*. Routledge.

Tronto, J. (2013). *Caring democracy—Markets, equality and justice*. New York University Press.

Twigg, J. (2000). Carework as a form of body work. *Ageing and Society, 20*(4), 389–411. https://doi.org/10.1017/S0144686X99007801

Utviklingsplan. (2017). *Kreftplan for AHUS (Oncology plan for AHUS)*. Akershus Universitetssykehus (Akershus University Hospital).

Vaajakallio, K., Lehtinen, V., Mattelmäki, T., Kuikkaniemi, K., & Kantola, V. (2010). Someone else's shoes: Using role-playing games for empathy and collaboration in service design. *Swedish Design Research Journal, 1*, 34–41.

van den Hoven, E., & Mazalek, A. (2009). Framing tangible interaction frameworks. *Artificial Intelligence for Engineering Design, Analysis and Manufacturing, 23*, 225–235.

Vargo, S., & Lusch, R. (2017). Service-dominant logic 2025. *International Journal of Research in Marketing, 34*(1), 46–67. https://doi.org/10.1016/j.ijresmar.2016.11.001

Vaughan, L. (2018). Design as a practice of care. In L. Vaughan (Ed.), *Designing cultures of care* (pp. 444–638). Bloomsbury.

Vink, J., Koskela-Huotari, K., Tronvoll, B., Edvardsson, B., & Wetter-Edman, K. (2021). Service ecosystem design: Propositions, process model, and future research agenda. *Journal of Service Research, 24*(2), 168–186. https://doi.org/10.1177/1094670520952537

Wartofsky, M. (1979). *Models: Representation in scientific understanding*. Reidel Publishing Co.

Weicht, B. (2016). The meaning of care: The social construction of care for elderly people. *Journal of Social Policy, 45*(3), 578–579.

Wellner, P., Mackay, W., & Gold, R. (1993). Back to the real world. *Communications of the ACM, 36*(7), 24–26. https://doi.org/10.1145/159544.159555

Wetter-Edman, K., Sangiorgi, D., Edvardsson, B., Holmlid, S., Grönroos, C., & Mattelmaaki, T. (2014). Design for value co-creation: Exploring synergies between design for service and service logic. *Service Science, 6*(2), 106–121. https://doi.org/10.1287/SERV.2014.0068CorpusID:167376913

Withagen, R., de Poel, H., Araúj, D., & Pepping, G.-J. (2012). Affordances can invite behavior: Re-considering the relationship between extaffordances and agency. *New Ideas in Psychology, 30*(2), 250–258. https://doi.org/10.1016/j.newideapsych.2011.12.003

Yu, E., & Sangiorgi, D. (2014). Service design as an approach to new service development: Reflections and future studies. In D. Sangiorgi, D. Hands & E. Murphy (Eds.) ServDes'14, *Proceedings of the 4th Service Design and Service Innovation Conference, Lancaster, 9–11 April 2014. Linköping Electronic Conference Proceedings*, Linköping, pp. 194–204. http://www.servdes.org/wp/wp-content/uploads/2014/06/Yu-E-Sangiorgi-D.pdf. Accessed 8 July 2021.

Zeithaml, V., & Bitner, M. (1996). *Service marketing*. McGraw-Hill.

Zimmerman, J., Stolterman, E., & Forlizzi, J. (2010). An analysis and critique of research through design: Towards a formalization of a research approach. In: *DIS'10, Proceedings of the 8th ACM Conference on Designing Interactive Systems*, Aarhus, 16–20 August 2010 (pp. 310–319). New York: ACM Press. https://doi.org/10.1145/1858171.1858228.

Karianne Rygh is an industrial designer and Service Design PhD fellow at the Institute of Design at The Oslo School of Architecture and Design (AHO). Her PhD thesis focuses on the role of tangibility in the intersection between Service Design and care in public health, investigating how multidisciplinary service development teams can be supported in the collaborative process of innovating healthcare services. The research is conducted in collaboration with Centre for Connected Care (C3) with the aim of accelerating the adoption and diffusion of patient centric service innovations within healthcare. C3 is an eight-year initiative started in 2015 by the Centre for Research-based Innovation (SFI), funded by the Norwegian Research Council.

Andrew Morrison is Professor in Interdisciplinary Design and Director of the Centre for Design Research at the Oslo School of Architecture and Design (AHO) in Norway. His research spans many domains in design including Service Design where his commitment has been to building and supporting a team of critically active doctoral students, connected to two Centres of Innovation. Andrew works in the emerging field of Anticipation Studies and Futures Design, and is interested in supporting long term sustainable and meaningful futures through design. This includes innovation in Service Design with cultural, technical, prospective, situated and collaborative qualitative inquiry and systemic change at its core.

A Speculation for the Future of Service Design in Healthcare: Looking Through the Lens of a Speculative Service Design Framework

6

Christopher Kueh, Fanke Peng, Philip Ely, and Gareth Durrant

Abstract

Service design (SD) is expanding from a discipline focussing on project-centred outcomes and developing toolkits into one that is used as a strategic and transformative driver in the public, social and health sectors. SD in healthcare continues to positively shape people's well-being and the organizational structure that supports health services. This chapter extends design discourse on 'Speculative Design' towards an analysis of service design in organizational and community success. We propose a speculative service design (SSD) framework that explores SD in healthcare through SD as a way of speculating on the future of community well-being. Through this future-focus perspective, we encourage service designers to unpack the complexity of organizational and community-based problems, and to approach SD as a platform to generate discursive dialogues with people (non-users, users and stakeholders) in the provision of health services.

C. Kueh (✉)
School of Arts and Humanities, Edith Cowan University, 2 Bradford Street, Mount Lawley, Perth, Western Australia 6050, Australia
e-mail: c.kueh@ecu.edu.au

F. Peng
UniSA Creative, University of South Australia, 61-68 North Terrace, Adelaide, SA 5000, Australia

P. Ely
The State of Design Research Network, School of Design and Built Environment, Curtin University, Kent St, Western Australia 6102, Australia
e-mail: philip.ely@curtin.edu.au

G. Durrant
DSIL Global, 408 Tampines Street 41#03-185, 520408 Republic of Singapore, Singapore
e-mail: gareth@disilglobal.com

© The Author(s), under exclusive license to Springer Nature Switzerland AG 2022
M. A. Pfannstiel et al. (eds.), *Service Design Practices for Healthcare Innovation*,
https://doi.org/10.1007/978-3-030-87273-1_6

6.1   Introduction

Healthcare is shifting rapidly from a biomedical care model to a people-centred and self-management care model (Malmberg et al., 2019). Design has played an important role in this shift by providing health systems with people-centred and creative approaches to rethink and reimagine health services (Cottam & Leadbeater, 2004; Pasman, 2016; Tsekleves et al., 2019). This chapter expands the role of service design in healthcare from one that provides service solutions for existing problems towards a more speculative practice that provokes the healthcare service sector to engage in dialogues that fundamentally challenge the status quo in current systems. We see that the future of service design in healthcare needs to be a platform to engage the communities in discursive dialogues about innovation, equality and sustainability.

Current approaches in service design include abstract, static and schematic representations of service strategies. Common techniques such as touchpoint matrices, service blueprints, customer journey maps and business model canvases involve service designers embodying the knowledge of providers, stakeholders, partners and patients in abstract graphic forms: the ubiquitous post-it note, sketched schematics and graphic or material forms. Whilst these approaches allow a service designer to create conceptual maps of the intended service and are primarily effective in the functional fulfilment of a service design brief, they do not provide enough opportunities for service designers and stakeholders to engage in critical dialogues about the future (Pasman, 2016, p. 511). Our view—as practising designers—is that the role of designer should therefore be one of a provocateur, in which we aim to envision a more radical future of healthcare service systems that allow people to genuinely shape their personal health (Ludden & Vallgarda, 2019). Such a speculative practice can be seen as complementary to the instrumentalist logic that dominates the application of service design in healthcare; a speculative practice that works to expand stakeholder's imagination to achieve both incremental change (in the short-term) and fundamental shifts in values and beliefs (Gerber, 2018, p. 33) in the longer term.

In the following pages, we set out a framework for this speculative service design and explore how this might be applied in real-life practical settings. Just as we suggest that service design should adopt more dialogical approaches to the creation of new health services, we adopted a similar approach in the development of the framework. We first explored contemporary shifts in service design practice and then proceeded to the analysis of a recent meaningful healthcare service design case study that one of the authors (Durrant) has been directly involved with. Emergent from this analysis is a model for speculative service designs that we believe is directly applicable to healthcare settings but may also be transferable to other domains.

6.2   From Service to Transformation

Service design is an expanding design practice that involves multi-disciplinary professions such as engineers, visual designers, psychologists, anthropologists and sociologists (Cottam, 2008; Stickdorn & Schneider, 2010; Sangiorgi & Junginger, 2015). Service design shapes people's experience through the strategic implementation of service touchpoints as part of overall service systems (Polaine et al., 2013). The early development of service design focussed on the practical tools necessary to develop services based on user's needs (Shostack, 1982). This user-centred focus has a strong presence in the subsequent development of the service design process and methods (see Curedale, 2013; Design Council, n. d.; Stickdorn & Schneider, 2010; Stickdorn et al., 2018). However, common service design methods—such as service blueprints and business model canvases—are schematic representations of complex design challenges and context that limits design's role in exploring and communicating experiences of services as a whole (Pasman, 2016).

Service design is expanding its role into that of a strategic and transformative driver (DeVylder, 2019). In the areas of public services, organizations and public are engaged in collaborative service modelling, resulting in transformations in interaction patterns and roles within service settings (Sangiorgi, 2011, p. 29; Schaminée, 2018). This shift means that the service designer's responsibility has expanded beyond applying creativity to produce service touchpoints; designers now need to apply design process and design ways of thinking to drive positive reform. Sangiorgi et al., (2017, pp. 25–30) explain that service design spaces include:

- Pre-design phase: where designers need to investigate and challenge pre-existing design practices and perceptions within an organization.
- During design: apart from contributing design skills to produce design outputs, designers must also contribute towards critical development in a creative and systemic process and adopt collaborative mindsets.
- Post-design: designers need to challenge an organization to move beyond its current situation by encouraging radical transformation through evaluation and reflection of service systems.

These phases expand the role of service design beyond simply the production and strategic implementation of service touchpoints to solve problems.

The transformative value of design, specifically in healthcare, is acknowledged by Burns et al. (2006) who coined the term "transformation design" during an effort to apply cross-disciplinary design to healthcare. According to Burns et al., (2006, pp. 20–22), the main characteristics of transformation design include:

- Defining and redefining the brief.
- Collaborating between disciplines.
- Employing participatory design techniques.

- Building capacity, not dependency.
- Designing beyond traditional solutions.

"Designing beyond tradition solutions" encourages designers to focus on imagining the future, rather than creating solutions based on current technology. This direction is especially important in highly complex healthcare service systems. As these complexities often involve generational problems in social, economic and cultural contexts, it is essential to critically examine and challenge the existing systems and apparent solutions. Healthcare service design therefore requires a future-focus approach that provides a platform for critical dialogues to take place.

6.3   From Service Solution to Speculation

Service design focuses on extracting insights from stakeholders to develop service touchpoints and systems that are useful in present contexts, whilst speculative design "projects" a future by detailing new ways for people to live, work and interact with each other through technology (Iadarola & Starnino, 2018, p. 49). The purpose of future projection is to use possible future scenarios to provoke and challenge current systems and therefore engaging people in conversations to think differently (Pasman, 2016). The contemporary service design practice and paradigm has a focus on solving problems within existing systems but appears to provide limited scope to users, stakeholders and providers to challenge the status quo. A future-focussed paradigm would provide designers—and the communities they serve—a platform to challenge and question these current systems (Gerber, 2018).

Speculative design encourages people to imagine scenarios about the future, prompting people to think, critique and question current situations (Dunne & Raby, 2013; Tharp & Tharp, 2018). Further, design fiction is a particular type of speculative design (Dunne & Raby, 2013) that provides a conceptual space where critical and discursive dialogues can be conducted through the giving of both form and context to cultural artefacts (Hales, 2013). However, it is important to understand that design fiction is a tool to allow discursive dialogues to take place not simply as a tool to predict preferential futures (Tsekleves et al., 2017, p. 8).

Probing future scenarios to provoke discursive dialogues requires the understanding of the nature of future. Dunne and Raby (2013, pp. 3–4) build on futurologist Stuart Candy's (2010, pp. 34–35) thesis in which he explores the "cone of possibility space" to explain different kinds of futures:

- Probable future: This refers to the events and things that are most likely to happen. This is where most traditional designers operate. Design activities include the application of design methods, processes, tools, production and evaluation.

- Plausible future: This is the field of practice where discoveries are made through science, technological, economic and political endeavours.
- Possible future: This field focuses on speculative efforts through writing, science fiction and social fiction.
- Preferable future: This is the intersection between probable and plausible futures.

The above categorization of future provides designers with heuristics by which to engage people in discussions.

Design fiction has expanded design's role from its traditional objective (a practice to converge on problems towards possible solutions) to a role where design is used to generate awareness, raise concerns or challenge values of new, emerging and future technologies, products and services (Pasman, 2016, p. 512). The use of narrative structure to explore and probe services through emerging and future technology allows service design to facilitate constructive dialogues (Pasman, 2016, pp. 512–513).

In recent years, speculative design has been applied in healthcare to engage communities in conversations about innovation (see Tsekleves et al., 2019; Voss et al., 2015). Speculative design and design fiction are applied as methods and tools in healthcare services to engage the broader community in discursive dialogues that critique current situations. For example, Tsekleves et al. (2017) applied design fiction as a tool to engage people in conversations that question the directions of future technologies and services in healthcare. The project applied design fiction to engage older citizens in the co-design of healthcare provision that considers ageing in place, loneliness and isolation. The authors found that a design fiction approach allowed people to accept future healthcare technologies and services, while raising potential ethical concerns surrounding new healthcare products and services (Tsekleves et al., 2017). By engaging the community in speculating on the future of aged care, this example demonstrates the role of design in a critique of current ethical frameworks and future health service and technology provision.

Design fiction also has the benefit of communicating complex healthcare information, such as self-care and channels of health care services, to the public. For example, Hoang et al. (2018) engaged patients with type 2 diabetes to co-create a fictional storybook of a person setting on a quest to explore a "healthcare universe" to learn more about their conditions. The book also presented questions that prompt readers to think about future healthcare scenarios and their lifestyle, habits and choices (Hoang et al., 2018, p. 471). This design fiction approach which engaged participants in fictional stories was less intrusive than ethnographic research (Hoang et al., 2018). It is an approach that leverages the future and imagination of design to stimulate dialogue on healthcare provision in the community.

6.4 Speculative Service Design Framework

We propose a speculative service design (SSD) framework that focusses on approaching service design as a speculative agent, placing itself outside of the normative, instrumentalist form of service design: the problem-solution binary. This framework (see Fig. 6.1) has the following elements:

- **Past**: Healthcare services have challenges that derive from the complexity that is formed through the years. Some of these challenges are intertwined; some are multi-faceted, while some are symptoms of other underlying challenges. To design a service would require designers to understand and pack the complexity of the past. This progress is recognized as "collective diagnostic", in which a critical lens is applied to unpack complexity that would have generated the need of the given service to be designed. This pre-design phase therefore is a discursive conversation with all stakeholders to thoroughly understand complexity. While the visual depiction of this phase is inspired by Newman's (2010) 'Process of design squiggle'—which captures the innovation process of understanding complexity, ideating and generating solutions—the adaptation of this "fuzzy front end" in our framework represents the need to understand the origin and development of complexity in healthcare services. In the context of a critical and speculative design, understanding complexity is important in generating future visions of healthcare services. This is different from unpacking complexity to generate solutions for immediate application. The idea here is to hold off a rush to "build" but to identify failures, paradoxes, prejudices, exclusions and assumptions made in the past.
- **Now**: This phase concerns ethical self-assessment for stakeholders to build empathy with the broader community. Empathy building is an important

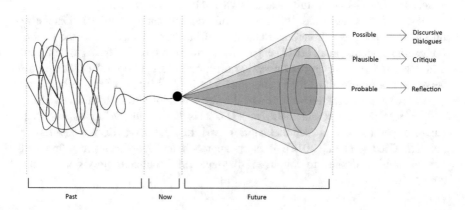

Fig. 6.1 Speculative service design (SSD) framework that focuses on generating discursive dialogues, critique and reflection on the future of healthcare services. *Source* Authors' own illustration (2021)

approach for service designers to help stakeholders to be critical of existing service systems. In current service design practice, this may be visualized as a rather simple and linear process (mapping entities, service functions and technologies). However, we see this as an ethical investigation phase for each stakeholder to self-assess their awareness of the community's needs against a backdrop of increasing complexity in social, political and technological life. We see that critiques in this phase are informed by insights from the past and visions from the future.

- **Future**: This phase adapts Candy's (2010) categorization of futures. We have contributed to this model by relating each future to design with specific roles:
  - **Probable/Reflection**: Probable future provides healthcare designers with a platform to reflect on new services that are more likely to be implemented. These new services could be the result of discursive dialogues taking place in the possible and plausible future. At the probable future level, design activities employed to generate outcomes need to involve or instigate critical reflections. Design processes, ideas and outcomes must reflect on their relevance towards the well-being and sustainability of social, environmental and economic development. This approach is in opposition to the fast pace "sprinting" approach that is commonly aimed at producing solutions to "solve" problems for the present time.
  - **Plausible/Critique:** Service design at this level provides an imaginative future that could contribute to system and process transformation. Plausible future includes discoveries from broad disciplinary advancement. Service design in healthcare must facilitate transformation in the healthcare system by providing an environment and a platform to critique existing policy and systems.
  - **Possible/Discursive Dialogue**: Possible future consists of a process of fictionalization as an outcome that provokes the community, providers and policymakers to rethink the boundaries of healthcare. Discussions in this level therefore concern social and cultural transformation that could drive service innovation. Service design here can bring to life a visualized fictional future that allows for discursive dialogues among healthcare service providers and the broader communities.

The SSD framework is therefore an integrative conceptual framework that combines Newman's design squiggle (2010) with Candy's future categories (2010) to expand service design outcomes in healthcare beyond service strategies and touchpoints. Under this framework, service design contributes by generating imaginative futures and engaging broad stakeholders in rethinking about the future of healthcare and well-being. To further explore and evaluate the SSD framework, the next section reflects on the SSD elements based on a speculative design project that applied a co-design process to imagine strategies to eradicate polio.

6.5   Case Study: Polio Eradication | Imagining the Future Without Polio

This case study analyses a speculative design workshop conducted by DSIL Global that had successfully created discursive dialogues surrounding polio eradication. We use this workshop as an example to reflect on the elements in the SSD framework.

In August 2019, DSIL GLOBAL (Designing for Systems Innovation and Leadership) was invited to a co-design workshop, following a technical advisory group (TAG) meeting for the eradication of poliomyelitis in Pakistan. During the meeting in Islamabad, Pakistan provincial representatives reported on—and shared progress—around vaccination programming and "Polio-plus activities": outreach activities that provide oral polio vaccine (as well as immunization against other childhood ailments) and other services such as nutrition.

The problem that generated the need for a TAG meeting was grounded in a complex service provision context. The existing service delivery model for vaccination campaigns was procedural at each stage of "pre-campaign", "during campaign" and "post-campaign". The formula involved first a coverage agenda to cover all households during the campaign, exemplified by a generic or sweeping "door-knock" approach. This was coupled with an extensive data collection and complex reporting processes that rarely supported quality decisions or allowed for real-time course correction or feedback.

Attendees of the TAG meeting were invited to spend an additional two days at a leadership retreat workshop delivered by DSIL. The participants were joined by "One Team", which included partner organizations such as Bill and Melinda Gates Foundation, WHO, Rotary International, UNICEF, N-STOP (National Stop Transmission of Polio) and Pakistan Government representatives. The workshop took a speculative design approach. The aim was to reconnect the leadership level and implementation level members of TAG on an individual level as well as inter-organizationally to expand conversations surrounding health delivery models from TAG meeting and to design more a collaborative and integrated approach to immunization service delivery and work towards effective polio eradication (Fig. 6.2).

6.5.1   How the Workshop Was Conducted

The workshop was scaffolded through three phases:

(1) Collective diagnostics of design situations that led participants to unpack complexity generated by the historical development of the problem;
(2) Understand the current situation through empathy building; and
(3) Encouraging discursive dialogues through a fictional future to critique and rethink about current possibilities.

Fig. 6.2 Day One Polio eradication leadership workshop with one team. *Source* Authors' own illustration (2021)

6.5.1.1 Unpacking Complexity of the Past

The first phase of the workshop reflects the "past" element of our SSD framework. Here, participants were led into a "collective diagnostics" phase to reflect and critique on the given design situation. Participants were aware of the Global Polio Eradication initiative by the World Health Organization and Rotary International in 1988. Unfortunately, Pakistan remains a final stronghold for polio. There is deep complexity in tribal areas and frontier regions within Pakistan, Islamist opposition to vaccination drives and propaganda against the polio programme steeped in a historical mistrust of the government.

Given the complexities of the past, an emergent facilitation process was used to diagnose the context. Participants were led to question:

What 'receptivity' is there likely to be for a particular service design output?

What kinds of work (including cultural work) is required alongside the design itself and what kind of service design process is needed?

This process successfully brought participants together as a community. It started with relationship building and then through various activities to elicit the needs of the group to form a direction for the remaining of the workshop (outlined below). The following sections discuss the flow of unpacking the past and present that led to the speculation of the future.

Polarities

To effectively pave the way for the various tensions in the recent past, DSIL offered a design primer activity called "Polarities". The team began this activity by creating an imaginary line through the room (facilitators can use a real one using chalk or masking tape on the floor). We then asked the group to decide if they needed more wisdom or creativity to eradicate polio. One end of the line represented "100% Creativity", while the other end stood for "100% wisdom". Participants positioned themselves along the line according to their views.

Participants were then invited to have a short conversation with the person on the other side of the spectrum to share their viewpoints and feelings. The aim was to invite participants to work with the tensions between wisdom and creativity, while engaging in dialogue with others with different viewpoints. Wisdom was discussed in terms of the science and expertise in the room which was deemed adequate. There was an acknowledgement that village workers and other junior staff might also have the wisdom to share, and that better consultation with frontline workers would result in more impact. Participants expressed the need to respond and refine strategies in real-time creatively, adjust the cadence or reframe messaging in response to hesitation in the community.

The activities described revealed that the challenges facing the programme were centred on the difficulties of reaching children with a vaccine in targeted areas. Health service delivery groups were combating increased community resistance and less-than-adequate preparation for high-quality mass immunization campaigns in particular areas. The vaccination programme also had the internal challenge of frontline worker fatigue and insufficient time for campaign preparation. Participants also reflected on the poor implementation of social mobilization and community engagement which was aimed at increasing vaccine demand. Additionally, the service delivery team also needed the space to discuss and critique the service delivery landscape that involved multiple stakeholders. These findings were observed through participants' engagement in insightful discussion about systemic and cultural challenges of the past that would also have resulted in problems in the present time.

6.5.1.2 What We Did to Bring in the Now

Understanding the complexity of the past is key to unpacking a problem in the present. To address the challenge of inter-agency collaboration, DSIL applied a design activity called "Empathy Wheel". This method allowed a group to walk in the shoes of the others in the room and speak to the work and tensions at play. The wheel is subsequently extended to consider the larger community that is impacted by and dedicated to eradication polio. The facilitators traced a large circle in the middle of the room with large masking tape and divided the pie into multiple spokes (e.g. UNICEF, WHO, Government, NSTOP, Rotary). Individuals were invited to enter the wheel, embody one stakeholder's perspective and respond to relevant questions (see Fig. 6.3). Questions included:

Fig. 6.3 Initial development and prototyping of the Empathy Wheel activity during the DSIL innovation and leadership course. *Source* Authors' own illustration (2021)

- What is the real problem/ the most challenging part of this challenge?
- What are your fears, concerns or doubts around it?
- What can you contribute to transforming the challenge?
- What do you need to say to other stakeholders that have not been said yet?

Empathy building was an appropriate tool to re-engage and realign stakeholders to understand the current complexity generated from the past. This aligns with our SSD framework's "Now" phase, which focuses on an ethical investigation through empathy building. Overall, there was a visible advocacy and care for frontline workers, the communities they work with this and an urge to understand frontline experiences.

The process also revealed that the leadership team was the one that needed more guidance to build empathy with others. The "One Team" was out of touch with understanding the given challenges from other stakeholders' perspectives. The "One Team" was being guided to come back to the basics of listening to others. This observation suggests that an empathy building process can at times be beneficial to mend relationship among stakeholders. (Re)building such a relationship is critical for a project to move forward into a speculative direction.

These challenges were observed to have a minor impact on the workshop. Overall, empathy building was important to unpack the complexity involved in the existing situations. More importantly, the realization of the lack of empathy in the leadership teams provided an opportunity to realign the project to a more holistic and inclusive one. This further reflects the importance of using empathy building to be critical to existing systems or ways of working through ethical investigation. Insights gathered in this phase were apparent in the projection of the future.

6.5.1.3 What We Did to Bring in the Future

After laying the foundation to unpack the tensions of the past and sharing honestly about the present, the last phase involved the participants engaging in critical dialogues about the future. This activity has conceptual links to eco-philosopher Joanna Macy's work (Macy & Brown, 2014). Macy's work in "Work that Reconnects" (WTR) largely relates to using these techniques and others to address ecological crises. It seeks to have groups play out (either through dialogue or movement) complex problems and situate those problems at different moments in time.

The adaptation of a WTR approach allowed the workshop to focus on the problem, user, need and insight rather than what a "solved problem" might look and feel like. These formats and approaches were chosen because the common direction of the design workshops tend to focus on ideation rather than creating a container in which a group can collectively envision. This sits within the "Possible/Discursive Dialogue" space articulated in our SSD framework. The design allows for an improvised retrospective where a positive possible fictional future is presented. Through these dialogues, participants and facilitators used the role "Historians of the avant-garde" as keepers of knowledge. The task of this role is to answer broad questions from "people of a future generation".

The discursive dialogue began as an imaginative conversation where the people from a possible future generation interview the historians of the avant-garde using the following prompts:

1. Historians, we have heard about the old days, times were hard. We heard that their intelligence, imagination, and creativity were in the work and hitting our collective targets was difficult. Why was work like this?
2. Historians, what was it like to work that way? How did you feel during that time? What gave you hope even when it was hard? Tell us.
3. Historians, we know the leaders were dedicated and committed to ending the transmission of Polio, and you were one of them. Your actions started a whole string of interventions and empowered those on the ground to continue to do good work. Over a matter of a few years things changed! Tell us one of the stories about you and your fellow change-makers, what first small steps did you take to create change? Tell us.
4. Historians, we know the leaders did not stop working to embody those minimum specs you build in Bhurban from the early days. Tell us, in what ways did you start to create that change right after that meeting? What did you realize then, that those before did not?

5. Historians, how did you do it!? How did you successfully invite an entire Nation into eradicating polio when they once held pockets of resistance?

With the questions and conversations, participants were shown an excerpt of a fictional future:

> The year is 2032. Polio is long gone. Children breathe well and walk freely. Play is unencumbered. Across the country of Pakistan, the social fabric is woven tighter than ever before …

> For years we thought our main and only concern was a final push against polio- the last mile. We worked so hard and when we reached it! However, the path was riddled with hopelessness, blame and ego - these were the quiet epidemics. At some point, we stopped celebrating each other's wins, recognizing each other's hard work or trusting each other to be doing this for the right reasons. It was only when we paused to reconnect and look inward in Bhurban after a TAG meeting and, decided something needed to change. There we committed to amplifying the wisdom and creativity of everyone around us, at all levels in this work and then we were able to reach every last child with polio vaccine.

> It didn't end there. We became an inspiration for the public health world. We were able to apply these learnings elsewhere, across other public health to work to wipe out other infectious diseases around the world, and even beyond into other areas like literacy and poverty.

> Now we thrive on collaboration. We know that failure is just learning and so we build our ideas and test them quickly so that solutions work and improve the lives of those living in Pakistan. Because we are grounded in collaboration, we see more opportunities than we ever did before, especially in our biggest challenges: In fact, it was one of our biggest challenges, eradicating polio, that taught us that. All of this happened because the people in this room were innovative at that time. Their courage showed the world what was possible through deep listening and honestly sharing. But they did much more than that too. Now, current generations know polio by history only. We are aligned and trust each other deeply- we have become old friends and even meet in Bhurban once a year to laugh and tell old stories.

Participants' engagement with the discursive dialogues based on a possible fictional future had successfully generated ideas and conversations surrounding plausible and feasible futures. Participants were observed to be involved in conversations that critique processes and systems surrounding the service delivery model. For example, participants proposed to support the Pakistan Polio Programme to work as part of "One Team" to define roles, partnership agreements and alignment of various organizational strengths, develop capacity building and retention plans at various levels. This workshop outcome suggests that the discussions surrounding plausible future derives from the broad discursive dialogues generated in a fictional possible future. A plausible future provides people with the opportunity of the critiquing system and process transformation.

Discursive dialogues generated from fictional possible future can also engage people in reflection about the probable future. Another core outcome from the workshop was the need to simplify the processes across campaigns designing more agile feedback loops, which would allow teams to experiment with solutions that can be tested quickly and iterated fast to better understand and respond to local trends as well as refocus efforts on areas that add the most value (building a range of micro-strategies to allow for even local -tailored household-level strategies which differentiate between first visits, refusals etc.). These approaches and recommendations are feasible and could be achieved in the near future. They were an outcome from participants' reflection on the current situation and based on discursive dialogues from fictional possible future.

6.6 Findings

The example explored above demonstrates that a fictional future provides opportunities for discursive dialogues to take place. This is especially important for highly complex healthcare service design projects. The example provides us with the platform to reflect on the SSD framework, an effective model to frame complex healthcare service design. Key findings include:

- Probable, plausible and possible futures are intertwined. As demonstrated through the polio eradication workshop, the broad discursive dialogues generated in the possible future allowed for ideas about the system and process transformation to take place at the plausible future level. The fiction-based comprehensive dialogues also helped people frame probable service ideas and strategies that could be implemented in the near future.
- SSD needs a solid foundation in understanding the past and the present. Standard practice in service design considers "ideas" as external to people and journey mapping as external to lived experiences "owned" and felt by patients. These methods also focus on generating solutions for existing problems. A speculative approach to service design generates meaningful dialogues in the projected future based on the in-depth understanding of complexity in the past and present. It is important to give time and energy to the past and the present before attempting speculative visioning. The architecture of the activities relating to the past, present and future are typical of empathy stage processes in design.
- To effectively engage participants in meaningful dialogues through future settings, it is essential to recognize the need to address the uncertainty and tensions that arise in non-linear iterative processes. Often, the designing for health systems are both technically and emotionally complex and an immediate focus on a "solutions" phase rarely works alone. As observed in the polio eradication workshop, the phrase "a world without Polio" seemed an empty slogan or broadly ill-defined problem. However, this fictional future created an opportunity for participants to engage directly with uncertainty—both in the unpacking of past complexity and acknowledging the various lived experiences of stakeholders. The discursive dialogue spoke more to what an ideal future "felt like" while still allowing the group an opportunity to envision how they (practically) might get there.

- SSD is not about predicting the future. Rather, it is to present a fictional future scenario juxtaposed with current realities, one which can be used to challenge, provoke and change current systems. By "walking back" from the speculative future and the present we encounter meaningful alternatives to narrow, instrumentalist and short-term solutions.

6.7 Conclusion

This chapter has argued the importance and benefit of expanding service design from touchpoints to a futurist/speculative approach to generate meaningful conversations surrounding health service systems. Service design commonly utilizes methods that involve schematic diagrams to depict high level planning of people's experience in using service touchpoints (Pasman, 2016). While these approaches are beneficial in solving service problems that exist during the time, they focus on critiquing and challenging systemic and policy-based problems. Meaningful conversations on service systems are critical in highly complex healthcare services that often involve social, cultural, political and economic factors.

Through the SSD framework, we encourage healthcare service designers to further the practice of speculative approaches to understand the complexity of service problems involved in the past and present and to probe future scenarios to engage people in discursive dialogues to critique and challenge the healthcare service system.

References

Burns, C., Cottam, H., Vanstone, C., & Winhall, J. (2006). Red Paper 02: Transformation Design. Design Council. London

Cottam, H., & Leadbeater, C. (2004). RED Paper 01: Health - Co-creating Services. Design Council. London

Curedale, R. (2013). Service Design: 250 essential methods. Design Community College Inc., Topanga, CA.

Candy, S. (2010). The futures of everyday life: Politics and the design of experiential scenarios. Honolulu: University of Hawaii at Manoa.

DeVylder, J. (2019, 17 November). *What service design is, and what it is not?* Meld Studio. Retrieved October 14, 2020, from https://www.meldstudios.com.au/what-service-design-is-and-what-it-is-not/.

Dunne, A., & Raby, F. (2013). Speculative everything: Design, fiction, and social dreaming. Cambridge MA: MIT Press.

Gerber, A. (2018). Radical futures: Designing for fundamental change. *Touchpoint, 10*(2), 31–33.

Hales, D. (2013). Design fictions an introduction and provisional taxonomy. *Digital Creativity, 24* (1), 1–10. https://doi.org/10.1080/14626268.2013.769453

Hoang, T., Khot, R. A., Mueller, F., & Waite, N. (2018). What can speculative design teach us about designing for healthcare services? OZCHI 18 (Ed.), Melbourne.

Iadarola, A., & Starnino, A. (2018). Speculative design and service design: A false dichotomy. *Touchpoint, 10*(2), 48–53.

Ludden, G. D. S., & Vallgarda, A. (2019). A design perspective on future healthcare services for the home environment. In M. A. Pfannstiel & C. Rasche (Eds.), *Service design and service thinking in healthcare and hospital management: theory, concepts, practice* (pp. 155–167). Cham: Springer Nature.

Macy, J., & Brown, M. Y. (2014). *Coming back to life: The guide to the work that reconnects.* Gabriola Island: New Society Publishers.

Malmberg, L., Rodrigues, V., Lannerstrom, L., Wetter-Edman, K., Vink, J., & Holmlid, S. (2019). Service design as a transformational driver toward person-centered care in healthcare. In M. A. Pfannstiel & C. Rasche (Eds.), Service design and service thinking in healthcare and hospital management: Theory, concepts, practice (pp. 1–18). Cham: Springer Nature.

Newman, D. (n.d.). *The Design Squiggle.* Retrieved May 31, 2021, from https://thedesignsquiggle.com/.

Pasman, G. (2016) Design fiction as a service design approach. In Georgraphies. In: Proceedings of the ServDes 2016. Issue 125 (pp. 511–515). Linköping. Schweden: Linkoping University Electronic Press. Linköpings universitet.

Polaine, A., Lovlie, L., & Reason, B. (2013). Service design: From insight to implementation. New York: Rosenfeld Media.

Sangiorgi, D. (2011). Transformative services and transformation design. *International Journal of Design, 5*(2), 29–40.

Sangiorgi, D., & Junginger, S. (2015). Emerging issues in service design. *The Design Journal, 18*(2), 165–170. https://doi.org/10.2752/175630615X14212498964150

Sangiorgi, D., Prendiville, A., & Jung, J. (2017). Expanding (Service) design spaces. In D. Sangiorgi & A. Prendiville (Eds.), Designing for services: Key issues and new direction. London: Bloomsbury.

Schaminée, A. (2018) Designing with-in public organizations: Building bridges between public sector innovators and design. Amsterdam: BIS Publishers.

Shostack, G. L. (1982). How to design a service. *European Journal of Marketing, 16*(1), 49–63.

Stickdorn, M., Lawrence, A., Hormess, M., & Schneider, J. (Eds.). (2018). This is service design doing. Sebastopol, California: O'Reilly Media Inc.

Stickdorn, M., & Schneider, J. (Eds.). (2010). This is service design thinking. BIS Publisher, Amsterdam.

Tharp, B., & Tharp, S. (2018). *Discursive design: Critical, speculative, and alternative things.* Cambridge MA: The MIT Press.

Tsekleves, E., Darby, A., Whicher, A., & Swiatek, P. (2017). Co-designing design fictions: A new approach for debating and priming future healthcare technologies and services. *Archives of Design Research, 30*(2), 5–21. https://doi.org/10.15187/adr.2017.05.30.2.5

Tsekleves, E., Yong, M. H., Lee, C. A. L., Giga, S., Hwang, J. S., & Lau, S. L. (2019). Rethinking how healthcare is concentualised and delivered through speculative design in the UK and Malaysia: A comparative study. *The Design Journal, 22*(Issue sup1). 429–444. https://doi.org/10.1080/14606925.2019.1595430

Voss, G., Revell, T., & Pickard, J. (2015). Speculative design and the future of an ageing population report 1: Outcomes. London: Government Office of Science.

Christopher Kueh is a design educator/researcher, practicing information designer and design strategist. He is currently a Senior Lecturer in Strategic Design at Edith Cowan University, Western Australia. His research and practice involve helping organisations to cultivate design abilities and to understand complexities through design.

Fanke Peng is an Associate Professor at UniSA Creative, Univeristy of South Australia. Her research focuses on design and health, cross-cultural design pedagogy, and service design for sustainability and social impact. She has worked on a range of interdisciplinary projects that were funded Australian Council for the Arts, UK research councils (AHRC, ESRC, EPSRC, TSB), the Museum of Australian Democracy, the Australian Department of Foreign Affairs and Trade Fund. Recent publications include Cross Cultural Design for Healthy Ageing (co-edited book 2020), and Service Design Thinking for Social Good (co-authored journal article 2020).

Philip Ely is Senior Lecturer at Curtin University where he is course director of the Master of Design. Philip is a design practitioner, educator, theorist and entrepreneur with over 20 years in industry. He founded The State of Design research network across Western Australia's five universities, exploring the impact and value of design in the region. In 2015, he was voted one of Britain's top business advisors by Enterprise Nation. Philip has served as a peer reviewer for the both the Australian and UK research councils and recently published work on the design value helix in the Design Management Journal and on differential design in the journal Design & Culture.

Gareth Durrant MPH is a public health practitioner turned designer. Gareth brings a wealth of field experience in design and health innovation having worked across Asia, the Pacific and Australia in medical and humanitarian emergency sector. He blends research and practice in his current role as a Creative Consultant with DSIL Global (Designing for Social Innovation and Leadership).

Crossing Asymmetries in Multistakeholder Service Design in Integrated Care

7

Anna Salmi, Outi Ahonen, and Päivi Pöyry-Lassila

Abstract

Designing for services to cater to clients with complex service needs in health and social care presents a tricky design challenge. Multiprofessional, cross-sectoral health and social care that involves multiple care system levels is a co-design context that requires context-specific knowledge, such as on evidence-based care and particular design competences to include the perspectives of diverse actors in design processes. Grounding on a literature review and reflecting on our experiences in a research project, we argue, that multistakeholder service design in health and social care involves knowledge asymmetries on various system levels that need to be crossed to reach new knowledge for design. In the project, we brought together diverse health and social care service ecosystem actors to co-design human-centered solutions for integrated care. To elaborate on how the knowledge asymmetries occur in multistakeholder service design for health and social care, and extend across different care system levels, we present an initial model of cross-level service design. Designing for services in this complex setting needs to strive to integrate evidence-based care and design practices and account for the knowledge asymmetries across levels.

A. Salmi (✉)
Laurea University of Applied Sciences, Ratatie 22, 01300 Vantaa, Finland
e-mail: anna.salmi@laurea.fi

O. Ahonen
Laurea University of Applied Sciences, Vanha maantie 9, 02650 Espoo, Finland
e-mail: outi.ahonen@laurea.fi

P. Pöyry-Lassila
Unit Information and Analysis, Finnish National Agency for Education, Hakaniemenranta 6,
P.O. Box 380, 00531 Helsinki, Finland
e-mail: paivi.poyry-lassila@oph.fi

© The Author(s), under exclusive license to Springer Nature Switzerland AG 2022
M. A. Pfannstiel et al. (eds.), *Service Design Practices for Healthcare Innovation*,
https://doi.org/10.1007/978-3-030-87273-1_7

7.1 Introduction

This paper deals with the timely and thorny problem in health and social care of how to serve people with multiple complex service needs while at the same time accounting for the broader benefit of the society and its citizens. In health economics topical debates, it is recognized that the care of a narrow part of the population brings most costs in industrialized societies. This is referred to as the 20/80 model of healthcare spending. The challenge does not limit itself to individual services or specific client groups but extends to multiple levels of care, social and health sectors and to the care system widely. At the heart of the dilemma are people in need of diverse and intense care. They are ordinary citizens in diverse life situations, concurrently going through multiple conditions, perhaps chronic, needing attention from a variety of actors in medical care, social support and benefits, employment, training services and sometimes even home care. At the same time, the care system is hampered by siloed ways of working, lack of up-to-date ICT systems and needed skills, supporting policies, laws and regulations and under constant budgetary pressures. Chronic care model provides one possible answer to person-centric multiprofessional care to clients with chronic illness and who have hard life situations. They need a great deal of support from professionals and an active approach to support their decision-making skills to enable them to make decisions that support well-being and health (Wagner et al., 2001). Responding to the pressing challenge calls for an ecosystemic approach and demands cooperative efforts from multiple stakeholders across sectors, organizations and professions, including citizens, public administrators, care professionals, companies, researchers, designers and developers.

Digitalization, streamlining of cooperation and harnessing knowledge across actors are seen as key in the resource balancing efforts. According to the rationale, the group of people with complex service needs is targeted indirectly by encouraging the rest, whose needs are less intensive to primarily use digital channels for care (Wagner et al., 2001; Ministry of Social Affairs & Health, 2015; Hujala & Lammintakanen, 2018).

The purpose of this book chapter is to describe and analyze multidisciplinary service design practices in the context of Nordic welfare model. We will focus on the identified asymmetries and their effect on co-design processes that target novel value co-creation in a multistakeholder social and health care service ecosystem. We will analyze the asymmetries reflecting on our experiences in the MORFEUS research project where we brought together diverse actors to co-design human-centered solutions for integrated care. By introducing the concept of asymmetry, we aim to highlight some of the tacit and escaping aspects of collaboration that affect design outcomes. We explore how the asymmetries of knowledge concerning different health system levels affected the stakeholders' capabilities to transform knowledge when engaging in co-design.

In our text, we combine theoretical perspectives and literature from design, service marketing research and health care and health informatics. Here, we see the contribution of design related to the pragmatic strategies and analytical tools it provides to catalyze change in the human and socio-material world. When focusing particularly on co-design, it helps to understand the implications of and supports the inclusion of diverse stakeholders' perspectives in processes of transformation (e.g. Sanders & Stappers, 2008). Importantly, service marketing research provides ways to understand the ways of value creation in services.

At same time, the context of health care is defined by evidence-based care (EBC) requirements. Health informatics gives tools to describe care processes. Patient's care plans are tools to communicate patient's care between them and different professionals. The patients' active role in negotiation and making decisions together with professionals supports commitment to care. Especially in chronic care, daily decisions play a crucial role in the outcomes of care.

The contribution of this chapter is related to the ways of identifying and the methods of crossing asymmetries, such as facilitation of cross-boundary collaboration. One of the conclusions is to describe how EBC in healthcare and co-design practices in the context of services can be successfully combined to include the people's and diverse stakeholders' knowledge and perspectives in the design for novel care services in service ecosystems. We argue that these practices need to be able to x the policy, law, regulatory requirements as well as the asymmetries at different system levels and genuinely account for them to reach new knowledge.

We adopt a design for services view to describe our design practice in the context of health and social care services. By committing to this strand, we aim to highlight the open-ended, co-creative premises of our approach that does not seek any particular outcome and is inclusive of the diverse views and contributions of the multiple stakeholders involved. In the context of care, our approach underlines the importance of doing with, instead of to or for, a rationale still dominating much of care services.

The recent debates in service marketing research on value co-creation emphasize the need for businesses to grasp and support the customers' own value generation processes (Heinonen & Strandvik, 2015), instead of focusing on what they can generate as an output (Lusch et al., 2007). This people-oriented, dynamic and distributed perspective is well in line with the key beliefs in design for services. It highlights design's "capacity to potentially create the right conditions for certain forms of interactions and relationships to happen" (Meroni & Sangiorgi, 2011, p. 82). Further, in search for the interface between design and service research, the concept of experience providers a lever. The stakeholders' value generation is a phenomenon of lived experience (Lehtimäki, Oinonen & Salo, 2018) and cannot be crafted, controlled or designed as such. Thus, value and experiences (Forlizzi & Ford, 2000) in the context of services can only be approached indirectly by providing ques and designing for favorable circumstances.

In this chapter, we mainly use the term client to refer to users of health and social care services and participants in co-design. We are aware that in service design and service marketing, the term customer is preferred. In discussing specific concepts of client experience measures in health care, we use the term patient which in that context is more appropriate considering the health care origin of the concepts. In using the term care professionals, we take it to refer to both health and social care professionals.

7.2 Theoretical Background

This work is concerned with how knowledge differences of the complex health system in co-design with multiple actors can downplay the opportunities for value co-creation in service ecosystems if not attended and addressed. In the following subchapters, we present theory relevant to analyze the case that is presented further on in this chapter.

7.2.1 The Nordic Care Model and Its Current Guidelines

The Nordic health care model is known worldwide as a concept of a high quality, effective and trustful evidence-based health care for all citizens. The three core dimensions to healthcare policy in the Nordic countries are access to care, treatment and public health care. Nordic health care model is based on the national public sector taking care of all citizens and managing the costs based on taxes. To simplify, the stronger make their share to take care of the weaker by paying more since it is thought that in the long term, it will pay back as increased collective well-being and lower costs. Nordic countries succeed in providing excellent health care to their entire population at a total relative cost. The proof of the model's effectiveness is that Nordic countries have healthy citizens based on statistics by the World Health Organization (Einhorn, 2019; Lyttkens, et al., 2016).

The system is not all trouble free. There are statistics that over 10 percent of the population are using almost 90 percent of expenses from the yearly budget. For now, all municipalities do not have appropriate processes to pick up the multi-morbidity citizens, support them and their relatives to have integrated services (Männikkö & Martikka, 2017). On the other hand, there is evidence that these multimorbidity citizens need care managers to help them coordinate and plan their own care. A named contact person in primary health care, written care plan and collaboration between health and social care services strengthen the client's decision-making about his/her well-being. At same time, there are special competences needed for professionals to manage large amounts of knowledge to support client's decision-making (Vehko et al., 2018).

Integrated care pathways from primary health care to specialized health care are at the root of high-impact health and social welfare services coordinated at the national and provincial level. In addition, pharmacies, social services, private and third sector are important actors in integrated care. The strategy in Finland is to support citizens' well-being by sharing available information for utilization and at the same time giving customer-centric guidance to services in multiprofessional cooperation.

The aim is that most of the citizens would manage well with self-care and prevention with the support of online services. At a second level, professional guidance is provided to citizens' self-service. On the third level comes the services implemented by a professional. At all levels, ICT solutions support the renewal of services. An effective health care ecosystem needs active cooperation between participants. At the heart of the ecosystems' operation is value co-creation that is based on producing effective services to the clients that meet their needs (Ministry of Social Affairs & Health, 2015, 2021).

Digitalization, having as its primary objectives increased public health through citizen empowerment, needs a lot of development work with all kinds of stakeholders (European Commission, 2018). Not least with the clients who are facing the crucial need of behavioral change. Co-design may offer potential to develop even more integrated care by engaging different stakeholders in designing for service.

7.2.2 Evidence-Based Care as a Base of Health and Social Care

The core of health care is always to give best care to clients, and evidence-based practice is the key element to effective care. Evidence-base has a long tradition in health care, and it is gaining acceptance globally (Di Censo & Cullum, 1989; Pearson et al., 2005, 2007). In Finland, evidence-based practice is also a demand of the law. Every patient needs to get effective care, based on high evidence (Ministry of Social Affairs & Health, 2010). In the social work and welfare sector, evidence-based culture is also growing, and it is increasingly taken into consideration in planning services to citizens (Kuusisto-Niemi, 2016, Paasio, 2014). In the future, services are co-created with an even larger number of citizens from different positions, and to enable that, responsible service developers need to provide new kinds of open platforms to build new services (Kiiski et al., 2018). The crucial sources of information for making EBC decisions are research-based recommendations, professional information, the clients' information about their own situation and environmental information (Di Censo & Cullum, 1989; Pearson et al., 2005).

It is a complex process to coordinate an evidence-based approach in the health care system so that all professionals know the right interventions and activities to take care of clients in a certain health care environment. There is a large amount of research, and there needs to be a common understanding of what kind of research is acceptable to count as evidence and to be included in evidence-based protocols. Large number of professionals recognize that collected evidence needs to be more than effective, it also needs to be feasible, appropriate and meaningful in order to achieve evidence-based healthcare practice. While evidence of effectiveness of various interventions is necessary, it is obvious that health professionals, customers and citizens need a large amount of information to facilitate change in practice for informed decision-making (Pearson et al., 2007).

High-quality care of chronic illness needs productive interactions between the interprofessional practice team and client. From a multiprofessional perspective, to ensure that each client's care is based on his/her needs, the care plan is an important communication tool. What is most important is that clients know their care plans, i.e., what are the next phases and targets on his/her care. At same time, professionals need to encourage people to use their self-management skills to make decisions considering their well-being. Integrated care plan is not only the tool for communication between professionals but also for client's communication with professionals. eHealth tools can be used to support professionals' and clients' communication (Wagner et al. 2001). Professionals need new competencies for empowering clients to communicate online, with different tools (Värri et al., 2020).

Communication with clients and how they see their feelings encountered by professionals is reflecting how they experience care (Wagner et al., 2001). Client experience data (PROM, PREM) and post-market monitoring data (PMS) are important measurements in quality work and developing new services. To support the realization of client goals in the health care system, it is important to consider the results of treatment reported by clients and their experiences of the effects of treatment. When patient-reported outcomes (PROMs) measure treatment health outcomes, patient-reported experience measures (PREMs) focus on patient experiences. PREMs can be divided into satisfaction and experience in relation to patient satisfaction or experience of structure (e.g., availability of services and comfort locations) and/or process (e.g., medical encounters and information needs/requests). In addition, PREMs may contain results; however, the PROMs measure outcomes as descriptions of the patient's health status at the point of reporting (treatment from the patient's perspective), PREMs include patients' assessment of treatment outcome (satisfaction with the treatment outcome). In Sweden, the system has been developed nationally (Nilsson, Orwelius, & Kristernson, 2016). In Finland, patients' assessments of treatment outcomes and experiences are not yet collected nationally, although the work is ongoing.

Ethical aspects are always important to consider when providing care and when developing care. Ethical aspects get a large amount of consideration even when there is no research-based information from new developed models (Sihvo et al., 2021).

7.2.3   Boundary Crossing in Innovation

A fair amount of innovation is claimed to occur at the boundaries of different fields (e.g., Dougherty & Takacs, 2004; Leonard-Barton, 1995). Boundaries emerge from differences, e.g., in stakeholders' professional identities, knowledge and expertise, and to reach novelty they need to be crossed. The practice-based view on knowledge management in organizations holds that integrating practices across various boundaries is key in bringing about novelty. For practices to be transformed the participating agents create a new joint field for reaching out to the shared objectives and crossing the boundaries (Levina & Vaast 2005). Facilitators of co-design can support boundary crossing by bringing their expertise on guiding the collaborative design process and choosing appropriate methods for creating shared vocabulary and new meanings (Salmi, Pöyry-Lassila, & Kronqvist, 2012).

7.2.4   Asymmetries

If approaching innovation and the problems related to collaboration from a critical angle, diversity may be seen as a source of asymmetry. Interest toward asymmetries has not been extensive in service research or co-design, with an exception on participatory design that has produced a great deal of research that goes into the power dynamics in cooperative design processes (e.g. Bratteteig & Wagner, 2012; Büscher et al., 2002). The concept of asymmetry refers to "the condition of not being equal or equally available between two people or groups" (Cambridge Dictionary, 2021), "lack of proportion between the parts of a thing" or "lack of coordination of two parts acting in connection with one another" (Merriam-Webster, 2021). Thus, in the context of our research, the critical perspective leads to questions of how diversity plays a role in the distribution of power among stakeholders, as well as in the accomplishment of the broader objectives in the system. In the next subchapters, we briefly walk through a few relevant perspectives.

7.2.4.1   Asymmetries in Value Co-Creation

The interest in service management and marketing research on asymmetries has focused on asymmetries of information between stakeholders in value co-creation where it has been seen as a complicating factor (e.g. Abea et al., 2019; Gallouj, 1997). Closest to our research topic in this field is a study that proposes an interpretative framework to extend the current understanding of information asymmetry in health care (Barilea et al., 2014). However, it is limited to dyadic service provider-patient relationships related to care and falls short in explaining how asymmetries play out in co-design in complex service ecosystems and at multiple care system levels influencing value co-creation.

In multistakeholder ecosystems, actors interact to collaborate to reciprocally bring value and benefit to its individual stakeholders collaborating in a network (Reypens et al., 2016). Value co-creation is theoretically rooted in service-dominant (S-D) logic in service marketing research and stresses the role of "intangibles, specialized skills, and processes (doing things for and with)" in service exchange (Vargo & Lusch, 2004, 1–2). Value co-creation necessitates interaction where value is generated when actors apply competences and integrate resources. In value co-creating constellations, no clear boundaries between providers and consumers exist (Vargo, Maglia, & Akaka 2008, 145, 146).

Following the thought pattern of customer-dominant logic of value creation, there is an underlying idea that the customers or the so-called end users of services are not only invited to take part in service development to come up to the experts but to participate on their own terms. When service-logic (e.g. Vargo & Lusch, 2008) meets customer-logic, there is a contrast. Service-logic highlights a provider-centric logic and easily dismisses the customer's value formation, which is much more fragmented, multi-contextual and affected by a multitude of other service processes and their associated value creation (Heinonen & Strandvik, 2015).

7.2.4.2 Asymmetries in Facilitation of Participatory Design

We take the asymmetries by Dahl and Svanæs (2020) as a starting point to our theoretical framing of asymmetries. Directing their contribution to the participatory design (PD) community, the key concerns of PD research, such as issues of power in design, democracy and tensions are crucial in their paper. They provide examples for their argument from facilitator performances in design cases in healthcare. For conceptualization of asymmetries, they use literature from PD and sociology (ibid).

Facilitation can play a role in how asymmetries are handled in discussions and negotiations between stakeholder groups and therefore, facilitators should be sensitive and self-reflective on their practice. They assert that inequalities can affect people's communicative behavior to the extent that it has a negative impact on their possibilities to influence. Their understanding of facilitation and the related asymmetries is situated and contextual, in the sense that it cannot be analyzed apart from method and its enactment, and participants in communication. As sources of asymmetry in care professional-patient interaction, they list professional knowledge, institutional knowledge, experiential relevance and power relations. As further, sources they note down social status, language and eloquence (Dahl et al., 2020, 676).

Authors explain the asymmetries following. They take professional knowledge to refer to the differences in the way ordinary people and health care practitioners understand and conceive of a medical condition. Institutional asymmetries they explain as differences in the participants' understanding of what kind of routines and how are performed in a particular institution. Experiential relevance touches on the different experience of an illness between care professionals and the patients. Knowing about an illness and the patients' experience are different from the experience of living with an illness. For the authors' power, asymmetries are associated with authority or the difference in decision-making power between people in a particular work hierarchy. The power difference is evident in doctor–patient relationships. Social status asymmetries compare the relative position of two or more actors in a society and make judgments based on their perceived differences. Lastly, the language and eloquence asymmetries bring attention to differences in language mastery and ways of communicating convincingly and persuasively (Dahl et al., 2020, 676). We suspect that these asymmetries apply to social care as well.

7.2.4.3 Attending to Asymmetries in Co-Design

In their framework of design choices, Lee et al. (2018) present choices that designers should consider when planning, conducting and analyzing co-creation.

They posit that systematic understanding of the different dimensions, attributes and alternatives benefits designers in making choices during planning and conducting co-design projects often characterized by dynamically changing conditions. The three aspects related to choices concerning participants in co-creation resonate with our study of asymmetries. Diversity in knowledge, differences in interests and distribution of power foreground these qualities for analyzing co-creation. Designers account for the asymmetries in practice by applying tools and settings that target participants with less power to engage on an equal footing (Lee et al., 2018, 23).

Concerning the diversity in knowledge, authors state that co-creation engagement should be planned along two dimensions: including people with relevant and diverse knowledge to the design process and including those people whose practices will be affected by the co-creation. In case examples concerning the dimension, they refer to professional, organizational and experiential knowledge differences. The differences in interests choice attends to the range of interests involved, possible conflicts that this entails and their effects to implementation of outcomes. Authors link responding to the differences in interests with choices of appropriate methods. Distribution of power refers to variation in participants' knowledge levels, interests, roles, societal and organizational backgrounds. Power matters manifest as differences in knowledge levels and social roles but also in facilitation approach (Lee et al., 2018, 22–23).

To sum up, we paralleled the asymmetries presented in Dahl et al. (2020) and Lee et al. (2018) to lay out an initial theoretical frame for our grounded theory inspired analysis. The authors' approaches are compared in Table 7.1. The key distinction between this study and the first-mentioned is that it examines asymmetries at the level of communicative interaction in facilitation and the latter one at the level of co-creation project. Both have recognized the role of different types of knowledge and the issue of power. However, the understanding of power as

Table 7.1 Mapping different authors' concepts of asymmetries

Dahl and Svanaes (2020)	Lee et al. (2018)
Asymmetries in PD communivative encounters due to inequalities in…	Asymmetries as differences in co-creation projects due to participants'…
Professional knowledge	Diversity in knowledge, Distribution of Power (knowledge levels, interests, roles, organizational status)
Institutional knowledge	Distribution of Power (organizational background)
Experiential relevance	Diversity in Knowledge, Differences in Interests and Distribution of Power (interests, roles, societal background)
Power relations	Distribution of Power (societal, organizational background)
Language proficiency	Distribution of Power (societal background)
Eloquence	Distribution of Power (societal background)

Source Author's own elaboration (2021)

authority in decision-making (ibid.) contrasts with the view that power difference is related to knowledge levels, interests, various roles, backgrounds and even the level of expertise in creative activities in Lee et al. (2018). Lee et al. (2018) take power difference to cover a range of asymmetries. We see that the language proficiency and eloquence do not directly map with any of the other authors' asymmetries but may be interpreted as a power difference that operates through societal or better, cultural background. Experiential relevance may partly overlap with aspects of differences in interests since people gain experiences by acting on their interests.

The asymmetries explained in previous subchapters provide a good starting point for understanding asymmetries in co-design. However, to be able to combine the ecosystem level goals with the local and global level requirements, a broader view on asymmetries is needed. Health and social care are rife with different kinds of care environments and the much needed evidence-based knowledge. In the wider context of the local environment, there are laws and regulations providing rules to care. To understand the whole context of health care, and to be fully able to support co-design in this setting, requires a significant amount of information of its legal and regulatory context and operating principles. At the same time, designers possess a wealth of knowledge on how to facilitate design processes so that patients and clients can have a stronger voice and influence what kind of services are created.

7.3 Case Description and Methods

Our analysis focuses on the MORFEUS research project and its four cases concerning service and solution development for different client groups and beneficiaries. They spanned different health and social care sectors and intersected the educational sector. Co-design was employed to increase the different stakeholders' knowledge and awareness of the key challenges and opportunities for cross-actor, cross-sector collaboration, to find ways to facilitate collaboration across boundaries and co-construct solutions for new value co-creation in the service ecosystem.

MORFEUS project (01/2015–06/2017) investigated cross-actor collaboration in health and social care in which one of the greatest and persistent challenges was siloed ways of working. The research on collaboration needed to respond to the very challenge. The complex and intricate phenomena necessitated cross-disciplinary research, collaborative inquiry and a multimethod approach. MORFEUS, a joint project of Laurea University of Applied Sciences and Aalto University, brought together knowledge from several fields including service design, health care, organization studies, law and contracting and future studies. The health service ecosystem consisted of participants from the citizen sector, including experts by experience, public health care from primary and specialized care levels, social work, IT and consulting companies and the education sector. The advisory board included specialists from knowledge producing organizations and foundations, such as centers for excellence. The citizen-driven approach adopted in the project focused on the whole service system around citizens with complex service needs and addressed the value creation dynamics among the ecosystem's multiple stakeholders.

The research project involved five intensive co-development cycles that closely engaged the ecosystem participants and the actual service users, either directly or represented using various methods and formats in design. Each of the cycles delved deeper into the cases that dealt with human-centered, holistic services for customers with mental health, addiction and substance misuse problems; integrated child welfare services for families with extensive service needs such as child protection; preventive, low-threshold mental health service for young men at high risk of social exclusion and service information modeling with specialists, professionals and scientific advisors.

Data was collected using various qualitative methods, such as interviews, video recordings and observations of collaborative workshops, photographing of co-created artifacts and user-testing of prototypes. Designers ensured the anonymity of participants by employing appropriate protocols. Diverse range of co-design methods were employed at different stages of the process, including stakeholder and ecosystem mappings, storytelling, design probes, customer personas and service process modeling, future scenarios, action plans, prototyping and testing with users.

The main result in the project was a service information modeling (SIM) that consisted of an ecosystem metamodeling and a service prototype for case management, service system management and decision-making. The SIM sought to provide ways to collect the needed information for procurement, production and development of more citizen-oriented and cost-effective services in the service ecosystem. It consisted of a metamodeling of the service ecosystem as well as a service prototype involving a digital service interface mock-up to support case managers and their clients' collaboration. The collaborative design engagements and SIM as its outcome provided research-based understanding on needs for policy, legal and regulatory level changes, the different stakeholders' information needs, resources and opportunities for combining resources as well as clarified roles and relationships within the service ecosystem. Also, valuable feedback for the digital service prototype was collected and insights gained on suitable methods and techniques for boundary crossing collaboration (Salmi & Pöyry-Lassila, 2020).

To analyze asymmetries and how they played out in co-design, we use our self-reflective accounts and written research material collected as a Wiki and shared in the designer team as data.

7.4 Analyzing Asymmetries in the MORFEUS Case

First, in analyzing asymmetries in MORFEUS, we use categories suggested by Lee et al. (2018) and lean on Dahl et al. (2020) where they extend the first mentioned. Due to its project-level focus, we found Lee et al. (2018) as more promising for our analysis of the ecosystemic collaboration.

The MORFEUS stakeholders had diversity in knowledge (Lee et al., 2018) which related to professional and institutional knowledge (Dahl et al. 2020). The IT and consulting company participants did not have professional knowledge from the health and social care practice, even though they had knowledge on IT development in health care. Health and social care professionals did not have professional knowledge on IT, but instead, they had legal knowledge. The other IT consulting company, a publicly owned, was partly specialized in development of health care management, quality and processes and, therefore, they had an advantage in health care institutional knowledge. In the multidisciplinary team of 8–10 researchers/designers, there were two with a professional background in nursing, but the others lacked health care professional knowledge. Many of the researchers/designers taught in health and social care leadership degree programs and had gained institutional knowledge through working with students and work life partners in educational settings. On the other hand, the researchers/designers had diverse professional knowledge on IT in health care, health care management, law and contracting in the public sector and creative co-design processes and business development also in health care.

The stakeholders' knowledge was diverse, and they broadly represented people who had relevant knowledge about the health care services and whose work was affected by the created services (Lee et al., 2018). The knowledge between participants was asymmetrical in the sense that their professional and institutional knowledge (Dahl et al., 2020) was anchored in different fields and organizations. In the multidisciplinary designer team, the professional and institutional knowledge (ibid.) was most diverse.

The most drastic asymmetry existed between the care clients, experts by experience and health and social care professionals. The asymmetry related to diversity in knowledge, difference in interests and distribution of power (Lee et al., 2018). It also touched on the asymmetry of institutional knowledge between the same groups. The asymmetry was by far the most complicating factor in co-design concerning the inclusion of different voices in design. There was resistance from the health and social care professionals' side on including clients in collaboration due to a preconception that some clients may tend to direct the attention of professionals to their own predicaments away from the broader challenge at stake. On the other hand, the asymmetry also challenged the recruitment of clients to co-creation. The events where medical professionals would have directly collaborated with clients were only few in the project.

The distribution of power (Lee et al., 2018) related to the asymmetry of expertise on creative activities. Not all service ecosystem participants had experience in participating in co-design or service design processes, not to say professional knowledge on innovation. Particularly, in the tightly scheduled work at the health care client interface, participation in external development projects is not a routine practice. However, in IT companies, service design is widely used and the professionals have related expertise. Also, the institutional research context of university was not familiar to all, except to those in health and social care and IT professionals who had conducted research or had a researcher education.

The stakeholders involved in co-design, in each case, had a variety of different interests (Lee et al., 2018) to participate in co-design. Designers were keen on the creation of new knowledge and experiment with methods and ways of engaging the diverse stakeholders. Care professionals in the public sector special health care were particularly interested in optimization of care processes, such as ways of improving treatment lead times and gaining ideas for preventive mental health care for young people. Third sector care service producers were after opportunities of collaboration with the public sector institutions to learn more about public procurement and to develop related processes. IT and consulting professionals were interested in gaining institutional knowledge from the care professionals about the challenges in health care. The reason for the clients and experts by experience participation was that they wanted to bring their care-related experiences to the design process and influence design.

Concerning distribution of power (Lee et al., 2018), participants' societal background was linked to educational background, its level and status and their organizational position varied from social care managers to medical doctors and administrative physicians, IT development managers to citizens. Between fields, such as medicine and social work, there were significant asymmetries in societal valuation. Experts by experience, even though trained, did not have a formal position in any organizational hierarchy and thus they were in asymmetrical position to employed stakeholders. An organizational asymmetry was obvious between physicians and social workers. On the other hand, between psychiatry and social work, there was mutual understanding on some of the key challenges of patients with multiple needs, and the asymmetry between their statuses did not seem to hamper cooperation.

Across sectors, asymmetries were not so salient, but they were related to the relative power in the health and social care service market. Citizen sector services could be thought of as an underdog due to their not-for-profit basis. However, the third sector service producers were found in expert discussions to be rather agile in shaping their services compared to their larger counterparts in the public sector. However, the public sector institutions were an important buyer and their changing purchase conditions and processes for procurement had a large effect on the third sector service producers. Also, the looming national health and social care reform was expected to significantly change the position of the public and private sector service producers, but at the point of the project, the specifics of the reform were not known. The private sector stakeholders in MORFEUS represented IT and consulting companies and were thus not directly in an asymmetric relation in the health and social care service market. Health care is a beneficiary of their IT solutions. However, the very reason for the engagement of the IT company and health and social care actors was to overcome the diversity in knowledge (Lee et al., 2018) about the opportunities of digital solutions in healthcare and the institutional knowledge on health and social care.

Our initial analysis of the asymmetries showed that the asymmetries cited in literature do not fully cover the knowledge differences influencing co-design in complex multistakeholder ecosystems and regulated settings such as health care. To account for the gap, we take a step further from the cited literature by suggesting two more knowledge-related asymmetries (see Table 7.2).

Based on our initial insights on the shortages of existing theory, we constructed a model (Table 7.2) to account for the knowledge asymmetries that extend the differences in knowledge in the multistakeholder service ecosystem. We also reworked the categories of experiential, professional and institutional knowledge (Dahl et al., 2020) to better respond to the requirements of the multistakeholder context and to consider the interdependent nature of knowledge and the practices that the stakeholders engage in their local contexts.

We explain the two additional categories covering guidelines and regulatory knowledge in the model (Table 7.2). In our case analysis, we noticed that there were differences between the stakeholders in the knowledge concerning guidelines such as EBC. Among the designers who did not have professional or institutional knowledge in health care, there was incomplete knowledge about how the model is implemented and where are the limits of the designers' influence. Overall, in the

Table 7.2 Integrated understanding (from Dahl et al., 2020; Lee et al., 2018) of cross-level asymmetries in ecosystemic co-design

Cross-level asymmetries in design			
Asymmetries as differences in actors' multilevel system knowledge in multiactor co-design in service ecosystem			
Ethical principles	Experiential knowledge	Person's level of education, socioeconomical and cultural background affects capacities to participate and influence. Training as expert by experience or having experience as a patient relative/advocate increases citizens' capacity to participate	Power relations
	Professional knowledge	Professionals in different roles have different knowledge. Associated asymmetries have an effect on collaboration and capability to participate	
	Institutional knowledge	Stakeholders' diversity in knowledge concerning different organizational levels in public, private and third sector organizations, enhanced with knowledge on multichannel digital services in health service ecosystems have an effect on participation. Knowledge about different institutional roles and responsibilities affects too	
	Guidelines knowledge	Stakeholders' diversity in knowledge about evidence-based care implementation model may misguide the focus of collaborative problem-saving and lead to outcomes that cannot be implemented in healthcare	
	Regulatory knowledge	Stakeholders diverse knowledge about public governance policies, laws and regulations affects stakeholders ability to take into account the legal and regulatory limits within which design takes place and may affect their ability of influence	

Source Author's own elaboration (2021)

model, the care environment and the ways in which the client experience is integrated as part of the care decision-making are the points that are the most accessible to the designers' input.

Concerning regulatory knowledge (Table 7.2), there was diversity in the stakeholders' knowledge concerning the national strategic guidance and legal requirements in health care. The relevant national strategies, such as the Information to Support Well-being Service Renewal Strategy (Ministry of Social Affairs & Health, 2015) and laws and regulations including EU fundamental rights (European Commission, 2012), the Constitution of Finland (Ministry of Justice, 1999), Act on the Status and Rights of a Patient (Ministry of Social Affairs & Health, 1992), Act on Health Care Professionals (Ministry of Social Affairs & Health, 1994), Social Welfare Act (Ministry of Social Affairs and Health, 1999), Act on Qualification Requirements for Social Welfare Professionals (Ministry of Social Affairs & Health, 2005), Act on the Status and Rights of Social Welfare Clients (Ministry of Social Affairs & Health, 2000) and Act on the Electronic Processing of Client Data in Healthcare and Social Welfare (Ministry of Social Affairs & Health, 2007) were not mastered equally among the stakeholders, which was an asymmetry in knowledge between them.

In our model (Table 7.2), we associated the knowledge asymmetries with power relations since in our analysis, we concluded that the knowledge differences are related to the stakeholders' capacities to engage in new transformative practice. For example, it was difficult for stakeholders to participate without sufficient knowledge on laws concerning the use of client health data (Ministry of Social Affairs & Health, 2007). Conforming to ethical principles in care, research and digitalization concerns the whole design process and all the stakeholders. Considering, e.g., ethics of care, design ethics or value sensitive design supports a broader consideration of human needs, not just the participating stakeholders.

7.4.1 Initial Model for Cross-Level Service Design

In Fig. 7.1, we describe the operating environment for design for services in multistakeholder setting, the different levels of the health and social care system in relation to it and the associated asymmetries or differences in knowledge. The designers need to have good skills in identifying and working with asymmetries across different levels. As they give a voice to each stakeholder, they also need to continuously (re) frame the challenge and integrate the emerging themes to the opportunities and limitations of the health care context. The differences in knowledge affect the stakeholders' capability to form a shared understanding of the challenge, preferences and needs, opportunities and priorities, and address them in co-design.

In a multistakeholder ecosystem, the asymmetries first affect co-design at the level of collaboration. Concerning the wider operating environment, the knowledge asymmetries extend to care provision and its design. Each professional and client is connected to a local level of services. When entering deeper into multidisciplinary exploration of the evidence-based care pathway, we find asymmetries in content knowledge of care, environment and research recommendations. Moreover, adding the client with complex service needs to the picture complicates it even further.

The different care pathways, environments and professional education are regulated by laws and policies. The dissemination of research-based recommendations is coordinated nationally and even internationally. The designer as a facilitator needs to consider all these aspects and to account for the fact that the evidence-based service is not totally open to design. However, in an ecosystem with multiple actors, there are a lot of needs and opportunities to design new ways for integrated care, engage the client and make his/her voice stronger.

In co-design, the designer helps the participants to collaborate and envision the solution. At the same time, the new solution may require actions on the law and policy to set new regulations or change existing ones. A good example could be digitalization and AI solutions, which transfer data that need new kinds of regulations, for example, laws concerning the uptake of medical devices. We envision that in future, the objectives of and implementation of the EBC model, design for service and policy design could be aligned, and the stakeholders would be better equipped to find their way through asymmetries in co-designing new services. Carr et al. (2011) propose interesting directions for incorporating experience-driven design and co-creation in evidence-based healthcare service design at a wider scale. (Carr et al., 2011).

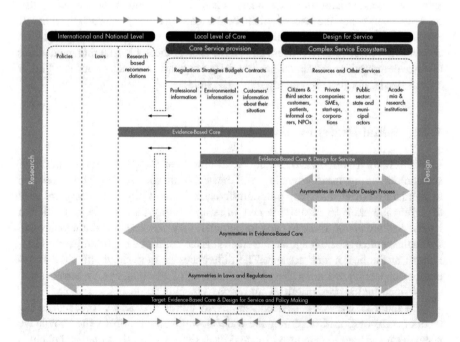

Fig. 7.1 Description of the operating environment for design for services and the asymmetries extending to different system levels. *Source* Author's own illustration (2021)

7.4.2   Initial Insights on Crossing Asymmetries

As the analysis of the data is still ongoing, we present some initial insights concerning actions and activities that helped cross knowledge asymmetries in MORFEUS.

In investigating the service ecosystem, we utilized a fictional case example about the collection of services that a family with complex service needs would use. In the case story, by employing a narrative format, we illustrated the family members' challenges and from the perspective of the people's experience.

We were aware that patient or client cases are commonly used in health and social care research and reporting and therefore deliberately tried to avoid field specific standards in our choice of format and wording. For us researchers acting as designers, it was a way to bypass the potential ethical problems associated with involving real service users. However, we found that it was a very useful way to share information about the characters' experiences in the service ecosystem that it conveyed the rich information about the design challenge in a way that was open to interpretation and easy to relate to independent of background. In the co-design engagements, we observed that the stakeholders made plentiful references to the story related to the characters by calling them with their names and discussed the family member life situations at an experiential level. The case story was used as a basis for stakeholder and ecosystem mapping. We think that the format of presenting client information to a multiprofessional group influenced the way the participants could make use of it in co-design. It helped cross-knowledge asymmetries between sectors, health and social care and between professions and institutions in the mapping exercise. Stakeholders' societal backgrounds did not come in the way because the story was easy to relate to at a human level.

We found the experiential knowledge asymmetry making the recruitment of young men in risk of social marginalization difficult. After tough attempts to reach suitable individuals, we managed to find four young men aged 16–19 who participated the study with their mothers. However, those that participated did so rather actively, which again may be a merit of the method.

Mobile probes worked well in engaging young people. The digital application used to collect data and communicate with the participants was an instant messaging solution that was easily accepted by the young people. The participants were asked about their everyday activities, relationships to friends, parents and important adults, resources and future expectations. One of the researchers commented in the notes that through using the method, it was easier to enter deeper conversations quicker and gain information that would be difficult to get through interviews. We interpret this as the method helping to cross asymmetry in experiential knowledge and societal background between the researchers and young people.

In involving experts by experience who were mental health services users in one of our workshops, we faced an asymmetry in institutional and regulatory knowledge related to permission to collect data. The participants raised concerns about how the recordings would be handled in the research and how anonymity could be preserved. From the position of the researchers, the intensity of the concerns came as a slight surprise. Despite the researchers' thoughtfulness on matters of research ethics, permissions and consents, the very suggestion of recording conversations concerning personal issues was, based on the reactions, experienced as an act of power on the participants' side. As representatives of science institution, we researchers may not always be aware of these kinds of asymmetries. In reflecting back this experience, we pondered if our regulatory knowledge about designing in the mental health care context was sufficient. Also, experiential asymmetry hindered us from preconceiving how they would respond to our requests to record the session.

When we pursued the SIM and service prototyping in the service ecosystem, we encountered asymmetry in regulatory knowledge. We designers ideated numerous ways how to improve the services by promoting the use of client data over boundaries. However, many of our ideas would not have been possible to implement by law. As the health care, social care and IT professionals daily deal with patient data and its handling, their regulatory knowledge in this area was much more thorough. Co-designing could have been more fluent had we designers had more symmetrical regulatory knowledge. Among the designer team, there were legal experts, but they were not trained in creative activities and needed to overcome that asymmetry.

7.5   Discussion and Conclusions

Innovative and future-oriented multistakeholder innovation needs to account for the uniqueness of the health and social care sectors' challenges and strive to integrate the evidence-based care and design practices. These practices need to be able to accommodate the law and regulatory requirements as well as the asymmetries at different system levels to reach new knowledge.

Fully acknowledging the impact of the national health care strategic objectives that in Finland promote the uptake of digital solutions in clients' self-care and their relation to the rationale of the 20/80 model in co-design will make the designers substantially better equipped in framing the design challenges. Also, the needs of the people with complex service needs, who are evidently in minority, sets an imperative for designers to carefully consider the balancing of stakeholders in including them in processes of design. This is one additional asymmetry to consider.

In co-design, it is not possible to know who has relevant knowledge, whose knowledge counts and how before the design process unfolds, as design problems and their solutions co-evolve (Dorst & Cross, 2001). The idea in co-design is that participants are provided suitable tools to share their knowledge and experiences as a basis for design. The use of appropriate methods can help diverse participants to express their views and understandings and thereby bridge knowledge differences. However, methods and their enactment may also introduce further asymmetries, such as the one described in (Dahl et al., 2020) on digital competences.

The project's main aim was to create an ecosystem which supports value co-creation based on customer logic. We created a digital service prototype: rethinking the idea of the one-stop-shop principle and customer coming to the service, toward a digital platform that the service provider, case manager and the client can access from their own context. It included views also to the service director for service planning and management. The platform offered a multi-channel service environment by forming an ecosystem that provided value to the client in the form of a seamless and reliable service. Co-designing the prototype required knowledge sharing across asymmetries in the service ecosystem. We may also ponder if knowledge on healthcare digitalization presents as one additional asymmetry since it required from us extensive desk research along discussions with IT professionals.

Health and social care have a long history of hierarchical culture and work has been hard to move on to a more modern leadership culture. Participatory design has developed strategies to lower tensions, but still, there are asymmetries in professional knowledge, power asymmetries, asymmetries in social status and language asymmetries. Design provides tools to open these blocks, increase communication and understanding of each other's work to design more integrated care.

Our analysis brought us to think about the relationship between tensions and how laying out them might inform us about the forces that are at work in co-design. This observation leaves room for further research. As is noted in (Dahl et al., 2020), in participatory design, asymmetries may be a source of tensions particularly in contexts where there are differences in values, interests and views between groups. In addition to the level of collaboration, tensions can be identified between the two states essential to design: the current or past and the aspired future situation (Steen, 2011). Designers need to balance between gathering research data and catalyzing, upholding and implementing change. We note a similar tension in integrating the evidence-based care and objectives of designs.

The ongoing developments in digital client data including the PROM and PREM present interesting opportunities for human-centered design and design for services. Integrating large sets of treatment outcome and experience data would enable a solid database for co-design of services. Also, it opens interesting avenues when extended with my data and citizen science approaches in health data production. This kind of secondary use of data culture is growing; this being one example how client-driven services could be designed when the laws and regulations reach the required level. The work is ongoing at the policy level.

Ethical questions of equality and equity are fundamental when talking about social and health care. The imperative is that we should be treated equally by the care system. The request for accountability in the Nordics is high as care is majorly funded by taxpayers. Furthermore, ethical principles concern designing for services and their role is accentuated, if there is not a strong evidence base for the context that we are designing for.

We found out that to cross boundaries and reach new knowledge in co-design, we need to consider the cross-level asymmetries. Knowledge about stakeholder engagement, design methods and how to apply them are core competences of designers, nevertheless, it is not enough. Especially in health and social care settings and when working with clients with complex needs, knowledge about the principles of the operating environment and power relations is necessary. In facilitating co-design, the different levels of knowledge of experiential, professional, institutional, guidelines related and regulatory asymmetries, and how they play out in people's discourse within and between the levels should be recognized. Accounting for them also calls for an awareness of the ethical principles in both design and health care. In the future, we will look forward to involving people all the way from citizens to policy makers and collaboratively finding ways to cross the asymmetries at different levels.

Acknowledgements Thank you for the creative research efforts of the project specialists and researchers at Laurea University of Applied Sciences and Aalto University, School of Science, Department of Industrial Engineering and Management, SimLab. The research was conducted as part of SHAPES—Smart and Healthy Ageing through People Engaging in Supportive Systems—that is funded by the Horizon 2020 Framework Programme of the European Union for Research Innovation. Grant agreement number: 857159 - SHAPES - H2020 - SC1-FA-DTS - 2018-2020. Part of the research was carried out in the MORFEUS project that was funded by the Finnish Funding Agency of Technology and Innovation (Business Finland) and the universities, which is gratefully acknowledged.

References

Abea, S., Tsutsuia, Y., Mitakea, Y., Sholihaha, M., Harab, N., & Shimomura, Y. (2019). An asymmetry analysis method to support value co-creation in product/service design. In Procedia CIRP 84, International Academy for Production Engineering (CIRP), pp. 442–446

Barilea, S., Savianob, M., & Polese, F. (2014). Information asymmetry and co-creation in health care services. *Australasian Marketing Journal, 22*(3), 205–217. https://doi.org/10.1016/j.ausmj.2014.08.008

Bratteteig, T., & Wagner, I. (2012) Disentangling power and decision-making in participatory design. In *Proceedings of the 12th Participatory Design Conference: Research Papers*, Vol. 1, August 2012, pp. 41–50. https://doi.org/10.1145/2347635.2347642 Corpus ID: 10901311

Büscher, M., Shapiro, D., Hartswood, M., Procter, R., Slack, R., Voß, A., & Mogensen, P. (2002) Promises, premises and risks: sharing responsibilities, working up trust and sustaining commitment in participatory design projects. In *PDC 02 Proceedings of the Seventh Biennial Participatory Design Conference*, 23.-25.06.2002, Malmö, Sweden, pp. 183–192.

Carr, V. L., Sangiorgi, D., Büscher, M., Junginger, S., & Cooper, R. (2011) Integrating evidence-based design and experience-based approaches in healthcare service design. *HERD: Health Environments Research & Design Journal, 4*(4), 12–33. https://doi.org/10.1177/193758671100400403. PMID: 21960190.

Cambridge Dictionary. (2021). Asymmetry. Cambridge Dictionary of English Language. Retrieved May 30, 2021, from https://dictionary.cambridge.org/dictionary/english/asymmetry.

Dahl, Y., & Svanæs, D. (2020). Facilitating democracy: Concerns from participatory design with asymmetric stakeholder relations in health care. CHI 2020, 25.-30.04.2020, Association for Computing Machinery, Honolulu, HI, USA. https://doi.org/10.1145/3313831.3376805.

Di Censo, A., & Cullum, N. (1989). Implementing evidence based nursing: Some misconseptions. *Evidencebased Nursing, 1*(2), 38–40. https://doi.org/10.1136/ebn.1.2.38CorpusID:72038657

Dorst, K., & Cross, N. (2001). Creativity in the design process: Co-evolution of problem–solution. *Design Studies, 22*(5), 425–437. https://doi.org/10.1016/S0142-694X(01)00009-6

Dougherty, D., & Takacs, C. (2004). Team play: Heedful interrelating as the boundary for innovation. *Long Range Planning, 37*(6), 569–590. https://doi.org/10.1016/j.lrp.2004.09.003

Einhorn, E. C. (2019). Health care in nordics. Healthcare in the Nordics. Retrieved June 15, 2021, from https://nordics.info/show/artikel/healthcare-in-the-nordic-region/.

European Commission. (2012). EU fundamental rights 2012/C 326/02. Retrieved June 21, 2021, from https://eur-lex.europa.eu/legal-content/EN/TXT/PDF/?uri=OJ:C:2012:326:FULL&from=EN.

European Commission. (2018). Communication from the Commission to the European Parliament, The Council, The European Economic and Social Committee and the Committee of the Regions on enabling the digital transformation of health and care in the Digital Single Market; empowering citizens and building a healthier society. Retrieved June 15, 2021, from https://eur-lex.europa.eu/legal-content/EN/TXT/PDF/?uri=CELEX:52018DC0233&from=EN.

Forlizzi, J., & Ford, S. (2000). The building blocks of experience: An early framework for interaction designers. In *Proceedings of Designing Interactive Systems 2000.* (pp. 419–423). Brooklyn, NY. https://doi.org/10.1145/347642.347800 Corpus ID: 207595864.

Gallouj, C. (1997). Asymmetry of information and the service relationship: Selection and evaluation of the service provider. *In International Journal of Service Industry Management, 8* (1), 42–64. https://doi.org/10.1108/09564239710161079CorpusID:167697935

Heinonen, K., & Strandvik, T. (2015). Customer-dominant logic: Foundations and implications. *Journal of Services Marketing., 29*(6/7), 472–484. https://doi.org/10.1108/JSM-02-2015-0096

Hujala, A. & Lammintakanen, J. (2018) Paljon sote-palveluja tarvitsevat ihmiset keskiöön. Kunnallisalan kehittämissäätiö julkaisu 12. Retrieved June 18, 2021, from https://kaks.fi/wp-content/uploads/2018/01/paljon-sote-palveluja-tarvitsevat-ihmiset-keskioon.pdf.

Kiiski, K. E., Laine, P., Jousilahti, J.,& Neuvonen, A. (2018). Hyvinvoinnin seuraava erä. Ihanteet, visio ja ratkaisut. 09.01.2018 Sitra muistio. Retrieved June 17, 2021, from https://media.sitra.fi/2018/01/05155811/hyvinvoinnin-seuraava-era-ihanteet-visio-ja-ratkaisut.pdf.

Kuusisto-Niemi, S. (2016). Tiedon hallinta sosiaalihuollossa. Tiedonhallinnan paradigma opetuksen ja tutkimuksen perustana. Väitoskirja. Kuopio: University of Eastern Finland. Retrieved June 17, 2021, from http://epublications.uef.fi/pub/urn_isbn_978-952-61-2279-3/urn_isbn_978-952-61-2279-3.pdf.

Lee, J.-J., Jaatinen, M., Salmi, A., Mattelmäki, T., Smeds, R., & Holopainen, M. (2018). Design choices framework for co-creation projects. *International Journal of Design, 12*(2), 15–31.

Lehtimäki, T., Komulainen, H., Oinonen, M., & Salo, J. (2018). The value of long-term co-innovation relationships: Experiential approach. *International Journal of Business Innovation and Research, 16*(1), 1–23. https://doi.org/10.1504/IJBIR.2018.091078

Leonard-Barton, D. A. (1995). Wellsprings of knowledge: Building and sustaining the sources of innovation. Boston: Harvard Business School Press.

Levina, N., s& Vaast , V. (2005). The emergence of boundary spanning competence in practice: Implications for Implementation and Use of Information Systems. *MIS Quarterly, 29*(2), 335. https://doi.org/10.2307/25148682

Lusch, R., Vargo, S., & O'Brien, M. (2007). Competing through service: Insights from service-dominant logic. *Journal of Retailing, 83*(1), 5–18. https://doi.org/10.1016/j.jretai.2006.10.002

Lyttkens, C. H., Christiansen, T., Häkkinen, U., & Kaarboe, O. (2016). The core of the Nordic health care system is not empty Article. *Nordic Journal of Health Economics, 4*(1), 7–27. https://doi.org/10.5617/njhe.2848

Meroni, A., & Sangiorgi, D. (2011). Design for services. Farnham: Gower Publishing, Ltd.

Merriam Webster. (2021). Asymmetry. Merriam-Webster.com Dictionary, Merriam-Webster (Ed.), Retrieved May 30, 2021, from https://www.merriam-webster.com/dictionary/asymmetry.

Ministry of Justice. (1999). The Constitution of Finland 731/1999. Retrieved June 21, 2021, from https://finlex.fi/fi/laki/kaannokset/1999/en19990731.pdf.

Ministry of Social Affairs and Health. (1992). Act on the Status and Rights of a Patient 17.8.1992/785. Retrieved June 21, 2021, from https://www.finlex.fi/fi/laki/kaannokset/1992/en19920785_20120690.pdf.

Ministry of Social Affairs and Health. (1994). Act on Health Care Professionals 28.6.1994/559. Retrieved June 21, 2021, from https://www.finlex.fi/fi/laki/kaannokset/1994/en19940559_20110312.pdf.

Ministry of Social Affairs and Health. (1999). Social Welfare Act 710/1982. Retrieved June 21, 2021, from https://www.finlex.fi/en/laki/kaannokset/1982/en19820710.

Ministry of Social Affairs and Health. (2000). Act on the Status and Rights of Social Welfare Clients 22.9.2000/812. Retrieved June 21, 2021, from https://www.finlex.fi/en/laki/kaannokset/2000/en20000812.

Ministry of Social Affairs and Health. (2005). Act on Qualification Requirements for Social Welfare Professionals 272/2005. Retrieved June 21, 2021, from https://finlex.fi/en/laki/kaannokset/2005/en20050272.

Ministry of Social Affairs and Health. (2007). Act on the Electronic Processing of Client Data in Healthcare and Social Welfare 159/2007. Retrieved June 30, 2021 from https://www.finlex.fi/en/laki/kaannokset/2007/en20070159.

Ministry of Social Affairs and Health. (2010). Health Care Act 1326/2010. Retrieved June 17, 2021, from https://www.finlex.fi/en/laki/kaannokset/2010/en20101326.

Ministry of Social Affairs and Health. (2015). Information to support well-being and service renewal. eHealth and eSocial Strategy 2020, Edita Prima, Helsinki, 2015. Retrieved June 17, 2021, from https://julkaisut.valtioneuvosto.fi/bitstream/handle/10024/74459/URN_ISBN_978-952-00-3575-4.pdf?sequence=1.

Ministry of Social Affairs and Health. (2021). Strategy 2030. Retrieved June 16, 2021, from https://stm.fi/en/strategy.

Nilsson, E., Orwelius, L., & Kristenson, M. (2016). Patient-reported outcomes in the Swedish National Quality Registers. *Journal of Internal Medicine, 279*(2), 141–153. PMID: 26306802. https://doi.org/10.1111/joim.12409.

Paasio, P. (2014). Näyttöön perustuva sosiaalityön käytäntö – järjestelmällinen katsaus vuosina 2010–2012 julkaistuista tutkimuksista. Lisensiaatintutkimus. Jyväskylän yliopisto. Retrieved June 16, 2021, from https://www.sosnet.fi/loader.aspx?id=ed6d31dd-6da0-4046-99e8-e9613b31714e.

Pearson, A., Wiechula, R., Court, A., & Lockwood C. (2005). The JBI model of evidence-based healthcare. *International Journal of Evidence-Based Healthcare, 3*(8), 207–215 PMID: 21631749. https://doi.org/10.1111/j.1479-6988.2005.00026.x.

Pearson, A., Wiechula, R., Court, A., & Lockwood, C. (2007). A re-consideration of what constitutes "evidence" in the healthcare professions. *Nursing Science Quarterly, 20*(1), 85–88. https://doi.org/10.1177/0894318406296306

Reypens, C., Lievens, A., & Blazevic, V. (2016). Leveraging value in multi-stakeholder innovation networks: A process framework for value co-creation and capture. *Industrial Marketing Management, 56*(2016), 40–50. https://doi.org/10.1016/j.indmarman.2016.03.005

Salmi, A., & Pöyry-Lassila, P. (2020). Systemic design addressing complexity in service ecosystems: Integrating empathic and systemic perspectives. In T. Hirvikoski, L. Erkkilä, M. Fred, A. Helariutta, I. Kurkela, P. Pöyry-Lassila, K. Saastamoinen, A. Salmi, & A. Äyväri (Eds.), *Co-creating and Orchestrating Multistakeholder Innovation* (pp. 23–36). Laurea ammattikorkeakoulu / Laurea University of Applied Sciences.

Sanders, E., & Stappers, P. (2008). Co-Creation and the new landscapes of design. *CoDesign, 4* (1), 5–18. https://doi.org/10.1080/15710880701875068

Salmi, A, Pöyry-Lassila, P., & Kronqvist, J. (2012). Supporting empathetic boundary spanning in participatory workshops with scenarios and personas. *International Journal of Ambient Computing and Intelligence, 4*(4) 21–39. https://doi.org/10.4018/jaci.2012100102

Sihvo, P., Vesterinen, O., Koski, A., Malkavaara, M., & Pasanen, M. (2021). Ethical operational model at the core of competence. Karelia University of Applied Sciences. Retrieved June 4, 2021, from https://www.theseus.fi/handle/10024/496170.

Steen, M. (2011). Tensions in human-centred design. *CoDesign, 7*(1), 45–60. https://doi.org/10.1080/15710882.2011.563314

Vargo, S., & Lusch, R. (2004). Evolving to a new dominant logic for marketing. *Journal of Marketing, 68*(1), 1–17. https://doi.org/10.1509/jmkg.68.1.1.24036

Vargo, S., & Lusch, R. (2008). Service-dominant logic: Continuing the evolution. *Journal of the Academy of Marketing Science, 36*(1), 1–10. https://doi.org/10.1007/s11747-007-0069-6

Vargo, S., Maglio, P., & Akaka, M. (2008). On value and value co-creation: A service systems and service logic perspective. *European Management Journal, 26*(3), 145–152. https://doi.org/10.1016/j.emj.2008.04.003

Vehko, T., Jolanki, O., Aalto, A.-M., & Sinervo, T. (2018). How do health care workers manage a patient with multiple care needs from both health and social care services?—A vignette study. *International Journal of Care Coordination, 21*(1–2), 5–14. https://doi.org/10.1177/2F2053434517744070.

Värri, A., Tiainen, M., Rajalahti, E., Kinnunen, U.-M., Saarni, L., & Ahonen, O. (2020) The definition of informatics competencies in finnish healthcare and social welfare education. Digital Personalized Health and Medicine, Studies in Health Technology and Informatics. In L. B. Pape-Haugaard et al. (Eds.), European Federation for Medical Informatics (EFMI) and IOS Press, Proceedings of MIE 2020. pp. 1143–1147. Retrieved June 16, 2021, from http://urn.fi/URN:NBN:fi-fe2020082563162. https://doi.org/10.3233/SHTI200341.

Wagner, E., Austin, B., Davies, C., Hindmarsh, M., Schaever, J., & Bonomi, A. (2001) Improving chronic illness care: Translating evidence into action. *Health Affairs, 20*(6), 64–78. PMID: 11816692. https://doi.org/10.1377/hlthaff.20.6.64.

Anna Salmi Doctoral Candidate in Design, MA, Senior Lecturer. Laurea University of Applied Sciences. Currently, she acts as a project specialist studying service design and co-creation in open ecosystems in the European SHAPES, The Smart & Healthy Ageing through People Engaging in Supportive Systems project and multistakeholder innovation in Co-Creation Orchestration (CCO) national project. She has conducted research in co-design in interorganizational settings in several domains, including social and health care. She acted as a researcher and designer in the MORFEUS project. She has over a decade of experience in teaching human-centered design, business development, and service design and innovation at universities in Master's programmes. Her research interests include design for services, and the application of design approach in facilitating collaboration in multistakeholder innovation ecosystems.

Outi Ahonen PhD, RN, Principal Lecturer. Laurea University of Applied Sciences. Currently, she acts as the project specialist in the project UUDO- Multidisciplinary competencies in developing digital health and social care services, specialization education. Recently she worked as project manager in the SotePeda 24/7 national project developing competences for eHealth and eWelfare Services in multiprofessional teams to health, social, IT and service designer students. Her PhD study content was: Developing Student Competence Assessment Tool for Developing Digital Health and Social Care Services in a Multidisciplinary Contexts University of Eastern Finland. She has 20 years' experience of higher education in the field of nursing sciences and higher education pedagogy based on the Learning by Development action model. She also acts as president of Finnish Society of Telemedicine and eHealth Association.

Päivi Pöyry-Lassila PhD, Head of Unit Information and Analysis, Finnish National Agency for Education. Currently she works as the head of unit producing and developing data and information related services in the field of education. Previously she has acted as a principal lecturer at Laurea University of Applied Sciences and as the scientific leader of the SotePeda 24/7 national project developing competences for eHealth and eWelface services in Finland. She has also researched service design practices in the context of digital social and health care services for marginalized customer groups in the DigiIN project (funded by Academy of Finland). She acted as a researcher, designer and project manager in the MORFEUS project. She has also taught service design and innovation in Master's programmes. She has 20 years' experience in research and teaching at universities in the fields of usability engineering, industrial engineering and management, and service design and innovation. Her special research interest is related to the practices of collaboration and facilitation in service design processes.

The e-Report System: Redesigning the Reporting in Turkish Healthcare Services

8

Çağdaş Erkan Akyürek, Şükrü Anıl Toygar, and Elif Erbay

Abstract

The healthcare industry is defined as a highly interdependent sector, one component of which often fails to compensate for efficiency that the other cannot provide. Today, comprehensiveness and digital transformation in healthcare services are two inseparable features. Therefore, one cannot aim to produce better results for patients in a health system without changing the way it works in an area that needs transformation. Accordingly, Turkey is working to make technology-based regulations to keep pace with this transformation taking place in the world. In this regard, "e-Report System" constitutes a basis for the study in order to ensure delivery of all reports (including birth, disability, driving license, sick leave, case notification reports, etc.) given by the healthcare organizations affiliated with the Ministry of Health in an electronic, e-signed format. Started to be implemented in 2010, the e-Report System consists of many components such as e-Birth Report, e-Disability Report, e-Driver Report, etc. With the implementation of this system, service processes have been redesigned. Thanks to this system, as access to data, is provided centrally, the control capacity is strengthened, expenses are reduced, the service process is shortened by reducing bureaucratic procedures, and ultimately, service quality and patient satisfaction are strengthened. In addition, thanks to this system, it is more possible to

Ç. E. Akyürek (✉) · E. Erbay
Department of Healthcare Management, Ankara University, Fatih Caddesi No:197/A, 06290 Keçiören/Ankara, Turkey
e-mail: ceakyurek@ankara.edu.tr

E. Erbay
e-mail: Elif.Erbay@ankara.edu.tr

Ş. A. Toygar
Department of Healthcare Management, Tarsus University, Takbaş Mahallesi Kartaltepe Sokak, 33400 Tarsus/Mersin, Turkey
e-mail: saniltoygar@tarsus.edu.tr

eliminate duplicate report writing, prevent irregular reports and facilitate sharing with relevant institutions. This study aimed to present how service processes are redesigned with the e-Report system implemented by the T.R. Ministry of Health and to compare the previous system with the new one in terms of their advantages and disadvantages. For this purpose, service design processes were explained by giving detailed information about the components of the system, and the effects of the system on service processes were discussed.

8.1   Introduction

Digitalization can be defined as developing business processes, increasing their competencies, adding value to their customers and the ecosystem during the transition of companies, organizations and brands to new thinking and modern ways of doing business by using information, technology and human resources to adapt to the digital age (Accenture, 2017). Improving the business processes, digitalization offers us more opportunities to get personalized services for our individual needs (Kuula & Haapasalo, 2017). As digitalization improves these processes, a growing number of people are demanding personalized services. This situation can also be observed in the health sector. It ranges from using data to understand meal preferences of a patient in hospital and delivering those meals exactly when they want them, to delivering information through the right channel based on selected preferences. In this way, digitalization can help support the delivery of healthcare whenever, wherever, and how people demand it (Accenture, 2019).

Healthcare service differs from other types of services because the evaluation of service delivery (diagnosis-treatment) and after-service output (discharge with full recovery and/or a state of complete well-being or seeking additional treatment) is predominantly done by the service provider (physician), and therefore the consumer (patient) remains passive in the process. In addition, the traditional debate about whether health is a marketable type of "service" where there is demand, supply and therefore competition or one of the fundamental rights of the people is moved to a different dimension as e-health services begin to be prominent during the diagnosis and treatment processes (Toygar, 2018). Before digitalized and therefore more personalized healthcare service provision, patients were passive in the healthcare service processes. However, with digitalization and improvements in e-health, patients are more involved in the service delivery and demanding more personalized healthcare.

On the supply side of the healthcare market, healthcare institutions should take advantage of these digital developments and harness digitalization as a means to transform themselves into smart service organizations (Rasche et al., 2017). Especially the digitization of healthcare data is important for data visualization, collaboration, and clinical decision support (Tresp et al., 2016). Since the healthcare industry is driven by cost efficiency, outcome-based compensation for treatments and patient well-being (KPMG, 2021), using healthcare information systems services is inevitable.

The practice of medicine is inseparable from the management of health information systems (Lin, 1993). Health information systems is the name given to all processes such as creating, organizing, and sharing the information and data that emerge in parallel with the developments in the field of healthcare, and determining and developing the diagnosis and treatment of patients. Health information systems are used to increase the effectiveness and efficiency of healthcare services (Göktaş et al., 2017: 127). Health information systems have many benefits to users. One of these benefits is that, by integrating computers into the health system, the practice of doing manual medical documentation is abandoned; thus, errors are reduced and faster access to the desired information is enabled (Toygar, 2018).

Transformation efforts in health services in Turkey started at the beginning of the 1990s. In 1990, the Health Project General Coordinatorship was established in order to prepare and coordinate the projects that will lead the transformation in healthcare services. In 1996, the Information Processing Department in the Ministry of Health was established and the foundation of Hospital Information Management Systems was laid (Işık, 2019). Since then, many health information systems have been used in Turkey: Physician Information Bank, Electronic Document Management System, Electronic Tuberculosis Management System, Examination Information Management System, Hospital Infections, Disabled Data Bank, Personnel Information System, Turkey Bone Marrow Information System, Turkey Dialysis Information Management System, Turkey Intensive Care Monitoring System, Turkey Organ and Tissue Donation Information System, Turkey Organ and Tissue Information System, Turkey National Hearing Screening Program, Auxiliary Health Personnel Information Bank, Green Card Information System. The e-transformation in health in Turkey will be summarized from this point forward and as the main focus of this chapter e-report system will be discussed in detail.

8.2   The e-Transformation in Health Systems in Turkey

The e-transformation in health consists of many systems and projects. National Health Information System (NHIS) is one of the main components of this transformation process. In NHIS, citizens can access their health information and their registries start from the prenatal period and cover all stages of life. The system includes a rapid connectivity backbone that covers the whole country and enables sharing of medical images. With NHIS it is aimed to ensure the standardization of health data, to establish data analysis support and decision support systems, to accelerate data flows between stakeholders, to create personal electronic health records, to ensure resource savings thus increase efficiency and to support scientific activities.

8.3 The Health.NET Project

Health.NET is an integrated, secure, quick, and extensible information system that intends to enhance the efficiency and quality of health services by gathering all types of data generated in healthcare institutions in accordance with standards and producing information suitable for all stakeholders. Health.NET collects and analyzes sufficient data to identify issues and priorities, implement solutions, organize sectoral resources and investments, and assess the quality of healthcare delivery in the healthcare sector. Health.NET has also undertaken a function to collect and process sufficient data to be used in scientific research and studies (Ministry of Health, 2021).

National Health Data Standards, Health Coding Reference Dictionary and online services are the three components of Health.NET. The Health.NET is able to transfer standard data from a variety of health institutions and also has a decision-making system that can retrieve data on the burden of disease, health expenditures, demographic analysis, etc. It allows for international data exchange and, follows and reports the indicators shared with international organizations like WHO, EUROSTAT and OECD. Health.NET allows citizens to access and manage their health records.

8.4 What is a "Health Report?"

There are many issues related to health which have to be determined, evaluated and documented from the beginning to the end of life. The final product of this determination, evaluation and documentation process is the health reports generated in accordance with the related laws, codes and directives. Health reports are officially valid documents that inform about a situation or a feature and organized by different healthcare providers according to the topic and content.

8.5 The Regulation of Health Reports

The processes of health reports in Turkey have been administered according to "The Procedures and Principles for Health Reports" which was firstly issued in April 2017. The purpose of this directive is to explain how health reports will be prepared by health service providers, to determine the format conditions for the reports, and to define how the processes of objection to health reports can be carried out. The Directive is binding on all public and private health service providers, private law legal entities and real persons. Legal basis of the directive which constitutes the provisions is the "Basic Law on Health Services" dated 7 May 1987 and numbered 3359, Articles 355 and 508 of the "Presidential Decree No. 1 on the Presidential Organization" published in the Official Gazette dated 10 July 2018 and numbered 30,474, dated 24 November 2004 and numbered 5258, the fifth article of the "Family Medicine Law" and the "Inpatient Treatment Institutions Management Regulation" that entered into force with the "Council of Ministers Decision" dated 10 September 1982 and numbered 8/5319.

Within the scope of the directive, health reports are handled in two separate groups depending on whether there are special legal regulations for that area or not. Reports prepared in connection with legal texts such as the Operating Regulation of Inpatient Treatment Institutions, the General Health Insurance Law No. 5510 and the Health Implementation Communiqué are classified under the title of "with special regulation." Health reports in this context are as follows:

- Rest and incapacity reports,
- Medical board reports of disability,
- Health reports of Turkish Armed Forces, Gendarmerie General Command, Coast Guard Command personnel,
- Health board report to be issued about students and civil servants to be submitted to the Police Department,
- Health committee report, which specifies the last status and the slice arranged in accordance with the Regulation on Health Conditions of the Police Organization,
- Driver and driver candidate's health reports,
- Health board report to be given for private security guard candidates,
- Health board report to be given for armed private security guard candidates,
- Health board report to be given to those who will obtain a license to own and carry a gun,
- Health board report, which is the basis for accrual of cash compensation,
- Forensic reports

"Reports without special regulation" are the reports that are not included in this first group and must be prepared in accordance with the form conditions specified in the annex of the directive. This includes reports to be issued by hospitals affiliated to the Ministry of Health, university hospitals, health institutions and organizations affiliated to other public institutions, private hospitals licensed by the Ministry of Health, private medical centers and primary healthcare providers. Reports in which a uniform format is specified for each report type are as follows:

- Sick leave report,
- Drug usage reports,
- Medical supplies reports,
- Health status reports by the health board,
- Single-physician health status reports.

Although the health reports are classified in this way within the scope of the directive, in this section, they have been classified into three main groups as "reports on the determination of disability in adults and children"; "status reports and special purpose reports" such as the driver/driver candidate, psychotechnics, recruitment and birth reports, and "post-sickness reports" on rest, incapacity, medication, medical devices and supplies. The reports in the third group are excluded from the scope of the section as they are prepared under the control of the Social Security Institution and within its own e-report system.

8.6 T.R. Ministry of Health e-Report System

Consisting of various components, T.R. Ministry of Health e-Report System was established to ensure that all reports issued by health institutions are provided electronically, with e-signature, and aimed to be integrated with the Health Information Management System and other information systems (e-Report System, 2021). The basic modules of the system which have been operational in different periods between 2018 and 2020 are as follows:

- e-Birth certificates,
- Psychotechnical reports,
- Reports for athletes,
- Driver reports,
- Statutory single-physician reports for bedridden people,
- Hospital books,
- Recruiting reports,
- Military reports,
- Single-physician status report,
- Medical board status reports,
- Disability medical board reports for adults,
- Special needs reports for children (ÇÖZGER).

8.6.1 Reports on the Detection of Disability in Adults and Children

These are the reports that evaluate the conditions of citizens aged 18 and over with disabilities and children under the age of 18 with special needs and only the specified public health institutions have the right to issue them. Within the e-Report system, it is carried out through two different modules: "Disability health board reports for adults" and "Special needs reports for children (ÇÖZGER)." In fact, although disability reports are also "status-reporting" in general terms, they are handled as a separate heading because the target audience is a "special" group and the privileges provided to this special group for social support are extremely open to abuse.

8.6.2 Medical Board Reports of Disability for Adults

Disability Health Board Report module for adults is regulated within the framework of the provisions of the "Basic Law on Health Services" numbered 3359, "Decree-Law on the Organization and Duties of the Ministry of Health and Affiliated Institutions" and "Inpatient Treatment Institutions Operation Regulation." In line with the "Regulation on Disability Assessment for Adults" published in the Official Gazette No.30692, It has been prepared in order to develop a common practice in areas where disability-related ratings, classifications and definitions are needed and to ensure the widespread use of international classifications and criteria, to determine the procedures and principles regarding the receipt, validity and evaluation of the "Disability Health Board Disability Report" for adults and the determination of authorized health institutions that can issue a health board report (Ministry of Health, 2020a).

8.6.3 Special Needs Reports for Children

The process of detecting and reporting the disability for children is carried out through a different terminology, a different legal ground, and therefore a different module due to the characteristics specific to the childhood situation. The main legal text of the process, the "Special Needs Report for Children (ÇÖZGER) Regulation," aims to identify the aforementioned needs of children with special needs, based on the difference that childhood shows from adulthood due to the developmental process, and provide access to health, education, rehabilitation and other social and economic rights and providing access to services. The "needs assessment" carried out for this purpose forms the basis of the reporting process. In the context of ÇÖZGER, "to have special needs for a child or a young person" and to participate in social life equally as individuals who do not have physical or developmental disability limitations means that they need health, education, rehabilitation, device, orthotics, prosthesis and other social and economic rights, services in different quality or quantity and environmental regulations for participation. This requirement is defined according to the rating principles in the annex of the relevant legislation. A child who can be defined to "have special needs," "have mild special needs," "have significant special needs" or "have special condition needs" is considered as "disabled" in legal regulations (Official Gazette, 2019).

8.7 Statutory and Ad Hoc Reports

There are nine different types of e-reports as Statutory and Ad Hoc Reports within the Turkish Ministry of Health. In this section, these nine e-reports will be described.

8.7.1 E-Birth Certificates

It is the module in which reports on births in hospitals are prepared and in communication with the General Directorate of Population and Citizenship Affairs. Reports of births in 2018 and later can be accessed via the module (Ministry of Health, 2020b).

8.7.2 Psychotechnical Reports

Psychotechnical reports, which are prepared for measuring the behavior, personality traits and motor skills of the drivers, are very important for the safety of other motor-vehicle drivers and pedestrians in traffic. Pursuant to item "e" of Article 34 of the "Road Transport Regulation" numbered 4925, a health report showing that they are physically and psychotechnically healthy in terms of the driving profession must be obtained from authorized health institutions and renewed every five years. This report is prepared after a one-hour test conducted by a psychologist in the simulator, which shows whether the physical and psychological conditions of the people are suitable for driving.

8.7.3 Reports for Athletes

It is the system that ensures the approval of the reporting processes of individuals carried out by all authorized health service providers from family physicians to health boards, established within hospitals, within the scope of primary healthcare, in order to participate in various sports branches as athletes and to become a referee and/or a coach within the scope of these sports branches (Ministry of Health, 2018a).

8.7.4 Driver Reports

It is the report that determines the situation regarding whether a person can be a driver or not and is obtained in order to have a driver's license which is a requirement for driving a personal vehicle without any professional aim. It is an application that aims to organize driver reports quickly and completely, starting from family physicians, similar to athlete reports, to hospital and commission processes at the highest point (Ministry of Health, 2020c).

8.7.5 Statutory Single-Physician Report for Bedridden People

The Report Component for Bedridden People allows citizens to apply to their family physicians and carry out health examinations. In case of detection of bed dependency, certain privileges are provided and financial care support can be provided to the said people in addition to providing certain services on site.

8.7.6 Hospital Books

The "Hospital Books" application aims to ensure that hospitals keep records of the files they want to archive in electronic form and with e-signature on a regular basis.

8.7.7 Recruiting Reports

With the "Military Check-up Health Examination Procedures" module developed on the e-Government, health examinations of obligatory persons through family physicians are carried out with a standard method and application within the scope of the "Health Capability Regulation," and the necessary codes and decisions are made in cases of diseases and malfunctions detected as a result of the examination. It is an e-Report module created for the purpose of issuing and writing the necessary referral letters for hospital referrals. Covers all "Military Attendance Health Examination Reports" issued throughout the country.

8.7.8 Military Reports

It is an online report module that covers the health examination and board processes required for military service. Reports required for the selection to special military classes such as commando, paratrooper, the diver, etc., is prepared through this module. Determining the procedures and principles regarding the receipt, validity and evaluation of the Ministry of National Defense (MoND) report and the determination of the authorized health institutions that can issue a health board report; The MoND Report Component was prepared on the e-Report application in order to develop a common application and to ensure the widespread use of international classification and criteria. It is planned to make fast and accurate integration with hospital information management systems (HIMS) in order to create the e-Report / MoND Report. The module covers the integration processes of all health institutions and organizations authorized to issue MoND Reports and HIMS software manufacturers throughout the country (Ministry of Health, 2018b).

8.7.9 Single-Physician and Medical Board Statutory Reports

There are two different modules to cover all the "Single-Physician Statutory Reports" issued throughout the country and all "Medical Board Statutory Reports" issued in the same context. Due to the significant differences between the scope and content of the reports that can be issued by a single physician and the reports that the health board is authorized to determine, they are managed through two different modules within the e-Report system. The e-Report System is developed according to the qualifications determined in the Directive on the Procedures and Principles Regarding Health Reports published by the Ministry of Health (Ministry of Health, 2020d).

8.8 The Assessment of e-Report System (Conclusion)

The e-Reporting system, which was put into operation gradually in the period between 2018 and 2020, reaches an annual average transaction volume of more than 3.5 million. Keeping a mass of documents of this size in an organized manner, in a way that can be accessed, queried and confirmed instantly is a real challenge. Despite all the difficulties, ensuring the sustainability of the existing health workforce with clear and understandable training materials prepared for users from all levels, and integration with other information systems by continuous development is an important development for the founders and users of the system. Perhaps the most appropriate way to better understand the point reached with the e-Report system is to make a "before-after" comparison within the scope of application. In order to make this comparison healthier, it would be correct to conduct it around certain headings.

In this context, when comparing the two processes, perhaps it is necessary to start from the most obvious benefit of the system. Before the transition to the e-Report system, the process of verifying a submitted report when necessary was extremely difficult as it required long-term correspondence and these correspondences were mostly stuck between bureaucratic obstacles. The verification process was carried out only in cases where the report was the subject of a complaint or requested by the judicial authorities. The difficulty of access and cumbersomeness in the verification process naturally hindered and weakened the control function the most. In the processes, where there was a control weakness, false statements, abuse, untrue transactions, forgery (fake seals, stamps, official document registration numbers, etc.) and information disinformation were experienced intensely. With the E-Report system (as a requirement of the electronic signature law), the reports prepared electronically can be confirmed instantly. The e-Report verification is open to all public and private administrations through the system. From the application, which is the first step of the preparation process of the report, to its approval at the last point, those involved in the process can be seen at each step, and the details of each transaction, especially the date and time, can be accessed. Thanks to this tremendous improvement in the control function, the security vulnerability has been significantly resolved and the abuses have been reduced.

Central control has extremely critical importance in terms of both nationally harmonizing the legal texts on the rights and privileges granted to the disabled in the global sense, and ensuring that the social assistance to be provided within the borders of the country within the scope of these rights and privileges can reach its target correctly, as well as to prevent abuses. Situational reports play a decisive role in providing support to population groups defined as socially disadvantaged. It is an inevitable necessity to strictly control certain privileges that should be unquestionably granted to those in need so that they are not subject to fraud and abuse. Failure to perform instant verification in the applications before the e-Reporting system, the cumbersome nature of the verification processes as well as bureaucratic obstacles caused many needy people not to reach the support they deserve, and to experience social inequality intensely due to the disadvantage they suffered.

Another dimension in which the two applications can be compared is related to the storage and access of the resulting mass of documents. Before the implementation of the e-Report system, the physical archive system created by each health service institution and organization authorized to issue reports, in line with their own resources, was a very limited structure in terms of access, and due to the lack of instant access, it burdened individuals with responsibilities such as storing, protecting and submitting reports when necessary. Damage to archives for different reasons or loss of the report caused significant grievances for individuals. Through the e-Report system, which works in integration with the e-pulse system, citizens have had the opportunity to easily access and submit their reports when necessary. Since the reports are stored electronically in the system, the disadvantages of keeping a physical archive are reduced.

Standardization processes play a decisive role in the sustainability of systems that appeal to large user groups and experience large amounts of data entry from many different service points. Although the e-Report system aimed at standardization in terms of process, it paved the way for an important standardization in terms of report formats. Prior to the implementation of the system, companies producing software for Hospital Information Management Systems were developing systems specific to each hospital that had customers, reflecting their own usage preferences and workflows, and the differences in preferences caused differences in the resulting reports. With the e-Report system, a significant standard has been achieved in report formats.

References

Accenture. (2017). Accenture digital health technology vision 2017. Retrieved June 14, 2021, from https://www.accenture.com/t20170524T014807%20__w__/us-en/_acnmedia/PDF-49/Accenture-Digital-Health-Technology-Vision-2017.pdf.

Accenture. (2019). Accenture Digital Health Technology Vision 2019. Retrieved June 14, 2021, from https://www.accenture.com/_acnmedia/PDF-102/Accenture-Digital-Health-Tech-Vision-2019.pdf.

e-Report System. (2021). e-Report. Retrieved May 20, 2021, from https://erapor.saglik.gov.tr/portal.

Göktaş, B., Önder, Ö. R., Duran, M., Şakar, S., Yılmaz, M., Güler, S., Çınar, İ., Çamlıdağ, Şenkal, Y., & Özdemir, G. (2017). A research on health information systems in Turkey. *Journal of Ankara Health Sciences*, 1-3, 125–138. https://doi.org/10.1501/Asbd_0000000066

Işık, T. (2019). Türkiye'de Sağlık Kurumlarında Dijital Dönüşüm Adımları. İçinde: *Sağlık Hizmetleri Uygulamalarında Dijital Dönüşüm*. In B. Eserler (Eds.). E. Y. Altıntaş. Konya: E. Yayınevi.

KPMG Türkiye. (2021). *Dijitalleşme Yolunda Türkiye 2021 Trendler ve rehber hedefler.* Retrieved March 11, 2021, from https://home.kpmg/tr/tr/home/gorusler/2021/04/dijitallesme-yolunda-turkiye-2021.html.

Kuula, S. & Haapasalo, H. (2017). Continuous and co-creative business model creation- models, strategies, tools. In M. A. Pfannstiel & C. Rasche (Eds.), *Service business model innovation in healthcare and hospital management*. models, strategies, tools (pp. 249–268). Springer Nature. Cham.

Lin, B. (1993). Health care information systems management: Structure and infrastructure. *Journal of International Information Management*, 2(1), Article 3, 27–39.

Ministry of Health. (2018a). *Reports for Athletes*. Retrieved December 20, 2020, from https://erapor.saglik.gov.tr/portal/detay/sporcu-raporlari-6.

Ministry of Health. (2018b). *Ministry of National Defense report*. Retrieved December 20, 2020, from https://erapor.saglik.gov.tr/portal/detay/askeri-raporlar-7.

Ministry of Health. (2020a). *Disability health board report integration guide for adults*. Retrieved December 20, 2020, from https://erapor.saglik.gov.tr/portal/documents/e-Rapor%20e-Eri%C5%9Fkinler%20%C4%B0%C3%A7in%20Engellilik%20Sa%C4%9Fl%C4%B1k%20Kurulu%20Raporu%20Entegrasyon%20K%C4%B1lavuzu.pdf.

Ministry of Health. (2020b). *Birth certificates*. Retrieved December 20, 2020, from https://erapor.saglik.gov.tr/portal/detay/dogum-raporlari-1.

Ministry of Health. (2020c). *Driver Reports*. Retrieved December 20, 2020, from https://erapor.saglik.gov.tr/portal/detay/surucu-raporlari-2.

Ministry of Health. (2020d). *Statutory Reports*. Retrieved December 20, 2020, from https://erapor.saglik.gov.tr/portal/detay/durum-bildirir-saglik-kurulu-raporlari-134.

Ministry of Health. (2021). *About Health.NET*. Retrieved February 14, 2021, from https://e-saglik.gov.tr/TR,6212/sagliknet-hakkinda.html.

Official Gazette. (2019). *Special needs report for children, special needs areas guide*. Retrieved May 20, 2021, from https://www.resmigazete.gov.tr/eskiler/2019/02/20190220-1-1.pdf.

Rasche, C., Margaria, T. & Floyd, B. D. (2017). Service model innovation in hospitals: Beyond expert organizations. In M. A. Pfannstiel & C. Rasche (Eds.), *Service business model innovation in healthcare and hospital management*. Models, strategies, tools (pp. 1–20). Cham: Springer Nature.

Toygar, ŞA. (2018). E-Sağlık Uygulamaları. *Yasama Dergisi, 37*, 101–123.

Tresp, V., Overhage, J. M., Bundschus, M., Rabizadeh, S., Fasching, P. A., & Yu, S. (2016). Going digital: A survey on digitalization and large-scale data analytics in healthcare. *Proceedings of the IEEE, 104*(11), 2180–2206. https://doi.org/10.1109/JPROC.2016.2615052

Çağdaş Erkan Akyürek is an Associate Professor at Ankara University Faculty of Health Sciences, Department of Healthcare Management. He received his PhD with the thesis tittled "Outsourcing in Heatlh Care System: Evaluation of Outsourcing Practices at T.R. Ministry of Health Hospitals" from Hacettepe University. His academic interest areas include Decision Making in Healthcare, Heatlh Policy and Planning, Strategic Management in Health Care and Operations Management. He also gives lectures in his academic interest areas both in graduate and postgraduate programs.

Şükrü Anıl Toygar is an Associate Professor at Tarsus University, Faculty of Applied Sciences, Healthcare Management Department. He received his PhD in Healthcare Management Gazi University. His research publications cover numerous areas of policy analysis, occupational health and disease, health policy and health technologies. He gives lectures on nursing management, health policy, health technologies and management. His articles have been published in both national and international journals.

Elif Erbay is a Research Assistant at Ankara University Faculty of Health Sciences, Department of Healthcare Management. She holds a master's degree in Healthcare Management. Her research interests include quantitative decision making in healthcare, healthcare policy, and social media management in healthcare. She is currently working on her PhD thesis titled "Forecasting the Demand for 112 Emergency Health Services and Selecting the Location of Ambulance Station: The Ankara Sample."

The Production and Use of Knowledge in the National Institutes of Health in Mexico–Designing the Healthcare System

9

Javier Jasso and Arturo Torres

Abstract

The aim of this work is to understand the processes of generation and mobilization of scientific and applied knowledge in health services to solve the health problems of the population. The study analyzes the scientific and inventive capacities of the 13 National Institutes of Health (NIH) as creators and users of knowledge. The study is based on bibliometric indicators of scientific publications and patents since the NIH emerged until 2019, complemented with interviews and data from the health institutes themselves to identify two fundamental aspects of the innovative process: a) the existence of scientific and invention patterns related to prevalent diseases and potential uses and b) the importance of the scientific and inventive collaboration of each institute with other agents. Publications and inventions in health services reflect the knowledge that is embodied in treatments, drugs, medical devices and vaccines that are used to improve the health of the population. To analyze scientific productivity, the search for authors affiliated with the NIH was carried out, using the SCOPUS Index data base, accessed through the portal to the year 2019. The patent data comes from the European Patent Office. Based on this information, the performance patterns of the institutes are characterized by considering the type and intensity of scientific production and the inventiveness and degree of collaboration with other agents. Inventions are grouped according to their potential uses and by the prevalent diseases in Mexico.

Present Address:
J. Jasso (✉)
Graduate School of Accounting and Management, National Autonomous University of Mexico (UNAM), Av. Universidad 3000, Mexico City 04510, México

A. Torres
Department of Economics, Metropolitan Autonomous University-Xochimilco (UAM-X), Calz. del Hueso 1100Villa Quietud, Coapa Coyoacán 04960, México

9.1 General Introduction

Concern for health is part of the development of mankind. Health is a biological resource that has an impact on human productivity and on a nation's economy; it is essential for sustainability (OECD, 2005). Adequate attention to improvements in health conditions results in the rise of the population's social welfare levels. Innovation is a collaborative and competitive social phenomenon in which various agents intervene to form a system. The innovation system involves companies, universities, research centers and the government, all of them interacting to generate and exchange scientific and applied knowledge. These innovation systems constitute the analytical framework for the understanding of the phenomenon of production and use of knowledge in the health area, where there are still few studies approaching the phenomenon from this perspective.

The use of this accumulation of knowledge implies the identification of the scientific and inventive capacities that have been developed by the various agents of the National Health Innovation System in Mexico. In areas of social impact, as is the case of health, the premise is that, although solutions exist in the world such as medicines, treatments, diagnostic methods, clinical technologies, nations need to build capacities and institutions to develop their own technologies and innovation processes that respond to their local health needs (Harris, 2004). The construction of these capacities or capabilities implies the development and strengthening of knowledge-generating centers, such as universities and Public Research Centers (PRC).

The health sector occupies a particular position, given its strong public and social component. Its development is strongly influenced by government policies, advances in technology, health care delivery and demographic changes. It is made up of a set of institutions that provide services, perform production activities and other activities complementary to medical practices. The institutions include public and private hospitals, physicians' offices, laboratories, pharmaceutical and medical equipment companies, universities and research centers, businesses and consumers. In general, studies have mostly focused on innovation in firms, and particularly on manufacturing, with still few studies focused on services (Jasso & Marquina, 2013). Even fewer have focused on healthcare (Torres & Jasso, 2014; Torres et al., 2015). In fact, innovation efforts in the health sector have been generally underestimated (Windrum & García-Goñi, 2008).

The reorientation of universities and PRC toward the commercialization of discoveries and inventions developed by their researchers has been praised by some as the new model to be followed by academic research, which would facilitate the economic and social returns of universities (Etzkowitz & Leydesdorff, 2000). This role of universities and PRC is part of the current debate that focuses on whether this participation should be maintained or whether it should be diversified to participate more actively in productive activities, either directly or by linking up with the productive and social sector. In this debate, collaboration, and the new role that universities and PRC are playing that are driving a new way of collaborating and integrating innovation systems in countries, where the capabilities of each of the agents in the system are strengthened: universities, research centers, companies and the government.

Within this systemic and collaborative vision among the actors of the health system, the role of service design, necessary for the improvement of processes and products aimed at solving health problems, should be highlighted. Design is a necessary tool to solve complex problems. The design of services encompasses transformation on several levels since services inherently involve the organization, employees and users (Malberg, 2017). As such, there is an interest in how service design, through its methods and approaches, transforms the systems where it is used (Rodrígues & Vink, 2016). It involves a process with the participation of various collaborative, interactive and iterative stakeholders (Meronj & San Giorgi, 2011).

The complexity of knowledge for innovation in the health sector requires cooperation between research groups from different scientific and technological disciplines and the participation of health service users. This interaction between users and knowledge producers generates a coordination process that creates value by solving a health problem in patients. Thus, the design of a health service is a system in which the producers and users of knowledge have an important role; the NIH can play a crucial role in service design through innovation activities. In the paper, we argue that health research centers such as the NIH support and drive innovation in services in this sector because of their scientific and inventive capabilities and the possibilities offered by the system and institutional environment. That is, the innovation process results from a complex of relationships and institutional arrangements, in which the NIH play an important role.

The aim of this work is to contribute to the understanding of the processes of generation and mobilization of scientific and applied knowledge in the health sector in Mexico, and of the innovation process in this sector. These processes are the result of accumulation of capabilities in areas and disciplines of knowledge related to the development of solutions, improvement, and attention to the health conditions of the population.

The questions guiding the work are the following:

- What is the magnitude and type of new scientific knowledge and inventions, in NIH?
- To what extent does the knowledge created correspond to the needs of the population according to the most prevalent diseases or causes of mortality?
- To what extent is the knowledge created in the NIH collaborative and with which agents?

The purpose is to characterize the production and use of knowledge in health in Mexico based on indicators related to the magnitude and type of knowledge produced and the type of diseases that this knowledge is aimed at combating, including the existence or not of collaboration and with which agents it has been carried out. This is based on bibliometric indicators of scientific publications and patents indicators since the NIH was founded, and up to 2018.

9.2   The Health Sector and Research Institutions in Mexico. The National Institutes of Health

The health sector in Mexico is made up of a set of public and private organizations in which the NIH are one of the most relevant agents in providing health services, training medical specialists and conducting cutting-edge biomedical research.

9.2.1   The Health Sector

The health sector occupies a particular position given its undeniable social utility. The use of practices and knowledge to treat diseases and improve health have been diverse and have been associated with scientific and traditional medicine. In the solution of problems and the improvement of the population's health levels, a set of public, private and community institutions, made up of universities, research centers and institutes, as well as hospitals, physicians and various health professionals, co-evolve and are configured.

Since the eighties of the twentieth century, the PRC have been subject to changes in institutional conditions and in the valorization of knowledge within what has been called "the knowledge society." In this new context, the PRC play a fundamental role in the creation of new knowledge and as basic institutions in the training of professionals and researchers. This leads to a reflection on the new role to be played, especially in those areas that are fundamental for the welfare of a society, such as health and therefore in the NIH. The relationship between economic development and the development of the health sector is widely recognized (Molina-Salazar et al., 1991). This sector has an important influence on economic and social welfare, derived from government policies, advances in technology and knowledge, the provision of health care, as well as demographic changes.

9.2.2   The Health Sector and Innovation Agents

The health sector is made up of a set of public and private organizations that provide services, carry out production activities and other activities complementary to medical practices. They include hospitals, medical practices, laboratories, pharmaceutical and medical equipment companies, universities and research centers, and consumers. Innovation occurs within a complex system of interactions between producers, intermediaries, and users of knowledge. The health innovation system includes key institutional components such as governments, service providers, resource institutions, institutional buyers, and other agents (Casells, 1995). Resource institutions include all organizations and institutions that produce the human and material resources for health care, including universities and other institutes of higher education, medical schools, schools of public health, public research centers, R&D departments of public and social security institutions, as well as those owned by private companies. In the health sector, resource institutions and in particular PRC and universities constitute a crucial part of the innovation system, as creators and disseminators of knowledge that participate to different degrees in product and process innovation processes (Jasso, 2015; Torres & Jasso, 2014).

In Mexico, health research activities are carried out in higher education institutions and PRC belonging to universities, as well as in PRC and specialized hospital facilities administered by the Ministry of Health and other health sector institutions such as Mexican Social Security Institute (IMSS), Institute of Social Security and Services for State Employees (ISSSTE), PEMEX Medical Services, among others.

It can be deduced that the actors related, directly and indirectly, to the solution of health problems on the supply side of knowledge are mainly the universities (at federal and local level), the PRC and Institutes (public and private), the NIH of the Ministry of Health, among others. In the Mexican health system, there are those who demand the knowledge generated, which are mainly the providers of health care services (public and private), starting from the second level of care (hospital and specialty services), as well as the manufacturers of health care goods. The Mexican Health System integrates various public, social and private schemes, with an extensive private market attended by hospitals and insurance companies. The private sector includes hospitals, doctors who perform private surgeries and others who practice alternative or traditional medicine. Most of the private hospitals operate also under health insurance schemes. They are not engaged in R&D activities, although some are involved in training and educational activities related to health care. Pharmaceutical firms producing and trading medicaments are also part of this segment. There are other organizations completing the system such as NGOs, health committees, and other agents affecting the health care of the population (Torres & Jasso, 2014). The sector is influenced substantially by national governmental policies, advances in healthcare delivery and technology and demographic changes (Fig. 9.1).

9.2.3   The National Institutes of Health

The NIH constitute a research subsystem administered by the Ministry of Health and composed of 13 institutes. The main objective of the NIH is scientific research in the field of health, the education and training of qualified human resources and the provision of high specialty medical care services with a scope of action that includes the entire national territory (DOF, 2019); that is, they address problems related to public health, disease control and prevention, medical assistance, and with teaching and training of specialized resources and health professionals with a social orientation. The services they provide are practically free of charge or according to the patient's income level.

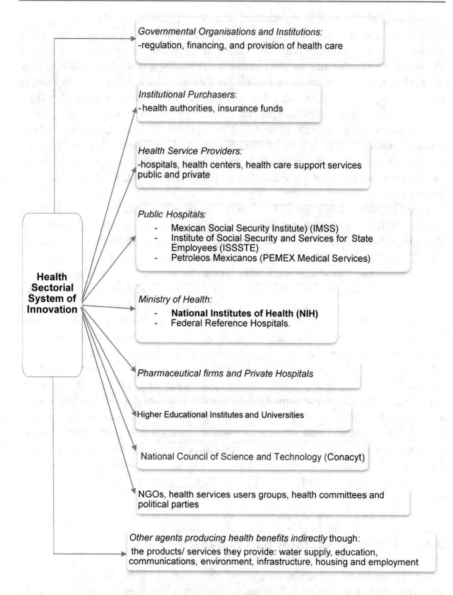

Governmental Organisations and Institutions:
-regulation, financing, and provision of health care

Institutional Purchasers:
-health authorities, insurance funds

Health Service Providers:
-hospitals, health centers, health care support services
public and private

Public Hospitals:
- Mexican Social Security Institute) (IMSS)
- Institute of Social Security and Services for State Employees (ISSSTE)
- Petroleos Mexicanos (PEMEX Medical Services)

Ministry of Health:
- **National Institutes of Health (NIH)**
- Federal Reference Hospitals.

Pharmaceutical firms and Private Hospitals

Higher Educational Institutes and Universities

National Council of Science and Technology (Conacyt)

NGOs, health services users groups, health committees and political parties

Other agents producing health benefits indirectly though:
the products/ services they provide: water supply, education, communications, environment, infrastructure, housing and employment

Health Sectorial System of Innovation

Fig. 9.1 Mexico. The Health Sectorial System of Innovation. *Source* Author's own illustration (2021)

The NIH are administered by the Ministry of Health. These NIH form a network of institutes, health centers and hospitals that provide specialized services, especially to the low-income population. The NIH are a reference in health care and scientific production not only in Mexico, but also in Latin America.

The first NIH was created in 1936 and from its origin it was envisioned to address public health problems, disease control and prevention, medical assistance, and to carry out teaching and research activities in which health professionals are trained by medical specialty areas and with a social orientation. They constitute a subsystem of medical and research units whose objectives have attended the health needs of users, regulations and scientific and technological advances, as well as technical and humanistic criteria. These NIH provide specialized care of greater complexity, as well as clinical and basic research by specialists and other professionals (Table 9.1).

Table 9.1 Mexico. National Institutes of Health, emergence and mission, 1936–2012. *Source* Own elaboration based on CCINSHAE (2020)

Num	Creation year	Name of the institute	Mission
1	1936	National Institute of Respiratory Diseases	To improve the respiratory health of individuals and communities through research, human resources training and specialized medical care
2	1943	Children's Hospital	To provide safe and quality high specialty medical care to children, train human resources and carry out scientific research of excellence
3	1944	National Institute of Cardiology	To provide high specialty cardiovascular care with quality to the population, preferably to those who lack social security; it also develops cutting-edge research and trains specialists in cardiology and related branches
4	1946	National Cancer Institute	To develop medical care, teaching and oncology research of excellence in Mexico
5	1946	National Institute of Nutrition	Improve health through specialized medical care, human resources training and biomedical research, with a comprehensive approach and excellence for the benefit of human beings and their environment
6	1964	National Institute of Neurology	To contribute to social welfare and equity in compliance with the right to health protection through scientific innovation, academic excellence, and the quality and safety of health services in the field of neurological sciences
7	1970	National Institute of Pediatrics	To develop models of care for children and youths through basic scientific, clinical and epidemiological research, applied to the prioritized needs of the population, through the training and development of human resources of excellence for health, as well as high quality specialty health care, constituting a world-class model of care
8	1973	National Institute of Rehabilitation	Institution dedicated to the prevention, diagnosis, treatment and rehabilitation of disability through scientific research, training of human resources and specialized medical care of excellence with a humanistic approach

(continued)

Table 9.1 (continued)

Num	Creation year	Name of the institute	Mission
9	1977	National Institute of Perinatology	Generate new knowledge, through innovation and quality research that impacts the population; training of human talent of high specialty and highly complex medical care, in the field of reproductive and perinatal health, to establish itself as a reference model of health nationwide, setting guidelines to contribute to the alignment of national health policies for the welfare of society
10	1978	National Institute of Psychiatry	To improve the mental health of the Mexican population through multidisciplinary research of excellence, specialized medical care and the training of human resources in the principles of quality and warmth
11	1987	National Institute of Public Health	To contribute to social equity and the full realization of the right to health protection through the generation and dissemination of knowledge, the training of human resources of excellence and innovation in multidisciplinary research for the development of evidence-based public policies
12	2004	National Institute of Genomic Medicine	To contribute to the health care of Mexicans by developing scientific research of excellence and training high-level human resources, leading to the medical application of genomic knowledge through an innovative culture, cutting-edge technology and strategic alliances, with adherence to universal ethical principles
13	2012	National Institute of Geriatrics	Promote healthy aging through the production of new knowledge, its dissemination and use; the development of human resources and the promotion of the necessary transformation of the National Health System

9.3 The Production and Use of Knowledge from the Agents' Perspective

Knowledge has always occupied a central place in economic growth and the progressive elevation of social welfare (David & Foray, 2002). Today's societies are experiencing an unprecedented increase in the rate of generation, accumulation and use of knowledge, which has led them to a new paradigm, known as the knowledge economy. A knowledge-based economy can be defined as one in which knowledge is created, transmitted and used effectively by businesses, government, universities, organizations, individuals and communities for greater economic and social development.

9.3.1 Scientific Productivity: Basic Science

Scientific productivity refers to the set of products derived from research activities. These products can be diverse. Scientific production is a process by which multiple inputs, such as knowledge base, physical and human equipment, are transformed into various outputs, e.g., publications, patents, university graduates, transferable technology (Nagpaul & Roy, 2003; Warning, 2004). Scientific research produces new knowledge, a fraction of which is expressed in new products and processes, or in the improvement of existing ones, i.e., it is expressed in innovations that can lead to the generation of significant returns (Kreiman & Maunsell, 2011). At the micro-economic level, universities and research centers have traditionally evaluated the performance of their researchers using as indicators the number of publications and the number of citations to published works (Gonzalez-Brambila & Veloso, 2007).

The discussion in the literature on scientific productivity has focused primarily on the usefulness of different indicators to assess the performance of individual researchers, groups of researchers and/or research organizations, as well as the impacts of that output, and the determinants of that performance. Many measures have been generated and discussed. Because much scientific output takes the form of publications in peer-reviewed journals, these measures focus on articles and citations, including a wide range of approaches, such as total number of citations, journal impact factors, electronic download statistics, and comments using social media (Garfield, 2006).

Scholars of this topic have focused on different units of analysis, including research areas or disciplines, academic institutions, groups of researchers, individual researchers, and have extensively explored related topics such as collaboration among researchers, and with other agents evaluating its impact on productivity. Quantitative studies have explored, among other topics, the relationship between characteristics such as age, reputation, membership in research groups, and the productivity of researchers; or the effects of collaboration between PRC and companies on the productivity of academics (Gonzalez-Brambila & Veloso, 2007).

To analyze scientific productivity, we searched for authors affiliated to the NIH, by using the SCOPUS data base.

9.3.2 The Production and Use of Health Knowledge

The production and application of knowledge is at the base of the current economic dynamics reflecting the constant innovations and technological development. In the area of health, the production and use of science-based knowledge blends knowledge from the cognitive function that is used to multiply scientific knowledge, with practical skills that feed the processes of knowledge application, embodied in methods and treatments.

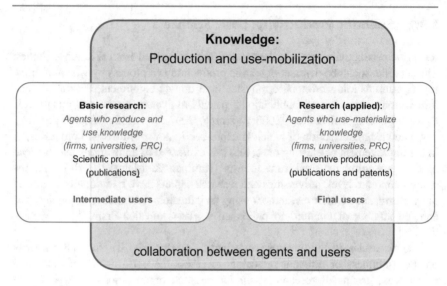

Fig. 9.2 Knowledge. Production and use. *Source* Author's own illustration (2021)

As mentioned before, the argument of the paper is that a fraction of knowledge is achievable to be materialized in an innovation. Thus, basic and applied research that is part of a patent may be materialized in a new product or process. Scientific publications and patents account for capabilities building (Fig. 9.2).

In the field of health, the premise is that although there are solutions in the world, nations need to develop their own technologies and processes that respond to their local health needs (Harris, 2004). Thus, for developing countries, it is important to generate capacities to create knowledge that can be used to improve the living conditions of the local population.

In the NIH, being part of the health subsystem, the purpose of generating patents is oriented to solve specific problems with a particular application aimed at attending or curing prevalent diseases in the national population; therefore, these patents would reflect a trajectory related to those needs, that is, with their potential use to solve them. In this sense, the use of knowledge in the creation of a patent is not conceived in the generalized sense that it must be applied and necessarily reach the market, but rather that the use refers to an additional intention to generate capabilities to contribute to solving health problems, even if only a fraction of these inventions eventually reaches the market. For example, in the health area, the use of knowledge from the basic research stage to the later phases implies an application or use, such as clinical trials, R&D and even production and ideas for commercialization, or even that different drugs or devices are tested by physicians, i.e., it would be an intermediate use of knowledge. Publications are basic research results that can feed new knowledge for patient care; laboratory results can support new treatments or forms of patient care (Figs. 9.2 and 9.3). This way of conceiving the use of knowledge has been addressed by translational research (see Lifshitz, 2009). Cooksey (2006) notes that translational research refers to the process of taking findings from basic or clinical research and using them to produce innovation in health care settings (Fig. 9.3). It leverages knowledge from basic science to produce new drugs, devices, and treatment options for patients. The end point is the production of something new that can be used clinically or brought to market, i.e., commercialized (Woolf 2008).

In the case of patents created by the NIH, these are directed. Hence, the areas in which NIH researchers patent are defined by the knowledge application objectives of the institutes, which are to address or solve a health problem, and which generate capabilities that accumulate in specific trajectories. In the production of scientific publications or patents, the NIH may or may not collaborate with other agents of the health innovation system such as universities, research centers, hospitals, companies and regulatory agents (Fig. 9.3). The co-creation of value in service design is carried out between the service deliverer and the user, within a given context (Yu & Sangiorgi, 2017).

In the design of the health service, various actors play roles that interact and exchange knowledge from which it is possible to offer a health service. This interaction or translation of knowledge is carried out at different levels mobilizing different types of knowledge that are articulated as they are from basic research,

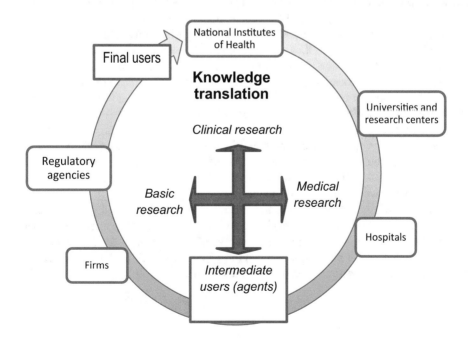

Fig. 9.3 Production and use of health knowledge. *Source* Author's own illustration (2021)

through clinical research and medical research. Knowledge users range from scientists to doctors and those who receive the health service who are patients or end users (Figs. 9.2 and 9.3).

9.3.3　Patent Production at National Institutes of Health: Technoscience

The research tools are composed of patent indicators and interviews applied to managers and researchers, and published NIH data to identify activities in collaboration with other research institutions and/or companies. One way to identify the degree to which knowledge is applied is through inventions. Inventions are new products or processes that may result from scientific or technical progress. In both cases creativity and continuity are important, although they can also be circumstantial. The diffusion of inventions and their use is what becomes innovation.

Invention can be measured by identifying patents. Patents are instruments of protection and also of dissemination of inventions and knowledge and is the most important and longest lasting intellectual property title (Van Dijk & Duysters, 1998). When patented, inventions are documented and published, achieving a wide dissemination. On the other hand, when protected, its use is restricted by legally ensuring a monopoly so that the holder can obtain an economic benefit from the use of his invention for a certain period of time, which does not necessarily coincide with the commercial life of the patented good. This intellectual property protection has boosted the development of knowledge mainly due to the increasing inventions related to the early development of new technology-based industries.

Granted patents are used as a proxy for production and overall for the potential of the use of knowledge, being an eminently inventive indicator that reflects the degree to which basic research is applied downstream to develop a new drug, device, method, or treatment that requires clinical testing before it is used by users in the end market as argued above (Figs. 9.2 and 9.3).

Patents are applied knowledge although only some of them will reach the market. The patent is a publication and is a source of knowledge that is used to create new knowledge. According to Van Dijk and Duysters (1998), companies with a basic research orientation were able to obtain a patent more easily than those companies more oriented to development.

Patent data are from the European Patent Office (EPO). Based on the patents obtained, innovation patterns are characterized considering the type of innovations and the degree of collaboration with other agents. The patent search and analysis period extend from the year of foundation of each research center to the year in which the latest registration appears, which is 2018.

9.3.4 Knowledge and Networks: Science and Technoscience

Technology in general and knowledge in particular have increased in complexity, raising the importance of relationships between companies and other organizations to acquire specialized knowledge. At this point, what is fundamental are the interactive processes that make it possible to generate and exchange such knowledge (OECD, 2005). Innovation is an interactive process, that is, a systemic process in which structure, strategies and routines make it possible to learn and disseminate technologies (Freeman, 1995; Lundvall, 1992; Nelson, 1993). Interaction involves different levels of linkage and/or collaboration between actors; the innovative performance of a country or sector depends to a large extent on how these actors relate to each other, as elements of a collective system that revolves around the production and use of knowledge and the technological or organizational solutions adopted (Jasso, 1998; Metcalfe, 1995). The role that universities and PRC as producers and transmitters of knowledge can play in innovation processes in developed and developing countries has been widely recognized (Arocena & Sutz, 2005; Cohen et al., 2002; Narin et al., 1997; Torres et al., 2011).

From a systemic perspective, innovation is a process that involves networks among diverse agents that acquire, share or assimilate knowledge to improve their processes, products and systems. In other words, it is a system and knowledge networks that form an environment of linkages between companies, research centers, universities and a diverse set of related institutions that participate in some way in research and development activities and in the processes of invention, innovation and dissemination of new products, services and production processes. The role of research centers is or can be relevant to boost innovation and technological entrepreneurship.

9.4 The National Institutes of Health. Production and Use of Knowledge

This section shows the results in the production and use of knowledge in the NIH of Mexico, based on indicators of scientific publications and patents.

9.4.1 The Scientific Trajectory

Scientific productivity in the NIH began in 1945, almost a decade after the opening of the first NIH (Respiratory Diseases). Although the scientific trajectory tended to increase, especially as new NIH appeared, it was not until the end of the 1980s that there was an upturn, as a result of public incentives when the National System of Researchers was created in 1984, which rewards publications. Currently, the NIH are among the institutions with the highest scientific production in health in the country (Torres & Jasso, 2014, 2019). This takeoff in scientific productivity

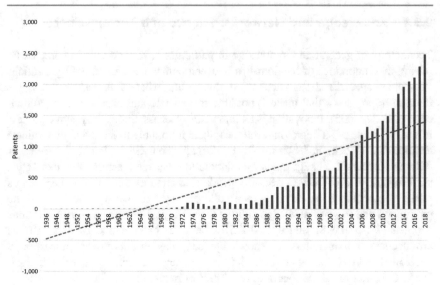

Fig. 9.4 Mexico. National Institutes of Health. Scientific trajectory, 1936–2018 (number of publications by NIH authors). *Source* Own elaboration with Scopus data (2021)

coincides with the appearance of the first patents in the 1990s, which, to some extent, is also the result of public policy measures increasingly aimed at promoting the application and use of knowledge (Fig. 9.4).

9.4.2 Scientific Production Intensity and Types

In 2018, the NIH had 832 researchers attached to the National System of Researchers. Among the institutes with the highest number of publications are the National Institute of Nutrition (21%), National Institute of Public Health (14%), National Institute of Cardiology (13%) and the National Institute of Neurology (8%); these are followed by the National Institutes of Cancerology, Pediatrics, Respiratory Diseases and the Children's Hospital with 7% each. The remaining five NIH account for the residual 16% (see Fig. 9.5).

9.4.3 Scientific Specialization Toward the Use of Knowledge

Scientific specialization is identified by areas of knowledge. As of 2018, they were medicine (56%), biochemistry, genetics and molecular biology (13%), immunology and microbiology (6%), neurosciences (5%) and pharmacology, toxicology and pharmaceutics (4%). These areas concentrate 84% of the scientific production (see Table 9.2). Considering the main area of expertise, which is medicine, it is shown that the effort to make scientific publications in the NIH has increased, by

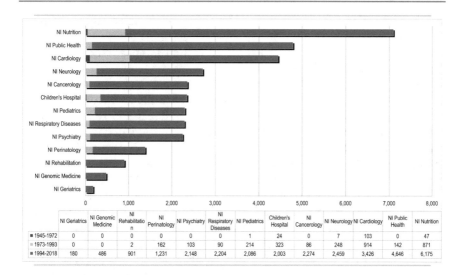

Fig. 9.5 Mexico. National Institutes of Health. Scientific production accumulated to 2018 (number of publications by NIH authors). *Source* Own elaboration with Scopus data (2021)

Table 9.2 Mexico, National Institutes of Health. Publications accumulated by area of knowledge to 2018 and 1980 (number and percentage of publications)

Area of knowledge	Total until 2018*	%	Total 1980	%
Total 28 areas	48,709	100.00	138	100.00
- Medicine	27,249	55.94	104	75.36
- Biochemistry, Genetics and Molecular Biology	6,309	12.95	12	8.70
- Immunology and Microbiology	2,699	5.54	12	8.70
- Neuroscience	2,181	4.48	2	1.45
- Pharmacology, Toxicology and Pharmaceutics	1,907	3.92	3	2.17
- Remaining 23 areas	8,364	14.06	5	3.62

Source Own elaboration with Scopus data (2021)
* *Note* The total number of publications shows a higher number, due to the Scopus registry in which a publication can be registered in more than one area of knowledge

increasing the presence of the research centers of this subsystem from three in 1980s that concentrated 85% (Cardiology, Nutrition and Pediatrics) to eight in 2018, adding those of Public Health, Neurology, Psychiatry, Cancerology, Respiratory Diseases. Over more than seven decades, the 13 NIH were created, focusing on areas of specialization that respond both, to the advances in science and to the diversity of areas required according to the health needs of the population. They articulate and complement basic and clinical research activities, medical practice and the preparation of highly specialized human resources. In accordance with this process of specialization and diversification, the scientific production of the NIH has grown significantly in the last four decades, from 138 publications in 1980 to almost fifty thousand in 2018.

As new specialized NIH were created, the scientific production related to the identified specialty areas of interest increased, as well as the diversity of knowledge areas and publications, all focused on the profile of diseases to be treated by the NIH. Thus, in the early 1940s–1950s, the areas of respiratory diseases, cardiology, cancerology and children's diseases prevailed, up to the new areas in the twenty-first century, such as genomic medicine, which also shows the advance in the frontier of knowledge to meet health needs. Thus, in 1980 the area of medicine concentrated a high share of publications (75%) and new areas such as neurosciences only 2%, and by 2018 the area of medicine was reduced to 56%, with greater participation in other areas such as neurosciences, which increased to 4.4% (Table 9.2). Finally, the publications of NIH without collaboration stand out, representing twice the number of NIH that collaborate with other agents. At the individual level, the magnitude of those who do not collaborate decreases to 54% of the total of those who publish in the NIH, which evidences the participation in research networks in at least half of the scientists with publications.

9.4.4 Magnitude, Trajectory and Inventive Specialization

Magnitude and trajectory

According to the search performed, of the 13 NIH, 12 have obtained at least one patent during the period analyzed. Graph 3 and Table 9.3 show the patents granted to the institutes from their creation in 1936 to 2018. Inventive productivity in the NIH began in 1990. A total of 49 patents have been granted to 12 NIH in which we have not included NIH Geriatrics, which has no patents (Fig. 9.6).

Inventive specialization by type of products

According to the type of technical solutions to health problems being developed by NIH, patents can be referred to three categories: medical devices, drugs/vaccines, and methods/treatments.

The NIH are very much oriented toward the development of new or improved methods and treatments (53%) such as diagnostics, clinical trials, and combating specific diseases or new or improved methods (e.g., methods for epilepsy diagnosis). Thirty-three percent is for medical devices and the remaining 14% for drugs and vaccines. Medical devices include portable testing equipment, surgical arm rests, electronic asepsis devices for surgical operating rooms, etc. Examples of vaccines are the intranasal vaccine against diseases caused by Escherichia coli. When collaboration exists, interconnections are mostly between NIH with other national or foreign PRC, and to a lesser extent with private companies (Table 9.3).

Table 9.3 Mexico. National Institutes of Health. Collaborative profile and inventive specialization, 1936–2018 (number and percentage of granted patents)

Institute/partnership/type of product	Medical devices	Medication/Vaccine	Method/Treatment	Total	
				Num	%
Total (Num.)	15	7	26	49	100.0
%	33	14	53		
Autarky	12	4	18	34	69.4
- Children's Hospital	1		2	3	
- National Institute of Cancerology			1	1	
- National Institute of Cardiology	5		2	7	
- National Institute of Respiratory Diseases			1	1	
- National Institute of Genomic Medicine	2		3	5	
- National Institute of Neurology	1		2	3	
- National Institute of Nutrition	1	1	3	5	
- National Institute of Pediatrics			3	3	
- National Institute of Perinatology	1			1	
- National Institute of Psychiatry		3		3	
- National Institute of Rehabilitation	1			1	
- National Institute of Public Health			1	1	
Network	4	3	8	15	30.6
University:		1	1	2	4.1
- National Institute of Neurology			1	1	
- National Institute of Nutrition		1		1	
University_Hospital:	1	1	2	4	8.2
- National Institute of Respiratory Diseases	1			1	
- National Institute of Nutrition		1	2	3	
University_Hospital_Inventor:			1	1	2.0

(continued)

Table 9.3 (continued)

Institute/partnership/type of product	Medical devices	Medication/Vaccine	Method/Treatment	Total Num	%
- National Institute of Neurology			1	1	
University Government:			1	1	2.0
- National Institute of Neurology			1	1	
Hospital:		1	2	3	6.1
- National Institute of Nutricion		1	2	3	
Universidad_Empresa:			1	1	2.0
- National Institute of Nutrition			1	1	
Inventor:	3			3	6.1
- National Institute of Nutrition	2			2	
- National Institute of Psychiatry	1			1	

Source Own elaboration based on EPO data base patent (2021)

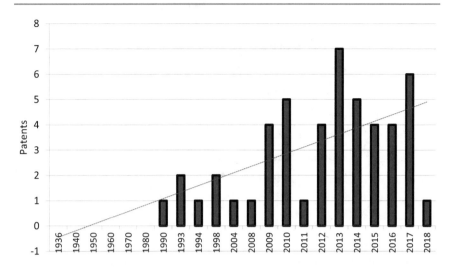

Fig. 9.6 Mexico. National Institutes of Health. Inventive trajectory, 1936–2018 (number of granted patents). *Source* Own elaboration based on EPO data base patent (2021)

Inventive specialization by type of disease

The knowledge reflected in patents had an application to diseases in which the NIH have specialized, with those of Infectious Diseases (27%), Development of Health Technologies (19%), Malignant Neoplasms (14%) and Chronic Diseases (10%) standing out. The remaining 30% are for the remaining five diseases: Psychiatric, Nutrition and Neurological Disorders, Reproductive Health and Accidents and Injuries. Of the patents granted, those for infectious diseases, chronic diseases, neurological disorders and accidents and injuries stand out as those with the greatest collaboration. This shows that the knowledge created by the NIH is being applied to address the main diseases of the Mexican population, such as heart disease, diabetes, tumors, liver disease, stroke and cerebrovascular diseases (Fig. 9.7 and Table 9.4).

9.4.5   Collaborative Invention in National Institutes of Health

Based on their patenting intensity and the existence or not of collaboration to develop patents, two groups of NIH can be identified: (a) those that patent in autarky and (b) those that patent in collaboration. The NIH in autarky patenting without networks correspond to eight NIH that have obtained patents at least since 1990, with a total of 34 patents, representing 69% of the total granted. Practically, all of the twelve NIH that patent do so in autarky, with the exception of four that also have patents in collaboration as detailed below (Table 9.5).

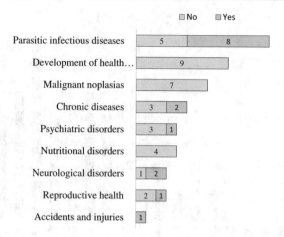

Fig. 9.7 Mexico. National Institutes of Health. Inventive specialization and collaborative profile 1936–2018 (number of granted patents). *Source* Own elaboration based on EPO (2021), CCINSHAE, (2020) and INEGI/Secretaría de Salud (2018)

Invention in autarky in the National Institutes of Health

Autarky prevails in the NIH that had a lower innovative intensity, which evidences the scarce work of the team in patenting and surely also in carrying out basic research with the possibility of scaling up and protecting itself intellectually. Although the scientific capacity in all NIH is outstanding and the recent patenting carried out by them in an eminently scientific trajectory is relevant, there are some NIH in which the inventive activity is still very low, such as the cases of Cancerology, Perinatology, Rehabilitation and Public Health. The NIH patents developed in autarky focus on developing or improving diagnostic and treatment methods, as well as medical devices such as diagnostic kits and improvements in medical equipment. The National Institute of Cardiology stand out with seven patents, those in Nutrition and Genomic Medicine with 5 patents each. These three NIH represent 50% of the patenting in autarky performed by 12 of the NIH (Tables 9.3 and 9.5).

The pattern of non-collaboration is far from the generalized practice and with greater applied results of basic research at the international level, characterized by collaborative work carried out in inter- and multi-disciplinary and internationalized teams and networks with an important national base, as is the case in many OECD countries and even in some emerging countries such as China or Brazil.

Collaborative invention at National Institutes of Health

Collaborative invention represents 31%, being most frequent with foreigners (21%); the remaining 10% is with Mexicans. The NIH that "patent in collaboration" correspond to four NIH: Respiratory Diseases, National Institute of Neurology, Medical Sciences and Nutrition, and Psychiatry. The institutions with which they

Table 9.4 Mexico. Causes of mortality, 2018

Cause	Rank	Deaths	%
Total		722,611	100.0
- Heart disease	1	149,368	20.7
- Diabetes mellitus	2	101,257	14.0
- Malignant tumors	3	85,754	11.9
- Liver diseases	4	39,287	5.4
- Assaults	5	36,685	5.1
- Cerebrovascular diseases	6	35,300	4.9
- Accidents	7	34,589	4.8
- Influenza and pneumonia	8	28,332	3.9
- Chronic obstructive pulmonary diseases	9	23,414	3.2
- Renal insufficiency	10	13,845	1.9

Source Own elaboration based on INEGI/Secretaría de Salud (2018)

collaborate are universities and hospitals (73%), the rest with companies and individual inventors (27%) (see Tables 9.3 and 9.6 and Graph 5).

As for the type of product, more than half of the total were for the introduction or improvement of methods for the diagnosis and care of certain diseases (53%), such as epilepsy, nervous system disorders, traumatic spinal cord disease, and for pediatric purposes, for the improvement of therapeutic methods and for medical devices 20% and drugs and vaccines 27%, especially anti-tuberculosis agents (Figs. 9.8 and 9.9).

NIH that patent in national and international networks have a solid track record in basic, applied, teaching and health care research in their areas of medical specialty. In the networks, the presence with various agents (23%), with health PRC (6%) and among inventors (2%) is outstanding. This result shows the peer-to-peer working teams of the NIH itself with other universities and PRC. The teams function and are organized through projects, and in some cases are maintained until patent registration as a group of inventors, which occurs mainly in the institutes of Nutrition, Neurology and Psychiatry. Collaboration between similar profiles of the health area itself, national and foreign, is present in a prominent way in the Nutrition NIH and to a lesser extent with universities, which reflects the importance of the complementarity of existing bodies of knowledge in different NIH and PRC. This result is paradoxical, given that there are close collaboration projects for the testing of new drugs, which require compliance with clinical trials in patients, and that this practice tends to encourage informal networks that are not reflected in institutionalized collaboration networks.

In summary, these results show the importance of how the production, use and access to knowledge in the area of health is vital for the improvement of conditions and care of existing and emerging diseases. However, in the subsystem analyzed, collaboration is still weak, and NIH that patent without collaborating show lower innovative intensity. The importance of collaboration is evident with the recent experience of the COVID-19 disease in which the importance of collaborative

Table 9.5 Mexico. National Institutes of Health by inventive profile, 1936–2018 (number of NIH and granted patents)

NIH Profile	Granted patents		NIH (Num)
	(Num.)	%	
Total	49	100	13
NIH with collaborative patenting activity	15	31	4
-National	5	10	
-International	10	21	
NIH with patenting activity in autarky (not collaborating)	34	69	8
NIH without patents*	–	–	1

Source Own estimates based on EPO data base patent (2021)
Note NIH without patents is National Institute of Geriatrics

Table 9.6 Mexico. National Institutes of Health. Profile of knowledge production and use as of 2018 (number and percentages)

Scientific magnitude (publications)		Magnitude of inventiveness (patents)	
Total	**33,556**	Total	**49**
1936-1972	182	1936-1972	0
1973-1993	3,115	1973-1993	3
1994-2018	30,219	1994-2018	46

Research personnel (2018). Total = 832

Production and use of knowledge

Scientific production by area of knowledge

Medicine ... 56%

Biochemistry, Genetics and Molecular Biology ... 13%

Immunology and Microbiology ... 6%

Neuroscience ... 4%

Pharmacology, Toxicology and Pharmaceutics ... 2%

Invention by product type

Methods/ Treatment ... 53%

Medical Devices ... 33%

Drugs/Vaccines ... 14%

Invention by disease attended

Infectious, infectious and parasitic diseases ... 27%

Health technologies ... 19%

Malignant neoplasms ... 14%

Chronic ... 10%

Psychiatric disorders ... 8%

Nutritional disorders ... 8%

Pattern of inventive collaboration

Autarchy 69%

Network 31%

Network collaboration, by type of actor

University 13%

University-Hospital 27%

University-Hospital-Inventor 6%

University-Government 7%

Hospital 20%

University-Company 7%

Inventor 20%

Source Own elaboration based on Tables 9.1 to 9.5 and Graphs 1 to 5

interaction at national and international level has been emphasized and not only to solve current diseases but potential diseases to appear (Jasso and Torres, 2020). It is very important to continue reflecting on which agents, which mechanisms promote production and collaboration to solve the pandemics to come, i.e., health is becoming an increasingly global problem that requires greater and more creative collaboration and greater inclusion at the global level. As warned by Jasso and Torres (2020), it is necessary to go beyond an immediate and conjunctural response to reduce the existing structural gaps in the world in terms of knowledge and technology, which should have an impact on reducing the exclusion of less developed countries.

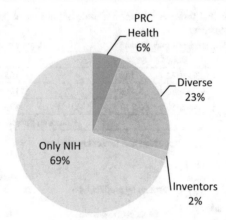

Fig. 9.8 Mexico. National Institutes of Health. Collaborative invention profile, 1936–2018 (number of granted patents). *Source* Own elaboration based on EPO data base patent (2021)

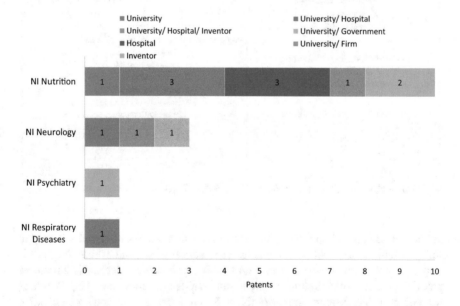

Fig. 9.9 Mexico. National Institutes of Health. Collaborative invention profile, 1936–2018 (number of granted patents). *Source* Own elaboration-based EPO data base patent (2021)

9.5 Summary and Conclusions

The text analyzed the production and use of knowledge in the NIH in Mexico. Based on indicators of scientific and inventive production of each NIH, the magnitude, intensity and type of inventive specialization were analyzed and characterized, as well as the patterns under which the NIH can be grouped to portray the production and use of knowledge. The creation of knowledge and its use is expressed in publications and in new products and production and problem-solving processes. Today, in a knowledge-based economy, PRC such as NIH, as creators and transmitters of new knowledge, play a key role in developing solutions available to end users. In this creation and dissemination, the collaboration of PRC with other agents such as companies, universities and governmental institutions, are of great support to exchange, obtain and develop different types of knowledge and other resources.

The results of the work suggest that the NIH have an important role in the generation and dissemination of knowledge to contribute to the solution of health problems in general. NIH do not invent just anything, but within their areas of interest, attention to diseases and the ways in which these can be controlled or solved. Collaboration with universities and PRC points to a collective effort in the pursuit of improving health care procedures and the quality of medical services. In summary, there is a notable impact of the production and use of NIH knowledge on the wellbeing of the population, highlighting its scientific, clinical and, above all, social role (Table 9.6).

The production of knowledge in health

The characteristics of scientific and inventive production in the NIH show that in the health sector, and it is relevant to have a scientific base, where the main source of technology are R&D activities that are carried out within the NIH and with other agents to link and complement or develop the knowledge created in these NIH, especially in new areas of health such as genomics, nanosciences, bioinformatics or to identify new diseases or to apply new drugs to new or old pathologies when facing the treatment of diseases considered incurable. Scientific progress in new areas such as biotechnology, enzymology, bioinformatics, robotics, combinatorial chemistry and digital technologies has allowed the introduction of new schemes for the discovery of vaccines, drugs and new devices, in which innovation became less a trial-and-error process and more based on incremental innovations.

Specialization and use of knowledge in health

Taking into account the epidemiological transition that the country is undergoing, the scientific and inventive capacities developed in Mexico have addressed the two epidemiological profiles that coexist in the country, both the traditional one where diseases typical of underdevelopment associated with infectious diseases and malnutrition predominate, as well as a more recent profile in which chronic diseases, typical of developed countries such as cancer, obesity, heart disease and diabetes, prevail. In the NIH, publication data between 1994–2018 indicate obesity, breast cancer, diabetes mellitus, HIV, hypertension as the most important topics.

The NIH have developed a scientific production directed in greater proportion to the profile where the majority of the population is found (diabetes mellitus and cancer), but their inventive capabilities are more oriented to the profile that includes diseases such as tuberculosis and parasitic infections.

Knowledge and its use imply solving health problems, so the NIH basic research is oriented to reinforce those other forms of research in the health area such as clinical and medical research and thus improve or create new forms of medical care and therefore to solve prevalent diseases in the country.

Patterns of collaboration

Two patterns of collaboration were identified. The first has to do with the magnitude and intensity of inventiveness and its collaboration (or not) with other agents in the system. The second pattern is related to the type of technical solutions to health problems being developed by the NIH such as medical devices, methods, or vaccines-drugs.

Consideration of both patterns of collaboration and their relationship with the types of technical solutions covered by patents shows that there are scientific developments that have been used (inventions) to address health problems. Collaboration among NIH researchers has had positive effects on the health care system by enabling the development of new methods and treatments, medical devices, vaccines and drugs. The results indicate that there is a clear lack of regular linkages between NIH and other economic and social actors. NIH tend to establish links with universities and other public PRC rather than with companies.

Service Design, and production and use of knowledge at NIH

The design of services at NIH is based on a framework in which physicians, patients as end users, as well as other agents are part. Thus, the production and use of knowledge have been approached from a service design perspective. The process of creation and use of knowledge in the health sector have been analyzed from a framework that places the interaction between the agents at the center. The framework is intended to constitute a platform for future research at the intersection of service design and the production and use of health knowledge. This will help health officials and service providers to generate a broad model, in which not only patients and doctors are part, but also producers and users of knowledge such as universities and PRC and in hybrid organizations such as the NIH.

Lines of research

The integration of knowledge generated in basic, applied and teaching research activities
    The production of knowledge and its use goes beyond considering them in stages that complement each other as suggested by several studies. The idea of considering knowledge with a dynamic of multiple diffusion by various agents implies the idea of mobilization and therefore the consideration of use, beyond market criteria, especially in developing countries. The functions assigned to universities and taken up again in a more integral model such as the NIH have shown the flexibility to intermingle these functions in an eminently applied idea, that of solving health problems.

In other words, it is not a linear vision, but is integrated to solve a problem (mission oriented), to provide solutions. It is a bidirectional flow. The recent experience with COVID showed how the capabilities of the universities were combined with those of the companies. This idea was already pointed out by Gibbons et al., 1994, when they suggested that knowledge should be articulated from the beginning in a transdisciplinary way, with the creation of knowledge directed to the solution of problems, in which its quality is not only measured by peers but by the diversity of agents involved in its creation, application and use.

Production and use in health. Access to users

Despite the results reflected in scientific production and inventions, there are still few experiences in which the knowledge generated reaches consumers either as new final products, processes or treatments, vaccines or drugs to solve health problems and clinical trials.

One of the ways for this solution is through collaboration with the productive sector and other agents which, as has been pointed out, is weak and it is considered that it should be encouraged to advance in its development and that users acquire it through the market or through the public health system.

In this regard, it is necessary to carry out additional studies to identify the obstacles to solving this weakness in collaboration, such as financial or institutional aspects.

Production and use in health. Mobilization and institutionalization in the network

The current debate in the literature on the production and use of knowledge is mainly focused on the collaboration between universities-PRC and companies, and the role of research and health care institutions is still little addressed.

Studies from the innovation approach are still scarcely addressing these aspects since its focus is mainly on companies. An evaluation of the positive effects of the interaction of professionals with companies and other actors in the health system requires a deeper discussion and analysis of the social role of universities, PRC and health institutes and hospitals, particularly in developing countries, and of the role of public policy.

The production and use of knowledge at the global level

The COVID-19 disease showed the weaknesses of the schemes to produce and use knowledge in an effective, timely and inclusive manner. Production is vital and so is collaboration. With the recent experience of COVID-19, the need for collaboration not only at the national but also at the international level became evident. COVID has shown the importance of collaboration going forward. More agents, more pandemics. Collaboration and the generation of mechanisms to ensure the use of medicines to the population without exclusions is crucial in the fight against global diseases.

References

Arocena, R., & Sutz, J. (2005). Latin American Universities: From an Original Revolution to an Uncertain Transition. *Higher Education, 50*, 573–592. https://doi.org/10.1007/s10734-004-6367-8.

Casells, A. (1995). Health sector reforms: Key issues in Less Developed Countries. *Journal of International Development, 7*(3), 329–347. https://doi.org/10.1002/jid.3380070303.

CCINSHAE, (2020). Comisión Coordinadora de Institutos Nacionales de Salud y Hospitales de Alta Especialidad (SSa). https://www.gob.mx/insalud/acciones-y-programas/institutos-nacionales-de-salud-27376. Accessed 9 Apr 2020.

Cohen, M., Nelson, R., & Walsh, J. (2002). Links and impacts: The influence of public research on industrial R&D. *Managment Science, 48*(1), 1–23. https://www.jstor.org/stable/822681.

Cooksey, D. (2006). *A review of UK health research funding*. London, UK: The Stationery Office.

David P. & Foray D. (2002). Fundamentos económicos de la sociedad del conocimiento. *Revista de Comercio Exterior*, Vol. 52, Núm.6., junio. 472–490. http://revistas.bancomext.gob.mx/rce/magazines/23/2/davi0602.pdf. Accessed 18 Jun 2021.

DOF (Diario Oficial de la Federación) (2019). *Ley de los Institutos Nacionales de Salud*. Cámara de Diputados del Congreso de la Unión, última reforma 14–11–2019, Ciudad de México. XXX, XXX, XXX.

Etzkowitz, H., & Leydesdorff, L. (2000). The dynamics of innovation: From national systems and "Mode 2" to a triple helix of university-industry-government relations. *Research Policy, 29*(2), 109–123. https://doi.org/10.1016/S0048-7333(99)00055-4.

European Patent Office, EPO. (2020). *Espacenet patent search*. http://worldwide.espacenet.com. Accessed March 21 Mar 2020.

Freeman, C. (1995). The 'National System of Innovation' in historical perspective. *Cambridge Journal of Economics, 19*(1), 5–24. https://www.jstor.org/stable/23599563.

Garfield, E. (2006). The history and meaning of the journal impact factor. *JAMA, 295*(1), 90–93. https://doi.org/10.1001/jama.295.1.90.

Gibbons, M., Limoges, C., Nowonty, H., Schwartzman, S., Scotty, P., & Trow, M. (1994). *The new production of knowledge. The dynamics of science and research contemporary societies*. Sage Publications Ltd.

Gonzalez-Brambila, C., & Veloso, F. (2007). The determinants of research output and impact: A study of Mexican researchers. *Research Policy, 36*(7), 1035–1051. https://doi.org/10.1016/j.respol.2007.03.005.

Harris, E. (2004). Building scientific capacity in developing countries. *EMBO Reports, 5*(1), 7–11. https://doi.org/10.1038/sj.embor.7400058.

INEGI/Secretaría de Salud. (2018). Principales causas de muerte según Lista Mexicana. México: INEGI/SS. https://www.inegi.org.mx/sistemas/olap/consulta/general_ver4/MDXQueryDatos.asp?#Regreso&c=. Accessed 28 May 2021.

Jasso, J. & Torres A. (2020). Nuevos mecanismos de colaboración público-privada para el desarrollo y acceso a la vacuna COVID-19: una perspectiva desde la teoría fundamentada. *Contaduría y Administración*, 65(4), 1–19. https://doi.org/10.22201/fca.24488410e.2020.3134.

Jasso, J., & Marquina, L. (2013). Innovación en los servicios. Problemática y reflexiones en el sector salud de la salud pública. En C. Del Valle, A. Mariño, & I. Núñez (Coord), *Ciencia, tecnología e innovación en el desarrollo de México y América Latina Tomo II Dinámicas de innovación y aprendizaje en territorios y sectores productivos* (págs. 179–221). México: Instituto de Investigaciones Económicas, Universidad Nacional Autónoma de México.

Jasso, J. (2015). Innovación y salud: agentes, redes y desarrollo. En A. Ranfla, M. Rivera, & R. Caballero, *Desarrollo económico y cambio tecnológico. Teoría, marco global e implicaciones para México* (págs. 175–204). México: Juan Pablos UNAM UABC.

Jasso J. (1998). De los sistemas nacionales a los suprarregionales y subnacionales de innovación. Propuesta analítica y conceptual, *Revista de Economía y Empresa*, 34(XII) 115–131.

Kreiman, G., & Maunsell, J. (2011). Nine criteria for a measure of scientific output. *Frontiers in Computational Neuroscience, 5*(48), 1–6. https://doi.org/10.3389/fncom.2011.00048PMCID: PMC3214728 PMID: 22102840.

Lundvall, B. (1992). *National system of innovation, towards a theory of innovation and interactive learning*. Pinter Publisher.

Lifshitz, A. (2009). Medicina traslacional (traduccional, traducida, traslativa, trasladada). *Medicina Interna De México., 25*(4), 251–253.

Malberg, L. (2017). *Building design capability in the public sector.expanding the horizons of development* (Vol. 1831). Linkoping: Linkoping University Electronic Press. https://www.diva-portal.org/smash/get/diva2:1074095/fulltext01.pdf.

Metcalfe, J. (1995). The economic foundations of technology policy: Equilibrium and evolutionary perspectives. In P. Stoneman (Ed.), *Handbook of the Economics of Innovation and Technological Change* (pp. 513–557). Blackwell Publishers.

Meroni, A., & Sangiorgi, D. (2011). *Design for services*. Gower Publising.

Molina-Salazar, R. E., Romero-Velázquez, J. R., & Trejo-Rodríguez, J. A. (1991). Desarrollo económico y salud. *Salud Pública De México, 33*(3), 227–234.

Nagpaul, P., & Roy, S. (2003). Constructing a multi-objective measure of research performance. *Scinciometrics, 56*(3), 383–402. https://doi.org/10.1023/A:1022382904996.

Narin, F., Hamilton, K. S., & Olivestro, D. (1997). The increasing linkage between US technology and public science. *Research Policy, 26*(3), 317–330. https://doi.org/10.1016/S0048-7333(97)00013-9.

Nelson, R. (1993). *National systems of innovation: A comparative study*. Oxford University Press.

OECD. (2005). *Reviews of health Systems-México*. https://www.oecd-ilibrary.org/oecd-reviews-of-health-systems-mexico-2005_5lh0hpphbqzt.pdf?itemId=%2Fcontent%2Fpublication%2F9789264008939-en&mimeType=pdf. Accessed 18 Jun 2021.

Pfannstiel, M. A. & Rasche, C. (2019). *Service design and service thinking in heathcare and hospital management. Theory, concepts, practice*. Springer Nature, Cham.

Rodrigues, V. & Vink, J. (2016). Shaking up the status quoin healtcare:Designing amld conflicting enacted social structures. In *Relating systems thinking and design symposium(RSD)*, 13–15 October, OCAD University Toronto, Canada. http://openresearch.ocadu.ca/id/eprint/1928/1/Vink_Design_2016.pdf.

Schumpeter, J. A. (1944). *Teoría del desenvolvimiento económico*, traducción española, Fondo de Cultura Económica, México, (1912).

Scopus. (2021). Scopus data base. https://www.scopus.com. Accessed 18 Jun 2021.

Torres, A., & Jasso, J. (2019). Capabilities and knowledge transfer: Evidence from a university research center in the health area in Mexico, *Contaduría y Administración. Especial Innovación, 64*(1), 1–16. https://doi.org/10.22201/fca.24488410e.2019.1808.

Torres, A., & Jasso, J. (2014). Knowledge and quality innovation in the health sector: The role of public research organisations. In: Al-Hakim, & Jin Ch. (Ed.), *Quality innovation knowledge, theory and practices* (pp. 159–188). s.l.: Hershey, PA: IGI Global Disseminator of Knowledge Editorial.

Torres, A., Jasso, J., & Calderón, G. (2015). Investigación científica y actividad inventiva en el sector salud en México: el caso del Instituto Mexicano del Seguro Social (pp. 213–236). In Corona J. (Coord) *Desarrollo Sustentable. Enfoques, políticas, gestión y desafíos*. UAM-X, México.

Torres, A., Dutrénit, G., Sampedro, J., & Becerra, N. (2011). What are the factors driving university-industry linkages in latecomer firms: Evidence from Mexico. *Science and Public Policy, 38*(1), 31–42. https://doi.org/10.3152/030234211X12924093660390.

Van Dijk, T., & Duysters, G. (1998). Passing the European patent office: Evidence from the data-processing industry. *Research Policy, 27*(9), 937–946. https://doi.org/10.1016/S0048-7333(98)00086-9.

Windrum, P., & García-Goñi, M. (2008). A neo-Schumpeterian model of health servicies innovation. *Research Policy, 37*(4), 649–672. https://doi.org/10.1016/j.respol.2007.12.011.

Yu, E. & Sangiorgi, D.(2017). Service design as an approach to implement the value cocreation perspective in new service development. *Journal of Service Research*, 21(1), 40–58.

Javier Jasso is a full time Senior Professor in the Graduate School of Accounting and Management at Universidad Nacional Autónoma de México (FCA, UNAM). He coordinated the Graduate Program in Management Sciences and he was also head of the Research Division at FCA, UNAM. He has a PhD in Economics from the Complutense University of Madrid, Spain. He is member of the National System of Researchers by Conacyt-Mexico. His research interest includes interaction of Science, Technology and Society, innovation, competitiveness and learning and technological capabilities at the firm level.

Arturo Torres is a professor and researcher in the Master's and PhD Programmes in Economics, Management and Innovation Policies at the Universidad Autónoma Metropolitana, Campus Xochimilco (UAM-X). He holds a DPhil in science and technology research studies from SPRU, University of Sussex, UK. He is member of the National System of Researchers by Conacyt-Mexico. His research interest includes university-industry linkages, learning and building of technological capabilities at the firm level, innovation in the health sector, entrepreneurship and innovation policy studies.

Using the Principles of the Holistic Wellness Concept in Designing and Developing Hospital Services: Case of Pärnu Hospital, Rehabilitation and Well-Being Centre

10

Heli Tooman, Marit Piirman, and Margrit Kärp

Abstract

The perceptions and attitudes of society, including both people and organisations, are changing along with the development of knowledge and technology. Several fundamental changes have taken place in healthcare in recent decades. Hospitals around the world are challenged to support patients' recovery and well-being by adding value to traditional medical treatments and developing new services. The holistic approach to health in developing and designing services based on patient well-being has become an integral part of hospital services. The development of Dunn's high-level holistic wellness concept was triggered by the World Health Organisation's definition of health in 1946, which carried the message that everyone is responsible for their own health. This broader understanding of health encouraged research and service development, including in the field of healthcare. By focusing on wellness as a continuous process that is never static, healthcare providers play a fundamental role in maintaining the vitality of a person. However, gaps can be found in the application of the holistic wellness concept in the design of healthcare services. This chapter will present an overview of implementing theoretical approaches of the holistic wellness concept in healthcare, noteworthy changes and trends in the design and development of hospital services, and the application of the concept in the

H. Tooman · M. Piirman (✉) · M. Kärp
University of Tartu Pärnu College, Ringi 35, 80012 Pärnu, Estonia
e-mail: marit.piirman@ut.ee

H. Tooman
e-mail: heli.tooman@ut.ee

M. Kärp
e-mail: margrit.karp@ut.ee

design of services. The experience of planning, targeting and developing a rehabilitation and well-being centre at Pärnu Hospital (Estonia) is described to explain how the wellness concept and wellness dimensions were the basis of the design and development of the centre's services.

10.1 Introduction

According to the World Health Organisation (WHO), "Health is a state of complete physical, mental and social well-being and not merely the absence of disease or infirmity". (Constitution nd) This definition which was introduced in 1946, can be considered to be the most important turning point in healthcare (World Health Organisation, nd). It is common to think about wellness in terms of illness and assume that wellness is the absence of illness only. However, there are many degrees of wellness, just as there are many degrees of illness.

According to Dunn (1959), a high level of well-being is equivalent to vitality, in which you experience joy of life, abundant energy and a feeling of "being alive clear to the tips of your fingers". Thus, vitality is often confused with a momentary sense of instant pleasure. Inspired by Dunn's philosophy, John Travis, an American author and medical practitioner composed the illness-wellness model (Fig. 10.1) in 1972 (Travis & Ryan, 2004) which pointed out two directions of health: the left arrow moves towards deteriorating health, while the right arrow moves towards an increasing level of health and wellness. In the centre of this continuum, the neutral point represents no noticeable illness or wellness. The left side of the neutral point

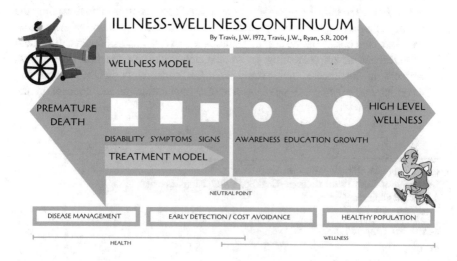

Fig. 10.1 Illness–wellness continuum. *Source* Travis and Ryan (2004)

is recognised as the zone of traditional treatment, where medical care is provided to ease the medical conditions until the danger to the patient's life is eliminated. Whereas the right side is seen as opportunities to take care of oneself to achieve personal well-being regardless of one's state of health, to take responsibility and contribute to one's health and holistic well-being.

Instead of being considered a static state, wellness means giving good care to the physical body, using the mind constructively, expressing emotions effectively, being creatively involved with those around, and being concerned about physical, psychological and spiritual environments (Travis & Ryan, 2004). Based on Prescott et al. (2019), vitality has lately become a measurable psychological construct and is associated with various health outcomes such as reducing non-communicable diseases, psychological well-being, and better health throughout the whole arch of life. While Dunn and Travis meant wellness mainly as each person's personal responsibility to have control over their health and well-being, the word *wellness* itself got very popular in the business world and was often exploited mostly for marketing purposes (Pilzer, 2001).

Subhedar and Dave (2016) suggest that utilising a perfect combination of the most advanced technological devices, highly skilled professionals and therapies including physiotherapy and holistically nurtured music therapy and a spiritually designed wellness setup will soon be a base for offering successful healthcare and rehabilitative services around the world. However, positive health for all is not achieved as long as the WHO does not include "spiritual health" in its definition of health and proposes including yoga and meditation in the primary healthcare as the best available methods to achieve positive health and holistic wellness (Ghiya, 2019).

In order to provide services that fulfil a person's individual needs, the customer (or patient, using the traditional health-care vocabulary) needs to be in the centre of all activities. Service design is a user-centric approach that uses different tools to systematically analyse, innovate and improve service processes from a customer's perspective (Stickdorn & Schwarzenberger, 2016). It helps to break down organisational "silos" and solve customers' problems with a co-creative and hands-on attitude using design as a toolset (Stickdorn et al., 2018). Service design is often also considered a mindset where customers' needs are the first priority, following 6 principles—human-centred, collaborative, iterative, holistic, sequential and real, meaning all the research and prototyping takes place in physical or digital reality (Stickdorn et al., 2018). There are several service design process models covering different stages of design process. Most known is Double Diamond model with four phases (Drew, 2019).

As one of the main principles of service design is focusing on customer and his or her needs, it might be said that involving patients' experience in the development of healthcare services is almost critical. The results of patient surveys, complaints and feedback can provide good input for developing services and maintaining service quality. However, by involving hospitalised or recently discharged patients, or their loved ones, into a real process of designing and creating services, the results can be much broader, involve more stakeholders and have a deeper impact on the patient (Castro et al., 2018).

Similar to other service sectors, service experience and value perception vary from individual to individual. Providing services in the field of medicine is particularly sensitive, since the treatments and support services that improve people's health and quality of life, as well as prevention activities that contribute to their well-being, are often provided during difficult periods of life. Therefore, co-creation plays extremely important role. Co-creation is a term used to describe the creation of common value between a company and a customer and it allows the customer to create a service experience according to their context. The concept of co-creation has been exploited in various service industries as a tool to encourage innovation and enhance customer satisfaction. It acknowledges that the success of any company depends not only on the expertise, assets and core competences of the service provider but also on the knowledge and perspectives of the target customer. Co-creating is not only consultation with or participation of consumers, it goes beyond that, by integrating customers into the process of product and service ideation (Palumbo, 2016). In the context of healthcare, relationships and trust are essential for meaningful patient engagement, since the experiences of patients can be used as a valuable source of ideas for transformation of services (Maher et al., 2017).

Besides, the increased patient satisfaction such a collaborative approach to medicine can ultimately also result in improved efficiency and outcomes. To have a common ground, ideation tools are good to use (Castro et al., 2018), for example, service design tools like patient journey mapping, experience-based surveys, and co-design workshops (Boyd et al., 2012). Co-creation can thus be considered to be the future method for quality improvement, research, intervention development and implementation (Castro et al., 2018). In recent decades, wellness and service design principles have been valued and are also used in traditional health institutions, including hospitals (Russell-Bennett et al., 2017).

This chapter introduces a true story of a large hospital on their journey to integrating the holistic wellness concept into their service development, from ideating and designing to creation and implementation. This strategic turnaround supports both the mission of a hospital to improve and support the health and quality of life of its patients and local habitants, as well as the principles of holistic well-being, by which each person will actively participate in protecting their health and in preventing diseases and will not leave all the responsibility to medication.

10.2 The Changing Role of Healthcare Institutions in Shaping people's Holistic Well-Being

Historically, patients have been considered passive recipients of services provided by the medical industry. The whole healthcare system has evolved relatively independently of patients, which is the opposite approach to customer–provider interaction that is approved and implemented in other service sectors. However, considering the high costs of healthcare services, as well the growing pressure for improved quality and increasing demand for more personalised care, the medical sector is facing the challenge to become more customer-centric and meet the needs of their most important stakeholders—their patients (Janamian et al., 2016).

Healthcare is evolving from sick care to preventive care, from care in the hospital to care anywhere, and from getting well to staying well (Glausier, 2018). The medical industry is moving towards preventive care and the role of hospitals is changing significantly. Ageing populations, technological advancements and illness trends all have an impact on where healthcare is headed.

Wellness principles may and should be used in the development of hospital services as well-being services, to move more towards high-level wellness, while acknowledging the six basic dimensions of personal wellness—physical, emotional, intellectual, environmental, spiritual and social. High-level wellness involves giving good care to the physical self, using the mind constructively, expressing emotions effectively, being creatively involved with those around, and being concerned about physical, psychological and spiritual environments. This argument is supported by defining wellness as a choice and a way of life, seeing it as a continuous process with balanced challenging energy, integrating body, mind, and spirit as well as having a loving acceptance of oneself.

10.3 Estonian Healthcare System and Development Opportunities of Healthcare Services in Hospitals

The current Estonian health system is a result of several healthcare reforms that took place before 2002. After Estonia regained independence in 1991, many changes took place in the healthcare system that were mainly related to closing or re-profiling small hospitals. To provide equal access to general healthcare services, family doctors and specialists, the co-operative network of hospitals was established by the state.

The provision of healthcare services in Estonia is regulated by the HealthCare Services Organisation Act 2001. According to the law, Estonian healthcare providers are considered legal entities that can make investments, buy and sell, and contract loans. They are responsible for their economic results and they keep the profits. Therefore, Estonian healthcare providers can make decisions about their future strategies, service development and work arrangement related issues.

A study focusing on Estonian health and wellness export possibilities found that, in addition to the general management of the health system, the big challenge for Estonia is to agree upon a common and far-sighted vision and implementation plan for the entire economy (Estonian Development Fund, 2010). If the knowledge-, service- and export-based economic model works for Estonia and can be applied to meet the growing demand for health and welfare services, it can be used support the economy. Formerly, medical spas were considered to be providers of paid medical services, but the previously mentioned study suggests looking at the wider picture, highlighting the great potential of Estonian healthcare service providers to develop additional income from international health tourism.

The report (Estonian Development Fund, 2010) also brings out connections between wellness and health services, where hotels and institutions offering relaxation-oriented services have added medical-related services to their portfolios, because clients are more aware of their health and are expecting those services. In principle, it is an old resort model brought into the modern day, where people wishing to improve their health take a few days or a week off, instead of month as they used to do. Therefore, considering the symbiosis between wellness and health service exports, the health sector can use the trust created by the wellness service providers to find users for their services. Likewise, wellness service providers can use the credibility and trustworthy images created by medical service providers to communicate that their services will provide value to their customers.

Heath tourism in Estonia began with medicinal sea mud in Saaremaa in 1824, when the first facility for mud treatment under medical supervision was opened. Following the successful example of Saaremaa, other treatment facilities were established in Haapsalu in 1825, Pärnu in 1838, Kuressaare in 1840 and Narva-Jõesuu in 1876. These medical healthcare institutions then boosted the development of the resort towns as they became desirable destinations for holidays and treatment. Thus, Estonia has a couple of hundred years of experience of using spa treatments for cardiovascular, nervous system and skin diseases, and even today spa treatments have an important role in modern rehabilitation treatments in Estonia.

Following the pattern of medical spas to design and provide wellness treatments along with medical treatments to enhance competitiveness and customer satisfaction, Estonian conventional healthcare institutions have also begun to consider the holistic approach to well-being in designing and developing processes. By opening the rehabilitation and well-being centre in 2013, Pärnu Hospital can be called a pioneer in combining traditional healthcare treatments with services based on the holistic wellness concept.

When considering implementing holistic wellness and service design principles into existing healthcare institutions, it is not only the new facilities, premises and services that should be addressed, but improvements to existing services and the service environment are also necessary. In terms of the future, the question of how to make people more interested in and contribute to their health and well-being is extremely important. The development of healthcare as an economic sector should lead to different technologies helping people to better manage their health. It is equally important that the healthcare system and institutions are willing and ready to introduce innovations, including adherence to the principles of the holistic wellness concept, and to participate in the design and provision of services that support people's quality of life and well-being.

10.4 From a Wanderer in the Hospital Network to the Cornerstone of the Health System: Pärnu Hospital's Health Campus in the Service of People's Health, Quality of Life and Well-Being

Pärnu Hospital (Fig. 10.2) was established by the city of Pärnu in 2000, following the guidelines set by the Estonian government in its Hospital Network Development plan, with an obligation to provide a wide range of health services. Located in the suburb of Pärnu, the hospital is surrounded by greenery and is easily accessible by any kind of transportation. The location was consciously chosen considering the surrounding environment, accessibility, aesthetic aspects and possibilities for expansion.

According to Pärnu Hospital's statutes, the main aim of the hospital is to provide high-quality care for both internal and external patients, emergency medical care and other related services to the citizens of, as well visitors to, the Republic of Estonia. The main service area consists of approximately 83,000 people, however, as a hospital in a tourism and resort town, the needs of visitors to the area should not be underrated.

When rehabilitation became an important subject in the European health system in the beginning of the 2000s, the European Union began funding the development of rehabilitation services and institutions. It could be said that the current Pärnu hospital is largely based on the strategy and support of the European Union.

To succeed in this competitive field of EU projects, something innovative, economically sustainable, and beneficial for peoples' health was needed in addition to rehabilitation related aspects. In preparation for this project, several ideas arose that led to the design of the holistic well-being centre next to the Pärnu Hospital. In the beginning of the design process, the name rehabilitation and wellness centre was given to the planned centre.

During the design process, however, this name was changed to the rehabilitation and well-being centre. This is because wellness often carries the image of luxury which was not set as a priority for the Pärnu Hospital. It was decided to incorporate the holistic wellness concept in the interior and service design and work arrangements, thus taking into account the objectives of the centre, customer groups and developed services. Therefore, it seemed suitable to call it the well-being centre. This approach is strongly supported by John Travis' illness–wellness continuum, where after medical treatment in hospital, the customer continues to improve their well-being.

According to the Chief Physician, Chairman and CEO of the Pärnu hospital, Urmas Sule (also Chairman of Estonian Hospitals Association, President of European Hospitals and Healthcare Federation (HOPE), and since 2020, the head of the COVID-19 Crisis Unit of the State Health Board), the focus of hospitals remains on the patients with severe medical conditions, such as stroke or heart attack, who cannot be treated in spas (Sule, nd). However, besides offering the necessary medical care for severe medical cases, a well-being centre provides services, and accommodation, for both rehabilitation patients and customers interested in

Fig. 10.2 Pärnu Hospital health campus with its rehabilitation and well-being centre. *Source* Pärnu Hospital (2021)

contributing to their personal well-being. Physical therapy, massages, water gymnastics, gymnasium facilities and counselling, etc. are all available to post-traumatic or post-surgery patients as well as to other customers for rehabilitation or prevention purposes. An important fact to note is that the institution offers several paid services for people without any medical complaints. These health and wellness supporting and illness preventing services are popular among both local residents and visitors to Pärnu (Figs. 10.3, 10.4, 10.5 and 10.6).

Fig. 10.3 Children's pool in Pärnu Hospital health campus. *Source* Pärnu Hospital (2021)

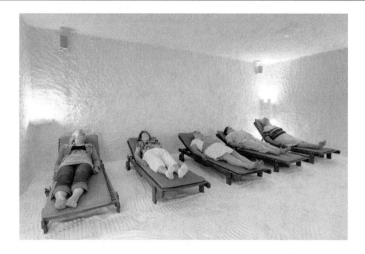

Fig. 10.4 Salt chamber in Pärnu Hospital health campus. *Source* Pärnu Hospital (2021)

Fig. 10.5 Light and music therapy with relaxing. *Source* Pärnu Hospital (2021)

Each of the last three strategic development plans of Pärnu Hospital have included one major building development. The first of these, the main hospital building was completed in 2005, followed by the rehabilitation and well-being centre in 2013, and the idea of a first level health centre integrated with hospital services to enable prompt diagnostics materialised in 2020, despite all the difficulties caused by the pandemic. The health campus on Pärnu Hospital was

Fig. 10.6 Training in the gym of Pärnu Hospital health campus. *Source* Pärnu Hospital (2021)

comprehensively developed and constructed, with a focus on effective management of facilities, customer-friendly services and environment, and services designed using holistic wellness principles to increase the satisfaction of both internal and external customers.

The last part of the Pärnu Hospital health campus—the Ristiku Health Centre—brings together into the collaboration family doctors and specialised doctors from the hospital. In the planning process for this centre, it was recognised that, to shorten the journey patients needed to take to access medical services and to provide the best expertise to treat the patients, locating the various services close together was essential. In comparison with the previous buildings of the Pärnu Hospital, the principles of the holistic wellness concept were more consciously considered and applied in the planning and construction of this new health centre. Hence, the layout of the premises, the interior design, and the services are all designed to meet the needs of the main target group—the customers or patients—as well as the needs of the personnel of the centre.

Performance and process management principles are used to achieve the strategic goals of the hospital, including service design and development, which are reflected through customers, processes, development and financial perspectives. The customer perspective aims to increase awareness in the local community about health and to make the Pärnu Hospital the first choice when people are deciding on treatment options, by providing the right services at the right time and in the right place, and services that are known to be safe.

The process perspective embraces the patient's needs—does the patient's journey respond to the patient's needs, are the diagnostics effective and reliable, do the treatments conform to contemporary treatment standards, is the therapy consistent with other similar therapies elsewhere, etc. Pärnu Hospital also aspires to be a trusted partner for other healthcare institutions and to apply the principles of quality management.

The perspectives of development include the desire for quality staff to work in the Pärnu hospital, the design of services and premises according to changing demand, effective, purposeful and secure management of big data, innovation, and up-to-date medical technology that meets the changing needs and is effectively used. From a financial point of view, the most important aspect for Pärnu Hospital is to ensure financial sustainability—the balance between income and expenditure.

Above all, the customer or patient is central—in planning all activities, developing new processes and services, and improving existing ones—the focus remains on the person for whom the activity creates value. There is an increasing emphasis on mapping the processes using service design principles and tools.

The mission of the Pärnu Hospital is to improve and support human health and life quality by providing interdisciplinary health and well-being services throughout the human life cycle—health and support services, improvement and support of human health, quality of life and well-being through prevention. Focusing on human health and desiring to accomplish the best possible result by being a reliable, innovative and caring medical team, creates favourable ground for raising customer awareness and achieving holistic well-being. Having such a rehabilitation and well-being centre next to the hospital is unique to Pärnu and is not found in any of the neighbouring countries. The fact it follows wellness principles in all of its development projects is also remarkable.

10.5 Using the Principles of the Holistic Wellness Concept in Designing and Developing the Services of the Pärnu Hospital Rehabilitation and Well-Being Centre

The Global Wellness Institute (GWI) defines wellness „the active pursuit of activities, choices, and lifestyles that lead to a state of holistic health " and refers to its multidimensionality–many dimensions should act in harmony to achieve the state of holistic health. By GWI the main six dimensions of holistic wellness are physical, social, environmental, emotional, intellectual and spiritual (GWI, 2019). These six dimensions were taken as the basis for the concept of the new rehabilitation and well-being centre. Due to the development of society over the decades, several other dimensions have been added to original six dimensions, such as financial, occupational, aesthetic, medical, multicultural, digital, creative, etc. However, these six dimensions are considered the most natural in the development of personal well-being.

The rehabilitation and well-being centre forms a complete complex by intertwining rehabilitation services, post-disease and post-surgery care, sports medicine and health related well-being services. Although the centre mostly serves patients from the hospital, using the national Health Insurance Fund (Eesti Haigekassa) to provide the services, several paid services are offered as well, such as laser, heat and cold, salt and light therapy, various body and mind exercises, services for athletes, etc. The important keyword for these services is prevention, and the thoughtfully designed services based on the needs of target groups are offered in collaboration with different departments and specialists.

Customers fall into two main categories depending on the path they use to access the centre. The largest group of customers comes from the hospital to recover from severe conditions, to prolong the effect of the medical intervention, and to improve and recover bodily functions faster and better, as much as possible. The services provided to this first group are mainly determined by contracts with the Health Insurance Fund, whereas the rest of capacity of the centre can be used to bolster the hospital's budget via the second type of customer. As the capacity to provide services is greater than the need to serve patients referred by their doctors, the second category of customers is recognised as those who take care of their own health and well-being by preventive activities.

The phase of planning the services for the innovative rehabilitation and well-being centre started with benchmarking the medical and wellness spas and comparing the experience of neighbouring countries. The population, geographical, demographical, and psychographic characteristics, as well as the numbers of yearly and seasonal tourists, were considered in the planning process.

With input from specialist doctors and rehabilitation specialists, the first version of the purpose of the well-being centre was described as being "in collaboration with specialists and doctors to ease the health issues of patients who need rehabilitation services or post hospital care, and support the overall well-being of customers who value their health". Using the expertise of some of the hospital's own doctors, physiotherapists, midwives, traumatologists, heart surgeons, orthopaedists, etc. the list of services necessary for rehabilitation was created. To plan the facilities and layout of the centre, the preliminary categories of services were identified as:

- Medical treatments (requiring a doctor's referral),
- Activities in the pool,
- Activities in the gym assisted by a physiotherapist,
- Group workouts,
- Family school.

In the next phase of development, the service design principles and methods were implemented, the customer personas for the rehabilitation and well-being centre were decided and created, and customer journeys were mapped. For persona creation, different target groups were considered—hospitalised patients, employees, and guests. Along with experiencing services within the hospital premises, the customer journey map covered booking services, accessibility both by public and private transportation, parking, eating, safety and the journey inside the hospital (Fig. 10.7).

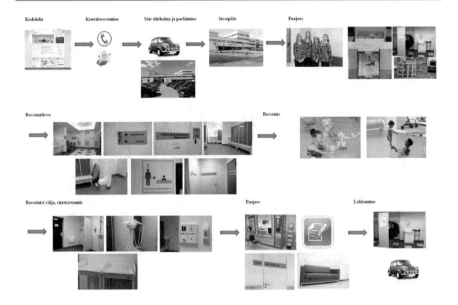

Fig. 10.7 An example of a customer journey map. *Source* Published with permission of Errit Kuldkepp

Based on the psychographic segmentation (by motivation, lifestyle, attitudes, health habits, and specific needs of customers—individuals with doctor's referrals, psychological indications, athletes, pregnant women and families, seniors, family doctors, etc.), various personas of Pärnu Hospital rehabilitation and well-being centre customers were created as follows:

- Future parent,
- Pregnant woman,
- Baby,
- Health-conscious person,
- Employee.

During the group work, every persona was analysed in depth by creating an empathy map for each one (Fig. 10.8). The aspects, such as what does the patient/customer say about the service when experiencing it, what is he/she thinking during the experience, what does he/she really do or how do they behave during the service, and what kind of feelings do they associate with the service, were interpreted on the empathy map. Additionally, problems and goals of the persona were identified during the workshop.

According to findings of previous service design phases, services were designed by considering people's needs. The list of services offered in the rehabilitation and well-being centre was formulated according to medical indications, experiences and

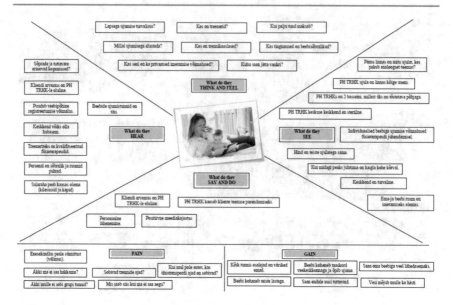

Fig. 10.8 An example of an empathy map. *Source* Published with permission of Errit Kuldkepp

expertise, facilities, created personas, and considering the findings of customer journeys and empathy maps.

QR-code that opens video of rehabilitation and well-being centre´s services. Source Author's own illustration (2021)

All the services of the centre, especially the activities, contribute to a person's well-being and are of a preventive nature.

In parallel with the design of the services, the interior design of the well-being centre was based on holistic wellness concept principles. The six main wellness dimensions—physical, emotional, spiritual, intellectual, environmental and social— were considered in the interior design. A colourful and clear house plan in the reception area, logical footpaths, a fresh non-medicinal smell, centrally selected

Fig. 10.9 Play-corner for children. *Source* Pärnu Hospital (2021)

background music, comfortable furniture that also meets special needs (e.g., after a hip replacement, a higher seat is needed), lights and decorations, wall colours, photos to attract attention, play-corners for children (Fig. 10.9), mind and skill games for adults, informative materials, interaction corners for social interaction, book shelves, blackboards to write down happy thoughts, a healthy menu in the café including vegetarian choices, and recycling opportunities—all of these aspects support a holistic view of well-being.

Physical well-being is supported and promoted via the health track which goes alongside the two main blocks of the health campus and the stairs of hospital main building through seven floors. Various specialists were involved in the design process of the track such as the architect, the marketing manager, nurses, physiotherapists and the administrative manager. For visual motivation, the butterfly-like symbol of Pärnu Hospital was transformed into butterfly motifs on the walls— different exercise stops along the health track are illustrated with butterfly images to encourage creativity and playful activities. The butterfly symbolises rebirth and stories of it activate intellectual wellness (Figs. 10.10 and 10.11).

Physical wellness has also been supported in a cafeteria, where healthy food is provided. Excellent service in centre's cafeteria supports emotional wellness, clean and safe environment contribute into environmental wellness. Intellectual wellness of visitors is supported with different exhibitions, that often present artwork of

Fig. 10.10 Health track in Pärnu Hospital. *Source* Author's own illustration (2021)

hospital employees, and spiritual with light-therapy combined with suitable music. Pärnu Hospital has taken a step further by using holistic wellness principles in providing conventional medical services, for example, by including family school classes at the Women and Children's Clinic to support families and prepare them for future parenthood. Prenatal classes help future parents to prepare for labour, birth and early parenthood. Some classes focus on labour and birth, while others on guidance through late pregnancy and life with a new-born baby. The topics covered in classes are versatile varying from the role of a support person, fathers' involvement, delivery, and relieving delivery pains to caring for the new-born, breastfeeding, and the postnatal period. Both parents are guided in how to maintain their own well-being as well as the baby's (Fig. 10.12).

The importance of including and involving future fathers into the whole expectance period has also been acknowledged. Family school provides essential knowledge and skills for future fathers about their family's development, during pregnancy, support during delivery, growing into a parent, sexuality and continuing everyday life after the child is born, and being a parent—all through the eyes of a man.

Fig. 10.11 Eye muscle exercise (part of the Health track) using the symbolic butterfly. *Source* Author's own illustration (2021)

Fig. 10.12 Family school in Pärnu Hospital. *Source* Pärnu Hospital (2021)

In addition to lectures, different various activities and classes are offered such as swimming in the pre and post delivery period, yoga and gymnastics for pregnant women, baby massage, infant/baby swimming classes, individual swimming and playschool for babies, and also, creativity classes for babies. The family school service is a complex and holistic well-being service covering all the dimensions of the holistic wellness concept. From the beginning of their pregnancy, future mothers are supported by special workouts and services for their physical well-being, connectedness to other persons experiencing a similar situation, getting to know midwives, doctors and trainers, and obtaining advice and information from specialists. They are encouraged to acquire new knowledge and share their experience with others. Beyond the need for medical support in monitoring the pregnancy and delivering the baby, the family school concept provides wider support for the major life changes that come with being a parent. This programme also provides social connectedness and through the programme the well-being centre is gaining new regular customers—infants, babies, mothers, fathers and even grandparents.

To market the services of the well-being centre, to raise awareness of the importance of preventive activities and personal contribution to health, and to encourage customers to actively participate in designing a healthy lifestyle, open house events are run twice a year at Pärnu Hospital. By introducing rehabilitation services, specialised doctors, family doctors and personnel to different customer groups, the variety of possibilities is presented. These events support the strategic perspective of increasing the awareness of a healthy lifestyle and support the understanding of everyone's role in shaping personal well-being throughout the arch of life. Moreover, these events are used as a channel for cross marketing the rehabilitation and well-being services.

At Pärnu Hospital, patient feedback is actively collected through annual customer satisfaction surveys. In addition to cross-hospital surveys, the patient experience is evaluated using feedback surveys from specific customer groups. All the complaints are analysed thoroughly using the methodology of grassroots analysis and, based on the results, necessary improvement projects are carried out.

To allow customers to give positive feedback to the hospital staff, special "Thank You" cards were designed. The card might be addressed to a specific hospital employee or to a whole department, giving the patient an opportunity to express their gratitude. This action can support the emotional and spiritual well-being of both the patient and the staff. To improve and to advertise its services, Pärnu Hospital has a practical collaboration with the University of Tartu Pärnu College, allowing international Wellness and Spa Service Design and Management Master's students evaluate its environment and services based on usage of wellness principles.

After the intensive development period and the superb opening, the rehabilitation and well-being centre was up and running, fulfilling the needs and expectations of its customers and patients. However, the knowhow of service design methodology and the mindset has gradually decreased in line with staff turnover in recent years. Therefore, the opening of the latest facility on the health campus in 2020, the

Ristiku Health Centre, brought with it a "new wave" of knowledge, service development ideas and motivation for action. Hospital staff participated in service design courses in the spring of 2020, from which a large number of new ideas emerged. The experience from developing the services for rehabilitation and well-being centre has shown how important it is to include employees to the design process.

The idea of co-creation has become more important and more meaningful than ever before. At the initiative of the hospital, a patients' council was established, and in cooperation with hospital expertise, the aim is to use the experience of patients in the development of hospital services, well-being support services and preventive activities. Service development has been in a stand-by mode for some time. Additionally, pandemic and related restrictions have had a strong impact on the attendance of the successfully operating rehabilitation and well-being centre. With the new hospital building completed, it is time for the hospital to renew its focus on innovative service development based on the principles of the holistic well-being concept that, are included in its operational plan. For better cooperation, new partner organisation has been established called patients' council. The patients' council is expected to bring a new vitality to this process and help to build the pillar of preventive well-being through the outputs from the rehabilitation and well-being centre. How to reach the target groups, what kind of communication is needed, what are the challenges inside the organisation and what attitudes should be shaped —these are the broader challenges the patients' council is facing and where the processes of co-creation need to be implemented.

10.6 Conclusions

Well-being and wellness will gain importance year by year and, as Eastern people have for thousands of years practiced holistic body-mind-spirit methods, the Western world is now taking steps to apply wellness dimensions into their everyday life and medical practices. Hospitals have always been mainly for people who wish to cure their illnesses, but for society to be sustainable in the long run, the aim of the medical system should be also to teach people about how they can prevent illness. Travis' wellness continuum has been around for decades, but the medical system has started paying attention to it only recently. Healthcare is slowly, yet consistently, moving in the direction that, in addition to treatment, increasing attention is paid to activities that support recovery and prevent diseases. More and more hospitals are providing supporting services for enhancing peoples' personal well-being throughout the entire life span. Taking care of personal well-being by following all the basic dimensions of the holistic wellness concept—physical, emotional, intellectual, spiritual, social and environmental—has become a fundamental part of a happy and healthy life.

Pärnu Hospital integrated the holistic wellness concept into the service design process almost ten years ago when they began the planning process for the rehabilitation and well-being centre. Using the collected experience from both the Pärnu Hospital and internationally, the principles of the holistic wellness concept were even more thoroughly considered in planning the most recent addition to the Pärnu health campus—the Ristiku Health Centre. The new health centre is continuing the journey of promoting holistic wellness principles to ensure the well-being of patients, customers and employees, and to provide the best service quality.

The experience of the Pärnu Hospital in implementing the principles of the holistic wellness concept, and in the use of service design thinking, principles and tools in the development of services and the entire hospital, will hopefully be a good support and inspiration for other hospitals as well (Fig. 10.13).

According to the case of the Pärnu Hospital and based on the literature, the following advice and recommendations can be given to the reader:

- Place the patient/customer and her or his needs and well-being first;
- Use the experience and wisdom of different the stakeholders (patients, their relatives, employees, customers, suppliers, network forces, etc.);
- Design services according to the customer's needs, general healthcare goals and holistic wellness principles;

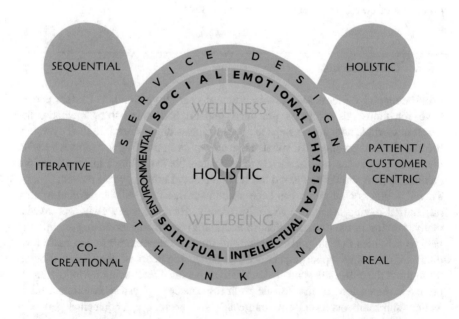

Fig. 10.13 Using the principles of the holistic wellness concept in designing and developing hospital services. *Source* Author's own illustration (2021), created based on GWI (2019) and Stickdorn et al. (2018)

- Keep in mind the service design thinking, principles, logic of the process and use suitable service design tools;
- Raise the awareness of holistic wellness among employees and involve them in the service design process;
- Be creative and playful;
- Educate members of community about healthy lifestyle and possibilities to increase personal wellness by offering related services, courses, etc.
- And remember, that as human beings, we all want to feel good and be healthy.

Combining wellness concept, service design logic and solving people's actual problems by applying the methodology of co-creation will, simultaneously, help to save resources and make the living environment better for everybody. This chapter has provided an overview of 20 years of development from a typical hospital into a holistic complex that will guide people through life helping to maximise their health, well-being and life satisfaction.

Acknowledgements The authors would like to thank Pärnu Hospital's Chief Physician Urmas Sule, Marketing and Communication Manager Kätlin Muru, Head of the Quality Management Department Teele Orgse, Customer Service Manager Lea Kalda, and former Marketing Manager for many years Errit Kuldkepp for providing valuable information and photos of the development of this unique well-being centre. Their enthusiastic attitude and will to contribute to the promotion of holistic well-being have had a great impact on health and well-being services offered in Estonia.

References

Boyd, H., McKernon, S., Mullin, B., & Old, A. (2012). Improving healthcare through the use of co-design. *New-Zealand Medical Journal, 125*(1357), 76–87. https://assets-global.website-files.com/5e332a62c703f653182faf47/5e332a62c703f6f7f92fde06_boyd.pdf. Accessed 1 Jun 2021.

Castro, E. M., Malfait, S., Regenmortel, T. V., Hecke, A. V., Sermeus, W., & Vanhaecht, K. (2018). Co-design for implementing patient participation in hospital services: A discussion paper. *Patient Education and Counseling, 101*(7), 1302–1305. PMID: 29602511 DOI: https://doi.org/10.1016/j.pec.2018.03.019.

Drew, C. (2019). Design council. The double diamond: 15 years on. https://www.designcouncil.org.uk/news-opinion/double-diamond-15-years. Accessed 31 May 2021.

Dunn, H. (1959). What high-level wellness means. *Canadian Journal of Public Health/Revue Canadienne de Santé Publique, 50*(11), 447–457. Canadian Public Health Association. DOI: https://doi.org/10.2307/41981469. https://www.jstor.org/stable/41981469.

Dunn, H. L. (1977). *High-level wellness*. Slack Publishing.

Estonian Development Fund. (2010). Tervishoiuteenused 2018: Eesti tervise- ja heaoluteenuste ekspordivõimalused (Health Services 2018: Export opportunities for Estonian health and welfare services). Accessed June 1, 2021, from http://www.arengufond.ee/upload/Editor/Publikatsioonid/Tervishoiuteenuste-eksport-2018.pdf.

Estonian Spa Association. (2012). Kuurortravi arengusuunad (Development trends of spa treatment). Kuurortravi arengukava 2013–2020 (Spa treatment development plan 2013–2020). Eesti terviseturismi klaster (Estonian Health Tourism Cluster, Ed.). Eesti Spaaliit (Estonian Spa Association, Ed.). http://healthrepublic.ee/wp-content/uploads/2013/09/KUURORTRAVI-ARENGUKAVA_2013_2020.Final_.pdf. Accessed 1 Jun 2021.

Ghiya, G. D. (2019). Promoting spiritual health and holistic wellness. *Journal of Health Management, 21*(2), 230–233. https://doi.org/10.1177/0972063419835104.

Glausier, G. (2018). The changing role of hospitals as healthcare evolves. https://scrubbing.in/the-changing-role-of-hospitals-as-healthcare-evolves/. Accessed 1 Jun 2021

Global Wellness Institute. (2019) Understanding wellness: Opportunities & Impacts of the wellness economy for regional development. Global Wellness Institute White Paper Series. Global Wellness Institute (Ed.). https://globalwellnessinstitute.org/industry-research/understanding-wellness-opportunities-impact-wellness-economy-for-regional-development/. Accessed 1 Jun 2021

Janamian, T., Crossland, L., & Wells, L. (2016). On the road to value co-creation in health care: The role of consumers in defining the destination, planning the journey and sharing the drive. *The Medical Journal of Australia, 204*(7), S12. https://doi.org/10.5694/mja16.00123.

Maher, L., Hayward, B., Hayward, P., & Dr, W. C. (2017). Increasing patient engagement in healthcare service design: A qualitative evaluation of a co-design programme in New Zealand. *Patient Experience Journal, 4*(1), 23–32. https://doi.org/10.35680/2372-0247.1149.

Palumbo, R. (2016). Contextualizing co-production of health care: A systematic literature review. *International Journal of Public Sector Management, 29*(1), 72–90. https://doi.org/10.1108/IJPSM-07-2015-0125.

Pärnu Hospital. (2019). Pärnu Haigla arengukava 2019–2023 (Pärnu Hospital Development Plan 2019–2023). Pärnu Hospital (Ed.). https://www.ph.ee/content/editor/files/SA%20P%C3%A4rnu%20Haigla%20arengukava.pdf. Accessed 1 Jun 2021

Pärnu Hospital. (2021). Family school. https://www.ph.ee/clinics_services/womens_and_childrens_clinic/family_school. Accessed 27 May 2021.

Pilzer, P. Z. (2001). The next trillion. Why the wellness industry will exceed the $1 trillion healthcare (sickness) industry in the next ten years. VideoPlus, Inc. Dallas. USA.

Prescott, S. L., Logan, A. C., & Katz, D. L. (2019). Preventive medicine for person, place, and planet: Revisiting the concept of high-level wellness in the planetary health paradigm. *International Journal of Environmental Research and Public Health, 16*(2), 238. https://doi.org/10.3390/ijerph16020238.

Riigi Teataja. (2021). Haiglavõrgu arengukava (Hospital network development plan). Riigi Teataja RT I 2003, 35, 223. https://www.riigiteataja.ee/akt/13353001. (https://www.riigiteataja.ee/en/). Accessed 1 Jun 2021.

Riigi Teataja. (2021). Tervishoiuteenuste korraldamise seadus (Health Care Services Organization Act 2001). RT I 2001, 50, 284. https://www.riigiteataja.ee/akt/110032011009. (https://www.riigiteataja.ee/en/eli/ee/Riigikogu/act/530042021002/consolide). Accessed 1 Jun 2021.

Russell-Bennett, R., Glavas, C., Josephine Previte, J., Härtel, C., & Smith, S. (2017). Designing a medicalized wellness service: Balancing hospitality and hospital features. *The Service Industries Journal, 37*(9–10), 657–680. https://doi.org/10.1080/02642069.2017.1354988

Stickdorn, M., & Schwarzenberger. K. (2016). Service design in Tourism. In H. Siller & A. Zehrer (Eds.), *Entrepreneurship und Tourismus* (pp. 261–275). Linde International. Wien. https://books.google.ee/books?hl=en&lr=&id=wNqOCwAAQBAJ. Accessed 1 Jun 2021.

Stickdorn, M., Hormess, M. E., Lawrence, A., & Schneider, J. (2018). *This is service design doing: Applying service design thinking in the real world.* O'Reilly. Sebastopol.

Subhedar, R., & Dave, P. (2016). Bombay hospital "Wellness Clinic": A Holistic concept in a Tertiary care multi specialty hospital for promoting "Global Wellness and Global Health" a scientific study on "The Holistic Physiotherapy Approach" In Rehabilitating Geriatric Community of Indore - India. *International Journal of Business and Management Invention, 5* (10), 22–31.

Sule, U. (nd). Pärnu Haigla—oluline nurgakivi Eesti tervisevõrgustikus (Pärnu Hospital—a cornerstone in the Estonian healthcare network). http://pol.parnumaa.ee/content/editor/files/Urmas%20Sule,%20P%C3%A4rnu%20haigla.pdf. Accessed 1 Jun 2021.

Travis, J., & Ryan, S. R. (2004). *The Wellness Workbook* (3rd ed). How to achieve enduring health and vitality. Celestial Arts, Berkeley. USA.

World Health Organization. (n. d.). Constitution. World Health Organization (WHO, Ed.). https://www.who.int/about/who-we-are/constitution. Accessed 27 May 2021.

Heli Tooman is an Associate Professor of Tourism Management at the University of Tartu, Pärnu College. She defended her doctoral thesis "Service society, service culture and conceptual starting points for customer service education" at the Tallinn Pedagogical University in 2003. Since 1997, she has worked as a lecturer. Her fields of study, research and guidance cover the themes of tourism and service economy, service philosophy, service culture, hospitality, quality management and health and wellness. She has written numerous articles and textbooks, is a member of the editorial board of several scientific and professional journals, participated in the activities of international organisations and conferences and research and development projects as an expert. She is a member of the Patients' Council of Pärnu Hospital.

Marit Piirman is a lecturer in Service Design and Destination Marketing in the University of Tartu, Pärnu College. Her main interest is service design, sustainable development, and tourism marketing. Her primary field of research has been tourism humour and she has previously been published in European Journal of Humour Research. She has been involved in several projects, conducted research, published chapters in handbooks and developed study programmes.

Margrit Kärp's field of expertise is mainly in spa management and wellness. With MBA in Service design and management and almost 15 years of experience as a spa manager she has been teaching wellness history and philosophy, wellness spa quality management and spa processes for 2 years in University of Tartu Pärnu College.

Design Thinking as Catalyst for a Hospital Operation Centre

11

Christophe Vetterli and Raphael Roth

Abstract

A mission control gathers all relevant decision makers in one room and provides them with real time data to anticipate the next few steps of the mission. This vision in healthcare helped to create a similar mission control or so-called Operations Centre at a major Swiss Hospital in Spring 2020 to assure stability in daily crisis management and beyond. Design thinking as the approach to develop a hospital mission control assured a tremendous development time of only 7 days to go live with a first version. Design thinking helped additionally to improve the mission control version day by day incorporating more and more needs of the users of this system. The elements that were embedded were: (1) a room with data-cockpits and relevant roles within, (2) a standardized data structure, (3) a standardized information flow, (4) centralized communication structures. Besides having fastened the problem-solving time, so that 80% of the problems were raised and solved within 90 min across all 5 hospital sites, this example also shows how design thinking helped to foster digitalization in healthcare in order to improve treatment quality and patient experience as well as how it fostered the creation of a completely new decision system to improve hospital leadership overall.

C. Vetterli (✉) · R. Roth
Vetterli Roth & Partners AG, Poststrasse 30, 6300 Zug, Switzerland
e-mail: christophe.vetterli@vetterlirothpartners.com

R. Roth
e-mail: raphael.roth@vetterlirothpartners.com

© The Author(s), under exclusive license to Springer Nature Switzerland AG 2022
M. Pfannstiel et al. (eds.), *Service Design Practices for Healthcare Innovation*,
https://doi.org/10.1007/978-3-030-87273-1_11

11.1   Introduction

What was the common approach of the NASA to fly Neil Armstrong and his two colleagues successfully to the moon and back in the late 60's and the Dragon Mission in Spring 2020? A mission control gathers all relevant decision makers in one room and provides them real-time data to anticipate the next few steps of the mission. This vision in healthcare helped to create a similar mission control or so-called Operations Centre at a major Swiss Hospital in Spring 2020 to assure stability in daily crisis management and beyond. During the Covid-19 pandemic, transparency and stability were key–however, the following explanations are less about the Covid-19 crisis itself but about creating sustainable agility in a hospital environment to address future challenges.

Many significant steps in technology developments could be achieved from the Apollo missions to Space X's Dragon Mission. However, the needs of having standardized procedures to initiate the right countermeasures, availability of (real-time) data to know what is fact and a passionate team which strives for excellence remain. Needs as we know, are lasting way longer than solutions. Hence, to know needs of stakeholders and patients/customers is helpful, not only for a short time view, rather more for a long-term perspective.

11.2   The Operations Centre

The hospital group in Switzerland which is used as an example was distributed over 5 different locations, each with their own procedures, teams and culture. In times of Covid-19 uncertainty in March 2020, this was toxic concerning transparency and quick (harmonized) reaction to daily occurring problems. Effective leadership was nearly impossible. Therefore, the leadership team, especially the military trained Chief Medical Officer, decided to initiate a centralized operations centre. They wanted to know the current status of capacity and demand in real time. Capacity discussion were about staff, in all their diversity, material, beds and respiratory machines. Demand was characterized by high uncertainty of how many patients in which condition were demanding care. Political authorities and the statisticians were continuously 1–2 days behind with their information. The hospital group needed real-time matching of the capacity and demand situations. The group started to embed different elements to enable the operations centre to come alive:

(1) The room. One room where the right constellation of staff was physically present to gather the right information. Each staff gathered the information of their own groups into the room to provide, e.g. logistic information, staffing planning status and demanded competencies, and so on.

(2) Standardized huddle structure. 35 different wards had to apply a harmonized so-called huddle structure to generate a very specific amount of data at specific times throughout the day. The huddle is gathering of interdisciplinary and

interprofessional staff members which bring together the right information at the right time.

(3) Data structure. The data structure was iteratively developed to provide the transparency needed to take the right action.

(4) Iterative evolution culture. The iterative approach which was part of the development provided an agility towards daily changing information and challenges.

11.3 The Development

The complete development was based on two main approaches which was combined to assure impact. First design thinking, as prototyping-based innovation approach that helped on very quickly provide first solutions and enter a continuous developing mode which helped to stay agile in the daily changing challenges. Second lean process principles that provided hints on how effective processes in healthcare could be defined and minimize waste, e.g. in gathering the right information or to structure interdisciplinary and interprofessional meetings to solve problems.

Both approaches already helped several hospitals in their independency to achieve impacts of more patient-centric processes or less waste in the value creation of care. However, the combination of both helped to leverage the effect even more. Even when lean processes in healthcare focus on eliminating waste in processes to maximize value creation towards patient flow (based on efficient organizational flows) there is no instruction on HOW to provoke new processes. Hints what are design principles are provided, but the real provoking of innovation is being provided by design thinking with its prototyping-based procedure. On the other way design thinking does not give hints on content—it is focusing on combining the right set of people, tools, mindset to provoke innovation. Therefore, combining lean principles with design thinking is very impactful in hospital environments and beyond.

11.4 Design Thinking as Prototyping Platform

Design thinking serves as prototyping-based innovation approach which integrates different elements to provoke human-centric innovation. One key element is the focus on needs as aspect which serves also long term as orientation of solution development. Another key element is the interdisciplinarity in design teams which is important to provide different perspectives on the same problem to tackle. Furthermore, the tangible approach to solution development which can be summarized as prototyping. The prototyping is one of the key steps in the iterative design cycle as shown in the next illustration (see Fig. 11.1):

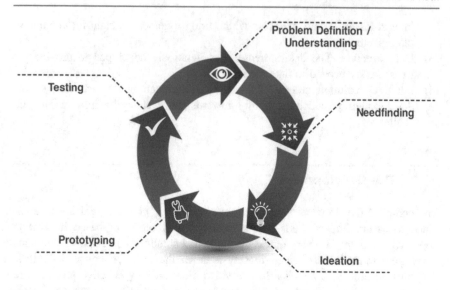

Fig. 11.1 The design thinking cycle. *Source* based on Stanford University (2021)

The problem definition, the identification of needs, the ideation process searching for many ideas, building tangible prototypes as previews of the solution as well as testing those are orientation points, which should be triggered within the design teams activity regularly. Finally, it is important to have an iterative approach and improve the design and the understandability of the problem, respectively, the solution iteration by iteration. The goal is to start with low-resolution prototypes and raise the resolution to high-resolution prototypes which provide a detailed preview of the future experience iteration by iteration.

Design thinking therefore provides a prototyping-based innovation platform with key elements together provoking sustainable innovations.

11.5   Lean Design Principles as Solution Hints

Lean design principles such as flow, standards and visual management have proven to provide effective environments for healthcare institutions. Especially, expert organizations benefit from the lean mindset of filtering the processes and environment for potential waste. The lean healthcare approach hence offers hints to good solutions which help expert organization to provide a more effective and efficient care based on team-medicine approaches. The hints can be derived from established lean design principles such as interdisciplinary daily huddling, unidirectionality of patient flow, immediate settlement, e.g. in terms of documentation, high competency at the front of processes to assure more efficient processes overall, visual management, etc.

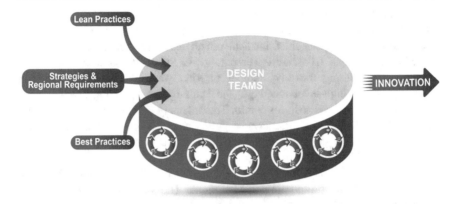

Fig. 11.2 The combination of design thinking and lean healthcare practices. *Source* Vetterli Roth & Partners AG (2021a)

The following illustration (see Fig. 11.2) shows the interdependency of design thinking and lean principles. Additionally, it is possible to integrate regional requirements such as specific regulatory specifications or strategic paths of the organization in such a setting. International best practices help to start into the prototyping activities as first "prototype" which the design team starts to adapt, test and redesign based on their specific experiences and ambition.

11.6   The Creation of an Operations Centre

Those key elements were applied to the hospital group of Switzerland starting on the very first day. The best practice of the already existing operations centres, such as the Humber River Command Centre in Toronto, helped to provide a first prototype to the design team on the ground. The design team was a team of leaders such as chief medical officer, chief nursing officer, head of logistics, IT, law, human resources and communication.

11.6.1   First Prototyping Phase

The first phase was led by the question: Which questions would you like to have answered after having designed a centralized operations centre that can help plan capacity, anticipate, and solve problems and act ahead of development and not only react? The first data points were defined as well as the necessity to gather information in a standardized way and bringing it to one room, one place where the responsible team can take action. Additionally, the team committed to a standard calendar to gather the relevant key players to specific times throughout the day. In a first version at 8:30 am in the morning, the core team consisting of the head of the emergency department, the head of infectiology, the head of nursing, the head of internal medicine and the chief medical officer analysed the gathered data and decided on next steps. To assure the preparation of the night and answer questions which emerged during the day, another meeting was defined for 3:30 pm. In addition to those high-level meetings, the team of the operations centre came together every 3 h to check-in for 5 min. This intensity of check-ins was based on needs identified in the very first days of prototyping the organization of an operations centre. After 7 days, the first operations centre as shown in the following figure (see Fig. 11.3) went live.

During the initial 7 days, the design team identified different targets which were directly addressed by prototyping the solutions. The solutions addressed needs within the current situation of different stakeholders that have been identified in parallel to prototyping and testing of the new operations centre elements. The following illustration (see Fig. 11.4) shows the continuous identification of new developing areas which is interlocked with the embedment of the new solutions.

The teams started with low-resolution prototyping; e.g. the first visualizations of data tables were excel- and powerpoint-based (see Fig. 11.5). Mainly, it was about patients, beds, staff and material. And the different detail information evolved along the development of the operations centre over the coming weeks.

The IT team started to develop more sophisticated, automatized processes and front-ends with higher certainty than the data gathered. The digitalization dynamism was fostered during that phase, and IT has reached another level of connected data from the core processes. This boost in IT development and data management helped the hospital group to reach another level of digitalization than before Covid-19.

Fig. 11.3 The operations centre room. *Source* Vetterli (2020a)

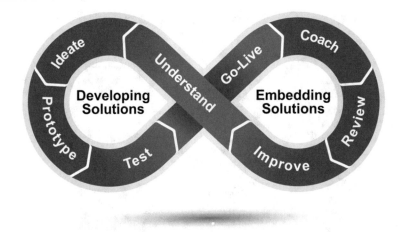

Fig. 11.4 Continuous development and embedment of solutions. *Source* Vetterli Roth & Partners (2021b)

🛏 Patients		⤢ Lits	Total		
34 Cas COVID-19[1]	**13** Cas suspects[2]	# de lits libres[10]	**140**	**95**	**45**
7 COVID-19 SI (total)[3]	**4** Décédés (total)[5]	# de lits SI libres avec resp.[11]	**20**	**20**	**0**
6 de celui-ci. intubé[4]	**0** Décédés aujourd'hui[6]				

⚙ Matériel	Quantité[12]	Capacité pour x jour[13]
Masques FFP2	2'400	9
Blouses de Protection	15'588	22
Ecouvillons	1728	8-34j
Désinfectants	1'050 l	18 jours
Oxygène	4'212 l O2 liquide	9.5 jours

👥 Personnel

22 14 infirmiers 5 médecins 3 ASSC	**15** 15 soins 7 Médecins	**56** 28 Méd. Ass. 28 CDC
Malade COVID-19[7]	Absente (total)[8]	Disponible (médecins)[9]

Fig. 11.5 First prototype of the operations centre dashboard view. *Source* Vetterli (2020b)

The constellation of people at the operations centre was an issue as well and iteratively evolved throughout the first days. The room was also called the place where the operations centre had its brain and finally consisted of the roles showed in the following illustration (see Fig. 11.6):

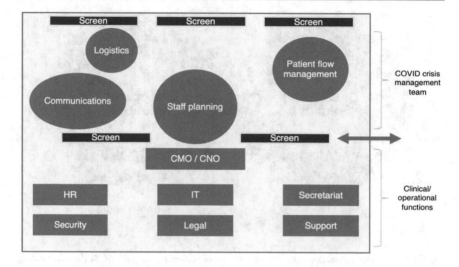

Fig. 11.6 Roles within the operations centre room. *Source* Vetterli (2020c)

The two groups (1) covid-crisis management team and (2) clinical operations function seamless cooperated and worked out countermeasures to problems occurring day by day.

11.6.2 Second Prototyping Phase and Partly Back to Old

The second phase was initiated after about 2 months of having professionalized the operations centre and its processes around the room itself, the huddle of the wards, the data management and the continuous improvement. The ambition was then defined by integrating other less Covid-19 focused operation processes into the operations centre such as e.g. elective interventions or the overall capacity management of wards. The pressure in the first phase was huge and helped to enable decisions which have not been possible in 10 years of hospital development. Some of the leadership team were highly motivated to keep this centralized transparency and quick decision process also for the post-covid-era. However, when the pressure of the Covid-19 was less present old dynamism around single exports started to gain power again. It became very clear that not every winning aspect of the embedded capacity management would survive into the new normal mode. So many of small changes were transferred to a second generation of this operations centre. However, the expert organization with some silo-characteristics was reactivated after the first serious phase of the pandemic era. What survived were the huddles for all the wards, structured gathering of data and the ambition to provide capacity transparency for centralized decisions through key players. This was in sum already a huge evolutionary boost in the development of the organization. One very specific effect summarized the impact of this evolution: Whereas before the crisis to create transparency of capacity many dozens of phone calls were necessary this was available and accepted at one click.

11.7 Conclusion

As summary the following benefits were mentioned from the key players who were involved from the very first moment to the transfer into the new normal situation:

(1) The iterative prototyping-based design sprints based on design thinking helped to be agile throughout the very ambiguous environment.
(2) The involvement of key staff in prototyping sprints was crucial to assure their commitment to the next version of the prototype (every development stage of the operations centre was seen as prototype).
(3) The provided design hints from similar centralized decision processes helped the design team to gain trust in the development of the own solutions.
(4) The external moderated development helped to keep distance in political difficult decisions.

This case focused on the application of design thinking and lean healthcare in a pandemic-driven environment. However, the effect and the approach demonstrate a proven way to start with capacity management, also outside of the Covid-19 environment. The Dragon Mission in 2020 and the Apollo 11 mission in the 60 s as well as many modern healthcare organizations use the operations centre as a hub of decisions and capacity management processes. However, the way to approach the different processes in expert organizations such as hospitals and clinics is still highly ambiguous. The need of having transparency in capacity and demand is omnipresent. Therefore, an agile approach is needed which incorporates the different experts as part of the development process. Many organizations in healthcare are being blocked by the complexity of their problems. Design thinking offers ways to address the complexity without being paralysed by it. The Just-do-it claim with the prototyping element helped many healthcare environments to continuously drive their development and stay agile for the current healthcare challenges. The transformation is on.

References

Stanford University (2021). *The design thinking cycle*. Retrieved, June 26, 2021, from https://web.stanford.edu/group/me310/me310_2018/.
Vetterli, C. (2020a). *The operations centre room*. Vetterli Roth & Partners (Eds.).
Vetterli, C. (2020b). *First prototype of the operations centre dashboard view*. Vetterli Roth & Partners (Eds.).
Vetterli, C. (2020c). *Roles within the operations centre room*. Vetterli Roth & Partners (Eds.).

Vetterli Roth & Partners (2021a). *Combination of design thinking and lean healthcare*. Vetterli Roth & Partners (Eds.).

Vetterli Roth & Partners (2021b). *Continuous development and embedment of solutions*. Vetterli Roth & Partners (Eds.).

Dr. Christophe Vetterli is fostering the embedment of Design Thinking into healthcare. He graduated from the University of St. Gallen with a PhD on Embedding Design Thinking and has published numerous scientific publications. During his PhD he worked closely at the intersection of science and business and collaborated with business partners as well as scientific partners from Stanford University. He was a year-long partner in a healthcare consulting firm before he co-founded his own consultancy company. Vetterli Roth & Partners Ltd. focuses on the transformation of healthcare, mainly hospitals and clinics, towards patient's and customer's needs. Thereby Vetterli enables the healthcare stakeholders to put patients & relatives at the core of their strategic & innovation work. The prototyping-based development of processes and solutions leads to patient & client centric solutions. He is co-responsible for a master's degree on healthcare real estate management and gives lectures at different international leading universities.

Raphael Roth is an international expert in lean healthcare and has a bachelor's degree in history and philosophy as well as a Master's degree in international Conflict Studies from the Kings College, London. Raphael has published several publications around applying the lean philosophy into healthcare environment and has transformed many core processes within hospitals into more patient-centric processes. He has co-founded his own consultancy firm with Dr. Christophe Vetterli. Vetterli Roth & Partners Ltd. focuses on the transformation of healthcare, mainly hospitals and clinics, towards patient's and customer's needs.

Mapping the Service Process to Enhance Healthcare Cost-Effectiveness: Findings from the Time-Driven Activity-Based Costing Application on Orthopaedic Surgery

12

Irene Schettini, Gabriele Palozzi, and Antonio Chirico

Abstract

The main goal for any healthcare delivery system is to improve the value delivered to patients. Particularly, to properly manage value, both outcomes and costs must be measured at the patient level; this requires the engagement of physicians, clinical teams, administrative staff and finance professionals in designing the process maps and estimating the costs involved in treating patients over the care cycle. Moreover, many scholars stated that Activity-Based Costing (ABC) strategies represent valid support in the decision-making process on healthcare management, by fostering corrective actions in the case of an inefficient process or low-quality outcomes. Accordingly, the goal of this work is to demonstrate how mapping processes, using the Time-Driven ABC approach, is a key for the improvement of the value created in health care, both in terms of better outcomes and cost reduction. To achieve this goal, a multi-centre experimental case study has been run on the field of orthopaedic surgery (hip and knee arthroplasty). The case study was designed on empirical observation, data collection and face-to-face interviews within three Italian Hospital Organizations. Findings confirm that mapping the surgery process allows clinical management to understand: (i) the whole clinical pathway (from pre to post patient's surgical path) and the associated resource consumption; (ii) which

I. Schettini (✉) · G. Palozzi · A. Chirico
Department of Management and Law, University Tor Vergata, Via Columbia, 2, 00133 Rome, Italy
e-mail: schettini@economia.uniroma2.it

G. Palozzi
e-mail: palozzi@economia.uniroma2.it

A. Chirico
e-mail: chirico@economia.uniroma2.it

clinical activities require more resources and time; and (iii) how phases of the surgery process could be improved in order to obtain best practice outcomes according to the NHS' necessity to lower costs and increase service quality.

12.1   Introduction

The aim of healthcare delivery in the Value Based Healthcare era is to provide high value to patients. This purpose is what matters to patients and bonds the interests of all system players; patients, payers and providers will all prosper as the healthcare system's economic sustainability improves. In this perspective, the system for performance improvement in health care should be defined by value creation and the best way to drive system change is through rigorous, disciplined assessment and enhancement of value (Porter, 2008). As a result, the healthcare delivery process has changed from quantity-based to value-based efficiency.

Within this system, the use of resources aimed at gathering valuable information for the overall activities performed by healthcare organizations are even more necessary. To this end, managerial accounting tools can be considered useful for information collection in the healthcare context. Several authors have defined Time-Driven Activity-Based Costing (TDABC) as a managerial tool (Kaplan & Porter, 2011) that fosters cooperation between clinicians and clerical staff by mapping the entire value creation process (Baratti et al., 2010; Demeere et al., 2009; Dombrée et al., 2014). Furthermore, because of the higher process standardization, TDABC is especially suitable for the surgical field (Akhavan et al., 2016). TDABC will provide more and better knowledge about timing, procedures and costs. According to (Moffitt & Vasarhelyi, 2013), accounting models should evolve and adapt to focus more on data quality, atomicity and data linkages; as a result, information gathering should shift from a periodic collection of data to a real-time flow.

This advancement in health care would be extremely beneficial for clinical managers (both physicians and administrative staff) in order to rapidly understand the effectiveness of a treatment and its resource consumption.

In the perspective of reorganizing the healthcare delivery process to achieve high value for the patient, through its process, TDABC mapping could generate information about which steps add the highest value and whether waste can be reduced or if resources are being under-utilized. TDABC application in orthopaedic surgery is particularly appropriate, as demonstrated by several authors (DiGioia et al. 2016; Akhavan et al., 2016; Pathak et al., 2019; Blaschke et al., 2020).

The aim of this study is to determine how knowledge obtained from the application of TDABC to the delivery process of two orthopaedic surgeries in separate hospitals can be used to enhance the delivery process. The orthopaedic surgical area was chosen because of its streamlined procedure and significant effect on healthcare system costs. The preference of total hip and knee arthroplasty (THA and TKA) is primarily due to the high frequency and demand for the two surgical procedures (Ministero della Salute, 2019).

Following this introduction, the paper has the following outline: the second section includes the key theoretical background; the third one reports on the method of the study, whilst the fourth section presents the research results. Section five discusses the results obtained and offers some implications on the role of accounting tools in the healthcare delivery process. The concluding section includes final remarks on the work.

12.2 Background

The healthcare sector has undergone significant improvements in the way it provides health care since the turn of the century. For example, rising healthcare costs, technological advances, cultural shifts and increased access to health information through the internet and digital media. These have led health care to a patient-centred approach to health and well-being (Francis, 2010; Frow et al., 2016), which involves new ways to lure patients to access services.

The patient-centred approach to care is a strategy of delivering care that aims to improve the quality of interactions between providers and customer institutions by putting consumers (and their families) at the centre of decisions that impact their well-being. This methodology entails patient involvement and attracting patients to a specific hospital.

Concerning patients' engagement, healthcare providers no longer regard patients solely as patients; they are increasingly regarded as healthcare customers (Levine, 2015). Furthermore, healthcare users are no longer passive recipients of care; rather, they are active participants in the design of their healthcare service experiences (Danaher & Gallan, 2016). In particular, in order to meet and surpass patients' desires and needs in this dynamic healthcare environment with patient consumerism, healthcare providers must consider what patients and families experience in their facilities, how they view healthcare service quality and what influences those expectations (Lee, 2011).

The healthcare industry has acknowledged the significance of servicescape (the organization's physical environment) in defining the service experience of its patients and families. The principle of patient-centred care is also closely related to the concept of service design; creating service encounters that are meaningful, functional and attractive from the client's point of view (Moritz, 2005). Healthcare providers have begun to incorporate critical techniques used in the guest services industry as they continue to emphasize the value of patient-centred care and work to increase the quality of that care (Lee, 2011).

As a consequence, in terms of attracting patients to the hospital, value creation for patients plays a critical role and is also a key for service design.

Porter (2010) defines value in health care as outcome over expense for a particular condition; an equation in which the patient outcomes obtained serve as the numerator and treatment costs serve as the denominator. As a result, in order to be more efficient, it is critical to maximize the quality of the process of healthcare delivery, whilst minimizing the cost expense for them.

Fundamental re-thinking (Clack & Ellison, 2019) of healthcare delivery is needed to increase value development. To provide a full cycle of treatment for a given health condition, care pathways must be reorganized around the patient's medical condition, which necessitates the formation of a dedicated multidisciplinary team that forms a common organizational unit (Porter, 2009).

Rehabilitative care, patient education and collaboration between a physician team leader and a care manager, who monitors each patient's care process and provides outcomes and cost indicators, are also part of the process improvement. Within the value-based healthcare system, healthcare costs are defined as the overall cost of patient care and are determined by the actual usage of resources involved in a patient's care process (personnel, facilities, supplies) (Porter, 2008). Accordingly, the study of the healthcare delivery process is the starting point to improve its process and cost efficiency. The Time-Driven Activity-Based Costing approach, a seven-step method that can be used to estimate the process and the cost of treatment for an individual patient treated along a care continuum for a specific illness, can perfectly respond to this information requirement (Kaplan & Porter, 2011). In this approach, clinical and nonclinical staff contribute to the creation of process maps that detail all of the activities required for a particular service or procedure. Based on surveys or direct observation, the TDABC team estimates the practical capacity (that is, the actual productive time) of each capacity-supplying resource (employee and equipment) and the average time required for each resource operation. It is a "bottom-up" approach that, through process mapping and time equations, captures the true complexity of activities at the patient level, whilst also accounting for the numerous care pathways amongst heterogeneous populations (Pathak et al., 2019). TDABC process maps, according to (Blaschke et al., 2020), provide the visibility needed to reveal high cost drivers, non-value-added measures and unused resource capability, which can then inform decision makers on how to maximize value through the care cycle. One of the model's main strengths is its ability to identify areas of variation or inefficiency in the care pathway by process mapping. The granular calculation of each process phase can then be used to advise strategic resource reallocation and care pathway restructuring to maximize value (Blaschke et al., 2020).

This technique has been used by many scholars in a variety of healthcare settings. (Demeere et al., 2009), for instance, employ the TDABC in an outpatient environment. This experience has enabled the medical directors to recognize the time required to carry out specific activities and analyze them. In particular, this study showed that the times for categorizing patients were twice as high in the Gastroenterology and Urology departments than in the other departments. At this point, managers, with the help of the various subjects involved, analyzed the methods of carrying out these activities and found that inefficiency was represented, in this case, by an incorrect distribution of roles and by a rotation of staff.

In the work of (Laviana et al., 2016), this methodology was used, instead, in order to determine the short- and long-term costs of localized prostate cancer. With the support of the TDABC, the delivery process was analyzed and the areas of inefficiency were identified in order to eliminate waste.

Concerning the surgery field, (Au & Rudmik, 2013) and (Akhavan et al., 2016) used the TDABC, respectively, for the cost of endoscopic breast surgery and for the calculation of the cost of arthroplasty surgery. In particular, (Akhavan et al., 2016) defined the entire process of patients undergoing THA and TKA from admission to the operating room to their transfer to the post care unit, distinguishing all the actors involved and time required. This allowed the authors to calculate and compare the cost information from traditional cost accounting with those obtained from the application of the TDABC, noting more accurate information from the use of the activity-based methodology.

All these authors also agree that the Activity-Based methodology is able not only to provide more information, but also to ensure greater detail and greater punctuality of the same, representing valid support to the decision-making process. Furthermore, the application of this methodology reduces the percentage of unspecified allocated overhead costs and, through process mapping, it is possible to effectively manage the entire process, resorting to corrective actions when necessary (Dombrée et al., 2014). In this way, the analysis of the healthcare delivery process is complete and correct as the resources used and the activities carried out are described with precision (Baratti et al., 2010). In addition, the information obtained and the ways in which it is detected, increases transparency in the management of companies and allows, as evidenced by the study by (Demeere et al., 2009), an internal analysis aimed at determining a reference benchmark.

To summarize, the following Fig. 12.1 reports a process map example of all pre-admission steps for a surgical patient within the hospital, according to his/her medical condition and/or situation.

The key to Fig. 12.1 and general roles for designing process maps:

– Rounded rectangles represent the start or the end of the process;
– Rectangles represent the activity performed;
– Arrows show the order of the activities within the process;
– The rhombus is the symbol for "decision turning-points". It represents where a decision is needed.

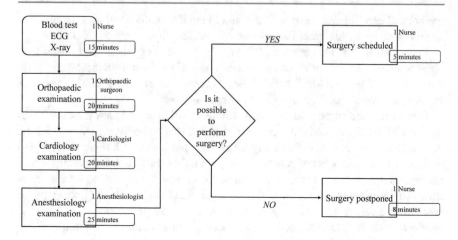

Fig. 12.1 Pre admission screening for patient undergoing elective surgery. *Source* Authors' illustration inspired by DiGioia et al. (2016), Akhavan et al. (2016), Pathak et al. (2019)

12.3 Method

A multi-centre case study (Yin, 2017) has been performed. Built as an experimental case (Scapens, 1990) applied to the service management field, this accounting inquiry has regarded the observation of a surgical team providing THA and TKA in three different hospitals.

Different scenarios of orthopaedic surgery in Italy have been analyzed. In particular, the following have been considered:

- A public hospital
- A university public hospital
- A private hospital

The hospitals are located in Italy, in two different Regions (Abruzzi and Latium).

Ninety procedures amongst the hospitals have been observed in order to map activities and resources involved in the surgeries analyzed. Table 12.1 below reports the detail about the procedures as per each organization participating in the case study.

Table 12.1 Number of observations. *Source* Authors' elaboration (2021)

	THA	TKA
Public hospital	15	15
University public hospital	15	15
Private hospital	15	15
Total number of observations	90	

Each surgery procedure observed corresponds to a patient eligible for THA or TKA. Only patients undergoing planned hip and knee replacement who did not have major comorbidities were included in the study. Consequently, all necessary interventions following traumatic events or in patients whose condition was particularly complex were excluded.

By using the Time-Driven Activity-Based Costing approach (Kaplan & Porter, 2011), built on seven steps of application (Keel et al., 2017), a process map of the whole healthcare services provided in a THA and TKA (from the patient's admission to his/her discharge) has been obtained.

The main activities and time spent on them during the delivery process, as well as the subjects involved, were identified using questionnaires collected through interviews and submitted to health professionals.

Process maps have been built including all the activities carried out and all the consumable goods needed in each phase of the care process.

The physicians', nurses' and technical staff's time spent on the specific procedures has been calculated. Time spent on each activity has been described by sample statistics.

The process maps have been reviewed by the main investigator (Klein et al., 2006) with key experts belonging to the three organizations included in the case study.

12.4 Results

The sequential process map related to THA is shown in Fig. 12.2, and the one related to TKA is shown in Fig. 12.3.

The diagram shows a process map outline of the arthroplasty operating day including anaesthesia preparation, surgical preparation and surgery. The large boxes represent activities with arrows indicating sequence. The colours correspond to different hospitals (see legend) with personnel ID in the upper smaller boxes (see legend). The numbers in the smaller boxes correspond to minutes used per activity.

The diagram shows a process map outline of the arthroplasty operating day including anaesthesia preparation, surgical preparation and surgery. The large boxes represent activities with arrows indicating sequence. The colours correspond to different hospitals (see legend) with personnel ID in the upper smaller boxes (see legend). The numbers in the smaller boxes correspond to minutes used per activity.

Except for the university hospital, every organization analyzed shows the same structure of patient pathway for THA and TKA. Except for the university hospital, where local anesthesia in the PACU is administered only for patients undergoing TKA, the main flows for the two surgical procedures observed are the same.

For both procedures, indeed, the activities regarding the operating room are equal in all the hospitals analyzed. They diverge only for time requirement and personnel involved.

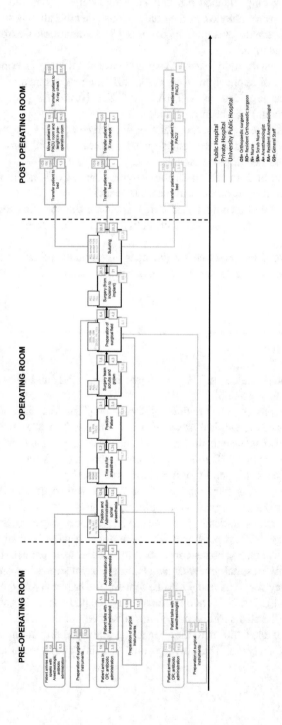

Fig. 12.2 Process map of total hip arthroplasty. OR = operating room; PACU = post anesthesia care unit. *Source* Author's own illustration (2021)

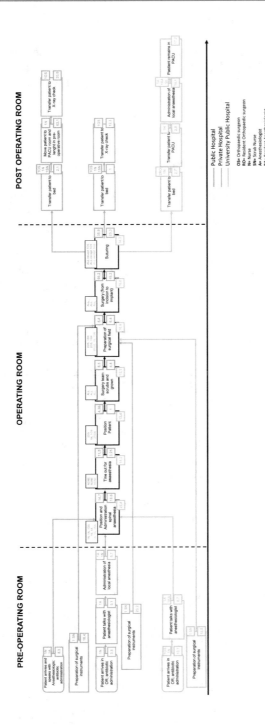

Fig. 12.3 Process map of total knee arthroplasty. OR = operating room; PACU = post anaesthesia care unit. *Source* Author's own illustration (2021)

Table 12.2 lists all the activities and the time required for them in every structure.

As we can note from the table, the main differences in times between the three hospitals, both in THA and TKA, are related to both the pre and post operating room activities. These differences are mainly concerned with the following key points of the surgical services:

Table 12.2 Mean time (minutes) required for all the activities. *Source* Authors' elaboration (2021)

Activity	Public hospital		Private hospital		Public university hospital	
	THA	TKA	THA	TKA	THA	TKA
Patient arrives in room Administer antibiotic	$\mu = 8,5$ $\sigma = 3,9$	$\mu = 8,3$ $\sigma = 3,8$	$\mu = 3,5$ $\sigma = 0,7$	$\mu = 3,8$ $\sigma = 0,8$	$\mu = 11,4$ $\sigma = 2,7$	$\mu = 10,7$ $\sigma = 2,4$
Patient speaks with anaesthesiologist			$\mu = 4,7$ $\sigma = 0,9$	$\mu = 5,1$ $\sigma = 1,0$	$\mu = 8,2$ $\sigma = 1,6$	$\mu = 8,7$ $\sigma = 1,1$
Administer local anaesthesia	NP	NP	$\mu = 4,8$ $\sigma = 0,8$	$\mu = 6,7$ $\sigma = 1,1$	NP	$\mu = 15,1$ $\sigma = 1,4$
Preparation of surgical instruments*	$\mu = 15,3$ $\sigma = 5,3$	$\mu = 16,4$ $\sigma = 5,7$	$\mu = 12,5$ $\sigma = 1,8$	$\mu = 23,2$ $\sigma = 3,3$	$\mu = 17,2$ $\sigma = 1,3$	$\mu = 18,5$ $\sigma = 1,2$
Position for spinal or general anaesthesia and administer anaesthesia	$\mu = 12,6$ $\sigma = 6,8$	$\mu = 14,7$ $\sigma = 8,0$	$\mu = 12,6$ $\sigma = 2,9$	$\mu = 18,6$ $\sigma = 4,3$	$\mu = 19,1$ $\sigma = 3,3$	$\mu = 22,4$ $\sigma = 3,05$
Time out for anaesthesia	$\mu = 8,3$ $\sigma = 3,4$	$\mu = 11,5$ $\sigma = 4,8$	$\mu = 1,25$ $\sigma = 0,5$	$\mu = 3,25$ $\sigma = 1,3$	$\mu = 14,7$ $\sigma = 0,4$	$\mu = 14,2$ $\sigma = 0,9$
Position patient	$\mu = 2,1$ $\sigma = 1,3$	$\mu = 4,36$ $\sigma = 2,9$	$\mu = 3,9$ $\sigma = 0,6$	$\mu = 1$ $\sigma = 0,1$	$\mu = 12,6$ $\sigma = 2,8$	$\mu = 13,4$ $\sigma = 1,4$
Surgery team scrubs and gowns	$\mu = 7,5$ $\sigma = 1,7$	$\mu = 8,5$ $\sigma = 2,0$	$\mu = 4,3$ $\sigma = 0,7$	$\mu = 4,4$ $\sigma = 0,7$	$\mu = 10,5$ $\sigma = 1,3$	$\mu = 12,1$ $\sigma = 1,2$
Preparation of surgical field	$\mu = 6,4$ $\sigma = 1,4$	$\mu = 5,4$ $\sigma = 1,2$	$\mu = 4,2$ $\sigma = 1,0$	$\mu = 6,4$ $\sigma = 1,5$	$\mu = 8,1$ $\sigma = 0,8$	$\mu = 10,9$ $\sigma = 1,2$
Surgery (from incision to implant)	$\mu = 38,5$ $\sigma = 12,6$	$\mu = 66,2$ $\sigma = 20,0$	$\mu = 31,0$ $\sigma = 3,83$	$\mu = 49,2$ $\sigma = 6,0$	$\mu = 65$ $\sigma = 6,4$	$\mu = 76,8$ $\sigma = 5,6$
Suturing	$\mu = 30,6$ $\sigma = 7,6$	$\mu = 38,9$ $\sigma = 9,4$	$\mu = 20,5$ $\sigma = 3,88$	$\mu = 25,3$ $\sigma = 6,6$	$\mu = 27,2$ $\sigma = 4,1$	$\mu = 34,3$ $\sigma = 3,9$
Transfer patient to bed	$\mu = 1,3$ $\sigma = 1,27$	$\mu = 2,1$ $\sigma = 0,7$	$\mu = 1$ $\sigma = /$	$\mu = 1$ $\sigma = /$	$\mu = 3,4$ $\sigma = 1,1$	$\mu = 2,7$ $\sigma = 0,9$
Total of time	**131,1**	**176,36**	**104,25**	**147,95**	**197,4**	**239,8**
Move patient to PACU	$\mu = 3,3$ $\sigma = 1,2$	$\mu = 2,2$ $\sigma = 1,0$	NP	NP	$\mu = 2,5$ $\sigma = 0,9$	$\mu = 2,6$ $\sigma = 0,8$
Patient stays in PACU	$\mu = 50,8$ $\sigma = 28,8$	$\mu = 60,9$ $\sigma = 40,2$	NP	NP	$\mu = 10$ $\sigma = 1,2$	$\mu = 17,2$ $\sigma = 2,1$
X-ray check	$\mu = 22,4$ $\sigma = 2,09$	$\mu = 20,6$ $\sigma = 2,3$	$\mu = 8,1$ $\sigma = 1,6$	$\mu = 12,3$ $\sigma = 2,4$	NP	NP
Transfer patient to ward	$\mu = 6,2$ $\sigma = 2,1$	$\mu = 2,9$ $\sigma = 1,3$	$\mu = 5,1$ $\sigma = 1,8$	$\mu = 5,5$ $\sigma = 1,6$	$\mu = 7,1$ $\sigma = 1,4$	$\mu = 6,9$ $\sigma = 1,2$
Total process time	**213,8**	**262,96**	**117,45**	**165,75**	**217**	**266,5**

*Not included in estimation; μ = mean, σ = standard deviation, NP = not performed

Table 12.3 Device and asset used in the three different structures

	Device	Asset	Public hospital	Private hospital	Public university hospital
Catheter	Yes	No	No	No	Yes
Echograph	No	Yes	No	Yes	Yes
Intraoperative x-ray	No	Yes	No	No	Yes
Post anaesthesia care unit	No	Yes	Yes	No	Yes

Source Authors' elaboration

- the steps performed by the patient;
- the device utilization; and
- the asset involved.

The different steps performed by patients have been shown by Figs. 12.2 and 12.3. The differences in asset and device utilization are reported in Table 12.3; in particular, private and university hospitals use the echograph for the administration of local anesthesia, specifically the first one in the pre operating room and the second one in the post operating room, whereas the public hospital requires the patient to be catheterized, which the other two structures do not.

12.5 Discussion

According to (Creswell & Clark, 2017), mapping the clinical pathway allows for the comprehension of connections between activities, actors, roles and responsibility of the service delivery process; additionally, the use of the Time-Driven Activity-Based Costing Method (TDABC) allows for the estimation of time consumed by various staff members involved in patient treatment during THA and TKA. It is fundamental to emphasize that as described by (Laberge et al., 2019), elective hip and knee surgeries are highly standardized procedures with identical clinical paths. Although these surgeries necessitate different materials and patient preparation, the processes are the same. This is confirmed by the findings of this study; therefore, both processes can be discussed as a whole.

The analysis of the process map discloses three main differences between the TKA and THA delivery processes between the three hospitals, in particular:

- Time required;
- Activity performed in pre and post operating room;
- Assets and devices involved.

The time required for the healthcare delivery process is higher for both procedures in university hospitals.

This could be mostly attributed to the "teaching" hospital's context, which requires residents' participation in the entire procedure; within this kind of hospital, it should also be noted that there are various levels of expertise in various fields, such as student nurses, radiologist technicians and residents of various medical fields (e.g., anesthesiology, orthopaedics). Thus, residents' involvement in several steps of the healthcare value chain is generally associated with greater, longer surgical time in total joint arthroplasties (Pugely et al., 2014).

The other explanation for the higher time required by university hospitals is the employment of a device (catheter) and assets (x-ray check in the OR) not found in the other structures.

The difference in activity performed in the pre and post operating room might be related to the different organization of the three structures. According to (Bhattacharjee & Ray, 2014), patient flow is influenced by seasonal and local variables, as well as the location of hospitals and the types of services provided.

Furthermore, within the context of the Italian National Health System, both public and private hospitals are structured in Operating Units or wards, clustered per specializations (e.g. Orthopaedics). The head of department is responsible for delivering organizational resources to ward staff as well as establishing a certain organizational climate, which includes unique policies (guidelines), processes and practices that may differ depending on the manager (Ancarani et al., 2019). Furthermore, clinical decisions addressing surgical strategies can be steered by the clinical staff background (e.g. current practices or specialist school legacy) and/or operating team adherence to scientific literature (e.g. evidence-based medicine or medical guidelines). This may explain why there is a different approach to using devices (e.g. catheter), assets (e.g. x-ray in OR) and activities performed pre and post operating theatre.

Instead, the activities performed in the operating room are equal in all the structures analyzed because, according to (Laberge et al., 2019), standardization of the prosthesis process was employed as a method for improving efficiency; i.e. patient safety. According to the author, this method allowed for the simplification of the supply procedure and the reduction of the strain on physicians to arrange for the proper materials for each surgery. Indeed, regardless of facility or surgeon volume, standardization is associated with improved processes and results for patients having THA or TKA (Bozic et al., 2010). It can also help to improve procedures, which increases productivity and the number of hip and knee replacement surgeries performed per operating room (Attarian et al., 2013).

From the mentioned findings, we can argue that the main differences in THA and TKA performed by the three organizations analyzed follow some organizational features that act as a "conditioning variable" for specific activities in the service processes.

Accordingly, Table 12.4 reports the activities that most differ in terms of time consumed between the three structures.

Table 12.4 The different activities and their conditioning variable. *Source* Authors' elaboration (2021)

	Activities	"Conditioning variable"
Operating room	Position patient	Different clinical approach
	Surgery	Surgeon's expertise
	Suturing	
Pre/post operating room	Length of stay in PACU	Organizational structure

Concerning the activity performed in pre and post operating room, they can diverge according to organizational structure; as shown in Table 12.4, the activity related to surgery can vary depending on the surgeon's expertise and background or training.

Accordingly, in order to define a benchmark of which clinical pathway of THA and TKA may be most suitable, university hospitals are excluded from the benchmark. These structures, in fact, perform teaching activity involving residents in all the delivery processes in order to improve their skills (Chung, 2005), probably extending the time required for the procedures (Tseng et al., 2011).

Performing joint replacement surgery necessitates several resources (operating input), which may be divided into two categories: equipment and labour. According to (Laberge et al., 2019), this research confirms that in order to increase the efficiency of joint arthroplasty, it is fundamental to monitor and measure: (i) the quantity of resources employed; and (ii) the mix of resources employed. Thus, this allows clinical management to manage performance obtained by the operating inputs involved in the clinical pathway.

As a consequence, the use of TDABC and the process map analyses are able to show the weak and strong points of various clinical pathways (Kaplan & Porter, 2011) related to THA and TKA; these points are compared to create a benchmark for patient satisfaction and cost reduction based on the time and personnel required for each activity.

12.6 Conclusion

This paper addresses the theme of the healthcare delivery process and how to increase its cost-effectiveness. Precisely, the work aims at understanding if and how the process mapping due to the application of TDABC can improve value creation and efficiency. Particularly, within the surgical sphere, the healthcare delivery process of knee and hip arthroplasty has been analyzed. To achieve the goal of this study, TDABC approach was employed in different hospitals in order to map the delivery process in different contexts.

The results allowed for:

- understanding the standard clinical pathway for patients undergoing THA and TKA;
- estimating the mean time required for each step of each activity, and so the mean cost too;
- confirming that the surgical process is a high-standard procedure and the patient pathway in THA and TKA differs only in pre and post operating room activities.

These findings seem particularly suitable for practitioners because they allow users to design an efficient surgical procedure. Particularly, the study shows a practical example of a useful process map that formalizes all the activities and resources required in providing surgery. Moreover, process mapping and time detection provide healthcare managers with a comparison between the planned performance and the actual one, according to their own business structure.

Accordingly, this is fundamental for the measurement of the efficiency in providing THA and TKA, by allowing comparisons with other providers' standards and with current practice achievements.

Furthermore, the findings show that the main operating differences in THA and TKA processes are not attributable to hospital ownership (private and public hospitals behave in the same way), but to the feature of being a teaching or non-teaching hospital. University hospitals, due to their institutional function, result in higher charges both for time and resource consumption in comparison with general hospitals.

The study confirms that by comparing standardized processes from different sources, it would be possible to design an optimal pathway for THA and TKA by keeping the best practices from each process analyzed. It would also be suitable for creating a standard process and related costs.

This is relevant also for scholars involved in Managerial Control tools applied in the Public Management field. Accordingly, the study could foster debate about the application of accounting tools, both for cost analyses and process design, following the new requirements of the NHS to increase access to services and quality together with reducing spending.

References

Akhavan, S., Ward, L., & Bozic, K. J. (2016). Time-driven activity-based costing more accurately reflects costs in arthroplasty surgery. *Clinical Orthopaedics and Related Research, 474*(1), 8–15. PMID: 25721575 PMCID: PMC4686520. https://doi.org/10.1007/s11999-015-4214-0.

Ancarani, A., Mauro, C. D., & Giammanco, M. D. (2019). Linking organizational climate to work engagement: A study in the healthcare sector. *International Journal of Public Administration, 42*(7), 547–557. https://doi.org/10.1080/01900692.2018.1491595

Attarian, D. E., Wahl, J. E., Wellman, S. S., & Bolognesi, M. P. (2013). Developing a high-efficiency operating room for total joint arthroplasty in an academic setting. *Clinical Orthopaedics and Related Research, 471*(6), 1832–1836. https://doi.org/10.1007/s11999-012-2718-4

Au, J., & Rudmik, L. (2013). Cost of outpatient endoscopic sinus surgery from the perspective of the Canadian government: A time-driven activity-based costing approach: Outpatient ESS cost for Canadian government. *International Forum of Allergy and Rhinology, 3*(9), 748–754. https://doi.org/10.1002/alr.21181

Baratti, D., Scivales, A., Balestra, M. R., Ponzi P., Di Stasi, F., Kusamura, S., Laterza, B., & Deraco, M. (2010). Cost analysis of the combined procedure of cytoreductive surgery and hyperthermic intraperitoneal chemotherapy (HIPEC). *European Journal of Surgical Oncology, 36*(5), 463–469. PMID: 20363094, https://doi.org/10.1016/j.ejso.2010.03.005.

Bhattacharjee, P., & Ray, P. K. (2014). Patient flow modelling and performance analysis of healthcare delivery processes in hospitals: A review and reflections. *Computers and Industrial Engineering, 78*(C), 299–312. https://doi.org/10.1016/j.cie.2014.04.016Corpus ID: 30965372.

Blaschke, B. L., Parikh, H. R., Vang, S. X., & Cunningham, B. P. (2020). Time-driven activity-based costing: A better way to understand the cost of caring for hip fractures. *Geriatric Orthopaedic Surgery and Rehabilitation*, 11, 1–6, PMID: 32974078 PMCID: PMC7495936. https://doi.org/10.1177/2151459320958202.

Bozic, K. J., Maselli, J., Pekow, P. S., Lindenauer, P. K., Vail, T. P., & Auerbach, A. D. (2010). The influence of procedure volumes and standardization of care on quality and efficiency in total joint replacement surgery. *Journal of Bone and Joint Surgery. American Volume, 92*(16), 2643–2652. https://doi.org/10.2106/JBJS.I.01477

Chung, R. S. (2005). How much time do surgical residents need to learn operative surgery? *The American Journal of Surgery, 190*(3), 351–353, PMID: 16105515. https://doi.org/10.1016/j.amjsurg.2005.06.035.

Clack, L. A., & Ellison, R. L. (2019). Innovation in service design thinking. In: M. A. Pfannstiel &C. Rasche (Hrsg.), *Service design and service thinking in healthcare and hospital management. Theory, concepts, practice* (pp. 85–92). Springer Nature.

Creswell, J. W., & Clark, V. L. P. (2017). *Designing and conducting mixed methods research.* Sage publications.

Danaher, T. S., & Gallan, A. S. (2016). *Service research in health care: Positively impacting lives.* Sage Publications.

Demeere, N., Stouthuysen, K., & Roodhooft, F. (2009). Time-driven activity-based costing in an outpatient clinic environment: Development, relevance and managerial impact. *Health Policy, 92*(2–3), 296–304. https://doi.org/10.1016/j.healthpol.2009.05.003 PMID: 19505741.

DiGioia, 3rd A. M., Greenhouse, P. K., Giarrusso, M. L., & Kress, J. M. (2016). Determining the true cost to deliver total hip and knee arthroplasty over the full cycle of care: Preparing for bundling and reference-based pricing. *Journal of Arthroplasty, 31*(1), 1–6, PMID: 26271543. https://doi.org/10.1016/j.arth.2015.07.013.

Dombrée, M., Crott, R., Lawson, G., Janne, P., Castiaux, A., & Krug, B. (2014). Cost comparison of open approach, transoral laser microsurgery and transoral robotic surgery for partial and total laryngectomies. *European Archives of Oto-Rhino-Laryngology, 271*(10), 2825–2834. PMID: 24906840, https://doi.org/10.1007/s00405-014-3056-9.

Francis, S. (2010). Plan for uncertainty: Design for change. In M. Kagioglou & P. Tzortzopoulos (Eds.), *Improving healthcare through built environment infrastructure* (pp. 40–52). Blackwell Publishing Ltd. https://doi.org/10.1002/9781444319675.ch3.

Frow, P., McColl-Kennedy, J. R., & Payne, A. (2016). Co-creation practices: Their role in shaping a health care ecosystem. *Industrial Marketing Management, 56*(2016), 24–39. https://doi.org/10.1016/j.indmarman.2016.03.007

Kaplan, R. S., & Porter, M. E. (2011). How to solve the cost crisis in health care. *Harvard Business Review, 89*(9), 46–52, 54, 56–61 passim. PMID: 21939127.

Keel, G., Savage, C., Rafiq, M., & Mazzocato, P. (2017). Time-driven activity-based costing in health care: A systematic review of the literature. *Health Policy. 121*(7), 755–763. PMID: 28535996. https://doi.org/10.1016/j.healthpol.2017.04.013.

Klein, K. J., Ziegert, J. C., Knight, A. P., & Xiao, Y. (2006). Dynamic delegation: Shared, hierarchical, and deindividualized leadership in extreme action teams. *Administrative Science Quarterly, 51*(4), 590–621. https://doi.org/10.2189/asqu.51.4.590

Laberge, M., Côté, A., & Ruiz, A. (2019). Clinical pathway efficiency for elective joint replacement surgeries: a case study. *Journal of Health Organization and Management, 33*(3), 323–338, PMID: 31122119. https://doi.org/10.1108/JHOM-03-2018-0087.

Laviana, A. A., Ilg, A. M., Veruttipong, D., Tan, J.-J., Burke, M. A., Niedzwiecki, D. R., Kupelian, P. A., King, C. R., Steinberg, M. L., Kundavaram, C. R., Kamrava, M., Kaplan, A. L., Moriarity, A. K., Hsu, W., Margolis, D. J. A., Hu, J. C., & Saigal, C. S. (2016). Utilizing time-driven activity-based costing to understand the short- and long-term costs of treating localized, low-risk prostate cancer: TDABC and Low-Risk Prostate Cancer. *Cancer, 122*(3), 447–455. PMID: 26524087. https://doi.org/10.1002/cncr.29743

Lee, S. (2011). Evaluating serviceability of healthcare servicescapes: Service design perspective. *International Journal of Design, 5*(2), 61–71.

Levine, S. (2015). We are all patients, we are all consumers. *NEJM Catalyst*, Retrieved June 29, 2021, from https://catalyst.nejm.org/we-are-all-patients-we-are-all-consumers/.

Ministero della Salute (2019). Tavole Rapporto SDO 2019 suddivise per capitoli. Retrieved June 6, 2021, from https://www.salute.gov.it/portale/documentazione/p6_2_8_3_1.jsp?lingua= italiano&id=34.

Moffitt, K. C., & Vasarhelyi, M. A. (2013). AIS in an age of big data. *Journal of Information Systems, 27*(2), 1–19. https://doi.org/10.2308/isys-10372

Moritz, S. (2005). Service design – Practical access to an evolving field. Service Design, 246. In S. Moritz (Hrsg.).

Pathak, S., Snyder, D., Kroshus, T., Keswani, A., Jayakumar, P., Esposito, K., Koenig, K., Jevsevar, D., Bozic K., & Moucha C. (2019). What are the uses and limitations of time-driven activity-based costing in total joint replacement? *Clinical Orthopaedics and Related Research, 477*(9), 2071–2081, PMID: 31107316 PMCID: PMC7000080. https://doi.org/10.1097/CORR. 0000000000000765.

Porter, M. E. (2008). Value-based health care delivery. *Annals of Surgery, 248*(4), 503–509, PMID: 18936561. https://doi.org/10.1097/SLA.0b013e31818a43af.

Porter, M. E. (2010). What is value in health care. *The New England Journal of Medicine, 363*(26), 2477–2481, PMID: 21142528. https://doi.org/10.1056/NEJMp1011024.

Porter, M. E. (2009). A strategy for health care reform — Toward a value-based system. *The New England Journal of Medicine, 361*(2), 109–112. PMID: 19494209, https://doi.org/10.1056/ NEJMp0904131.

Pugely, A. J., Gao, Y., Martin, C. T., Callagh, J. J., Weinstein, S. L., & Marsh, J. L. (2014). The effect of resident participation on short-term outcomes after orthopaedic surgery. *Clinical Orthopaedics and Related Research, 472*(7), 2290–2300, PMID: 24658902 PMCID: PMC4048420. https://doi.org/10.1007/s11999-014-3567-0.

Scapens, R. W. (1990). Researching management accounting practice: The role of case study methods. *The British Accounting Review, 22*(3), 259–281. https://doi.org/10.1016/0890-8389 (90)90008-6,CorpusID:153690192

Tseng, W. H., Jin L., Canter, R. J., Martinez, S. R., Khatri, V. P., Gauvin J., Bold, R. J., Wisner, D., Taylor S., & Chen, S. L. (2011). Surgical resident involvement is safe for common elective general surgery procedures. *Journal of the American College of Surgeons, 213*(1), 19–26, PMID: 21493108, https://doi.org/10.1016/j.jamcollsurg.2011.03.014.

Yin, R. K. (2017). *Case study research and applications: Design and methods*. Sage publications.

Irene Schettini is a PhD Student in Management—Business Management and Accounting at the University of Rome Tor Vergata—Italy, Department of Management and Law. Her research interests fit into healthcare management, with a focus on application of accounting tools in the healthcare sector. In particular, her research project concerns Time-Driven Activity-Based Costing as a relevant tool for healthcare providers in order to reduce waste, improve value and decision-making processes of both managers and physicians.

Gabriele Palozzi is a Research Fellow in Management at the University of Rome Tor Vergata—Italy, Department of Management and Law. He received his PhD in Management from the University of Rome Tor Vergata. He is Lecturer of Managerial Control. His studies address the sphere of Managerial Accounting, Strategic Controlling and Performance Management. Particularly, his researches focus on economic, social and clinical joint impacts connected to the digital transformation and new technologies in healthcare.

Antonio Chirico is Associate Professor of Accounting at the University of Rome Tor Vergata—Italy, Department of Management and Law. He received his PhD in Banking and Finance from the University of Rome Tor Vergata. He is Associate Professor of Accounting and Managerial Accounting. Nowadays, he is Coordinator of the Master of Science Degree in Management. His main research interests include Financial Reporting & Analysis, Managerial Accounting, Performance Management, both in the Public and Private sectors.

Healthcare Design Practice for Humanizing the Patient Journey

13

Cecilia Xi Wang, Craig M. Vogel, and Shaun A. Wahab

Abstract

Design practitioners should play a critical role in shaping a human-centered healthcare experience through innovative empathic solutions. The chapter explains the value of the humanized patient journey and how to foster it in the hospital environment by healthcare design practice. The content retrieves from several collaborative healthcare service design projects from the Live Well Collaborative, the University of Cincinnati Health, and GE Health. The multidisciplinary team used the approach to identify the challenge of outpatients and families not fully understanding the radiology department's processes and workflow. Humanizing the radiology patient journey was distinguished as an essential issue. The projects engaged multidisciplinary students in holistic patient experience throughout the design practice process by incorporating research, identification, and refinement. Benchmarking, site observations, co-design activities, and in-depth interviews merged with data and insights drawn from scholarly evidence-based design literature reviews. Using a human-centered design practice process, motivated the multidisciplinary team

C. X. Wang (✉)
University of Minnesota, 240 McNeal Hall, 1985 Buford Avenue, St. Paul, MN 55108, USA
e-mail: ceciw@umn.edu

C. M. Vogel
DAAP School of Design - 0016, Aronoff Center, 5420, University of Cincinnati, Cincinnati, OH, USA
e-mail: vogelcg@ucmail.uc.edu

S. A. Wahab
Department of Radiology, University of Cincinnati, 234 Goodman St, Cincinnati, OH 45267-0761, USA
e-mail: shaun.wahab@uc.edu

© The Author(s), under exclusive license to Springer Nature Switzerland AG 2022
M. A. Pfannstiel et al. (eds.), *Service Design Practices for Healthcare Innovation*,
https://doi.org/10.1007/978-3-030-87273-1_13

to be more engaged in the project. Therefore, it facilitated the creation of a new and original toolkit for humanizing the patient journey. The toolkit was innovative and impactful in supporting all stakeholders in the outpatient radiology journey.

13.1 Introduction

Design practitioners should play a critical role in shaping a human-centered healthcare experience through innovative empathic solutions, by centering on eco-stakeholder, including patient, family members, care team, empathic design help to affirming life and build a contemporary holistic healthcare culture. Human-centered healthcare design can and should inform the design practice and bring design solutions into the needs and desires of patients and the care team. Healthcare design, guided by empathic design process and principles, offers solutions to inspire the healthcare experience.

This chapter shares a new way of designing experience and physical journey for patients and all the relevant stakeholders using the design practice process, tools, and principles. This approach offers a unique perception to enhance compassion for people grounded in healthcare evidence-based design (HEBD) principles, thus, connecting the individual experience with subject ways of experiencing. The humanizing the radiology patient journey case study focuses on designing an outpatient CT and MRI experience in the radiology department using human-centered empathic design thinking methodology within a senior-level design institution collaboration with hospital and healthcare industries. Within this context, humanizing the patient experience and physical journey became a vehicle for the multidiscipline design team to explore dimensions of empathetic design practice from stakeholders' perspectives. This process involved exploring patient experience through three models of design practice process, including research, ideation, and refinement, to inspire empathic design thinking. Humanized patient journey, told in the first person, situated the role of the design practice within the radiology outpatient CT and MRI experience. We argue that the grant-winning result of this project invites a brand new design practice process, one that integrated humanizing the patient journey with HEBD.

Background and Context

The Live Well Collaborative is a non-profit design institution founded by the University of Cincinnati (UC) and Procter and Gamble (P&G) in 2007 located in Cincinnati, Ohio, dedicated to leading-edge human-centered user experience (UX) research which is translated into ideal solutions that fit the complexities of well-being across the lifespan. Collaborating academia and industry model with

Live Well's empathic design thinking and practice process, they co-create meaningful, designed solutions for all the stakeholders. A unique multidisciplinary team structure of faculty and students from UC's top ranking collaborates with industry partners' design expertise.

UC Health Radiology and Live Well Collaborative are parties to a Strategic Member Agreement dated January 23, 2018. UC Health Radiology is dedicated to improving lives through empathy, expertise, and innovation in radiology. The vision of UC Health Radiology is to be a nationally recognized center of imaging excellence known for best-in-class patient experience, with a nationwide referral base, and innovative research and teaching. Through a collective effort, UC Health Radiology, the Live Well Collaborative, and GE Healthcare are committed to helping UC Health Radiology achieve those objectives.

During the Summer 2018 Scoping Project, the Live Well Collaborative team identified the challenge of patients and families not fully understanding the processes and workflow of UC Radiology. Humanizing radiology is identified as a top priority. Patients stated that they were not fully aware of what to bring to their appointments, how long wait times were at the hospital, what to expect during the imaging process, and what happens with their images between the imaging test and their results being delivered to their medical chart.

This project addresses previously stated patient concerns by developing a tool addressing expectations of their imaging appointment. This tool will visually communicate to patients how to navigate their way through an appointment and set expectations for their visits. The tool will also give patients a global view of the imaging process at UC Health Radiology. The project aims to,

- Understand patients' entire current imaging process and communication of process to patients (verbal, analog, digital), beginning with imaging referral and ending with results delivery from both the patient and staff perspectives, and defining the minimum viable product.
- Understand other successfully mapped processes by benchmarking similar and other industrial processes.
- Create the preferred patient experience, identify the preferred method of receiving information, and create a minimum viable product.

The chapter explains the value of the humanizing the patient journey and how to foster it in the hospital environment by healthcare design practice. The content retrieves from several collaborative healthcare service design projects from the Live Well Collaborative, the University of Cincinnati Health, and GE Health. The multidisciplinary team attempted to identify stakeholders and pain points in the radiology department's processes and workflow. Humanizing the radiology patient journey was distinguished as an essential issue.

13.2   Empathic Design Practice in Healthcare

Leonard and Rayport's empathic design techniques "require exceptional collaborative skills, open-mindedness, interview and observation skills, and inquisitiveness." The use of visual information entails an understanding of the user. In short, build a new observation in the user's familiar contexts (Leonard and Rayport, 1997). Of course, we cannot experience the way others experience, but with supportive tools, we can attempt to get as close as possible and without pre-judgment and pre-conception.

Empathic design practice is a collaboration of tools to facilitate the design team in obtaining a deeper understanding of the problem and stakeholders they are designing for. It requires designers to uncover a user's emotional and physical needs and how users see, understand, and interact with the world around them to manage their interactive behaviors and build a better experience. Empathic design is not concerned with facts about users but more about their desires and motivations. For instance, why an outpatient prefers to get instructions before a CT or MRI scan.

"Empathies" is the first stage of the design practice process. The following stages can be summarized as research, ideation, and refinement. The goal is to gather an in-depth empathic understanding of users and the problem context. In order to interpret the user's experience and motivations, empathic design thinking involves observing, empathizing with all the relevant stakeholders, and stepping into their physical environment to have a holistic understanding of the challenges. The most commonly used empathic design methods,

- Set up a beginner's mindset
- Ask what-how-why
- Design and conduct interviews with empathy
- Use personal photograph and video journals
- Engage with all the relevant stakeholders
- Stories tell-and-capture
- Use journey maps

The quality of care influenced by empathy design practice shows improved patient experience and clinical outcomes (Kim et al., 2004) and reduced maloperation medical activities and errors (Haslam, 2007). The evidence suggests that understanding patient experience is critical, influenced by communications between the care team and patients and organization or institution development outcome enhancement.

Healthcare ecosystem stakeholder team including physicians, technologists, nurses, social workers that have the chance to be empathetic during each clinical interaction. Caregivers can change roles from information providers to internal innovators by empathy activities with compassion to their patients. Empathy empowers patients and attempts to give them a more holistic experience, reduce uncertainty, and become more informed of their healthcare decision-making.

Scholarly communication among the multidisciplinary team in design practice, education, and industry required by the next generation of UX designers recognizes the critical of empathy.

To communicate more efficiently, reduce patient anxiety and uncertainty and improve patient collaboration, leading to better results (Halpern, 2007), and eventually, engagement encourages the continuum of healthcare. Research literature, including psychology, social science, psychotherapy, and healthcare communication, all echo the importance of healthcare empathetic design practice and processes.

Scholars also emphasize that healthcare teams improve individual experience levels when they are empathetic to patients (Larson & Yao, 2005). Empathy builds a holistic system of caring, helping, and healing between physicians and patients. Empathy makes patients more informed of their concerns and facilitates communication with the care team, collects critical information during the whole healthcare journey, and is more engaged in their therapy by increasing self-awareness and encouraging interactions with the care team that influence patient recovery (Larson & Yao, 2005).

Human-centered healthcare promotes individual interaction; supports patient education, shared decision-making, and responsibility; encourages family member involvement; incorporates a systematic approach to caring and the influence of the surrounding environment, and considering the multistakeholders (Guastello & Frampton, 2014). Empathy is at the core of human-centered design thinking and practice, and arguable should be at the center of design education and research.

13.3 Healthcare Design Practice Process

Apart from creating an innovative culture, institutions need to know how to proceed: fully understand a problem and then solve it by creating something relevant for their customers or stakeholders. The "designer's way of thinking" has been identified as a fruitful approach to user-centered innovation (Dunne & Martin, 2006).

Design thinking (DT) is a systematic design methodology that provides a solution-based approach to frame and solve problems. The problems designers and design researchers face are more complex or ill-defined by tackling the human-centered needs involved. Understanding these three stages of human-centered empathic design thinking will enable anyone to apply design thinking methods to frame and solve problems that occur every day.

Design thinking is a nonlinear, iterative process that teams use to build an empathic understanding of users problems, reframe them, and create innovative solutions to change behaviors and improve the experience. The three stages of design thinking are as follows: research, ideation, and refinement. Let us take a closer look at the three different stages of design thinking (see Fig. 13.1).

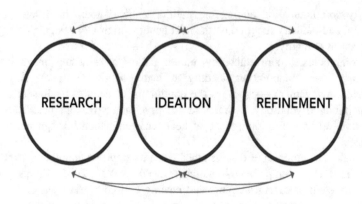

Fig. 13.1 Design thinking process. *Source*: Live Well Collaborative (2021)

13.3.1 Research Phase

Design thinking research systematically studies all the relevant stakeholders and their requirements, adding contexts and collecting insights to design thinking processes. It is the steppingstone toward defining the requirements for the product are about to design. Design researchers adopt various methods to uncover problems and design opportunities. Doing so, they reveal valuable information which can feed into the design process.

Research is an essential step across the entire design thinking process. It will most likely happen every time a new idea is framed or improve existing ones. The primary value of the pre-development research phase is defining the initial direction that the product/service will take moving forward. The majority outcome from the research phase includes:

- Who are the stakeholders, and what are their relationships?
- What are the stakeholders trying to achieve and desire?
- What are the pain points, and how to solve these problems?
- Who are the competitors?

The main outcomes from the humanizing the radiology patient journey project are the (1) UC Health Radiology stakeholder system map which illustrated the radiology ecosystem and relationships between referring physicians, patients, and the radiology department team. (2) Human-centered radiology outpatient journey map which covers key steps of the imaging journey (see Fig. 13.2). The pain points are,

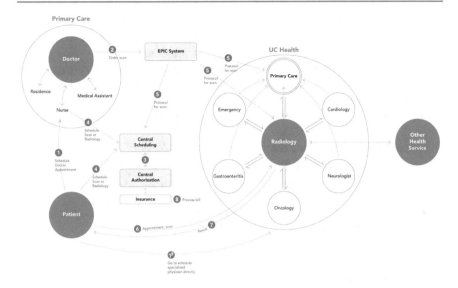

Fig. 13.2 UC Health Radiology stakeholder system map. *Source* Author's own illustration (2021)

- Not feeling informed about the scan
- Instructions not clearly captured by patients
- Biased information from unreliable resources online
- Patient not following key prep. instructions
- Struggling with wayfinding from the patient garage to the radiology department
- Not being able to provide accurate personal information
- Increased anxiety due to uncertainty
- Unexpected needs during preparation
- Unanticipated fear of the scanner
- Lack of information to navigate to their next appointment
- Inadequate explanations from MyChart

13.3.2   Ideation Phase

The goal of ideation is to create ideas that the team can test with stakeholders then prepare down to the most suitable, most practical, and innovative solutions. More specifically, ideation is interested in the activity whereby designers are exteriorizing stakeholder's internal mental images, engaging in a conversation of sorts with them. By widening the solution scope, the design team will look beyond the usual methods of solving problems to find better, more elegant, and satisfying solutions to problems that affect a user's experience of a product or service.

The ideation stage often follows the research stages with significant over-lap. Understanding the user, interpreting data/information, and frame/reframe the problem(s), and ideation drive the generation of solutions.

The methods the design team incorporates in the two stages are overlapping as well. For example, co-creation activities and usability tests are often used in both of these stages. Ideation will help the design team,

Mapping stakeholder and bring together perspectives.

- Increase the innovation of potential of solutions
- Uncover unexpected areas of innovation.
- Create volume and variety of innovative options

The key outcomes from the humanizing the radiology patient journey project are themes of opportunity areas,

- Improved patient care
  - Patient consult service
  - Physician consult service
- Making the radiologist visible

  - Radiology Web site redesign
- Improving stakeholder communication

  - Individualized FAQ
- Understanding radiology report

  - Interactive imaging report

13.3.3 Refinement Phase

This stage helps the design team to develop ideas and concepts and deliver them to stakeholders. Once the team or designer is confident that the proposed solution will work for users after research and ideation, the project transitions into build and launch mode. For designers, this can involve producing a high-fidelity prototype for the development team, working with a visual designer, and being involved during the implementation phase to ensure that the design intent is being carried through to the final product. This may mean providing feedback to the development team or doing usability testing on beta versions of a product to check whether interactions are as intended. The main focus of this phase is,

- Develop, incorporating early end-user consideration as much as possible.
- Test and debug.
- Deploy.

Refinement phase key result is the ideal humanizing radiology patient journey map. The team translated research insights into an ideal human-centered radiology outpatient journey. Following the journey steps (refer Table 13.1), the team listed expectation/pain points, protentional solutions, and existing tools through the whole imaging process to set up the goals and principles for the final deliverables (refer Fig. 13.3).

13.4 Methods: Humanizing the Patient Journey

To implement empathy design practice in the healthcare context, this case study involved designing prototypes for an outpatient radiology CT/MRI experience using a humanized patient journey method. A unique aspect of the humanizing radiology patient journey project was the support provided by UC Health and GE healthcare, industry leaders in healthcare UX design. Their support gave the Live Well multidisciplinary team the resources to conduct empathic design research and practice. This partnership facilitated behind the scenes tours in their organization system and also provided the Live Well team with an opportunity to learn from their empathy design process and methods providing compelling insights for the characters used in research in design (refer to Table 13.2).

The project involved designing a radiology outpatient imaging toolkit including two educational videos about the CT and MRI patient journeys, a radiology service pamphlet including the radiology outpatient journey map and a 2.5D navigation map. The project was completed by a multidisciplinary team including faculty and students at the University of Cincinnati. Seven team members from visual communication design, biomedical engineering to digital media majors participated in the 15-week project during the Spring semester of 2019. The majority of participants in the project were seniors in the College of Design, Architecture, and

Table 13.1 Human-centered radiology outpatient journey, *Source*: Author's own compilation (2021)

Referral	Arrival	Check-in	Imaging	Leaving radiology	Results
Initial appointment	Leaving home	Check-in	Preparation	Check out of radiology	Waiting period
Scheduling	Transportation to appointment	Register	Imaging	Head to next appointment	Follow-up appointment
Waiting (at home)		Waiting room		Transportation to home	

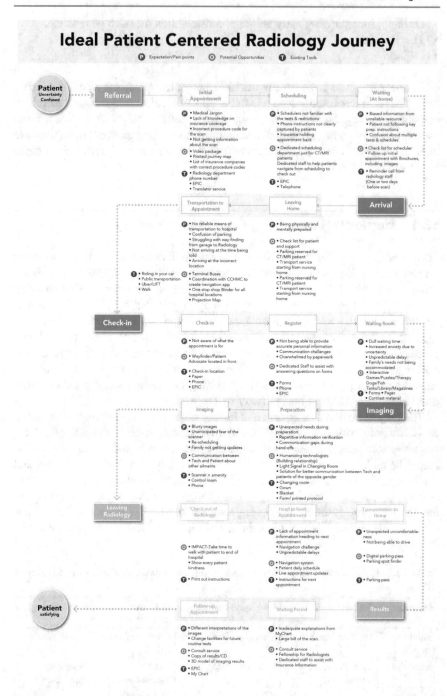

Fig. 13.3 Humanizing radiology patient journey map. *Source* Author's own illustration (2021)

Table 13.2 Project engagement and development. *Source* Author's own compilation (2021)

Multidisciplinary team	
Member	Title/company
Linda Dunseath	Executive Director, Live Well
Craig Vogel	Executive Director/Founder, Live Well
Bain Butcher	MD Associate Professor, DAAP, UC
Jocelyn Jia	Master of Design, DAAP, UC
Cecilia Xi Wang	Post-doc Fellow, DAAP, UC
Kellen Crosby	Biomedical Engineering, CEAS, UC
Ariel Swift	Communication Design, DAAP, UC
Chauyie Wei	Video Production, DMC, UC
Engaged Experts	
Mary Mahoney	MD, FACR, FSBI, Professor of Radiology; Chair, Department of Radiology, UC Health
	MD, MS, Professor of Radiology, UC Health
Achala Vagal	MD, Assistant Professor of Radiology, UC Health
Shaun A. Wahab	MD, MS, Associate Professor of Radiology, UC Health
Seetharam Chadalavada	MD, Assistant Professor of Radiology, UC Health
Ann L. Brown	DO, Assistant Professor of Radiology, UC Health
Rifat A. Wahab	MD, Assistant Professor of Radiology, UC Health
Bruce Mahoney	RT, Quality Coordinator, UC Health
Shari S. Lecky	RT, CT Manager, UC Health
Erica Washburn	RT, Director of Imaging, UC Health
Becky Allen	
Co-creation activities	
Core team ideation workshop	
Feasibility matrix activity	
Lotus diagram	
Card sorting activity	
Empathic design thinking workshop CT/MRI	
Site visits	
Physician's office observation and interview	
Radiology office observation	

Planning. This group had diverse design research and practice experience but had either completed training or UX design study experience before joining the project. The 15-week project was divided into three sections (research, ideation, and refinement). Each section had five weeks to facilitate collaboration and completion of the project. Each student had 20 h working load each week. The project focused on the radiology outpatient experience.

The project involved an iterative phased dedicated to research, ideation, and refinement. The research phase consisted of capturing the current situation of the radiology outpatient experience and pain points throughout the imaging journey. The ideation phase converted the research insights into design solutions to test and co-create with stakeholders and the radiology team. In the refinement phase, an effective implementation plan was created with the final concepts. First, the team focused on the extant secondary research through literature review. The literature addressed patient experience, information gathering and sharing behaviors, caregiver needs, patient education, and design principles and factors. Next, the team engaged in competitive research and benchmarking, site observation, and interviews, gathering primary research data and insights from radiology patients and care teams. The design team also conducted at least one co-creation session with radiologists, technologists, and nurses with intimate knowledge of the radiology patient journey.

In addition, the team analyzed the existing humanizing patient journey tools among healthcare institutions nationally and internationally. These research, ideate, and refinement activities and experiences facilitated the development of the radiology outpatient experience toolkit including two educated videos illustrated the CT and MRI patient journeys and a radiology experience pamphlet including the humanizing patient-centered radiology journey map and the physical navigation map.

Incorporating healthcare evidence-based design (HEBD) research and practice, humanizing patient journey was coupled with the empathic design process. The team was tasked with mapping the patient experience journey to capture emotions, expectations, and pain points. This not only facilitated human-centered design but also enhanced the teams' empathic design thinking capabilities. Humanizing the imaging patient journey forced the team to make design decisions beyond the visual or purely esthetic dimensions to consider the human needs, desires, expectations, judgements, and experiences within the healthcare context.

13.5   Conclusion

A human-centered empathic design approach motivated the multidisciplinary team to be aware of the possibilities and massive potential in contemporary healthcare design. It inspired the generation of innovative ideas to address the pain points in the radiology outpatient CT and MRI experience. The ecosystem design solutions were innovative, meaningful, and most importantly, integrated the perspectives of all the relevant stakeholders. They recognized that people full of challenges and expectations for the CT/MRI journey illustrated a commitment to HEBD. It was incorporated humanizing the patient journey as the majority content of the empathy design thinking and practice methods and strategies. The human-centered empathic design practice process involved both HEBD and humanizing patient journey. The design team was immersed in the perspectives of the patient and all relevant stakeholders; attempting to truly understand their expectations, desires, and experiences.

In this chapter, we advocate the use of human-centered empathic design to achieve inspired healthcare experience design. Humanizing the patient journey enables the design team to gather insights about stakeholders for whom they design. The humanizing journey offers one way to cultivate empathy in the design team and help develop a perception of elevating human-centered healthcare.

The healthcare provider team becomes more aware of patient experience, including activities, desires, and values to facility shared healthcare decisions (Institute of Medicine, 2001b, p. 40). The humanizing patient journey focuses on the individual patient perspective and expands to incorporate the input of all stakeholders, which helps to bridge the gap between patients, families, and healthcare providers.

Humanizing patient journey has the potential to highlight empathy within the human-centered design practice process and finalized product or service system unlocking human-centered healthcare design:

Designing a humanizing patient journey and empathic design practice process helped identify empathy for the patient or all the relevant stakeholders. Sometimes, in a design practice process, the user can easily ignore or forget—a humanizing user journey forces the team to concentrate on the holistic user experience map.

Implications for Practice

1. Integrating the insights of all stakeholders is essential in promoting multidisciplinary collaboration and fostering a more humanized patient journey.
2. Designer can and should play a critical role in a multidisciplinary team to develop innovative human-centered healthcare design products/services.
3. Humanizing the patient journey provides a context to patient experience within the healthcare system which can in turn be utilized and integrated in human-centered experience design practice to create more optimal results.
4. Humanizing user journey maps can be used as an empathic human-centered design practice tool and integrated into UX design research, practice, and in final empathetic solutions.

Acknowledgements These authors would like to thank UC health, and GE Healthcare for their generous supports. The radiology department of UC Health greatly contributed to the project and helped shape this study. The project team Linda Dunseath, Dr. Bain Butcher, Jocelyn Jia, Kellen Crosby, Ariel Swift, Chauyie Wei, Shari Lecky, Dr. Achala Vagal, Dr. Seetharam Chadalavada, Dr. Rifat Wahab, Dr. Bruce Mahoney, Dr. Ann L. Brown, and Dr. Mary Mahoney are recognized for their contributions to this study. The authors also wish to recognize all students and radiology faculty of UC health for their works on the project.

References

Dunne, D., & Martin, R. (2006). Design thinking and how it will change management education: An interview and discussion. *Academy of Management Learning & Education, 5*(4), 512–523. https://doi.org/10.5465/AMLE.2006.23473212CorpusID:18904407

Garrett, J. J. (2010). *The elements of user experience: User-centered design for the web and beyond.* Pearson Education.

Guastello, S., & Frampton S. B. (2014). Patient-centered care retreats as a method for enhancing and sustaining compassion in action in healthcare settings. *Journal of Compassionate Health Care, 1*, Article number 2, 1–6.

Halpern, J. (2007). Empathy and patient–physician conflicts. *Journal of General Internal Medicine, 22*(5), 696–700. https://doi.org/10.1007/s11606-006-0102-3

Haslam, N. (2007). Humanising medical practice: The role of empathy. *Medical Journal of Australia, 187*(7), 381–382. https://doi.org/10.5694/j.1326-5377.2007.tb01305.x

Kim, S. S., Kaplowitz, S., & Johnston, M. V. (2004). The effects of physician empathy on patient satisfaction and compliance. *Evaluation & The health Professions, 27*(3), 237–251. PMID: 15312283, https://doi.org/10.1177/0163278704267037.

Larson, E. B., & Yao X. (2005). Clinical empathy as emotional labor in the patient-physician relationship. *JAMA, 293*(9), 1100–1106. PMID: 15741532, https://doi.org/10.1001/jama.293.9.1100.

Leonard, D., & Rayport, J. F. (1997). Spark innovation through empathic design. *Harvard Business Review, 75*(6), 102–113. PMID: 10174792.

Live Well Collaborative (2021). Hompage. Live Well Collaborative (Ed.). Our Process Model. Retrieved July 28, 2021, from https://www.livewellcollaborative.org/who-we-are.

Cecilia Xi Wang is a design researcher, educator, and practitioner focusing on service design, user experience design, digital media collaborative, visual communication design, interaction design, healthcare design, and multidisciplinary design research and practice. Dr. Cecilia Xi Wang's primary research interests lie in the overlap of design philosophy, user experience design, healthcare design, service design, visual communication design, and multidisciplinary design. With the underlying of an increasingly complex and dynamic social and culture, we must rethink the value of design. The critical near-term challenge is understanding how better design thinking can help achieve an organic flow of experience in concrete situations, making such experiences more intelligent, meaningful, and sustainable. Dr. Wang is interested in discovering designers' ability to find new relationships among signs, things, actions, and thoughts take advantage of design thinking, the challenge is to reconsider and reconstruct the relationship between design research and practice. With her visual communication and user experience design and research experience, she feels well-placed to recognize how to exploit new design thinking philosophy and methods for ever more meaningful and valuable experience in concrete situations.She got her PhD of design in the School of Design at Jiangnan University in June 2018. She studied communication design for her BS and MS at the Zhengzhou University of Light Industry and Jiangnan University. She is working as an assistant professor at the Graphic design department, College of Design at the University of Minnesota at present.

Craig M. Vogel is professor and the Director of the Digital Media Collaborative at the University of Cincinnati. He has served for the past twelve years as Associate Dean of Graduate Studies and Research for the College of DAAP. He is also a professor in the School of Design with an appointment in Industrial Design, and co-founder of the Livewell Collaborative in Cincinnati and Singapore. He is a Fellow, Past President Elect and Chair of the Board of the Industrial Designers Society of America (IDSA). Vogel is co-author of the book, Creating Breakthrough Products, Financial Times, Prentice Hall, with Professor Jonathan Cagan. He is one of three authors of the book on innovation and organic growth, Design of Things to Come. During the last 25 years Professor Vogel has been a consultant to over 20 companies and advised and managed dozens of research projects and design studios collaborating with industry. He has also been a visiting scholar in China for the past two decades. Vogel is recognized as one of the most admired professors in architecture and design in the United States by Design Intelligence for 2008 and 2011. In 2015 he was recognized as one of 50 most Notable IDSA Members in the last 50 years.

Shaun A. Wahab, M.D., is an assistant professor with UC Health and University of Cincinnati College of Medcine in the Department of Radiology where he also serves as the Body Imaging Fellowship Director. Dr. Wahab is an academic abominal imaging radiologist by training but has co-authored design thinking manuscripts in the radiology literature with the multidisciplinary team from Live Well, UC DAAP, GE Healthcare, and UC Health. He completed his radiology residency with Michigan State University followed by a Fellowship in Body Imaging with Vanderbilt University.

While-U-Wait: A Service-Based Solution for Emergency Room Overcrowding

Joshua O. Eniwumide, Patrick O. Akomolafe, and Christoph Rasche

Abstract

Prolonged waiting and overcrowding at hospital emergency departments remain problematic. In spite of much effort from high-ranking hospital directors and policy makers, the time patients spend in hospital emergency departments awaiting treatment is on a continuous rise. An increase in the demand for the emergency department's service, in addition to the high complexity of the hospital and healthcare systems is thought responsible for the difficulty in finding sustainable solutions for the rise. Rather than focusing on how to reduce the prolonged waiting time and overcrowding, the present paper looked at altering the perception of patients waiting to receive medical treatment with respect to their waiting time. In doing so, the aim was to reduce the much observed waiting associated stress and hence improve their overall experience and satisfaction with the received healthcare service. A Web-based virtual waiting platform was developed, which communicated individual waiting times

J. O. Eniwumide (✉)
Senior Research Fellow, Department für Sport- und Gesundheitswissenschaften, Lehrstuhl für Management, Sportökonomie & Professional Services, Universität Potsdam, Humanwissenschaftliche Fakultät, Wirtschafts- und Sozialwissenschaftliche Fakultät, Karl-Liebknecht-Straße 24-25, Haus 24, Raum 126, 14476 Potsdam, Germany
e-mail: jeniwumide@uni-potsdam.de

P. O. Akomolafe
Lecturer, Computer Science Department, University of Ibadan, Ibadan 200213, Oyo, Nigeria
e-mail: op.akomolafe@ui.edu.ng

C. Rasche
Professor, Department für Sport- und Gesundheitswissenschaften, Lehrstuhl für Management, Sportökonomie & Professional Services, Universität Potsdam, Humanwissenschaftliche Fakultät, Wirtschafts- und Sozialwissenschaftliche Fakultät, Karl-Liebknecht-Straße 24-25, Haus 24, Raum 126, 14476 Potsdam, Germany
e-mail: chrasche@uni-potsdam.de

to its users as well as other relevant messages. The waiting information was obtained through the platform's ability to interface with an organization's queueing management systems, while the other sets of information were added manually by the users and emergency department employees. As future scope, a two-part clinical utility study is laid out, which would answer the questions of adoptability and impact. Finally, the platform's adaptability to all sectors where waiting is unavoidable, undesired, and prolonged is described. In which, the platform would enable its users to queue for multiple services and products simultaneously. Users will be able to optimize their day, transiting from one appointment to the next, and arriving at points of service just in time. This embodies the principle of off-site queueing and just-in-time arrival.

14.1   The Impact of Outpatient Waiting Times on Clinical

Outcomes

Hospital emergency departments (EDs) are the first point of contact when seeking attention and ultimately treatment for acute medical needs. Thus, they serve as the gateway to the utilization of hospital services. While in the ED, patients will often experience wait times lasting four, often longer hours on average. Despite a lack of standard definition for wait time in the ED, the present work defines ED wait time as the time laps between a patient's arrival at the ED and their initial contact with a physician, physician assistant, or nurse practitioner. Excessively long wait time leads to overcrowding of the ED, which itself has been attributed to a substantial negative impact on quality-of-care, patient satisfaction, and a hospital's financial health (Bernstein et al., 2009; Davenport et al., 2017; Ranney et al., 2012; Trout et al., 2000). The phenomena of long ED wait times and indeed, overcrowding has been the focus of discussions globally with much published and readily available scientific research on healthcare systems of Taiwan (Hu, 1994), The United Kingdom (Bagust et al., 1999), Spain (Miro et al., 1999), and Australia (Richardson et al. 2002; Sprivulis et al., 2005). The consequences of long wait times have been demonstrated in EDs based both in developed and developing countries (Goodman et al., 2017; Knight et al., 2013).

Excessively long wait times lead to higher health risks, as well as patients leaving the ED without being treated. Patients leaving the ED without being seen by the physician risks delayed diagnosis and treatment of their conditions, and therefore, a worsen morbidity than their original medical issue (Clarey et al. 2012; Vieth & Rhodes, 2006; Baker et al., 1991). Long wait time and crowding have been shown to negatively impact several domains of healthcare quality such as timeliness, safety, and patient centeredness (Hing and Bhuiya, 2012; Moskop et al., 2009; Pines et al., 2008). For this reason, ED wait time-related data are essential quality metric (Lucas et al., 2014) employed both at the department level as well as the hospital level. To this extent, hospitals commonly advertise their wait times on their

Website, not only to help manage patients' expectations, but also as to demonstrate service quality. Essentially, this practice serves as a marketing strategy that is aimed to help steer patients to a hospital's ED, thereby potentially increasing its revenue. However, the strategy may also help to bring about a relief to overburdened EDs, as patients with less acute problems may, in theory take the extra time to go to a hospital with a less wait time, despite it not being the closest to them. Furthermore, some hospitals post wait times of other local EDs in its waiting room, thereby offering the patients, the ability to choose to leave and go to nearby affiliated hospital with a shorter wait time. This has the potential to smoothen the daily peaks and troughs of ED waiting times at local levels. In describing this phenomena, SG Weiner (2013) suggested that advertising wait times may encourage patients to self-triage in a dangerous way. Additionally, the published times may be inaccurate, given the dynamic nature of the hospital EDs. Furthermore, the lack of a standardized definition of wait time (Hwang & Concato, 2004) may lead to misunderstandings on the side of the patient. As a conclusion, caution was advised on the use of advertised wait time, pending more evidence.

Factors Contributing to Outpatient's Waiting Times

The length of time a patient spends waiting to be seen affects not only the patient's perception and ultimately their satisfaction with the treatment received, but also the utilization of healthcare services. Fears of a prolonged waiting times have been implicated as barrier to patients seeking medical attention. Prolonged waiting times and crowing of emergency departments are a reflection of larger supply and demand mismatches in the healthcare system. The cause of prolonged wait in the emergency department has been subject to much research. Factors contributing to patient waiting times have been studied both in developed and developing healthcare systems. In general, authors point to both intrinsic as well as extrinsic factors. For example, Hemmati et al. (2018) conducted a cross-sectional study of patients waiting times in the emergency departments of two teaching hospitals in Tehran. Their study demonstrated that a large number of patients needing medical attention, long distance between emergency units, poor communication, and the low hospital manpower to be the major causes of waiting times. In addition, their results showed the patient waiting time to significantly depend on daily duty shift, the day of the week, and insurance coverage. Meanwhile, a large demand on the healthcare facilities compounded by staff shortage had been described as a main factor in a study by Oche and Adamu (2013) who had focused on the general outpatient departments in north western Nigeria. The impact of the increase in the demand for emergency services on patient waiting times has been reported for healthcare systems over the globes. In fact, studies of extrinsic influences on waiting times in the US health systems have sought to provide some insight into the causes of the increased demands and ultimately, the way in which patients waiting times are impacted. For example, Billings et al. (2000) reported that a general dissatisfaction with the quality of local primary care has contributed to the surge in the demand for emergency service. This in turn leads to overcrowding of the emergency departments and ultimately prolonged patient waiting times. Interestingly, social demographic represented a double whammy on the increased demand for emergency healthcare. On the one hand, the limited accessibility to local health services by uninsured citizens drove the increase in demands for emergency services, on the other hand, the privately insured seeking a "one-stop" healthcare source similarly contributed to the increased demand, which has been associated with increased waiting time in the emergency departments (Cunningham and May, 2003).

In addition to these, healthcare systems within developed societies have been reported to suffer from intrinsic factors such as staffing shortages, lack of attention given to measuring and managing patient flow, and beds shortages (Pate & Puffe, 2007).

Asplin et al. (2003) developed a conceptual model of ED crowding to help understand its causes and develop potential solutions. In their concept, ED crowding was partitioned into three interdependent components, namely input, throughput, and output. The schematic in Fig. 14.1 depicts the interconnectivity of the three components.

Their description of input factors is quite similar to other research, representative of extrinsic factors, which contribute to the demand on the emergency services. Specifically, they highlighted the role of the emergency departments within the community in the treatment of seriously ill and injured patients; often serving as a referral site for other providers in situations where patient stabilization and hospital admission are deemed necessary. Particularly, for complex patients, the emergency departments enable for the stabilization, triage, and an initial diagnostic evaluation before admission. In addition to emergency care, the ED also provides a significant amount of unscheduled emergency care. In this capacity, the inadequacy of the local care and or an exacerbation of a chronic health issue or simply due to convenience prompts patients to opt for demanding the cervices of emergency departments. Rather than endure the long wait for a doctor's appointment or sometimes even a problem may worsen while waiting for the appointment, patients will typically seek the service of the ED. Moreover, the fact that the hospital ED service is available around the clock and offers an all-inclusive, same-day service, removes conflicts with employments, and other personal responsibilities. This attracts patients to the ED and causes crowding. Finally, the emergency department acts as a safety net to individuals who face significant barriers be it cost or access to regular healthcare (Gallagher & Lynn, 1990). In fact, 2003 reports from the Institute of Medicine and the general accounting office suggest crowding of emergency departments to be more severe in communities with higher numbers of uninsured residents (Institute of Medicine, US, 2003).

The throughput part of their model looks at the efficiency and effectiveness of the ED's internal processes. The authors described the need to standardize the patient triaging and set goals for time required to place patients into specific waiting rooms and for the provision of the initial evaluation. The phase accounting for the majority of patients waiting time lies in the throughput part, namely the diagnostics testing and treatment. Some of the factors, which contribute to the long wait during this phase includes the layout of the ED and the physical proximity of the different units, the appropriateness of the nursing, physician and specialty consultations ratio

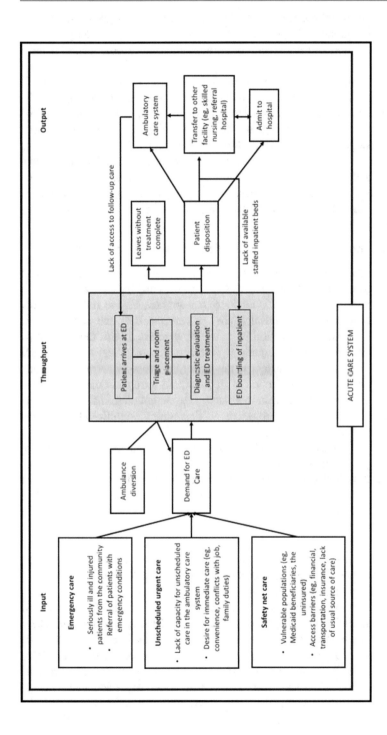

Fig. 14.1 Input-throughput-output conceptual model of ED crowding. *Source* Adapted from Asplin et al. (2003)

and the cohesiveness of the team dynamics, the efficient use of diagnostic testing facilities such as laboratory or medical imaging technologies, the quality of information documentation and the access to thorough medical records, just to name a few.

While the throughput part of the model is intrinsic in its nature, the output is rather extrinsic, often a result of insufficiency downstream. For example, quite often, ED patients who are to be admitted unto specialty wards for further care end up being boarded in the ED long after the decision for the admission had been reached (US general accounting office, 2003). Their continual boarding often results from a lack of inpatient bed at their destination. This boarding of patients effectively reduces the emergency departments' capacity for new patients and has been reported to have even further downstream consequences such as ambulance diversion, which ultimately prolongs waiting times of other emergency departments.

The Adverse Effects of Prolonged Outpatient Waiting Times

Among others, the most frequently researched consequence of prolonged patient waits is its negative impact on patient satisfaction with the care they receive. Although the totality of the available evidence has not been able to statistically link patient satisfaction with the technical quality of care received, the body of work demonstrates that patient satisfaction is, however, associated with the concept of overall quality as perceived by the patient. To this end, satisfaction as a parameter has been studied in various outpatient settings over the years. For example, Huang et al. (2004) compared the satisfaction of frequent and infrequent emergency care users with the care they received. In their study, the authors found factors such as their discharge instructions and subjective waiting time to significantly influence patient satisfaction with emergency care.

In their study to assess the impact of waiting time on patient satisfaction with not only the quality of care but also with their physician's abilities, Bleustein et al. (2014) analyzed 11,352 survey responses returned by patients over the course of one year across 44 ambulatory clinics within a large academic medical center. The authors concluded that essential metrics such as the likelihood to recommend and the overall satisfaction with the experience were negatively impacted by longer wait times. Additionally, increased wait times affect the perceptions of information, instructions, and the overall treatment provided by physicians and other caregivers. Specifically, the patient's perception of the provider's competence was also affected by a prolonged waiting time.

The focus on patient satisfaction as a metrics stems from the believe that satisfied patients are least likely to complain or file a legal suit. Rather, they are more likely to recommend the emergency department and are more likely to return in future emergencies and not exacerbate symptoms through procrastination or delay (Rydman et al., 1999). On an even more practical note, even earlier studies such as by Waggoner et al., 1981 and Björvell & Stieg, 1991 suggested that satisfied patients are more likely to comply with their discharge instructions.

A further consequence of prolonged waiting time is its association with frustration, aggression, and often violence toward the hospital staff. This greatly impacts the department's atmosphere, ultimately leading to increased tension, and pressure experienced by the medical staffs. In a retrospective review of 218 incident report forms in an urban UK emergency department, James et al. (2006) identified long waiting time as well as influence of drugs or alcohol to be a contributing factor for triggering violence toward emergency staffs. Similarly, Morphet et al. (2014) employed the Adelphi technique, a consensus-building method to identify and compare what nurse unit managers, triage and non-triage nurses believed to be the prevalence, and nature of violence and aggression in the emergency department. The common consensus was violence, resulted from drugs and alcohol, as well as long waiting times. Most recently, Johnsen et al. (2020) conducted a study in ten emergency primary healthcare clinics in Norway over the period of a year, in order to determine the nature and causes of aggressive incidents. The authors found that specifically for verbal assaults, which accounted for 31.6%, waiting time is a central provocation.

A perhaps quite obvious consequence of prolonged waiting time is the exacerbation or the worsening of a patient's medical condition. This is often more noticeable in cases where pain or bleeding is involved. Using ambulance diversion and emergency department crowding as a measure of prolonged patient waiting time, Sun et al. (2013) performed retrospective cohort analysis of patients admitted in 2007 through the EDs of non-federal and acute care hospitals. Focusing on inpatient mortality and hospital length of stay, their findings from 995,379 admissions to 187 hospitals revealed that patients who were admitted on days with high ED crowding experienced 5% greater odds of inpatient death, 0.8% longer hospital length of stay, and 1% increased costs per admission.

Analyzing the mean occupancy of an emergency department between 2002 and 2004, Richardson (2006) was able to quantify the relationship between emergency department overcrowding and patient mortality at ten days. In this study, patients were stratified by the status of the emergency department at the time they were brought in which were characterized as either overcrowded or non-overcrowded. In a total of 34 377 overcrowded and 32 231 non-overcrowded presentations at 736 shifts each, there had been 144 deaths in the overcrowded cohort and 101 deaths in the non-overcrowded cohort, equating to 0.42% and 0.31%, respectively. The relative risk of death at ten days was, therefore 1.34.

In an earlier study, Krochmal and Riley (1994) categorized patients admitted into their hospital over a three-year period, categorizing them into whether they had spent less than one day or more than one day in the ED, after they had been admitted to the hospital and were waiting for a bed assignment. The physicians found that during the three years, patients who had spent more than one day waiting in the ED had 11%, 13%, and 10% increase in total hospital length of stay.

Liew et al., 2003 were able to directly correlate the length of time spent in the emergency department with the length of inpatient hospital stay. While assessing 17,954 hospital admission, the group found that patients who spent 4, 4–8, 8–12, and greater than 12 h in the emergency department ended up spending an average of 3.37 days, 5.65 days, 6.6 days, and 7.2 days, respectively.

An exacerbation of the patient's condition has also been found to have economic consequences for the clinic. A 2020 paper published by Woodworth and Holmes (2020), estimating the effect of emergency waiting time on the cost of treatment found that prolonging the wait of a patient who arrives with a serious condition by ten minutes will increase the hospital's cost to care for the patient by an average of six percent. Notably, this effect was found to be less pronounced for patients with less serious conditions.

Current Strategies for Managing Outpatient Waiting Times

In most industries, when a business perpetually fails to deliver on its essential performance indicators, pressure is applied both internally and externally, forcing the organization to a point of bending or breaking. Internal pressures could come from managers to implement major changes to ways of working, in order to improve performance, efficiency or both. Meanwhile, external pressures could come in the form of market pressures, with customers choosing to go to competitors, which offer better services. The hospital emergency department is, however, too complex a system to simply fold to these types of pressures. For one thing, inappropriate attempts to squeeze more efficiency out of a hospital emergency department could have major impacts on patient safety. Moreover, the concept of shopping for alternative options or better competitors is rarely an option when a patient has an urgent medical need. The following section uses the conceptual model developed by Asplin et al. (2003) mentioned earlier to describe how some of the ED crowding solutions are designed to target the different aspects of the healthcare system as a whole.

Asplins et al. conceptualized model categorized the cause and cure of ED crowding into three parts, namely input, throughput, and output. On this wise, Arain et al. (2015) performed a survey to determine the impact of having a nearby GP-led walk-in center in Sheffield, England on the demand for emergency department care. Their interviews of over 500 patients demonstrated a 26% monthly reduction in adult "PG-type" of ED visits. Albeit, the 7% drop in the pediatric groups proved to be statistically insignificant, as did the 8% drop in the total ED visits. A few years prior, a similar observation on the other side of the world by Sharma and Inder (2011) had demonstrated that the availability of locally-accessible GP clinics offered non-urgent patients more choice and thereby diverted these categories of patients to an alternative care model and ultimately resulted in a 19% drop in waiting times for patients with urgent needs. By contrast, Anantharaman (2008) could not demonstrate an impact of alternative clinics on public ED attendances in Singapore, arguing that these types of clinics tend to be highly priced and attract their own type of patients.

A not too dissimilar strategy saws a 26% decrease in ED admission following a pilot program, which extended the opening hours of its nearby GPs and increased their availability days to seven days a week service (Dolton & Pathania, 2016; Whittaker et al., 2016). In addition to the aforementioned strategies, several other social interventions have also been reported. These include public education campaigns, financial consequences for nonemergent cases, as well as transfer of nonemergency patients to alternative hospitals. The impact of these measures on ED waiting times was, however, found to be variable. Some were positive, but unsustainable, while others were met with resistance from the public Anantharaman (2008).

The most obvious place to make changes that will reduce patients waiting time is within the emergency department itself. Hence, it is without surprise that over half of published works on this subject are report on strategies to improve the operational efficiency of the emergency department. For the most part, these strategies aimed to get the patient in front of a physician at the quickest possible time. A large body of work has looked at the advantages of involving the doctors earlier in the patient journey. Particularly, at the triaging phase (Holroyd et al., 2007; Burstrom et al. 2016). While some of these studies focused on the lengths of time spent at the emergency department (Jarvis et al., 2014; White et al., 2012), some observed its impact on how many patients left the emergency room without being seen by the physician (Burke et al., 2017; Shetty et al., 2012). Another strategy readily published on was the incorporation of a fast-track system for patients with lower acuity presentations (Arya et al., 2013). While this strategy reportedly led to a reduction in the length of time spent at the emergency department (or emergency department length of stay (EDLOS)), a closer scrutiny revealed that the reduced waiting time and reported improvement was rather limited to the triage category, which had been fast-tracked (Copeland & Gray, 2015).

Some targeted strategies have focused on specific parts of the patients' ED journey. In particular is the length of time patients spent waiting for their test results. In this regards, Elizabeth Lee-Lewandrowski et al. () reported a mean EDLOS declined from 8.46 to 7.14 h for diagnostic tests, performed at the point of care, compared with those performed in a central laboratory. Additionally, a clinical satisfaction survey revealed patients dissatisfaction with central laboratory testing times as compared with tests, which were performed at the point of care.

Another strategy related to this is the employment of dedicated staff. For instance, Singer et al. (2008) reported on the implementation of a purposefully dedicated stat laboratory made available to the ED on a 24/7 basis. The ensuing was a reduction in median EDLOS of 64 min from the pre-dedicated stat lab phase. In line with this, several reports describe the success of having a purposely dedicated nurse, assigned to manage the flow of the patient journey within the ED. These nurses focus on identifying the delay to patients being seen by a doctor (Tenbensel et al., 2017). These have been shown to be pretty successful, helping EDs achieve their waiting time targets (Asha & Ajami, 2014).

Following the conceptual model developed by Asplin et al. (2003), strategies exist, which primarily target the output phase of the emergency services in order to reduce emergency department crowding. While some of these solutions look at expediting patient receipt of their prescription medications and their discharge notice in order to free up the emergency room, most of the studies within this remit focus on getting patients admitted into an inpatient ward as soon as possible. For the most part, this is being achieved by removing the blockage downstream. An example of this was described by Howell et al. (2008), who assessed the efficacy of the implementation of a proactive bed manager. This manager by making regular daily rounds of the emergency department monitors the bed availability, emergency department congestion, and flow in real time. The said manager had the freedom to facilitate the transfer of admitted patients from the emergency department to their destined inpatient ward. Moreover, these managers had the buy-in and support of assigned bed directors, who in turn could call for additional resources from other departments to augment the emergency department. This intervention got patients who had been admitted out of the emergency department on average 98 min faster. However, it had no impact on patients who had not been admitted. Similar strategies, which dedicated resources to the identification and allocation of beds, were reported by Barrett et al. (2012) to have improved the waiting time in a Midwest medical center with 59,000 annual ED visits from an average of 216–103 min. This allowed the staff at the hospital to care for an additional 2,936 patients. Just as the bed managers are able to recruit help from bed directors, several studies have shown the importance of management or leadership support in tackling ED crowding. This top-down approach usually manifests in some sort of management-led initiatives, monitoring programs, changes to working cultures, among others. An example of such was a study by Patel et al., 2014, where leaders from both the emergency departments and the main hospital collaborated to track and monitor hospital-wide inpatient bed availability and emergency department crowding. Their goal was to increase the percentage of patients who were admitted to inpatient beds within 60 min from the time, the beds were requested and ED boarding time. This outcome measure was increased by 16%. To achieve this, top managers had to actively intervene in real time by contacting staff whenever delays occurred to expedite immediate solutions to achieve the 60 min goal.

The adoption of targets and goals has also been associated with reduced patient waiting times and crowding of the emergency departments, particularly when it is a national guideline. However, close scrutiny of the achievements of externally placed mandates and legislation shows that care is needed when interpreting the results or assessing the true impacts. For example, a study reported on by Perera et al. (2014) described an increase in clearance from the emergency department from 49.0% to 53.2% in response to a Government-imposed National Emergency Access Target. However, while length of stay was reduced in the emergency department, it increased in the inpatient wards, pretty much suggesting that the problem was simply shifted down the stream, rather than be solved, since the Government's target had been solely focused on decongesting the emergency department.

Objective Waiting Time: An Alternative Approach to Tackling the Problems Associated With Emergency Room Waiting

While a large amount of collective efforts has gone into reducing patient waiting times in order to quantifiably improve their satisfaction, some researchers have approached the issues of patient dissatisfaction (as brought on by prolonged waiting times) directly, and from a psychological perspective, looking at their needs (Hostutler et al., 1999). It had long since been demonstrated that the perceived wait time is a more compelling indicator of patient satisfaction than actual wait time (Thompson et al., 1996). Moreover, while studying the effect of waiting time on patient satisfaction, Pruyn et al. (1998) found an interrelationship between the perceived waiting time and patients' emotional state. Therefore, researchers have tried to address the fear, anxiety, stress, and perception of pain which have all been tied to patient waiting experience of the ED (Gordon et al., 2010).

Both the patient's perception and psychology have been the focus in these attempts. The simplest examples were providing more information to the patients (Oermann et al., 2003; O'Neill et al. 2004). This information includes queuing information such as how long they may have to wait (Levesque et al., 2000), the number of cases in front of them (Dansky & Miles, 1997), or even process information such as the patient journey, and where they are along that journey. These information help to manage the patient's expectations, influencing more so a patient's psychology and their perception, and yet contributes to patient satisfaction (Oermann et al., 2002). In a Web-based survey of 5030 patients, Anderson et al. (2007) found that getting to spend longer time with the doctors could counteract the patient dissatisfaction with long waiting times, finally arguing in alignment with earlier research (Feddock et al. 2005) that shortening patient waiting times at the expense of time spent with the patient would be counterproductive in terms of patient satisfaction.

Service Design Practices

It is in light of this latter approach, namely the psychological that the present work proposes a change in the service and practices of the hospital emergency departments. All patients are at least to some extent cognizant of the fact that waiting for a service is unavoidable. However, being aware of its necessity has not made the experience of waiting in the emergency department for medical attention any less unpleasant. Rather, it is said to fuel aggression among those waiting to receive the service (Anderson et al. 2000; Sprague et al., 2011). The aggression, in turn, has been reported to elicit feelings of anger and frustration in the target of the aggression (Demsky et al., 2014), and thus reduces well-being (Spielberger et al. 2009). To summarize, the declining patient satisfaction with emergency care with increased waiting times has a downstream effect on the emotional and psychological state of the medical staff and that of the emergency department. Therefore, tackling the patients waiting from a psychological standpoint not only improves patient satisfaction but also that of the working environment for the medical staffs.

Rather than reducing the length of time patients spent waiting in the ED to receive healthcare, the present study aims not to reduce the negative impact of said waiting time on the psychological and emotional well-being of the patients.

Employing a Web-based single-patient virtual waiting portal, patients will be provided regularly updated information about their ED-journey and an estimated waiting time. In addition, the portal will provide a mean of communication between patients and ED staff. Finally, the platform will offer information and entertainment activities, which are aimed to help the patients wile away their waiting time. As the platform will be online, this affords the patients flexibility and mobility, enabling them to go out for fresh air, rather than being glued to the monitors in the waiting rooms.

It is expected that the communication of their waiting time, the entertainment provided on the waiting platform and the ability to move around and not be confined to a waiting room will positively influence the patients' perception of their waiting times, and ultimately improve their satisfaction with the received healthcare.

Proposal

The employment of a Web-based, virtual queuing, and communication platform may improve the perception of patients, and ultimately, their overall satisfaction with the received healthcare within a hospital's emergency department.

While-U-Wait: A Virtual Queueing Platform

The while-u-wait service concept centers around a Web-based, individual virtual queuing, and information portal, which enables patients triaged within an emergency services ward to monitor and stay up-to-date with their journey through the medical care facilities. The platform provides constantly updated information to the patients about their waiting times, place in queue, unexpected delays, and even a communication channels, where ED staffs may ask medically-relevant question or make requests, without requiring patients' physical presence at their reception desk. This affords the patients mobility, and subsequently, the freedom to go out for fresh air, to eat, use other hospital facilities, or other forms of distraction, rather than be confined to the queuing monitoring screens in the waiting rooms. In doing so, the virtual waiting platform aims to combat waiting-associated stress and its impact on patient satisfaction and ultimately clinical outcomes. For the sake of context-driven description, the term while-u-wait platform will be synonymously used with the virtual waiting platform or the virtual queueing platform.

Rational: The Psychology of Waiting

As described in the previous sections of this work, patient satisfaction with emergency department care declines as the time spent waiting for it increases. Decades of tireless efforts by physicians, ED specialists, Government regulations, guidelines, and targets have not succeeded to eliminate or significantly reduce the long waiting times in the ED. On this wise, the present work focuses on improving the patient journey, regardless of the persistent long waiting time. Concisely, given that endeavors to reduce the ED waiting time have failed, the present service concept aims to reduce the negative impacts of prolonged waiting on the patients.

The present work exploits the key principles of the psychology of waiting. Several of these principles were discussed by David Maister (1985), who studied some psychological considerations involved in managing customer's acceptance of waiting time. In this chapter, "The Psychology of Waiting Lines," the former Harvard business school professor examined how waits are experienced by customers, and offered practical suggestions on how to address specific customer perceptions, in order to enhance customer satisfaction. Although the publication was by no means exhaustive in its listing of customer perception of waiting time, it did, howeve, r identify very key principles of psychological perceptions, namely.

1. Unoccupied time feels longer than occupied time
2. Preprocess waits feel longer than in-process waits
3. Anxiety makes waits seem longer
4. Uncertain waits are longer than known, finite waits
5. Unexplained waits are longer than explained waits
6. Unfair waits are longer than equitable waits
7. The more valuable the service, the longer the customer will wait
8. Solo waits feel longer than group waits.

The following study will address principles 1, 3, 4, and 5, namely unoccupied time feels longer than occupied time, anxiety makes waits seem longer, uncertain waits are longer than known, finite waits and unexplained waits are longer than explained waits, in that the virtual waiting platform will help occupy the patient time, providing mild distractions, even entertainments. In doing so, it aims to help take patients focus away from their predicament of physical discomfort and having to wait outside their natural comfort zone. Thirdly, the platform will provide regularly updated estimation of their remaining waiting times, what they are waiting for, and information on unexpected causes of delays.

Platform Design

The virtual waiting platform facilitates the provision of individual queueing information to patients awaiting healthcare, through a responsive Website accessed via patients' own mobile devices. Once patients have been received by a triage staff, they are assigned a unique two-part case/patient identification. This information need not be attributable to the patient, nor must it be able to identify an individual. Rather, two randomly generated sets of numbers, which when used together allows the user to receive information pertaining to their ED process. In the background, the virtual waiting platform interfaces with the hospital's own queueing system retrieves the waiting information pertaining to the said user which would have also been displayed on the monitors in the waiting room. This information is sent directly to the user's personal login on the virtual waiting platform. Unlike the display monitors in the waiting room, the virtual waiting platform offers a one-to-one interface between the patient and the ED team. Therefore, information may be shared and updated.

The primary role of the virtual waiting platform is to display the remaining waiting time for the user. However, the platform could also be used to pass on more sophisticated information to the patients such as the reasons for the delay, changes to waiting times, follow-up questions, and instructions for the subsequent stages of the user's ED journey. Furthermore, the system could also be used to provide information and even distract and entertain by way of games and media.

The while-u-wait platform aims improve the patients' experience and perception of their personal ED journeys by emerging them in a useful and user-friendly design, which ensures security and privacy.

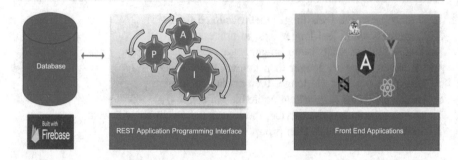

Fig. 14.2 Architecture of the virtual waiting platform, front-end development framework for 2021. *Source* Author's own compilation (2021)

The Essential Components

Figure 14.2 shows a schematic representation of the architecture of the virtual waiting platform. The system is principally a processing unit, which transmits waiting times, retrieved from the hospital's own waiting system directly to patient's individual digital waiting space. The platform was built as a three-tier application consisting of

1. The database tier: This was built with a flexible and scalable NoSQL document database system (Cloud Firestore)
2. The API: This is the server end of the application, it was built with firebase, a serverless framework, and the code was written in TypeScript
3. The front which is the while-u-wait application has two-part

    a. The hospital end
    b. The patient end

These were both written in with angular, a single page application development framework.

Use Case Scenario

Patient Experience

The schematic diagram in Fig. 14.3 describes the features and activities which the virtual waiting platform offers the patients, namely;

1. The platform verifies the patient's hospital-generated ID. This is important because the platform only enables the patient to see their own waiting information and not those of others in the queue. Therefore, it is essential that the patient is seeing the correct waiting information
2. The platform allows patients to log in and remain logged in, until otherwise logged out by the patient or the hospital has closed their case. This is important

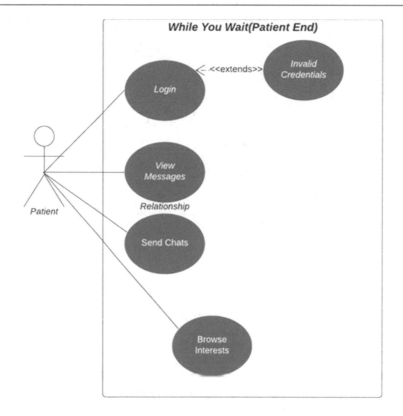

Fig. 14.3 Schematic representation of the patients use case scenario on the W-U-W platform. *Source* Author's own illustration (2021)

because patients may feel that their waiting time is affected by having interruptions in their login status
3. The platform shows the patients, their waiting information possibly the next activities on their patient journey, where they need to present themselves, and any other information, the hospital wishes to relay to the patients
4. The platform allows a bilateral communication between the hospital staffs and the patient. This is useful when there are follow-up questions or requests by the ED team members, without the patient having to present themselves at the ED reception desk.
5. Patients have the opportunities to initiate a conversation with the hospital staffs. This is equally important, for example, to report medically-relevant changes in their condition
6. Patients have the option of browsing the Internet or be entertained by multimedia, which may later include local radio stations and advertisements of local facilities.

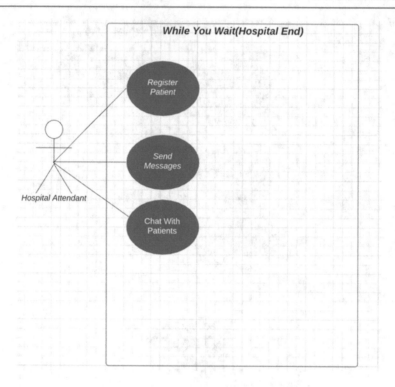

Fig. 14.4 Schematic representation of the hospital's use case scenario on the W-U-W platform. *Source* Author's own illustration (2021)

Hospital View

The schematic diagram in Fig. 14.4 describes the features and activities which the virtual vaiting platform offers the hospital, namely;

1. The hospital staff registers the patient on the platform
2. The hospital server connects with that of the virtual waiting platform and transmits patients individual waiting information
3. The virtual waiting platform server regularly requests waiting time updates from the hospital server and sends the updates and messages to patients' individual Web-based waiting space
4. The hospital staff may communicate ad hoc with the patients via the virtual waiting platform as needed.

The Patient Journey and Virtual Waiting

The following section describes the sequence of events, which ensues a patient presenting himself at the emergency department and using the virtual waiting platform to manage their queueing.

The journey begins with the registration of the patient and their triaging. During this phase, the patient is allocated a system-generated identification code. In emergency departments with a televised queueing system, this identification code would be shown, with those of other patients in the waiting rooms, once their turn has come to present themselves to the next stage of their ED journey. However, within the hospitals queueing system exists already other information, pertaining to the patient's approximate waiting time, prioritization, and target treatment time, among others.

The virtual waiting system requests some of this information at the patient level and presents them to the patient on an individualized Web-based waiting platform. The platform is accessed by the patient, by logging into an Internet browser using the hospital generated patient ID, plus an additional password.

Whereas, the monitors in the hospital waiting lounge present neither a patient's estimated waiting time nor their priority level, the virtual platform has the ability to constantly present these information and update them at regular intervals.

Proposed Benefits

A major benefit is that the phenomenon of "waiting fatigue," whereby patients are constantly staring at the screen not knowing when their number will be called or afraid to stretch their legs or use the toilets or other facilities for fear of missing their number being called, can be prevented.

Additional benefit of the virtual waiting platform is that it could be used by the clinical team to communicate with the patients about things specific to their case, without having to call them into the reception desk. Further benefits include the possibility of additional activities, such as light reading, multimedia or games, which could proof a positive distraction for the patients to while away the time. Not least of all is the possibility to reduce the overcrowding in the hospital waiting room, due to the fact that the patients are no longer bound to the waiting room monitor. This may potentially improve the mood in the waiting room and improve the working conditions of the clinical staff.

14.2   Conceptualization of Clinical Benefits

Measurability of Benefits

In order to assess the benefits offered by the virtual queuing management platform to the patients and potentially the clinical staff, proof-of-concept studies will be required, which will answer the following questions:

1. Adoption: Will patients be prepared to log onto the system and use it?
2. Efficacy: Will the use of the system influence the patients' perception of their waiting time and or their satisfaction with their ED experience.

Upon their arrival at the ED and having been triaged, the patients will be informed of the W-U-W service concept and its potential benefits to the waiting patients and the clinical staff. The patients will then be invited to use their given triage number to log themselves onto the virtual waiting platform in order to access and monitor their waiting time. Once their ED journey is over, the patients will be invited to fill out a simple questionnaire.

Platform Adoption

The adoption test is based on the assumption that patients waiting for their treatments will place a high value on receiving more information about their ED journey than they currently do. In this phase, the number of patients who were approached and invited to use the platform will be compared with the actual number of patients who indeed proceeds to use the platform. A distinction will be drawn between those who logged onto the platform, and those who used it to the end and filled out the test questionnaire. These data will be stratified according to patient triage number, in order to assess any correlation between a patient's willingness to use the platform and ability to use the platform. This will help identify and eliminate potential barriers to adoption.

Hypotheses:

- Patients waiting in a hospital emergency department will recognize the potential value of a virtual waiting platform in reducing waiting associated stress and will endorse its usage.
- Patients will log onto the platform, in order to gain early access to their waiting times

Success Criteria

A substantial number of patients who have the opportunity to log onto the platform will log on.

Efficacy: Patient Perception and Satisfaction Questioner

To demonstrate the platform's effectiveness at helping to manage the waiting times of those who log onto and use the system, patients will be handed a short questionnaire after their treatment. The questionnaire will ask questions relating to their perception of their waiting time, namely how long they feel to have been waiting? Whether they feel that it is too long or appropriate? Finally, the patients will be asked about their level of satisfaction with the received treatment. Their questionnaire results will be matched with patients, who present with similar seriousness as demonstrated by their triage number, or physical capability, in order to balance out the influence of a patient's circumstances such as pain and emotional stress level.

Hypotheses:

- Patients who log onto and use the platform during their waiting time will develop a more positive perception of their waiting time. Precisely, these patients will perceive their waiting times as having been shorter than those who had not use the platform.
- Patients who log onto and use the platform during their waiting time will report a higher level of satisfaction with their received treatments than those who did not use the platform.

Success Criteria

A higher gross difference perceived waiting time and actual waiting time, for patients who logged onto and used the platform compared with patients who did not.

The higher degree of treatment satisfaction reported by patients who logged onto and used the platform compared with patients who did not.

Patient Information and Informed Consent

A very brief information page regarding the W-U-W service concept and the virtual waiting platform and the test being conducted will be provided to all patients entering the emergency department. The information page will inform the patients of how to log onto the Web-based platform. It will also ensure that they understand that the system will require and hence place an additional burden on their device battery life and mobile data. An informed consent form will be incorporated into the patient information sheet. The consent form is to be signed by the patients, documenting their willingness to participate in the study, and to fill out the short questionnaire at the end of their treatment.

Data Handling and Privacy

For its operation, the virtual waiting platform requires information from the hospital system pertaining to a patient waiting times. However, patient-identifiable information is not required and therefore will not be exchanged between the hospital queue management system and the W-U-W platform.

Summary

The utility studies are designed to help assess possible impact of the virtual queueing platform on patients awaiting healthcare services. The study is divided into two or at least designed to answer two questions, namely,

1. Will patients use the platform?
2. Will those who use the platform get the desired benefits?

In both cases, the information gained by the platform users will be compared to patients received by the ED at similar periods and having similar triage number. A success here will be defined as a high proportion of people logging onto and using the platform and patients, who use the platform reporting a more positive perception of waiting time.

14.3 Conclusion

The present work studied ways in which technology could be used to manage waiting and anticipation, particularly for patients while awaiting much medical care. A focus was placed on the hospital's emergency department, because it represents an environment where the phenomenon of prolonged waiting is not only common-placed, but also persists, despite much effort from hospital managers, directors, and government policy makers globally.

The researched literature summarized the available knowledge on prolonged waiting and overcrowding in the hospital's emergency department. Some of the major causes for prolonged waiting and overcrowding were briefly described along with unavoidable consequences associated with waiting too long for healthcare treatment. Subsequently, key strategies and systems put in place to combat prolonged waiting and emergency department overcrowding were briefly delved into. With the understanding that the collective effort to combat prolonged waiting has neither eliminated it nor is it likely to, the concepts of objective waiting and perceived waiting time were introduced.

The while-u-wait platform proposed an alternative service-based strategy to help hospitals manage the hospital overcrowding, and the patient to help deal with waiting associated stress. The technology itself which is the virtual waiting platform was developed and tested. The platform comprises of two interfaces. One for the waiting patients and the other for the hospital or the waiting manager, who had the possibility of viewing all waiting clients simultaneously. The platform was able to register users and communicate within itself.

To realize its full functionality, the platform would have to interface with a hospital's already established waiting platform. Moreover, it would allow for the determination of its adoptability by and impact on its target audience. This latter hypothesis was designed as two-part study, which posed the questions will patients waiting for healthcare understand the value of receiving regularly updated information about their waiting time and whether the access to such information will positively influence their perception of the time spent waiting and ultimately their perception of the healthcare they receive.

Finally, the future scope of the platform describing its versatility and adaptability to all sectors, where waiting is unavoidable, undesired, and prolonged was proposed. Within the remit of this future scope, the maturity of the platform into a mobile application, which would manage multiple virtual queueing and waiting, essentially allowing its user to queue for multiple services and products simultaneously. Essentially, its users would be able to optimize their day, transiting from one appointment to the next, and arriving at the points of service just in time. This embodies the principle of off-site queueing and just-in-time arrival.

References

Anantharaman, V. (2008). Impact of health care system interventions on emergency department utilization and overcrowding in Singapore. *International Journal of Emergency Medicine, 1*(1), 11–20. https://doi.org/10.1007/s12245-008-0004-8. PMID: 19384496; PMCID: PMC2536176.

Anderson, C. A., & Dill, K. E. (2000). Video games and aggressive thoughts, feelings, and behavior in the laboratory and in life. *Journal of Personality and Social Psychology, 78*(4), 772–790. https://doi.org/10.1037/0022-3514.78.4.772

Anderson, R. T., Camacho, F. T., & Balkrishnan, R. (2007). Willing to wait? The influence of patient wait time on satisfaction with primary care. *BMC Health Service Research, 7*(31), 1–5. https://doi.org/10.1186/1472-6963-7-31. PMID: 17328807; PMCID: PMC1810532.

Arain, M., Campbell, M. J., & Nicholl, J. P. (2015). Impact of a GP-led walk-in centre on NHS emergency departments. *Emergency Medicine Journal, 32*(4), 295–300. https://doi.org/10.1136/emermed-2013-202410 PMID: 24406328.

Arya, R., Wei, G., McCoy, J. V., Crane, J., Ohman-Strickland, P., & Eisenstein, R. M. (2013). Decreasing length of stay in the emergency department with a split emergency severity index 3 patient flow model. *Academic Emergency Medicine, 20*(11), 1171–1179. https://doi.org/10.1111/acem.12249 PMID: 24238321.

Asha, S. E., & Ajami, A. (2014). Improvement in emergency department length of stay using a nurse-led "emergency journey coordinator": A before/after study. *Emergency Medicine Australasia, 26*(2), 158–163. https://doi.org/10.1111/1742-6723.12201 PMID: 24708005.

Asplin, B. R., Magid, D. J., Rhodes, K. V., Solberg, L. I., Lurie, N., & Jr, C. C. A. (2003). A conceptual model of emergency department crowding. *Annals of Emergency Medicine, 42*(2), 173–180. https://doi.org/10.1067/mem.2003.302 PMID: 12883504.

Bagust, A., Place, M., & Posnett, J. W. (1999). Dynamics of bed use in accommodating emergency admissions: Stochastic simulation model. *BMJ, 319*(7203), 155–158. https://doi.org/10.1136/bmj.319.7203.155 PMID: 10406748; PMCID: PMC28163.

Baker, D. W., Stevens, C. D., & Brook, R. H. (1991). Patients who leave a public hospital emergency department without being seen by a physician. *Causes and Consequences. JAMA, 266*(8), 1085–1090. PMID: 1865540.

Barrett, L., Ford, S., & Ward-Smith P. (2012). A bed management strategy for overcrowding in the emergency department. *Nursing Economics, 30*(2), 82–5, 116. PMID: 22558725.

Bernstein, S. L., Aronsky, D., Duseja, R., Epstein, S., Handel, D., Hwang, U., McCarthy, M., John McConnell K., Pines, J. M., Rathlev, N., Schafermeyer, R., Zwemer, F., Schull, M., & Asplin, B. R. (2009). Society for academic emergency medicine, emergency department crowding task force. The effect of emergency department crowding on clinically oriented outcomes. *Academic Emergency Medicine, 16*(1), 1–10. https://doi.org/10.1111/j.1553-2712.2008.00295.x. PMID: 19007346.

Billings, J., Parikh, N., & Mijanovich, T. (2000). Emergency department use in New York City: A substitute for primary care? *Issue Brief (common Fund), 433*, 1–5.

Björvell, H., & Stieg, J. (1991). Patients' perceptions of the health care received in an emergency department. *Annals of Emergency Medicine, 20*(7), 734–738. https://doi.org/10.1016/s0196-0644(05)80833-9 PMID: 2064093.

Bleustein, C., Rothschild, D. B., Valen, A., Valatis, E., Schweitzer, L., & Jones, R. (2014). Wait times, patient satisfaction scores, and the perception of care. *The American Journal of Managed Care, 20*(5), 393–400. PMID: 25181568.

Burke, J. A., Greenslade, J., Chabrowska, J., Greenslade, K., Jones, S., Montana, J., Bell, A., & O'Connor, A. (2017). Two hour evaluation and referral model for shorter turnaround times in the emergency department. *Emergency Medicine Australasia, 29*(3), 315–323. https://doi.org/ 10.1111/1742-6723.12781 PMID: 28455884.

Burström, L., Engström, M. L., Castrén, M., Wiklund, T., & Enlund, M. (2016). Improved quality and efficiency after the introduction of physician-led team triage in an emergency department. *Upsala Journal of Medical Sciences, 121*(1), 38–44. https://doi.org/10.3109/03009734.2015. 1100223. PMID: 26553523; PMCID: PMC4812056.

Clarey, A. J., & Cooke, M. W. (2012). Patients who leave emergency departments without being seen: Literature review and English data analysis. *Emergency Medicine Journal, 29*(8), 617–621. https://doi.org/10.1136/emermed-2011-200537 PMID: 21890863.

Copeland, J., & Gray, A. (2015). A daytime fast track improves throughput in a single physician coverage emergency department. *CJEM, 17*(6), 648–655. https://doi.org/10.1017/cem.2015.41 PMID: 26063177.

Cunningham, P., & May, J. (2003). Insured Americans drive surge in emergency department visits. *Issue Brief (center for Studying Health System Change), 70*, 1–6. PMID: 14577417.

Dansky, K. H., & Miles, J. (1997). Patient satisfaction with ambulatory healthcare services: Waiting time and filling time. *Hospital & Health Services Administration, 42*(2), 165–177. PMID: 10167452.

Davenport, P. J., O'Connor, S. J., Szychowski, J. M., Landry, A. Y., & Hernandez, S. R. (2017). The relationship between emergency department wait times and inpatient satisfaction. *Health Marketing Quarterly, 34*(2), 97–112. https://doi.org/10.1080/07359683.2017.1307066 PMID: 28467280.

Demsky, C. A., Ellis, A. M., & Fritz, C. (2014). Shrugging it off: Does psychological detachment from work mediate the relationship between workplace aggression and work-family conflict? *Journal of Occupational Health Psychology, 19*(2), 195–205. https://doi.org/10.1037/ a0035448 PMID: 24635738.

Dolton, P., & Pathania, V. (2016). Can increased primary care access reduce demand for emergency care? Evidence from England's 7-day GP opening. *Journal of Health Economics, 49*, 193–208. https://doi.org/10.1016/j.jhealeco.2016.05.002. PMID: 27395472.

Feddock, C. A., Hoellein, A. R., Griffith, C. H. 3rd, Wilson, J. F., Bowerman, J. L., Becker, N. S., & Caudill, T. S. (2005). Can physicians improve patient satisfaction with long waiting times? *Evaluation and the Health Professions, 28*(1), 40–52. PMID: 15677386.

Gallagher, E. J., & Lynn, S. G. (1990). The etiology of medicalgridlock: Causes of emergency department over-crowding in New York City. *Journal of Emergency Medicine, 8*(6), 785–790. https://doi.org/10.1016/0736-4679(90)90298-a

General Accounting Office. (2003). *Hospital emergency departments: Crowded conditions vary among hospitals and communities.* General Accounting Office.

Goodman, D. M., Srofenyoh, E. K., Olufolabi, A. J., et al. (2017). The third delay: Understanding waiting time for obstetric referrals at a large regional hospital in Ghana. *BMC Pregnancy and Childbirth, 17*, 216. https://doi.org/10.1186/s12884-017-1407-4

Gordon, J., Sheppard, L. A., & Anaf, S. (2010). The patient experience in the emergency department: A systematic synthesis of qualitative research. *International Emergency Nursing, 18*(2), 80–88. https://doi.org/10.1016/j.ienj.2009.05.004 PMID: 20382369.

Hemmati, F., Mahmoudi, G., Dabbaghi, F., Fatehi, F., & Rezazadeh, E. (2018). The factors affecting the waiting time of outpatients in the emergency unit of selected teaching hospitals of Tehran. *Electronic Journal of General Medicine, 15*(4), em66. https://doi.org/10.29333/ejgm/ 93135.

Hing, E., & Bhuiya, F. (2012). Wait time for treatment in hospital emergency departments: 2009. *NCHS Data Brief, 102*, 1–8. PMID: 23101886.

Holroyd, B. R., Bullard, M. J., Latoszek, K., Gordon, D., Allen, S., Tam, S., Blitz, S., Yoon, P., & Rowe, B. H. (2007). Impact of a triage liaison physician on emergency department overcrowding and throughput: A randomized controlled trial. *Academic Emergency Medicine,* *14*(8), 702–708. https://doi.org/10.1197/j.aem.2007.04.018 PMID: 17656607.

Hostutler, J. J., Taft, S. H., & Snyder, C. (1999). Patient needs in the emergency department: Nurses' and patients' perceptions. *Journal of Nursing Administration, 29*(1), 43–50. https://doi. org/10.1097/00005110-199901000-00007 PMID: 9921148.

Howell, E., Bessman, E., Kravet, S., Kolodner, K., Marshall, R., & Wright, S. (2008). Active bed management by hospitalists and emergency department throughput. *Annals of Internal Medicine, 149*(11), 804–811. https://doi.org/10.7326/0003-4819-149-11-200812020-00006 PMID: 19047027.

Hu, S. C. (1994). Clinical and demographic characteristics of adult emergency patients at the Taipei Veterans General Hospital. *Journal of the Formosan Medical Association, 93*(1), 61–65. PMID: 7915584.

Huang, J. A., Lai, C. S., Tsai, W. C., Weng, R. H., Hu, W. H., & Yang, D. Y. (2004). Determining factors of patient satisfaction for frequent users of emergency services in a medical center. *Journal of the Chinese Medical Association, 67*(8), 403–410. PMID: 15553800.

Hwang, U., & Concato, J. (2004). Care in the emergency department: How crowded is overcrowded? *Academic Emergency Medicine, 11*(10), 1097–1101. https://doi.org/10.1197/j. aem.2004.07.004 PMID: 15466155.

Institute of Medicine (US) Committee on the Consequences of Uninsurance. (2003). A shared destiny: Community effects of uninsurance. Washington (DC): National Academies Press (US). PMID: 25057645.

James, A., Madeley, R., & Dove, A. (2006). Violence and aggression in the emergency department. *Emergency Medicine Journal, 23*(6), 431–434. https://doi.org/10.1136/emj.2005. 028621 PMID: 16714500; PMCID: PMC2564335.

Jarvis, P., Davies, T., Mitchell, K., Taylor, I., & Baker, M. (2014). Does rapid assessment shorten the amount of time patients spend in the emergency department? *British Journal of Hospital Medicine (london, England), 75*(11), 648–651. https://doi.org/10.12968/hmed.2014.75.11.648 PMID: 25383437.

Johnsen, G. E., Morken, T., Baste, V., Rypdal, K., Palmstierna, T., & Hjulstad, J. (2020). Characteristics of aggressive incidents in emergency primary health care described by the Staff Observation Aggression Scale—Revised Emergency (SOAS-RE). *BMC Health Services Research, 20*(33), 1–8. https://doi.org/10.1186/s12913-019-4856-9

Knight, H. E., Self, A., & Kennedy, S. H. (2013). Why are women dying when they reach hospital on time? A systematic review of the "third delay." *PLoS ONE, 8*(5). https://doi.org/10.1371/ journal.pone.0063846 PMID: 23704943; PMCID: PMC3660500.

Krochmal, P., & Riley, T. A. (1994). Increased health care costs associated with ED overcrowding. *American Journal of Emergency Medicine, 12*(3), 265–266. https://doi.org/10.1016/0735-6757 (94)90135-x. PMID: 8179727.

Lee-Lewandrowski, E., Corboy, D., Lewandrowski, K., Sinclair, J., McDermot, S., & Benzer, T. I. (2003). Implementation of a point-of-care satellite laboratory in the emergency department of an academic medical center. Impact on test turnaround time and patient emergency department length of stay. *Archives of Pathology and Laboratory Medicine, 127*(4), 456–460. https://doi. org/10.1043/0003-9985(2003)127<0456:IOAPSL>2.0.CO;2. PMID: 12683874.

Lee-Lewandrowski, E., Nichols, J., Van Cott, E., Grisson, R., Louissaint, A., Benzer, T., & Lewandrowski, K. (2009). Implementation of a rapid whole blood D-dimer test in the emergency department of an urban academic medical center: Impact on ED length of stay and ancillary test utilization. *American Journal of Clinical Pathology, 132*(3), 326–331. https://doi. org/10.1309/AJCP6US3ILGEAREE. PMID: 19687307.

Levesque, J., Bogoch, E. R., Cooney, B., Johnston, B., & Wright, J. G. (2000). Improving patient satisfaction with time spent in an orthopedic outpatient clinic. *Canadian Journal of Surgery, 43* (6), 431–436. PMID: 11129831; PMCID: PMC3695198.

Liew, D., Liew, D., & Kennedy, M. P. (2003). Emergency department length of stay independently predicts excess inpatient length of stay. *Medical Journal of Australia, 179* (10), 524–526. https://doi.org/10.5694/j.1326-5377.2003.tb05676.x PMID: 14609414.

Lucas, J., Batt, R. J., & Soremekun, O. A. (2014). Setting wait times to achieve targeted left-without-being-seen rates. *American Journal of Emergency Medicine, 32*(4), 342–345. https://doi.org/10.1016/j.ajem.2013.12.047 PMID: 24582605.

Maister, D. (1985). The psychology of waiting lines. In J.A. Czepiel, M.R. Solomon & C.F. Surprenant (Eds.) *The Service encounter: managing employee/customer interaction in service businesses* (pp. 3–16). Lexington, MA: D. C. Heath and Company, Lexington Books.

Miró, O., Antonio, M. T., Jiménez, S., De Dios, A., Sánchez, M., Borrás, A., & Millá, J. (1999). Decreased health care quality associated with emergency department overcrowding. *European Journal of Emergency Medicine, 6*(2), 105–107. https://doi.org/10.1097/00063110-199906000-00003 PMID: 10461551.

Morphet, J., Griffiths, D., Plummer, V., Innes, K., Fairhall, R., & Beattie, J. (2014). At the crossroads of violence and aggression in the emergency department: Perspectives of Australian emergency nurses. *Australian Health Review, 38*(2), 194–201. https://doi.org/10.1071/AH13189 PMID: 24670224.

Moskop, J. C., Sklar, D. P., Geiderman, J. M., Schears, R. M., & Bookman, K. J. (2009). Emergency department crowding, part 1–concept, causes, and moral consequences. *Annals of Emergency Medicine, 53*(5), 605–611. https://doi.org/10.1016/j.annemergmed.2008.09.019 PMID: 19027193.

Oche, M., & Adamu, H. (2013). Determinants of patient waiting time in the general outpatient department of a tertiary health institution in north Western Nigeria. *Annals of Medical and Health Sciences Research, 3*(4), 588–592. https://doi.org/10.4103/2141-9248.122123 PMID: 24380014; PMCID: PMC3868129.

Oermann, M. H., Masserang, M., Maxey, M., & Lange, M. P. (2002). Clinic visit and waiting: Patient education and satisfaction. *Nursing Economics, 20*(6), 292–295. PMID: 12567931.

Oermann, M. H., Webb, S. A., & Ashare, J. A. (2003). Outcomes of videotape instruction in clinic waiting area. *Orthopaedic Nursing, 22*(2), 102–105. https://doi.org/10.1097/00006416-200303000-00006 PMID: 12703393.

O'Neill, E., Woodgate, D., & Kostakos V. (2004). Easing the wait in the emergency room: Building a theory of public information systems. DIS2004—Designing Interactive Systems: Across the Spectrum, Cambridge, MA, USA, 01.-04.08.2004, Association for Computing Machinery, New York, NY, United States, pp. 17–25. https://doi.org/10.1145/1013115.1013120.

Pate, D. C., & Puffe, M. (2007). Special report: Quality of care survey Improving Patient Flow. *Physician Executive, 33*(3), 32–36. PMID: 17539560.

Patel, P. B., Combs, M. A., & Vinson, D. R. (2014). Reduction of admit wait times: The effect of a leadership-based program. *Academic Emergency Medicine, 21*(3), 266–273. https://doi.org/10.1111/acem.12327 PMID: 24628751.

Perera, M. L., Davies, A. W., Gnaneswaran, N., Giles, M., Liew, D., Ritchie, P., & Chan, S. T. (2014). Clearing emergency departments and clogging wards: National emergency access target and the law of unintended consequences. *Emergency Medicine Australasia, 26*(6), 549–555. https://doi.org/10.1111/1742-6723.12300 PMID: 25332129.

Pines, J. M., Iyer, S., Disbot, M., Hollander, J. E., Shofer, F. S., & Datner, E. M. (2008). The effect of emergency department crowding on patient satisfaction for admitted patients. *Academic Emergency Medicine, 15*(9), 825–831. https://doi.org/10.1111/j.1553-2712.2008.00200.x PMID: 19244633.

Pruyn, A. T. H., & Smidts, A. (1998). Effects of waiting on the satisfaction with the service: Beyond objective time measures. *International Journal of Research in Marketing, 15*(4), 321–334. https://doi.org/10.1016/S0167-8116(98)00008-1

Ranney, M. L., Choo, E. K., Wang, Y., Baum, A., Clark, M. A., & Mello, M. J. (2012). Emergency department patients' preferences for technology-based behavioral interventions.

Annals of Emergency Medicine, 60(2), 218–27.e48. https://doi.org/10.1016/j.annemergmed. 2012.02.026 PMID: 22542311.

Richardson, D. B. (2002). The access-block effect: Relationship between delay to reaching an inpatient bed and inpatient length of stay. *Medical Journal of Australia, 177*(9), 492–495. https://doi.org/10.5694/j.1326-5377.2002.tb04917.x PMID: 12405891.

Richardson, D. B. (2006). Increase in patient mortality at 10 days associated with emergency department overcrowding. *Medical Journal of Australia, 184*(5), 213–216. https://doi.org/10. 5694/j.1326-5377.2006.tb00204.x PMID: 16515430.

Rydman, R. J., Roberts, R. R., Albrecht, G. L., Zalenski, R. J., & McDermott, M. (1999). Patient satisfaction with an emergency department asthma observation unit. *Academic Emergency Medicine, 6*(3), 178–183. https://doi.org/10.1111/j.1553-2712.1999.tb00152.x PMID: 10192667.

Sharma, A., & Inder, B. (2011). Impact of co-located general practitioner (GP) clinics and patient choice on duration of wait in the emergency department. *Emergency Medicine Journal, 28*(8), 658–661. https://doi.org/10.1136/emj.2009.086512 PMID: 20668112.

Shetty, A., Gunja, N., Byth, K., & Vukasovic, M. (2012). Senior Streaming Assessment Further Evaluation after Triage zone: A novel model of care encompassing various emergency department throughput measures. *Emergency Medicine Australasia, 24*(4), 374–382. https:// doi.org/10.1111/j.1742-6723.2012.01550.x PMID: 22862754.

Singer, A. J., Viccellio, P., Thode, H. C., Jr., Bock, J. L., & Henry, M. C. (2008). Introduction of a stat laboratory reduces emergency department length of stay. *Academic Emergency Medicine, 15*(4), 324–328. https://doi.org/10.1111/j.1553-2712.2008.00065.x PMID: 18370985.

Spielberger, C. D., & Reheiser, E. C. (2009). Assessment of emotions: Anxiety, anger, depression, and curiosity. *Applied Psychology. Health and Well-Being, 1*(3), 271–302. https://doi.org/10. 1111/j.1758-0854.2009.01017.x

Sprague, J., Verona, E., Kalkhoff, W., & Kilmer, A. (2011). Moderators and mediators of the stress-aggression relationship: Executive function and state anger. *Emotion, 11*(1), 61–73. https://doi.org/10.1037/a0021788 PMID: 21401226.

Sprivulis, P., Grainger, S., & Nagree, Y. (2005). Ambulance diversion is not associated with low acuity patients attending Perth metropolitan emergency departments. *Emergency Medicine Australasia, 17*(1), 11–15. https://doi.org/10.1111/j.1742-6723.2005.00686.x PMID: 15675899.

Sun, B. C., Hsia, R. Y., Weiss, R. E., Zingmond, D., Liang, L. J., Han, W., McCreath, H., & Asch, S. M. (2013). Effect of emergency department crowding on outcomes of admitted patients. *Annals of Emergency Medicine, 61*(6), 605–611.e6. https://doi.org/10.1016/j.annemergmed. 2012.10.026. PMID: 23218508; PMCID: PMC3690784.

Tenbensel, T., Chalmers, L., Jones, P., Appleton-Dyer, S., Walton, L., & Ameratunga, S. (2017). New Zealand's emergency department target—Did it reduce ED length of stay, and if so, how and when? *BMC Health Services Research, 17*(1), 678. https://doi.org/10.1186/s12913-017-2617-1. PMID: 28950856; PMCID: PMC5615466.

Thompson, D. A., Yarnold, P. R., Williams, D. R., & Adams, S. L. (1996). Effects of actual waiting time, perceived waiting time, information delivery, and expressive quality on patient satisfaction in the emergency department. *Annals of Emergency Medicine, 28*(6), 657–665. https://doi.org/10.1016/s0196-0644(96)70090-2 PMID: 8953956.

Trout, A., Magnusson, A. R., & Hedges, J. R. (2000). Patient satisfaction investigations and the emergency department: What does the literature say? *Academic Emergency Medicine, 7*(6), 695–709. https://doi.org/10.1111/j.1553-2712.2000.tb02050.x PMID: 10905652.

Vieth, T. L., & Rhodes, K. V. (2006). The effect of crowding on access and quality in an academic ED. *American Journal of Emergency Medicine, 24*(7), 787–794. https://doi.org/10.1016/j.ajem. 2006.03.026. PMID: 17098098.

Waggoner, D. M., Jackson, E. B., & Kern, D. E. (1981). Physician influence on patient compliance: A clinical trial. *Annals of Emergency Medicine, 10*(7), 348–352. https://doi.org/ 10.1016/s0196-0644(81)80234-x. PMID: 7018328.

Weiner, S. G. (2013). Advertising emergency department wait times. *The Western Journal of Emergency Medicine, 14*(2), 77–78. https://doi.org/10.5811/westjem.2012.8.13147 PMID: 23599836; PMCID: PMC3628484.

White, B. A., Brown, D. F., Sinclair, J., Chang, Y., Carignan, S., McIntyre, J., & Biddinger, P. D. (2012). Supplemented triage and rapid treatment (START) improves performance measures in the emergency department. *Journal of Emergency Medicine, 42*(3), 322–328. https://doi.org/10.1016/j.jemermed.2010.04.022 PMID: 20554420.

Whittaker, W., Anselmi, L., Kristensen, S. R., Lau, Y. S., Bailey, S., Bower, P., Checkland, K., Elvey, R., Rothwell, K., Stokes, J., & Hodgson, D. (2016). Associations between extending access to primary care and emergency department visits: A difference-in-differences analysis. *PLoS Medicine, 13*(9). https://doi.org/10.1371/journal.pmed.1002113 PMID: 27598248; PMCID: PMC5012704.

Woodworth, L., & Holmes, J. (2020). Just a minute: The effect of emergency department wait time on the cost of care. *Economic Inquiry, 58*(2), 698–716. https://doi.org/10.1111/ecin.12849

Joshua O. Eniwumide is a senior research fellow at the sports and healthcare-economics department of the university of Potsdam. With a primary interest on Stakeholder-driven remodelling, Dr. Eniwumide focusses on the impact of "patientcentricity" on healthcare systems of developed and developing economies. Having obtained a PhD in tissue engineering and regenerative medicine, and a MBA in innovative healthcare, Dr. Eniwumide works in medical affairs within the pharmaceutical sector, while consulting with international pharma and biotech companies.

Patrick O. Akomolafe lectures at the Department of Computer Science, University of Ibadan, Nigeria.His research interests include Pervasive and Mobile Computing, Mobile Agent Technology, Cloud Computing, Context Aware Computing and Data Science. A former visiting researcher at the Hasso-Plattner-Institute, University of Potsdam, Dr. Akomolafe also runs a technology consulting company, which provides platform services for higher and further education institutes across Nigeria.

Christoph Rasche heads the chair of professional and corporate services at the University of Potsdam. He adopted visiting professorships at the Universities of Innsbruck, Alcalá de Henares as well as the Hochschule Osnabrück. He teaches strategic and general management in national and international MBA programmes with special respect to subjects connected with the healthcare and hospital industry. Formerly, he consulted with Droege International AG and was co-founder of Stratvanguard and the General Management Institute Potsdam. Prof. Rasche's research subjects circle around the field of strategic and general management in the healthcare and hospital sector, which witnesses an era of professional value creation by means of a strong management and leadership focus. Practically, he consults with healthcare players and is actively involved in executive trainings—ranging from corporate universities to MBA and PhD programmes for healthcare professionals.

RETRACTED CHAPTER: Use of Causal Loop Diagrams to Improve Service Processes

15

Bertil Lindenfalk, Andrea Resmini, Konstantin Weiss, and Wilian Molinari

The authors have retracted the contribution "Use of Causal Loop Diagrams to Improve Service Processes" by Bertil Lindenfalk, Andrea Resmini, Konstantin Weiss, Wilian Molinari, published in the book "Service Design Practices for Healthcare Innovation", pages 295–313, DOI https://doi.org/10.1007/978-3-030-87273-1_15 due to the alleged unauthorized use of company data by a contributing author. The chapter has now been removed.

M. A. Pfannstiel et al. (eds.), *Service Design Practices for Healthcare Innovation*,
https://doi.org/10.1007/978-3-030-87273-1_15

RETRACTED CHAPTER

RETRACTED CHAPTER

RETRACTED CHAPTER

RETRACTED CHAPTER

RETRACTED CHAPTER

RETRACTED CHAPTER

RETRACTED CHAPTER

RETRACTED CHAPTER

A Holistic Framework of Strategies and Best Practices for Telehealth Service Design and Implementation

16

Pavani Rangachari

16.1 Introduction

Telehealth refers to the use of electronic media to support a broad range of remote services such as patient care, education, and monitoring (Schwamm, 2014). It helps to overcome two barriers that patients face when seeking health care: distance and time. Telehealth has been found to deliver a range of benefits, including improved access to healthcare, more timely interactions between providers and patients, leading to improved continuity of care, and more efficient use of providers' time, to name a few. Proponents of telehealth have argued that it has the potential to transform healthcare delivery by reducing costs and increasing quality of care and patient satisfaction (Schwamm, 2014; Taylor, 2013).

In the United States, although telehealth was a "hot topic" before the COVID-19 pandemic, its use was far from widespread and was limited to certain medical specialties (Adler-Milstein et al., 2014; Andrus, 2017; Kane & Gillis, 2018; Lin et al., 2018; Schwamm, 2014). With the arrival of the pandemic, however, there has been a massive acceleration in the use of telehealth, not only because of physical (social) distancing requirements, but also due to the temporary removal of regulatory barriers to telehealth use. Nevertheless, the questions that do not yet have definitive answers are: Is telehealth here to stay? Will providers find it to be an effective method for providing care? Will patients prefer it over traditional in-person visits? Will policy and regulatory barriers to telehealth use be permanently lifted? (Perry, 2020; Shachar et al., 2020). Although there is much uncertainty about the future of telehealth in the post-pandemic era, one point of consensus is that the elimination of policy-level barriers to telehealth use by itself,

P. Rangachari (✉)
Department of Interdisciplinary Health Sciences (CAHS), Department of Family Medicine (MCG), The Graduate School, Augusta University, 987 St. Sebastian Way, Augusta, GA 30912, USA
e-mail: prangachari@augusta.edu

© The Author(s), under exclusive license to Springer Nature Switzerland AG 2022
M. A. Pfannstiel et al. (eds.), *Service Design Practices for Healthcare Innovation*,
https://doi.org/10.1007/978-3-030-87273-1_16

would not suffice to enable widespread, sustainable use of telehealth services. Instead, the literature has emphasized the need for healthcare organizations and providers to make concerted efforts to design and implement telehealth services for successful and sustainable use (Failed, 2014; Hebert, 2001; Kho et al., 2020; Moehr et al., 2006; Schwamm, 2014).

Purpose of this Chapter

Drawing upon the "design thinking" or "systems thinking" framework, a holistic approach to telehealth service design would be one that takes into consideration the multiple, interdependent dimensions of telehealth services, including processes, user-experience, and sustainability (Dovigi et al., 2020; Taylor, 2013). Likewise, drawing upon the "consolidated framework for implementation research (CFIR)" a holistic approach to telehealth service implementation would be one that involves extensive planning and stakeholder engagement BEFORE service design, and substantial investment in execution, reflection, and evaluation, AFTER service design (Bobinet & Petito, 2020).

The information technology infrastructure library (ITIL) is a well-known framework of best practices in IT service management (Damschroder et al., 2009; Greene, 2020; White & Greiner, 2019). However, as a stand-alone resource, it is limited in being able to provide a meaningful set of strategies for telehealth service design and implementation for clinicians and healthcare leaders (as discussed in the next section). In other words, there is a gap in the literature with respect to a "holistic framework" of strategies and best practices for the design and implementation of telehealth services, which could be meaningful to clinicians, healthcare leaders, and IT service managers alike. This paper seeks to address this gap.

As discussed in the next section, the ITIL framework emanated from an industry-based approach to identifying best practices for IT service management (Damschroder et al., 2009; White & Greiner, 2019). This paper takes an organizational theory-based approach to developing strategies for telehealth service design and implementation. These strategies are then integrated with practices put forth by the existing ITIL framework, to develop a holistic framework of strategies and best practices for telehealth service design and implementation.

In summary, the primary purpose of this paper is to integrate theory-based "design thinking" and "CFIR" frameworks, with the existing industry-based ITIL framework, to develop a holistic framework of strategies and best practices for telehealth service design and implementation. A supplemental purpose is to apply the holistic framework to cases of success and failure in telehealth services and discuss implications for future research and practice in telehealth service design and implementation.

16.2   Limitations of the ITIL Framework in Informing Telehealth Service Design and Implementation

In the 1980s, the U.K. Government's Central Computer and Telecommunication Agency developed the information technology infrastructure library (ITIL) in an effort to improve standards for IT service quality (Damschroder et al., 2009; Greene (n. d.), 2020; White & Greiner, 2019). Since then, the ITIL has not only gained international popularity but has also evolved into a widely-used framework of best practices for IT service management. Version 3 of ITIL (released in 2007) included a detailed description of practices arranged along the service lifecycle: service strategy, service design, service transition, service operation, and continual service improvement. Version 3 also described itself as a three-dimension model of (1) people, (2) process, and (3) technology, while version 4 (released in 2019) included a fourth dimension of (4) partners and supplies in an effort to market itself as a comprehensive framework of best practices for IT service management (Greene, 2020).

On the face of it therefore, ITIL may come across as the "ultimate solution" for designing and implementing any IT-enabled service including telehealth services. However, despite its popularity in the IT industry, the ITIL by itself is not designed to be meaningful to clinicians and healthcare managers looking to get started with a new telehealth service and establish a successful and sustainable telehealth infrastructure. Having originated in the IT industry, the ITIL utilizes considerable industry-level jargon and terminology to describe practices in each service lifecycle stage (Greene, 2009). For example, the stage of service design includes jargon-based practices like service catalog management, service continuity management, etc., which may be meaningful to an IT service manager but not necessarily to a clinician or healthcare leader (Wiki, 2020). On the other hand, applying "design thinking" theory to telehealth service design suggests that the first step to designing an effective telehealth service is to view the service in the context of the clinician-patient interaction, i.e., the social system in which it is embedded, which in turn is a broad strategy that would be meaningful to clinicians and healthcare leaders (Taylor, 2013; Wiki 2020).

Similarly, although ITIL discusses steps to be followed BEFORE and AFTER the service design stage to ensure successful service implementation, it utilizes considerable IT jargon to describe the implementation steps. For example, terms like service portfolio management and business relationship management are used to describe practices in the lifecycle stage of service strategy (which comes BEFORE service design) (Taylor, 2013; Wiki 2020). On the other hand, applying the "CFIR" framework to telehealth service implementation suggests that service design must be preceded by a planning and engagement phase that takes into consideration characteristics of the intervention (e.g., telehealth technology), the inner and outer settings of the healthcare organization, and characteristics of individuals being impacted, to effectively engage a multidisciplinary and inter-sectoral set of stakeholders (e.g., providers, patients, IT vendors, economists, and policymakers) in telehealth service implementation (Bobinet & Petito, 2020). This in turn is a broad strategy that clinicians and healthcare leaders would be able to relate to. In other words, integrating theory-based frameworks like "design thinking" and "CFIR" with the industry-based ITIL framework has the potential to generate a holistic framework of strategies and best practices for the design and implementation of telehealth services, that is, relevant and meaningful to clinicians, healthcare leaders, and IT service managers alike.

16.3   Dimensions of Telehealth Services

The first step toward developing a holistic framework of strategies and best practices for telehealth service design and implementation would be to understand the multiple, interdependent dimensions of telehealth services: (1) processes; (2) user-experience; and (3) sustainability (Dovigi et al., 2020; Kho et al., 2020; Taylor, 2013; Wiki 2020).

1. **Processes**: When telehealth is used to artificially eliminate distance between the provider and patient, it changes the processes associated with provider-patient interactions. However, the design of telehealth services cannot simply be a linear sum of processes changes. Instead, many process changes are interdependent one change may impact other parts of the solution. For example, process changes may necessitate risk assessments to ensure that they do not compromise quality of care (Tang et al., 2006; Taylor, 2013). Process changes may also create additional requirements for clinician, staff, and patient training to support the transition to a new model of care. In some instances, such requirements may add significantly to the costs, which may have the potential to compromise the proposed process and erode the value of telehealth services. Importantly, process changes would need to be supported by integral mechanisms to collect data to demonstrate improvements to care and outcomes. This would be essential for making a case for sustainability of process changes (Wiki 2020; Tang et al., 2006). In summary, process changes resulting from introduction of telehealth, demand a more holistic approach to service design.

2. **User-experience**: Telehealth service design needs to be directly responsive to the needs, expectations, and experience of its users, including providers and patients (Dovigi et al., 2020; Wiki (n. d. e) 2020). A telehealth encounter must be accessible, reliable, convenient, efficient, and must accommodate sudden modifications. It should integrate with the patient's preferred electronic media, such as messaging or e-mail, with formal records and updates that could be saved and retrieved. It should push or pull appropriate information at the right times in the care pathway and provide information at the most appropriate point in the encounter (e.g., preregistration). Concurrently, the needs and expectations of providers must be taken into consideration, e.g., their guidelines for which symptoms and conditions can and cannot be managed virtually, their need for

real-time access to patient data, their checklist of considerations for safety and quality, support for the regulatory restrictions they face in clinical practice, etc. Patients in turn would expect to have clear instructions how to prepare for the telehealth encounter and how they could provide feedback, e.g., through a post-visit survey. These types of "usability" considerations are typically identified when developing a prototype of the telehealth service design (Dovigi et al., 2020; Taylor, 2013).

3. **Sustainability**: Since telehealth changes the provider-patient interaction, it has been argued that success and sustainability of a new telehealth service ultimately depends on how the new telehealth offering changes the distinct value proposition for each key stakeholder (e.g., clinicians, patients, and administrators). In other words, it has been argued that success and sustainability of telehealth services depends far more on managing the provider and patient's expectations and behavior than on technology (Taylor, 2013; Wiki 2020; Tang et al., 2006). However, technology considerations in telehealth service design become most relevant when planning for the sustainability of the telehealth service. New telehealth services become self-sustaining when they effectively transition their demands for resources from project funding to "business as usual" operations. This transition needs to be an integral part of the scope of telehealth service design. Early attention to design considerations such as interoperability has potential to increase sustainability in the face of inevitable change. Similarly, integration with upstream and downstream systems such as scheduling systems, billing and administration, record keeping, and planned clinic sessions also has potential to boost sustainability. Importantly, integrating performance indicators into telehealth projects from the outset will ensure that each project is designed to meet specific measurable objectives (Brown, 2008; Senge, 1992; Tang et al., 2006). This in turn can help to provide a quantifiable basis for defining the effectiveness of telehealth services for future funding and investment, to satisfy key stakeholders.

16.4 Identifying Effective Strategies and Practices for Telehealth Service Design

The above discussion related to the dimensions of telehealth services helps to understand that telehealth service design requires a comprehensive approach to working with participants (e.g., providers and patients), to identify the key forces and factors at play, and address them through a holistic design solution. Some telehealth projects may effectively design "parts" of a new service, however, such design may not sufficiently account for the role of other critical forces in the problem context (Brown, 2008; Senge, 1992; Tang et al., 2006; Taylor, 2013). A holistic design solution for telehealth services, would seek to resolve all of the significant forces in the problem's context to create a new balance, requiring designers of telehealth services to take a "systems" view of the context for provider-patient interaction (Wiki, 2020; Tang et al., 2006). The need for a holistic design solution in turn provides the rationale for a "systems thinking" or "design thinking" approach to developing strategies for the design of telehealth services.

"Design thinking" has been described as "a discipline that seeks to match people's needs with what is technologically feasible and what a viable business strategy can convert into customer value and market opportunity." (Tang et al., 2006; Taylor, 2013). It is similar to "systems thinking" in that, it recognizes the role of the target for design (i.e., service) within a larger socio-technical system. The approach involves extensive in-situ observation and end user participation to identify potential interventions, and often employs prototyping and mock-ups to rapidly evaluate these in context. Such an iterative approach in turn has potential to highlight implications of the proposed intervention to all stakeholders and deliver a solution that is co-designed and has broad buy-in through end user participation. The backbone of this process, therefore, is the understanding of end user behavior, including the needs and motivations of end users. Service designers could obtain this information through a variety of fact-finding techniques, including ethnography, end user interviews, or shadowing of end users. In summary, such an approach to designing telehealth service focuses design effort on the actual service offered by the clinician/provider to the patient, and provides a key perspective on user experience (Tang et al., 2006; Taylor, 2013).

Since the understanding of end user behavior is integral to the "design thinking" approach, the literature has discussed the importance of integrating design thinking with behavioral economics, the science of individual decision-making in a variety of everyday settings (Dyk, 2014; Singh et al., 2010; Thaler & Sunstein, 2009). Studies in this field have indicated that people make more decisions reactively (in-the-moment) than analytically, drawing on arbitrary factors such as product packaging, convenience of access, simplicity, or brand familiarity, and as the primary basis of decisions or choices (Thaler & Sunstein, 2009). The literature in turn, has discussed how service designers could leverage these insights about end user behavior to create opportunities for "nudging" or selecting defaults to achieve desired behaviors, i.e., to influence choices for both individual and common good. Examples of "nudging" include setting savings plan enrollment and risk profile defaults to "on" and placing healthy food options at eye level. From the perspective of telehealth service design therefore, behavioral economics or "nudging" can offer useful insights into low-friction design of services, particularly in situations where complexity is not avoidable at the user interface (Singh et al., 2010).

The above discussion provides insights into strategies for telehealth service design that could be highly relevant to clinicians and healthcare leaders (Taylor, 2013). A holistic approach to designing telehealth services would incorporate the following elements based on principles of "design thinking:"

(1) It would begin with in-situ observation, to capture the nuances of clinical practice, clinician-patient interaction, and patient preferences.
(2) It would be based on the principle of co-design in which clinicians and patients (end users) work together with service designers to determine the objectives

and develop the service design; a co-design approach in turn would enable clinicians to contribute expert insights and patients to offer practical suggestions, while designers facilitate the process but do not dictate the results.

(3) It would be highly iterative, recognizing that insight must be vigorously tested and refined and that a viable telehealth service must resolve complex forces in many dimensions at once.

(4) It would recognize the socio-technical system in which the clinician-patient interaction occurs and would pursue the boundaries of the service design until the new service could be justified in the context of a complete and balanced system.

(5) It would seek to stabilize patient behaviors rather than enforce process compliance. It would incorporate an awareness of the different techniques in telehealth services for influencing productive choices through defaults that act in the interest of both parties, and the provision of "just enough" information to efficiently support the clinician-patient interaction at each step.

Each of the aforementioned strategies in turn, represents a rich source of techniques for telehealth service design. To come full circle with the design process, it is essential to discover which techniques are most relevant and how they could be structured into a methodology, that is, practical and accessible to clinicians and patients (Taylor, 2013). The strategies for telehealth service design (discussed above) in turn could be synergized with existing ITIL "best practices" for service design, to develop a comprehensive set of strategies and best practices for telehealth service design, for use by clinicians, healthcare leaders, and IT service managers alike. The ITIL framework includes the following 11 best practices for service design: (1) Design coordination, (2) service catalog management (SCM), (3) service level management (SLM), (4) risk management, (5) capacity management, (6) availability management, (7) IT service continuity management (ITSCM), (8) information security management, (9) compliance management, (10) architecture management, and (11) supplier management (11). Each of these IT service design best practices could integrated into the overall strategy for telehealth service design informed by principles of "design thinking" and behavioral economics.

16.5   Identifying Effective Strategies and Practices for Telehealth service Implementation

The service lifecycle stages put forth by ITIL help to understand that the service implementation cycle begins well BEFORE service design (with service strategy) and extends to well AFTER service design, to service transition, service execution, and continuous service improvement. The existing telehealth literature has consistently emphasized the importance of recognizing the complexity in implementing telehealth services (Taylor, 2013; Yellowlees, 2005). In addition to the need to consider multiple interdependent dimensions (of processes, user-experience, and sustainability), by definition, telehealth services are delivered over a distance and often span multiple organizational entities with varying cultures, practices, and business models. Correspondingly, the design and implementation of telehealth services often involves the engagement of stakeholders from a variety of disciplines from both inner and outer settings of the organization. In view of this complexity, a considerable portion of the telehealth literature has paid attention to determinants of failure or success of telehealth implementation initiatives (Almathami et al., 2020; Attewell, 1992; Batsis et al., 2020; Broens et al., 2014; Buchachi & Pakenham-Walsh, 2007; Christie et al., 2018; Cilliers & Flowerday, 2013; Damschroder et al., 2009; Dyk, 2014; Finch et al., 2006; Foster & Sethares, 2014; Garavand et al., 2019; Hadjistavropoulos et al., 2017; Khoja et al., 2007a, 2007b, 2013; Koivunen & Saranto, 2018; Pelletier-Fleury et al., 1997; Tanriverdi & Iacono August, 1998; Warner et al., 2018).

Within the last decade, van Dyk (2014) conducted a comprehensive review to identify and compare existing frameworks on telehealth service implementation to identify common themes and areas for future development (Yellowlees, 2005). A total of nine frameworks related to telehealth use and implementation were reviewed, including: (1) barriers to the diffusion of telemedicine, which emphasizes technical, behavioral, economic, and organizational barriers (Khoja et al., 2007a); (2) telehealth readiness assessment tools, which emphasize core (planning), technological, learning, societal, and policy readiness (Cilliers & Flowerday, 2013; Khoja et al., 2007b); (3) telehealth applications of the unified theory of acceptance and use of technology (UTAUT), which describes the interaction among several variables influencing technology acceptance, including perceived importance of standardization (Finch et al., 2006; Garavand et al., 2019); (4) seven core principles for the successful implementation of telemedicine (discussed earlier) (Broens et al., 2020); (5) lessons in telemedicine service innovation, which identifies factors contributing to telehealth success, including the policy context, evidence gathering, outcomes monitoring, perceived benefit, reconfiguring services, professional roles, and willingness to cross boundaries (Buchachi & Pakenham-Walsh, 2007); (6) framework for assessing health system challenges to scaling up for telehealth, which includes consideration for policy, organizational, technological, and financial challenges (Buchachi & Pakenham-Walsh, 2007; Cilliers & Flowerday, 2013); (7) comprehensive model for the evaluation of telemedicine, which considers several issues related to telehealth implementation, including cost of education, quality of clinical services, community access to services, among others (Pelletier-Fleury et al., 1997); (8) layered telemedicine implementation model, which identifies determinants of success associated with each lifecycle phase of telemedicine (Khoja et al., 2007b); and (9) the Khoja-Durrani-Scott (KDS) evaluation framework, which also considers telehealth lifecycle stages and incorporates various themes of evaluation, including readiness and change, policy, technological, behavioral, economic, and ethical (Damschroder et al., 2009). Overall, the review by van Dyk (2014) concluded that a holistic approach is needed to telehealth implementation, which includes consideration for organizational structures, change management, technology, economic feasibility, societal impacts, perceptions, user-friendliness, evidence and evaluation, and policy and legislation (Attewell, 1992).

In more recent years, the consolidated framework for implementation research (CFIR) (Bobinet & Petito, 2020). has been leveraged to guide telehealth service implementation initiatives (Bardosh et al., 2017; Batsis et al., 2020; Hadjis-tavropoulos et al., 2017; Warner et al., 2018; Weinstein et al., 2014). Since its introduction in 2009, the CFIR has gained considerable popularity and recognition as an influential theoretical framework to inform both "implementation science" and "implementation strategy." (Bobinet & Petito, 2020). The CFIR comprises five major domains (characteristics of the intervention, the outer setting, the inner setting, characteristics of the individuals involved, and the process by which implementation is accomplished). Each domain in turn is mapped to an array of constructs informed by existing implementation theories and conceptual models. The five domains (and constructs) in the CFIR in turn interact in rich and complex ways to influence implementation effectiveness.

To elaborate, the CFIR domain of intervention characteristics has been mapped to the following constructs: (1) intervention source, (2) evidence strength and quality, (3) relative advantage, (4) adaptability, (5) trialabilty, (6) complexity, (7) design and packaging, and (8) cost. The domain of outer setting has been mapped to the following constructs: (1) patients' needs and resources; (2) cos-mopolitanism (or degree of networking with external organizations); (3) peer pressure; and (4) external policies and incentives. The domain of inner setting has been mapped to the following constructs: (1) structural characteristics, (2) networks and communication, (3) culture, including norms and values of an organization, and (4) implementation climate or the absorptive capacity for change. Six sub-constructs contribute to a positive implementation climate for an intervention: readiness for implementation, compatibility, relative priority, organizational incentives and rewards, goals and feedback, and learning climate. Readiness for implementation in turn includes three sub-constructs, leadership engagement, available resources, and access to information and knowledge. The domain of individual characteristics has been mapped to the following constructs: (1) knowledge and beliefs about the intervention, (2) individual self-efficacy; (3) individual stage of change, (4) individual identification with organization, and 5) other personal attributes. Lastly, within the domain of implementation process, the CFIR describes four essential activities of that are common across organizational change models: planning, engaging, executing, and reflecting and evaluating (Bobinet & Petito, 2020).

Each of the core activities associated with the CFIR implementation process in turn could be mapped to the PRE-service design and POST-service design stages of the ITIL service lifecycle. For example, the activities of "planning" and "engaging" in the CFIR domain of implementation process could be mapped to the service strategy phase of the ITIL service lifecycle (PRE-service design). Likewise, the CFIR activity of "executing" could be mapped to the service transition and service operation phases of the ITIL service lifecycle (POST-service design), while the CFIR activity of "reflecting and evaluating" in the domain of implementation process could be mapped to the continual service improvement phase of the ITIL service lifecycle. Overall, the CFIR is a pragmatic meta-theoretical framework with a comprehensive taxonomy of domains and constructs that could be used to guide formative evaluation of implementation efforts over three phases of evaluation (Bobinet & Petito, 2020), including:

(1) Implementation capacity/needs assessment (prior to implementation, in the planning and engaging phases of the CFIR implementation process or the service strategy phase of the ITIL lifecycle).
(2) Implementation/process evaluation (during implementation, in the executing phase of the CFIR implementation process or the service transition and service operation phases of the ITIL lifecycle).
(3) Implementation outcome/impact evaluation (post implementation, in the reflecting and evaluating phase of CFIR or the continuous service improvement phase of the ITIL lifecycle).

Prior to implementation (i.e., in the planning and engaging phases of implementation), the CFIR can be leveraged for capacity/needs assessment to identify potential barriers and facilitators to implementation from the perspective of the individuals and organizations involved in the implementation. For example, in a recent study (Warner et al., 2018), the CFIR was used to assess barriers and facilitators to implementing a telemedicine-delivered healthy lifestyle program for obesity management in a rural obesity clinic. Elements of consolidated framework for implementation research (CFIR) provided a basis for assessing intervention characteristics, inner and outer settings, and individual characteristics using surveys and semi-structured interviews. In this study, the reach, effectiveness, adoption, implementation, and maintenance (RE-AIM) framework was used in concert with the CFIR to assess staff barriers to success for future scalability. While CFIR can be used to explain why implementation succeeded or failed, the RE-AIM provides a practical framework for planning and evaluating practice change interventions to assure their external validity. Using CFIR, the intervention was found to be valuable from both patient and staff perspectives. A significant barrier limiting sustainability was physical space for intervention delivery and privacy and dedicated resources for staff. The study concluded that it was crucial to engage staff, enhance organizational culture and increase reach, for rural health obesity clinics to be able to enhance sustainability of using telemedicine for the management of obesity.

In a similar vein, the CFIR could be leveraged during implementation (i.e., in the executing phase) for monitoring progress for unanticipated influences and progress toward implementation goals. For example, in a recent study, the CFIR was used to conduct a process evaluation of the implementation of Internet-delivered cognitive behavior therapy (ICBT) within community mental health clinics (Bardosh et al., 2017). The process evaluation was designed to understand facilitators and barriers impacting the uptake and implementation of ICBT. The study found that ICBT implementation was perceived to be most prominently facilitated by intervention characteristics (namely the relative advantages of ICBT compared to face-to-face therapy) and implementation processes (namely the use of an external facilitation unit that aided with engaging patients, therapists, and managers and ICBT implementation). The inner setting was identified as the most significant barrier to implementation as a result of limited resources for ICBT combined with greater priority given to face-to-face care.

Finally yet importantly, the CFIR could be leveraged in the post-implementation (reflecting and evaluating) phase, for impact evaluation, to guide exploration into the question of what factors influenced implementation of the intervention. For example, a recent study examined contextual factors influencing implementation effectiveness and potential for scale-up of an evidence-based mHealth intervention (Weinstein et al., 2014). A comparative qualitative case study design was used, which drew on multiple key informant interviews with stakeholders involved in six projects (utilizing the same health intervention). The CFIR was used to compare findings (implementation effectiveness) across projects.

A two-fold approach to ensuring sustainability of telehealth services.

It would be relevant to note that although sustainability of telehealth services can be provided for as part of service design, the true test for telehealth service sustainability would arise in the service transition and service operation phases (i.e., in the executing phase of CFIR) (Bobinet & Petito, 2020). In regard to the "sustainability" dimension in telehealth services, it would be important to distinguish between:

(1) Sustainability issues associated with people, processes, and technology and
(2) Sustainability issues associated with funding support beyond the pilot period.

Although the first could be addressed through application of theory-informed strategies and best practices for telehealth service design and implementation (e.g., the holistic framework) developed in this paper, the second would need to be addressed separately by the providers and organizations involved in the telehealth implementation depending on the nature of services and specialties involved. In this regard, it would be relevant to note that the likelihood of longer term funding sustainability of a telemedicine program is known to increase when it offers: (1) gap service coverage, e.g., teleradiology; (2) urgent service coverage, e.g., telestroke, teleburn, teletrauma, etc.; (3) mandated services, e.g., correctional telemedicine; or (4) Video-enabled multi-site group chart rounds (Hailey & Crowe, 2003). The extension for community healthcare outcomes (ECHO®) program developed group chart clinical rounds that are managed over telemedicine networks. The underlying concept is that specialists in the management of specific chronic diseases can maximize their effectiveness by mentoring a group of primary care physicians on how to manage these diseases (Hailey & Crowe, 2003).

For example, in cardiology (one of the higher telehealth using specialties), telehealth has been leveraged extensively for urgent service coverage, e.g., for percutaneous coronary intervention (Hailey & Crowe, 2003). To boost the potential for sustainability of telehealth offerings, lower telehealth using specialties like allergy immunology could learn from the cardiology experience by utilizing telehealth for mandated services, e.g., telehealth for asthma management in the correctional health setting. Also, given the anticipated shortage of allergists nationwide, the field could benefit by aligning with project ECHO®, i.e., enabling medical education to be integrated with clinical practice to facilitate the connection between allergy specialists and primary physicians in rural areas. Additionally, allergy providers could be proactive in attracting sustained funding support for telehealth from hospitals and payers through initiatives aligned with the triple aim of healthcare: (1) improve patient experience, (2) lower costs, and (3) promote population health. For example, allergy providers could undertake initiatives to utilize remote monitoring for asthma management to prevent unnecessary emergency and inpatient visits for asthma, reduce costs, and promote population health. Such efforts would be highly relevant to hospitals and payers seeking to expand the provision of telehealth services, in an era of value-based reimbursement.

16.6 A Holistic Framework of Strategies and Practices for Telehealth Service Design/Implementation

Following from the discussion in the last two sections, i.e., (1) effective strategies and practices for telehealth service design and (2) effective strategies and practices for telehealth service implementation, Fig. 16.1 summarizes a holistic framework of strategies and practices for telehealth service design and implementation. As indicated, the framework integrates theory-informed strategies, i.e., "design thinking" or "CFIR" theory-based strategies with industry-based ITIL best practices across each of the five stages the telehealth service lifecycle. In the next section, the "holistic framework" is applied to cases of success and failure in telehealth to discuss implications for future research and practice.

16.7 Discussion

Applying the "holistic framework" to cases of success and failure in telehealth.

The international conference on successes and failures in telehealth (SFT) which has been held annually for nearly 20 years, attracts a diverse group of stakeholders. The unique focus of the SFT is to provide an engaging forum to share both positive (successes) and the more challenging (failures) experiences in telehealth, to help promote the increasing uptake of telehealth and digital healthcare on a national and international scale. Over the years, papers presented at the SFTs have made a helpful contribution to understanding and overcoming the practical challenges of using implementing telehealth. Presentations at the conferences have covered a variety of health systems and telehealth applications. To address the question of what the papers presented tell us about the successes and failures in telehealth, a review was carried out of the papers from selected SFT conferences, the proceedings of which were published as supplements to the journal of telemedicine and telecare (Gilman & Stensland, 2013). This review helped to identify some common

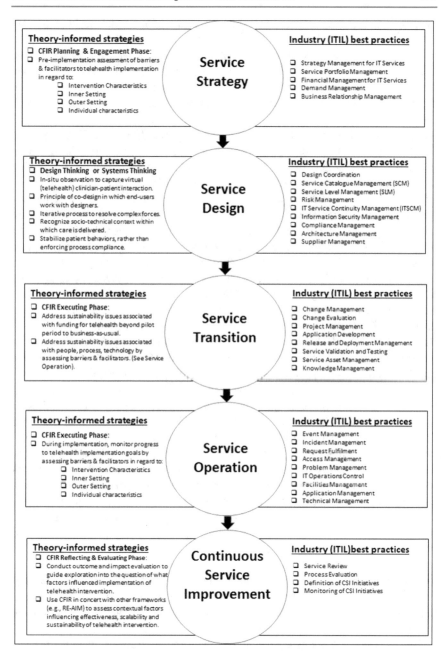

Fig. 16.1 A Holistic Framework of Strategies & Best Practices Spanning Telehealth Service Lifecycle. *Source* Author's own illustration (2021)

themes on challenges or determinants of success and failure of telehealth, including the involvement of stakeholders in planning, health professionals' attitudes toward training, changes in responsibility, autonomy, perceived need for telehealth, the stability of management structures, the turnover of personnel and cooperation between organizations, the reliability of equipment, adequacy of technical support, the reliability of vendors, and policy and budgetary issues (Gilman & Stensland, 2013).

Each of the challenges identified in review of papers from the SFT conferences could be addressed through application of the "holistic framework" developed in this paper. For example, the challenge of stakeholder involvement, health professional attitudes, perceived need for the telehealth intervention, and reliability of vendor could be addressed at the service strategy or planning and engaging (pre-implementation) stage of the telehealth lifecycle. At this stage, the CFIR could be used to assess barriers and facilitators to telehealth implementation from the perspective of individuals involved. Likewise, during the service design phase, these challenges could be addressed through a "design thinking" approach to telehealth service design, based on in-situ observation, principles of co-design, and thorough understanding of the socio-technical context within which clinician patient interaction occurs. Likewise, in the service transition and service execution phases, the CFIR could be leveraged to monitor progress from the perspective of individuals involved. Also, in the post-implementation phase, the CFIR could be leveraged to conduct and impact and process evaluation to understand why the implementation failed from the perspective of individuals involved.

In a similar vein, challenges associated with stability of management structures, turnover of personnel, and cooperation between organizations, could be addressed by leveraging CFIR to assess barriers and facilitators associated with the inner setting, through constructs of (1) structural characteristics, (2) networks and communication, (3) culture, and (4) implementation climate or the absorptive capacity for change. As discussed earlier, a positive implementation climate requires readiness for implementation, which in turn includes three sub-constructs, leadership engagement, available resources, and access to information and knowledge. This assessment of barriers and facilitators associated with inner setting in turn could be conducted pre-implementation, during pre-implementation and post-implementation. Likewise, challenges associated with reliability of equipment and adequacy of technical support could be addressed by leveraging the CFIR to assess barriers to implementation from the perspective of intervention characteristics in the service strategy phase. Moreover, in the service design phase, systems thinking principles could be used to identify and address all training needs from the perspectives of telehealth service users.

Lastly, policy and budgetary challenges could be addressed by assessing barriers to implementation on CFIR domain of outer setting which in turn could be accomplished pre, during, and post implementation. During the service design phase, consideration for the policy and budgetary issues could be incorporated into the socio-technical context used to inform the design of telehealth services. As discussed earlier, although sustainability issues associated with people, process, technology, and partners/suppliers could be addressed using the holistic framework, sustainability issues associated with funding would need to be addressed separately by providers and organizations involved in implementation, to ensure that funding constraints do not adversely affect service transition and service execution phases. In the continuous service improvement phase, the CFIR could be combined with the RE-AIM framework, to assess potential for scalability and sustainability of the intervention. In summary, appropriate utilization of the "holistic framework" can provide clinicians, healthcare leaders, and IT service managers alike with a comprehensive approach to addressing barriers to the effective design and implementation of telehealth services.

16.8   Implications for Practice and Future Research

As discussed in the Introduction, a key concern in the current telehealth literature is the widespread sustainability of telehealth use across multiple specialties in the post-pandemic environment. Considering the example of the United States (US), recent (pre-pandemic) studies in the US have reported wide variation in telehealth use across medical specialties. This is intriguing, because the US lacks a nationwide standardized set of telehealth reimbursement policies, which in turn, has historically posed a barrier to telehealth adoption in all specialties (Brown, 2006; Spivak et al., 2020). Despite these macro (policy-level) constraints experienced by all medical specialties, some specialties have been able to normalize telehealth to mainstream practice (e.g., psychiatry, cardiology); while others are just getting started during the COVID-19 pandemic (e.g., allergy-immunology) (Brown, 2006; Spivak et al., 2020).

Calling upon the "macro-meso-micro" three-layer framework, three levels of factors, including macro (societal or policy level), meso (group or organizational level), and micro (individual-level) factors can help to explain behavior (e.g., telehealth use in a medical specialty). Since macro (policy-level) factors (barriers) by themselves do not help to explain the wide variation in telehealth use across specialties, it would be important to examine the meso (organizational level) and micro (individual-level) factors (barriers or facilitators) influencing telehealth use in medical specialties, to better understand reasons for the variation across specialties, and identify implications for widespread sustainability of telehealth use in the post pandemic era.

The "holistic framework" developed in this paper can provide healthcare organizations at the meso level and individual providers at the micro level, with a foundation for getting started with designing and implementing a successful and sustainable telehealth service. Future research on other meso (group or organizational-level) factors and micro (individual provider and patient-level) factors could help to supplement the strategies and insights gained from this paper for effective telehealth design and implementation, to provide additional implications for ensuring widespread sustainability of telehealth services. For example, if research shows that specialty society organizations at the meso level could have substantive role to play a role in promoting telehealth use within their respective specialties (for example, by educating providers on how to get started with telehealth, providing opportunities for telehealth training, or advocating for telehealth training in medicine residency curriculum), then the "holistic framework" developed in this paper could provide a strong foundation for specialty societies to develop organized provider-training (within the specialty), on designing and implementing a successful and sustainable telehealth service infrastructure.

Future research may also reveal that specialty societies in the US are in a unique positon to influence macro (policy-level) factors influencing telehealth use (e.g., reimbursement and coverage), through advocacy for consistent payment policies from public and private payers. In other words, specialty societies may be in a unique position to influence both meso-level factors (e.g., provider tech-training and culture within a specialty) and macro-level factors (telehealth reimbursement policies). Correspondingly, specialty societies could play a substantive role in alleviating sustainability issues associated with people, process, and technology (e.g., by leveraging the holistic framework to develop organized training for telehealth design and implementation) and sustainability issues associated with funding support for telehealth (by influencing macro-level factors like payment policies). In regard to the latter, specialty societies could play a significant role in supplementing independent provider efforts to ensure funding sustainability (e.g., by facilitating provider alignment with the triple aim framework).

Following from the above discussion, two lines of future research could help further enrich the strategies, practices, and insights gained from the "holistic framework" for telehealth design and implementation: (1) research on improving telehealth implementation effectiveness (e.g., systematic evidence on the relationships among the key domains and constructs of CFIR to influence implementation effectiveness) and (2) research on promoting telehealth implementation sustainability, e.g., future research on strategies for reducing variation in telehealth use across medical specialties to enable widespread sustainability in telehealth use in a post-pandemic era.

16.9 Conclusion

Telehealth changes the established patient-clinician interaction. As such, the success of a new telehealth service is known to depend more on changing the expectations and behavior (and the resultant clinician-patient relationship) than on technology. Success in telehealth projects is highly dependent on understanding how the new telehealth offering changes the distinct value proposition to each of the parties—clinicians, patients, and administrators. Successful and sustainable telehealth services will not be created by addressing the needs of one party or by focusing on one part of the problem.

Although existing theories and frameworks for telehealth design and implementation do echo these realities at a broad level, the practical strategies emanating from these theories remain fragmented and divorced from industry-level best practice frameworks for telehealth design and implementation. The latter in turn have limited relevance to key telehealth implementation stakeholders like clinicians and healthcare leaders. This paper synthesizes strategies for telehealth service design and implementation emanating from the existing theoretical literature and integrates them with industry-based (ITIL) best practices, to develop a "holistic framework" of strategies and best practices for telehealth service design and implementation. In doing so, the paper addresses a key gap in the telehealth literature. Additionally, the framework is applied to cases of success and failure in telehealth to discuss implications for future research and practice. Overall, the strategies, best practices, and insights for sustainability gained from the "holistic framework," could be used to shape a contemporary method for design and implementation of telehealth services that has potential to improve the outcomes of telehealth implementation projects. They can also enable telehealth project champions to avoid misconceptions that might lead to unintended and expensive consequences.

References

Adler-Milstein, J., Kvedar, J., & Bates, D. W. (2014). Telehealth among US hospitals: Several factors, including state reimbursement and licensure policies, influence adoption. *Health Aff (millwood)., 33*(2), 207–215. https://doi.org/10.1377/hlthaff.2013.1054 PMID: 24493762.

Almathami, H. K. Y., Win, K. T. & Vlahu-Gjorgievska, E. (2020) Barriers and Facilitators That Influence Telemedicine-Based, Real-Time, Online Consultation at Patients' Homes: Systematic Literature Review. J Med Internet Res., 22(2):e16407

Andrus B. (2017) 5 Healthcare Specialties Leading the Way In Telemedicine, E-visit (Ed.), Accessed December 1, 2020, from https://blog.evisit.com/virtual-care-blog/top-specialties-for-telemedicine

Attewell, P. (1992) Technology diffusion and organizational learning: The case of business computing. Organ. Sci., 3(1), 1–19. from https://doi.org/10.1287/orsc.3.1.1

Bardosh, K. L., Murray, M., Khaemba, A. M., Smillie, K., & Lester, R. (2017). Operationalizing mHealth to improve patient care: A qualitative implementation science evaluation of the WelTel texting intervention in Canada and Kenya. *Global Health., 13*(1), 87. https://doi.org/10.1186/s12992-017-0311-z.PMID:29208026;PMCID:PMC5717811

Batsis, J. A., McClure, A. C., Weintraub, A. B., Sette, D., Rotenberg, S., Stevens, C. J., Gilbert-Diamond, D., Kotz, D. F., Bartels, S. J., Cook, S. B., & Rothstein, R. I. (2020). Barriers and facilitators in implementing a pilot, pragmatic, telemedicine-delivered healthy lifestyle program for obesity management in a rural, academic obesity clinic. *Implement Sci Commun., 1*(83), 1–9. https://doi.org/10.1186/s43058-020-00075-9.PMID:33015640;PMCID: PMC7526351

Bobinet, K. & Petito, J. (2020) Designing The Consumer-Centered Telehealth & eVisit Experience. The Office of National Coordinator for Health Information Technology U.S. Department of Health & Human Services, Accessed November 10, 2020, from https://www.healthit.gov/sites/default/files/DesigningConsumerCenteredTelehealtheVisit-ONC-WHITEPAPER-2015V2edits.pdf

Broens, T. H., Vollenbroek-Hutten, M. M., Hermens, H. J., van Halteren, A. T. & Nieuwenhuis, L. J. () Determinants of successful telemedicine implementations: A literature study. J. Telemed. Telecare, 13(6), 303–309. doi: https://doi.org/10.1258/135763307781644951.

Brown, N. A. (2006). State Medicaid and private payer reimbursement for telemedicine: An overview. *Journal of Telemedicine and Telecare, 12*(2), S32–S39. https://doi.org/10.1258/135763306778393108 PMID: 16989672.

Brown, T. (2008) Design Thinking. Harvard Business Review, Brighton, MA, USA.

Buchachi, F., & Pakenham-Walsh, N. (2007). Information technology of health in developing countries. *Chest, 132*(5), 1624–1630. https://doi.org/10.1378/chest.07-1760

Christie, H. L., Bartels, S. L., Boots, L. M. M., Tange, H. J., Verhey, F. J. J., & de Vugt, M. E. (2018). A systematic review on the implementation of eHealth interventions for informal caregivers of people with dementia. *Internet Interventions, 13*(2018), 51–59. https://doi.org/10.1016/j.invent.2018.07.002.PMID:30206519;PMCID:PMC6112102

Cilliers, L. & Flowerday, S. V. (2013) Health information systems to improve health care: A telemedicine case study. SA J. Inf. Manag., 15(1):1–5, Art. #541, doi:https://doi.org/10.4102/sajim.v15i1.541.

Damschroder, L. J., Aron, D. C., Keith, R. E., Kirsh, S. R., Alexander, J. A., & Lowery, J. C. (2009). Fostering implementation of health services research findings into practice: A consolidated framework for advancing implementation science. *Implementation Science, 4*(50), 1–15. https://doi.org/10.1186/1748-5908-4-50.PMID:19664226;PMCID:PMC2736161

Dovigi, E., Kwok, E. Y. L. & English, J.C. 3rd. (2020) A Framework-Driven Systematic Review of the Barriers and Facilitators to Teledermatology Implementation. Curr Dermatol Rep. 1–9. doi: https://doi.org/10.1007/s13671-020-00323-0. Epub ahead of print. PMID: 33200042; PMCID: PMC7658914.

Dovigi, E., Kwok, E. Y. L. & English, J.C. 3rd. (2020b) A Framework-Driven Systematic Review of the Barriers and Facilitators to Teledermatology Implementation. Curr Dermatol Rep. 1–9. doi: https://doi.org/10.1007/s13671-020-00323-0. Epub ahead of print. PMID: 33200042; PMCID: PMC7658914.

Finch, T., Mair, F., & May, C. (2006). Teledermatology in the UK: Lessons in service innovation. *British Journal of Dermatology, 156*(3), 521–527. https://doi.org/10.1111/j.1365-2133.2006.07608.x

Foster, M. V. & Sethares, K. A. (2014) Facilitators and barriers to the adoption of telehealth in older adults: an integrative review. Comput Inform Nurs. 32(11):523–533; quiz 534–535. doi: https://doi.org/10.1097/CIN.0000000000000105. PMID: 25251862.

Garavand, A., Samadbeik, M., Nadri, H., Rahimi, B., & Asadi, H. (2019). Effective Factors in Adoption of Mobile Health Applications between Medical Sciences Students Using the UTAUT Model. *Methods of Information in Medicine, 58*(4–05), 131–139. https://doi.org/10.1055/s-0040-1701607 PMID: 32170717.

Gilman, M., & Stensland, J. (2013). Telehealth and Medicare: Payment policy, current use, and prospects for growth. *Medicare & Medicaid Research Review, 3*(4), E1–E14. https://doi.org/10.5600/mmrr.003.04.a04.PMID:24834368;PMCID:PMC4011650

Greene J. (n. d.) The Essential Guide to ITIL Framework and Processes; Accessed November 5, 2020, from https://www.cherwell.com/it-service-management/library/essential-guides/essential-guide-to-itil-framework-and-processes/

Hadjistavropoulos, H. D., Nugent, M. M., Dirkse, D., & Pugh, N. (2017). Implementation of internet-delivered cognitive behavior therapy within community mental health clinics: A process evaluation using the consolidated framework for implementation research. *BMC Psychiatry, 17*(1), 331. https://doi.org/10.1186/s12888-017-1496-7.PMID:28899365;PMCID:PMC5596488

Hailey, D., & Crowe, B. A. (2003). profile of success and failure in telehealth–evidence and opinion from the Success and Failures in Telehealth conferences. *Journal of Telemedicine and Telecare, 9*(2), S22–S24. https://doi.org/10.1258/135763303322596165 PMID: 14748344.

Mended Hearts (n. d.) Telemedicine's expanded role in cardiac care, Mended Hearts (Ed.), Accessed September 2, 2020, from https://mendedhearts.org/story/telemedicines-expanding-role-in-cardiac-care/

Hebert, M. (2001). Telehealth success: Evaluation framework development. *Stud Health Technol Inform., 84*(Pt 2), 1145–1149. PMID: 11604908.

Kane, C. K., & Gillis, K. (2018). The Use Of Telemedicine By Physicians: Still The Exception Rather Than The Rule. *Health Aff (millwood)., 37*(12), 1923–1930. https://doi.org/10.1377/hlthaff.2018.05077 PMID: 30633670.

Kho, J., Gillespie, N., & Martin-Khan, M. (2020). A systematic scoping review of change management practices used for telemedicine service implementations. *BMC Health Services Research, 20*(1), 815. https://doi.org/10.1186/s12913-020-05657-w PMID: 32873295.

Khoja, S., Scott, R. E., Casebeer, A. L., Mohsin, M., Ishaq, A. F., & Gilani, S. (2007a). e-Health readiness assessment tools for healthcare institutions in developing countries. *Telemedicine Journal and E-Health, 13*(4), 425–431. https://doi.org/10.1089/tmj.2006.0064 PMID: 17848110.

Khoja, S., Scott, R., Casebeer, A., Mohsin, M., Ishaq, A., & Gilani, S. (2007b). E-health readiness assessment tools for healthcare institutions in developing countries. *Telemed. e-Health, 13*(4), 425–432. https://doi.org/10.1089/tmj.2006.0064

Khoja, S., Durrani, H., Scott, R., Sajwani, A., & Piryani, U. (2013). Conceptual framework for development of comprehensive e-Health evaluation tool. *Telemed. e-Health, 19*(1), 48–53. https://doi.org/10.1089/tmj.2012.0073 Epub 2012 Sep 7.

Koivunen, M., & Saranto, K. (2018). Nursing professionals' experiences of the facilitators and barriers to the use of telehealth applications: A systematic review of qualitative studies. *Scandinavian Journal of Caring Sciences, 32*(1), 24–44. https://doi.org/10.1111/scs.12445 Epub 2017 Aug 3 PMID: 28771752.

Lin, C. C., Dievler, A., Robbins, C., Sripipatana, A., Quinn, M., & Nair, S. (2018). Telehealth In Health Centers: Key Adoption Factors, Barriers. *And Opportunities. Health Aff (millwood), 37* (12), 1967–1974. https://doi.org/10.1377/hlthaff.2018.05125 PMID: 30633683.

Moehr, J. R., Schaafsma, J., Anglin, C., Pantazi, S. V., Grimm, N. A., & Anglin, S. (2006). Success factors for telehealth–a case study. *International Journal of Medical Informatics, 75* (10–11), 755–763. https://doi.org/10.1016/j.ijmedinf.2005.11.001 Epub 2006 Jan 4 PMID: 16388982.

Nguyen, M., Waller, M., Pandya, A., & Portnoy, J. (2020). A Review of Patient and Provider Satisfaction with Telemedicine. *Current Allergy and Asthma Reports, 20*(11), 72. https://doi.org/10.1007/s11882-020-00969-7.PMID:32959158;PMCID:PMC7505720

Pelletier-Fleury, N., Fargeon, V., & Lano'e, J. & Fardeau, M. (1997). Transaction costs economics as a conceptual framework for the analysis of barriers to the diffusion of telemedicine. *Health Policy, 42*(1), 1–14. https://doi.org/10.1016/s0168-8510(97)00038-9 PMID: 10173489.

Perry A. (2020) Institute for Healthcare Improvement. Recommendations for designing high quality telehealth, Institute for Healthcare Improvement (ihi, Ed.), Accessed August 15, 2020, from   http://www.ihi.org/communities/blogs/recommendations-for-designing-high-quality-telehealth

Schwamm, L. H. (2014). Telehealth: Seven strategies to successfully implement disruptive technology and transform health care. *Health Aff (millwood)., 33*(2), 200–206. https://doi.org/10.1377/hlthaff.2013.1021 PMID: 24493761.

Senge, P. M. (1992). *The Fifth Discipline: The Art and Science of the Learning Organization.* Random House Business Books.

Shachar, C., Engel, J., & Elwyn, G. (2020). Implications for Telehealth in a Postpandemic Future: Regulatory and Privacy Issues. *JAMA, 323*(23), 2375–2376. https://doi.org/10.1001/jama.2020.7943 PMID: 32421170.

Singh, J., Lutteroth, C., & Wünsche B. C. (2010) Taxonomy of usability requirements for home telehealth systems. in Proceedings of the 11th International Conference of the NZ Chapter of the ACM Special Interest Group on Human-Computer Interaction. CHINZ, Association for Computing Machinery (ACM, Ed.), Auckland, New Zealand, July 8–9, pp. 29–32.

Spivak, S., Spivak, A., Cullen, B., Meuchel, J., Johnston, D., Chernow, R., Green, C. & Mojtabai, R. (2020) Telepsychiatry Use in U.S. Mental Health Facilities, 2010–2017. Psychiatr Serv., 71 (2):121–127. doi: https://doi.org/10.1176/appi.ps.201900261. Epub 2019 Oct 16. PMID: 31615370.

Tang, Z., Johnson, T. R., Tindall, R. D., & Zhang, J. (2006). Applying heuristic evaluation to improve the usability of a telemedicine system. *Telemedicine Journal and E-Health, 12*(1), 24–34. https://doi.org/10.1089/tmj.2006.12.24 PMID: 16478410.

Tanriverdi, H., & Iacono, C. S. (August 1998). (1998) Knowledge Barriers to Diffusion of Telemedicine. *In Proceedings of the International Conference of the Association for Information Systems, Helsinki, Finland, 14–16,* 39–50.

Taylor, P. R. (2013) An approach to designing viable and sustainable telehealth services. Stud Health Technol Inform. 188(XXX):108–113. PMID: 23823297.

Thaler, R. & Sunstein, C. (2009). NUDGE: Improving Decisions about Health, Wealth, and Happiness. Penguin, London, UK. ISBN: 9780141040011 29.Briggs L. (2007) Changing Behaviour: A Public Policy Perspective, from https://legacy.apsc.gov.au/changing-behaviour-public-policy-perspective Australian Public Service Commission, Australian Government, Accessed February 5, 2021

Van Dyk L. (2014) A Review of Telehealth Service Implementation Frameworks. Int. J. Environ. Res. Public Health, 11(2), 1279–1298. PMID: 24464237 PMCID: PMC3945538.

Warner, G., Lawson, B., Sampalli, T., Burge, F., Gibson, R., & Wood, S. (2018). Applying the consolidated framework for implementation research to identify barriers affecting implementation of an online frailty tool into primary health care: A qualitative study. *BMC Health Services Research, 18*(1), 395. https://doi.org/10.1186/s12913-018-3163-1.PMID:29855306; PMCID:PMC5984376

Weinstein, R. S., Lopez, A. M., Joseph, B. A., Erps, K. A., Holcomb, M., Barker, G. P., & Krupinski, E. A. (2014). Telemedicine, telehealth, and mobile health applications that work: Opportunities and barriers. *American Journal of Medicine, 127*(3), 183–187. https://doi.org/10. 1016/j.amjmed.2013.09.032 Epub 2013 Oct 29 PMID: 24384059.

White, S. K., & Greiner, L. (2019) What is ITIL? Your guide to the IT Infrastructure Library, Accessed November 10, 2020, from https://www.cio.com/article/2439501/infrastructure-it-infrastructure-library-itil-definition-and-solutions.html#:~:text=ITIL%20is%20a% 20framework%20of,for%20growth%2C%20scale%20and%20change

Wiki (n. d. a) ITIL Service Strategy. Accessed November 5, 2020, from https://wiki.en.it-processmaps.com/index.php/ITIL_Service_Strategy

Wiki (n. d. b) ITIL Service Design. Accessed November 5, 2020, from https://wiki.en.it-processmaps.com/index.php/ITIL_Service_Design

Wiki (n. d. c) ITIL Service Transition. Accessed November 5, 2020, from https://wiki.en.it-processmaps.com/index.php/ITIL_Service_Transition

Wiki (n. d. d) ITIL Service Operation. Accessed November 5, 2020, from https://wiki.en.it-processmaps.com/index.php/ITIL_Service_Operation;.

Wiki (n. d. e) ITIL Continual Service Improvement. Accessed November 5, 2020, from https:// wiki.en.it-processmaps.com/index.php/ITIL_CSI_-_Continual_Service_Improvement

Wikipedia (n. d.) ITIL; Accessed November 5, 2020, from https://en.wikipedia.org/wiki/ITIL

Yellowlees, P. (2005). Successfully developing a telemedicine system. *Journal of Telemedicine and Telecare, 11*(7), 331–336. https://doi.org/10.1258/135763305774472024

Dr. Pavani Rangachari is a tenured Professor of health management, informatics, and public health at Augusta University, USA. She holds an MS and PhD in Health Management & Policy from the State University of New York at Albany, USA. Her scholarly interests are in health services research, with a special interest in studying the implementation of change and innovation in healthcare organizations. Dr. Rangachari has received research funding as Principal Investigator, from the Agency for Healthcare Research and Quality (AHRQ), USA, and recently completed a four-year term as standing member of a study section for AHRQ. She currently serves as Associate Editor for BMC Health Services Research.

Physical Activity Based on M-Health Tools: Design a New Strategy for the Prevention of Cardiovascular Diseases

17

Gianluca Antonucci, Gabriele Palozzi, Francesco Ranalli, and Michelina Venditti

Abstract

Cardiovascular Disease (CVD) represents 31% of global deaths; the cost for Europe was estimated at €122.6 billion in 2020, with an increase in €20.5 billion over 6 years. It has been demonstrated that leisure-time physical activity reduces the risk of CVD regardless of age and gender. Nevertheless, the use of physical activity as a "treatment" in health care is still scarce. According to the WHO, this under-usage is due to: (i) difficulty in monitoring patients' activities; (ii) absence of guidelines; and (iii) lack of competences in sport activity prescription. New technologies have been implemented to promote physical activity. Innovation in this field offers, nowadays, several different tools to boost physical activity to prevent CVD. Being drawn into the emerging relevance of the diffusion of m-health services, this work intends to investigate the role of the public sector in addressing the specific strategies needed to favor the adoption of a m-health system to boost physical activity for CVD prevention. We depicted our investigation starting from the fuzzy zone between the time in which an innovation is available, and the time when a public service can be effectively affected by this innovation. The study examines which factors foster the

G. Antonucci · M. Venditti
DEA—Department of Business Administration, "G. d'Annunzio" University of Chieti—Pescara, Viale Pindaro 42, 65127 Pescara, Italy
e-mail: gianluca.antonucci@unich.it

M. Venditti
e-mail: m.venditti@unich.it

G. Palozzi (✉) · F. Ranalli
Department Management and Law, University Tor Vergata, Via Columbia 2, 00133 Rome, Italy
e-mail: palozzi@economia.uniroma2.it

F. Ranalli
e-mail: ranalli@uniroma2.it

337

planning and implementation of a m-health service as a booster of well-being behaviors among patients and practitioners. Particularly, this chapter reports on the initial deducing findings coming from an exploratory pilot study targeted on qualitative interviews with privileged experts in the areas of CVD and Kinesiology. Findings appear to claim for a change in the framework of intervention in the general public policy setting, pushing for a change in vision, approach, institutional framework, and cultural setting. Aspects such as: absence of guidelines, lack of specific physical training as well as the necessity to rethink the governance to access services have been found as challenges to be faced, at policy level, toward the realization of value co-creation schemes in health care.

17.1 Background and Research Aim

The use of mobile computing resources in health care has been growing since the end of the last century (Criswell & Parchman, 2002; Gillingham et al., 2002). These tools add value to clinical practice because they facilitate access to clinical information, improve the exchange of information, and provide clinical decision support (Bates & Gawande, 2003; Ruland., 2002). The technological development of these tools led academics to study benefits and barriers regarding their practical, effective adoption (Lu et al, 2005). On the one hand, it was indeed clear, since the beginning, that there were benefits, such as cost saving (Silva et al, 2003), time saving (d'Hemecourt, 2001; Rothschild et al., 2002), error reduction (Barrett et al., 2004; Lapinsky et al., 2001), and improvement of medical practice Schneider, 2001; McAlearney et al, 2004). On the other hand, it was clear that there were also barriers hindering their practical adoption, such as personal factors (i.e., discomfort in using the tool) (McAlearney et al, 2004), non-integrated systems (Barrett et al., 2004), physical design and data entry problems (McAlearney et al, 2004), fragility and maintenance problems (Brody, 2001), and technical difficulties (Beasley, 2002; Lyon, 2002). Apart from these specific barriers, related to the technological components of the tools, there were "other barriers" (Lu et al., 2005). They pertained to the broad organizational and managerial support, such as: lack of institutional support (Lu et al., 2003), inadequate availability of the tools and lack of support in choosing among competing technologies (McAlearney et al, 2004), and lack of needs or motivation and insufficient personnel training (Lapinsky et al., 2001).

Over the years, the technical barriers have been tackled because advances in mobile technologies enabled devices to perform functions that had not even been imagined a few years before (Putzer & Park, 2010). This evolution has been possible thanks to the development of a new field, known as mobile health or m-health (Gagnon, et al., 2016). A m-health system improves healthcare service delivery processes by offering support and services to healthcare providers or targeting communication between healthcare services and consumers (Free et al, 2013); thus changing the traditional modes of information sharing and dissemination (Elwood et al., 2011). Nowadays, m-health constitutes a central component of pervasive healthcare (Zhang et al., 2010) and represents an important instrument to increase: health promotion, disease prevention, provision of care, and monitoring (Heerden et al., 2012).

While m-health tackled the technical barriers, the "other" barriers (namely, institutional, organizational, and managerial) increased, and now represent the main aspect to be tackled (Gagnon et al, 2012). The point is that despite the technical relevance of the information and communication technology tools, the success of m-health depends on its adoption by healthcare providers (Gagnon et al, 2012). This adoption must address specific aspects. Differently from other information technologies, it is mainly consumer-centered and consumer-driven (Akter & Ray, 2010). M-health interventions are a patchwork of small-scale projects (Heerden et al., 2012). Most m-health apps work as black boxes with little use of the theoretical basis (Tomlinson et al., 2013).

In synthesis, in spite of the pervasiveness of mobile devices in most everyday activities: "the use of m-health applications to provide health information and care is particularly challenging and calls for specific strategies" (Gagnon et al., 2016: 212).

Starting from the above considerations, this paper intends to investigate the role of the public sector in addressing the specific strategies required to favor the adoption of a m-health system. It, therefore, aims to answer the following research question:

What should be the role of the public sector in favoring m-health adoption for increasing citizens' health and wellbeing?

Particularly, we decided to focus our attention on the public initiatives that should be implemented to overcome the above described "other" barriers, which are non-technical, and deal with institutional organizational and managerial issues.

In order to avoid the risk of being too vague in directing our research aims, we decided to concentrate our analysis on the relevance of m-health in addressing one specific relevant disease. We chose to frame our investigation upon aspects related with m-health initiatives to contrast Cardiovascular Diseases (CVDs).

CVDs are the number one cause of death globally, representing 31% of all global deaths (WHO, 2020). In 2017, the American Heart Association accounted CVDs' cost in the USA as $555 billion (Bernick & Devis, 2014), the study by shows that the total costs of CVDs in main European economies were estimated at €122.6 billion in 2020, with an increase in €20.5 billion over 6 years. These impressive costs are due to the fact that CVD also represents a leading cause of disability (WHO, 2017).

Most CVDs could be prevented by addressing risk factors, such as tobacco use, unhealthy diet and obesity, physical inactivity, and harmful use of alcohol (WHO, 2017). That is why people with CVD, and especially those who are at high cardiovascular risk, need early detection and management, using counseling and medicines, as well as behavioral changes (WHO, 2018a). Effective behavioral changes could, indeed, prevent 75% of cardiac events (Wang et al., 2014).

Among the behavioral changes able to prevent CVD, there is the practice of amateur sport and leisure-time physical activity, which shows a linear negative correlation with the risk of CVD, regardless of age and gender (Cheng et al., 2018). Physical activity is much more effective than many medical prescriptions (WHO, 2017) because its practice positively affects the quality of life of people at risk (Abu-Omar et al., 2017).

The practice of physical activity as a therapeutic preventive factor is, nonetheless, still lacking (Abu-Omar et al., 2017), and levels of inactivity in high-income countries are even increasing (Benjamin et al., 2017; AHA, 2016). To this end, the major barrier for prescribing physical activity as therapy, as underlined by WHO (2018a), is the difficulty in monitoring patients during their performance. This problem can be addressed by the use of wearable technology, which could allow clinicians to evaluate activities carried out, gesture accuracy, and several biomedical data. The following Figs. 17.1 and 17.2 show two real examples of wearable technology systems for detecting biomedical parameters during patients' exercises.

Clearly, the highest potential of wearable technologies in health care can be expressed when patients and clinicians are not in the same place; this is possible through the implementation of models based on the Internet of Health Things (Terry, 2016), which makes it possible to monitor the patient from a distance.

Accordingly, a new frontier to promote amateur sport and physical activity is represented by the use of m-health (Xiong et al, 2019). New technologies have been implemented to promote physical activity (Duncan et al, 2014; Gao & Lee, 2019;

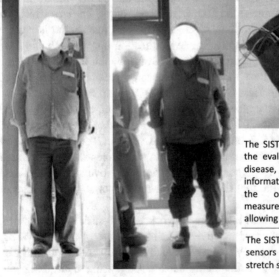

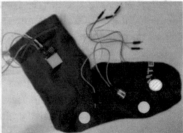

The SISTINE, a telemonitoring system for the evaluation of patients with vascular disease, is able to provide useful information that can be used directly by the operator carrying out the measurement and at the same time allowing remote monitoring by the doctor.

The SISTINE socks are equipped by: force sensors (Yellow); inertial sensor (Blue); stretch sensor (Red).

Fig. 17.1 The SISTINE system: sensorized socks for vascular disease monitoring. *Source* Author's illustration from Lucangeli et al. (2021)

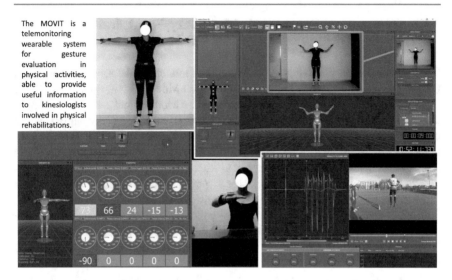

The MOVIT is a telemonitoring wearable system for gesture evaluation in physical activities, able to provide useful information to kinesiologists involved in physical rehabilitations.

Fig. 17.2 The MOVIT system: telemonitoring avatar for activity tracking and gesture correctness analysis. *Source* Author's illustration from Captks s.r.l., Italy, http://www.captiks.com (2021)

Zhang et al, 2015). Innovation in this field offers several different tools to boost physical activity to prevent CVDs (Gao, 2017; King et al, 2015).

M-health in the domain includes: exergaming (active video games); social media; mobile device apps; health wearables; mobile games; augmented reality games; global positioning and geographic information systems (GPS/GIS); and virtual reality (Pope et al., 2019).

Starting from the above-reported considerations, our study intends to investigate the issue, at a public policy level, looking at the role of the public sector in designing proper strategies for the adoption of innovative m-health systems in this field. It, therefore, investigates aspects regarding public health design, legal frameworks and general services to favor the adoption of m-health as a booster for physical activity to prevent CVD.

The paper is structured as follows: after this introduction, the Sect. 17.2 depicts the theoretical framework regarding the fuzzy front end of digital innovation in the public sector. The Sect. 17.3 describes the research methodology, while the Sect. 17.4 illustrates the findings of the qualitative inquiry carried out. The Sect. 17.5 discusses the results. To conclude, the Sect. 17.6 draws some final remarks about the usefulness of the study in the perspective of healthcare services design.

17.2 Theoretical Framework: The Fuzzy Front End of Digital Innovation in the Public Sector

While health studies about the use of technology influenced theories on its adoption (Fox et al., 2018)—like the Technology Adoption Model (Davis et al, 1989) or the Unified Theory of Technology Acceptance and Use Model (Venkatesh et al, 2003)—the role of the public sector in favoring (or not) m-health implementation is still under-investigated (Boonstra & Offenbeek, 2010; Kruse et al, 2014). This lack of investigation also reflects a scarcity in distinctive frameworks to explore the issue (Boonstra & Offenbeek, 2010; Gagnon et al., 2016; Kruse et al, 2014). We, therefore, had to find a suitable reference model, able to give us indications on how to frame our study in the specific context related to our aims.

After considering the above, we decided to look at a methodology that has been properly developed to study digital innovation in the public sector in general; we then adapted it to the specific context of m-health to boost physical activities to prevent CVD.

We started by considering that in the last 20 years, digitalization has changed public administration and public policy (Fishenden et al., 2013). However, this transformation has not been as huge as initially thought and, most of all, it did not lead to such a great re-design in all sectors and countries. Nowadays, there is indeed a patchy situation (Bekkers et al., 2011).

The main issue appears to be the fact that in studying any innovation in the public sector, it is necessary to consider that it is not achieved per se in a blink. It is rather the result of a process locally embedded: in a specific context (such as a specific policy sector with specific state and governance traditions); in a specific time; and within specific power relations (Bekkers et al., 2011). More explicitly, it must be noted that differently from private sector innovation, the public sector's is typically aimed at services rather than products, thus requiring more interaction, negotiation and dispute resolution with stakeholders (Cunningham & Kempling, 2009). It is, therefore, necessary to tackle aspects like: inflexible cultures, legal requirements, a need for inclusiveness and diversity, and the lack of a policy framework (Lee et al., 2012).

All the above considered, we depicted our investigation referring to the methodology that Tate et al. (2018) developed for analyzing digital innovation in public services. According to their analysis, every digital innovation has to face what has been named the fuzzy front end (FFE). Namely, it is the fuzzy zone between the time in which an opportunity (or need) is known, and the time when serious effort is devoted to the development project, where there is the challenge of analyzing good ideas for deciding which one to pursue (Gassmann et al., 2004).

Within this FFE, the authors depict the different barriers and constraints to effective innovation and identify the opportunities to be aligned to address these barriers. Moreover, they show how to draw insights, from existing methodologies, to create a purpose-built method. In synthesis, they "present a methodology for

Table 17.1 Analyzed factors within FFE. *Source* Authors' elaboration

Challenges	Barriers
Proactive services	Digitizing without transforming
Design-led innovation and agile services	Lack of shared standards
Translational roles	Internal culture barriers

carrying out open innovation for digital public services, concentrating on the FFE" (Tate et al., 2018: 187).

Therefore, we decided to have Tate et al.'s (2018) framework as a reference point to depict our study, concentrating the analysis upon: governance innovation; process innovation; communication innovation (De Vries et al., 2016; EU, 2020).

Particularly, we focused our investigation on the relevance of barriers to be mitigated and opportunities to be enabled. Thus, from among those drawn by Tate et al. (2018), we intended to identify the specific barriers and opportunities in the field we were investigating. Among the fifteen factors identified by Tate et al. (2018) we, therefore, identified the following six, as illustrated in Table 17.1, as more suitable for our research aims.

Hence, being aligned with Tate et al.'s (2018) framework, we reframed our investigation according to the design and methods, which could be, as shown in the following paragraph, more suitable for our research aims.

17.3 Research Design and Methodology

Aiming at investigating how public administration could overpass some dimensions of the FFE in designing m-health policy to foster physical activity for CVD prevention, we ran a case study addressing 'why' and 'how' issues (Yin, 2014) of public service (Osborne & Strokosch, 2013).

In particular, at a preliminary stage of investigation, we executed exploratory targeted qualitative interviews (Bailey, 1987) with privileged witnesses, who were able to be informative as experts in the area (Weiss, 1995).

Coherently, with the qualitative "explorative case sampling" (Patton, 2002), we investigated the feasibility within a real-life context of using digital innovations to promote public health policies aimed at enhancing citizens well-being through amateur sport and physical exercise.

Thus, with the purpose of capturing some insights from information-rich informants, the research has been designed for "face to face" interviews (El Said et al., 2017) with 5 experts, who can be considered as highly skilled specialists in the clinical fields of cardiovascular disease and motor rehabilitation. The interviewees were clustered into two groups: i) CARDIOLOGIST; ii) KINESIOLOGIST.

The following shows the interviewees' job-position within their organization:

Group 1—Cardiologists:

- Head of the Dept. of Cardiology of Umberto I General Hospital, Rome, Italy— Full Professor of Cardiology at University "La Sapienza" of Rome (E1).
- Head of the Dept. of Cardiology of Casilino General Hospital, Rome, Italy— Aggregate Professor of Sport Cardiology at University "Foro Italico" of Rome (E2).
- Cardiologist at the Dept. of Cardiology of SS Annunziata, Chieti, Italy—Full Professor of Sport Cardiology at University "G. d'Annunzio" of Chieti—Pescara (E3).

Group 2—Kinesiologists:

- Researcher of Kinesiology at University "G. d'Annunzio" of Chieti—Pescara (E4).
- Researcher of Kinesiology at University "G. d'Annunzio" of Chieti—Pescara (E5).

Even if only five, in the authors' opinion, these interviewees represent a good depiction of clinical experience about sport and physical activity application in service implementation aimed at health status enhancement.

Particularly, interviewees E1, E2, and E3 are responsible for their business units, and they are the main coordinators of the decision making for their working teams with the power to develop new streams of intervention in patients' management; interviewees E4 and E5 are experts in physical rehabilitation techniques and new technologies applied to motor physical activities.

In order to disentangle and discuss Tate et al.'s (2018) six chosen dimensions of the FFE (Table 17.1), as explained in the previous section; two interview protocols have been designed, respectively, for the two groups, according to the following branches of enquiry:

- how digital technologies could actually contribute to prescribing physical activities and exercises as a "therapy" for CVD management–health policy dimension.
- how digital technologies could actually work in the current clinical practice of rehabilitation techniques
- operating dimension.

Accordingly, we developed the main theoretical rationales for the interview protocols starting with the following main barriers, recognized by the WHO (2018b), as being responsible for the under-usage of sport activities as a "tool" for health improvement:

(i)   Tracking: difficulty in monitoring of patients' activities;
(ii) Guideline: absence of guidelines;
(iii) Know-how: lack of competences in sport activity prescription.

Additionally, we integrate the interview protocols with Schreckling and Steiger's (2017) pillars of digital innovation evaluation. The framework considers the following key dimensions related to the impact of digital transformation within the business environment, and which have been considered as perspectives of service-change management:

(a) Customer centricity: issues related to customer-patient engagement;
(b) Leadership and strategy: reasons why organizations should focus on digital initiatives;
(c) Culture: people mindset for digital adoption;
(d) People: skills and obstacles for digital business;
(e) Structure and governance: roles and authority mechanisms;
(f) Processes: objects of digitalization;
(g) Technology foundation: value of new technology;
(h) Business model: the importance of innovating business by new offerings.

The following Tables 17.2 and 17.3 report the interview protocols.

Interviews were run between January and August 2020 and conducted in the interviewers' and interviewees' native language (Italian). The average interview lasted about 30 min each. The records transcriptions were analyzed through content analysis (Bauer & Gaskell, 2000) developed through a deductive thematic analysis, having a theoretically driven coding (Braun & Clarke, 2006), following the highlighted dimension of Tate et al.'s (2018) framework. Considering that we had no previous data to facilitate coding, we decided not to use any specific assisted computer software. The content analysis results were then translated into English, and finally re-analyzed for the redaction of this work.

The findings of the research are reported in the next section.

17.4 Findings

In the following sections, we illustrate what emerged from the analysis of each of the considered factors; how the results of the content analysis confirm both their presence and relevance. In subsequent paragraphs, we discuss the results, presenting how to address the identified barriers and challenges of the FFE in the adoption of m-health to foster amateur sport and physical activities to prevent CVD.

17.4.1 Proactive Services: The Necessity to Challenge the Lack of Preliminary Facilitating Factors

The first aspect we investigated regards the possibility of developing, thanks to the use of m-health, a much more proactive prevention service, especially for people at risk of CVD. According to the scheme developed by Tate et al. (2018), being

Table 17.2 Interview protocol for cardiologist group–health policy dimension. *Source* Authors' elaboration

Issue	Questions	References	
		WHO (2018b)	Schreckling and Steiger (2017)
Physical activity monitoring	– How would it be possible to verify if patient/user regularly actually performs physical activity? – How would it be possible to monitor his/her correct progress?	Tracking	– Customer centricity
Physical activity prescribing	– In your opinion, would it be possible to develop "standard" programs and guidelines (suitable for cardiologists, general practitioners [GPs], other specialists) aimed at spreading the prescription of physical activity for therapeutic/preventive strategy in CVD management? – Would it potentially be possible to introduce "standards" based on generic parameters of patients (e.g.: age, sex, weight, pathology, use of drugs, etc.)? Otherwise, would there be a need for a precise `calibration' on the single patient?	Guidelines	– Processes
Education	– In the education of clinicians, would it be advisable to include programs/courses/refresher courses (e.g., university courses, Master's, etc.) aimed at training on the potential of physical activity as therapeutic support for the treatment/prevention of CVDs?	Competences	– People – Culture
Innovative service implementation	– Based on your experience, which type of CVD would be effectively treated/prevented through the use of sports activities? Do you recognize a specific cluster of patients (sex, age, pathology)? – Based on your experience, could digital technologies foster physical activity carried out for the purpose of reducing cardiovascular risk? In particular, would they have any impact in terms of monitoring and prescribing physical exercise? If so, how?	All	– Structure and governance – Business model

Table 17.3 Interview protocol for Kinesiologist group–operative dimension. *Source* Authors' elaboration

Issue	Questions	References	
		WHO (2018b)	Schreckling and Steiger (2017)
m-health affordability	– Based on your experience, how reliable do you consider m-health tools in measuring the "performance" of motor and sports activities carried out by the users? – Are there any technologies more affordable than others? Are there, consequently, important cost differences?	Tracking	- Technology foundation
m-health accessibility	– Do you think there is a problem of ˋaccessibility' to m-health tools? – Are they user-friendly or should the user receive preliminary instruction? – Do you recognize specific technical digital issues or digital divide?	Competences	– People – Culture
m-health efficacy	– Could the "sole" technology ˋpush a patient's behavioral change or is there always a need for continuous and constant monitoring and support from specialized personnel to ensure correct use of the tool? – Is there a risk that the use of m-health tools by the user will decrease over time (e.g., at the beginning, I see the novelty and use it as a 'new game`, then, with the passage of time, the frequency of use decreases, thus affecting its effectiveness as a preventive therapy)? – Do you think that technicians and clinicians can easily learn the correct use of m-health tools to monitor the activity carried out by users? – Do you think it possible to have an effective recognition of these tools as preventive therapies?	– Tracking – Guidelines	– Leadership and strategy – Process

proactive means to develop services that are able to respond when and where appropriate, and also being able to anticipate citizens' needs. In our specific case, prevention is fundamental and the promotion of physical activity represents (as highlighted in the Sect. 17.1) a valid effective factor. So, the ability to define a proactive service represented, in our opinion, the first aspect to be investigated.

According to the results of our content analysis, the promotion of physical activity already represented a challenge, even before the development of m-health; and it still does.

All the interviewed cardiologists revealed that the challenge still lays on the relevance of a change in the design of CVD health prevention services. Specifically, they state that before talking about the use of digital tools, there should be a definition on how to "prescribe" physical activity; and to whom, according to the different clusters of people at risk. Although the validity of physical activity is not new, there have never been defined specific protocols to be followed.

> E1 even affirmed: "the topic is not new at all, I remember that since I was still a student, my professor talked about the importance of physical activity (...) Nowadays, thanks to digital tools, we could really develop precision medicine using physical activity to prevent CVD risks (...) There should be agreed guidelines, not only for cardiovascular specialists, but also and especially for GPs who in close contact with the patients." E3 highlighted: "there should be a real promotion of continuing education and training courses, for medical doctors in general, about the relevance of physical activity as a preventive factor for health in general, not only to prevent CVD." E3 even affirmed: "There should be a state 'marketing campaign' to promote physical activity as a preventive factor, especially in young adults, with slogans like: 'physical activity is cool; who does physical activity is healthy (...).'"

In synthesis, it appears that there is, from the medical side, recognition of the validity of developing proactive services, but before thinking about the development of them, a change in the framework of intervention for CVD prevention is needed. Particularly, the lack lays at policy level; when designing the services, physical activity and m-health should be included as encoded, recognized therapies–first of all, through the definition of specific guidelines.

17.4.2 Design-Led Innovation and Agile Services: The Gap Between Trials and Actual Wide Use of Tools

Design-led innovation was defined, in Tate et al. (2018) framework, as an opportunity-based approach to innovation. According to this vision, early versions of new design artifacts, and their business vision and models, co-evolve; thus, focusing on customer's empathy, ideation, experimentation, constant evaluation, and prototyping (Hildenbrand et al., 2012).

In our specific case, it seemed that such a kind of tool suffers in reaching its aim, resulting in the lack of users' wide and long-lasting participation. In this case, the interviewed kinesiologist researchers underlined the existence of a great gap between successful trials and actual mass production. In particular,

> E4 highlighted: "Look, there are really a lot of academic articles showing the importance and validity of these electronic tools. Nevertheless, one thing is to have participants in a trial (...), another thing is to have patients that follow the prescriptions (...) And few possible users do not push companies to invest in developing these tools."

In this sense, the difficulty in leading users toward behavioral change, as will be described in Sect. 1.4.6, appears to be one of the greater aspects to be faced.

From the views of the cardiovascular specialists, it was once again affirmed that GPs should favor the change because they are in very close contact with their patients.

E1 affirmed, "First of all, it is necessary to sensitize (…) It is different if you are a healthy person or one at risk of CVD, you should teach patients to never reach a pain threshold."

In synthesis, it appeared that it is fundamental that GPs, together with motor and physical activity specialists, teach people how to do physical activity. The m-health tool is introduced afterward, as a valid tool to favor, monitor, and measure physical activity. However, in this sense,

E3 affirmed: "But could you imagine GPs prescribing sport and physical activity? Do you think that they could then easily work in reading patients' data developed by digital tools? They have not been trained to do that; and it is not an easy process to be developed." E2 even affirmed: "Discussion about the lack of education and training are becoming profuse. There is still nothing! Sport-therapy should be a subject to be studied, not only by medical doctors, but within all the degrees related with health sciences and beyond."

To synthesize, the distance that divides effective trials from a mass use of the tools affirm the "guiding" of both GPs and patients in changing their mood toward continuous and committed use of the tools; as if they were pills to be prescribed by the GP and taken by the patient.

17.4.3 Translational Roles: A Challenge at the Governance Level

The last challenge we considered was what Tate et al. (2018) named translational roles. It is described as the possibility to have trustworthy facilitators in different environments; thus, being able to bridge boundaries.

In our specific case, this appeared to be the hardest challenge to be faced. Indeed, both at the educational training level, but especially at the policy one, it seems that there are two different frameworks that are very far one from each other. At the educational level, health operators (from medical doctors to nurses) are very far from sport and physical activity specialists and trainers. On this aspect,

E1 affirmed: "there ought to be integration, within physiology courses, on the possibilities to develop treatments for gray patients [meaning: the person at risk is possibly going to face an acute event]." Apart from education, it seems there is a lack at the institutional level. E4 affirmed: "It is not easy to involve, around the same table, medical doctors and sport and physical activity specialists as we are (…) When you plan and then apply to develop an experimental trial, ethical commissions do not easily agree because of this admixture of medical doctors together with physical activity specialists in dealing with patients' personal data."

Indeed, despite the evidence, in the last decade, of the importance of boosting m-health physical activity within public health policies, the discussions about the political issues in this field appear to be still at a preliminary stage. While there is an established corpus of policy-orientated research articles on public health and life-style factors, including physical activity, its promotion together with grassroots sport is remarkably absent from the public health research agenda (Mansfield et al., 2016). Running a research on national governments of EU countries, we found that the two paradigms are seen as very far from one another. Health policies are, most of the time, under the jurisdiction of a specific Ministry or, if not, they are usually under the specific authority within Welfare Ministries. On another side, there are sport and physical activities, which most of the time are included within educational ministries and sometimes within cultural heritage and tourism. This aspect appears to be evidence of how distant, at the government level, the two fields are. It is a matter of governance and policy design.

> E1 affirmed: "The Health Ministry should do more to favor amateur sport and physical activity (…) there should be communication campaigns, as the ones developed to prevent cancer through periodical screening." From the side of motor and physical activity specialists, E4 declared: "You see now the point because you are running a research, but you have to consider that, at policy level, sport is not seen much in the value of grassroots sport and physical activity for people wellbeing. It is rather seen as the possibility to grow elite athletes as well as for its relevance in the education of youngsters, being in this last case, closer to social policies rather than to health ones."

In synthesis, the point appears to be that in our specific case, before thinking about the way to favor the wide use of digital tools, there are preliminary aspects to be faced at the policy design level that should find a bridge between the two fields.

17.4.4 Digitizing Without Transforming: Problems in Tool Reliability and in Users' Commitment

A major barrier found by Tate et al. (2018) was referred to the fact that many e-government initiatives were simply digitizing, without transforming services' design and delivery. In our specific case, looking at an initiative inspired by the development of e-health services, three main obstacles were found in the possibility of using digital tools to promote sport and physical activities as a preventive therapy against CVD.

All the aspects were highlighted by the kinesiology researchers. First of all, they highlighted that there is still a digital divide. Most people at risk of CVD are more than 60 years old, and thus, not so used to a daily-connection with high profile digital tools. This first aspect appears, anyway, to be decreasing in the last years, thanks to the possibility of using more friendly developed tools, which are able to easily interact with common smartphones. This fact requires, from the users' side, neither specific, complicated, expensive tools to be acquired, nor particular knowledge for interacting and using the tool in a proper way.

What appeared to be a positive factor to solve the first problem, revealed itself as a new barrier. Indeed, we were told that these new friendly technologies (mobile apps, smartwatches, etc.) are not completely reliable. In particular,

E4 affirmed, "Few of these friendly commercialized tools own a scientific certification about their effectiveness and reliability. You absolutely have to avoid errors and an approximation in measurement efficacy. A light imprecision of these instruments might become a risk for the person."

In essence, the first two obstacles could be overcome, through favoring only the use of reliable and friendly tools, although they can be expensive.

Our interviewees told us about a further barrier named the Behavioral Change Technique. This aspect deals with the possibility, for a specific tool of intervention, to really modify the high-risk behavior of the patient. Indeed, it has been seen that in the majority of the users, these tools are effective only for a few months. After the initial period, there is a kind of disaffection in using them. This reflects itself in a slow decrease of physical activity by the patient, or even in inconstant activity, and this is riskier than not doing sport and physical activity at all. At a practical level, these tools are used and thus effective at the beginning, as if the users were experiencing a new game. With the passage of time, inner wrong risk behavior takes over again, conveying the history of the patient. This problem is common to most preventive therapies based on the necessity to stop risky behaviors (e.g., quit smoking, following a correct diet, etc.). In the case of digital tools to promote physical activity, the new frontier is represented by the possibility of linking activity trackers to the achievement of results and prizes.

E4 affirmed: "like if you were playing a digital competition (...) The possibility to interact, through linked social media channels, with other people facing the same problem can positively affect behavioral change." In this sense, E2 affirmed, "ICT tools could develop a system of monitoring with inducements. There should be prizes and also possibilities to have fair 'competitions' with other patients, in order to motivate people. There are motivating apps on smartphones."

17.4.5 Lack of Shared Standards: A Problem of Certification and Accountability

If the first barrier might be overcome in the near future, the other two appear very far from being tackled. They, indeed, require a change in the way of thinking, both at the policy level and that of practitioners and users.

Particularly, a great obstacle is represented by the lack of shared standards. Thus, it appears to be strictly linked with the challenges to be faced, as described in the previous paragraphs of this section. A common point is indeed that, at this stage, stating the absence of guidelines and the lack of specific training for most practitioners (from GPs to nurses, as well as motor and physical activities trainers), physical activity cannot be prescribed as a medicine. In the case of a drug, there is always a protocol to be followed for prescribing it to a patient. International and specific national institutional bodies (e.g., European Medicines Agency in the EU; Food and Drug Administration in the USA; Agenzia Italiana del Farmaco in Italy, etc.) certify both its efficacy for treatment as well as a low risk for what is regarded as possible side effects. Moreover, in the case of drugs prescriptions, as well as in an intervention by a specialized team on an acute patient, both private insurance systems and national health services can account costs. In this case, they refer to what is agreed for the medicine and/or to the specific diagnosis-related group cost for a clinical intervention. Can we imagine the same setting for the possibility of prescribing the use of a digital tool to favor amateur sport and physical activity as a preventive factor to reduce CVD risk? According to E2 we are far from this, but it is not impossible to achieve such a target.

> He stated, "There should be the possibility to prescribe physical activity as a therapy. Sport is a therapy, but it is not perceived as such; both by policy makers and health professionals (...) We should arrive at standard prescriptions, as if we had a medical handbook for prescribing physical activity according to different clusters of typologies of patients."

17.4.6   Internal Culture Barriers: The Barrier of the Barriers

The last barrier we depicted from the analysis of our interviews, through the lens of the FFE methodology, regarded internal cultural barriers. We found them not only from the public delivery side, as found by Tate et al. (2018) (risk aversion, lack of incentives to change), but also even from the users' side.

As appeared clear in all the above sections, challenges to be faced and barriers to be overcome involve a change in governance and planning. There should firstly be a bridging of the boundaries between the health intervention and the motor and physical activities settings. The use of digital tools appears to have the potential to reach this aim. Proper certified digital tools able to favor exergaming, thus also being effective as Behavioral Change Techniques, can really achieve such an important target. In this case, there might be positive results both in people's quality of life as well as in health spend reduction. The problem is represented by the fact that such an achievement should firstly face a cultural change in approaching the issue. According to the analysis of our interviews, this outcome is still far from being reached. In this sense, E1 affirmed:

> One might check from a distance if the patient is doing physical activity, but medical doctors continue to lag behind in using e-health services and digital tools." E2, reinforcing the necessity for a change of vision, declared: "Medicines are seen as a therapy. The prescription of physical activity is not considered as such." Moreover, E3 said: "In many cases it is "safer" for a medical doctor to prescribe a medicine because the prescriptions follow specific protocols and the responsibility to take the right dosage at the right time, as prescribed, is up to the patient (...) With regard to the use of digital tools, you firstly need a change of vision.

Our interviewees told us that the cultural barrier was present also on the patient's side. She/he is not able to perceive the prescription for the use of a tool to monitor his/her physical activity as a therapy. E3 said in this sense:

> In most of the cases, it is the patient that interrogates about the relevance of physical activity and asks for a medicine; an aspect which represents more of a therapy from his/her

point of view." E5 made an explanatory last example: "Do you know which was found, at the academic level, the most powerful digital tool to change behaviors, thus promoting physical activity? (…) One which was not thought for this reason: Pokémon Go (…) even very lazy youngsters started doing physical activity to participate in the game." Regarding a possible "evolution" of the system, E2 stated: "You should use e-tools, like telephone apps, to give incentives which also represent monitoring (…) Goals to be achieved, instead of taking [let's say] 5 pills. You have a system asking you: 'Have you achieved the level?' [the minimum prescribed physical activity per week] (…) There should be 'motivating apps' that are low cost and integrate simple wearable tools with telephone data storage and analysis.

17.5 Discussion

According to the results of our interviews, the six components (three challenges and three barriers as defined in Tate et al.'s (2018) framework were found as relevant. They, indeed, constituted the FFE that still involved the implementation of an effective m-health prevention strategy for tackling CVD risks. We summarize, in the following chart depicted in Fig. 17.3, the different insights that came from our analysis, indicating the different relations among the components.

The lack of monitoring and prescription of physical activities as preventive therapies are the principal enabling factors for affording the challenge of having proactive services (WHO, 2018b). This challenge represents the ability to anticipate the patients' needs (Benincasa et al, 2020). According to our interviews—although the efficacy of amateur sport and physical activity has been recognized for decades —there is not yet a 'prescription' of these activities. In summary, at this stage, it seems that the challenge has not been accepted yet, at a policy level dimension.

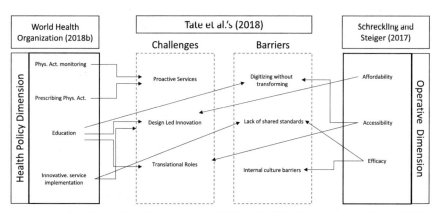

Arrows connect issues included in the interview protocols with Tate et al.'s (2018) selected challenges and barriers of FFE

Fig. 17.3 Interactions among challenges and barriers in the health policy and operative dimensions. *Source* Author's own illustration (2021)

The lack of education (O'Donoghue et al., 2012), although considered important, as confirmed by all the cardiologists, has two negative consequences. First of all, it does not allow tackling the challenge related with design led innovation because there are no interactions for improving the tools. Secondly, it reflects itself both in the lack of translational roles and, especially, in creating the barrier of digitalizing without transforming. The absence of role integration and continuing education—although hoped for by both cardiologists and kinesiologists—does not allow the birth of translational roles able to bear new proactive preventive m-health services. As a consequence, we have a scenario in which there are tools, but there is no change; that is: there is a digitalization without any actual transformation. The digitalization without any transformation is a barrier which, according to our interviews, is related also with accessibility. The indication of a digital divide, especially for older people, seems to be an obstacle to be overcome. This could be done thanks to the use of easily wearable tools, connected with smartphones, accessible and fairly inexpensive (Godinho et al., 2020). However, this aspect refers to the reliance of taking the challenge of translational roles, thus having collaboration among the different fields, from medical to ICT, passing through the sport (Anderson et al., 2018). According to our interviewees, this challenge has not been taken yet, and the collaboration among the fields does not yet seem around the corner.

The greatest barriers, which also preclude the possibility of tackling the challenges, concern cultural barriers and the lack of shared standards. Both these barriers are connected with the efficacy of the system as considered by the operative dimension. This appears to be the closure of a vicious circle. Indeed, the lack of shared standards, expressed by all the interviewees in all the dimensions, appears to be an aspect weighted on the operative side, attached to the health service, but not yet agreed and implemented at policy level. This deficiency influences actual implementation, reflected also by low investment for increasing the development of the different tools already tested at the pilot study level (Kampmeijer et al., 2016). This leads, as a consequence, to the low reliability of some of these tools, as expressed on the operative side. The point is that as long as there are cultural barriers (the barrier of the barriers as defined in Sect. 4.6) that do not allow the consideration of sport and physical activity as a preventive therapy, at a generalized level, it will be nearly impossible to implement an effective strategy for m-health services to prevent CVD.

17.6 Conclusion

Starting from the consideration that the success of m-health depends on its adoption by healthcare providers (Gagnon et al., 2012), this chapter aimed at studying the public sector's role in the adoption of m-health services to promote physical activities and amateur sports as a preventive factor for CVDs.

Knowing that the use of m-health applications is particularly challenging and calls for specific strategies (Gagnon et al, 2016), we concentrated our analysis on public health design, public frameworks and general services to favor the adoption of m-health.

Since this aspect is still under-investigated (Boonstra & Van Offenbeek, 2010), there are not yet any specific models to explore the issue (Kruse et al, 2014). We, therefore, decided to frame our investigation looking at a properly developed methodology to study digital innovation in the public sector. We chose the one depicted by Tate et al. (2018). This methodology considers the relevance of the FFE, identifying barriers to be mitigated and opportunities to be enabled for favoring digital innovation in the public sector.

We developed our research through a deductive thematic analysis, having a theoretically driven coding inspired by the WHO (2018b) physical activities promotion guideline, and Schreckling and Steiger's framework (2017) for digital adoption. We executed exploratory, targeted, qualitative interviews with privileged witnesses, who were able to be informative as experts in the area. We, therefore, ran a content analysis making a specific categorization of the factors individualized by Tate et al. (2018), interpreting them through the analysis of the records of the interviews.

Summarizing the findings from the interviewees, we draw the following flow-chart (Fig. 17.4) for a general framework of monitoring prescribed physical activities as a preventive factor for CVD. The flow-chart shows how digital technologies allow for development of a preventive service for CVDs by connecting clinicians and patients.

This way, m-health could trigger a feedback model, where the clinician can assess the improvements of patients by tracking the level of the quality and accuracy of their activities and exercises. Indirectly, the monitoring of physical activities carried out by a patient means the enhancement of the patient's health.

From the analysis of our findings, it appears clear that the recognition of the validity of the m-health tools is support for physical activity prescription as a therapy (Siedler et al., 2020), but its actual adoption appears not so easy. Indeed, interviewees underlined that before thinking of an actual effective adoption, a change in the general public policy setting is needed. They told us about the problems in the standard prescription of physical activities and how patients carry them out, rather than about the actual efficacy or the deficiencies of the digital tools. Indeed, the absence of guidelines and the lack of specific training for most practitioners (from GPs to nurses, as well as motor and physical activity trainers) requires a rethinking of governance and accountability frameworks for managing new ways to deliver healthcare services (Bergerum et al., 2020).

In this sense, the relevance of the public policy context in public health appears to be predominant. Indeed, while mobile technologies are influencing the private sector and private organizations, public agencies are under increasing pressure to apply digital technologies to renew and transform their business models (Kohli et al., 2019) thus, m-health adoption is still challenging (Gagnon et al, 2016; Heerden et al., 2012; Aktera and Ray, 2010; Tomlinson et al, 2013).

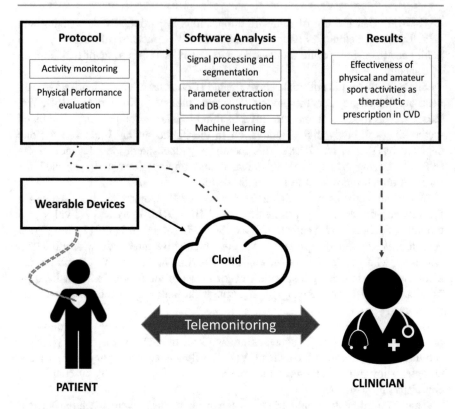

Fig. 17.4 General telemonitoring framework for prescribing physical activities as CVD prevention. *Source* Authors' illustration inspired by D'Angelantoni et al. (2021)

Our findings confirm that the public sector requires more interaction, negotiation and dispute resolution with stakeholders (Cunningham & Kempling, 2009), having to tackle aspects like: inflexible cultures, legal requirements, a need for inclusiveness and diversity, and lack of a policy framework (Lee et al, 2012) Concerning CVD care and prevention, present clinical practices and culture seem to represent one of the main obstacles to be addressed before thinking about an actual adoption of m-health to promote physical activities for CVD prevention. Indeed, all the interviewees reported problems in prescribing the digital tools rather than in clearly assessing their validity and effectiveness.

In this sense, the actual adoption of prevention policies, based on physical activities tracked by m-health, appears to be impeded by the lack of managerial frameworks as well as traditions in this sense.

Generally speaking, for designing new healthcare services following the technology availability, this study confirms that the main barrier is the cultural legacy of healthcare administrations. Particularly, public agencies should take up the challenge of a cultural transformation toward:

- providing updated guidelines and education for new technology employment in healthcare;
- fostering the debate among different policy fields (e.g., technical, clinical, managerial, legal, etc.) addressing the same health necessity;
- stimulating patient involvement in the service.

These topics seem to be perfectly fitting within the debate about new strategies for creating public value in health care, following the citizenship's changing needs. Particularly, this concerns performance governance (Bouckaert and Hallington, 2007) toward the design of co-produced services (Osborne & Strokosch, 2013) based on patients' participation fostered by digital innovation availability.

References

Abu-Omar, K., Rütten, A., Burlacu, I., Schätzlein, V., Messing, S., & Suhrcke, M. (2017). The cost-effectiveness of physical activity interventions: A systematic review of reviews. *Preventive Medicine Reports, 8*, 72–78. https://doi.org/10.1016/j.pmedr.2017.08.006.

AHA—American Heart Association. (2016). *What is cardiac rehabilitation?* http://www.heart.org/HEARTORG/Conditions/More/CardiacRehab/What-is-Cardiac-Rehabilitation_UCM_307049_Article.jsp#.Wp31Y6huaUk. Accessed Jan 2021

Akter, S., & Ray, P. (2010). mHealth-an ultimate platform to serve the unserved. *Yearbook of Medical Informatics, 19*(1), 94–100. https://doi.org/10.1055/S-0038-1638697CorpusID: 36383669 PMID: 20938579.

Anderson, S., Nasr, L., & Rayburn, S. W. (2018). Transformative service research and service design: Synergistic effects in healthcare. *The Service Industries Journal, 38*(1–2), 99–113. https://doi.org/10.1080/02642069.2017.1404579

Bailey, D. B. (1987). *Methods of social research*. Free Press.

Barrett, J. R., Strayer, S. M., & Schubart, J. R. (2004). Assessing medical residents' usage and perceived needs for personal digital assistants. *International Journal of Medical Informatics, 73*(1), 25–34. PMID: 15036076. https://doi.org/10.1016/j.ijmedinf.2003.12.005.

Bates, D. W., & Gawande, A. A. (2003). Improving safety with information technology. *New England Journal of Medicine, 348*(25), 2526–2534. https://doi.org/10.1056/NEJMsa020847

Bauer, M. W., & Gaskell, G. (2000). *Qualitative researching with text*. London, Sage Publishing.

Beasley, B. W. (2002). Utility of palmtop computers in a residency program: a pilot study. *Southern Medical Journal, 95*(2), 207–212. PMID: 11846246. https://doi.org/10.1097/00007611-200202000-00010. Corpus ID: 19293399.

Bekkers, V. J. J. M., Edelenbos, J., & Steijn, B. (2011). *Innovation in the public sector: Linking capacity and leadership*. London, UK: Palgrave Macmillan. PMID: 31866635. https://doi.org/10.1253/circj.CJ-19-0879.

Benincasa, G., Marfella, R., Della Mura, N., Schiano, C., & Napoli, C. (2020). Strengths and opportunities of network medicine in cardiovascular diseases. *Circulation Journal, 84*(2), 144–152. PMID: 31866635. https://doi.org/10.1253/circj.CJ-19-0879.

Benjamin, E. J., Blaha, M. J., Chiuve, S. E., Cushman, M., Das, S. R., Deo, R., de Ferranti, S. D., Floyd, J., Fornage, M., & Gillespie, C. (2017). On behalf of the American Heart Association Statistics Committee and Stroke Statistics Subcommittee. Heart Disease and Stroke Statistics—2017 Update: *A Report from the American Heart Association. Circulation, 135*(10) e146–e603. PMID: 28122885; PMCID: PMC5408160. https://doi.org/10.1161/CIR.0000000000000485.

Bergerum, C., Engström, A. K., Thor, J., & Wolmesjö, M. (2020). Patient involvement in quality improvement–a 'tug of war'or a dialogue in a learning process to improve healthcare? *BMC*

Health Services Research, 20(1), 1–13. PMID: 33267880; PMCID: PMC7709309. https://doi.org/10.1186/s12913-020-05970-4.

Bernick, S., & Devis, A. (2014). *The economic cost of cardiovascular disease from 2014–2020 in six European economies.* Cebr.

Boonstra, A., & Van Offenbeek, M. (2010). Towards consistent modes of e-health implementation: Structurational analysis of a telecare programme's limited success. *Information Systems Journal, 20*(6), 537–561. https://doi.org/10.1111/j.1365-2575.2010.00358.x

Bouckaert, G., & Halligan, J. (2007). *Managing performance: International comparisons.* Routledge.

Braun, V., & Clarke, V. (2006). Using thematic analysis in psychology. *Qualitative Research in Psychology, 3*(2), 77–101. https://doi.org/10.1191/1478088706qp063oa

Brody, J. A., Camamo, J. M., & Maloney, M. E. (2001). Implementing a personal digital assistant to document clinical interventions by pharmacy residents. *American Journal of Health-System Pharmacy, 58*(16), 1520–1522. PMID: 11515349. https://doi.org/10.1093/ajhp/58.16.1520.

Cheng, W., Zhang, Z., Cheng, W., Yang, C., Diao, L., & Liu, W. (2018). Associations of leisure-time physical activity with cardiovascular mortality: A systematic review and meta-analysis of 44 prospective cohort studies. *European Journal of Preventive Cardiology, 25*(17), 1864–1872. PMID: 30157685. https://doi.org/10.1177/2047487318795194.

Criswell, D. F., & Parchman, M. L. (2002). Handheld computer use in US family practice residency programs. *Journal of the American Medical Informatics Association, 9*(1), 80–86. PMID: 11751806; PMCID: PMC349390. https://doi.org/10.1136/jamia.2002.0090080.

Cunningham, J. B., & Kempling, J. S. (2009). Implementing change in public sector organizations. Management Decision.

D'Angelantonio, E., Lucangeli, L., Camomilla, V., Mari, F., Mascia, G., & Pallotti, A. (2021). Classification-based screening of phlebopathic patients using smart socks. In *2021 IEEE International Symposium on Medical Measurements and Applications (MeMeA)*, 23–25 June 2021, in print.

d'Hemecourt, P. (2001). Assistance in the palm of your hand. *Healthcare Informatics, 18*(6), 102–103. PMID: 11419330.

Davis, F. D., Bagozzi, R. P., & Warshaw, P. R. (1989). User acceptance of computer technology: A comparison of two theoretical models. *Management Science, 35*(8), 982–1003. https://doi.org/10.1287/mnsc.35.8.982

De Vries, H., Bekkers, V., & Tummers, L. (2016). Innovation in the public sector: A systematic review and future research agenda. *Public Administration, 94*(1), 146–166. https://doi.org/10.1111/padm.12209

Duncan, M., Vandelanotte, C., Kolt, G. S., Rosenkranz, R. R., Caperchione, C. M., George, E. S., Ding, H., Hooker, D., Karunanithi, M., & Maeder & Mummery, W. K. (2014). Effectiveness of a web-and mobile phone-based intervention to promote physical activity and healthy eating in middle-aged males: Randomized controlled trial of the ManUp study. *Journal of Medical Internet Research, 16*(6). https://doi.org/10.2196/jmir.3107PMCID:PMC4090375 PMID: 24927299.

El Said, G. R. (2017). Understanding how learners use massive open online courses and why they drop out: Thematic analysis of an interview study in a developing country. *Journal of Educational Computing Research, 55*(5), 724–752. https://doi.org/10.1177/0735633116681302

Elwood, D., Diamond, M. C., Heckman, J., Bonder, J. H., Beltran, J. E., Moroz, A., & Yip, J. (2011). Mobile health: Exploring attitudes among physical medicine and rehabilitation physicians toward this emerging element of health delivery. *Pm & R, 3*(7), 678–680. PMID: 21777869. https://doi.org/10.1016/j.pmrj.2011.05.004.

EU—European Union. (2020). Public sector innovation concepts, trends and best practices, EU Parliament Briefings. https://www.europarl.europa.eu/RegData/etudes/BRIE/2020/651954/EPRS_BRI(2020)651954_EN.pdf. Accessed 16 June 2021.

Fishenden, J., & Thompson, M. (2013). Digital government, open architecture, and innovation: Why public sector IT will never be the same again. *Journal of Public Administration Research and Theory, 23*(4), 977–1004. https://doi.org/10.1093/JOPART/MUS022CorpusID:16859670

Fox, G., & Connolly, R. (2018). Mobile health technology adoption across generations: Narrowing the digital divide. *Information Systems Journal, 28*(6), 995–1019. https://doi.org/10.1111/isj.12179

Free, C, Phillips, G & Watson, L. (2013). The effectiveness of mobile-health technologies to improve health care service delivery processes: a systematic review and meta-analysis. *PLOS Medicine, 10*(1), e1001363, 1–26. PMID: 23458994; PMCID: PMC3566926. https://doi.org/10.1371/journal.pmed.1001363.

Gagnon, M. P., Desmartis, M., & Labrecque, M. (2012). Systematic review of factors influencing the adoption of information and communication technologies by healthcare professionals. *Journal of Medical Systems, 36*(1), 241–277. PMID: 20703721; PMCID: PMC4011799. https://doi.org/10.1007/s10916-010-9473-4.

Gagnon, M. P., Ngangue, P., Payne-Gagnon, J., & Desmartis, M. (2016). m-Health adoption by healthcare professionals: a systematic review. *Journal of the American Medical Informatics Association, 23*(1), 212–220. PMID: 26078410; PMCID: PMC7814918. https://doi.org/10.1093/jamia/ocv052.

Gao, Z. (2017). *Technology in physical activity and health promotion.* Routledge Publisher; London.

Gao, Z., & Lee, J. E. (2019). Emerging technology in promoting physical activity and health: Challenges and opportunities. *Journal of Clinical Medicine, 8*(11), 1830. https://doi.org/10.3390/jcm8111830

Gassmann, O., & Enkel, E. (2004). Towards a theory of open innovation: Three core process archetypes. In Paper presented at the R&D Management Conference (RADMA), 07-09.07.2004, Lisbon.

Gillingham, W., Holt, A., & Gillies, J. (2002). Hand-held computers in healthcare: What software programs are available? *New Zealand Medical Journal, 115*(1162), U185. PMID: 12386664.

Godinho, M. A., Jonnagaddala, J., Gudi, N., Islam, R., Narasimhan, P., & Liaw, S. T. (2020). mHealth for integrated people-centred health services in the Western Pacific: A systematic review. *International Journal of Medical Informatics, 142*, 104259. PMID: 32858339. https://doi.org/10.1016/j.ijmedinf.2020.104259.

Heerden, A. V., Tomlinson, M., & Swartz, L. (2012). Point of care in your pocket: a research agenda for the field of m-health. *Bulletin of the World Health Organization, 90*(5), 393–394. PMID: 22589575; PMCID: PMC3341694. https://doi.org/10.2471/BLT.11.099788.

Hildenbrand, T., & Meyer, J. (2012). Intertwining lean and design thinking: software product development from empathy to shipment. In *Software for People* (pp. 217–237). Berlin: Springer Verlag.

Kampmeijer, R., Pavlova, M., Tambor, M., Golinowska, S., & Groot, W. (2016). The use of e-health and m-health tools in health promotion and primary prevention among older adults: A systematic literature review. *BMC Health Services Research, 16*(5), 467–479. PMID: 27608677; PMCID: PMC5016733. https://doi.org/10.1186/s12913-016-1522-3.

King, A. C., Glanz, K., & Patrick, K. (2015). Technologies to measure and modify physical activity and eating environments. *American journal of preventive medicine, 48*(5), 630–638. PMID: 25891063; PMCID: PMC7155784. https://doi.org/10.1016/j.amepre.2014.10.005.

Kohli, R., & Melville, N. P. (2019). Digital innovation: A review and synthesis. *Information Systems Journal, 29*(1), 200–223. https://doi.org/10.1111/isj.12193

Kruse, C. S., DeShazo, J., Kim, F., & Fulton, L. (2014). Factors associated with adoption of health information technology: A conceptual model based on a systematic review. *JMIR Medical Informatics, 2*(1), e9. PMID: 25599673; PMCID: 4288077. https://doi.org/10.2196/medinform.3106.

Lapinsky, S. E., Weshler, J., Mehta, S., Varkul, M., Hallett, D., & Stewart, T. E. (2001). Handheld computers in critical care. *Critical Care, 5*(4), 227–231. PMID: 11511337; PMCID: PMC37409. https://doi.org/10.1186/cc1028.

Lee, S. M., Olson, D. L., & Trimi, S. (2012). Co-innovation: Convergenomics, collaboration, and co-creation for organizational values. *Management Decision., 50*(5), 817–831. https://doi.org/10.1108/00251741211227528

Lu, Y. C., Lee, J. J. K., Xiao, Y., Sears, A., Jacko, J. A., & Charters, K. (2003). Why don't physicians use their personal digital assistants? In *AMIA Annual Symposium Proceedings* (Vol. 2003, p. 405), 8–12 November 2003. Washington, DC: American Medical Informatics Association.

Lu, Y. C., Xiao, Y., Sears, A., & Jacko, J. A. (2005). A review and a framework of handheld computer adoption in healthcare. *International Journal of Medical Informatics, 74*(5), 409–422. PMID: 15893264. https://doi.org/10.1016/j.ijmedinf.2005.03.001.

Lucangeli, L., D'Angelantonio, E., Camomilla, V. Pallotti, A. (2021). SISTINE: Sensorized socks for telemonitoring of vascular disease patients. In *IEEE International Workshop on Metrology for Industry 4.0 & IoT*, 7–9 June 2021, in print.

Lyon, D. M. (2002). The dilemma of PDA security: An overview. Information Security Reading Room https://www.sans.org/reading-room/whitepapers/pda/paper/257. Accessed 16 June 2021.

Mansfield, L., & Piggin, J. (2016). Sport, physical activity and public health. *International Journal of Sport Policy and Politics, 8*(4), 533–537. https://doi.org/10.1080/19406940.2016.1254666

McAlearney, A. S., Schweikhart, S. B., & Medow, M. A. (2004). Doctors' experience with handheld computers in clinical practice: qualitative study. *BMJ, 328*(7449), 1162. PMID: 15142920; PMCID: PMC411090. https://doi.org/10.1136/bmj.328.7449.1162.

O'Donoghue, G., Cusack, T., & Doody, C. (2012). Contemporary undergraduate physiotherapy education in terms of physical activity and exercise prescription: practice tutors' knowledge, attitudes and beliefs. *Physiotherapy, 98*(2), 167–173. PMID: 22507368. https://doi.org/10.1016/j.physio.2011.04.348.

Osborne, S. P., & Strokosch, K. (2013). It takes two to tango? Understanding the co-production of public services by integrating the services management and public administration perspectives. *British Journal of Management, 24*(S1), S31–S47. https://doi.org/10.1111/1467-8551.12010

Patton, M. Q. (2002). *Qualitative evaluation and research methods*. Sage Publishing, Inc.

Pope, Z. C., Barr-Anderson, D. J., Lewis, B. A., Pereira, M. A., & Gao, Z. (2019). Use of wearable technology and social media to improve physical activity and dietary behaviors among college students: A 12-week randomized pilot study. *International Journal of Environmental Research and Public Health, 16*(19), 3579. PMID: 31557812; PMCID: PMC6801802. https://doi.org/10.3390/ijerph16193579.

Putzer, G. J., & Park, Y. (2010). The effects of innovation factors on smartphone adoption among nurses in community hospitals. Perspectives in Health Information Management/AHIMA, American Health Information Management Association, 7(Winter). PMCID: PMC2805554; PMID: 20697467.

Rothschild, J. M., Lee, T. H., Bae, T., & Bates, D. W. (2002). Clinician use of a palmtop drug reference guide. *Journal of the American Medical Informatics Association, 9*(3), 223–229. PMID: 11971883; PMCID: PMC344582. https://doi.org/10.1197/jamia.m1001.

Ruland, C. M. (2002). Handheld technology to improve patient care: evaluating a support system for preference-based care planning at the bedside. *Journal of the American Medical Informatics Association, 9*(2), 192–201. PMID: 11861634; PMCID: PMC344576. https://doi.org/10.1197/jamia.m0891.

Schneider, T. (2001). Easy access to a world of information: Using a handheld computer. *Journal of Emergency Nursing, 27*(1), 42–43. PMID: 11174270. https://doi.org/10.1067/men.2001.112978.

Schreckling, E., & Steiger, C. (2017). Digitalize or drown. In *Shaping the digital enterprise* (pp. 3–27). Cham: Springer.

Siedler, M., Murad, M. H., Falck-Ytter, Y., Dahm, P., Mustafa, R. A., Sultan, S., & Morgan, R. L. (2020). Guidelines about physical activity and exercise to reduce cardiometabolic risk factors:

protocol for a systematic review and critical appraisal. *BMJ, 10*(1).e032656. PMID: 31980508; PMCID: PMC7044951. https://doi.org/10.1136/bmjopen-2019-032656.

Silva, M. A., Tataronis, G. R., & Maas, B. (2003). Using personal digital assistants to document pharmacist cognitive services and estimate potential reimbursement. *American Journal of Health-System Pharmacy, 60*(9), 911–915. https://doi.org/10.1093/ajhp/60.9.911 PMID: 12756942.

Tate, M., Bongiovanni, I., Kowalkiewicz, M., & Townson, P. (2018). Managing the "Fuzzy front end" of open digital service innovation in the public sector: A methodology. *International Journal of Information Management, 39*(2018), 186–198. https://doi.org/10.1016/j.ijinfomgt.2017.11.008

Terry, N. P. (2016). Will the internet of things transform healthcare. *Vanderbilt Journal of Entertainment and Technology Law, 327*(19), 327–352.

Tomlinson, M., Rotheram-Borus, M. J., Swartz, L., & Tsai, A. C. (2013). Scaling up mHealth: Where is the evidence? *PLoS Medicine, 10*(2). https://doi.org/10.1371/journal.pmed.1001382

Venkatesh, V., Morris, M. G., Davis, G. B., & Davis, F. D. (2003). User acceptance of information technology: Toward a unified view. *MIS Quarterly, 27*(3), 425–478. https://doi.org/10.2307/30036540. https://www.jstor.org/stable/30036540.

Wang, W., Lau, Y., Chow, A., Thompson, D. R., & He, H. G. (2014). Health-related quality of life and social support among Chinese patients with coronary heart disease in mainland China. *European Journal of Cardiovascular Nursing, 13*(1), 48–54. PMID: 23382534. https://doi.org/10.1177/1474515113476995.

Weiss, R. S. (1995). *Learning from strangers: The art and method of qualitative interview studies.* Free Press.

WHO. (2017). Cardiovascular diseases (CVDs)—Keyfacts. World Health Organization (WHO, Ed.)   https://www.who.int/news-room/fact-sheets/detail/cardiovascular-diseases-(cvds). Accessed 16 June 2021.

WHO. (2018a). Global action plan on physical activity 2018–2030: More active people for a healthier world. World Health Organization (WHO, Ed.), Switzerland.

WHO. (2018b). Promoting physical activity in the health sector (2018). World Health Organization (WHO, Ed.), Switzerland. https://www.euro.who.int/en/health-topics/disease-prevention/physical-activity/data-and-statistics/physical-activity-fact-sheets/promoting-physical-activity-in-the-health-sector-2018. Accessed 16 June 2021.

WHO. (2020). The top 10 causes of death. https://www.who.int/news-room/fact-sheets/detail/the-top-10-causes-of-death. Accessed 16 June 2021.

Xiong, S., Zhang, P., & Gao, Z. (2019). Effects of exergaming on preschoolers' executive functions and perceived competence: A pilot randomized trial. *Journal of Clinical Medicine, 8*(4), 469. https://doi.org/10.3390/jcm8040469

Yin, K. R. (2014). *Case study research: Design and methods* (V). Sage Publishing.

Zhang, H., Cocosila, M., & Archer, N. (2010). Factors of adoption of mobile information technology by homecare nurses: A technology acceptance model 2 approach. *CIN: Computers, Informatics, Nursing, 28*(1), 49–56. PMID: 19940621. https://doi.org/10.1097/NCN.0b013e3181c0474a.

Zhang, J., Brackbill, D., Yang, S., & Centola, D. (2015). Efficacy and causal mechanism of an online social media intervention to increase physical activity: Results of a randomized controlled trial. *Preventive Medicine Reports, 13*(2), 651–657. PMID: 26844132; PMCID: PMC4721409. https://doi.org/10.1016/j.pmedr.2015.08.005.

Gianluca Antonucci (MSc London School of Economics and PhD University of Rome Tor Vergata) is Assistant Professor at "G. d'Annunzio" University of Chieti—Pescara, where he is tenure of the courses: "Corporate Social Responsibility" (Master degree in Economics and Management); "Management of Sports Organisations" (degree in Sport Sciences); "Business Economics of building Sector" (degree in Building Construction) His research focuses on, co-production, public accountability, sport management.

Gabriele Palozzi is a Research Fellow in Management at the University of Rome Tor Vergata— Italy, Department of Management and Law. He received his PhD in Management from the University of Rome Tor Vergata. He is Lecturer of Managerial Control. His studies address the sphere of Managerial Accounting, Strategic Controlling and Performance Management. Particularly, his researches focus on economic, social and clinical joint impacts connected to the digital transformation and new technologies in healthcare.

Francesco Ranalli is Full Professor of Accounting at the University of Rome Tor Vergata—Italy, Department of Management and Law. He is the Head of the Department of Management and Law and the former Coordinator of the PhD Course in Public Management and Governance for the University of Rome Tor Vergata. Author of several publications, his main research interests include Financial Reporting and Analysis, Control, Governance and Management both in the Public and Private sectors.

Michelina Venditti is Full Professor of Business Administration at "G. d'Annunzio" University of Chieti—Pescara. She holds Planning and Controlling courses in Business Administration Bachelor and Master degrees in "G. d'Annunzio" University. She is Director of the Department of Business Administration (DEA) of "G. d'Annunzio" University and delegate of the Rector to represent the University in the National Network of Sustainable Universities. Her main research interest regards the aspects related with Sustainability, Circular Economy, Health and Social Inclusion.

Seven Practices for Innovation in Healthcare Products

18

Patricia E. Alafaireet, Chintan Desai, and Howard L. Houghton

Abstract

The successful delivery of precision medicine or that which is personalized to an individual patient's health needs will increasingly be highly dependent on information technology and information systems designed to support the delivery of clinical and nontraditional health services. Innovation and extensive development of the required technology products represent a significant financial investment, much of which will be borne by healthcare enterprises and, ultimately, by patients. This chapter presents seven practices to support innovative healthcare product design. These practices include leveraging case-based patient and physician/provider centered requirements gathering to help ensure end product efficacy, even when end users cannot accurately specify their needs for solutions that may not yet exist. Also introduced is the rational approach of capture and use of data from atypical sources to offset product development decision-making errors that commonly result in product failure post market introduction. Preemptive concept development as a tool to ensure that development teams are confident in their ability to select the best solution when divergent solutions present as a function of the variability intrinsic in the development process is described, along with the use of ethno-graphic tool-based workflow analysis and cognitive analysis as product cost-effective evaluation strategies. Lastly, this chapter proposes the use of guideline

P. E. Alafaireet (✉)
University of Missouri, 734 CS&E Building, Columbia, MO 65212, USA
e-mail: alafaireetp@umsystem.edu

C. Desai
Ascension, All Saints, 3809 Spring Street, Racine, WI 53405-1690, USA
e-mail: chintan.desai@ascension.org

H. L. Houghton
University of Missouri, DC067.00 MUPC Room PC3002, Columbia, MO 65212, USA
e-mail: Houghtonh@umsystem.edu

© The Author(s), under exclusive license to Springer Nature Switzerland AG 2022   363
M. A. Pfannstiel et al. (eds.), *Service Design Practices for Healthcare Innovation*,
https://doi.org/10.1007/978-3-030-87273-1_18

evaluation tools and technology enabled observation as preemptive strategies to reduce design errors. This chapter delivers practical approaches that can be used by individuals across the spectrum of healthcare product development to meaningfully contribute to efficacious technology products at lower development costs.

18.1 Introduction

If clinical decision support systems (CDSSs) are to meet their promise to shift the paradigm of health and healthcare delivery, their core function (augmentation of the complex clinical decision-making process) increasingly will be dependent on the use of information technology and information systems (Sutton et al., 2020). This dependence is especially true of CDSS designed to support genetically guided personalized medicine (Kim et al., 2020; Welch & Kawamoto, 2013). The long development curve required to move baseline research to full clinical implementation is further exacerbated by clinician unfamiliarity with genomics (Balas & Boren, 2000; McGlynn et al., 2003).

The successful delivery of precision and/or personalized medicine will increasingly be highly dependent on information technology and information systems designed to support the delivery of clinical and nontraditional health services (Downing et al., 2009).

Innovation and extensive development of the required technology products represent a significant financial investment, much of which will be borne by healthcare enterprises, and, ultimately, by patients. Costs include those for technology development and for the large time commitments made by physicians and other clinicians as part of the CDSS development cycle, including the time needed to create the clinical information underpinning (Field et al., 2008).

This chapter presents seven relatively accessible practices which can be used by healthcare organizations to support innovative, lower cost, and healthcare product design. These practices include leveraging case-based patient and physician/provider centered requirements gathering to help ensure end product efficacy, even when end users cannot accurately specify their needs for solutions that do not yet exist. Also introduced is the rational approach of capture and use of data from atypical sources to offset product development decision-making errors that commonly result in product failure post market introduction. This chapter also introduces preemptive concept development as a tool to ensure that development teams are confident in their ability to select the best solution when divergent solutions present as a function of the variability intrinsic in the development process. The use of ethno-graphic tool-based workflow analysis and cognitive analysis as tools for establishing a baseline for subsequent, cost-effective evaluation strategies are covered. This chapter proposes the use of guideline evaluation tools and technology enabled observation as preemptive strategies to reduce design errors. This chapter delivers practical approaches that can be used by individuals across the spectrum of healthcare product development to meaningfully contribute to efficacious technology products at lower development costs.

18.2   Practice 1-Patient and Physician/Provider Centered Requirements Gathering

The development of any information system is complex, costly, and critical to the success of many organizations (Reddy et al., 2003). Many information system development efforts, including whose output is to create CDSSs fail (The Standish Group, 1994, 2020). The Standish Group's research (first published in 1994 and latest published in 2020) shows a continued trend of failure (The Standish Group, 1994, 2020). Consistently, only about 35% of IT projects are fully successful with respect to time and budget, 19% of projects will be canceled before completion, and 47% are challenged by being over budget, behind schedule, and by production of low-quality deliverables (The Standish Group, 1994, 2020). One reason for these failures, especially in the healthcare arena, is a mismatch between traditional constructs of requirements and the richness of the settings in which computer systems are typically deployed (Reddy et al., 2003).

A key step in ensuring a successful software development process is the development and analysis of requirements (the qualities and features that the software must have) (Robertson & Robertson, 1999).

Traditional "requirements analysis" is based on a set of assumptions, including the assumptions that the application domain is stable, that information is fully available and known, and that most work is routine (Reddy et al., 2003). These assumptions often break down in dynamic, real-world settings, such as the settings found in healthcare (Reddy et al., 2003). Healthcare, especially at the bedside, is typically a highly collaborative, exception-filled, domain that fails to exhibit the underlying assumptions of traditional requirements analysis (Reddy et al., 2003). These assumptions would have validity if clinical IT systems were only used as repositories for patient information, but the collaborative nature of medical work embeds the need for information access within a richer and more varied system of work practice and healthcare workers interact more frequently with each other than in other industries (Reddy et al., 2003). Research suggests that any weakening of collaboration among healthcare workers can result in poor patient outcomes (Reddy et al., 2003). Traditionally, the practice in software development has been to ignore the application domain and focus on system functions on the "presupposed" system boundaries and to privilege system functionality over the actual work of the users (Reddy et al., 2003). Designers of healthcare applications, including decision support systems, must broaden their focus from only the technical system to include the work carried out and the collaboration needed to capture these interactions (Reddy et al., 2003). Examining and understanding an individual's work are a nontrivial task; this is especially true in healthcare which is characterized by the need for an intensely collaborative process that incorporates an unpredictable combination of routines and exceptions, and one in which the motivations, and concerns of different providers can be quite different (Reddy et al., 2003).

Sociotechnical requirements analysis offers a potential solution (Reddy et al., 2003). Sociotechnical requirements analysis reveals that it is impossible to separate the organizational and/or social issues from the technical concerns. Furthermore, it focuses on how the technology will be incorporated into work activities. Under sociotechnical requirements analysis the focus is on how implementing a successful technology requires a thorough understanding of the organizational context, including the organization's structure, work, and employees (Reddy et al., 2003). Ethnographic techniques are particularly effective at gathering requirements that are derived from the way in which people actually work (rather than the way in which process definitions say they ought to perform the work) and those requirements that are derived from cooperation and awareness of other people's activities (Reddy et al., 2003). Sociotechnical requirements analysis addresses the concern that, in many cases in healthcare, the most needed information is information about the activities of other healthcare workers and the improved coordination that arises when providers know about one another's activities, including the timing of those activities (Reddy et al., 2003). The effective coordination of diverse activities requires people to interpret each other's actions and includes the need to communicate both directly and indirectly to ensure that activities mesh effectively (Reddy et al., 2003). Coordination is an important feature of collaboration that is often only noticed if or when it fails (Reddy et al., 2003).

In a heterogeneous work environment such as that found in healthcare, providers' activities, and knowledge are diverse and need tailored views of identical underlying information (Reddy et al., 2003). These differing views should be oriented to the specific needs of the different groups of providers who use them. The need for these different views must be balanced by the need for shared information. These different perspectives must then be synchronized to reflect changes made to the underlying information by a user as part of the work process (Reddy et al., 2003).

Sociotechnical requirements analysis also offers a potential solution to the problem of ensuring that GUI esthetics and requirements are adequately considered and planned for. Capturing end user opinion regarding GUI esthetics is difficult, but important (Akoumianakis et al., 2001). GUI characteristics that should be considered include but are not limited to (1) use of color and underlining to inform users of additional information displayed elsewhere, (2) preferred color of text, (3) preferred navigation mechanisms, (4) preferences in the display of function icons, (5) preferred form of graphical representation, (6) preferences in screen balance, unity, equilibrium, complexity, and regularity, (7) references in list item order, and (8) preferred position of important information on the screen (Alafaireet, 2006).

To achieve improved patient and provider-centered requirements gathering, further interdisciplinary research is needed around: (1) organizational level research into the design of healthcare systems, processes, and workflow, (2) computable knowledge structures and models needed to make sense of available patient data, including preferences and health behaviors, (3) human–computer interaction in a clinical context (Stead & Lin, 2009).

Federal and State Governments can improve the situation by incentivizing clinical performance gains rather than acquisition of IT per se by encouraging: (1) initiatives that empower iterative process improvement and small-scale optimization, (2) the continuing development of standards and measures of healthcare IT performance, and (3) efforts to aggregate data about healthcare people, processes, and outcomes (Stead & Lin, 2009). They can also support additional education and training efforts at the intersection of healthcare, computer science, and health/biomedical informatics (Stead & Lin, 2009).

The computer science community can help by engaging as coequal intellectual partners and collaborators with practitioners and experts in health/biomedical informatics and other relevant disciplines in an ongoing relationship to understand and solve problems of importance to healthcare. (Stead & Lin, 2009) They can also work to develop academic institutional mechanisms for rewarding work at the healthcare/computer science interface and support educational and retraining efforts for computer scientists to explore research in healthcare (Stead & Lin, 2009).

Healthcare organizations can help improve effective requirements gathering by creating incentives, roles, workflows, processes, and supporting infrastructure to encourage, support, and respond to opportunities for clinical performance gains (Stead & Lin, 2009). They can work to balance their IT portfolios among automation, connectivity, decision support, and data-mining capabilities and focus on developing the necessary data infrastructure by aggregating data (Stead & Lin, 2009). Healthcare organizations can also insist that vendors supply systems permit the separation of data from applications and those that facilitate data transfers to and from other non-vendor applications in sharable and generally useful formats (Stead & Lin, 2009).

18.3 Practice 2-Use of Nontraditional Data Sources to Improve Evidence Base

Most CDSSs currently used in healthcare are primarily underpinned with data that originate solely within the clinical care delivery process. This data, often drawn from electronic medical records, computerized ordering systems, pharmacy systems, and other similar information tools are by necessity a limited data source and one that is not primarily accumulated for the purpose of creating decision support tools. Clinical data, while useful in that care provision process, are often extremely limited in its applicability to the entirely of health itself. This bias toward the clinical utility of data creates gaps in the evidence base available to underpin useful decision support systems.

Recent research on the fundamental causes of lack of health, both at the individual person level and the population level, demonstrates that a number of factors, outside of access to and use of traditional clinical health services, contribute heavily to being healthy (Alafaireet & Houghton, 2019). These social determinants of health include social circumstances, individual behavior, and the physical environment (Alafaireet & Houghton, 2019). Data around social circumstances that impact health includes data regarding type of employment held, occupation, and working conditions and income as well as data regarding educational level, language(s) spoken, and literacy/numeracy. Data regarding cultural, community, and familial norms including religiosity, civil participation, and the quality and quantity of support from family and friends are often elusive but may be obtained from sources outside of the clinical realm (Alafaireet & Houghton, 2019). Data regarding specific status markers, such a military or veterans' status and history of incarceration, are valuable when creating holistic decision support systems for is in the delivery of health (Alafaireet & Houghton, 2019). Data around systemic discrimination and acts of violence (whether perpetrated against an individual or societal) are also essential to the complete understanding of health (Alafaireet & Houghton, 2019). Determinants, such as gender identity, sexual orientation, sexual activity, and intimate partner violence, while extremely sensitive and requiring of substantial security, are often quite critical to health decision making (Alafaireet & Houghton, 2019).

Data regarding individual behavioral characteristics are also valuable in supporting a holistic health decision support system. Individual behaviors such as tobacco and alcohol use, diet, exercise, and sleep patterns, and the availability and use of firearms can be critically important to health. Mental health-related data such as that related to depression, stress level, and satisfaction with life is often not available but is especially helpful when making health decisions.

While the health implications associated with the physical environment may be more generalizable to the population than to individuals, their use in health decision making remains important. Such determinants as crime level, exposure to toxins and pollutants, and air quality impact health. Limited access to educational opportunity, safe housing, and recreational/exercise opportunities are all drivers of health for which data are not optimally captured in most clinical data systems.

In addition, certain nonclinical, but associated determinates, such provider availability, health literacy accommodation, quality of healthcare available, insurance or payment ability status, and travel distance to healthcare and health-related services, play a large role in the health of individuals and of populations (Alafaireet & Houghton, 2019). Data regarding these determinants is often not available from clinical data sources.

Practically, the entities that collect, manage, and use data regarding social circumstances, individual behavior, and the physical environment are not typically considered healthcare entities, although they may deliver significant health benefits. The entities most likely to be able to provide these types of data include social services agencies, school systems, government agencies, including city governments, and law enforcement.

Healthcare users of decision support tools can employ several strategies to shift the focus away from CDSSs that are predicated solely on clinical data in several ways. Perhaps the most obvious strategy is to tailor their purchasing behavior toward CDSSs that are capable of using a variety of health data. Market pressure is conditional on the purchaser's understanding of the value of nontraditional and nonclinical data to the delivery of health. Much education regarding the use of CDSS needs to occur within the social service, education, governance, and law enforcement communities. This educational effort needs not be a one-way transaction. The utilization of community level health CDSSs; those designed to support coordination and collaboration across a wide array of health situations can be invaluable in health delivery. Partnerships to enable community level use of CDSS can reduce overall costs through improved service coordination and non-duplication of services offering. Fundamentally changing the way health is paid for and healthcare is carried out is another mechanism of change toward the use of more holistic decision support systems. Value-based service provision and reimbursement models such as the accountable community for health (ACH) can be used to enable this shift (Alafaireet & Houghton, 2019). Economic strategies such as those described in donut economics hold promise to reframe and right size priorities regarding health in new and exciting ways (Olakotan & Yusof, 2021). At the most granular level, providers of clinical healthcare services can expand the knowledge base needed to use effective health decision support by deliberately cultivating partnership and data exchange with nonclinical providers of health.

18.4   Practice 3-Preemptive Concept Development to Support Design Decision Making

Healthcare and health-related enterprises do not commonly support the development of CDSSs with preemptive concept development. Concepts can be thought of as the underlying characteristics that are important to users of products and services. Take, for example, the "concept car." These vehicles are created and shown at large, often international, venues with the express purposes of creating market demand and demonstrating design skills and innovation. Concepts, such as "sleek," "futuristic," and "innovative," are on display. The concepts chosen for a particular vehicle are carefully selected to create an emotional reaction in potential customers (and occasionally to inspire envy in the hearts and minds of design competitors). Many of these prototype vehicles will never be mass produced, but they provide, via retrospective analysis, a wealth of information about the response of potential customers to a particular design feature. Built up, over time, these analyzes provide a useful window into the wants, needs, and desires of the target customers.

Some enterprises effectively engage in concept development before any product or service begins the design process. This purposeful development of key concepts underpinning a specific market offering can be effectively used to establish priorities in the design process and support decisions around cost of development when a limited development budget is in place or when different design choices require differing levels of resource expenditure.

When healthcare CDSSs are developed for the market, the concepts of "safety" and "quality" are the primary concept substrate for development, even when these concepts are ill undefined. To improve the design and development of healthcare CDSS and to reduce associated costs, preemptive concept development should be the norm. Healthcare needs to move beyond the use of mission, vision, and values statements as criteria for CDSS design development and evaluations.

Part of the reason healthcare enterprises do not leverage concept creation is that the industry, as a whole, does not view the provision of healthcare as a commodity. Another part of this concept disuse is the lack of infrastructure by which the concept may be developed. Another part of the disuse of concepts lies in the very intent of eliciting an emotional response. For all of the inherently emotional nature of the delivery of healthcare, the expression of emotion and outside of occasional bursts of anger that are the nominally accepted purview of physicians, emotion is curiously and regularly suppressed. So, healthcare CDSSs are not designed to bring joy to the user or to support confidence building or to provide positive reinforcement for a job well done. And that lack (something that would never be tolerated in video games, for example) impedes both the cost-effective production of CDSSs and user-orientated evaluation of their use (Fig. 18.1).

So, what does healthcare need to change? First of all, producers of CDSS should decide well in advance of any design work, what "gut feeling" they want to engender in primary users (typically physicians and other providers) and secondary users (patients and their caregivers) when the CDSS is used. Critical decisions about concepts, such as trustworthiness, convenience, and ease of use, should be made early in the development process by soliciting input from a wide representation of potential users. Cross discipline focus groups, interviews, and structured survey tools are effective in gathering the needed input, especially if the power differentials that are a part of the healthcare command structure can be neutralized using Delphi techniques or similar strategies. CDSSs that include patients and caregivers as potential primary or secondary users should always have patient and caregiver representation in the concept development process.

With a sound set of concepts in place, healthcare enterprises have improved ability to make informed decisions about development costs (and perhaps also purchase costs). Inevitably, in the design and development process or in the purchase process, a variety of options will be presented often with widely different associated costs. One effective way to select from alternative options and differing

---

Concepts healthcare organizations may wish to consider:

Rewarding, Supportive, Joyful, Exciting, Easy, Perceptive, Adaptable, Time saving, Flexible, Intuitive

---

Fig. 18.1 Concepts. *Source* Authors' own illustration (2021)

costs is to measure alignment with the concepts. Does one option do a better job of meeting user needs, even when those needs cannot be captured in specific elements of information system functionality? Can the organization justify more costs because including an important concept leads to higher user satisfaction and improved decision support utilization?

The degree to which a CDSS meets the wants, needs, and desires of the user population is an invaluable baseline for any evaluation strategy and is relatively easy to incorporate and typically low cost.

With rising costs for healthcare and the increasing demands on physicians and providers that are consequent in precision medicine, effective CDSSs are critically important. Aligning, CDSSs so they best support the wants, needs, and desires of users though preemptive concept development, is a cost-effective enabler for those who design and develop or purchase these systems.

18.5   Practice 4-Use of Workflow Analysis as an Evaluation

There are three main predictors of CDSS efficacy (Zaidi et al., 2008). These include how easy the CDSS is to learn, how helpful it is to the learning needs of its users, and the level to which it is integrated into the daily workflow (Zaidi et al., 2008). Workflow analysis was belatedly identified as a useful tool to enable electronic health record implementation. In many instances, the matching of a CDSS with the intended user's workflow as part of the selection and acquisition process has remained elusive. Preemptive workflow analysis can also create useful foundations for evaluation of the decision support system, by creating a baseline understanding of the workflow from which further analysis of the likelihood of successful implementation and use of a CDSS can occur. Construction of accurate workflow and measurement of the proportion of workflow supported by the information system product can be used as a means of evaluating the potential use rate of the decision support system (Fig. 18.2).

Some important understandings of the nature of CDSSs in relation to workflow should be established early in the process of obtaining a decision support system, as should the evaluation of the decision support system. Typically, a CDSS should not be used, primarily, to redefine a workflow, but rather must be functionally integrated into the workflow and its use should lead to time-savings for its users (Wong et al., 2000). Organizations that plan to utilize a CDSS as a workflow modifier must

---

Rule of Thumb:

A decision support system should support at least 80 percent of the workflow

Fig. 18.2 Rule. *Source* Authors' own illustration (2021)

be careful to ensure that any changes to the workflow are comprehensively monitored and evaluated for both acceptance by end users and for efficacy. Failing to do so, organizations can create a situation that necessitates the use of work-arounds in the care delivery process and introduce potential opportunities for care provision failures such as adverse drug events and missed diagnosis.

There are a number of elements that should be evaluated when matching a CDSS to a workflow. First of all, comprehensive workflow analysis is needed to ensure that key pieces of information are incorporated seamlessly and sensitively into the context of the work being done (Sittig et al., 2008). The intrusiveness of the CDSS into the workflow (alerts, for example) should be proportional to the importance of the information being provided (Sittig et al., 2008). Information presented to physicians and other providers via the use of a CDSS should be time, location, and context specific and should be evaluated to ensure that its placement in the workflow makes it easy for the end users to take action, including take action as to recommended treatment (Kawamoto et al., 2005; Sittig et al., 2008).

When developing a prospective evaluation of a CDSS, organizations should incorporate workflow considerations as a major part of the evaluative process. Useful workflow considerations include:

- The ability of the CDSS to provide access to a wide array of current information in the shortest amount of time (Feied et al., 2004).
- The ability of the CDSS to help clinicians/users see the right amount of the right type of data wherever and whenever needed, including 24/7/365 access, through a variety of interfaces and devices (Feied et al., 2004).
- Provider access to clinical data/information should not be unnecessarily restricted as a function of workflow (Feied et al., 2004).
- The ability of the decision support system to reduce to a reasonable minimum number of steps required to obtain any information, including access to data aggregated from disparate sources whenever possible (Feied et al., 2004).
- The ability of the CDSS to meet the regularly recurring data needs of the users, preferably without extensive formal training (Feied et al., 2004).

Alerting is rightly considered a major dissatisfier of the use of decision support systems because of its intrusive nature into the workflow (Sijs et al., 2009). Organizations seeking to prospectively evaluate the likelihood of decision system nonuse should create evaluation plans that seek to measure the potential fit of alerts into the workflow. Considerations should include:

- The extent to which the alerts presented are clinically important and pertain to a specific patient (Sijs et al., 2009). Alerts should not be of minor importance or of little importance to a specific patient (Sijs et al., 2009).
- The extent to which alerts are followed with clinical and contextually appropriate and informationally current suggested actions that are clear, unambiguous, and useful to both the clinical specialty and the level of training/experience held by the physician or other clinical provider. (Karsh, 2009; Sijs et al., 2009).

- The extent to which entering exceptions or mitigating circumstances is easy to complete within the workflow, except in the case of alerts done to prevent fatalities, where the seriousness of the alert should be clear and where overriding the alert requires justification. (Sijs et al., 2009).
- The extent to which use of the CDSS allows its users to proceed with acceptable speed through the clinical workflow (Sijs et al., 2009).
- Alerts should be directed to the right person and should promote action rather than stopping intended action (Sijs et al., 2009).
- The CDSS should respond with reasonable speed and should be configured so as to reduce the need for additional data entry and minimize the need for additional navigation efforts (scrolling, mouse clicks, etc.) (Sijs et al., 2009).
- The use of the CDSS should not exceed the time and effort required to provide care without its use (Karsh, 2009).

Effective use of workflow analysis in the prospective and on-going evaluation of CDSS can help expose and prevent design or configuration errors and workflow/CDSS correspondence mismatches that disrupt clinical workflow, undermine provider ability to provide timely care, and allow opportunity for negative impact on patient safety (Olakotan & Yusof, 2021).

Successful incorporation of workflow into evaluation of clinical CDSS can address important process-related factors and lead to increased provider and patient satisfaction, improved education regarding the most current therapies and treatments, and ultimately, lead to improvement in the design, production, implementation and use of much needed healthcare technology (Olakotan & Yusof, 2021).

18.6   Practice 5-Cognitive Analysis as a Product Development Tool

The complexity of human-information interaction stems from the variability of individual human cognitive processes and the obtrusive and unwaveringly dynamic work environment in which providers must operate. With the continued advancements in information systems, information technology, clinical and bench research, and the complexity of patient presentations and management, the bedside providers can be readily overwhelmed. While this has led to more information and data being available, it has also resulted in a greater cognitive workload for the provider; all of the new data and information has to be processed, analyzed, and acted upon. This increase in cognitive load can lead to errors and poor patient outcomes.

The study of ergonomics has been historically relevant in the fields of aviation, air traffic control, nuclear power, oil and gas, and the military. These industries rely on safety–critical protocols that require high reliability processes, frameworks, and mental models to thrive. These same principles are readily used to describe the healthcare industry, however, the use of ergonomics, specifically cognitive ergonomics, and cognitive flow analysis have been overtly underutilized. The cognitive elements of work, which include situational awareness, reasoning, knowledge and information integration, decision making, etc., are thought to be ingrained in the root causes of human error. This is impressively true of the complex sociotechnical system that is healthcare. We look to introduce cognitive task analysis in the context of the design and implementation of healthcare products and services (Lawler et al., 2011; MacLeod, 2004).

There has always been a focus of physical ergonomics in the workplace, however, cognitive science and the foundational principles and applications of cognitive ergonomics have been otherwise absent. The design of information systems and technologies with an emphasis on human cognition can help to mitigate some of this cognitive workload. Cognitive task analysis (CTA) methods can be used to guide healthcare service and product development by incorporating human cognition, memory, automaticity, and situational awareness.

Implementation of CTA methods in service and product design has been shown to improve our understanding of macro cognition but can also potentially help alleviate the constraints of micro cognition in complex systems. Macro cognition is defined as the "study of cognitive processes affecting people such as firefighters, pilots, nurses, and others who [have] had to wrestle with difficult dilemmas in complex settings under time pressure and uncertainty" (Klein & Wright, 2016). In the healthcare context, this equates to the clinical, administrative, and organizational cognitive workflows and heuristics providers are continuously forced to balance. CTA methods such as task diagramming, concept mapping, critical decision method, simulation interviewing, knowledge audits, cognitive demands analysis, and many others can help healthcare service and product design to improve satisfaction and safety. We look to briefly introduce several fundamental CTA methods concepts that can have an immediate impact on the iterative design process (Christensen et al., 2005; Hollnagel, 1997; Potworowski, 2013).

Task analysis serves as the first step in evaluating the macro cognition [responsibilities] of the end user. This is done by interviewing end users that range from the expert, intermediate, and novice user as defined by the Rasmussen skills-rules-knowledge taxonomy (Kahneman, 2011). The interviewing process is done in phases which helps to break down the tasks into three to seven subtasks. The next step involves further breaking down these subtasks into those that require active cognition such as assessing a patient, using clinical judgement, decision making, situational awareness, and in general, rational and deliberate thinking (as described by Daniel Kahneman) (Kahneman, 2011). The last step is to diagram the subtasks in by their sequence and the type of cognitive skills required in relation to the parent task. This diagram produces a framework that can be used, at last, to wireframe and prototype a redesign of the current processes and workflows.

Many of the CTA methods build on each other to provide a complete picture of the task(s) and the cognitive load required. The next step in task analysis is concept mapping and critical decision method (CDM). Concept mapping refers to a graphical schema of decision making and performance by experts in the field. The result of this activity is a network of mental models of how topics, activities, and concepts are [worked through] by subject-matter experts. While concept mapping focuses on the gestalt of an activity in relation to the system, it ignores the tacit knowledge gained by clinical, administrative, and organizational experience. The CDM interview helps to fill this void. The questions during the CDM interview are targeted toward specific, atypical, and rare situations where the expertise of the user highlights the successful resolution of that instance. When both of these methods are used in conjunction, the spectrum of macro cognition is analyzed and engineered to improve the conceptual framework of current design processes (Potworowski, 2013; Thordsen, 1991).

The medical literature has described the effects of cognitive science on errors, provider burnout, organizational outcomes, medical training, and the overall delivery of healthcare services. For example, Joeres et al. used CTA to ascertain the perioperative information needs of surgeons performing partial nephrectomies (Joeres et al., 2019). This right information at the right time will lead to a safer perioperative clinical course. CTA methods have also been used in simulation training of orthopedic residents and procedures. Medical devices, clinical decision support tools, teamwork, communication, are a few of the many other applications of the various CTA methods to improve patient care and safety.

18.7   Practice 6-Use of Guideline Evaluation Tools to Reduce Design Errors

Many CDSSs currently used in healthcare incorporate one or more (sometimes many more) clinical guidelines. These evidence-based guidelines are most often based on results from multiple randomized controlled trials, although guidelines based on expert clinical opinion may also be used, in part, or as a whole. Typically, these guidelines are created as a way to diminish inappropriate clinical practice, as a way to improve health outcomes, and as a way to control the costs of clinical care delivery (Shiffman et al., 2007). The guidelines are often published in a paper-based prose format, or a digital version of a paper-based prose document, and sometimes as algorithmic flowcharts (Shiffman et al., 2007). In this format, these guidelines are often inconveniently accessible (at best) in the clinical practice workflow (Shiffman et al., 2007). While digital or electronic dissemination can sometimes help solve the accessibility issue, access to the actual knowledge embedded in the guideline can still be very problematic (Shiffman et al., 2007). It is vitally important to both developers of CDSSs and to those organizations who purchase and deploy them that these clinical guidelines can be accurately programmed so as to avoid undue user/patient risk.

There are a number of tools available to enable the use of clinical guidelines in decision support systems, but many were not developed expressly for use in healthcare. Knowledge modeling of guidelines is an effective tool for measurement of the potential programmability of an effective clinical guideline. An ideal guideline knowledge model is comprehensive and capable of expressing all the knowledge contained in the guideline (Shiffman et al., 2007). This is particularly necessary in healthcare applications because guidelines must adequately express the complexity of knowledge and detail needed to facilitate translation into the electronic mode to enable point of care usage (Shiffman et al., 2007). Likewise, an ideal knowledge model must be expressively adequate and able to convey the complexities and nuances of clinical medicine while remaining fully informationally equivalent to the original guideline (Shiffman et al., 2007). It is especially important that knowledge modeling used for the development of healthcare CDSSs be flexible so as to be able to accurately deal with the variety of complex guidelines used in healthcare (Shiffman et al., 2007). It should also permit modeling at both high and low levels of granularity (Shiffman et al., 2007). Knowledge modeling should be comprehensible in that it should match the stakeholders' (usually physicians and other clinical providers) normal problem-solving language and it should allow the healthcare domain experts to describe their knowledge with little effort (Shiffman et al., 2007). It is useful to note that the knowledge model should lead to CDSS that is easily learned by nonprogrammers (Shiffman et al., 2007). Given the high costs associated with the development of clinical CDSSs, knowledge modeling should be sharable across institutions and enterprises and should provide for cross-platform compatibility (Shiffman et al., 2007). Because the clinical guideline landscape is constantly shifting at a rapidly accelerating rate knowledge models should be reusable across all phases of the guideline life cycle, including those instances where rapid change is necessary as a function of the emergence of new disease or when approved treatment rapidly changes (Shiffman et al., 2007). Finally, it is important that knowledge modeling used for healthcare can be used for all types and formats of guidelines (Shiffman et al., 2007).

18.8 Practice 7-Use of Socio-Ethnographic Tools for Design Error Reduction

Historically, a large percentage of healthcare-related software development projects are never completed and of those that are developed, about fifty percent successfully meet user needs (The Standish Group, 1994, 2020). Information system development, including the development of CDSS intended for use in healthcare is a complex and often costly process that is, in many cases, critical to the success of many organizations (Reddy et al., 2003). A key part of the software development process is the development and analysis of user requirements which help establish the context in which designers and developers have an in-depth understanding of the required qualities and features (Robertson & Robertson, 1999). Understanding the context and environment in which the software application will be used is also critical if design errors are to be eliminated. Part of the reason for these failures lies in a mismatch between the traditional constructs and methods of requirements gathering and the settings in which the resulting software applications are ultimately deployed (Reddy et al., 2003). Conveying the richness and sometimes chaotic, nonroutine nature of healthcare delivery is essential. Assumptions made in the user requirements gathering phase, such as those made around the routineness of work and domain stability often lead to the development of software that is either significantly degraded or totally degrades in dynamic, real-world clinical settings, often because of the chaotic collaborative and exception filled process of care (Reddy et al., 2003).

To be more successful reducing design errors, developers of software for healthcare use can enhance the use of socio-ethnographic tools to record and analyze both the actual work be carried out by physicians and others and the level and type of collaboration such work requires so they can lessen the design approach that is predominantly focused on the technical features and constraints of the software (Reddy et al., 2003).

Social-ethnographic tools and methods are more used in the social sciences and include structured observation, use of video recordings, and use of information from social media) (Morgan-Trimmer & Wood, 2016). In general, there are three approaches to gaining insight into user requirements (experimental, simulation, and naturalistic) and social-ethnographic techniques can be used in all three approaches. The use of social-ethnographic tools all a practical way to separate organizational specific issues and/or social issues from the technical issues in design and development (Kushniruk, 2002). They allow a strong first look at how technology can or will be incorporated into work flow and work activities (Reddy et al., 2003). Socio-ethnographic tools are particularly effective when gathering requirements that reflect the way in which people actually work (rather than the work processes as they are defined in policies and operating procedures) and requirements that are focused on the cooperation needed to carry out the care process, including the awareness of other people's activities that are part of that care process (Reddy et al., 2003).

Social-ethnographic tools and methods with applicability to healthcare and healthcare decisions support systems include, but are not limited to, capture of workflow for analysis, job analysis, capture and analysis of decision-making strategies, and cognitive task analysis. Specific activities including interviews, questionnaires, holding of focus groups, as well as more ambient data collection, such as security camera footage analysis, design walk-throughs that occur is the actual use environment, are also helpful as is shop-floor development (when possible while maintaining patient privacy standards).

While the use of socio-ethnography can help identify and analyze unexpected issues and are very useful to uncover user attitudes and emotions about and toward decision support systems, their success is critically dependent on the skill set of the ethnographer and their ability to ensure the study is representative, accurate, and fair (Logan, 2020). Carried out with trained ethnographers, healthcare organizations can use socio-ethnographic tools to address design errors that negatively affect decision support.

18.9 Conclusion

This chapter outlines seven not commonly used practices that can be employed by healthcare organizations to enhance the design, development, implement, and use of clinical CDSS to their advantage. Effective CDSS is increasingly required as enablers of personalized medicine (Downing et al., 2009; Kim et al., 2020; Welch & Kawamoto, 2013). CDSSs promise to improve nearly all aspects of present care delivered, including the quality of care offered, and will be increasingly important as new treatments and pharmaceuticals become available (Feied et al., 2004; Field et al., 2008; Frueh & Gurwitz, 2004; McGlynn et al., 2003). Barrier free clinical CDSSs also hold promise to help address physicians (and other care providers) burnout (Khairat et al., 2020; Melnick et al., 2020; Sinsky & Privitera, 2018).

References

Akoumianakis, D., Grammenos, D., & Stephanidis, C. (2001). *User Interface Adaption: Evaluation perspectives user interfaces for all: Concepts, methods and tools* (pp. 339–354). Lawrence Erlbaum Associates.

Alafaireet, P. (2006). Information processing in the service of mankind and health. In *ICICT- GUI Design Characteristics Needed for Physicians Use IEEE CCC Code*: 0-7803-9770-3/06 December

Alafaireet, P., & Houghton, H. (2019). It takes more than a village-leveraging globalized information, knowledge and resources to design services tailored to an accountable health community for mental health. In: M.A. Pfannstiel & C. Rasche (Eds.), *Service design and service thinking in healthcare and hospital management. Theory, concepts, practice* (pp. 259–277). Springer Nature.

Balas, E. A., & Boren, S. A. (2000). Managing clinical knowledge for health care improvement. *Yearbook of Medical Informatics, 2000*(1), 65–70.

Christensen, R. E., Fetters, M. D., & Green, L. A. (2005). Opening the black box: Cognitive strategies in family practice. *The Annals of Family Medicine, 3*(2), 144–150.

Downing, G. J., Boyle, S. N., Brinner, K. M., & Osheroff, J. A. (2009). Information management to enable personalized medicine: Stakeholder roles in building clinical decision support. *BMC Medical Informatics and Decision Making, 9*(44), 1–11. https://doi.org/10.1186/1472-6947-9-44

Feied, C. F., Handler, J. A., Smith, M. S., Gillam, M., Kanhouwa, M., Rothenhaus, T., Conover, K., & Shannon, T. (2004). Clinical information systems: Instant ubiquitous clinical data for error reduction and improved clinical outcomes. *Academic Emergency Medicine, 11*(11), 1162–1169.

Field, T. S., Rochon, P., Lee, M., Gavendo, L., Subramanian, S., Hoover, S., Baril, J., & Gurwitz, J. (2008). Costs associated with developing and implementing a computerized clinical CDSS for medication dosing for patients with renal insufficiency in the long-term care setting. *Journal of the American Medical Informatics Association, 15*(4), 466–472. https://doi.org/10.1197/jamia.M2589

Frueh, D., & Gurwitz, D. (2004). From pharmacogenetics to personalized medicine: A vital need for educating health professionals and the community. *Pharmacogenomics, 5*(5), 571–579.

Hollnagel, E. (1997). Cognitive ergonomics: It's all in the mind. *Ergonomics, 40*(10), 1170–1182.

Joeres, F., Schindele, D., Luz, M., Blaschke, S., Russwinkel, N., Schostak, M., & Hansen, C. (2019). How well do software assistants for minimally invasive partial nephrectomy meet surgeon information needs? A cognitive task analysis and literature review study. *PLoS One,* *14*(7), e0219920. https://doi.org/10.1371/journal.pone.0219920.

Kahneman, D. (2011). *Thinking, fast and slow* (1st ed.). Farrar.

Karsh B. T. (2009). Clinical practice improvement and redesign: How change in workflow can be supported by clinical decision support. *AHRQ,* Publication No. 09-0054-EF. Agency for Healthcare Research and Quality.

Kawamoto, K., Houlihan, C. A., Balas, E. A., & Lobach, D. F. (2005). Improving clinical practice using clinical decision support systems: A systematic review of trials to identify features critical to success. *BMJ, 330*(7494), 1–8. https://doi.org/10.1136/bmj.38398.500764.8F

Khairat S., Coleman C., Ottmar P., Jayachander D. I., Bice T., & Carson S. S. (2020). Association of electronic health record use with physician fatigue and efficiency. *JAMA Network Open, 3* (6), e207385, pmid: 32515799, https://doi.org/10.1001/jamanetworkopen.2020.7385.

Klein, G., & Wright, C. (2016). Macrocognition: From theory to toolbox. *Frontiers in Psychology,* *7*(54), 1–5. https://doi.org/10.3389/fpsyg.2016.00054

Kim, H. J., Kim, H. J., Park, Y., Lee, W. S., Lim, Y., & Kim, J. H. (2020). Clinical Genome Data Model (cGDM) provides interactive clinical decision support for precision medicine. *Science and Reports, 10*(2020), 1414. https://doi.org/10.1038/s41598-020-58088-2

Kushniruk A. (2002) Evaluation in the design of health information systems: Application of approaches emerging from usability engineering. *Computers in Biology and Medicine, 32*(3), 141–149, https://doi.org/10.1016/s0010-4825(02)00011-2.

Lawler, E. K., Hedge, A., & Pavlovic-Veselinovic, S. (2011). Cognitive ergonomics, socio-technical systems, and the impact of healthcare information technologies. *International Journal of Industrial Ergonomics, 41*(4), 336–344.

Logan, B. (2020). *When and how to use ethnographic research.* Retrieved May 28, 2021, from https://www.spotless.co.uk/insights/ethnography-when-and-how/.

MacLeod, D. (2004). Cognitive ergonomics: Making sense with design. *Industrial Engineer, 36* (3), 26–31.

McGlynn, E. A., Asch, S. M., Adams, J., Keesey, J., Hicks, J., DeCristofaro, A., & Kerr, E. A. (2003). The quality of health care delivered to adults in the United States. *New England Journal of Medicine, 348*(26), 2635–2645.

Melnick, E. R., Dyrbye, L. N., Sinsky, C. A., Trockel, M., West, C. P., Nedelec, L., Tutty, M. A., & Shanafelt, T. (2020). The association between perceived electronic health record usability and professional burnout among US physicians. *Mayo Clinic Proceedings, 95*(3), 476–487. https://doi.org/10.1016/j.mayocp.2019.09.024.pmid:31735343

Morgan-Trimmer, S., & Wood, F. (2016). Ethnographic methods for process evaluations of complex health behaviour interventions. *Trials, 17*(232), 1–11. https://doi.org/10.1186/s13063-016-1340-2

Olakotan, O. O., & Yusof, M. (2021). The appropriateness of clinical CDSS alerts in supporting clinical workflows: A systematic review. *Health Informatics Journal, 27*(2), 1–22. https://doi.org/10.1177/14604582211007536

Potworowski, G. (2013). Cognitive task analysis: Methods to Improve patient-centered medical homemodels by understanding and leveraging its knowledge work. *AHRQ,* Publication No. *13-0023-EF,* 1–12.

Reddy, M., Pratt, W., Dourish, P., & Shabot, M. M. (2003). Sociotechnical requirements analysis for clinical systems. *Methods of Information in Medicine, 42*(4), 437–444.

Robertson, S., & Robertson, J. (1999). *Mastering the requirements process.* ACM Press.

Shiffman, R. N., Karras, B. T., Arawal, A., Chen, R., Marenco, L., & Nath, S. (2007). GEM: A proposal for a more comprehensive guideline document model using XML. *Journal of the American Medical Informatics Association, 7*(5), 488–498.

Sinsky, C. A., & Privitera, M. R. (2018). Creating a "Manageable Cockpit" for Clinicians: A shared responsibility. *JAMA Internal Medicine, 178*(6), 741–742. https://doi.org/10.1001/jamainternmed.2018.0575.pmid:29582080

Sittig, D. F., Wright, A., Osheroff, J. A., Middleton, B., Teich, J. M., Ash, J. S., Campbell, E., & Bates, D. W. (2008). Grand challenges in clinical decision support. *Journal of Biomedical Informatics, 41*(2), 387–392. https://doi.org/10.1016/j.jbi.2007.09.003.pmid:18029232

Stead, W. W., & Lin, H. S. (2009). *Computational technology for effective health care: Immediate steps and strategic directions.* The National Academies Press.

Sutton, R. T., Pincock, D., Baumgart, D. C., Sadowski D. C., Fedorak R. N. & Kroeker K. I. (2020). An overview of clinical decision support systems: Benefits, risks, and strategies for success. *npj Digital Medicine, 3*(17), 1–10. https://doi.org/10.1038/s41746-020-0221-y.

The Standish Group. (1994). *The chaos report.* Retrieved May 28, 2021, from http://www.pm2go.com/sample_research/chaos_1994_1.asp.

The Standish Group. (2020). *The chaos report.* Retrieved May 28, 2021, from https://standishgroup.myshopify.com/.

Thordsen, M. L. (1991). A comparison of two tools for cognitive task analysis: Concept mapping and thecritical decision method. *Proceedings of the Human Factors Society Annual Meeting, 35*(5), 283–285.

Van der Sijs, H., Aarts, J., Vulto, A., & Berg, M. (2009). Overriding of drug safety alerts in computerized physician order entry. *Journal of the American Medical Informatics Association, 13*(2), 138–147.

Welch, B. M., & Kawamoto, K. (2013). Clinical decision support for genetically guided personalized medicine: A systematic review. *Journal of the American Medical Informatics Association, 20*(2), 388–400. https://doi.org/10.1136/amiajnl-2012-000892

Wong, H. J., Legnini, M. W., & Whitmore, H. H. (2000). The diffusion of CDSS in healthcare: Are we there yet? *Journal of Healthcare Management, 45*(4), 240–249.

Zaidi, S. T. R., Marriott, J. L., & Nation, R. L. (2008). The role of perceptions of clinicians in their adoption of a web-based antibiotic approval system: Do perceptions translate into actions? *International Journal of Medical Informatics, 77*(1), 33–40.

Patricia E. Alafaireet has a broad background in biomedical informatics and health information technology in the delivery of healthcare, especially in rural environments. Her current research interests focus on the use of big data in predictive modeling, GUI aesthetics for physician use and the application of informatics tools to day- to-day clinical operations with a focus on mental health care. She is involved in the formulation of national level policy and standards development for usability and physician supplied data. Dr. Alafaireet is an associate professor at the University of Missouri and currently oversees the Missouri Health IT Assistance Center.

Chintan Desai is a practicing Internal Medicine Hospitalist and the Medical Director at Ascension All Saints in Racine, WI. He is also a dual-Masters (MHA/MHI) student at the University of Missouri. His current research interests focus on the application of human factors, systems engineering, product development and service delivery to improve quality of care and enhance patient safety.

Howard L. Houghton is a practicing psychiatrist and is an associate professor of clinical psychiatry at the University of Missouri. His research interests focus on treatment noncompliance and recidivism prevention in mental health care as well as innovative treatments and pharmaceuticals.

Design of Robotic Care: Ethical Implications of a Multi-actor Perspective

19

Martina Čaić, Stefan Holmlid, Dominik Mahr, and Gaby Odekerken-Schröder

Abstract

The topic of ethically-sound robotic design is timely and societally relevant as service robots have roles with increasingly social demands in diverse service contexts. Robots fill caregiving roles for vulnerable consumers, including older adults and children. This chapter presents an empirical study investigating social and ethical ramifications of robotic elderly care from the perspective of those receiving and those providing care. Consequently, 36 actors (i.e., older adults, informal, and formal caregivers) were interviewed through generative phenomenographic interviews. This approach leveraged data-rich narratives and informant-made visualizations of future networks of care to uncover their expectations and concerns. A multi-actor perspective on the ethical implications of robotic care is captured with three thematic maps built around: (1) assistance, (2) monitoring, and (3) companionship. The results indicate that care robots

M. Čaić (✉)
Department of Design, School of Arts, Design and Architecture, Aalto University, Otaniementie 16, 02150 Espoo, Finland
e-mail: martina.caic@aalto.fi

S. Holmlid
Department of Computer and Information Science, Linköping University, E-huset Campus Valla, 581 83 Linköping, Sweden
e-mail: stefan.holmlid@liu.se

D. Mahr
Department of Marketing and Supply Chain Management, Maastricht University, Tongersestraat 53, 6211 LM Maastricht, Netherlands
e-mail: d.mahr@maastrichtuniversity.nl

G. Odekerken-Schröder
Department of Marketing and Supply Chain Management, Maastricht University
Tongersestraat 53, 6211 LM Maastricht, Netherlands
e-mail: g.odekerken@maastrichtuniversity.nl

© The Author(s), under exclusive license to Springer Nature Switzerland AG 2022
M. A. Pfannstiel et al. (eds.), *Service Design Practices for Healthcare Innovation*,
https://doi.org/10.1007/978-3-030-87273-1_19

could improve the wellbeing of older adults and wider care-providing networks through service, constant presence, and increased reliability. However, the visualizations of future robotic care uncovered informants' latent fears, in addition to ethical concerns found (e.g., decline in agency, loss of privacy, and delusion). For example, formal caregivers who emphasized that they do not fear robots replacing their jobs would not place the robot close to the older person in the visualization of future care constellations. This suggests that although formal caregivers tend to give "desirable" responses in interviews, they are still reluctant to accept robots as care co-providers.

19.1   Robots in Service Contexts

Robots and other artificial intelligent (AI) agents are becoming ubiquitous in diverse service contexts. While decades ago, robots and automation were mainly employed in industrial settings (e.g., factories), nowadays, robots are introduced in various public (e.g., classrooms, museums, hotels, hospitals) and private (e.g., homes) service settings (e.g., Engwall et al., 2021; Tung & Au, 2018). It is becoming increasingly common for humans to cross paths with service robots in a restaurant, in an office building on their way to work or at an elderly care facility (KPMG, 2016). Robots are not only reserved for automating repetitive, dangerous, and tedious tasks performed in structured industrial environments but are also interacting with humans in chaotic and highly unstructured customer-facing settings, in which they are expected to perform socially sensitive roles. This brings many challenges for the technology developers since state-of-the-art AI still lack the ability to handle chaos and context-ambiguity (Charisi et al., 2017). As robots become integrated in the service frontline, they disrupt institutionalized social structures and cause many economic, social, and ethical ramifications. Thus, robot engineers, designers, and developers need to leverage socially- and ethically-sound design principles (Fjeld et al., 2020) to minimize negative unintended consequences of their created robotic artifacts.

Robots are embodied technologies capable of moving, sensing, information processing, and responding (Singer, 2009). To serve the networks of actors, robots need to be endowed with social value propositions, comprising capability to engage in conversations, gesticulate, perceive, and respond to emotional cues, and other human-like traits (Breazeal, 2002; Čaić et al., 2019b). The care robots need to adopt ethical norms of conduct (The IEEE Global Initiative on Ethics of Autonomous and Intelligent Systems, 2017) and grow into rule-abiding agents to become well-integrated into the human society which thrives on social interactions.

The need to integrate ethical dimensions into the robotics developments was first introduced by the novelist Isaac Asimov in his three laws of robotics emphasizing that robots (1) should not injure or harm humans in any way, (2) should obey orders by humans (except when they violate the 1st law), while (3) protecting their own existence (when not conflicting with the previous two laws) (Asimov, 1950). Today, with the proliferation of AI technologies with a desirable value co-creation potential, the requirement of ethical conduct in robotics seems more relevant than ever before and serves as one of the key drivers of battling robotic hesitancy in actor networks.

However, many technology developers innovate relying solely on their vision of what the technology should look like, feel like, and be capable of doing. In that way, they impose their idea of the solution to users who might have different needs, fears and hopes, and ethical concerns regarding the future technology-enhanced services. In this chapter, we advocate for human-centered, generative research approaches which tap into both explicit and tacit knowledge of users in development and design of robotic care. By doing so, we fill in the gap in extant literature by offering a future user's perspective which helps in balancing technical, social, and ethical aspects of the design of robotic care.

19.2 Machine Morality and Ethics

The debate about robot's ability to make ethical decisions remains inconclusive. While humans act on moral prescriptions (right vs. wrong) which they learn through social and cultural immersion, robots demand algorithms to analyze various contextual situations and then apply matching ethical principles to guide their actions (Charisi et al., 2017). Utilitarianism (or consequentialism) and deontology (or duty-based ethics) are the most commonly discussed ethical theories (e.g., Charisi et al., 2017; Kuipers, 2016; Veruggio & Operto, 2008). While utilitarianism stresses that individual rights can be violated for the benefit of the overall societal welfare, deontology prioritizes the individual rights relative to overall welfare concerns (Kuipers, 2016). To implement these moral capacities, Wallach and Allen (2008) offer two different ways: A top-down approach uses a set of ethical norms, rules, and principles of a chosen ethical theory and defining a decision-making algorithm around it, while the bottom-up draws on an AI-based learning about the norms and morally acceptable behavior without a predefined ethical theory.

19.2.1 Robot Ethics

Rather than following developments in machine ethics, the field of "robot ethics" attempts to address potential ethical implications of current and prospective robotic developments (e.g., Lin et al., 2011; Veruggio & Operto, 2008). When discussing the economic and social consequences, debated topics are consumer privacy concerns, consequences for user wellbeing, threats to employment, data security concern or deepening the digital divide (e.g., Calo, 2011; Wisskirchen et al., 2017). We argue that human-centricity is an essential principle to design robots aiming at coexistence and interaction with humans. Crucially, robots should respect basic human values and rights, not do harm to humans due to malfunction and be accountable for their activities (The IEEE Global Initiative on Ethics of Autonomous and Intelligent Systems, 2017).

19.2.2 Robot Ethics in Elderly Care

Designing ethically sound robots is especially important in a service setting which involves vulnerable customers with a potential dependence on technology which can further erode their personal agency. The elderly care setting falls within this category and provokes brisk academic and public policy discussions (Sorell & Draper, 2014; Sparrow, 2016; Vandemeulebroucke et al., 2020). Especially, the wellbeing of the elderly segment and their care-providing networks heavily relies on advancements in robotics and AI. However, there is disagreement about robots being a panacea for the challenges facing the elderly care. In anticipation of robots taking increasingly complex social roles, we cannot say with certainty whether their introduction leads to utopian or dystopian future service scenarios. Nevertheless, by employing human-centered and value-sensitive design (Friedman et al., 2013), engineers and service designers can signal their endeavors toward future robotic services that enhance the wellbeing of careers and the cared-for.

Within the context of elderly care, robots differ depending on their social and assistive capabilities (e.g., Čaić et al., 2018; Fong, 2003). Socially-assistive robots, which combine these two value co-creation capabilities and embody companion and collaborator roles to build close relationships with users, raise the most critical social and ethical challenges (Malle et al., 2017). Extant literature (e.g., Sharkey & Sharkey, 2012) suggests several areas needing special ethical consideration: (i) assistance, (ii) monitoring, and (iii) companionship. First, the assistance domain is concerned with the variety of tasks that robots should take over. In other words, allowing for older adults' prolonged independence without jeopardizing their personal autonomy. Second, the robot's ability to monitor plays an invaluable role for safety and quick reaction in case of an emergency yet raises discussions about potential privacy violation and prevalence of virtual over real visits. Third, while the role of social companion offers a novel value proposition for elderly people and can positively affect their propensity to adopt robotic services, it also puts robots in a unique position to manipulate and deceive users through their "enhanced" human-like traits (e.g., perfect memory, negotiation and persuasion skills, no embarrassment or guilty conscious; Calo, 2011; Sparrow, 2016).

All the outlined ethical considerations demand a strategic approach to avoid a long-term decline in older adults' wellbeing through loss of human dignity and autonomy, detachment from the real world, increased dependency, and misplaced trust (Veruggio & Operto, 2008). While academics and public strongly discuss on whether robots lead to human flourishing or deterioration and whether is ethical or unethical to introduce robots in elderly care networks, little is known on how older adults and their care-providers perceive disruptive effects and ethical ramifications of robotic care and roles of the care robots in their care networks (Sorell & Draper, 2014).

19.3 Method

As a part of a larger study investigating future robot-enhanced elderly care service, we collected prospective users' expectations of both positive (value enhancing) and negative (value hindering) consequences of introducing robotic caregiving. We interviewed twenty older adults, seven formal caregivers, and nine informal caregivers using in-depth interviewing technique (context disruption interviews; Čaić et al. 2019a) leveraging visualizations of future service scenarios generated by informants themselves (see Table 19.1). This approach allowed us to collect both "what they say" (narratives containing informants' expectations of the future robotized care) and "what they make" (visualizations utilizing specifically designed network actor cards) (Sanders, 2000). Informants were prompted to imagine and elaborate on the future in which robots will assist the elderly in their daily activities (e.g., sending medication reminders, safeguarding, engaging in social interactions) and coordinate the entire caregiving network (e.g., updating caregivers on elderly person's medical status, alerting in case of an accident, mediating virtual visits). The objective was to learn about the hopes and fears concerning future robotic care from a multi-actor perspective.

19.4 Analysis

To analyze the data, we engaged in a rigorous process of thematic analysis (Braun & Clarke, 2006). First, we transcribed and reviewed the interviews and got familiarized with the data. We drew upon collected visualizations to get a richer understanding of the meaning of the collected narratives. Second, in a joint analysis session, we generated the initial coding scheme by identifying recurring patterns in the raw data. Third, we inspected for repeating ideas and similarities in coded insights in search of overarching themes. Finally, we reviewed the themes and established relationships between codes and themes by reviewing the existing literature. In this step, we matched the codes and themes with the three ethical considerations identified in the literature (i.e., assistance, monitoring, and

Table 19.1 Context disruption interview protocol, *Source* adapted from Čaić et al. (2019a)

Step	Name	Description
1	Contextual value network mapping: Current service	Mapping the care-based value network before the introduction of the service robot
2	Active immersion	Sensitizing to new technology usage
3	Introducing disruption	Introducing, assessing, and prioritizing service robot's functions
4	Contextual value network mapping: Future service	Mapping the care-based value network after the introduction of the service robot

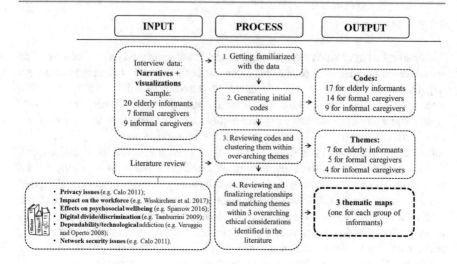

Fig. 19.1 Thematic analysis approach. *Source* Author's own illustration (2021)

companionship). Throughout the process, we identified 17 initial codes for the elderly segment of informants, 14 codes for the formal caregivers, and nine codes for the informal caregivers (see Fig. 19.1). These initial codes were then clustered within seven themes (the elderly informants), five themes (formal caregivers), and four themes (informal caregivers). Finally, we comprised three thematic maps.

19.5 Results

A multi-actor perspective on the ethical ramifications of robotic elderly care is captured by the three thematic maps (see Figs. 19.2, 19.3, and 19.4). Each of the three maps is organized according to three ethical considerations identified in the literature (1) assistance, (2) monitoring, and (3) companionship (e.g., Calo, 2011; Sharkey & Sharkey, 2012).

19.5.1 Narratives—Elderly informants

Assistance: The elderly informants recognize the robot's value-creating potential and welcome its assistance through offered reminders, advice, and a more general (cognitive) support. As explained by one of the informants: *"With time, maybe I will not be able to remember every time [to take his medication]. And that is why this function [medication reminder] is really important."* (E4) At the same time, older adults have some concerns that have certain ethical implications:

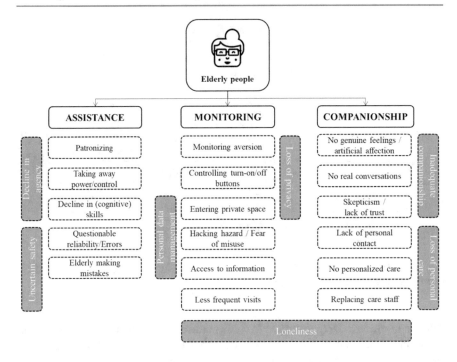

Fig. 19.2 Thematic map 1—elderly people's perspective. Note: ▭▭▭ represent ethical concern themes. *Source* Author's own illustration (2021)

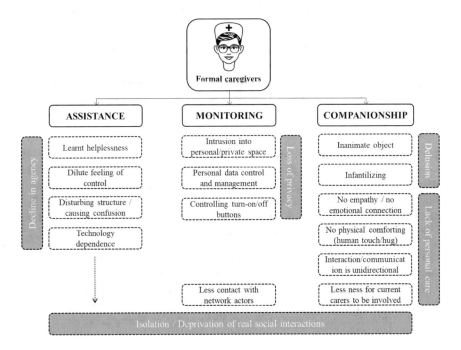

Fig. 19.3 Thematic map 2—formal caregiver's perspective. Note: ▭▭▭ represent ethical concern themes. *Source* Author's own illustration (2021)

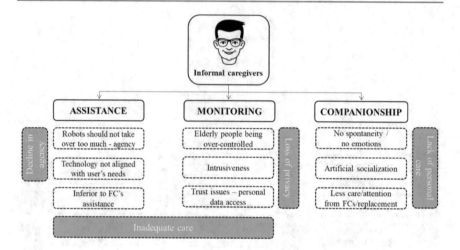

Fig. 19.4 Thematic map 3—informal caregiver's perspective. Note: ▭▭▭represent ethical concern themes. *Source* Author's own illustration (2021)

Decline in agency: The informants from this critical stakeholder group fear that the robot might take too much control out of their hands and hence negatively affect their feeling of independence. The following quote emphasizes their desire to stay in charge: *"I am just telling you that for now I do not need it [the robot]. I want to do it myself [track her medication intake]...I know exactly when to take each pill. And how do I know it? I have that box that says «morning», «noon», etc.... I want to keep practicing my brain."* (E5).

Uncertain safety: The elderly people also fear that the robot might fail to provide proper assistance and jeopardize their safety, either because of the robot's technical problems or seniors' lack of technical skills: *"I have some fears! Whatever I touch, I break it somehow. (Laughs) ... Yes! The only thing I would like to avoid is that I need to set up the robot myself or anything like that ... in order not to break it."* (E3).

Monitoring: This segment of informants repeatedly emphasizes a trade-off between certain privacy violations in return for lifesaving alertness: *"If I fall down, I'm in a need of help. And privacy in the bathroom... Naked or not, I'm in need of help... Privacy could be life threatening in my case."* [E9] Despite their general openness toward monitoring due to its value creating potential, the elderly informants indicate three main areas of ethical concern:

Loss of privacy: Interviewed elderly informants fear that by granting the robot access to their private spaces, it would record what they permit and what they wish to keep for themselves. For example, one informant explained: *"Well, I would not feel comfortable [being monitored]. Maybe I would get accustomed with time, but it would be rather unusual at the beginning. No one likes to be monitored at all times.*

With TV and other devices it is easy, you turn them off when you do not 'want them… but for a robot to monitor you when it should and should not. When you want and do not want…" (E8) Another informant added: *"I do not want the robot around me all the time. I would turn its power off!"* (E10).

Personal data management: Another ethical concern the elderly informants vocalize is a lack of control over and potential misuse of their personal data: *"As much as the robot would be helpful, in case of hacking it could become an enemy."* (E2) Collected narratives include information about different layers of access to the information stored in the robot. As explained by one of the informants: *"I would not want everyone [in her care-based network] to access the information from the robot. I would need to choose carefully to whom to grant access."* (E6).

Loneliness: The elderly welcome the possibility to connect with their family and friends via the robot's communication and information-sharing platform. However, they share a concern that virtual visits might exceed real visits and leave them deprived of social contact: *"They [her children] would still visit, but they would not be around for daily help."* (E3) *"I'm afraid it will take a lot of my contacts from me…"* (E10).

Companionship: When assessing the robot as a companion, the elderly informants foresee how it could (in future) alleviate their solitude. *"It [the robot] would be ideal for keeping me company. And it would listen to me. It would not judge me. And it would not have any agenda in it. And I would not be alone."* (E6) However, the role of a social companion also raises the following ethical concerns:

Inadequate companionship: The elderly informants do not believe that the robot's current skills can fulfill their need for socialization. They are skeptical about the robot's capability to develop genuine feelings and real conversations. As explained by one of the informants: *"It [the robot] does not interest me. It is not a living creature. It is like a dead person. No, not for me. I do not believe in that thing. For the short time I have left, give me real people who are alive."* (E15).

Loss of personal care: Another concern with ethical implications are that the introduction of social robots might lead to less personal interactions with the professional caregivers, and consequently, decrease the personalized care they are currently receiving. *"People really know me; the robot does not know me. Understand me. Yes… the care staff over here knows me and knows what I want and need. They have emotions."* (E9).

Loneliness: Finally, the elderly segment fears that as the robot takes the tasks from formal and informal caregivers, they will slowly be replaced and the old people will be left alone with a metal box. *"Yes, I think it will affect my contact with all of them [other network members]…Because they are less needed."* (E16).

19.5.2 Narratives—Formal Caregiver

Assistance: While the formal caregivers welcome different ways of cognitive assistance offered by the robot (e.g., medication and agenda reminders, nutritional advice), they worry about the robot's intrusiveness and the consequences of overconsuming robotic services. As explained by one of the informants: *"He [the elderly] likes to be notified about his activities. He would appreciate being notified to take his medication... But I can imagine he might feel a bit like a robot interfering too much..."* (FC2) The formal caregivers emphasize the following two ethical considerations needing special attention within the assistance category:

Decline in agency: The formal caregivers fear not only that the robot would be annoying and intruding but also that it would increase the technology dependence and in the long-term decrease elderly persons' wellbeing. As the following quote indicates: *"It's a shame the robot would take these things [autonomy, agency, control] out of their hands. There are things they [elderly people] can do themselves that stimulate them. I don't think the robot should take everything out of their hands."* (FC4).

Isolation / Deprivation of real social interactions: While receiving AI assistance may decrease the need for support from other network actors and hence unburden careers of some of their responsibilities, it may lead to an isolated life for the elderly, which has shown to be a risk factor for developing dementia (Fratiglioni et al., 2000) or Alzheimer's disease (Wilson et al., 2007): *"As the robot is more reliable, he [the elderly] would not be in contact with his neighbor [currently the first contact person] so often."* (FC6).

Monitoring: This segment of informants insists that the elderly need to preserve their right to control their personal data and, if desired, keep it private: *"I think this [monitoring] does not bother him [elderly patient], for as long as he has control over the information. If he knows that the information will only be shared when he wants and with whom he wants."* (FC6) While formal caregivers acknowledge that monitoring can enhance the wellbeing of multiple network actors (i.e., providing feeling of security, unburdening, reassuring), they suggest two areas rising ethical concerns:

Loss of privacy: The formal caregivers emphasize that the robot needs to respect human dignity and not record and share what it is not authorized to. They accentuate privacy regulations as a top priority: *"How privacy would be handled, needs to be discussed thoroughly."* (FC4) They fear that some older adults will need longer adjustment periods in which they might obstruct the robot's functioning by requesting frequent moments of privacy: *"There will be moments that she [the elderly] will put the power off. She's very keen on her privacy and she already told me before that she does not want the Robot in her bedroom or bathroom. She will use the robot, but only if she wants to."* (FC3).

Isolation/Deprivation of real social interactions: Similarly, as for assistance (and companionship), the formal caregivers fear that too much reliance on technology (e.g., video communication via the robot) might lead to social deprivation and isolation: *"If she communicates through Skype, it could be that she does not leave her room anymore to visit her friends."* (FC3).

Companionship: In the media, there is a lot of discussion about robots replacing the professional caregivers. Our informants do not seem to share the same dystopian forecasts about the future robotized care: *"Well, there are also people that are afraid that it [the robot] would substitute what we do. But I do not think so. I see it as a complementary!"* (FC4) However, the formal caregivers do emphasize that there needs to be a balance between human and robotic care: *"If there is a high level of robotization, it becomes dehumanizing and there must be a limit."* (FC6) According to this stakeholder group, there are three alarming ethical ramifications:

Delusion: While the majority believes that the elderly will not develop attachment with the robot, some indicate that the elderly might start confusing robots for something they are not: *"I know some elderly people might forget that the robot is a machine and might think the robot is their friend, their buddy."* (FC2).

Lack of personal care: Most commonly emphasized is the belief that robots will not be able to replace human care and love because they cannot experience affection and empathy which are integral to care provision: *"The technology does not replace anything. As much as it helps, the robot will never hug or caress him [the elderly]. They [old people] give a lot of importance to the touch or hug, and I do not know how the robot will satisfy them in these emotional terms!"* (FC7).

Isolation/Deprivation of real social interactions: Another thing the formal care-givers fear is that this simulacrum of social companionship might have detrimental consequences for the elderly person's psychosocial health: *"I think she [the elderly] would prefer the robot to people in future. And I think that's very dangerous for her… because she will isolate herself. So, for her, a robot is a very interesting thing, but also, in my opinion, a very dangerous thing for her."* (FC1).

19.5.3 Narratives—Informal Caregivers

Assistance: The informal caregivers believe that we are still far from the "robotic care" in a true sense. "This is still not a complete, holistic solution for the elderly care. It is only additional help, like an advanced mobile phone with some additional useful functions." (IC2) They suggest that the introduction of the robot-assisted services might lead to:

Decline in agency: The informal caregivers share a worry that the robot will be met with some resistance, which can be explained as elderly people's way of fighting for their independence: "Keeping in mind my father situation, I do not know if he will happily accept having a machine there to tell him things… he only does what he wants. I think it's going to bother him, because he's going to feel a bit controlled.

I don't know if having a machine next to him would seem like a loss of independence to him." (IC6).

Inadequate care: A commonly emphasized ethical theme is "personalization of care:" "...because they [elderly people] also differ...the ones that are 65 and 75 and 85." (IC1) The informal caregivers foresee a decline in the quality of care due to the robot's inability to genuinely understand human needs. As explained by one of the informants: "I think, for my mom, it is actually those moments of contact with people that are important. And especially with medication it is not possible [for robots to replace caregivers] since she is in a wheelchair. The robot can say "you have to take your medication," but if she cannot reach it..." (IC5).

Monitoring: This segment of informants mainly believes that their loved ones (e.g., their parents, family members or friends) will not be bothered by the robot's monitoring capabilities. As exemplified in these quotes: "I think mom would not have a problem with the robot being here [and monitoring]." (IC5) and "I think my dad would be glad that the robot can watch him." (IC8) However, they do indicate how the introduction of monitoring can lead to certain ethical considerations:

Loss of privacy: The informal caregivers acknowledge that it would take some time for the elderly to adapt to the feeling of being constantly watched: "Maybe she [her mom] will have a feeling that we are controlling her even more. Will she get a feeling that now we can check her all the time, and that we will control her, I don't know... But after a short adaptation period, she would be fine." (IC3) "I do not know whether the access is pushed by the robot or fetched by the people? If the robot pushes the info, then it needs to decide what info is for whom. And I think it is a completely different thing if everybody can access the robot in order to find out what she is doing, because then she [his mother-in-law] will become observed...but then I guess everybody should have different authorities, because she would not want everyone to know everything." (IC4).

Companionship: There is a prevalent disbelief that the robot could replace the companionship of human caretakers. As suggested in the following quotes: "It [the robot] could take a bit from each one of us. But not in a sense that she [his mom] would rather talk to Robi [a name he gave to the robot] than with her neighbor or friends. That not, for sure!" (IC9) "I still think that the robot cannot take over human interaction." (IC3) Since the informants within this stakeholder group share the view that robots are incapable of developing genuine emotions and personalized care, they fear that this might lead to negative outcomes for the elderly, foremost:

Lack of personal care: As emphasized in the following quote: "You know, they already have so little face-to-face contact with the caretakers and I think that we need to preserve that little that they have now. And not all of those, robots, just walking around here. Nobody wants no people around...no because that's something... the warmth of people, the voice of people, the emotions of people, I think that's important especially for that generation." (IC5) These concerns raise the commonly emphasized question of whether it is ethical or not to let the elderly engage in artificial socialization.

19.5.4 Visualizations

As a last step in a four-step "context disruption" interview protocol (Čaić et al., 2018, 2019a), informants were asked to map out the elderly care-based actor networks, as they anticipate them to take form after the introduction of the care robot. The mapping was done using a set of network actor cards specifically designed to depict the focal actor (i.e., elderly person) and various care-providing actors (i.e., formal and informal caregivers). Cards were chosen as a method because of their ability to spark discussions and their tangibility (Brandt, 2006; Clatworthy, 2011). In this section, we investigate the visual data in addition to the narratives already analyzed and focus on the position of the robot card relative to the elderly person card (i.e., the focal actor card).

The majority of the informants chose to place the robot card close to the elderly person, indicating the importance of assistance, monitoring, and companionship as capabilities of the robot and the necessary quick alerts pushed toward the caregivers in case of an emergency. However, our analysis shows that there were differences between the types of actors, with respect to the position of the robot card relative to the elderly person card (i.e., "prioritized position" right next to the elderly person card vs "further away" from the elderly person, with formal or informal caregivers having a closeness priority). We found a relatively high number of formal caregivers placing the robot card further away from the elderly person (three out of seven formal caregivers of the interviewed sample; 43%). At the same time, only one out of nine informal caregivers decided to place the robot card further away the elderly person (11%). Finally, four out of 20 elderly people (20%) placed their formal and/or informal caregivers closer than the robot (see Fig. 19.5).

In (service) design, mapping techniques, as the one used in this study, help designers collect and summarize (tacit) knowledge together with users (Blomkvist & Segelström, 2014). Visualizations of current and future care-providing networks help designers to develop value-sensitive insights, communicate insights with others, and maintain empathy with informants (Segelström, 2013). By analyzing the act of placing the robot card further away from or closer to the focal care-receiving actor together with accompanying narratives, we find that:

- The elderly who voice the greatest number of ethical concerns and are reluctant to accept robotic care are the ones who place the robot card further away from the card representing themselves.
- The formal caregivers who repeatedly emphasize that they do not fear the robots replacing their jobs are the ones who place the formal caregiver card closer to the elderly than the robot card.
- The informal caregivers recognize the unburdening potential of the care robot the most, hence also place the robot card very close to the elderly person card.

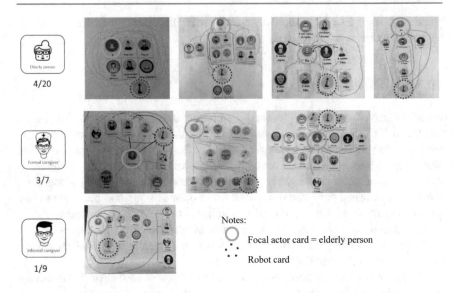

Fig. 19.5 Visualizations of future care networks showing how the robot is placed further away from the elderly person. *Source* Author's own illustration (2021)

19.6 Discussions and Conclusion

Robotic technologies can be seen as a potential solution for ensuring the wellbeing of elderly people and their care-providing networks through improved service, constant presence, and reliability. Still, the introduction of robots within the elderly care setting provokes brisk academic and public policy discussions (e.g., Sorell & Draper, 2014; Sparrow, 2016; Vandemeulebroucke et al., 2020) moving from dystopian (e.g., fear of losing human touch, human obsolescence, privacy concerns) to utopian (e.g., panacea for social problems, unburdening of the overworked care staff, prolonged independent living) projections.

In this chapter, we show how by acknowledging multiple network actors as experts of their own experiences (Visser et al., 2005) and by leveraging their narratives and visually-created insights, yields an important input for the design of future robotic care. By combining the two types of collected data and visualizing the findings in a matrix format (see Fig. 19.6)—with the y-axis representing the amount of vocalized ethical concerns (few/many) and the x-axis indicating the position of the care robot in the user's network visualization (closer to/away from the focal actor)—we show the importance of collecting both "what informants say" and "what informants do:"

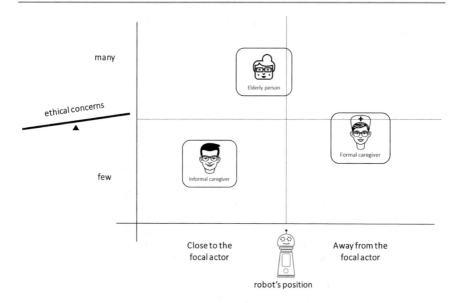

Fig. 19.6 Mapping of vocalized ethical concerns against the "act of placing the robot card close to/away from the focal actor". *Source* Author's own illustration (2021)

- For informal caregivers, the findings are straightforward. We can map them in the lower left quadrant of the matrix, indicating a low number of ethical concerns voiced by this group of informants and their inclination to place the care robot in the close vicinity of the elderly people (i.e., the focal network actor).
- The elderly (upper left quadrant) shared the greatest number of ethical concerns with regards to robotic care, however, by placing the care robot close to themselves in their network visualizations, they are indicating that the benefits of having the care robot might outweigh these if handled in a good way.
- Finally, the most interesting is the group of formal caregivers (lower right quadrant) who did not share a lot of ethical concerns, and also, when asked if they fear being replaced by care robots they unanimously said "No." However, their act of placing the robot card further away from the elderly person does communicate either their reluctance to accept robots as co-care-providers or their superiority over the inanimate caregivers.

References

Asimov, I. (1950). *Runaround. I, Robot.* New York City: Doubleday.

Blomkvist, J., & Segelström, F. (2014). Benefits of external representations in service design: A distributed cognition perspective. *The Design Journal, 17*(3), 331–346. https://doi.org/10.2752/175630614X13982745782849

Brandt, E. (2006). Designing exploratory design games: A framework for participation in participatory design? In *Proceedings of the Ninth Conference on Participatory Design: Expanding Boundaries in Design* (Vol. 1, pp. 57–66). Trento, Italy, ACM. https://doi.org/10.1145/1147261.1147271

Braun, V., & Clarke, V. (2006). Using thematic analysis in psychology. *Qualitative Research in Psychology, 3*(2), 77–101. https://doi.org/10.1191/1478088706qp063oa

Breazeal, C. L. (2002). *Designing sociable robots.* MIT press.

Čaić, M., Holmlid, S., Mahr, D., & Odekerken-Schröder, G. (2019a). Beneficiaries' view of actor networks: Service resonance for pluralistic actor networks. *International Journal of Design, 13* (3), 69–88.

Čaić, M., Mahr, D., & Oderkerken-Schröder, G. (2019b). Value of social robots in services: Social cognition perspective. *Journal of Services Marketing, 33*(4), 463–478. https://doi.org/10.1108/JSM-02-2018-0080

Čaić, M., Odekerken-Schröder, G., & Mahr, D. (2018). Service robots: Value co-creation and co-destruction in elderly care networks. *Journal of Service Management, 29*(2), 178–205. https://doi.org/10.1108/JOSM-07-2017-0179

Calo, M. R. (2011). 12 Robots and privacy. *Robot ethics: The ethical and social implications of robotics* (pp. 187–201). Cambridge, Massachusetts: The MIT Press.

Charisi, V., Dennis, L., Lieck, M. F. R., Matthias, A., Sombetzki, M. S. J., Winfield, A. F., & Yampolskiy, R. (2017). Towards moral autonomous systems. arXiv:1703.04741.

Clatworthy, S. (2011). Service innovation through touch-points: Development of an innovation toolkit for the first stages of new service development. *International Journal of Design, 5*(2), 15–28.

Engwall, O., Lopes, J., & Åhlund, A. (2021). Robot interaction styles for conversation practice in second language learning. *International Journal of Social Robotics, 13*(2), 251–276. https://doi.org/10.1007/s12369-020-00635-y

Fjeld, J., Achten, N., Hilligoss, H., Nagy, A., & Srikumar, M. (2020). Principled artificial intelligence: Mapping consensus in ethical and rights-based approaches to principles for AI. *Berkman Klein Center Research Publication,* (2020–1). Retrieved July 1, 2021, from https://dash.harvard.edu/bitstream/handle/1/42160420/HLS%20White%20Paper%20Final_v3.pdf?sequence=1&isAllowed=y.

Fong, T., Nourbakhsh, I., & Dautenhahn, K. (2003). A survey of socially interactive robots. *Robotics and Autonomous Systems, 42*(3–4), 143–166. https://doi.org/10.1016/S0921-8890(02)00372-X

Fratiglioni, L., Wang, H. X., Ericsson, K., Maytan, M., & Winblad, B. (2000). Influence of social network on occurrence of dementia: A community-based longitudinal study. *The Lancet, 355* (9212), 1315–1319 (PMID: 10776744). https://doi.org/10.1016/S0140-6736(00)02113-9

Friedman, B., Kahn, P. H., Borning, A., & Huldtgren, A. (2013). Value sensitive design and information systems. In *Early engagement and new technologies: Opening up the laboratory* (pp. 55–95). Dordrecht: Springer. https://doi.org/10.1007/978-94-007-7844-3_4 (Corpus ID: 8176837).

IEEE Standards Association. (2017). The IEEE Global Initiative on Ethics of Autonomous and Intelligent Systems. IEEE. org. Retrieved March 12, 2021, from http://standards.ieee.org/develop/indconn/ec/autonomous_systems.html.

KPMG (2016). *Social robots: 2016's new breed of social robots is ready to enter your world.* KPMG Advisory N.V., Arnhem.

Kuipers, B. (2016). Toward morality and ethics for robots. In *Ethical and Moral Considerations in Non-Human Agents, AAAI Spring Symposium Series.* 21.-23.03.2016, Palo Alto, California. Corpus ID: 17719469.

Lin, P., Abney, K., & Bekey, G. (2011). Robot ethics: Mapping the issues for a mechanized world. *Artificial Intelligence, 175*(5–6), 942–949. https://doi.org/10.1016/j.artint.2010.11.026

Malle, B. F., Scheutz, M., & Austerweil, J. L. (2017). Networks of social and moral norms in human and robot agents. In *A world with robots* (pp. 3–17). Cham: Springer. https://doi.org/10. 1007/978-3-319-46667-5_1.

Sanders, E. N. (2000). Generative tools for co-designing. In *Collaborative Design* (pp. 3–12). London: Springer. https://doi.org/10.1007/978-1-4471-0779-8_1.

Segelström, F. (2013). *Stakeholder engagement for service design: How service designers identify and communicate insights.* Doctoral dissertation, Linköping University Electronic Press (Ed.), Linköping. https://doi.org/10.3384/diss.diva-97320.

Sharkey, A., & Sharkey, N. (2012). Granny and the robots: Ethical issues in robot care for the elderly. *Ethics and Information Technology, 14*(1), 27–40. https://doi.org/10.1007/s10676-010-9234-6

Singer, P. W. (2009). *Wired for war: The robotics revolution and conflict in the 21st century.* Penguin Press.

Sorell, T., & Draper, H. (2014). Robot carers, ethics, and older people. *Ethics and Information Technology, 16*(3), 183–195. https://doi.org/10.1007/s10676-014-9344-7

Sparrow, R. (2016). Robots in aged care: A dystopian future? *AI & Society, 31*(4), 445–454. https://doi.org/10.1007/s00146-015-0625-4

Tamburrini, G. (2009). *Robot ethics: A view from the philosophy of science.* Ethics and Robotics (pp. 11–22). Corpus ID: 12023653.

Tung, V. W. S., & Au, N. (2018). Exploring customer experiences with robotics in hospitality. *International Journal of Contemporary Hospitality Management, 30*(7), 2680–2697. https://doi.org/10.1108/IJCHM-06-2017-0322CorpusID:158470246

Vandemeulebroucke, T., Dierckx de Casterlé, B., Welbergen, L., Massart, M., & Gastmans, C. (2020). The ethics of socially assistive robots in aged care. A focus group study with older adults in Flanders, Belgium. *The Journals of Gerontology: Series B, 75*(9), 1996–2007. https://doi.org/10.1093/geronb/gbz070.

Veruggio, G., & Operto, F. (2008). Roboethics: Social and ethical implications of robotics. In *Springer handbook of robotics* (pp. 1499–1524). Berlin: Springer. https://doi.org/10.1007/978-3-540-30301-5.

Visser, F. S., Stappers, P. J., Van der Lugt, R., & Sanders, E. B. (2005). Contextmapping: Experiences from practice. *CoDesign, 1*(2), 119–149. https://doi.org/10.1080/15710880500135987

Wallach, W., & Allen, C. (2008). *Moral machines: Teaching robots right from wrong.* Oxford University Press.

Wilson, R. S., Krueger, K. R., Arnold, S. E., Schneider, J. A., Kelly, J. F., Barnes, L. L., et al. (2007). Loneliness and risk of Alzheimer disease. *Archives of General Psychiatry, 64*(2), 234–240. PMID: 17283291. https://doi.org/10.1001/archpsyc.64.2.234.

Wisskirchen, G., Biacabe, B. T., Bormann, U., Muntz, A., Niehaus, G., Soler, et al. (2017). Artificial intelligence and robotics and their impact on the workplace. *IBA Global Employment Institute* (Ed.). London.

Martina Čaić is Assistant Professor in Strategic Service Design at Aalto University (Finland) and associate researcher at Hanken School of Economics (Finland). Her research addresses customer value, experience, and wellbeing in value constellations (e.g., elderly care), with a particular focus on how emerging technologies (e.g., AI, social robotics, assisted living technologies) disrupt existing practices of care. She has published her conceptual and empirical studies in the Journal of Service Management, Journal of Services Marketing, International Journal of Design, and International Journal of Social Robotics.

Stefan Holmlid is Professor in Design at Linköping University (Sweden), focusing on developing knowledge in the meeting between design practices and practices in service systems, in the public realm as well as with industrial corporations. His main research interests are design from a situated cognition perspective, mediated action in complex adaptive systems, and design on new arenas, such as service and policy. He heads the Interaction and Service design research group, the MSc programme in Design at LiU, and cofounded the ServDes conference in 2008, and the international Service Design Network in 2003.

Dominik Mahr is Professor for Digital Innovation & Marketing at Maastricht University (The Netherlands). He is also Scientific Director of the Service Science Factory bringing together academia and practice of Service Design. His research focuses on digital technologies, customer co-creation, service design, and service innovation, among others, and has been published in high impact journals. Prior to his academic career, Dominik worked for several years in different management and marketing consultancies, operating in the high-tech and automotive industry.

Gaby Odekerken-Schröder is Professor of Customer-Centric Service Science at Maastricht University (The Netherlands). Her main research interests are service innovation, service design, relationship management, customer loyalty, and service failure and recovery. She is one of the co-founders of Maastricht University's Service Science Factory (SSF) and Brightlands Institute for Supply Chain Innovation (BISCI), as she loves to bridge theory and practice. Her research has been published in Journal of Marketing, MISQ, Journal of Retailing, Journal of Service Research, International Journal of Social Robotics, Journal of the American Medical Doctors Association, Journal of Service Management, Journal of Services Marketing and many more.

Impact of Chinese Traditional Art Training as an Emotional Therapy for Older People with Cognitive Impairment in the UK

20

Yuanyuan Yin and Lesley Collier

Abstract

Providing activity for older people with dementia within the homecare sector is challenging and requires innovative service delivery to capture the skills and capacities of residents. Chinese traditional art is an unconventional but forward-thinking way of engaging older people with dementia. This research aims to investigate the impact of emotional art therapy on people with dementia using Chinese traditional art. This study explores whether Chinese traditional art therapy interventions can be used to promote healthy ageing in British older people. A mixed methodology, using the Pool Activity Levels Engagement Measure to assess engagement and the Neurobehavioral Rating Scale assessment to explore the impact on mood and behaviour, was employed to obtain an understanding of older people's engagement with the Chinese Traditional Art (CTArt) programme, and it is the impact on their behaviour. The CTArt programme took place over six weeks with 15 participants. Based on the research findings, it has been found that the CTArt intervention has a positive impact on the participant's engagement, concentration and fine motor control. Overall, it was noted that individuals with different levels of ability were able to engage with this activity from single water ink on reusable paper through to free style Xieyi painting.

Y. Yin (✉)
Winchester School of Art, Faculty of Arts and Humanities, University of Southampton, Park Avenue, Winchester SO23 8DL, England
e-mail: Y.Yin@soton.ac.uk

L. Collier
Faculty of Health and Well-Being, School of Llied Health Professions, University of Winchester, Sparkford Road, Winchester SO22 4NR, England
e-mail: Lesley.Collier@winchester.ac.uk

© The Author(s), under exclusive license to Springer Nature Switzerland AG 2022
M. A. Pfannstiel et al. (eds.), *Service Design Practices for Healthcare Innovation*,
https://doi.org/10.1007/978-3-030-87273-1_20

399

20.1 Introduction

Providing activity for older people with dementia is challenging within the homecare sector and requires innovative service delivery to capture the skills and capacities of residents. Chinese traditional art is an unconventional but forward-thinking way of engaging older people with dementia. By nature of its origins, it is an art form that is largely unfamiliar to individuals living in the UK but as such, does not place individuals with an artistic advantage. The free-flowing movements required to create an image embrace a mindful perspective and encourage both gross and fine motor control, communication with others and periods of time to be fully engaged. The activity can be structured to meet the needs of those with different levels of dementia and has been shown to be accessible for those with limited abilities. This chapter will describe the challenges experienced in engaging people with dementia in meaningful activity and will discuss a study that was undertaken to explore the feasibility of the intervention.

20.2 Existing Services at Care Homes

Despite the challenges of engaging people with dementia in care homes, it is well recognised that the need to participate in activity is innate for health and well-being (Martyr et al., 2018; Farina et al., 2017). Many of the therapies currently available in care homes, such as reminiscence therapy and validation therapy, endeavour to facilitate participation in activity by addressing some of the challenges presented by people with dementia but the absence of challenges does not necessarily suggest that well-being has been achieved (Björk et al., 2017). The concept of well-being is complex and many existing activities are not necessarily structured in such a way that is accessible or even suitable to each individual. Indeed, a systematic review by Curtis et al. (2018) reported that despite activities being present in care homes evidence of benefit on quality of life and well-being was limited. However, the use of arts-based activities and music appeared to have some impact (Liu et al., 2014; Camic et al., 2013).

These interventions are undertaken to increase well-being but often the activities themselves are not necessarily structured in a way that is accessible to older people. Therefore, it is necessary to consider what is achieved by offering purposeful activity.

20.3 Contribution of Activity in Maintaining Function

There is a general consensus that activities for older people with dementia maintain psychological and physical health. However, the progressive nature of the dementia disease process can lead to a reduction in activity and increased levels of dependency. This dependency is enhanced by carers within the care home environment, where carers staff often find removing activities a solution for time-consuming one-to-one supervision. These activities range from basic activities of daily living such as bathing, dressing and eating through to occupational pursuits such as gardening, cooking and socialising with others (Baum, 1995). This disruption in activity is reflected in the person's behaviour. Wandering and searching may reflect a level of boredom whilst aggression and agitation may indicate frustration at not being able to take part in activity (Shiells et al., 2020; Cohen-Mansfield & Jensen, 2018). These ideas support the need for occupation both to maintain function and to moderate mood and behaviour.

The relationship between occupation and function has been explored in association to engagement and maintenance of performance. Baum (1995) examined the role of occupation in maximising functional performance and reducing disturbed behaviours. 34 women and 38 men with mild-to-moderate Alzheimer's disease were randomly selected from the Washington University Alzheimer's Disease Research Centre database. Inclusion criteria also included being married and living in the community. Once informed consent had been gained from the participants, a baseline measure was taken using the Clinical Dementia Rating (CDR). Further data were collected by Occupational Therapists, Psychologists and a Research Assistant using the Kitchen Task Assessment and the Short Portable Mental Status Questionnaire. Data were collected from the carers using the Memory Problems Behavioural Checklist, Activity Card Sort and the Zarit Burden Interview. Variance was measured using a regression equation to determine that other neurological deficits did not contribute. Following analysis of the results using covariance analysis of linear structural equations the following interpretations were made:

- An increase in executive skills would result in the person giving up less occupational activity, this would lead to
- A decrease in the amount of help needed to perform basic self-care.
- An increase in memory would result in the person giving up less activity.
- An increase in activity would lead to a decrease in disturbing behaviour.
- An increase in disturbed behaviour increases demand stress and emotion focused stress in carers.

These results suggest that activity is an intervening variable between cognitive level and disturbing behaviour. However, it does not address whether continued engagement prevents decline in executive skills and memory deficits. This study underpins the need for occupation performance to manage behavioural disturbance both for the person with dementia and their carers.

Many studies have explored the relationship between activity and rate of cognitive decline; however, three are of particular interest (Guure et al., 2017; Karr et al., 2018; Scarmeas et al., 2001). These three longitudinal studies suggest that there is an association between the frequency of cognitive activity and the rate of cognitive decline. Scarmeas et al. (2001) were particularly interested in exploring whether participation in activity reduced the risk of Alzheimer's disease. In their study, 1772 participants aged 65 years or older were recruited. These participants had no diagnosis of dementia. They were assessed at baseline for participation in leisure activity. The group was followed longitudinally for a period of up to 7 years (mean 2.9 years). Levels of participation in leisure activity and incidence of dementia were recorded. After adjustment for age, ethnic group, education and occupation, the results indicated that the risk of dementia was reduced in participants who engaged in high levels of leisure activity.

Although these studies provide support for the notion of 'level of activity influences risk/rate of cognitive decline', little justification has been given to why particular activities may have been chosen. Activities selected for the above studies may have a different effect on the participant both by the level of complexity they offer, as well as the challenge demanded by the participant (is it something they are interested in?). This balance has been explored by Csikszentmihalyi (1988). Csikszentmihalyi (1988) suggest that behavioural disturbance is directly related to the person's ability to cope with environmental demand. How individuals interact with activities is dependent on whether the task is within their capabilities. Csikszentmihalyi suggested that there needs to be a balance between anxiety and boredom. If the task is too demanding the person experiences stress (anxiety), if the task is not challenging the person will experience boredom. He described this balance as 'flow', the balance between environmental demand and sustained occupational performance.

Finally, activity also may have the potential to increase a sense of well-being. Chung (2004) explored the patterns of activity and the state of well-being in a group people with dementia in long-term care. Participants were recruited from six nursing homes that specialised in care for people with dementia. Each nursing home had a part-time Occupational Therapist who managed functional problems such as eating. The Occupational Therapist also coordinated activity programmes such as multi-sensory stimulation and reminiscence therapy. Inclusion criteria included a clinical diagnosis of dementia or dementia-related disorder and residency at the nursing home for at least 6 months. Data were collected from 43 nursing home participants. The average age of participants was 81 years, 67% were female, 54% had not received any formal education and the average length of stay at the nursing home was 27 months. Participants were assessed using the Clinical Dementia Rating (CDR) which revealed 50% of participants had a severe level of impairment. Baseline assessments were carried out using the Dementia Care Mapping tool (DCM). This tool revealed the activity patterns engaged in by participants as well as their state of well-being during the activity. The results suggested:

- Participants spent 51% of time in type ll activities (uninvolved, passive, withdrawn, sleeping, distressed, self-stimulating, talking to self) 48% of time in type l activities (leisure activities, activities of daily living, interacting with others).
- Most participants' experienced fair (27.9%) to poor (34.9%) well-being with 20% experiencing an overall state of ill-being.
- Significant positive correlations were found between the states of well-being and time spent in type l activities.

Although this study clearly advocates the use of constructive activity in order to increase the level of perceived well-being, there are a number of points that need to be considered. Whilst a number of participants were able to take part in constructive activity there were a significant group who, due to the severity of their dementia, were unable to participate. The study offers no suggestions of how this group may be engaged. Also, no reference was made to the environments in which the activities took place. According to Lawton (1986), successful engagement must be supported by the right environment.

Key points from the studies above suggest.

- As the dementia disease process progresses, there is a reduction in activity and an increase in dependency.
- An increase in activity can lead to a decrease in disturbed behaviour.
- Risk of dementia may be reduced in participants who engaged in high levels of leisure activity.
- There is a positive relationship between constructive activities and sense of well-being.

These key points are often the driving points for activities facilitated by healthcare professionals for older people with dementia. The challenge is how to tap into the person's potential and maximise their remaining capabilities.

20.4   Art Training as One Type of Activity, Benefits of Art Training for Older People with Cognitive Impairment in the UK

The increase in older people with moderate to severe dementia with decreasing functional abilities has implications for service provision and healthcare costs (Prince et al., 2015). The National Services Framework for Older People (Department of Health, 2001) set out a ten-year plan to improve services for older people. Particular features of the plan, which was of relevance to older people with dementia, included person-centred care and improved standards of service provision. Person-centred care was identified by the Department of Health as a particular concern as it was felt that current service provision was limited in what was available for this group. However, the plan is limited in that it gives no suggestion of how service provision may be improved. The Care Management Approach for Older people with Serious Mental Health Problems (Department of Health, 2002) also endeavoured to address the challenges presented by older people with severe dementia, but offered limited guidance with the main emphasis being on assessment rather than on intervention. Whilst improved assessment is the cornerstone to improved management, the lack of clear direction in management is problematic.

With the increasing trend to conceptualise dementia from a more psychological perspective, more therapeutic options for care have become available (Nyman et al., 2016) and psychological therapies have been recommended as a first line treatment for people with dementia (Nyman et al. 2016). Although there has been a lack of direction, service providers have recognised the need to be more inclusive of different models of disease management, in order to provide a more holistic approach to care. Köttl et al. (2021) also acknowledged that there are an increasing number of treatments available, and psychological approaches provide some benefit in the care of people with moderate to severe dementia. The more common interventions used specifically with people with moderate to severe dementia are Reality Orientation, Validation Therapy and Reminiscence Therapy. More non-specific activities include activity groups, music groups, cookery groups, art groups and so forth. These latter groups focus more on the social components of the activity with subgoals being to increase concentration, mood and participation. The use of art-based activities is more limited.

Although these activities have been well introduced and applied with older people groups through local community centres and ageing-related NGOs (such as Age UK) and have received positive feedback in improving people's health and well-being, very few older people in the UK have tried Chinese traditional art in their activities due to cultural differences.

20.5 Art Training with Chinese Traditional Art Painting

Chinese traditional art training activities for older people have been well established and are popular in China. It normally includes Chinese Calligraphy, Gongbi Painting and Xieyi Painting (Jiang et al., 2006). Chinese calligraphy is the writing of Chinese characters by hand using a soft-tipped brush pen; it has been used historically as a means of communication (Kao et al., 2018). It involves visual perception of the character, spatial structuring of the character, cognitive planning and manoeuvring of the brush pen to follow specific character configurations (Fig. 20.1). For each individual Chinese character stroke, it has a specific way to move the brush pen in painting. Figure 20.2 shows moving tracks of a brush pen when painting different stroke.

Gongbi (skilled brush) painting and Xieyi (freehand strokes) painting are the two main forms of Chinese Traditional painting. Gongbi painting (detailed painting) requires higher drawing skills and patience (Fig. 20.3). Because it attempts to capture the fine details of the botanical specimen, it usually takes hours or even days to finish a painting. Before photography was invented, this style of painting allowed accurate and even scientific records to be kept. Xieyi painting refers to painting in freestyle (Fig. 20.4). Even without formal training in drawing, everyone can draw an orchid by following some simple steps. It is quite easy to learn, but difficult to excel.

Fig. 20.1 Chinese calligraphy. *Source* static.yczihua.com (2021). Accessed June 30, 2021, from https://static.yczihua.com/images/202007/goods_img/16886_P_1594067176589.jpg; stor.calligra phy-museum.com (2021). Accessed June 30, 2021, from https://stor.calligraphy-museum.com/source/image/News/2020/06/sw1.jpg

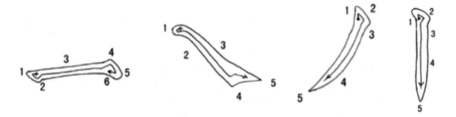

Fig. 20.2 Chinese calligraphy painting techniques. *Source* adapted from Plaza.ufl.edu (2021). Accessed June 30, 2021, from http://plaza.ufl.edu/haishicui/techniques.html

Fig. 20.3 Gongbi painting. *Source* Chinashj.com (2021a). Accessed June 30, 2021, from http://www.chinashj.com/sh-ddsh-tjzppdy/3713.html

Fig. 20.4 Xieyi painting. *Source* chinashj.com (2021b). Accessed June 30, 2021, from http://www.chinashj.com/yssc/zhanlan/2020/0108/17447.html

Comparing with western art painting, Chinese traditional art practice requires an integration of the mind, body and character/pattern interwoven in a dynamic painting process (Kao, 2010). For example, in Chinese Calligraphy, the organisation of the character entails certain geometric properties, including the topological principles of connectivity, closure, orientation, symmetry, etc. In writing, these properties cause the writer's perceptual, cognitive and bodily conditions to engage in corresponding adjustments and representations (Chen, 1982; Kao, 2010). For beginners, people normally use 'Miaohong' (tracing) to start their Calligraphy learning (Fig. 20.5). In Miaohong, the task of the writer is to move the brush pen to track the established stroke patterns by following preprinted outlines. The participants can then move from tracing to copying and then freehand (Shek et al., 1986). Some researchers have confirmed that the writer's perceptual, cognitive and motor activities are feedback regulated and are integrated in a dynamic writing task with the writer's body interfacing the character in an interactive process (Kao et al., 2019). Another key feature of Chinese traditional art is the soft brush pen (Fig. 20.6). Because of the softness of the brush tip, the Chinese traditional art painting involves a 3D motion, which generates a powerful source of impact on the practitioner's perceptual, cognitive and physiological changes during its practice. Furthermore, Chinese traditional painting encourages older people to not only use their hands and fingers but also arms, shoulders and upper body for the painting. In this way, they will be able to engage more body movements and exercise with more body muscles during painting. From painting style and presentation aspects, Chinese traditional painting is more interpretive and freely expressive for people to reveal the spirit or soul of the subjects they do and share the view and understandings of life and nature with viewers. This will provide a new way to express emotion for older residents in the UK.

There is evidence shown that Chinese traditional art training can improve people's behavioural, psychosomatic, as well as clinical conditions (Kao et al., 2019). For example, these include attention and concentration, physical relaxation and

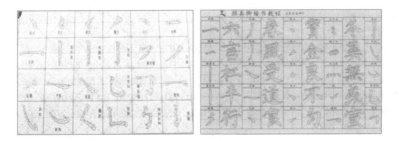

Fig. 20.5 Miaohong. *Source* Author's own illustrations (2021)

Fig. 20.6 Chinese painting brush pen. *Source* xiewenyin.com (2021). Accessed June 30, 2021, from https://www.xiewenyin.com/449.html

emotional stabilisation. Successful treatments with this intervention have been obtained for people with stroke,3,6 Alzheimer's disease,3 cancer,7 and post-traumatic stress disorder.

20.6 Research Aim and Research Question

This research aims to investigate impact of emotional art therapy for people with dementia using Chinese traditional art. This study explores whether Chinese traditional art therapy interventions can be used to promote healthy ageing in British older people.

The research question is:

Can Chinese traditional art can be used as an emotional art therapy to improve well-being and engagement in older people with dementia living in the UK?

20.7 Methodology Design

A mixed study methodology, which included PAL Engagement Measure based observations and conversation-based Neurobehavioral Rating Scale assessment, was employed to obtain an understanding of older people's engagement with the Chinese Traditional Art (CTArt) programme and its impact on their behaviour (such as concentration, cognition, communication, positive/negtive emotional expression and control of body).

20.7.1 Research Design

The CTArt programme took place over six weeks, to balance the richness of data collection and the feasibility of high-quality participant engagement. The CTArt programme took place in a Care Home located in the South of the UK. All participants gave their consent to participate in the study. Ethics approval was granted by the University of Southampton (Ref. 19,789).

During the CTArt programme, participants were invited to join an interactive learning session (1.5 h) once a week. There were six sessions in total and the researchers taugh participants how to do CTArt which included four steps: 1) Chinese calligraphy miaohong with reusable water writing cloth, 2) Chinese calligraphy miaohong with black ink and rice paper, 3) Xieji paintingn with black ink and rice paper and then 4) goingbi painting with colour ink and rice paper (Table 20.1). The researcher provided all materials for the CTArt learning sessions.

Table 20.1 Four stepes of CTArt programme, *Source* Author's own elaboration (2021)

Activities	Tasks	Materials
1. Chinese calligraphy miaohong with reusable water writing cloth	Tracing outlines of Chinese charactoers on a piece of reusable water writing cloth by using water as ink	Brush pen, water (as ink), reusable water writing cloth with Chinese charactoers outlines on it
2. Chinese calligraphy miaohong with black ink and rice paper	Tracing outlines of Chinese charactoers on a piece of rice paper by using black ink	Brush pen, black ink, Chinese calligraphy rice paper with Chinese charactoers outlines on it
3. Goingbi painting with colour ink and rice paper	Detailed style painging on a piece of rice paper with Gongbi painting outlines (three designs). Step 1: draw outline of the painting by using black ink; Step: add colour into the painting outline	Brush pen, black ink, colour ink, rice paper with Gongbi painting outlines on it
4. Xieji paintingn with black ink and rice paper	Free style painging on a piece of rice paper by using black ink	Brush pen, black ink, a blank rice paper

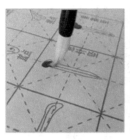

Fig. 20.7 Chinese calligraphy on reusable water writing cloth with tracing outlines on it. *Source* Author's own photographs (2021)

Participants joined the sessions either by themselves or with the support from a staff member from the Care Home.

Each participant was coached on how to undertake each activity. The coaching was tailored to meet the different cognitive and physical needs of each participant. During the CTArt programme, each participant is progressed through Gongbi painting and then Xieyi painting. For the Chinese calligraphy exercise, participants started with calligraphy with water on reusable water writing cloth (Fig. 20.7) and then calligraphy with black link on rice paper (Fig. 20.8). On both writing cloth and rice paper, there was printed outline of Chinese characters so participants could trace the characters. Participants started with Chinese calligraphy to learn how to use a soft brush pen in their drawing, writing and painting.

Once Chinese writing was mastered, the researchers introduced Gongbi painting which is a detailed painting design (Fig. 20.9). Gongbi painting required the participants to carefully trace a thin outline of a painting by using a smaller size soft-brush pen and black ink and then use colour inks to add colours to the paint. This will also require the participant to plan their design of colour for the paint.

Finally, Xieyi painting was undertaken. Xieyi is a freestyle painting style with a soft brush pen, but also it is the most difficult one. Participants were encouraged to draw with their emotions to paint flowers and flowing shapes (Fig. 20.10).

20.7.2 Data Collection Narrative

All participants were assessed using the Pool Activity Level Instrument for Occupational Profiling (Pool, 2012). This baseline assessment determined how the training session was to be structured based on cognitive ability, physical ability and social interaction. Levels within the instrument include the Planned Level—able to undertand the concept of the activity and follow the steps with minimal guidance, able to notice and correct errors; Exploratory Level—able to understand the concept of the activity but may fail to remember the steps, may become distracted. Sensory Level—More concerned with the sensory components of the activity, does not

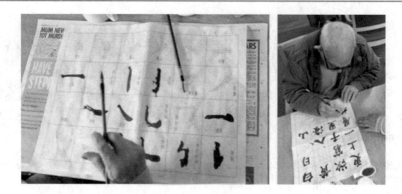

Fig. 20.8 Chinese calligraphy rice paper water with tracing outlines on it. *Source* Author's own photographs (2021)

Fig. 20.9 Participant Gongbi painting: chose design, outlining, adding colour and final outcome. *Source* Author's own photos (2021)

Fig. 20.10 Participant Xieyi painting. *Source* Author's own photographs (2021)

demonstrate an awareness of the potential outcome; Reflex level—unable to engage with activity without considerable support, does not initiate engagement.

During the training sessions, the researchers observed how the participants engaged with the painting activities using the PAL Engagement Measure (Pool & Collier, In press). The PAL Engagement Measure uses cognitive ability, physical ability, social interaction and emotional well-being as predictors of engagement. Observations under each of these four domains were undertaken during each of the sessions by an independent rater. Outcomes included 'not observed during the activity', 'observed at times but not consistently', and 'engaged consistently in keeping with the activity'.

One small video recorder was used to further explore how paticipants engaged in the CTArt programme as well as capturing emotional responses without disturbing the participant. A Content analysis approach was employed to analysis the video data.

The Neurobehavioral Rating Scale (Sultzer et al., 1992) was used to establish mood and behaviour during the sessions. During the sessions observations were made regarding levels of anxiety, fatigability, expression, communication, and mood. Factors determined by the assessment include cognition and insight, agitation and disinhibition, behaviour and spped of movement, anxiety and depressions, verbal output, and psychosis.

20.7.3 Participants' Backgrounds

In this study, participants were recruited through our research partner, a care home in the South of England, which had provision for both nursing care and residential care. All care-home residents who were aged 65 + and demonstrated an interest in joining the CTArt programme were invited to participate. Details of the activity and the signing of consent forms was undertaken. Family members were also involved in this process.

There were 15 participants who joined the CTArt programme, 6 male participants and 9 female participants (Table 20.2). Due to participant health and other planned activities during the CTArt period, only 5 participants attended more than 5 training sessions. Thus, the data analysis in the paper focuses on the 5 participants who attended more than 5 training sessions.

20.8 Findings

The following sessions present key research findings from both quantitative and qualitative presptives. The quantitative analysis utilised descriptive and parametric anaysis to consider the relationship between variables. A qualitative case study presents evidences of the positive impact of CTArt programme on a participant's behaviour from concentration, cognition, communication, Emotion and satisfaction, and control of body prespectives.

Table 20.2 Participant background, *Source* Author's own elaboration (2021)

NO	PAL level	Gender	Age	Long term illness	No of attendance
001	Exp	M	93	Yes	4
002	Sensory	F	90	Yes	1
003	Planned	M	77	Yes	5
004	Reflex	M	92	Yes	1
005	Exp	F	93	Yes	2
006	Planned	F	95	Yes	1
007	Planned	F	81	Yes	6
008	Sensory	F	89	Yes	1
009	Sensory	M	95	Yes	1
010	Exp	F	88	Yes	5
011	Exp	F	90	Yes	5
012	Exp	M	94	Yes	5
013	NK	M	85	Yes	1
014	NK	F	NK	NK	1
015	NK	F	NK	NK	1

20.8.1 Quantitative Results

Participants were recruited from a social services care home in the south of England. Demographics of the participant group are illustrated in Table 20.3.

Participants were assessed at baseline using the Neurobehavioural rating scale (NRS; Sultzer et al., 1992), the Pool Activity Level Instrument for Occupational Profiling (PAL; Pool, 2012), and the Pool Activity Outcome Measure (PALOM; in press). Baseline data are recorded in Tables 20.4, 20.5 and 20.6.

T Tests were undertaken to explore whether baseline data improved in terms of mood, behaviour and engagement. The PAL engagement scores improved over time, t (3) = 14.03, p = 0.001, suggesting there was an improvement in engagement scores. In particular cognitive abilities including goal awareness, initiation, attention, concentration, exploration and response improved. Additionally, physical ability including co-ordination, manipulation, and handling of objects improved. Scores for the NRS did not change significantly except for cognitive / insight, which included relating to others, increased speed of movement, and increased emotional tone and intensity of emotional response, t (3) = 5.51, p = 0.012.

Table 20.3 Demographics of participants, *Source* Author's own elaboration (2021)

n = 13	Range	Mean	Standard deviation
Age	77–95 years	89 years	6 years
n = 13	*Male*	*Female*	
Gender	5	8	

Table 20.4 PAL baseline scores, *Source* Author's own elaboration (2021)

PAL criteria	Planned	Exploratory	Sensory	Reflex
Nos of participants	3	6	3	1

Table 20.5 NRS baselines scores, *Source* Author's own elaboration (2021)

NRS criteria	Mean	Standard deviation	Skewness
NRS-A (Cognition/Insight)	18	8.78	0.54
NRS-B (Agitation/Disinhibition)	8.54	9.19	1.77
NRS-C (Behavioural retardation)	2.38	2.84	1.87
NRS-D (Anxiety/Depression)	2.54	4.96	2.90
NRS-E (Verbal output)	0.92	1.18	1.58
NRS-F (Psychosis)	2.31	4.27	1.99

Table 20.6 PALOM baseline scores *Source* Author's own elaboration (2021)

PALOM criteria	Mean	Standard deviation	Skewness
PALOM cognitive ability	15.08	4.42	−0.14
PALOM social interaction	8.38	2.50	0.01
PALOM physical ability	11.46	3.20	−0.21
PALOM emotional well-being	7.85	2.99	0.08
PALOM total score	42.77	11.41	0.001

20.8.2 Qualitative Case Study

Participant 007 was aged 81 when she joined the CTArts programme and attended all 6 sessions. She had two long-term illnesses including stroke. These long-term illnesses caused tremor, especially for her hands, leading to poor motor control. She had fixed flexion deformity of her middle finger, ring finger and little finger, and only thumb and index fingers could move with flexibility. Her PAL level was found to be at the Planned level.

Concentration

During the 6-week CTArt programme, the participant's concentration improved. In Week 1, her concentration level with the calligraphy painting was on average around 2–3 min. Concentration time increased to 20 min by the end of the session in the Week 2, then 30 min in Week 4 and 5, and 20 min in Week 6. In Week 2, the participant started with water Chinese calligraphy stroke painting and then progressed to painting with black ink. Once the researcher demonstrated how to use black ink for painting to her, she worked on the calligraphy stroke worksheet for

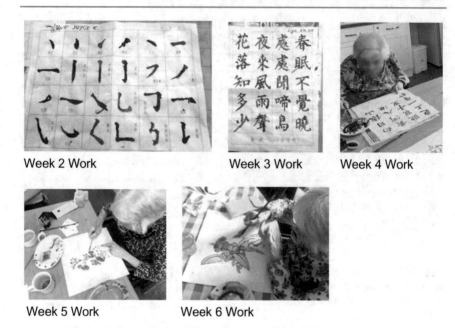

Fig. 20.11 Participant 007's works during the CTArt programme. *Source* Author's own photographs (2021)

around 20 min (Fig. 20.11 image of Week 2 work). In Week 4, the participant used black ink for her calligraphy painting, and she had a sheet with 28 Chinese characters. She continued painting for 30 min to complete the whole sheet. In Week 5 and 6, the sessions progressed to Gongbi outline and colouring. The participant engaged well in these sessions and her longest concentration time was 30 min in Week 5, and 20 min in Week 6. From the image of Week 6 work, we can see she used her left hand to support her right hand.

Another sign of concentration was demonstrated by her reluctance to disturb others. In the beginning of Week 2, when asked if she wanted a hot drink, the participant did not respond and did not stopping painting even when the staff member asking her was stood beside her. She was concentrating on controlling her hand to stop it shaking and continued her water ink painting until she had finished that calligraphy character. After that, she responded to the staff for her drink order. Similarly, in Week 4, one of the care home staff was dancing and entertaining participants near her table, but she did not stop painting.

Cognition

Participant 007 demonstrated cognitive skills in terms of understanding and following instructions, learning and problem solving during the 6 CTArt programme sessions.

Her engagement with the CTArt activities during the programme included:

- Chinese calligraphy with water ink on reusable water writing cloth
- Chinese calligraphy with black ink on rice paper
- Gongbi outline with black ink on rice paper
- Gongbi colouring on the same rice paper with painting outline
- Freestyle Xieyi painting

Each of these activities increases in complexity in both motor control as well as creative design.

It was difficult for her to start Chinese calligraphy at the beginning of the programme due to the novelty of the activity However, she quickly picked up the technique of Chinese character design and stroke painting principles following the researcher's demonstration. In Week 1, she worked well with the stroke painting with water ink on the cloth but found it difficult to initiate the next stroke in the Chinese character formation. When she moved to painting with black ink, she was not confident and said, 'I don't know what I am doing now' and 'I don't know why I am so shaking today'. The researcher encouraged her and suggested her to start with a stroke which was relatively easy to begin with. After that, she was motivated to continue. In Week 3 and 4, the participant showed good understanding of the next level of complexity when the researcher taught her about how to use the soft brush pen to paint Chinese characters stroke by stroke by using her hand, arm and upper body as a harmony, and how to add colour to her Gongbi outlines. She followed the demonstration well and was keen to practise by herself. For example, when the researcher suggested she need a bit more ink to paint, she immediately responded to dip her pen into the water pot and then soak the top of the pen into coloured ink. Her action was slow but smooth. When she worked with her second Gongbi outline painting during Week 4, she did not need any additional support. In Week 5 and 6, she also performed well in Gongbi colouring and also tried free style Xieyi painting (Fig. 20.12).

Fig. 20.12 Free style Xieyi painting in the Week 6. *Source* Author's own photographs (2021)

Communication

This participant had good communication skills and enjoyed talking with the researchers, care home staff and other participants. She was friendly and always spoke to other participants in the sessions. She was confident to ask questions whenever needed. For instance, she asked the researcher to repeat information, when necessary, as she was absorbed in the activity and sometimes missed the instructions. During the activity she frequently used positive statements about her abilities and challenges she faced such as 'come on' and 'I shake and roll today', 'It will be better tomorrow, I'm sure'. The participant also used facial expression and body language in her communication. For example, she raised up her elbow and waved her hands to express her happiness or to emphasis what she wanted to say. Sometimes, when her speaking was not that clear, she spoke slowly and repeated herself. During the 6 weeks of the CTArt programme, her communication skills remained good consistently. She demonstrated great interesting in the activity and was keen to have a better understanding of the structure and meanings of Chinese characters.

Emotion and satisfaction

During the 6 weeks CTArt programme, the participant expressed both positive and negative emotions. Positive emotion mainly focused on her satisfaction with the painting activities, her achievements and interactions with other people in the sessions (researchers, staff and other participants). Negative emotion was mainly due to her shaking hands, ambitions, high self-demand and tiredness.

When she first tried Chinese calligraphy painting with black ink, she was very happy and confident (Week 2). In the Week 3, when she completed her first Chinese pome calligraphy painting, she was elated (Fig. 20.13). She also expressed happiness when she received encouraging feedback from the researchers and care home staff (Fig. 20.14, 20.15). For example, the researcher asked for her feedback on the sessions, she said 'it's has been very interesting' (Week 1) and 'I am very enjoyed it' (Week 4).

Fig. 20.13 Completion of her first Chinese pome calligraphy painting in the Week 3. *Source* Author's own photograph (2021)

Fig. 20.14 Participant 003 pleased with her works in the Week 5. *Source* Author's own photgraphs (2021)

Fig. 20.15 Participant 003 pleased with her works in the Week 6. *Source* Author's own photographs (2021)

At the beginning of Week 2, it was difficult for the participant to hold the soft brush pen by her hand and finger. So, she used her right hand to hold the brush pen and left hand to support the right hand and to control the shaking. The shaking caused her concern and impacted on her enjoyment.

In the Week 4, the participant was not very happy when she joined the session (Fig. 20.16). She looked tired and mentioned her 'wobbling' hands several time during the session. After she finished her Gongbi outline painting, she used a tissue to cover her eyes for a few seconds and was tearful.

Another negative emotion was expressed in the Week 5, when she felt her performance was not as good as the other participants. In that session, another participant shared the same table with her and did a great job in Gongbi colouring. From the video, it was seen that she stopped painting and looked at the other

participant when the research commented positively on his painting. When the researcher came to ask her about her painting progress, she said it was not a good day today, and she pointed out that the participant did very well. From Fig. 20.17, we can see other participant has completed two Gongbi painting and she was still working on her first Gongbi painting.

Moreover, when she felt tried, she was less confident with her work and worried more about her hand shaking. Also, she complained of her eyes watering when she felt tried. In Week 4, after finishing the Chinese calligraphic painting, the participant felt tired, and her hand was shaking more. When the researcher brought a flower Gongbi painting paper for her to try, she said, 'I don't think I can do flowers today' and 'I am wobbly today'. The staff encouraged her and helped her to start the flower painting.

Fig. 20.17 Participant 007 and 012 were sharing a table in the Week 5. *Source* Author's own photograph (2021)

Control of body

Due to her tremor, it was difficult for her to hold the soft brush pen for painting at the beginning of the programme (Week 1 and 2). She needed to reposition the pen in her fingers and take regular breaks. She always had to stop painting when her hands were shaking. She encouraged herself 'it's a good job to use these two fingers (index and middle fingers), isnt it?'. Later on, she commented that the brush pen could not keep her hand steady. She needed to use both hands to hold the water bowl to dip water. Also, her left hand could not hold the paper steady, so that the paper moved around on the table when she tried to use her right hand to write. It was difficult for her to put her glasses on. When she was holding the soft brush pen in her right hand, her left hand would shake making it difficult for her put her glasses on. As a result, she would put the pen down, then put her glasses on with both hands.

In Week 3, there was a clear improvement of the participant's dexterity. She commented 'it's a bit better than last week'. In Week 4, the participant was not in an active mood. She had difficulty with her tremor at the beginning of the training session. It was difficult for her to move the brush pen to a better position with her right hand, she had to use her left hand to help (Fig. 20.18). She used her left hand to position the pen into her right hand. Occassionally, she used her left hand to support her right hand when dipping the brush pen into the small water bowl (Fig. 20.19).

As the participant had a 'wobbly' hand in Week 4, to start with, she did not want to paint. She had difficulty controling her tremor, and encouraged herself saying 'come on', this appeared to motivate her and she started to paint the flowers. Although her hands were still shakey in Week 5 and Week 6, it was clear that she had some improvment in controlling her tremor.

In terms of managing painting mateirals, in Week 1, she needed to use both hand to manage painting materials such as water bowl and painting paper. In Week 2, when she used the rice paper for Chinese caligraphy painting, it was more difficult for her. She used her left hand to hold and steady the paper, but her left index finger caught the paper during painting, causing the rice paper to fold. She required assistence to flatten the paper back out (Fig. 20.20).

Fig. 20.18 It was hard to position of the brush pen—Week 3. *Source* Author's own photographs (2021)

Fig. 20.19 She used her left hand to hold her right arm when dipping brush pen into the small water bowl, as her right hand was shaking. *Source* Author's own photographs (2021)

Fig. 20.20 The researcher helped the participant to flatten the painting paper. *Source* Author's own photographs (2021)

In the Week 4, she was ready to try real ink to paint. She found it difficult to move the paper up after she finished the top lines of Chinese characters, as her arm could not reach the far side of the table when she seated in her wheelchair (Fig. 20.21). She also struggled due her eyesight, initially holding the brush the wrong way up until a staff member pointed out her mistake. She smiled and said, ' oh boy, do I need a pair of new glasses' oh dear. She cleaned the ink on the pen and said, 'wasn't that silly?' 'wasn't that stupid thing to do'.

Fig. 20.21 Difficult to move paper. *Source* Author's own photographs (2021)

Fig. 20.22 Participant was holding the brush pen upside down. *Source* Author's own photographs (2021)

Fig. 20.23 Participant dragged the paper to move colouring palette. *Source* Author's own photograph (2021)

By Week 5 and 6, she could manage the materials on the table well. One example of her ability to problem solve was where she found it hard to move the colouring paper due to the palette resting on the top of the paper. She moved the palette with her right hand and manipulated the paper with her left (Fig. 20.23).

20.9 Conclusion

In conclusion, the CTArt intervention demonstrated an increase in engagement amongst the participants, over the sessions. Elements of note were an increase in initiation, attention and concentration. Ability to manipulate the brush also improved over time. These changes were illustrated in the case study described. Although the case study participant demonstrated some difficulty with motor control, she was able to improve her dexterity with the brush, in order to produce an output she was pleased with. Overall, it was noted that individuals with different levels of ability were able to engage with this activity from single water ink on reusable paper through to free style Xieyi painting.

References

Baum, C. M. (1995). The contribution of occupation to function in persons with Alzheimer's disease. *Journal of Occupational Science, 2*(2), 59–67. https://doi.org/10.1080/14427591.1995.9686396

Björk, S., Lindkvist, M., Wilmo, A., Juthberg, C., Bergland, A., & Edvardsson, D. (2017). Residents engagement in everyday activities and its association with thriving in nursing homes. *Journal of Advanced Nursing, 73*(8), 1884–1895. https://doi.org/10.1111/jan.13275

Camic, P. M., Myferi Williams, C., & Meeton, F. (2013). Does a 'Singing Together Group' improve the quality of life of people with a dementia and their carers? A pilot evaluation study. *Dementia, 12*(2), 157–176. PMID: 24336767. https://doi.org/10.1177/1471301211422761.

Chen, L. (1982). Topological structure in visual perception. *Science, 218*(4573), 699–700. https://doi.org/10.1126/science.7134969

Chung, J. C. C. (2004). Activity participation and well-being of people with dementia in long-term care settings. *OTJR-Occupation Participation and Health, 24*(1), 22–31. https://doi.org/10.1177/153944920402400104

Cohen-Mansfield, J., & Jensen, B. (2018). Attendance in recreational groups for persons with dementia: The impact of stimulus and environmental factors. *American Journal of Alzheimer's Disease & Other Dementiasr, 33*(7), 471–478. https://doi.org/10.1177/1533317518788158

Csikszentmihalyi, M. (1988). Atheoretical model for enjoyment. In M. Csikszentmihalyi (Ed.), *Beyond Boredom and Anxiety* (pp. 35–54). Jossey-Bass.

Curtis, A., Gibson, L., O'Brien, M., & Roe, B. (2018). Systematic review of the impact of arts for health activities on health, well-being and quality of life of older people living in care homes. *Dementia, 17*(6), 645–669. https://doi.org/10.1177/1471301217740960

Department of Health. (2002). *Care Management of Older People with Serious Mental Health Problems.* Retrieved May 31, 2021, from www.dh.gov.uk.

Department of Health. (2001). *National Services Framework for Older People.* Retrieved May 31, 2021,from https://www.gov.uk/government/publications/quality-standards-for-care-services-for-older-people.

Farina, N., Page, T. E., Daley, S., Brown, A., Bowling, A., & Basset, T. (2017). Factors associated with the quality of life of family carers of people with dementia: A systematic review. *Alzheimers Dement, 13*(5), 572–581. PMID: 28167069. https://doi.org/10.1016/j.jalz.2016.12.010.

Guure, C. B., Ibrahim, N. A., Adam, M. B., Said, S. M. (2017). Impact of Physical Activity on Cognitive Decline, Dementia, and Its Subtypes: Meta-Analysis of Prospective Studies, BioMed Research International, Vol, 2017.Guure, C. B., Ibrahim, N. A., Adam, M. B., & Said, S. M. (2017). Impact of physical activity on cognitive decline, dementia, and its subtypes: Meta-analysis of prospective studies. *BioMed Research International,* 2017, 13 pages. Article ID 9016924. https://doi.org/10.1155/2017/9016924.

Jiang, S., Huang, Q., Ye, Q., & Gao, W. (2006). An effective method of detect and categorize digitized traditional Chinese paintings. *Pattern Precognition Letters, 27*(2006), 734–746. https://doi.org/10.1016/j.patrec.2005.10.017

Karr, J. E., Graham, R. B., Hofer, S. M., & Muniz-Terrera, G. (2018). When does cognitive decline begin? A systematic review of change point studies on accelerated decline in cognitive and neurological outcomes preceding mild cognitive impairment, dementia, and death. *Psychology and Aging, 33*(2), 195–218. PMID: 29658744 PMCID: PMC5906105. https://doi.org/10.1037/pag0000236.

Kao, H. S. (2010). Calligraphy therapy: A complementary approach to psychotherapy. *Asia Pacific Journal of Counselling and Psychotherapy, 1*(1), 55–66. https://doi.org/10.1080/21507680903570334

Kao, H. S., Lam, S. P., & Kao, T. T. (2018). Chinese calligraphy handwriting (CCH): A case of rehabilitative awakening of a coma patient after stroke. *Neuropsychiatric Disease and*

Treatment, *2018*(14), 407–417. PMID: 29440902 PMCID: PMC5798538. https://doi.org/10. 2147/NDT.S147753.

Kao, H. S., Wang, M., Yu, S., Yuan, S., Fung, M. M. Y., Zhu, L., Lam, S. P. W., Kao, T. T., & Kao, X. (2019). Treatment effects of acupuncture and calligraphy training on cognitive abilities in senile demented patients. *Chinese Medicine and Culture*, *2*(2), 95–98. https://doi.org/10. 4103/CMAC.CMAC_18_19

Köttl, H., Fallahpour, M., Hedman, A., Nygård, L., & Kottorp, A. (2021). Depression, everyday technology use and life satisfaction in older adults with cognitive impairments: a cross-sectional exploratory study. *Scandinavian Journal of Caring Sciences*, *35*(1), 233–243. PMID: 32200561. https://doi.org/10.1111/scs.12838 .

Lawton, M. (1986). *Environment and Aging* (2nd ed.). Albany.

Lui, X., Niu, X., Feng, Q. & Liu, Y. (2014). Effects of five element music therapy on elderly people with seasonal affective disorder in Chinese nursing home. *Journal of Traditional Chinese Medicine*, *34*(2), 159–161. PMID: 24783926. https://doi.org/10.1016/s0254-6272(14) 60071-6.

Martyr, A., Nelis, S., Quinn, C., Wu, Y., Lamont, R., Henderson, C., & Clare, L. (2018). Living well with dementia: A systematic review and correlational meta-analysis of factors associated with quality of life, well-being and life satisfaction in people with dementia. *Psychological Medicine*, *48*(13), 2130–2139. PMID: 29734962. https://doi.org/10.1017/S0033291718000405 .

Nyman, S. R., & Szymczynska, P. (2016). Meaningful activities for improving the wellbeing of people with dementia: beyond mere pleasure to meeting fundamental psychological needs. *Perspectives in Public Health*, *136*(2), 99–107. PMID: 26933079. https://doi.org/10.1177/ 1757913915626193.

Pool, J. (2012). *The Pool Activity Level (PAL) Instrument for occupational profiling* (3rd ed.). Jessica Kingsley Publishers.

Pool, J., & Collier, L. (in press). Pool activity levels outcome measure.

Prince, M., Wimo, A., Guerchet, M., Ali, G.-C., Wu, Y.-T., & Prina, M. (2015). *World Alzheimer Report 2015 – The Global Impact of Dementia: An Analysis of Prevalence, Incidence*. Cost and Trends. Alzheimer's Disease International.

Scarmeas, N., Levy, G., Tang, M., Manly, J., & Stern, Y. (2001). Influences of leisure activity on the incidence of Alzheimer's disease. *Neurology*, *57*(12), 2236–2242. PMID: 11756603 PMCID: PMC3025284. https://doi.org/10.1212/wnl.57.12.2236.y

Shek, D. T. L., Kao, H. S. R., & Chau, A. W. L. (1986). Attentional resources allocation process in different modes of handwriting control. In: Kao H. S. R., van Galen G. P., & Hoosain R. (Eds.) *Graphonomics: Contemporary research in handwriting* (pp. 289–304). Elsevier Science Publilshers B.V., North-Holland. Amsterdam.

Shiells, K., Pivodic, L., Holmerová, I., & Van den Block, L. (2020). Self-reported needs and experiences of people with dementia living in nursing homes: A scoping review. *Aging & Mental Health*, *24*(10), 1553–1568. PMID: 31163987. https://doi.org/10.1080/13607863.2019. 1625303.

Sultzer, D. L., Levin, H. S., Mahler, M. E., High, W. M., & Cummings, J. (1992). Assessment of cognitive, psychiatric and behavioural disturbance in patients with dementia: The neurobehavioural rating scale. *Journal of the American Geriatric Society*, *40*(6), 549–555. https://doi. org/10.1111/j.1532-5415.1992.tb02101.x

Yuanyuan Yin is an Associate Professor at the Winchester School of Art, University of Southampton. Her research has been concentrated on promoting business performance through developing design and brand strategies, understanding customers and users, supporting design collaboration, and improving innovation in product design. In recent years, she focused on research in inclusive service design for the ageing population. She has received more than 556 k grants income from ESRC, British Council, Confucius Institute Headquarter and the University of Southampton.

Lesley Collier is Head of Department at the Faculty of Health and Well-being, University of Winchester. Her research focuses on the use of sensory approaches with people with dementia and the effect of the environment on performance. Her work has resulted in collaboration with International Ministries of Health, NGOs, and industry.

Service Design Methods: Re-Envisioning Infection Practice Ecologies in Nursing to Address Antimicrobial Resistance (AMR)

21

Alison Prendiville, Colin Macduff, and Fernando Carvalho

Abstract

Antimicrobial resistance (AMR), whereby antibiotics no longer work against bacterial infections, poses a global threat to human health. Within healthcare practices, nursing has been highlighted for its under-utilisation to prevent the advancement of AMR, particularly given the multiple responsibilities nurses have within clinical environments and in community settings. Concurrently, international and national institutions have recognised that to deal with the complexity of AMR, interdisciplinary collaborations are required that extend beyond the medical sciences to incorporate not only the social sciences but also arts and humanities. This chapter presents the role of service design methods in a UKRI AHRC funded research project re-envisioning practice ecologies in nursing (RIPEN) with community and hospital nurses to explore the co-development of interventions to prevent the spread of AMR. The work focuses on the use of co-design as visual storytelling, mappings and provocations, integrated with material from historical archives, and guided by the Design Council's Double Diamond process model. Drawing specifically on four workshops delivered from the London Lab, this chapter reveals the

A. Prendiville (✉)
Elephant and Castle, LCC, University of the Arts London (UAL), London 1 6SB, England
e-mail: a.prendiville@lcc.arts.ac.uk

C. Macduff
87 Hammerfield Avenue, Aberdeen, Scotland AB10 7FD, UK
e-mail: colinmacduff@talktalk.net

F. Carvalho
School of Design, San Francisco State University, San Francisco, USA
e-mail: fcarvalho@sfsu.edu

opportunities for service design methods, to uncover the implicit knowledge and creativity that nurses use in their daily practices. By adopting these innovative practices, we were able to harness new ways of giving agency to the nurses, questioning the issues of AMR whilst also imaging new futures to inform policy.

21.1 Introduction

Design's role within healthcare settings has a long and established history (Tsekleves and Cooper, 2017) culminating in the recent launch in 2017 of the Design for Health Journal, a specialist publication presenting and critically engaging with design's role in delivering not only the tangible elements of healthcare communications and products but increasingly focusing attention on the design of healthcare service experiences and examining its more transformational and organisational role as a facilitator for innovation (Wolstenholme et al., 2017). Sangiorgi, (2011) identified early on in service design's emergence, the changing role of SD practitioners in 'moving from providing solutions to a specific problem to supporting organisations with the tools and capabilities for human centred service innovation' (p.31). Equally, since its arrival in 2005–2006, Experience-Based Co-Design (EBCD) (Bate & Robert, 2006) has been widely adopted as a design informed approach to healthcare quality improvement, that borrows from participatory and user experience (Donetto et al., 2015).

Core to the ambit of service design in healthcare settings is the use of co-design visualisation methods that are central to facilitating collaborations between multiple stakeholders as a mode of knowledge co-production that reveals insider perspectives (Sevaldson, 2013). Initially offered as a set of tools and methods for collaboration (Stickdorn & Schneider, 2010), co-design is increasingly viewed as an experiential phenomenon that amplifies ways of knowing (Akama & Prendiville, 2013) and which crosses-over into design anthropology (Kilbourn, 2013). Central to these interdisciplinary ways of working is the enactment of disruption, whereby creative practices and research enquiry actively seek to defamiliarise and make strange, our assumptions and to open up new ways of seeing or thinking (Akama, Pink & Sumartojo, 2018). This disruption is recognised by the authors as 'inviting participants and research collaborators to journey into new ways of questioning what is happening, what can be imagined and what is possible' (p.49). Such creative knowledge forming interactions have particular relevance in health care where empathy, listening and capturing lived experiences within complex socio-material and I would add biological entanglements, do not offer linear or off the shelf responses. Thus, to capture and render visible the quotidian experiences and knowledge that are recursive and often implicit, requires Service Design to initiate collaborative forms of inquiry that are creative, dialogical and reflexive so to enable the participants to question assumptions in order to meaningfully envision new futures.

For Shove (2007), practices themselves bring knowledge and competencies to the fore with these in themselves being social products (Law, 1992). For De La Cadena and Blaser (2018), knowledge is revealed by making conceptual or material through procedures that need to be recognisable. Thus, methods and tools so intrinsic to service design are in themselves knowledge making, meaning they have the potential to enact and make visible forms of knowledge such as those relating to AMR, microbes and nursing. To be truly impactful, Vink, (2019) advocates for a more strategic practice in the form of service eco-design that extends well beyond service design's focus into actors everyday lives. Instead, she proposes a focus on building knowledge and the ability of the actors 'to intentionally adapt social structures and recognize their own agency in influencing the service systems they are part of'(135).

With this in mind RIPEN—re-envisioning infection practice ecologies in nursing —aimed to collaborate and co-design with a range of nurses and related healthcare practitioners, to address the challenge of AMR through the use of Service Design methods as part of a broader Arts and Humanities Research approach. This chapter focuses on the four workshops undertaken at the London Lab over a 12 month period, which informed and led to the culmination of a shared policy workshop with our Glasgow Lab partners, at the Royal College of Nursing (RCN) in London with 38 healthcare and related practitioners.

21.2 Background

AMR and Nursing

Antimicrobial resistance is a global concern with the UK's previous Chief Medical Officer Dame Sally Davies reporting (2011) on the rapid increase of resistant strains of bacteria and the catastrophic threat that this poses to the long-term sustainability of public health. She notes the misuse and overuse of antimicrobials in both human and animal health that has led to the current crisis, and presents this as a major threat to modern health systems of all types, as treating infections and undertaking routine operations are all dependent upon effective antibiotics. One of the many recommendations to come out of the report was is the importance placed on engagement with key stakeholders particularly the public, patient organisations and healthcare workers.

As the largest professional healthcare workforce globally, nurses should be actively engaged and have extensive influence on this issue. Nurses have numerous daily interactions with healthy and ill individuals, family members, community groups and other care professionals (Macduff et al., 2020). As such, they have many potential opportunities to enact antimicrobial stewardship practices such as education to help lessen inappropriate demand for antibiotics or ensuring that these drugs are prescribed and administered optimally (Macduff et al., 2020). Additionally, the effective use of Infection, Prevention and Control (IPC) measures as highlighted in the WHO (2013) report also lends itself to the daily practices of nurses and AMR, in hospital environments and in the community.

However, to date, the profession has been under-utilised to actively engage in the prevention of AMR advancing or to countenance the consequences of failure (Macduff et al., 2020). The authors also point to Survey research in the UK and beyond (e.g. NHS Education for Scotland 2014; (Mostaghim et al., 2017)) that indicates that nurses often struggle to substantively develop antimicrobial stewardship (AMS) practices within their roles, with low levels of understanding of AMS, time/workload constraints and ingrained habits and attitudes all cited as impeding factors. Although the authors recognise a number of AMR toolkits developed for staff (e.g. TARGET Public Health England 2015), they further highlight that many of the AMR initiatives covering nursing so far have had a top-down tendency, in effect instructing the staff what to do offering them very little agency. For Macduff et al. (2019), this situational analysis points to a relative lack of engagement with, and ownership of, this agenda contributing to a lack of meaningfulness of the espoused AMR agenda for enactment in practice.

Chandler et al. (2016:6) recommends that consideration for AMR needs to go beyond the 'remit of behaviour of patients, prescribers and to embrace broader social material and other lives that make up the problem of AMR'. The authors further state, the importance of knowing how AMR is enacted (debated, discussed, identified and acted upon) and what forms these take in different settings, as this will increase our understanding of AMR. For RIPEN, AMR was framed as an ecological issue involving the conjunction of people, places and pathogens with the work of nurses typically located at this nexus and manifested in ecologies of practice (Macduff et al., 2020). Concomitantly, the invisibility of pathogens resistant to antibiotics through their entanglement and movement with people and places means that they can be difficult to conceptualise by individuals and can thus be a key causative factor in healthcare-associated infections (HAIs) (Macdonald et al. 2017). Similarly, AMR and some of its consequences are normally invisible, and this is true generally across everyday work in healthcare settings (Macduff et al., 2020; MacDonald et al. 2017). For Macduff et al. (2020), the invisibility further extends to the antibiotics themselves following injection or ingestion, and within community settings their storage, accessibility and disposability may be determined by multiple care staff or family members. Thus, AMR, in hospital and community care service delivery, can be an abstract and messy concept that contrasts with the many manifest and pressing demands on staff. Because of these practice ecologies, the following research questions were formulated to scaffold the workshop activities and the co-design activities.

Research Questions

How can relevant arts and humanities-based approaches help nurses to re-envisage their infection control practice ecologies in response to antimicrobial resistance? For the purposes of this paper, we specifically focus on the four London workshops with the focus on service design methods to investigate the following subsidiary questions:

(1) How do groups of hospital and community-based nurses understand and respond to the priorities and consequences of antimicrobial resistance (AMR) within the context of their everyday working lives?

(2) How can co-design and visualisation-based approaches help these nurses to identify and construct sets of meaningful practices that optimise present prevention of AMR?

(3) How can co-design, visualisation, history and other relevant arts and humanities approaches help nurses to re-imagine and re-envisage their infection control practice ecologies in a future with minimal or no effective antibiotics?

(4) What priority issues and other questions does this initial enquiry raise, and how can these best inform policy and planning, education and further research?

21.3 Methodology

To fully contextualise the four workshops, the following provides a logistical summary of the complete workshop programme undertaken between June 2018 and July 2019 at both the London and Glasgow Labs, plus the final policy workshop delivered at the Royal College of Nursing (RCN).

- 8 Workshops 4 × Glasgow and 4 × London, plus a final and joint policy workshop in London. In total 20 nurses from different backgrounds, community, hospital and IPC participated at the two sites.
- Each workshop was approximately 4–4.5 h long.
- Pre-workshop participation on a VLE in preparation of the workshops.
- For each workshop collectively 32 person/hours in total was committed.
- In total, 256 hours of participation were given to the RIPEN project by the nurses at the two locations.
- A final policy workshop in London with an interdisciplinary group of healthcare practitioners was delivered with 38 participants in October 2019.

Each of the workshops corresponded to the Discovery, Define, Develop and Deliver frame to scaffold the design of the activities to the research questions as a process of iterative learning, Fig. 21.1. By working with the same group of participants over a year, the workshops were designed to be responsive and provide continuity as the different teams, explored ideas, built-up dialogical relationships and shared ways of knowing.

The research had a 'dual Lab' structure whereby the team's London-based researchers had backgrounds primarily in design and collaborated predominantly with community-based nurses over the course of the year with the nurses having the following experiences and roles: District nurse team manager; community mental health nurse; community nurse/district nursing student; rehabilitation nurse case manager; community nurse (medical screening); community occupational health nurse; health advisor nurse; IPC consultant nurse (hospital groups); IPC nurse (Ministry of Defence).

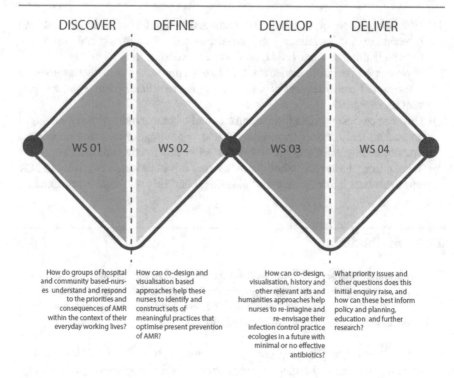

Fig. 21.1 Prendiville, MacDuff and Carvalho. *Source* Author's own illustration (2021)

Concurrently, the team's Glasgow-based researchers had backgrounds in nursing and health service research and worked predominantly with hospital-based staff. This approach afforded opportunities for each Lab to explore the research questions from a range of nursing perspectives, whilst following and maintaining an overall continuity of approach. Through these parallel sessions, divergent and convergent thinking, directed through specific activities scaffolded the exploration of nursing within the context of AMR and IPC. Workshop 1 (WS01) Table 21.1 and Workshop 2 (WS02) Table 21.2 addressed the first two research questions which align with the 'discover and define' stages of the Double Diamond with Workshop 3 (WS03) Table 21.3 and Workshop 4 (WS04) Table 21.4 responding to the 3rd and 4th research questions. The focus of this chapter is on the 4 London workshops as these collaborative encounters specifically utilised Service Design with the combination of historical archives in WS3 to explore practice ecologies of nurses and AMR. The following section provides four summary tables, presenting the structure and activities for each of the workshops and corresponding to the following headings:

- the research questions that the workshop was linked to;
- the rationale for its use in re-envisioning practice ecologies in nursing;

- the overall objectives of the workshop
- the activities used to scaffold the thinking.

Summary Tables of the 4 London Lab Workshops (Tables 21.1, 21.2, 21.3, and 21.4).

Table 21.1 Summary of Workshop 01, including the research question, raiontale, objectives and activities

Workshop 01 London: Visualising Narratives around AMR/IPC from a Personal and Professional Perspective	
Research Questions:	How do groups of hospital and community based nurses understand and respond to the priorities and consequences of antimicrobial resistance (AMR) within the context of their everyday working lives?
Rationale:	To use creative, co-design methods to elicit the participant's understandings of, and responses to, the priorities and consequences of AMR within their everyday working and personal lives.
Objectives:	• Collect your initial thoughts on how antimicrobial resistance and antibiotics impact on your daily life outside the work setting and your definition of AMR; • Gain insights into the main activities and contexts which make up your typical working day; • Understand your perspective of infections and AMR hotspots; • Identify how infections and AMR practices feature in your daily routine; • Gather your opinion on the cause and effect of infection and AMR practices.
ACT 01: Quick fire questions	Using prompt questions to obtain a snapshot of how the participants see and use antibiotics in their everyday lives, within and outside the work setting;
ACT 02a: My role and routine	Participants were asked to complete the 8-box storyboard template to represent a day in the life of a district nurse including encounters relating to antibiotics;
ACT 02b: Infection hotspots on the storyboard	Using red stickers, participants needed to highlight on their storyboard where they encounter particular AMR and IPC practices. Then, were then required to provide and explanation for their choices;
ACT 03a: AMR as a concern in your daily practices	In pairs, participants were then asked to use a marker to prioritise on a spectrum issues of high to low concerns, providing the rationale for the positioning of each AMR, IPC-related issue;
ACTO 03b: Cause and effect of AMR	Participants were asked to create a visual narrative (comprising six steps) around the cause and effect of AMR, using and images (collage, drawings, diagrams, etc.);
ACT 04: Have I got Infection Control News for you	Encouraging people to complete the missing words on provocative newspaper headlines.
Final	Facilitated group discussions and evaluation of works

Source Author's own illustration (2021)

Table 21.2 Summary of Workshop 02, including the research question, raiontale, objectives and activities.

Workshop 02 London: Defining individual and Collective Priorities to Think about Solutions for AMR and the Role of Nurses	
Research Questions:	How can co-design and visualisation based approaches help these nurses identify and construct sets of meaningful practices that optimise present prevention of AMR?
Rationale:	Building from the results of Workshop 1, participants were required to use creative, co-design methods to support the development of interventions of ideas to address key AMR issues, previously identified by the group. This workshop aimed at highlighting the roles placed by nurses in the development, enactment and implementation of interventions. The participants were expected to undertake the following:
Objectives:	•Discuss different approaches to solving AMR-related issues, according to individual and collective points of view; •Support the participatory development of intervention ideas around previously identified AMR issues; •Explore the ways in which interventions could be materialised in relation to four specific modes of delivery: policy making, social prescription; technology-based; and education and training; •Facilitate the establishment of agreed-upon priorities of action, considering the different roles of nurses with the community and the hospital environments.
ACT 00: VLE Themes and issues – Intervention ideas—Role of nurses	Working from a template, sent via e-mail, participants started identifying areas and themes of priority to nurses and how they would initially envision change to the practice
ACT 01: Introduction to Workshop 02	Team deliver a brief presentation in order to bring participants back to the project via establishing a shared platform regarding timeline, objectives, information and plans.
ACT 02: Initial intervention ideas presentation	Each participant presents their individual work, giving other participants an opportunity to learn about the proposals their colleagues have had generated.
ACT 03: Prioritise (and rationale for choice)	Groups determine which issues and ideas individually developed are relevant or urgent and why, according to their shared perspective.
ACT 04a: Giving shape to the group's ideas	One intervention solution per group is developed and described, based on the prompting questions to provide a common basis for intergroup comparison to complement and critique.

(continued)

Table 21.2 (continued)

Workshop 02 London: Defining individual and Collective Priorities to Think about Solutions for AMR and the Role of Nurses	
Research Questions:	How can co-design and visualisation based approaches help these nurses identify and construct sets of meaningful practices that optimise present prevention of AMR?
ACT 04b: Provocation	Groups explore how interventions manifest differently when considering specific means to support the enactment or implementation of the interventions.
ACT 05: Feedback and reflection, plus prioritising final ideas	All participants discuss the ideas proposed by each group and select the top 2 intervention proposals that are most relevant and urgent and why?
Final	Closing remarks, next steps, participants' feedback.

Source Author's own illustration (2021)

Table 21.3 Summary of Workshop 03, including the research question, raiontale, objectives and activities.

Workshop 03 London: Historical Reflections and Future Projections on AMR/IPC Nursing Practices	
Research Questions:	How can co-design, visualisation, history and other relevant arts and humanities approaches help nurses to reimagine and re-envisage their infection control practice ecologies in a future with minimal or no antibiotics?
Rationale:	To reflect upon how various artefacts, standards and practices have contributed to past and present changes to nursing practice by selecting and reflecting on 2–3 images from a choice of 13 selected from the Kings College London and Wellcome Trust online archives. To, then, look at how these may further contribute to changes to the profession in a future with minimal or no effective antibiotics. The workshop aims at exploring how these issues manifest across different levels of change identified from Workshop 1: - Policy (Nation, Councils, white papers); - System (NHS, CCGs, hospitals, clinics, community care); - Practice (wards, departments, teams, individuals)
Objectives:	• Elicit reflection on how artefacts, standards and innovations have impact and changed past nursing practices (focusing on AMR/IPC); • Explore how some selected historical artefacts and innovations contributed to determine the expectations and aspirations of nursing practice in the past; • Explore how some current artefacts and innovations contribute to the nursing practice of today and how some imagined artefacts and innovations can

(continued)

Table 21.3 (continued)

Workshop 03 London: Historical Reflections and Future Projections on AMR/IPC Nursing Practices	
Research Questions:	How can co-design, visualisation, history and other relevant arts and humanities approaches help nurses to reimagine and re-envisage their infection control practice ecologies in a future with minimal or no antibiotics?
	contribute to the nursing practice in a future with limited availability of effective antibiotics; • Reflect on how innovations across different levels of change interact to facilitate meaningful improvements to the nursing profession in the past, present and particularly, in a future with limited availability of effective antibiotics
ACT 00: The past of nursing practice and AMR/IPC	Participants are required to choose 2–3 images from a selection hosted on the project's website to reflect on how artefacts, standards and innovations have impacted and changed past nursing practices. Participants were asked to consider two questions in relation to the selection: • How does the image, and what it represents to you, portray issues that have contributed to change in the healthcare system broadly, as well as specifically in relation to AMR? • In what ways do the images elicit relevant aspects of current IPC/AMR nursing practices?
ACT 01: Mapping of selected images	Each participant used stickers to identify the images they have chosen from the website on a visual board. Participants are required to draw lines connecting the images selected using markers.
ACT 02: Rationale for choice, and reflections	To get a sense of how the participants saw the artefacts and other innovations affecting/changing past and present nurses' practice, each was asked to talk about the choice of their images
ACT 03: Historical Perspectives on nursing practice	Participants are divided into groups of 2 and 3 people to further explore how the selected historical artefacts and innovations have contributed to determine the expectations and aspirations of nursing practices (with a focus on AMR/IPC)
ACT 04: Looking back at the levels of change in practice	Participants are required to plot historical artefacts and innovations onto a large map divided into three levels: policy/systems/practices; to, then reflect on how these levels interact to facilitate meaningful changes to the nursing profession in the past
ACT 05: Future Perspectives on nursing practice	Participants are supplied with template tools to explore the context and use of certain artefacts, standards, practices and professional relationships concerning present future nursing practice
ACT 06: Looking forward to the levels of change in practice	Participants are required to plot the artefacts they analysed in ACT05 onto the same template of ACT 04
Final	Closing remarks, next steps, participants' feedback

Source Author's own illustration (2021)

Table 21.4 Summary of Workshop 04, including the research question, raiontale, objectives and activities.

Workshop 04 London: Translating Process and Practice into Policy on AMR and IPC	
Research Questions:	*What priority issues and other questions does this initial enquiry raise, and how can these best inform policy and planning?*
Rationale:	Working from the lessons learnt and the accumulated developments of all the previous workshops, we applied a variety of creative and analytical methods to identify priority areas, targeted at diverse groups of stakeholders across the healthcare service environment. The purpose was also directed as proposing improvements, thinking about how assessment and evaluation would change, as well as to design and enact policies focused on improving nursing practices, education and future AMR/IPC research
Objectives:	• Select individual and group priority areas for policy change and action, looking into the future role and practices of nurses concerning AMR/ICP within a context with limited effective antibiotics; • Identify key stakeholder within a comprehensive landscape of healthcare service provision (government agencies, politicians, practitioners, members of the public, etc.); • Outline the specifics of what changes need to be implemented, along with clear guidelines for assessing key indicators of change • Identify what is needed to be done by whom in order to enable policies to become effective; • Design policy pathways to enable future actions concerning the demands, opportunities, roles and responsibilities of nurses and other stakeholders in order to improve AMR/ICP practice and the quality of the healthcare services provided to patients; • Draft statements that communicate the policy pathways to their specific audiences
ACT 01: Selecting areas of priority	From a selected list (taken from previous workshop activities) participants were asked to select and cut—first individually then in groups—the priority AMR and IPC areas to focus on
ACT 02: Identifying key stakeholders and ambitions for change	Participants were then required to identify the main stakeholders affected or involved within a comprehensive landscape of healthcare service provision connected to the priority areas. The groups were required to pair their chosen priorities and stakeholders to ambitions set by the UK government in its plan to tackle AMR (Tackling antimicrobial resistance, 2019–2024; The UK's National Action Plan).

(continued)

Table 21.4 (continued)

Workshop 04 London: Translating Process and Practice into Policy on AMR and IPC	
Research Questions:	*What priority issues and other questions does this initial enquiry raise, and how can these best inform policy and planning?*
ACT 03: Making and assessing change	The next step was for groups to think of interventions and how change will be assessed, considering: What needs to change? What does change look like? What are the indicators of change?
ACT 04: Enabling changes to become effective	Once the group had determined the nature, shape and form of change (and how changes will be evaluated), participants were asked to consider: Who needs to do what? What other provisions and resources are required?
ACTO 05: Designing policy pathways	Each group was required to design a policy pathway using the supporting templates by combing areas of priority and key stakeholders, ambitions for change, innovations and evaluations, and necessary enablers
ACT 06: Writing policy statements	This final activity required the participants to draft a policy statement for a time when the use of antibiotics would have limited of no effect. The statements needed to account for an overarching approach to action and change
Final	Final: Discussion, closing remarks, participant's feedback.

Source Author's own illustration (2021)

21.4 Findings

Workshop 1

The activities for Workshop 1 focused on creating a shared understanding amongst all the participants on the personal and professional use of antibiotics. By prompting questions on the use and disposal of antibiotics within these frames, the participants shared their knowledge and experience of using antibiotics. Visualisation of daily practices was explored through storyboards, with the nurses creating rich descriptive visual narratives of their encounters with AMR and how they enacted practices to manage the complexity of IPC and antibiotic use, Fig. 21.2.

The analysis of the visual materials from the first London workshop identified emerging themes, recurring concerns and areas for future development. AMR and IPC were considered by most to be of high priority, with the nurses identifying three levels; affecting society in general (macro-level—policy, national councils, white papers) as well as healthcare organisations and services (meso-level—NHS, Care Commissioning Groups CCGs, clinics, community care); and individuals (micro-level—wards, departments, teams and individuals).

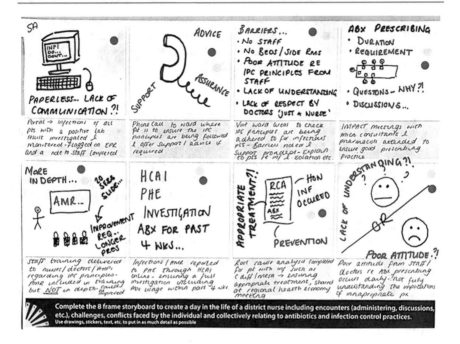

Fig. 21.2 Storyboard generated from Workshop 01, providing a visual narrative representing the challenges and encounters of dealing with AMR. The storyboard also includes activities 2a and 2b, showing the location of AMR hotspots and IPC for a participant nurse, and the complexity of dealing with AMR in their daily activities. *Source* Participant Workshop 01 (2021)

The misuse or overuse of antibiotics and the resulting resistance to the positive effects of such drugs is also seen as a complex issue, which, in the perception of the participants, is related to, or aggravated by, multiple factors including (but not limited to): an ageing population with comorbidities and chronic conditions; an increase in international travelling and mobility; and differences in knowledge and practice around AMR across the health system and professional specialisations. Routines and embeddedness of antibiotic use within healthcare practices were acknowledged for their entanglement in their daily use. Some participants also made connections between their everyday practice, their home lives, and the wider economic, political and social drivers of AMR. Importance was also given to how boundaries are conceptualised and managed. Imagined and real physical boundaries were highlighted by a number of the participants, including managing 'microbiological boundaries' and 'macro' boundaries between care settings and among professionals and the public.

These results informed the planning and structuring of the activities of Workshop 2, which aimed at using creative, co-design methods to support the development of intervention ideas to address some pressing AMR issues, previously identified by the participants.

Reflections

The role of co-design in Workshop 1 began a process of transformation for the participants. As a group of nurses who were unfamiliar with each others personal and work experiences, each activity was designed to facilitate a coming together as a collective and creative endeavour to share stories and practices relating to AMR. The visual story boarding and sharing experiences were highlighted as enhancing knowledge exchange and reflection with one participant noting the most valuable moment in the workshop:

'Listening to others' viewpoints 'the day in the life of' (visual exercise) because it strongly illustrated the clinical struggle of frontline nurses.'

Reflecting on what had been learnt from the first workshop a participant responded:

'I learnt to be creative and imaginative at story-telling, I increased my knowledge about AMR'.

Workshop 2

This workshop focused on visualisation-based approaches in assisting nurses to identify and construct meaningful practices that optimise present prevention of AMR. Three priority areas were identified from Workshop 1 and these included: health literacy work; improving surveillance and handover processes for people returning from international travel who have health issues that may increase AMR. To respond to these a series of activities facilitated the development of individual and collective ideas to tackle primary AMR-related concerns of nurses and those previously identified in the first workshop. These priorities were structured into a template, in order to support the development of interventions, with consideration given to the role of nurses in the proposed changes. The aim was to start identifying areas and themes of individual priority to participants, and how they initially envision changes in their practice. These formed the basis of Workshop 2 and took the participants on a journey of collective creativity to draw on their insights from practice to offer and interrogate solutions.

By working through their interventions in groups applying collage and drawing, the participants were able to envision how they would work and the changes that they would promote, Fig. 21.3. The participants jointly prioritised four ideas and collectively developed these considering: the respective target populations for the interventions: how they would work: and what changes they would promote. The four intervention ideas are summarised follows:

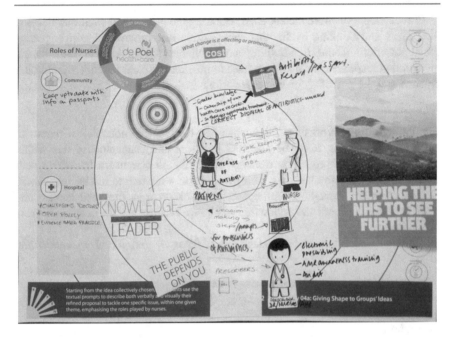

Fig. 21.3 In Activity 4a, a design tool template supported the collective development of chosen interventions to tackle AMR. *Source* Author's own illustration (2021)

(1) A 'My health App/Health Passport'. This idea would make of technology and data to support patients and carers.

(2) An electronic prescribing and prompt system. This idea builds on the difficulties experienced by some of the participating community nurses concerning acess and consulting patients' antibiotic prescribing status and history.

(3) A disposable antibiotic record. Aiming to address broader concerns around the correct disposable of antibiotics, this idea would make use of the integrated patient data to build a historical record of the patient's antibiotic intake whilst including a service solution whereby collection and correct disposal of antibiotics and other drugs are controlled and accounted for.

(4) A home Starter Health Kit. The Kit targeted at older patients and patients with chronic conditions in homecare, would include a number of materials, (such as a measuring cup, a medicine/antibiotic calendar, recording book) to facilitate and increase active participation of patients, families and carers. The Kit would also include features to facilitate monitoring and communication, mediating interactions with health staff during routine visits and when patients go to GP appointments or clinic appointments.

Provocation tools were then applied, requiring the participants to further develop their ideas and thinking by framing them within one of four categories: policy, social prescription, education/training and a technology. The visual enactments and provocation responses enabled the nurses to imagine different realities around their practice and the potential for implementation.

Reflections

The findings from Workshop 2 demonstrated the creative potential of nurses to enact change relating to AMR and IPC practices and conceptualise this within different frames. The process also elicited some of their current frustrations of their own limited agency in managing their own practices relating to minimising AMR. Reflecting on the workshop, participants fed back on what they had learned and what had been valued, the following responses encapsulate the responses from participants:

'*Creativity, plasticity and representation of ideas* via *design and communication tools*',

'*Working collaboratively, with colleagues, brain storming, defining and materialising one particular project idea*'.

Workshop 3

Building from extensive analysis of historical images from the Kings College Nursing archive and the Wellcome Trust collection, thirteen historical artefacts relating to five eras of AMR/IPC from 1870 onwards were selected for participants to consider how their practice might manifest in 2030 and any related implications for current practice, Fig. 21.4.

The explanation for their choice provoked discussions on what had been lost in current nursing practices compared to different points in time and also what could be learnt to tackle AMR/IPC. In 'the capacity of design to envision and give shape to new possibilities' (Halse et al. 2019), these artefacts acted as reflexive catalysts to revisit AMR and IPC within different historical frames and interrogate what this meant for nursing practices.

Once the interpretations had been negotiated, the participants considered their choice of artefacts at the different levels of change Fig. 21.5.

The related boards detailed many issues and opportunities including:

- A need to reconsider contexts for care, with much more prevention and treatments in the community;
- Hospitals being used more for complex cases and isolation;
- Changes to hospital architecture to support IPC;
- The need for changing our healthcare workforce composition and skills set accordingly (e.g. development in cleaning roles so this is recognised as a professional role);
- The 'pharmaceuticalisation' of products aimed at promoting a healthy mirobiome;

Fig. 21.4 Workshop 03 outputs for activities 01 and 02, mapping the connections between the nurses choice of images relating to AMR and IPC, and providing a rationale to explaine the choice and linkage between the images. *Source* Author's own illustration (2021)

- More use of technology to facilitate patient care, record keeping and televisual communication;
- Change in how we relate to other species e.g. domestic animals may no longer be possible if antibiotics are unavailable to treat, for example cat bites.

Reflections

The activities and support templates developed for this workshop articulated a combination of analytical reflection of past and current practice with the creative exploration of future possibilities. The workshop further sough to position this approach within an encompassing perspective of change making framed by three levels: practice (micro), systems (meso) and policy (macro) levels. This structuring enabled consideration to be given to moving current priority ideas towards policy Fig. 21.5.

When asked about the most valuable moments in the workshop and what did you value and why? The following feedback was given:

The poster/collage allowed reflection on cause and effect with good discussion.

'I found it valuable hearing about other participant's practices and what is most challenging for them'.

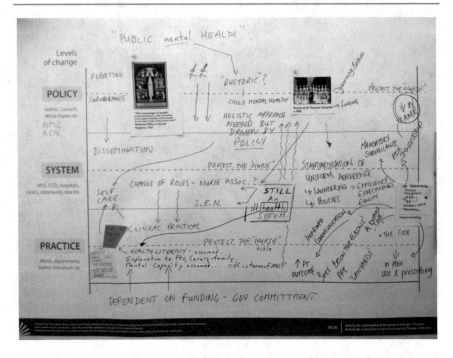

Fig. 21.5 Workshop 03 outputs for activity 04 and 06, converging the historical reflections on AMR and nursing on different levels of the nursing system. *Source* Author's own illustration (2021)

Workshop 4

Design tools and activities were once again informed from the previous workshops as an iterative process, with a synthesis of the outputs, for the identification of stakeholders, priority areas and improvements. In addition, the 'UK Government's Tackling antimicrobial resistance (2019–2024): The UK's five-year national action plan (2019)' report was used to frame Workshop 4 to address the Government's ambitions for change, as defined by the UK 2040 AMR vision, policy paper. To direct the workshop, a policy design wheel was used to represent the process.

In this final London workshop, participants engaged with tools that aimed at facilitating the construction of policy pathways and policy statements. The activities of this workshop were conceptualised as a result of the combined work from the three previous workshops. Priorities and relevant key stakeholders were singled-out and paired with the national ambitions for change. This led to an exploration of proposals for change, along with a reflection on the agendas and resources that would enable such change to be enacted. A stepwise template was then used to assist participants (practitioners, not policy-makers) to devise policy proposals, attuned to specified target audiences.

London participants further combined, defined and developed their priority ideas through a structured process to identify key considerations and produce related policy statements. Policy statements were conceived within a patient-centred approach, with the idea that they would reflect the priorities and ambitions in relation to the relevant stakeholders previously identified. The resulting policy statements were focused on:

- AMR: is everybody's business and everybody's responsibility
- AMR: National/local priority and emergency plan.

This exercise encapsulated the ultimate ambition of this project, which aimed at empowering practitioners, through the use of service design methods, by manifesting their value and expertise and lived experiences as tangible forms, to inform the making of effective policy and facilitate and enable real change to AMR/IPC, Fig. 21.6.

Reflections

The six activities designed around three design tools, scaffolded a process of change around a priority area identified from the earlier workshops. The purpose of each of the activities was to make tangible what change would look like and how it could be enacted through understanding the stakeholders, how it aligned with government

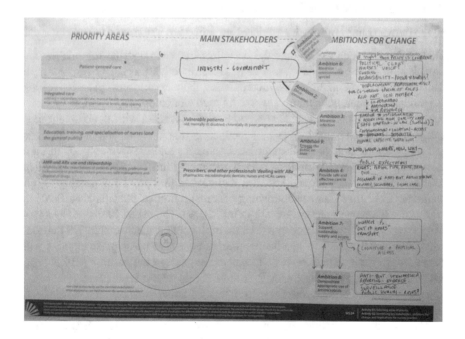

Fig. 21.6 Workshop 04 outputs for activity 01 and 02 shows how an earlier idea for a 'Health Passport' is aligned within broader government priorities and ambitions on the template as a form of making interventions responsive to Government action plans and tangible at a policy level. *Source* Author's own illustration (2021)

policy and also how change would be resourced and assessed. Once this had been identified and mapped the participants consolidated the information into a policy statement. By scaffolding this process of change as a further iteration from earlier workshops, the participants were able conceptualise change around AMR and IPC at a macro- and more strategic level.

'It was really interesting looking at bringing ideas together using different methods to what would usually have been used. I particularly enjoyed creating the story boards from the first session and seeing how everything linked together by the end. I also liked the pre-session exercise which involved looking at photographs and linking ideas together from them'.

'Brought a different depth to it (AMR / IPC) in terms of understanding and meant ... a lot more involved than in other research because the focus is different rather than just tick-sheets'.

'Discussion/ thought process of priorities and stakeholders; the importance of priorities and stakeholders in the change processes leading to policy. The change processes allowed clinical expertise / thought processes to be explored and developed'.

'I feel more aware of my own practice and feel able to advocate in a more informed way. Being exposed to some of the old photographs and news articles that other participants brought along also made me think about things in a different way, and equipped me with different methods to advocate regarding AMR. Overall, the whole process was really enjoyable and 'different' which enlightening'.

Reflections on SD Role in Re-envisioning Infection Practice Ecologies

Throughout the four workshops, the design of the tools and the formulation and organisation of the activities was a continuous, iterative process of responding to the proposals of the participants, incorporating their experiences, perspectives and the products of their collaborative work. As each workshop progressed, the creative confidence of the participants also grew as they interacted with the different tools and visualisations, so that by WS3 the facilitation was minimal, and the teams were self-propelled in their own interactions, discussions and creative outputs. In these instances, we observed co-design as a personal transformative process where relationships are made around complex and challenging problems, leading to 'eudaimonic wellbeing (human flourishing and realisation of potential) and hedonic well-being (happiness and pleasure)', (Vink, 2019). The visual forms of enactment from WS1 through to the conceptualisation of the policy statements in WS4 created what Vink (2019) notes as a collective designing where participants connect with others to establish shared interests to collaborate and in the case of RIPEN enact meaningful change relating to AMR at three levels within health care.

A key aspect of our approach was to engage with participants in the messiness of antibiotics usages and AMR not exclusively in relation to the nurse's professional roles but by also extending reflexivity into domestic and personal spheres. Donald (2016) notes how many AMR studies fail to acknowledge that professionals have multiple identities, including family life and citizenship. This was evident in many of the discussions including the use of antimicrobials in the home, promotion of health literacy and probiotics. This strengthened an emergent theme that AMR nursing is more than antibiotics and embraces multiple forms, such as microbial citizens (as recommended by Roe, Veal, and Hurley, 2019), creatively negotiating borderlands (Hinchliffe et al. 2013) and spanning contexts within the community such as the home and social care settings and in healthcare environments from hospitals to GP practices. Furthermore, we believe that by engaging in the use of visual methods to facilitate participants own perceptions of relevant AMR-related content has particular value, by rendering tangible the many contexts, conceptions, individual roles, team activities, materialities, porous and fluid boundaries, power relations and uncertainties that tend to characterise practice. The work of Olans et al., (2016) and Broom et al., (2017) suggest that such elements of AMR related to nursing can often be invisible or hidden from sight, marginalising nursing's presence and voice. Thus, the RIPEN approach centred on how to visually amplify practices relating to AMR and IPC in nursing, with it culminating in a policy workshop with the Glasgow Lab, to support the development of an updated government paper by the Professional Lead Infection Prevention and Control for AMR, at the Royal College of Nursing (RCN).

21.5 Conclusion

Nurses are at the front line of AMR and IPC praxis but are often overlooked in creating meaningful change when addressing the complex challenge of overuse and inappropriate use of antibiotics in hospitals and community settings. Such challenges are more than just medicines they are conceived within time pressures, existing infrastructures, complex human needs and power structures. Until recently AMR was very much seen as an area of attention for the biosciences with the interdisciplinary potential of the social sciences and lately Arts and Humanities only emerging since 2014. By using service design methods, with a diverse group of nurses, to visualise and to enact daily practices and reimagine new futures, we were able to demonstrate the creative potential of the group to re-envision and explore change in tackling AMR and IPC. Through these sessions, not only were the nurses able to co-produce knowledge on AMR as a shared experience, and make visible their tacit knowledge and experience this also gave the participants a sense of their own agency to enact change and to understand how policy may be informed through these experiences.

Acknowledgements This chapter is drawn from the London Lab work of the RIPEN Re-envisioning Practice Ecologies in Nursing research project, https://www.ripen.org.uk/. RIPEN was funded by the UK Research Arts and Humanities Research Council (AH/R002126/1). Special thanks must be made to all the nurse participants in the project and the supporting partners.

References

Akama, Y., Pink, S., & Sumartojo, S. (2018). Uncertainty and Possibility. New Approaches to Future Making in Design Anthropology. Bloomsbury, London.

Akama, Y., & Prendiville, A. (2013). A phenomenology of co-designing services: The craft of embodying, enacting and entangling design. *10th European Academy of Design Conference: Crafting the Future, April 17–19* (pp. 1–16). Gothenburg.

Bate, P., & Robert, G. (2006). Experience-based design: From redesigning the system around the patient to co-designing services with the patient. *Quality and Safety in Health Care, 15*(5), 307–310. https://doi.org/10.1136/qshc.2005.016527

Broom, A., Broom, J., Kirby, E., & Scambler, G. (2017). Nurses as antibiotic brokers: Institutionalized praxis in the hospital. *Qualitative Health Research, 27*(13), 1924–1935. https://doi.org/10.1177/1049732316679953

Contained and Controlled (2019). UK's 20-year vision for antimicrobial resistance. Policy Paper. HM Government Department of Health and Social Care (Ed.), London. Retrieved June 8, 2021, from https://www.gov.uk/government/publications/uk-20-year-vision-for-antimicrobial-resistance.

Chandler, C. Hutchinson, E., Hutchinson, C. (2016) Part 1. Applying social theory to antimicrobials in practice. In: Addressing antimicrobial resistance through social theory. An anthropologically oriented report London: London School of Hygiene & Tropical Medicine, supported by the Wellcome Trust. https://doi.org/10.17037/PUBS.03400500. Retrieved June 8, 2021, from https://researchonline.lshtm.ac.uk/id/eprint/3400500/1/Addressing%20Antimicrobial%20Resistance%20Through%20Social%20Theory%20GOLD%20VoR.pdf.

Davis, D. S. (2011). Annual of the chief medical officer (Vol. 2). Infections and the rise of antimicrobial resistance. Retrieved June 8, 2021, from https://www.gov.uk/government/publications/chief-medical-officer-annual-report-volume-2.

De La Cadena, M., & Blaser, M. (2018). Pluriverse, proposal for world of many worlds. In M. De La Cadena & M. Blaster (Eds.), *World of many wolrds* (pp. 13–60). Duke University Press.

Donetto, S., Pierri, P., Tsianakas, V., & Robert, G. (2015). Experiencebased co-design and healthcare improvement: Realizing participatory design in the public sector. *Design Journal, 18*(2), 227–248. https://doi.org/10.2752/175630615X14212498964312

Kilbourn, K. (2013). Tools and movements of engagement: Design anthropology's style of knowing. In W. Gunn, T. Otto, & R. C. Smith's (Eds.), *Design Anthropology* (pp. 68–82). Theory and Practice, Bloomsbury.

Law, J. (1992). Notes on the theory of the actor network: Ordering strategy and heterogenity. *Systems Practice, 5*(4), 379–393.

Macduff, C., Marie Rafferty, A., Prendiville, A., Currie, K., Castro-Sanchez, E., King, C., et al. (2020). Fostering nursing innovation to prevent and control antimicrobial resistance using approaches from the arts and humanities. *Journal of Research in Nursing, 25*(3), 189–207. https://doi.org/10.1177/1744987120914718

Macdonald, A., Macduff, C., Loudon, D., et al. (2017). Evaluation of a visual tool co-developed for training hospital staff on the prevention and control of the spread of healthcare associated infections. *Infection, Disease and Health, 22*(3), 105–116.

Mostaghim, M., Snelling, T., McMullan, B., Konecny, P., Bond, S., Adhikari, S., et al. (2017). Nurses are underutilised in antimicrobial stewardship – Results of a multisite survey in paediatric and adult hospitals. *Infection, Disease and Health, 22*(2), 57–64. https://doi.org/10.1016/j.idh.2017.04.003

Olans, R. N., Olans, R. D., & Demaria, A. (2016). The critical role of the staff nurse in antimicrobial stewardship - unrecognized, but already there. *Clinical Infectious Diseases, 62*(1), 84–89. https://doi.org/10.1093/cid/civ697

Roe, E., Veal, C., & Hurley, P. (2019). Mapping microbial stories: Creative microbial aesthetic and cross-disciplinary intervention in understanding nurses' infection prevention practices. *Geo: Geography and Environment, 6*(1), 1–20. https://doi.org/10.1002/geo2.76.

Royal College of General Practitioners (2015). TARGET Antibiotics Toolkit. Retrieved June 8, 2021, from https://www.rcgp.org.uk/clinical-and-research/resources/toolkits/amr/target-antibiotics-toolkit.aspx.

Sangiorgi, D. (2011). Transformative services and transformation design. *International Journal of Design, 5*(2), 29–40.

Sevaldson, B. (2013). Systems Oriented Design: The emergence and development of a designerly approach to address complexity. In: *Drs Cumulus 2013, 2nd International Conference for Design Education Researchers, Oslo, May, 14–17.* Retrieved June 8, 2021, from http://designforpublicservices.com/s/DRScumulusOslo2013_birger_sevaldson.pdf.

Shove, E., Watson, M., & Hand, M. (2007). *The Design of Everyday Life.* Berg Publishers.

Stickdorn, M., & Schneider, J. (2010). *This is service design thinking, basic, tools, cases.* Amsterdam: BIS.

Tackling Antimicrobial Resistance: UK's five year national action plan. January 2019. HM Government Department of Health and Social Care, Policy Paper. Retrieved June 8, 2021, from https://www.gov.uk/government/publications/uk-5-year-action-plan-for-antimicrobial-resistance-2019-to-2024

Tsekleves, E., & Cooper, R. (2017). *Design for health, design for social responsibility series.* Routledge Oxford: A Gower Book.

Vink, J. (2019). Visible- conceptualizing service ecosystem design. Retrieved June 8, 2021, from http://www.diva-portal.org/smash/record.jsf?pid=diva2%3A1313628&dswid=7912.

WHO (World Health Organisation) Advanced Infection Prevention and Control Training. Infection Prevention and Control (IPC) to combate antimicrobial resistance (AMR) in health care settings: trainer's guide. World Health Organization (WHO, Ed.). Retrieved June 8, 2021, from https://www.who.int/infection-prevention/tools/trainer-guide_AMR-prevention.pdf.

Wolstenholme, D., Grindell, C., & Dearden, A. (2017). A co-design approach to service improvement resulted in teams exhibiting characteristics that support innovation. *Design for Health, 1*(1), 42–58. https://doi.org/10.1080/24735132.2017.1295531

Alison Prendiville is Professor of Service Design at LCC University of the Arts London. Her research and practice are situated within human and animal health, where she draws on her expertise in co-design, participatory methods and anthropology, to engage communities, experts and policy makers in service development and transformation. Currently, she is working on the global health challenge of antimicrobial resistance (AMR) in the Global South as part of a One-Health Approach. Alison's work has been published in books and journals including Designing for Health, Gower publishing (2017) and Design Issues. She has recently edited with Daniela Sangiorgi 'Designing for Service: Key Issues and New Directions, published by Bloomsbury (2017).

Colin Macduff formerly a Senior Research Fellow at Glasgow School of Art, has a clinical background in mental health and general nursing. He has a longstanding interest in the development and application of the expressive arts in nursing and health services. This has manifested in a range of initiatives and publications. He is recently completed two Arts and Humanities Research Council-funded studies that use arts and humanities approaches to address the problems of antimicrobial resistance and healthcare-associated infections.

Fernando Carvalho is a Lecturer in Product Design at Nottingham Trent University, UK, where he leads modules and teaches undergraduate and graduate courses. His main professional and research projects include healthcare services, systems' change, and medical devices with a focus on quality improvement and participatory behaviour change. Dr. Carvalho's design practice and scholarship include works in Latin America, Europe, the USA and the UK. He has presented his research in international conferences, published and acted as guest editor and reviewer for academic journals.

Co-designing Tools to Support Self-mastering of Multiple Sclerosis— A Serious Chronic Disease

22

Charlotte J. Haug and Ragnhild Halvorsrud

Abstract

Patients with chronic diseases such as multiple sclerosis (MS) are seen perhaps biannually by a specialist, where a 30-min consultation could encompass the following: make an account of their condition, the effect of a number of prescription drugs, medical and social needs, etc. While this evaluation is important, patients with chronic conditions must take care of themselves most of the time in order to have a good life. This chapter presents the background and preliminary findings from a project with the overall goal of supporting self-mastering of multiple sclerosis. The project will provide tools for documenting and communicating patient functions, needs, and preferences. Due to the coronavirus pandemic, we had to change our planned method of using in-person co-design workshops. While this had its disadvantages, we also describe how carefully planned digital workshops can replace in-person workshops and in some ways even improve the outcome.

22.1 Background

Sara Riggare (born 1971) is an engineer and doctoral student in health informatics at Karolinska Institutet in Stockholm, she is a teenage mother and has had Parkinson's disease for almost 30 years. She is a proponent of real patient participation as a tool to improve the management of chronic diseases (Riggare, 2018).

C. J. Haug (✉) · R. Halvorsrud
SINTEF Digital, Box 124 Blindern, N-0314 Oslo, Norway
e-mail: Charlotte.Johanne.Haug@sintef.no

R. Halvorsrud
e-mail: ragnhild.halvorsrud@sintef.no

449

She argues that patients' own, systematic observations in all the time they are not in contact with the health service will be able to provide invaluable information both to the patient himself and to health personnel. She describes her way of thinking best herself—see text box below.

Figure 22.1 "I see my neurologist twice a year, about half an hour every time. That's one hour per year in healthcare for my Parkinson's disease. During the same year I spend 8,765 h in selfcare, applying my knowledge and experience together with what I get from my neurologist to manage a difficult condition as best I can. Only during the one hour per year (the red circle in the image to the left) am I in direct contact with neurological specialty care and its clinical practise and guide-lines. And it's also during this one hour that my condition is evaluated by my neurologist and my treatment is prescribed. But it's during the 8,765 h of selfcare (the blue circles in the image, and yes, there are 8,765 blue circles, I am that nerdy) that the I put my treatment into action. I take 6 prescription drugs, 6 times a day, in 5 different combinations, with 6 different time intervals. Because let's face it, my doctor doesn't even know if I take my medications or not. It is also during my 8,765 h of selfcare that I can observe the effects of my treatment. And what if I could register my observations in a systematic way and bring to my next neurol-ogists' visit? Guess what? I already am! I am not saying I want more time in healthcare. I really don't think I need more time with my neurologist. However, I am saying that healthcare needs to acknowledge the work we patients do in selfcare and also start working to make use of our observations for their own knowledge. Just imagine what we could achieve if we start working together—as equals with different but complementary areas of expertise!" (Sara Riggare, 2018).

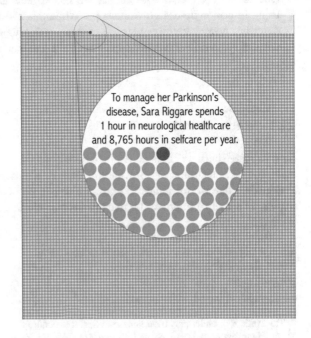

Fig. 22.1 Proportion of hours a person with a chronic illness is in self-care per year: 1 h versus 8765 h, according to Sara Riggare (2018). *Source* Author's own illustration (2021), inspired and redrawn after Riggare (2018)

Our project "EgenMS" (in Norwegian) or "MyMS" (in English)—self-mastery measures for people with MS—is inspired by this way of thinking. We want to make Sara Riggare's idea of registering "how you are doing" in a systematic and continuous way a reality for patients with chronic disorders.

We want to develop this tool in collaboration with people with MS, but the tool we want to develop will not be specific to this patient group. On the contrary, we want to develop a tool that can potentially be useful for all patients with chronic diseases both in coping with their own everyday lives and in communication with the health service, relatives, social network, and other patients.

People with chronic diseases and complex disorders have a lot in common: They have a diagnosis—maybe several—that they have to live with for a long time, maybe the rest of their lives. They are, of course, dependent on the best possible medical treatment. But first and foremost, they have a life they want to live as rich and complete as possible. Medical tests such as blood tests and X-rays are important, but it is the perceived quality of life in everyday life that really counts. It does not help much that the blood pressure is under control, if you feel so powerless that you cannot go to the store or play with the (grand)children. It does not help much that the MRI image shows stable disease development of your MS (radio-logically speaking), if you have become more depressed and isolate yourself socially.

If you have several chronic diseases at the same time, it is extra important to assess the entirety of the treatment. If the cardiologist adjusts his treatment according to results from ECG, echocardiography and blood tests, the pulmo-nologist adjusts chronic lung disease treatment according to spirometry results and the neurologist adjusts MS treatment according to MRI results—then the specialists each do an excellent job. But for the person concerned, the various treatments as a whole can give a suboptimal result. In addition to specific medical treatment of illnesses, the perceived quality of life is naturally most affected by a number of conditions outside the medical sphere: Family life, work life, social and societal conditions, personal finances, diet and activity—to name a few.

Paradoxically, today there is no systematic registration of how people with chronic diseases feel in everyday life between meetings with the healthcare service. Of course, everyone gets the question "How have you been since last visit?" But it is actually a very difficult question to answer when you sit in the doctor's office after a few months with a state of health and a quality of life that has varied—often quite a lot. Sometimes, especially for research purposes, patients fill out ques-tionnaires to try to capture "how they have been doing since the last visit" (SF-36, WHO-5, etc.). These are good and validated tools, but they have the weakness that they are retrospective, and require the patient to remember how they felt, how active they were, etc., back in time. It is difficult for everyone—both healthy and sick.

In addition to the fact that it is difficult to remember how things really were a few weeks ago, most patients are very careful and reluctant to "burden" the specialist healthcare service in particular with their more general problems. "You don't call your neurologist to tell about your mental problems", said an MS patient in a project we at SINTEF recently carried out (Røhne et al., 2018). Patients select the information they pass on to healthcare professionals and others, not because they want to withhold this information, but because the time they have with healthcare professionals is very limited. Thus, health professionals do not receive information that could be useful to them when giving advice to patients with chronic diseases. It is usually only the patient himself and/or close relatives who have and can have a comprehensive overview of various treatments and follow-ups.

If information about the quality of everyday life could be collected continuously and in a way that was not experienced as tiring and intrusive for the patients, and at the same time could be presented in an understandable way, it would be of great help both for the person/patient and those who are to help him/her. This is the information this project aims to develop.

22.1.1 Related Work

SINTEF has extensive experience of working with user experiences in general and MS patients in particular and has also studied how such experiences are important in large, multinational projects. We believe that patient involvement is essential to meet the needs of a population that lives longer, but with more chronic diseases. Self-mastery is essential for the health service—both in Norway and other countries—to be able to meet these needs (Riggare, 2018). As Sara Riggare also points out, it is absolutely necessary that people with chronic diseases receive the necessary training, follow-up and support to be able to handle their own condition. This applies first and foremost to all the days they do not have contact with the health service, but it also applies in the meetings with the health services: Patients often experience being the weak party who has difficulty documenting how everyday life goes, who has difficulty coming up with objections to the specialists' recommendations, and who may not receive help with important issues that are "on the side" of what the health services can or have a tradition of caring about.

In the case of MS, we have recently mapped how people with MS experience their everyday life over a period of 4–6 weeks (Halvorsrud et al., 2019). The purpose of that study was to establish knowledge about how digital aids can be of help and support for people with MS. One of the most important findings is that people with MS have many of the same challenges as Parkinson's patient Sara Riggare: health and quality of life vary from day to day, and most days there is no health service to get help from. However, there are many digital aids that are now becoming advanced enough, user-friendly enough, and possible to reconcile with a normal life. For example, PCs/tablets/mobile phones are in daily use by the vast majority, many also use activity bracelets, and the technology to be able to communicate with computers via "chat" and speech is becoming ubiquitous. By taking these experiences further and putting patients in the driver's seat themselves, we want to develop digital support tools that enable people with MS to register how they feel in ways that do not make users sick, but rather help them focus on what they have/can, and offer support and help based on needs.

22.1.2   Objectives of the Project

The overall goal of the project is for people with MS (and eventually other chronic diseases) to get a tool that makes it easier to live with the disease and easier to communicate how they feel toward relatives and the health service.

We want to establish knowledge about, develop and test digital tools that can register, and make available health and wellness-related user experiences in people with MS. The aim is to develop a research prototype for a digital assistant that semi-continuously registers well-being/quality of life and function and that shows the result of the registrations in a user-friendly way both to the patient himself and to those the patient wants to share the data with (relatives, healthcare professionals, fellow patients, and others).

22.2   Planned Methods

The target group in this project is people with MS and their relatives and caregivers. People with MS are the most important target group. The project is based on a co-design methodology with strong user involvement and management. There are many ways in which to involve users and stakeholders—from collecting their thoughts and insights, to letting them take a more active role in the development process of systems, products, and services. The benefits of involving users in system development are more precise system requirements, higher system quality, and improved user satisfaction (Kujala, 2003). Many branches of user involvement have evolved over the years, e. g., participatory design, co-design, contextual design, and co-creation. The delineations between some of these forms are often blurred. In participatory design, users are involved in every stage of design, from early discussions focusing on needs and challenges, to brainstorming and concept development, and evaluation and refinement (Schuler & Namioka, 1993).

In "MyMS" we chose to adopt participatory design as a development method since a profound understanding of the patients' situation is required, and at the same time, the course of the disease is highly variable for the individual patient over time. Our methodology has previously been explored in system design for stakeholders in crisis management (Stiso et al., 2013), but not in the case of virtual workshops.

Users will be the main informants in the insight/problem mapping work and priorities of what the development project should be based on the users' perceptions. Development, testing, and evaluation will take place in several short iterations where users are involved and provide feedback in each new round of development. Such close user participation helps to ensure convergence toward good, customized solutions.

In the first phase of the project, only people with MS will be defined as "users". It is their experience and description of everyday life with the disease that will be at the center. In the second phase of the project, people with MS will still be the key premise providers, but because we are here to investigate how information can best be shared with relatives, other caregivers, the primary and specialist health services, representatives of these groups will also participate in the project as "users".

22.2.1 Workshops

The workshop method is based on experience from user participation in crisis management, and it takes some principles known from design thinking methodology (Stiso et al., 2013). The workshop method mainly consists of three parts which in short include:

- Current practice, user needs, and barriers (User needs session).
- Future-oriented wishful thinking, brainstorming, and concept sketches (Blue sky-session).
- Concept development and co-design session.

Acknowledging that the users in this project are people living with a serious, chronic condition, we wanted to create the best possible conditions for the user groups and their special needs and preferences.

22.2.2 Changes Introduced by COVID-19

After the definition of the project's methodology, the COVID-19 pandemic arrived in early 2020. This imposed changes in the methodology with an increased reliance on digital services. Originally planned as physical workshops, the pandemic has greatly affected the way we have carried out the co-design sessions, which in our case have been conducted as Microsoft Teams meetings. The data collection was originally planned as physical workshops.

Due to COVID-19, we changed the method to virtual workshops. One of the challenges was how to exchange personal, sensitive information through digital channels. Virtual workshops posed a number of concerns but turned out to be advantageous in many ways. For example, it was easier to join some short virtual session compared to traveling to a meeting location to participate in a one-day in-person workshop. Observing the efforts the MS patients made to participate— several of them could only participate from a horizontal position—we realize that it would have been impossible for many of them to take part in a long in-person workshop.

Challenges when replacing physical meetings with virtual meetings include:

- No opportunities for quick-and-dirty sketching on paper and whiteboard
- Less opportunity for group work and break-out sessions
- Increased difficulty in picking upon "body language", and therefore, to respond to user reactions
- Face-to-face conversations missing, easier to drop out of discussions

- `Digital fatigue" and more time consuming to establish and verify details
- Possible unwillingness to share information or engage in discussion because of concern around unexpected recording.

22.3 Methods Used

In the following section, we describe the modified method we used when we had to replace the in-person workshops with virtual workshops. The main modifications were fewer participants per workshop and multiple short workshops instead of a full day workshop. In addition, we had much more interaction with the participants before and in between the workshops.

An introductory meeting was arranged to inform the participants about the project, followed by an extended preparatory phase. A series of four subsequent workshops formed the core, creative phase of the project. The first three workshops were carried out over a period of 1 week, and the last workshop followed 4 weeks later. In the first workshop, the aim was to explore the user needs, their daily practices in coping with the disease, the interaction with healthcare services, and mapping of the general "MS landscape". The second workshop focused on brainstorming and blue-sky thinking, ignoring any practical, economic, and technological limitations. The last two workshops were dedicated to co-design of specific concepts and tools.

22.3.1 Privacy by Design

Developing a digital assistant with functions as described has potentially great utility value but is complicated both methodologically and with regard to data security and privacy. Moreover, even if the tool is intended for personal use, when used in communication with the health service, it can be used both diagnostically and to follow up and adjust treatment. In that case, the tool will fall into the category of "medical equipment" or possibly "medical intervention". Then there are very specific requirements for study design and the quality and scope of documentation. The aim of this project is to develop and test this tool so far that at the end of the project you have sufficiently durable documentation to start validation studies (cf. "Phase 2" clinical studies) as well as studies of generalizability (i.e., upscaling possibilities) and testing of commercial potential.

We develop this tool according to the principles of Privacy by Design as described in GDPR (Haug, 2018).

22.3.2 Recruitment of Participants

Participants were recruited by the Norwegian MS Society (www.ms.no). The MS society announced the project on its Web site. Interest in participation was the only inclusion criteria. There were no exclusion criteria. So, obviously, we had very motivated participants and not a random selection of people living with MS. For this pilot project that was our intention. When the announcement was made in July 2020, we said we would be interested in many different forms of engagement and participation.

- Participation in in-person co-design workshops in September 2020
- Interviews
- Testing later on.

More than 40 people signed up before we had to close recruitment.

22.3.3 Introductory Meeting

In late August 2020, we realized that the prospect of arranging in-person workshops with people with a serious chronic disease would be unrealistic even if we postponed the project for six months. We needed to find a way to proceed with the project using digital tools. We did not know exactly how to do that and decided—in the spirit of the project—to involve the participants in our discussions about how to proceed. We invited everybody who had signed up to an information/introductory meeting in September 2020 on Microsoft Teams: One meeting in the morning and one meeting in the afternoon to allow for individual preferences. At this meeting we informed about the project and its goals, and the challenges we faced due to the pandemic. We told the participants that the workshops had to be virtual/digital, that we did not have any experience with that and needed to spend the next couple of months to figure out how to do that in the most efficient and safe (with respect to privacy) way.

About half of the participants who had originally signed up showed up for the introductory meeting. Most of them have participated in this pilot project.

At that meeting we introduced the participants to the concept of "personas" and told them that we thought using such personas in the months to come would be crucial for the progress of the project. We asked them to participate in the creation of many more personas than we had originally planned for (see below).

22.3.4 Co-creation of Personas

Personas is a pragmatic tool in marketing and user research to represent fictional customers, users, or customer segments (Goodvin, 2009). The advantages for "MyMS" were evident from the start:

- Privacy: the participants can share information while preserving privacy
- Creativity: may encourage imagination and creativity
- Perspective: the collection of personas encourages a wider focus and perspective.

Usually, participants are presented with predefined personas at a co-design workshop. In this case, we decided to involve the participants in the creation of the personas.

Immediately after the introductory meeting, the participants received an e-mail containing information about the personas we had presented at the introductory meeting and an invitation to contribute to more and more detailed personas. We sent out a template by e-mail and received input for seven more personas between October and December 2020. Some very detailed and personal, some more sketchy.

The personas were systemized and compared, then adjusted and modified to obtain a common level of detail and structure. The personas were collated and anonymized by adjusting, e.g., age, gender, symptoms, work profession to ensure that there were no way to link the persona with the author. This resulted in a set of six personas, as shown in Fig. 22.2.

22.3.5   Preparation for workshops

In early January, invitations to the workshops were sent out. The participants received a folder by post and e-mail that contained:

- Information about the project
- Consent form (again)
- Program for the first workshop (user needs)
- A rich description of the personas (one page each):
  - Family situation and professional career
  - Onset and diagnosing of their MS
  - Development of the disease and how they tackle it
  - Use of digital tools
  - Healthcare actors involved in treatment and follow-up of the disease
- Sticky notes and pen for drawing and brainstorming
- "Homework" to be completed before the workshop
  - What factors are important in the daily life of Mike, Tracy, Evelyn, Jenny, Frank, and Rose?
  - Which challenges do they face?
  - What do they need?

Mike (33) *"I am not sick, but I have an illness"*

Mike is a family man and was recently diagnosed with MS after an optic nerve infection. The disease was discovered at an early stage, and he quickly returned to full-time work as a researcher. Mike has no physical manifestations of MS, but reads a lot about prognoses and preventive measures. He does everything he can to keep the disease at distance: He has changed his diet, exercises systematically and purposefully. He has also become more aware of what is good in life.

Tracy (65) *"Bitterness and melancholy is a part of my everyday life"*

Tracy is single and works 40% in a fishing company. When she was diagnosed as a 25-year-old, she chose not to start a family so that the disease would not affect anyone but herself. She regrets this sometimes. For several years she has dragged on one leg, and lately she has had to give up playing the piano. Tracy has always refrained from offerings of support and aids. Difficulty sleeping and depression make everyday life difficult, and Tracy has no energy for social activities.

Evelyn 52) *"I have MS only from the waist down"*

Evelyn is married, has two grown children and runs a full-time agency. Evelyn was diagnosed with MS at the age of 25 and became dependent on a wheelchair at an early age, but this does not prevent her from living a very active life. Her hobbies are hunting and skydiving. Evelyn is a distinctly surplus person and also finds room for volunteer work. She has MS "only from the waist down" and loves to explore the limits of what she can achieve with a wheelchair.

Jenny (39) *"My husband thinks I'm reacting too late to the signals of fatigue"*

Jenny is married, has three school children and is working full time as a GP. She was diagnosed with MS 10 years ago, right after giving birth for the first time. The treatment she receives every 4 weeks keeps the disease stable. Only her family and a few close friends know she has MS. Jenny uses all her energy at work, and this gives her a constant bad conscience towards the family. A couple of times a year she experiences fatigue, becomes depressed, and may be on sick leave for several weeks.

Frank (57) *"You have to be strong to be sick"*

Frank is married to Pete and works 50% as the manager of a store. He was diagnosed with MS at the age of 37. Frank is an outdoor person. He spends a lot of time in the mountains even though he has been dependent on a wheelchair for the last 10 years. Frank finds it difficult to live with reduced functional ability and is unable to motivate himself for exercise. He has large mental fluctuations and in difficult periods he misses a low-threshold offer to get help to cope with the mental.

Rose (29) *"I feel I am sole responsible for the disease"*

Rose is married and has a 2-year-old. She is a nurse and currently works 70%. She developed symptoms of MS as a 20-year-old, but was constantly rejected by her GP. When she finally went to the neurologist, she was quickly diagnosed with MS. Rose is often bothered by invisible symptoms such as fatigue and difficulty concentrating. She knows the healthcare system well, and experiences a lot of routine failure around follow-up and treatment of her own illness. This makes her worried and resigned.

Fig. 22.2 Consolidated personas after interaction with the participants. *Source* Author's own illustration

22.3.6 Digital Workshops

The four subsequent workshops were carried out with two groups of patients, both groups going through the same procedure. The group size was small to allow ample opportunity to hear individual reflections and opinion sharing.

Although informed consent was obtained prior to the workshop, each workshop was initiated by reminding about the privacy policy, the participants rights to withdraw, information about data collection and data storage, and asking if the participants were comfortable with screen recording.

The workshops had the following structure:

- Welcome, privacy statement, and introduction (10 min)
- **First trigger question**
  - Individual reflection (10 min)
  - Facilitated walkthrough of reflections (15–20 min)
- Break
- **Second trigger question**
  - Individual reflection (10 min)
  - Facilitated walkthrough of reflections (15–20 min)
- Concluding remarks and preparation for next step (5 min).

22.3.7 Workshop 1: User Needs

In this virtual workshop the aim was to answer the question "what is important to me as a person living with MS?".

The personas were presented briefly again. Then the participants were asked to think about one or more of the personas, or themselves, and reflect on the following question:

Trigger question 1.1: What is it important to communicate to your neurologist at the next visit?

We muted everyone during the individual work, and the short version of the personas was kept on the screen.

Trigger question 1.2: What is it important to communicate to your family and friends about how your health and well-being varies?

Concluding session: encourage everyone to submit their notes by e-mail. Also things they were thinking about after the workshops. The workshop was finalized by informing about the next workshop and prepare the participants for blue-sky thinking.

22.3.8 Workshop 2: Blue-Sky Thinking

In this virtual workshop, the aim was to answer the question "if anything was possible what would you like to have in your environment to function as well as possible with your MS diagnosis?".

The goal was to generate ideas and concepts without being constrained or limited (ignore current practice, practical, economical, and technological constraints), to generate new concepts and build further on each other's ideas.

The participants were encouraged to make use of the toolkit. Also this time, they were encouraged to use one or more of the personas, or themselves.

Trigger question 2.1: If everything were possible—what would an ideal offer from the healthcare services look like?

Trigger question 2.2: If everything were possible—how could everyday life be better?

22.3.9 Workshop 3: Concept Development I

In this workshop we presented the participants with the "MS ecosystem" that we had developed based on the two previous workshops and asked them trigger questions to further develop these concepts (Fig. 22.3).

Trigger question 3.1: Think about your previous input. Do you feel that your concepts are included in the ecosystem? Don't think too detailed!

Trigger question 3.2: Please choose two of the main concepts to further develop. How would you prefer to work from now on?

22.3.10 Workshop 4: Concept Development II

In preparation for this workshop, the researchers used the "MS ecosystem" presented in workshop 3 and the feedback from workshop 3 to develop the concepts into a "MS toolkit" (Fig. 22.4).

During workshop 4, the participants were given trigger questions to further develop two of the concepts/tools (Fig. 22.5).

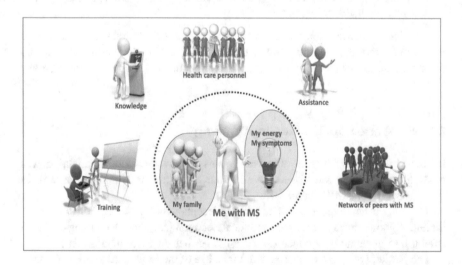

Fig. 22.3 MS ecosystem. *Source* Author's own illustration (2021)

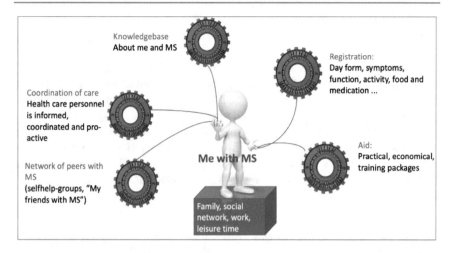

Fig. 22.4 MS toolkit. *Source* Author's own illustration (2021)

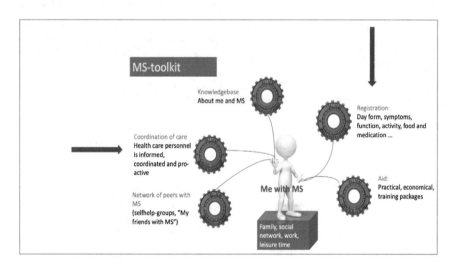

Fig. 22.5 Extra workshop to concretize two of the concepts. *Source* Author's own illustration (2021)

22.4 Results

Basically, our results can be categorized as follows:

1. We co-created PERSONAS
2. We developed a method for feedback and interaction in and in-between digital workshops

3. We developed CONCEPTS and an ECOSYSTEM (where the concepts could be positioned).

The co-creation of personas is decribed in Sect. 1.3.4. During the "User needs" workshop all participants said they based their input on several of the personas, and that they could recognize several personal aspects in some of them. Some participants said they mixed their own experience with the persona experience.

During the "Blue Sky-session" the participants answered the trigger-questions individually by sketching thoughts and wishes on paper at home, taking a photograph of the sketches and sending the photograph to the facilitator. The facilitator then shared the photographs using the "share document" function in Microsoft Teams (Figs. 22.6 and 22.7).

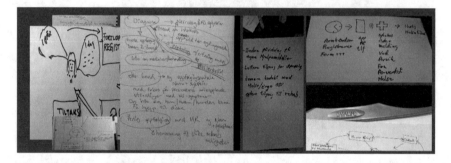

Fig. 22.6 Text and drawings made by the participants, photographed, and shared with the facilitator during the "Blue Sky"-session. *Source* Author's own illustration (2021)

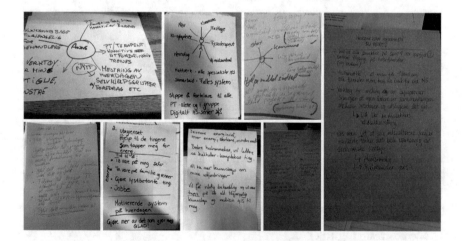

Fig. 22.7 Text and drawings made by the participants, photographed and shared with the facilitator during the "Blue Sky"-session. *Source* Author's own illustration (2021)

Based on the concepts shared and the discussion among the participants, the researchers developed the "MS Ecosystem" and the "MS Toolkit" (Figs. 22.3 and 22.4) and further developed two of the concepts in the toolkit (Fig. 22.5).

22.5 Conclusions and Lessons Learned

We have used a set of different instruments and techniques to engage with the participant/patient group as summarized in Fig. 22.8.

The original aims of this phase of our project were to determine if it was.

1. possible to use a co-design methodology with people living with a serous chronic disease (in this case multiple sclerorisis (MS)) as research participants (not only informants), and
2. use this method to determine what was important to them in their daily life living with this disease, and then

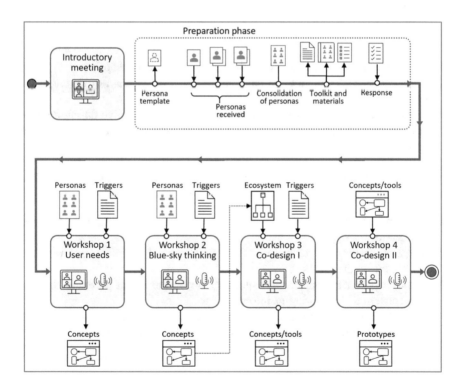

Fig. 22.8 Engagement with the participant/patient group through the first phase of our project. *Source* Author's own illustration (2021)

3. start devolping concepts that would be helpful in designing tools to improve their function and quality of life and improve their communication with family, caregivers, and the healthcare system.

As described above, this was not only possible, but the expert opinion from MS patients gave us much more to work with going forward than we could have hoped for.

In addition, due to the coronavirus pandemic, we had to develop a modified, virutal version of our methology more or less from schratch. As researchers, we were initially very disappoited that we could not meet in person, but as it turned out we got a lot more out of this way of conducting workshops than we had expected. Probably more than we would have achieved through in-person workshops.

The lessons we learned from this were these.

1. It was possible to create a productive and including atmosphere even if we did not physically meet, and we got very many ideas worth to pursue in the future.
2. We got a balanced input because of thorough planning, scripts for what to say, and a clear and effective facilitation (ensuring everyone got to say something and nobody dominated).

The use of personas was a success criterion:

1. It engaged the participants to contribute prior to the workshops
2. It mitigated the "cold start" problem and lowered the concern of sharing own, sensitive information.
3. It was a support to maintain a broad and inclusive perspective during concept development, taking into account differences in degree of sickness and personalities.

Observed advantages when replacing physical meetings with virtual meetings include.

1. Lowering the threshold to participate, since participants did not have to leave their home
2. Increased opportunity to include those with reduced mobility, and who are hardest hit by the disease
3. Willingness to share information, possibly due to the use of personas (to mitigate concern about sharing of information)
4. Increased efficiency during the workshops since we did not have to physically relocate and move groups of people during sessions and breaks.

References

Goodvin, K. (2009). *Designing for the digital age: How to create human-centered products and services.* Wiley.

Halvorsrud, R., Røhne, M., Celius, E. G., Moen, S. M., & Strisland, F. (2019). Application of patient journey methodology to explore needs for digital support: A multiple sclerosis case study. In *Proceedings of the 17th Scandinavian Conference on Health Informatics (SHI 2019)* (pp. 148–153). Oslo, Norway. . Accessed 8 June 2021 from https://ep.liu.se/ecp/161/025/ecp19161025.pdf.

Haug, C. J. (2018). Turning the tables—The new European general data protection regulation. *The New England Journal of Medicine, 379*(3), 207–209. https://doi.org/10.1056/NEJMp1806637. PMID: 29874143.

Kujala, S. (2003). User involvement: A review of the benefits and challenges. *Behaviour and Information. Technology, 22*(1), 1–16. https://doi.org/10.1080/01449290301782

Riggare, S. (2018). E-patients hold key to the future of healthcare. *BMJ. 360*, k846. https://doi.org/10.1136/bmj.k846. PMID: 29483151.

Røhne, M., Halvorsrud, R., Strisland, F., Moen, S. M. & Celius, E. G. (2018). Digital follow-up and support for people with multiple sclerosis. Experiences from the MS-DOS project (in Norwegian). SINTEF Report. Stiftelsen for industriell og teknisk forskning (SINTEF, Ed.). Trondheim.

Schuler, D. & Namioka, A. (1993). *Participatory design: Principles and practices.* Hillsdale, NJ: Lawrence Erlbaum Associates (Ed.).

Stiso, M. W., Eide, A. W., Halvorsrud, R., Nilsson, E. G. & Skjetne, J. H. (2013). Building a flexible common operational picture to support situation awareness in crisis management. In: *10th International ISCRAM Conference* (pp. 220–229), Baden-Baden, Germany. Accessed 2 June 2021, from http://idl.iscram.org/files/stiso/2013/976_Stiso_etal2013.pdf.

Charlotte J. Haug is a senior researcher at SINTEF Digital in Oslo, Norway. She is a MD, PhD from the University of Oslo, Norway, and holds a MSc in Health Policy and Research from Stanford Unversity, USA. Her current research interests include development of tools to help empower patients with chronic diseases to handle their daily life and interactions with the healthcare system better while protecting sensitive personal data.

Ragnhild Halvorsrud is a senior researcher at SINTEF Digital in Oslo, Norway. Her research interests include service research, human-computer interaction, analysis of service processes, and empirical investigation of human experiences. She managed the VISUAL project, which produced the Customer Journey Modelling Language. She holds a PhD in physics and has also 10 years of industrial experience from Telenor, a global telecommunication company. She developed a company-wide toolbox for customer journeys, which has been in active use since 2006.

Self-fulfilling Prophecies in Service Design: Strategies to Address Virtuous and Vicious Circles for Mental Healthcare Transformation

23

Alessandra Sara Cutroneo, Daniela Sangiorgi, and Fabio Lucchi

Abstract

The self-fulfilling prophecy can be best described as an assumption that, only because of the fact of being believed, provokes certain expectations and patterns of behavior that eventually make the initial assumption come true. This phenomenon has been long studied in a variety of applied settings, including the one of mental health care: in this regard, the concepts of stigma and self-stigma have been proven to be, in part, self-fulfilling. Service design has been working in the field of mental health care to address these issues by promoting service co-production and a recovery-oriented approach. However, shared beliefs and norms within organizations, rooted in unquestioned and taken-for-granted ways of operating, may hinder this transformational process. In fact, these shared beliefs and norms may result in unconscious self-fulfilling prophecies, that are, positive and negative feedback loops of thinking and acting in the form of virtuous and vicious circles. Recent studies in service design identify institutional theory at the macro-level and mental models' theory at the micro-level as promising practices to prompt individual and collective reflexivity to overcome these barriers. This chapter aims to further develop this research stream to address both virtuous and vicious circles at the micro-level, in order to reveal,

A. S. Cutroneo (✉)
Customer Experience Design e Canali Digitali, Generali Italia S.P.A, Piazza Tre Torri 1, 20145 Milano, Italy
e-mail: alessandrasara.cutroneo@generali.com

D. Sangiorgi
Dipartimento Di Design, Politecnico Di Milano, Via Candiani 72, 20158 Milano, Italy
e-mail: daniela.sangiorgi@polimi.it

F. Lucchi
Centro Di Salute Mentale Rovereto, APSS Trento, UOP 4, 38068 Provincia Autonoma di Trento, Italy
e-mail: fabio.lucchi@apss.tn.it

© The Author(s), under exclusive license to Springer Nature Switzerland AG 2022
M. A. Pfannstiel et al. (eds.), *Service Design Practices for Healthcare Innovation*,
https://doi.org/10.1007/978-3-030-87273-1_23

question, and transform them if necessary to foster change at the macro-level, too. Through an experimental work within a Northern-Italy department of mental health care, this chapter reflects on which kinds of service design reflexivity tools can help to enable transformational processes across service systems.

23.1 Introduction

Healthcare systems and organizations are in need of profound transformations to address the consequences of changing demographics, that are shifting care from dealing mainly with the treatment of acute conditions to managing a growing demand for chronic and long-term care (Bodenheimer et al., 2002); also a more articulated and comprehensive understanding of care is pointing toward the need to acknowledge the wider social determinants of health and their impact on non-communicable diseases (Kaplan, 2006). These transitions are all demanding paradigmatic changes in the approaches to health care, embracing a biopsychosocial perspective at the core for the implementation of patient-centered care (The Health Foundation, 2016). However, they can face significant resistance given the competing cultures implied in the process, informed by conflicting ontologies with very different philosophical convictions that can challenge "the most basic assumptions within current medical thinking" (Anjum, 2016: p. 425). Also, dealing with chronic and long-term care demands the reorganization of large care systems that should be understood with the lenses of complexity studies, given the dynamic, interdependent, and emergent qualities of their development and evolution (Greenhalgh & Papoutsi, 2018). Instead of linear and predictable models of actions and innovation, these perspectives call for different models of research and design that acknowledge the multi-level context of the interventions (i.e., micro-meso-macro) (Greenhalgh et al., 2017). While considering the multiple dimensions interplay within extensive system transformation, radical changes in healthcare systems must therefore take into account the fundamental values, beliefs, and assumptions that characterize different professional practices and might dominate specific healthcare organizations (Willis et al., 2016).

As a human-centered, holistic, and iterative approach to the creation of new services, service design has been recently investigated as a promising approach to catalyze healthcare service systems' transformation (Patricio et al., 2020). While reinforcing the importance of multi-level service design approaches (Patricio et al., 2011), particular attention has been given to the hidden layers, often unconscious, that inform an organizational culture (Schein, 2010). In this regard, studies in service design have underlined a correlation between such organizational dynamics and individual actors, proposing different levels of depth of design inquiries (Junginger & Sangiorgi, 2011). As such, when aiming for transformational changes (Sangiorgi, 2011), service design must explore ways to challenge standardized and universally accepted ways of operating that originate from norms, values, and beliefs rooted in each individual (Vink et al., 2018). Particularly mental models—cognitive representations of how the environment works that shape how individuals act and learn—can be shared intersubjectively as part of ideologies and institutions (Denzau & North, 1994); challenging these deep beliefs and representations is at the basis of cognitive shifts essential for strategic change (Guiette & Vandenbempt, 2013) and possibly for larger system transformation (Vink et al., 2021).

As mental models are primarily unquestioned and taken for granted, these fundamental assumptions are mainly enacted passively and unconsciously, perpetuating over time. Understanding how these dynamics operate, inform and sustain certain behaviors and practices, or how they can be made explicit and questionable to initiate a more paradigmatic transformation, is still a crucial question in service design.

To shed some light on these dynamics, the authors have been exploring the concept of the "self-fulfilling prophecy" (Merton, 1948). Intended as a socio-psychological process through which an assumption about something or someone can affect a person's expectation and behavior in a way that leads that assumption to become a reality (ibid), a self-fulfilling prophecy (SFP) can lead to the enactment of so-called vicious or virtuous circles, perpetuating belief over time and reinforcing both positive and negative outcomes. More specifically, the recursive and interpersonal nature of the SFP can play a critical role in designing for transformational change, as it manifests between the system's actors at different aggregation levels, that are strongly intertwined and sometimes constrained by each other.

This chapter will elaborate on this initial hypothesis, focusing on mental health care as an experimental setting, given the strong call for paradigmatic and systemic change toward recovery-oriented and community-based service models, that are actively and repeatedly counteracted by deep-seated professional, organizational and societal cultures reinforcing medicalized and stigmatized systems of care. These intangible and invisible structures and beliefs should be revealed, questioned, and transformed to stimulate a more radical transformation.

This chapter will review the concept of SFP and its specific application in the context of mental health care to illustrate an experiment conducted within a Department of Mental Health in Northern Italy, testing reflexivity tools and processes to initiate virtuous circles in the overall organization. This first experiment will then be used to reflect on a design-informed viral approach to larger-scale transformation, based on the model of self-fulfilling circles, that will be discussed within the field of service design and health care.

23.2 Defining Self-fulfilling Prophecies

The idea behind the self-fulfilling prophecy (SFP) has its origins traced back to 1928, when the American sociologist William Thomas stated that, "If men define situations as real, they are real in their consequences" (Thomas & Thomas, 1928: p. 572). However, the SFP had been officially theorized by the American sociologist Robert Merton, who first coined the term in 1948 to describe "a false definition of the situation evoking a new behavior which makes the originally false conception come true."

Nevertheless, this research stands apart from Merton's original interpretation and agrees with subsequent studies (e.g., Watzlawick, 1984), arguing that the initial assumption could either be true or false, as long as it is believed to be true. This prerequisite proves fundamental to create the assumed reality: if there is no element of belief or conviction, the prophecy will not fulfill. Accordingly, the SFP can be best described as a socio-psychological process through which a belief about something or someone can affect one's expectations and behavior in a way that leads that belief to eventually become a reality—thus, turning the individual who produced it into a "prophet."

The SFP can be either positive, when a desirable outcome follows a favorable prediction, or negative, when an unfavorable prediction fulfills a consequent undesirable outcome.

In rare cases, the SFP cycle might just come to an end once the assumed reality has been created and the prophecy fulfilled. However, as shown in Fig. 23.1, it more often acts as a reinforcing feedback loop, described as a reflexive (i.e., recursive) system in which an action leads to an outcome that produces more of the same action, resulting in either growth or decline (Bellinger, 2004). Within this perspective, a positive SFP is likely to generate what is known as a virtuous circle, that is, a reflexive structure producing and reinforcing a desirable result. On the contrary, a negative SFP is likely to develop a vicious circle, a reflexive structure producing and reinforcing an undesirable result (Masuch, 1985).

The fascinating aspect of this phenomenon lies in the idea that a single assumption, if it is rooted in someone's belief system, may alter the course of events, and as previously mentioned, this does not only concern the so-called prophet but who and what surrounds them, too.

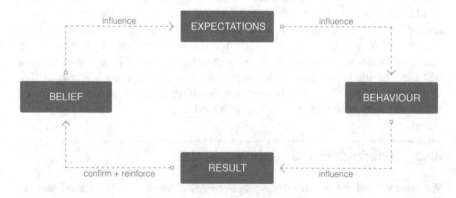

Fig. 23.1 Circular and recursive dynamics characterizing the SFP. *Source* Author's own illustration (2021)

In this regard, SFPs can be categorized as self-imposed or other-imposed (Adler et al., 2012) and are not mutually exclusive. In a self-imposed SFP, one's expectations, arising from one or more beliefs, constitute the actual cause for one's thoughts and actions. This type of prophecy lies on the concept of self-expectancy, that is, the expectations a person has directly of themselves.

On the contrary, other-imposed SFP arises when one's expectations affect the actions of another individual. This type of prophecy lies instead on the concept of interpersonal expectancy, that is, the expectations a person has of another person (Jussim & Eccles, 1995).

In the case of other-imposed SFPs, a standard paradigm is generally used, that is, the dyad composed by the perceiver (the person who holds expectations of another person) and the target (the person on which expectations have been laid on) (Stukas & Snyder, 2016).

For example, a doctor (A) and an intern (B) may be considered. The intern may produce a thought, such as "I will never be a good doctor." This thought can result in the expectation of failing, potentially generating anxiety over typical tasks a doctor carries out—such as intravenous injections (IV). When that same intern is required to insert an IV, he might experience negative feelings leading to a lousy procedure, thus reinforcing the initial thought of never becoming a good doctor. Therefore, the belief in failing generated failure indeed. In different circumstances, the doctor (A) may be convinced that the intern (B) will never become a good doctor. Because A imposed this expectation on B, A will behave in a way that may lead B to believe it and act accordingly.

Nevertheless, as previously mentioned, these two types of SFPs are not mutually exclusive but rather have the potential to influence and even cause one another (Biggs, 2009). Following this logic, A and B may be experiencing a dysfunctional relationship that they both believe to be the other's fault, considering their behavior only as a reaction to that of the other. A fears B is not good enough at inserting IVs, which B admits, but because A is intimidating and never leaves space for practicing. For A, this is not true: B's behavior is the cause of A's justified fear against B's incompetence.

Because the behavioral pattern between the two people has been repeating itself for too long, it developed a vicious circle, and the question of who originated the SFP in the first place becomes meaningless (Fig. 23.2).

Fig. 23.2 Example of SFP characterized by interpersonal expectancy. *Source* Author's own illustration (2021)

As demonstrated, initial assumptions may play a primary role in the development of SFPs. Considering these assumptions are believed to be accurate, it comes as a direct result that most of the time, they turn out to be generally accepted and unquestioned by first of all perceivers and consequently targets. In this regard, it is not uncommon that beliefs arising at an individual level end up having significant repercussions on collectivity. As such, even though the assumption usually stems from a simple thought, it can gradually transform into a profoundly rooted belief or even stereotype and prejudice (e.g., Merton, 1948). Of course, stereotypes, even if inaccurate initially, may become accurate through SFP, which would then create "both social and conceptual problems" (Jussim et al., 1996: p. 323).

In this regard, stigmatization is not a new issue: it has long been researched on how discriminated groups may fall victim to self-fulfilling stereotypes and prejudice from the dominant group. Often and unfortunately, it is the victims themselves who are blamed for their own condition, rather than the social expectations and prejudices that in large part led to that condition (Merton, 1948). These dynamics can be easily detected at the individual, societal, and even organizational level for what concerns mental health care, as we elaborate in the following section.

23.3   Self-fulfilling Prophecies in Mental Health Care

Social psychology describes stereotypes as to how members of one social group (in-group) categorize information about people belonging to other groups (out-groups) (Major & O'Brien, 2005). In this regard, negative stereotypes often associated with mental illness can be remarkably harmful to individuals who are battling one—the most common pejorative stereotypes about mental illness include blame, dangerousness, and incompetence (Corrigan et al., 2009), together with a sense of chronicity linked to helplessness, especially regarding most severe illnesses such as schizophrenia (McGorry & Mei, 2020). Moreover, when people endorse these pejorative stereotypes, they turn them into prejudice and generate adverse emotional reactions, leading to discrimination (Corrigan et al., 2009; Major & O'Brien, 2005). This chain of stereotypes, prejudice, and discrimination is known as public stigma (Corrigan & Rao, 2012).

In addition to being publicly stigmatized by others, people with mental illness may also stigmatize themselves (Manago, 2015); this happens when they internalize these public prejudices toward their condition (Corrigan et al., 2009), developing what is known as self-stigma. Self-stigma, in particular, constitutes a dangerous mechanism, laying the foundation for the "Why Try" Effect, that is, the interference of self-stigma with the achievement of life goals (Corrigan et al., 2009). As such, the "Why Try" Effect has been demonstrated to potentially harm self-concept (everything one knows and thinks about oneself), self-esteem (how one evaluates the self-concept), and eventually self-efficacy (one's belief in one's ability to succeed) (Yu et al., 2021).

For example, an individual may internalize highly negative stereotypes about their mental illness (e.g., "People with schizophrenia are incapable of leading a normal social life"), and then projecting them on themselves through self-stigma (Pasman, 2011); this may act as an SFP, and the individual may behave more defensively or less confidently, eventually avoiding social interaction. In turn, this may lead the individual to think he is not capable of social interaction at all, thus affecting self-concept, self-esteem, and eventually self-efficacy (Link et al., 2001).

Throughout the decades, many studies have investigated the role of stigma and self-stigma in relation to being diagnosed with mental illness. In this regard, Scheff's Labelling Theory (1966) claimed that the stigma of being labeled mentally ill could cause someone to become mentally ill due to a particular kind of SFP, generally known as a self-fulfilling diagnosis. As such, if an individual is aware of what others expect of him as a mentally ill person, that individual has no other choice than to act out to those expectations, actually becoming mentally ill (Perkins et al., 2018). However, subsequent studies (Link et al., 1989) have adopted a less absolute position and instead argued that labeling could not develop mental illness but may worsen the course of existing mental illness and lead to the "Why Try" Effect.

The overall negative reputation of the diagnosis, seen as a potential threat for effective recovery, has often led to inadequate and incomplete care of mental illness within the healthcare organization (Benoit et al., 2019), in favor of a somewhat optimistic regimen that often relies on undertreatment rather than overtreatment (McGorry & Mei, 2020). Within these circumstances, it is not uncommon for vicious circles to develop and perpetuate. In fact, service models which encourage late intervention sometimes lead individuals to access care only when their symptoms are too severe for a compelling prospect of recovery (ibid). As a result, the sense of helplessness embedded in the diagnosis gets reinforced, causing increasing dismay of the patient and sometimes medical professionals in any possibility of recovery.

This modus operandi most likely stems from what is known as "clinician's illusion," described as a phenomenon "that leads to health professionals maintaining a distorted and excessively pessimistic perception of an illness" (McGorry & Mei, 2020: p. 333). In other words, as clinicians fear the possibility of self-fulfilling diagnoses, mental illness is treated as taboo until symptoms become unavoidable. Nevertheless, it should be underlined how medical professionals often adopt these procedures under the weight of the dominant biomedical model of care (UN Human Rights Council, 2017), which relies on a top-down, evidence-based approach primarily focused on the alleviation of psychiatric symptoms rather than on the individual experience of each patient (Roberts, 2000).

A direct consequence of this biomedical paradigm is power imbalances. Because of it, health professionals retain almost all responsibilities within the healthcare system, meaning they are entirely responsible for the consequences of a diagnosis, treatment, and prognosis. At the same time, users often find themselves disempowered and not allowed to make decisions about their health conditions (UN Human Rights Council, 2017). As a result, a vicious circle perpetuates where clinicians are burdened by their medical and legal accountability while users adopt a passive and pessimistic attitude. These dynamics altogether encourage healthcare systems in general and mental health services in particular to favor defensive and risk-aversive practices through the employment of standardized guidelines and protocols, based on the assumption that traditional models are safer against eventual disputes arising from users, managers, and public opinion (Mullen et al., 2008).

To counterbalance the traditional biomedical model of care, a more experience-based approach relying on the importance of individual narrative has recently been developing (Roberts, 2000), known as Recovery Model (Leamy et al., 2011). This perspective underlines the essential complementarity between clinical recovery and personal recovery, the latter intended as "a way of living a satisfying, hopeful and contributing life, even within the limitations caused by illness. [...] Recovery involves the development of new meaning and purpose in one's life as one grows beyond the catastrophic effects of mental illness" (Anthony, 1993: p. 527).

The Recovery Model establishes an equal relationship between the clinician and the patient by giving importance both to professional experience (expert and technical knowledge belonging to clinicians) and lived experience (individual and personal experience of each patient), thus aiming to reduce power asymmetries (Boyle & Harris, 2009).

Moreover, the integration of lived experiences within the dominant biomedical model allows for the employment of both a quantitative and qualitative approach, where personal narrative preserves individuality and humanity, while evidence-based protocols offer a reliable and scientific foundation for treatment (Roberts, 2000). As such, the service becomes co-produced, constituting a prolific environment for virtuous circles to arise, based on the restoration of hope, self-determination, and personal empowerment (Nakanishi et al., 2021). As Roberts (2000: p. 438) points out, "This very different perspective enables the prospect of recovery to become a realistic goal for every patient, and it is one of the inspirational dynamics of rehabilitation."

Within this perspective, early intervention, combined with high-quality, tailored, and effective care at every stage of the illness, would be the most promising way to achieve both clinical and personal recovery (McGorry & Mei, 2020), reaching far more satisfying results. Unfortunately, however, this model of care is struggling to become the norm. We argue that the deep beliefs associated with opposite modi operandi might be the primary cause of this issue, raising multiple barriers which impede the effective coexistence of evidence-based and experience-based medicine.

These rooted and mainly unconscious beliefs are at the core of the vicious circles arising within the healthcare organization and need to be revealed, questioned, and transformed to favor a smoother integration of these approaches, thus fostering a better service experience for everyone involved in the system. Recent interest in reflexivity in service design is the starting point for this exploration on how to make SFPs evident in mental healthcare systems.

23.4 Building Reflexivity in Service Design

Designers are generally described as "reflective practitioners," adopting two approaches regarding reflection: reflection-on-action, when they learn from an experience completed in the past, and reflection-in-action, representing the ongoing conversation with the situation, informing the design process (Schön, 1984). These forms of reflection, though, are focused on the individual practitioners and their work without considering other issues at stake, such as the political implications of participatory design processes or bias associated with values, assumptions, and power embedded in design (Pihkala & Karasti, 2016).

Reflexivity can be defined as the capacity of any entity to turn back on itself, to make itself its object of investigation (Steier, 1991). For example, in qualitative research, "personal reflexivity" is the ability of the researcher to reflect on their own values, beliefs, attitudes, and aims to influence the overall research process and make them as explicit as possible (Gray, 2017). In addition to this, researchers should constantly reflect on their work's power dynamics and positionality and how this affects the relationship with the research context and participants (Sultana, 2007).

Design in general, and service design in particular has felt the urge to develop more reflexivity in designers' practice over the last years, given the increasing complexity and scale of design interventions and the emphasis placed on the participatory and transformational aims of design work (Sangiorgi, 2011). Moreover, a call for more social responsibility of designers has been there for some decades now (Maldonado, 1990; Margolin, 1998; Manzini, 1994). However, only recently, a growing stream of research has attracted attention to the hidden consequences of a lack of attentiveness toward, for example, issues of heterogeneity promoted by the decolonizing design movement (Schultz, 2018), especially when designers work in international or community development projects. This growing sensitivity has been particularly evident within recent Participatory Design studies, recognizing the complexity and plurality of participation and the positionality of the design researchers (Pihkala & Karasti, 2016); instead of an idea of design from nowhere (Suchman, 2002), these studies encourage designers to recognize their "embodied, and therefore partial, perspective" and to be accountable for it (ibid: p. 96).

To support designers' reflexivity, some tools have been proposed: for example, "tools for reflection" to keep track of how the participants' situation in designing can change over time (Kraff, 2018), "reflective design documentation" to support and document a shared decision-making process (Dalsgaard & Halskov, 2012), or the "practice notation" tool to visualize and reflect on long-term collaborations and infrastructure processes (Agid & Akama, 2020).

Apart from being discussed as a fundamental attitude to better address design and research's ethical dilemmas, lately, reflexivity has been examined as a crucial lever to promote more profound and large-scale transformations in organizations, service systems, and society starting from individuals' worldviews (Lu &

Sangiorgi, 2021). More established examples can be traced back to critical, associative, or speculative design (Malpass, 2012), using design as an investigation practice to raise sensibility in the public (Malpass, 2013). Moreover, design has been looking into ways to promote individual and collective reflexivity to challenge existing social norms that might perpetuate discriminatory solutions and prevent change and innovation.

Norm Creative Innovation is an approach with the primary intent to help reveal and challenge hidden social norms, intended as the set of values, mental models, and worldviews that guide our everyday actions and may contribute to inequality and social exclusion (Nilsson & Jahnke, 2018). This methodology is described as made of two main stages: a norm-critical design and a norm-creative design, where the identified criticalities are exploited to inform the development of ideas (ibid). Combining a critical ethnographic perspective with norm-creative design tactics, this approach can provide the participating stakeholders with the tools to promote social and organizational change (Isaksson et al., 2019).

Another approach considers the potential of organizational change adopting a neo-institutional theory perspective that defines reflexivity as "an individuals' general awareness of the constraints and opportunities created by the norms, values, beliefs and expectations of the social structures that surround them" (Suddaby et al., 2016: p. 229). As such, while social structures create conformity and inertia, individuals with a high level of "social position" and "social skills" can recognize the surrounding institutional environment and promote change processes (ibid). Changes at the individual levels are therefore potentially connected with change at a larger scale, from single organizations to service ecosystems, intended as a "relatively self-contained, self-adjusting system of resource-integrating actors connected by shared institutional arrangements and mutual value creation through service exchange" (Vargo & Lusch, 2016: pp. 10–11). Here institutions are intended as the humanly devised rules and beliefs that enable and constrain actions, the so-called rules of the game (Scott, 2008), while institutional arrangements are "interrelated sets of institutions that together constitute a relatively coherent assemblage that facilitates coordination of activity in value-cocreating service ecosystems" (Vargo & Lusch, 2016: p. 18). With the novel notion of service ecosystem design, a less reductionist view of service design has been therefore advanced, recognizing the "complexities of catalyzing intentional, long-term change in service systems" (Vink et al., 2021: p. 15). Here, the need for new service design methods has highlighted the necessity to foster the capability for reflexivity and reformation in service design collective processes (ibid). Examples are practices explicitly designed to stage "aesthetic experiences" via prototyping, engaging participants in new ways of working, or helping people reflect on the implications of preferred futures (Vink et al., 2017a, 2017b). Alternatively, visual tools such as the "Iceberg Model" can be taken into consideration, representing the hidden layers of existing social structures in order to stimulate design participants to identify and understand which social structures or "institutional arrangements" might need to change when aiming for a preferred future situation (Vink, 2019). This latest evolution regarding the employment of reflexivity within service design practice has been taken as inspiration for the co-design experiment carried out within a Northern-Italy department of mental health.

23.5 A Co-design Experiment into SFPs and Mental Healthcare Transformation

The experimentation regarding the notion of SFPs was implemented in collaboration with the Centre of Mental Healthcare (CMH) of Rovereto in Trentino Alto-Adige, Northern Italy. The CMH operates within the Ospedale Santa Maria del Carmine of Rovereto, following a traditional way of promoting mental well-being through evidence-based medicine and expert knowledge; however, it has been recently integrated with the bigger Mental Health Department of Trento, well known for being the first one in Italy to have introduced peer-support, expert users, and a strong orientation toward the co-production of mental healthcare services in its ordinary practice about twenty years ago (De Stefani et al., 2008).

Although this paradigm shift has undoubtedly brought positive change within the CMH, attempting to eliminate power asymmetries toward a more recovery-oriented approach, it also led to several frictions caused by the cultural clash between the two models of care, each one anchored to its beliefs and modi operandi.

In this sense, the CMH of Rovereto represented an interesting environment to investigate the role these rooted, and often unconscious beliefs can play in the development of SFPs, limiting or fostering the positive transformation of services. Against the above backdrop, the CMH agreed to collaborate with this research to explore how service design reflexivity tools could reveal and acknowledge such beliefs to foster a more recovery-oriented approach within the current service ecosystem.

Accordingly, two reflexive and consequential co-design workshops were planned to help the CMH's actors to reveal existing SFPs, oscillating between individual and collective reflexivity, present and future activities, and micro-meso-macro service system levels. More specifically, the first workshop focused on individual reflexivity, encouraging each participant to reflect on their personal beliefs and potential virtuous or vicious circles, which had to be shared with others to spark conversation and gain empathy toward a multiplicity of perspectives. The second workshop focused on collective reflexivity instead, encouraging participants to explore how individual beliefs and related SFPs that emerged during the first workshop could shape the positive or negative outcome of collective situations happening within the service ecosystem. Participants would then imagine and value the implications of possible future scenarios where everyone's vicious circles would be challenged and transformed into virtuous ones (see Table 23.1).

Table 23.1 Overview of the co-design workshops

Title	Focus	Main aim	Duration	People involved	Activities
Workshop 01	Individual reflexivity	Reveal participants' unconscious beliefs, foster discussion, and empathy toward a multiplicity of perspectives	3 h and 30 min	2 patients (01. 02) 2 nurses (01, 02) 1 psychiatrist 1 psychologist 1 educator 1 psychiatric rehabilitator	- Recovery map - Systemic-self matrioska - Map of circles - Mini-diary
Workshop 02	Collective reflexivity	Reflect on the findings from the previous workshop, imagine a preferable future scenario, identify steps to achieve it	3 h and 30 min	2 patients (01. 02) 2 nurses (01, 02) 1 psychiatrist 1 psychologist 1 educator 1 psychiatric rehabilitator	- Mini-diary outcome - Situation cards - Systemic scenario - Role-play loop

Source Author's own illustration (2021)

Following the two co-design workshops, evaluative semi-structured interviews (Silverman, 2013) have been carried out with each participant to assess how the workshop activities were perceived and what they helped to reveal about interviewees' beliefs and ordinary practice.

To better aid reflexivity and openness, the participants were already acquainted with each other, and all belonged to the same service organization: six staff members were chosen to represent the main professional service backgrounds (one educator, two nurses, one psychiatrist, one psychiatric rehabilitator, one psychologist), while two patients who were more comfortable and used to sharing their experiences with others were engaged.

23.5.1 Co-design Workshop 01

As previously mentioned, the first workshop primarily focused on individual reflexivity, intending to reveal participants' unconscious beliefs and related virtuous or vicious circles to foster discussion and empathy toward a multiplicity of perspectives. As such, the workshop was mainly informed by the concepts of recovery, virtuous and vicious circles, and systemic self, defined as "a schematic diagram that depicts a systematic arrangement of the psychological constructs and postulates of the self" (Massey-Hicks & Altmann, 1979: p. 197).

In particular, the activities of this workshop drew inspiration from three main sources: reflexivity tools (i.e., Iceberg Model), service design tools (i.e., brainstorming map, storyboard, empathy map, user journey), and self-reporting psychology techniques (i.e., personal diary). These have been re-interpreted, ideating new tools that aimed to encourage both individual and collective reflexivity in the specific context of mental healthcare services (see Table 23.2).

Table 23.2 Overview of the activities included in the first workshop

Activity	Type	Duration	Purpose	Specifics
Recovery map	Group icebreaking exercise	30 min	Make participants feel more at ease, gather an initial collective perspective on the concept of recovery	Participants were asked to think about keywords and service situations they immediately associate with the concept of recovery; these thoughts had to be written on post-its, stuck on a map, and discussed in the group
Systemic-self matrioska (SSM)	Semi-individual two-steps exercise	1 h and 30 min	Compare the self-perception on one participant with others' perception of that participant, to spark reflection and discussion and let hidden beliefs emerge	Each participant had to fill in the first part of the tool by describing their typical day through text and illustrations. Participants then had to pass their SSM clockwise for other participants to complete the second part, imagining what that participant's thoughts, beliefs and pressures might have been; eventually, each participant got back their own SSM and discussed the findings
Map of circles	Individual	1 h	Reveal and visualize hidden personal virtuous/vicious circles and the related beliefs that	Focusing on one specific service situation of their choosing (e.g., patient–doctor appointment), each

(continued)

Table 23.2 (continued)

Activity	Type	Duration	Purpose	Specifics
			may cause them; reflect on possible strategies to maintain or transform them	participant had to identify and list on a map their prominent virtuous or vicious circles and beliefs that may cause them, to then imagine possible ways to deal with them
Mini-diary	Individual take-away exercise	10 min + time required to complete the exercise in-between the two workshops	Actively and consciously try to break one personal vicious circle; reflect on what this change would imply	Each participant was required to select a single vicious circle from their Map of Circles and try to break it before the next workshop by taking track of possible strategies, difficulties, and lessons learned on a small diary

Source Author's own illustration (2021)

More specifically, tools such as the Iceberg Model (Vink, 2019) and A Day in the Life (Sturdivant & Gouillart, 1994) have been revisited and combined with service design tools such as the storyboard and the empathy map to develop the Systemic-Self Matrioska.

As shown in Fig. 23.3, the stories emerging from the daily routine of each participant were employed as a starting point to iteratively gather impressions from other participants following the different levels of depth and introspection suggested by the Systemic-Self Matrioska (i.e., responsibilities, social pressures, thoughts, feelings, values, and self-concept). As a result, this would enable participants to confront their self-perception with external perception, fostering empathy and discussion while promoting a more vertical and systemic understanding of individuals.

23.5.2 Findings from Workshop 01

Overall, the workshop succeeded in its goal of promoting individual reflexivity by revealing vicious and virtuous circles of participants, stimulating empathy and a sense of surprise. Interestingly, several SFPs related to mental health emerged, such as defensive routines, lack of proactive involvement, information asymmetry, and

Fig. 23.3 Systemic self-matrioska. *Source* Author's own illustration (2021)

self-stigma. Moreover, the workshop confirmed the complexity of mental health care, as vicious and virtuous circles originating both from the service system and mental illness were revealed.

In particular, the Systemic-Self Matrioska exercise encouraged participants to reflect on themselves and others in vertical terms, letting assumptions and beliefs emerge (Fig. 23.4). For example, the psychiatrist described their typical day in such a professional and neutral way that other participants claimed they could not get any

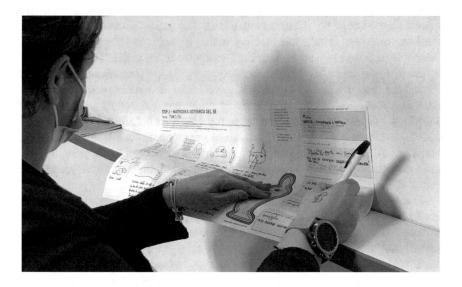

Fig. 23.4 Participant completing the second half of the systemic-self matrioska. *Source* Author's own illustration (2021)

idea of his thoughts or feelings; as a result, they collectively wondered if this attitude may be present when interacting with patients, too, which may then perceive the psychiatrist as distant and cold. The psychiatrist acknowledged this possibility and kept it in mind for the following exercises.

On the other side, the Systemic-Self Matrioska of patients confirmed the presence of self-stigma and the "Why Try" Effect. For example, when other participants described a patient as an excellent student and a good daughter with many creative hobbies, the patient said, "yes, it could be true, but only if it wasn't for my depression." This sparked a reflection in her, and she concluded that "maybe this is all in my head…and maybe I should focus more on what others wrote on this piece of paper."

Regarding the Map of Circle activity, it confirmed the presence of context-specific SFPs related to both organizational dynamics and mental illness.

For example, a nurse's dominant vicious circle was "we always worked like this, and nothing will ever change," which she claimed made her feel "small" and pushed her not to express her opinion during meetings, being passive toward "pre-packed solutions." She acknowledged this was a risky vicious circle, as things will only never change if nobody takes a move. As such, a strategy she suggested was to "speak up more during professional meetings." When talking about group activities with patients, another nurse claimed that sometimes she only focuses on "calming and sedating the symptoms," grounded in the belief that the medical model is illness-centered rather than person-centered. As such, she realized how the institution was becoming embedded in her, and her strategy was to "always remember that a patient is also a person, a daughter, a friend."

It was also interesting to see how dyadic perspectives on the same situation sparked dialogue. For example, both the psychiatrist and a patient focused on "the appointment between psychiatrist and patient." The patient claimed that one of his dominant behaviors during this meeting is that he tends to "always ask the psychiatrist if he is sure of what he is doing," grounded in the belief "I do not trust my psychiatrist very much" and that their relationship "is too professional and there is not enough time available." In turn, the psychiatrist shared his perspective of the same situation, more specifically focusing on "when the patient asks me to do something I do not agree with." As such, his dominant beliefs and vicious circles were "it is too risky," "choices which are too autonomous can lead to failures of which I could feel responsible for," or "it did not work once, it is not going to work this time either." "Valuing openness, curiosity and humility" has been recognized as one of the main strategies to overcome these barriers.

As regards patients, their vicious and virtuous circles were not linked to the service system but rather to aspects of everyday life. For example, vicious circles grounded in the "Why Try" Effect such as "Nobody will hire me for a job if I am mentally ill" were the most common. On the other hand, virtuous circles mainly constituted part of good daily routines, such as "exercise to get rid of intrusive thoughts" or "force myself to take long walks when I feel sleepy or sad."

23.5.3   Co-design Workshop 02

The second workshop focused on collective reflexivity instead, considering how the transformation of individual beliefs and related virtuous and vicious circles could positively or negatively influence existing situations within the service ecosystem, and what individual and collective steps could be taken in order to favor a positive transformation toward a recovery-oriented approach.

This workshop was developed building on the concepts of recovery, virtuous and vicious circles, and future scenarios, while the tools were informed by existing methods, particularly Scenario Building (Jonas, 2010) and Role Play (Curedale, 2013), revisited following a systemic and circular structure (see Table 23.3).

Table 23.3 Overview of the activities included in the second workshop

Activity	Type	Duration	Purpose	Specifics
Mini-diary outcome	Linking exercise	20 min	Gain empathy and spark reflection by sharing personal struggles, lessons learned and insights	Each participant had to share the vicious circle they chose to break, highlighting how that affected their daily routine, behaviors, and interpersonal relationships
Situation cards	Small group exercise	30 min	Identify a specific service situation to work on for the rest of the workshop	Divided into small groups, participants had to select a specific service situation, possibly choosing one of the situations emerged in previous activities (i.e., Recovery Map and Map of Circles); after this, each group had to briefly describe and illustrate this situation on a paper card
Systemic scenario	Small group exercise	55 min	Compare the present situation with a potential preferable future of that situation, and identify possible steps to achieve that future	Based on the specific situation selected, each group had to reflect on the dynamics (i.e., virtuous/vicious circles) that characterize it and the actors most involved in that situation; after this, groups were required to think about how that situation could be improved in the future and what that would imply

(continued)

Table 23.3 (continued)

Activity	Type	Duration	Purpose	Specifics
Role-play loop	Small group exercise	1 h and 15 min	Perceive multiples points of view, reflect on how individual behaviors can have an impact on collectivity	The two groups were required to improvise their situation three times in a row after defining exchanged roles (e.g., the nurse impersonating the patient); at the end of each improvisation, they had to think about what behaviors each participant could change and then improvise again, improving that behavior, noting down reflections on a map

Source Author's own illustration (2021)

More specifically, the future scenarios were developed to be confronted with the present time to value the in-between steps to reach that preferable future. At the same time, the Role Play was designed to be enacted multiple times in a loop, each time transforming individual negative behaviors into positive ones, to demonstrate how small individual steps could gradually improve collective service situations.

23.5.4 Findings from Workshop 02

Overall, the workshop succeeded in its goal of promoting collective reflexivity by sparking discussion on a possible preferable future for specific situations within the service system, also helping to visualize possible steps to achieve it. Unlike the previous workshop, this proved less demanding on a psychological level, as the focus was not on the person but instead on service dynamics. In this regard, the co-design workshop enabled participants to collectively discuss and analyze what is usually not taken into consideration, as it is traditionally accepted and taken for granted.

This discussion was firstly enabled by what emerged from the Mini-Diary exercise from the first workshop. For example, a nurse admitted she could not transform her vicious circle, that was, "speaking up more during professional meetings." When asked why she said that hierarchical pressures were "huge," and when she felt like suggesting alternative perspectives, she heard a voice in her head saying, "it is not going to matter." Nevertheless, she admitted the exercise made her experience "positive anger," as she was less passive during meetings: "I think this is the first step to make things change, but of course it is a long journey." Building on these statements, participants started a collective discussion on traditional ways of operating and actively reflected on which dynamics in the service system were working out or not.

Fig. 23.5 Participants completing the systemic scenario activity. *Source* Author's own illustration (2021)

This preliminary discussion proved helpful to complete the Systemic Scenario exercise (Fig. 23.5), where both groups chose a similar situation: the group meeting involving staff members, patients, and families. However, they gave very different interpretations of it. For example, when asked to identify who was more involved during the chosen situation, the first group put the doctor at the first place, claiming that "it is him who starts and leads the conversation…it is a historical thing, where the doctor is seen as the most responsible for the patient" (patient 02). On the other hand, the second group (which counted more professionals in its participants) put the patient first. This sparked a discussion on how different perceptions may be present within the service, specifically in certain situations. As a result, all participants imagined how this situation could be improved in the future, finding a good compromise for everyone involved.

Regarding the Role-Play Loop, both groups actively participated. While role-playing a typical clinician–patient–family appointment, participants showed great interest in knowing what personal behaviors could be improved for each specific role. For example, one group noted that the psychologist often kept her arms folded, which may be perceived as a sign of closure. As a result, she acknowledged this unconscious behavior and said she would keep it in mind for the future. At the same time, a patient has been advised to act less defensively during meetings and better work on his sense of trust toward medical professionals. In this regard, the exchanged-role feature was particularly appreciated as it helped to put participants "in the shoes of someone else" and at the same time "do not have that much pressure" on themselves and their behaviors.

23.5.5 Data Analysis

Each workshop has been documented with field notes, audio recordings, photographs, and the outcomes of each tangible tool. Together with the data collected from the workshops, individual semi-structured interviews were carried out with the eight participants. These interviews, which lasted about 30–40 min, were held via phone or video call and audio recorded and focused primarily on three key aspects: general feedback on the overall understanding, usefulness, impact, and accessibility of the tools and process employed; reflections on the level of personal change considering lessons learned, difficulties, and any noted behavioral variation; reflections on service level change valuing the role of SFPs for the transformation of the service system.

23.5.6 Overall Feedback

Although some participants were already familiar with the topics dealt with during the workshops, the majority expressed enthusiasm toward how these were approached and discussed in a "less traditional and more engaging" way (psychiatric rehabilitator), "focusing on specific situations and not in general, which can be confusing" (patient 01).

Some difficulties in completing the exercises on an emotional and cognitive level were reported. The majority of interviewees identified the Systemic-Self Matrioska, the Map of Circles, and the Mini-Diary as the most demanding, involving a deeper level of psychological introspection.

The Systemic-Self Matrioska had been considered the more complicated tool as it required to "get out the comfort zone, getting rid of the fear of being judged and saying potentially uncomfortable things," and "reflect on people we think we know but actually, we do not" (nurse 02). On the other hand, The Map of Circles and the Mini-Diary were primarily focused on auto-analysis, which is something "not everybody is used to doing" (educator). The Mini-Diary especially required participants to note down their reflections and accomplish small tasks every day: "as adults, we are lost in our frantic life, and most of the time we forget the importance of sitting down at a table and take some time to reflect…it is challenging" (psychologist).

Generally, staff members also admitted they had some initial difficulties opening up about their thoughts and feelings given the presence of patients at the workshops. Some of them were "afraid of saying inappropriate things," but also admitted how this feeling gradually diminished once they went on completing the exercises: "I felt a sense of relief…it makes you realize that there is so much more you can tell and share than you think" (nurse 02).

Concerning usefulness, some of the interviewees categorized activities as applicable on a personal and service level. However difficult, the activities mentioned above (i.e., Systemic-Self Matrioska, Map of Circles, and Mini-Diary) have been recognized as very useful on a personal level, as they helped to "not only perceive and being perceived by others but also to reflect on how we can better express ourselves more clearly and sincerely" (psychologist). Interestingly, a patient (02) admitted she created a Mini-Diary of her own to keep working on her vicious circles.

On a service system level, the Role-Play Loop has been particularly appreciated, as it involved "physical, mental and emotional elements" that allowed participants to "fully commit to the activity" (patient 01). Interviewees also enjoyed the exchanged roles feature, as it allowed them to "see things from a different perspective" (nurse 02). Moreover, the exercise proved helpful as "changing little things one at a time can really affect the future scenario" (nurse 01).

The Systemic Scenario has been perceived as functional as it facilitated discussion on topics and situations traditionally taken for granted and uncontested, prompting collective reflexivity. In this regard, the majority of interviewees acknowledged the importance of focusing on one specific situation at a time, as it allowed for a more targeted and effective reflection: "looking at the big picture can make you feel lost and overwhelmed but working on the small things first makes it easier to act…and then you put these things together, and change can be fostered" (nurse 02).

23.5.7 Reflections on Personal Change

Interviewees reported a change in the way they view certain things, both in their everyday life and within the service system—one participant claimed she perceived these workshops as "a possible innovative form of therapy" (educator), as they prompted her to acknowledge that alternative mindsets exist and can be embodied.

Furthermore, participants said they tended to notice more their potential enactment of virtuous and vicious circles and did the same with other people's—for example, the psychologist admitted she has been more attentive to hers and her patients' virtuous and vicious circles during appointments. Nevertheless, it has been acknowledged how the worst vicious circle of all, that is, the deep-rooted conviction that "nothing will ever make a difference," could potentially affect this change of mindset.

23.5.8 Reflections on Service Change

Overall, most interviewees believed that this kind of activities could bring effective change on a service and organizational level if they are embedded in the organization and happen regularly. As such, they claimed more people belonging to the service system should be involved in these activities (i.e., family members, friends, more patients, and staff members), as well as external associations belonging to the network.

On a more systemic level, a possible next step that has been identified is to include in this process both the Quality Department and the Training Department of the Hospital, so that these activities could be integrated into the system as "training programs" (psychiatrist). Moreover, the role of the facilitator (i.e., the service designer) has been recognized as fundamental for the effective implementation of this transformative process.

The most considerable resistances identified were of organizational and cultural nature: "I think that as long as the majority of people feel comfortable in the status quo, fostering change can be extremely difficult" (psychiatric rehabilitator). In this regard, most participants feared the potential consequences that may arise from challenging higher organizational levels and related traditional modi operandi, even if it was recognized as "not impossible to achieve," suggesting how "change should start together, from the bottom" (psychiatrist).

23.6   Discussion

Based on what emerged from the interviews, it can be stated that the field experimentation has generated positive feedback. Overall, the methodology employed was effective and appreciated, as it succeeded in prompting both individual and collective reflexivity. In this regard, it revealed rooted thoughts, behaviors, and rules that are often taken for granted and unquestioned, both on a personal and service level, and sparked open collective discussion on the latter.

As a result, it constituted an input for a change of mindset in participants, also favored by the opportunity of coming in contact with different people and mental models—in this sense, the reflexivity tools utilized enabled the activity of "perceiving multiples" (Vink et al., 2018). As such, heterogeneity (i.e., individuals with diverse backgrounds, roles, personalities) has been recognized as essential for reflexivity practices. At the same time, reflexivity tools nudged participants to implement new approaches of dealing with certain attitudes and situations, building awareness of the fact that alternative ways of acting exist and are possible—in this sense, enabling the activity of "embodying alternatives" (Vink et al., 2018).

In this regard, it is relevant to mention another key point emerging from the interviews: the possibility of working on specific situations within the service rather than on the whole system. Like SFPs on an individual level, these "service situations" can be collectively revealed, questioned, or transformed for the whole service to gradually get closer to the overall transformational aim. As already mentioned, this may favor a more targeted and effective kind of change.

Furthermore, it appeared how the alternated focus on individual reflexivity first and collective reflexivity afterward increased the awareness of one's own potential vicious/virtuous circles and one's role in the service situation, suggesting how this oscillation between individual and collective reflexivity should be maintained throughout the process.

At the same time, the workshops mainly focused on SFPs and situations that could be adjusted or reshaped while paying less attention to defining ways to maintain and develop what is already "virtuous." As such, it represents a partial view of the so-called institutional work intended as "the sets of practices through which individual and collective actors create, maintain and disrupt the institutions of organizational fields" (Lawrence & Suddaby, 2006: p. 220).

While the experiment had positive feedback, two co-design workshops are, however, not enough to generate a relevant, tangible, and long-lasting change within the service organization; in fact, they acted as a prototype and should be seen as an integral part of a bigger circular and self-adjusting process fostering transformation.

Furthermore, as the evaluation has shown, transformation must take place both horizontally and vertically. From a horizontal perspective, the transformational process should gradually involve actors external to the service, who nevertheless play a fundamental role in the overall process (i.e., other departmental units and external associations belonging to the network). From a vertical perspective, the transformational process should instead gradually involve people belonging to different levels of the service system (i.e., engaging both users and personnel with more managerial and leadership roles). We recognize that the nature of the reflexive tools might need to change, depending on the levels of considerations on the service system development.

Also, as previously mentioned, a transformational process certainly requires a long-term perspective and may hide several limitations and constraints, especially of cultural and organizational nature (i.e., cultures clash, preservation of the status quo, defensive routines). To overcome these barriers, the organizations could look for, both horizontally and vertically, potential role models: a concept theorized by Merton describing individuals open to change and discussion and capable of providing a good example (Holton, 2004), thus facilitating the gradual inclusion of other actors in the transformational process and encouraging a distributed cultural contamination. In this sense, the transformation has to start from individuals who can enact reflexivity to create, maintain, or transform both their personal vicious/virtuous circles and collective service situations at different levels of aggregation to encourage tangible and distributed change within the organization.

Eventually, while this pilot project proved effective in provoking reflexivity in the workshop's participants, it should be underlined that it may have lacked other dimensions of reflexivity, such as the designer's personal reflexivity. In this regard, the "protected positionality" deriving from relatively privileged conditions (i.e., research developed within a MA thesis, ongoing support of medical professionals belonging to the CMH) should be pointed out. In the eventuality of shifting from single one-off interventions to longer processes of change, we reckon the necessity of reflexivity tools targeted to the designer, too, to better track and reflect on the ongoing collaboration process and the actual conditions of participation. With this in mind, tools such as the "reflective design documentation" (Dalsgaard & Halskov, 2012) or the "practice notation" (Agid & Akama, 2020) presented earlier would become an important addition.

23.7 Conclusion

The field of mental health care is amid a confrontation among different cultures and practices, which seems to be still far away from an agreed landing point. In this regard, the biopsychosocial approach essential for the implementation of patient-centered care has been consistently challenged by more biological models of care, which in turn limit the application of community-oriented perspectives such as co-production, lived experience, and recovery, even though they have proven potential to improve mental health services by not only making them more responsive to users' needs and values, but also by redistributing power. As such, a more integrative approach to mental healthcare comprehensive of both evidence-based and experience-based medicine would be the most promising way to achieve satisfying results in this field. However, as demonstrated, this complementary model of care is struggling to become the norm due to organizational cultures and related modi operandi that may conflict with each other.

Stressing the embedded systemic and multi-level characterization of services, we illustrated how organizational cultures are generally the result of the shared mental models belonging to individual actors (Vink et al., 2018), consisting of deeply rooted beliefs, assumptions, and values. Further exploring this research stream, we argued how these individual beliefs might perpetrate SFPs within the organization in the form of virtuous or vicious circles, having a tangible impact on fostering or limiting transformational change.

More specifically, it was pointed out how the field of mental health care is characterized by specific SFPs, mostly perpetrating vicious circles, often resulting in stigma and self-stigma, power imbalances, and defensive practices. On the other side, it was suggested how introducing a more recovery-based approach may instead foster the perpetration of virtuous circles based on the restoration of hope, self-determination, and personal empowerment.

In this regard, we stressed the need to reveal the rooted and often unconscious beliefs at the basis of these circles in order to break the vicious ones while consciously maintaining the virtuous ones, thus favoring a smoother service experience for everyone involved in the system.

We suggested how this revelation could be possible through the employment of reflexivity, recently identified as a crucial lever to promote more profound and large-scale transformations in organizations and service systems starting from individuals' worldviews.

In particular, we delineated how reflexivity could be employed to develop service design tools to be used during co-design workshops among service actors (micro-level) by oscillating between individual and collective reflexivity, present and future scenarios, and focusing on one specific service situation at a time. Specifically, the experimentation, which took place within a Northern-Italy department of mental health, concentrated on how vicious circles could be gradually transformed into virtuous ones while also illustrating how to acknowledge what was already virtuous more consciously.

In this sense, this chapter has pointed out the importance of focusing on actors' mental models at the micro-level of aggregation, implementing research in this subfield which has until now been marginalized, underestimated, and neglected (Vink et al., 2018), stressing its potential to enable organizational transformation at the macro-level, too. As such, it has reflected on the importance of service design practices as collective activities in which all actors collaborate at the micro-level in a unique form of institutional work, prompting individual and collective reflexivity in a multiplicity of perspectives.

Furthermore, it sheds light on the complex and contentious dynamics which characterize the field of mental health care, highlighting the presence of SFPs of dual nature (organization and illness-caused) and constituting an input for a change of mindset in the actors involved, building awareness of the fact that alternative ways of thinking and acting exist and are possible.

However, as already said, this experimentation should be considered a prototype as it constituted the first iteration of a much longer and ongoing transformation process, whose interest lies in the potential to be embedded in the organization's strategic and training infrastructures to leverage the reflexivity and reformation potential. The concept of working in interrelated circles across the service system could be explored further as a transformational service design process, spurring a tangible and distributed cultural contamination, alternating interventions at different levels of the service system, and eventually expanding to the broader ecosystem.

References

Adler, R. B., Rosenfeld, L. B., & Ii, R. P. F. (2012). *Interplay: The process of interpersonal communication* (12th ed.). Oxford University Press.

Anthony, W. A. (1993). Recovery from mental illness: The guiding vision of the mental health service system in the 1990s. *Psychosocial Rehabilitation Journal, 16*(4), 11–23. https://doi.org/10.1037/h0095655

Agid, S., & Akama, Y. (2020). Reflexive account-giving through "practice notations": Plural dimensions and dynamics of infrastructuring. In *Proceedings of the 16th Participatory Design Conference 2020-Participation(s) Otherwise* (pp. 164–169), Manizales, Colombia. https://doi.org/10.1145/3384772.3385136, Corpus ID: 219844669.

Anjum, R. L. (2016). Evidence based or person centered? An ontological debate. *European Journal for Person Centered Healthcare, 4*(2), 421–429.

Bellinger, G. (2004). Systems thinking: "A journey in the realm of systems". Accessed 14 June 2021, from: http://www.systems-thinking.org/index.htm.

Benoit, L., Russo, T., Barry, C., Falissard, B., & Henckes, N. (2019). ". You have to believe in something: Risk of psychosis and psychiatrists' beliefs in the self-fulfilling prophecy. *Social Science and Medicine, 230*, 20–29. https://doi.org/10.1016/j.socscimed.2019.03.035

Biggs, M. (2009). Self-fulfilling prophecies. In *The Oxford handbook of analytical sociology* (pp. 294–314). Oxford: Oxford University Press. https://doi.org/10.1093/oxfordhb/9780199215362.013.13.

Bodenheimer, T., Wagner, E. H., & Grumbach, K. (2002). Improving primary care for patients with chronic illness. *JAMA, 288*(14), 1775–1779. https://doi.org/10.1001/jama.288.14.1775

Boyle, D., & Harris, M. (2009) The challenge of co-production. In *How equal partnerships between professionals and the public are crucial to improving public services*. London: Nesta (Ed.).

Corrigan, P. W., Larson, J. E., & Rüsch, N. (2009). Self-stigma and the "why try" effect: Impact on life goals and evidence-based practices. *World Psychiatry, 8*(2), 75–81. https://doi.org/10. 1002/j.2051-5545.2009.tb00218.xPMCID:PMC2694098 PMID: 19516923.

Corrigan, P. W., & Rao, D. (2012). On the self-stigma of mental illness: Stages, disclosure, and strategies for change. *Canadian Journal of Psychiatry, 57*(8), 464–469. https://doi.org/10. 1177/070674371205700804

Curedale, R. (2013) *Design thinking: Process and methods manual*. Design Community College Inc (Ed.), Topanga.

Dalsgaard, P., & Halskov, K. (2012). Reflective design documentation. In *Proceedings of the Designing Interactive Systems Conference, DIS'12* (pp. 428–437), Newcastle, UK. https://doi. org/10.1145/2317956.2318020. Accessed 11–15 June 2021.

De Stefani, R., Torri, E., Bertotti, K. (2008). Il coinvolgimento attivo di utenti e familiari nel Servizio di salute mentale di Trento. L'approccio del "fareassieme" e gli Utenti Familiari Esperti (UFE). In *Salute e Società* (pp. 170–180), Milano, Italy. https://doi.org/10.3280/ SES2011-002014.

Denzau, A. T., & North, D. C. (1994). Shared mental models: Ideologies and institutions. *Kyklos, 47*(1), 3–31. https://doi.org/10.1111/j.1467-6435.1994.tb02246.x

Gray, D. (2017). *Doing research in the real world*. SAGE Publications.

Greenhalgh, T., Wherton, J., Papoutsi, C., Lynch, J., Hughes, G., A'Court, C., Hinder, S., Fahy, N., Procter, R., & Shaw, S. (2017). Beyond adoption: A new framework for theorizing and evaluating non adoption, abandonment, and challenges to the scale-up, spread, and sustainability of health and care technologies. *Journal of Medical Internet Research, 19*(11), e367. https://doi.org/10.2196/jmir.8775.

Greenhalgh, T., & Papoutsi, C. (2018). Studying complexity in health services research: Desperately seeking an overdue paradigm shift. *BMC Medicine, 16*(1), 4–9. https://doi.org/10. 1186/s12916-018-1089-4

Guiette, A., & Vandenbempt, K. (2013). Exploring team mental model dynamics during strategic change implementation in professional service organizations: A sensemaking perspective. *European Management Journal, 31*(6), 728–744. https://doi.org/10.1016/j.emj.2013.07.002

Holton, G. (2004). Robert K. Merton (4 July 1910–February 2003). *Proceedings of the American Philosophical Society, 148*(4), 505–517. Retrieved May 28, 2021, from http://www.jstor.org/ stable/1558145.

Isaksson, A., Börjesson, E., Gunn, M., Andersson, C., & Ehrnberger, K. (2019). Norm critical design and ethnography: Possibilities, objectives and stakeholders. *Sociological Research Online*. https://doi.org/10.1177/1360780417743168.

Jonas, W. (2010). A scenario for design. In R. Buchanan, D. Doordan & V. Margolin (Eds.). *The designed world: Images, objects, environments* (pp.37–52). Oxford: Berg. Oxford. Retrieved May 27, 2021, from https://doi.org/10.5040/9781350096004.ch-003.

Junginger, S., & Sangiorgi, D. (2009). Service design and organizational change: Bridging the gap between rigour and relevance. In: *IASDR09 Conference, Seoul* (pp. 4339–4348). Accessed on June 14, 2021, from http://www.iasdr2009.org/ap/Papers/SpecialSession/ AdoptingrigorinServiceDesignResearch/ServiceDesignandOrganizationalChange-BridgingtheGapBetweenRigourandRelevance.pdf.

Jussim, L., & Eccles, J. (1995). Naturally occurring interpersonal expectancies. In N. Eisenberg (Ed.), *Review of personality and social psychology, social development* (Vol. 15, pp. 74–108). Sage Publications, Inc. Thousand Oaks, CA, US.

Jussim, L., Eccles, J., & Madon, S. (1996). Social perception, social stereotypes, and teacher expectations: Accuracy and the quest for the powerful self-fulfilling prophecy. *Advances in Experimental Social Psychology, 28*, 281–388. https://doi.org/10.1016/S0065-2601(08)60240-3

Kaplan, G. A. (2006). *Social determinants of health* (2nd edn). In M. Marmot & R.Wilkinson (Eds.). Oxford: Oxford University Press, pp. 1111–1112.

Kraff, H. (2018). A tool for reflection—On participant diversity and changeability over time in participatory design. *CoDesign, 14*(1), 60–73. https://doi.org/10.1080/15710882.2018.1424204

Lawrence, T. B., & Suddaby, R. (2006). Institutions and instiutional work. In R. Clegg, C. Hardy, T. B. Lawrence, & W. R. Nord (Eds.) *Handbook of organization studies* (Vol. 5, 2nd edn, (pp. 215–254). London: Sage.

Leamy, M., Bird, V., Le Boutillier, C., Williams, J., & Slade, M. (2011). Conceptual framework for personal recovery in mental health: Systematic review and narrative synthesis. *British Journal of Psychiatry., 199*(6), 445–452. https://doi.org/10.1192/bjp.bp.110.083733 PMID: 22130746.

Liberati, E. G., Gorli, M., Moja, L., Galuppo, L., Ripamonti, S., & Scaratti, G. (2015). Exploring the practice of patient centered care: The role of ethnography and reflexivity. *Social Science and Medicine*, 133, 45–52. https://doi.org/10.1016/j.socscimed.2015.03.050. PMID: 25841094.

Link, B. G., Struening, E., Cullen, F. T., Shrout, P. E., & Dohrenwend, B. P. (1989). A modified labeling theory perspective to mental disorders: An empirical assessment. *American Sociological Review, 54*(3), 400–423. https://doi.org/10.2307/2095613

Link, B. G., Struening, E. L., Elmer, L., Neese-Todd, S., Asmussen, S., & Phelan, J. C. (2001). Stigma as a barrier to recovery: The consequences of stigma for the self-esteem of people with mental illnesses. *Psychiatric Services, 52*(12), 1621–1626. https://doi.org/10.1176/appi.ps.52.12.1621. PMID: 11726753.

Lu, P. & Sangiorgi, D. (2021). Exploring implications for designing for sociotechnical transitions: Taking reflexivity as a matter of scale, Nordes 2021, Matters of Scale. In *Conference: NORDES 2021, the 9th Nordes Design Research Conference*, Kolding, Demark.

Major, B., & O'Brien, L. T. (2005). The social psychology of stigma. *Annual Review of Psychology.* 56, 393–421 https://doi.org/10.1146/annurev.psych.56.091103.070137.

Maldonado, T. (1990). *Cultura, democrazia ambiente: Saggi sul mutamento*. Milano: Feltrinelli Editore.

Malpass, M. (2012). *Contextualising Critical design: Towards a taxonomy of critical practice in product design*. Ph.D. thesis, Nottingham Trent University (Ed.), Nottingham.

Malpass, M. (2013). Between wit and reason: Defining associative, speculative, and critical design in practice. *Design and Culture, 5*(3), 333–356. https://doi.org/10.2752/175470813X13705953612200

Manago, B. (2015). Understanding the social norms attitudes, beliefs, and behaviors towards mental illness in the united states. In *Proceedings of the National Academy of Sciences*, Indiana University (Ed.), Bloomington, IN, US.

Maniatopoulos, G., Hunter, D. J., Erskine, J., & Hudson, B. (2020). Large-scale health system transformation in the United Kingdom: Implementing the new care models in the NHS. *Journal of Health Organization and Management, 34*(3), 325–344. https://doi.org/10.1108/JHOM-05-2019-0144

Manzini, E. (1994). Design, environment and social quality: From "Existenzminimum" to "Quality Maximum." *Design Issues, 10*(1), 37–43. https://doi.org/10.2307/1511653

Margolin, V. (1998). Design for a sustainable world. *Design Issues, 14*(2), 83–92. https://doi.org/10.2307/1511853

Massey-Hicks, M., & Altmann, H. (1979). *The Journal of Educational Thought (JET)/Revue de la Pensée Éducative, 13*(3), 168–171. Werklund School of Education (Pub.), University of Calgary. Calgary, Canada.

Masuch, M. (1985). Vicious circles in organizations. *Administrative Science Quarterly, 30*(1), 14–33. https://doi.org/10.2307/2392809

McGorry, P. D., & Mei, C. (2020). Why do psychiatrists doubt the value of early intervention? The power of illusion. *Australasian Psychiatry, 28*(3), 331–334. https://doi.org/10.1177/1039856220924323 PMID: 32436728.

Merton, R. K. (1948). The self-fulfilling prophecy. *The Antioch Review, 8*(2), 193–210. http://doi.org/https://doi.org/10.2307/4609267.

Mullen, R., Admiraal, A., & Trevena, J. (2008). Defensive practice in mental health. *The New Zealand Medical Journal, 121*(1286), 85–91. PMID: 19098951.

Nakanishi, M., Kurokawa, G., Niimura, J., Nishida, A., Shepherd, G., & Yamasaki, S. (2021). System-level barriers to personal recovery in mental health: Qualitative analysis of co-productive narrative dialogues between users and professionals. *BJPsych open, 7*(1), e25. https://doi.org/10.1192/bjo.2020.156.

Nilsson, Å. W., & Jahnke, M. (2018). Tactics for norm-creative innovation. *She Ji: The Journal of Design, Economics, and Innovation, 4*(4), 375–391. https://doi.org/10.1016/j.sheji.2018.11.002

Pasman, J. (2011). The consequences of labeling mental illnesses on the self-concept: A review of the literature and future directions. *Social Cosmos, 2*, 122–127. Corpus ID: 142218724.

Patrício, L., Fisk, R. P., Cunha, J. F. E., & Constantine, L. (2011). Multilevel service design: From customer value constellation to service experience blueprint. *Journal of Service Research, 14*(2), 180–200. https://doi.org/10.1177/1094670511401901

Patrício, L., Sangiorgi, D., Mahr, D., Čaić, M., Kalantari, S., & Sundar, S. (2020). Leveraging service design for healthcare transformation: Toward people-centered, integrated, and technology-enabled healthcare systems. *Journal of Service Management. Ahead-of-Print.* https://doi.org/10.1108/JOSM-11-2019-0332

Perkins, A., Ridler, J., Browes, D., Peryer, G., Notley, C., & Hackmann, C. (2018). Experiencing mental health diagnosis: A systematic review of service user, clinician, and carer perspectives across clinical settings. *The Lancet. Psychiatry, 5*(9), 747–764. https://doi.org/10.1016/S2215-0366(18)30095-6

Pihkala, S., & Karasti, H. (2016). Reflexive engagement—Enacting reflexivity in design and for "participation in plural." In *PDC '16: Proceedings of the 14th Participatory Design Conference: Full papers in ACM International Conference Proceeding Series* (Vol. 1, pp. 21–30). https://doi.org/10.1145/2940299.2940302.

Roberts, G. A. (2000). Narrative and severe mental illness: What place do stories have in an evidence-based world? *Advances in Psychiatric Treatment, 6*(6), 432–441. https://doi.org/10.1192/apt.6.6.432

Sangiorgi, D. (2011). Transformative services and transformation design. *International Journal of Design, 5*(2), 29–40.

Sangiorgi, D., Farr, M., McAllister, S., Mulvale, G., Sneyd, M., Vink, J. E., & Warwick, L. (2019). Designing in highly contentious areas: Perspectives on a way forward for mental healthcare transformation. *Design Journal, 22*(sup1), 309–330. https://doi.org/10.1080/14606925.2019.1595422

Scheff, T. J. (1966). *Being mentally Ill: A sociological theory.* Aldline.

Schein, E. H. (2010). *Organizational culture and leadership.* Jossey-Bass.

Schön, D. A. (1984). *The reflective practitioner: How professionals think in action.* Basic Books (Pub.), New York City, NY, US.

Schultz, T. (2018). Decolonising techno-colonising indigenous design futures. *Strategic Design Research Journal, 11*(2), 79–91.

Scott, W. R. (2008). *Institutions and organizations: Ideas and interests.* Sage.

Silverman, D. (2013). *Doing qualitative research: A practical handbook.* Sage.

Steier, F. (1991). *Research and reflexivity.* Sage.

Stukas, A.A., & Snyder, M. (2016). Self-fulfilling prophecies. In *Encyclopedia of mental health* (2nd edn, (pp. 92–100). Elsevier Inc., Amsterdam. https://doi.org/10.1016/B978-0-12-397045-9.00220-2.

Sturdivant, F. D., & Gouillart, F. J. (1994). Spend a day in the life of your customers. *Harvard Business Review, 72*, 116–125.

Suddaby, R., Viale, T., & Gendron, Y. (2016). Reflexivity: The role of embedded social position and entrepreneurial social skill in processes of field level change. *Research in Organizational Behavior, 36*(C), 225–245. https://doi.org/10.1016/j.riob.2016.02.001.

Suchman, L. (2002). Located accountabilities in technology production. *Scandinavian Journal of Information Systems, 14*(2), Article 7. Sultana Corpus ID: 15307022.

Sultana, F. (2007). Reflexivity, positionality and participatory ethics: negotiating fieldwork dilemmas in international research. *ACME: An International Journal for Critical Geographies, 6*(3), 374–385.

The Health Foundation. (2016). Person-centred care made simple. What everyone should know about person-centred care. In *The health foundation (Ed.)* (pp. 1–45). Accessed 14 June 2021, from https://www.health.org.uk/sites/default/files/PersonCentredCareMadeSimple.pdf

Thomas, W. I., & Thomas, D. S. (1928). *The child in America.* Knopf (Ed.), New York, NY, US.

UN Human Rights Council. (2017). Report of the special rapporteur on the right of everyone to the enjoyment of the highest attainable standard of physical and mental health. UN Human Rights Council A/HRC/35/21 2017. Accessed on June 14, 2021, from https://digitallibrary.un.org/record/1298436?ln=en.

Vargo, S. L., & Lusch, R. F. (2015). Institutions and axioms: An extension and update of service-dominant logic. *Journal of the Academy of Marketing Science, 44*(2016), 5–23. https://doi.org/10.1007/s11747-015-0456-3

Vargo, S. L., & Lusch, R. F. (2016). Institutions and axioms: An extension and update of service-dominant logic. *Journal of the Academy of Marketing Science, 44*(1), 5–23. https://doi.org/10.1007/s11747-015-0456-3

Vink, J. (2019). In visible—Conceptualizing service ecosystem design (p. 217). Accessed 14 June 2021, from http://www.diva-portal.org/smash/record.jsf?pid=diva2%3A1313628&dswid=7912.

Vink, J., Edvardsson, B., Wetter-Edman, K., & Tronvoll, B. (2018). Reshaping mental models—Enabling innovation through service design. *Journal of Service Management, 30*(1), 75–104. https://doi.org/10.1108/JOSM-08-2017-0186

Vink, J., Koskela-Huotari, K., Tronvoll, B., Edvardsson, B., & Wetter-Edman, K. (2021). Service ecosystem design: propositions, process model, and future research agenda. *Journal of Service Research., 24*(2), 168–186. https://doi.org/10.1177/1094670520952537

Vink, J., Tronvoll, B., Edvardsson, B., Wetter-Edman, K., & Aguirre, M. (2017a). Service ecosystem design: Doing institutional work through service design. In *Proceedings of the 5th Naples Forum on Service* (pp. 1–15), Sorrento, Italy.

Vink, J., Wetter-Edman, K., & Aguirre, M. (2017b). Designing for aesthetic disruption: Altering mental models in social systems through designerly practices. *The Design Journal, 20*(sup1), S2168–S2177. https://doi.org/10.1080/14606925.2017.1352733

Watzlawick, P. (1984). Self-fulfilling prophecies. In *The social production of reality, essays and readings on social interaction* (pp. 392–408).

Willis, C. D., Saul, J., Bevan, H., Scheirer, M. A., Best, A., Greenhalgh, T., Mannion, R., Cornelissen, E., Howland, D., Jenkins, E., & Bitz, J. (2016). Sustaining organizational culture change in health systems. *Journal of Health, Organisation and Management, 30*(1), 2–30. https://doi.org/10.1108/JHOM-07-2014-0117

Yu, B. C. L., Chio, F. H. N., Mak, W. W. S., Corrigan, P. W., & Chan, K. K. Y. (2021). Internalization process of stigma of people with mental illness across cultures: A meta-analytic structural equation modeling approach. *Clinical Psychology Review, 87*, 102029. https://doi.org/10.1016/j.cpr.2021.102029 PMID: 34058604.

Alessandra Sara Cutroneo has recently completed her Master's Degree in Product Service System Design from Politecnico di Milano, where she also obtained a Bachelor's Degree in Communication Design. Moreover, she has participated in the Master of European Design, studying at Köln International School of Design and The Glasgow School of Art. She has worked with the International Society of Service Innovation Professionals (ISSIP) and CILAB research laboratory from Politecnico di Milano and has attended projects in collaboration with NHS Scotland. She now works as a Junior Service Designer for Generali Italia. Her research interests focus on implementing service design approaches to favor organizational change, especially when applied to the public sector.

Daniela Sangiorgi a PhD in Design, is an Associate Professor at the Design Department of Politecnico di Milano, Italy. She has been one of the first researchers investigating the area of Service Design. From 2007 to 2015, she has worked at the research group Imagination at Lancaster University, UK. Her research interest focuses on the role of design in the development of services, with a particular focus on public-sector innovation. Her research has been published in the Journal of Service Research, Journal of Service Management, The Design Journal, International Journal of Design, and Design Studies.

Fabio Lucchi is a psychiatrist responsible for the Mental Health Department at Azienda Provinciale Servizi Sanitari (APSS), Provincia Autonoma di Trento, Trentino Alto-Adige, Italy. His practice focuses on integrating a more recovery-oriented approach within the dominant biomedical model of care.

Co-creation in Health Services Through Service Design

24

Birgit Mager, Anna-Sophie Oertzen, and Josina Vink

Abstract

Integrating co-creation in health services is increasingly acknowledged to improve health outcomes and service quality. To support co-creation in this context, service design is leveraged as a process. However, there often remains a superficial understanding of what co-creation entails, its benefits, and how it can be meaningfully supported through service design. In this chapter, we detail how service design is being leveraged in the health sector to drive co-creation and catalyze a variety of beneficial outcomes. We illuminate the dynamics and challenges of co-creation through service design by presenting a case of a service design project conducted by Experio Lab in Sweden. In doing so, this chapter helps to provide a more nuanced understanding of how service design contributes to co-creation in health services.

24.1 Introduction

The healthcare sector increasingly recognizes the need to support co-creation opportunities for patients, families, service providers, and other community stakeholders to enhance service quality and catalyze innovation (Aghdam et al.,

B. Mager (✉)
University of Applied Sciences Cologne, Köln, Germany
e-mail: mager@service-design.de

A.-S. Oertzen
Düsseldorf, Germany

J. Vink
Oslo School of Architecture and Design (AHO), Oslo, Norway

© The Author(s), under exclusive license to Springer Nature Switzerland AG 2022
M. A. Pfannstiel et al. (eds.), *Service Design Practices for Healthcare Innovation*,
https://doi.org/10.1007/978-3-030-87273-1_24

497

2020). As part of this development, service design is increasingly being integrated in health systems around the globe to support the co-creation process in the form of labs, commissioned projects, capacity building programs, and others. However, there remains some ambiguity around what co-creation in health care facilitated by service design entails. Without this more in-depth understanding there are risks that the co-creation process is superficial or tokenistic and not embracing its full transformative potential. Accordingly, there is a need for a more nuanced understanding of co-creation and how to thoughtfully support it within a service design process in health care.

To support this knowledge building, we start by positioning service design in relation to a broader understanding of design and highlight the ways in which it is being taken up in the health sector internationally, particularly to support co-creation. We then draw from research to build a more holistic understanding of co-creation and its potential benefits in the healthcare context. To contextualize this understanding, we provide a case example of co-creation through service design conducted by Experio Lab in Sweden, in a project focused on youth mental health. This case also illuminates some of the critical challenges associated with co-creation in health care that need to be considered in such service design processes. As such, this chapter can aid practitioners in gaining a deeper knowledge of co-creation and a foundation from which they might strategize to support respectful co-creation processes in healthcare service design.

24.2 Positioning Service Design

Herbert A. Simon defines design as an activity "aiming at changing existing conditions into preferred ones" (Simon, 1969). This is what people do all the time—when they get up in the morning and make their bed, when they sort their clothes by color in order to find something suitable more quickly, and when they prepare a mash from a raw potato. Seen this way, every person is a designer, and design is a driver of change and innovation. There are differences in the intensity of the design that is being done: the basic level is "doing," then comes "adapting," followed by "making," and on the most advanced level it is "creating." The level of creating is what professional design is aiming at (Sanders & Stappers, 2012).

Design connects the needs of people with the business models of providers and the technological possibilities of the present and the future. Design has traditionally been profoundly oriented toward humans—considering people as consumers, as users, as employees, as co-creators. Design embraces the natural capability of humans to be creators. Design aims at solutions within systems that create value for the different actors, that are thoughtful in form and function.

While in the past design was anchored in the material, visible world, during the last three decades it has moved into the world of the invisible. Service design has established itself as a new field of practice—as a response to economic and social transformations. Service design brings with it a radical shift: away from product and applications toward the system, the users, and their journeys through the system. Not "tayloristic" organizational interests and silo thinking but people with their needs and holistic experiences are the focus of service system design.

Service design choreographs people, technologies, and processes within complex service systems to co-create value for relevant stakeholders. This definition, which at first seems simple, has a lot going for it. After all, the term choreography (ancient Greek χορός "dance" and γράφειν "to write"), whose roots lie in the performing arts and especially in dance, refers to the demand for a perfectly formed, even artful interplay between different actors, technologies, different channels, and, of course, the interplay between efficiency and elegance.

The positioning of service design in the context of complex systems underlines that designers work in networked structures of self-dynamic subsystems (Weisser et al., 2018) that cannot be controlled, but only influenced and steered. This work with living systems is particularly challenging and requires a healthy mix of self-awareness and humility. It requires co-creation with users, providers, experts in all phases of the design and the delivery of services.

24.3 Service Design and the Health Sector

In 2015, the project "Redesigning Breast Cancer Diagnostics," conducted by Designit, was awarded with the Service Design Award. This project redefined the way Oslo University Hospital handles the referral and diagnostic process. "The result of the project was a 90% reduction in waiting time from a patient's first visit with her general practitioner through to her final diagnosis at the hospital: From up to 12 weeks, down to an average of seven days. This represents a dramatic improvement in efficiency, a huge improvement in quality of life for patients in a tremendously stressful period of time, and potentially saved lives" (Nisbett, 2017).

In the year 2016, the award went to a project conducted by Philips Service Design in the Netherlands. "Focusing on the most complex and highest cost patients, the eIAC program Intensive Ambulatory Care is designed to support chronically ill patients manage their condition at home. Enabling all stakeholders in the clinical and social management of a patient to identify and address root causes of patients' frequent admissions. Overall costs of care were reduced by 34.5%. Hospitalizations were reduced by 49.5%. Number of days in hospital were reduced by 50%" (Nisbett, 2017).

These are just two examples from an abundance of cases that show how service design helps to make change happen: "Never before has there been so much opportunity for design to make a positive impact on the well-being and health of citizens. Governments worldwide recognize that patients' expectations are rising fast and there is a need for a fundamental change in how people interact with health services and professionals. The nature of the global challenge is hugely complex, distinctly human, systemic and intertwined, and the scope of the opportunity hugely broad, involving stakeholders from government agencies, non-profits, insurance companies, hospitals, pharmacies, patients, caregivers, and doctors. Crucially though, it is the underlying framework of policies and regulation that need to offer the springboard for radical transformation" (Collmann, 2017).

Service design today goes far beyond the project level—it helps to make strategic change happen and to create policies for a better future, and it does this in collaboration and co-creation with relevant stakeholders. In a study conducted by the Service Design Network in 2017, five key areas of impact for service design in the health sector were identified: organizational change, cultural change, patient engagement, education and capacity building, and policy making (Mager, 2017). Further, this study showed that more than 170 organizations were active in 680 projects focused on healthcare service design, with 40% of these projects being implemented and scaled. A key focus of the service design projects profiled in the Service Design Network's 2017 Healthcare Impact was engagement of stakeholders in the process including in the design of new service offerings and their implementation, and the need and value of moving beyond tokenistic engagement in this space. In particular, this work highlighted the benefit of service design building on the ongoing tradition of peer support and expert users in health care. This highlights a need to deepen the understanding of the importance and benefits of meaningful co-creation in healthcare service design.

24.4 The Benefits of Co-creation in Healthcare Service Design

The concept of co-creation has gained increasing traction across many industries, for instance in the form of open idea contests for new services in the utilities sector (Verrinder, 2012), users submitting and voting on designs in retail (Russo-Spena & Mele, 2012), or partnering with patients to innovate diabetes services in health care (Freire & Sangiorgi, 2012). Co-creating services involve collaborative activities between two or more people, influenced by a multi-actor network (Oertzen et al., 2018). Co-creation may be leveraged across the entire service process—from designing and developing services all the way through to delivering and consuming services. The duration of collaboration can vary, such that co-creation may occur during a one-time workshop or in the form of a partnership during a participatory design project over the course of many months. A broad range of beneficial outcomes may ensue co-creation efforts that can be of personal, social, hedonic, cognitive, economic, or pragmatic nature (For a detailed typology see Oertzen et al., 2018; Verleye, 2015). Personal benefits may include increased well-being and empowerment (Engström & Elg, 2015; Vahdat et al., 2014), while social benefits may be in the form of more trust and better engagement (Dabholkar & Sheng, 2012; Hoyer et al., 2010). Hedonic benefits can make the service interaction more enjoyable and lead to positive moods (Chen et al., 2016; Sheng & Zolfagharian, 2014) and cognitive benefits foster new knowledge and skills (Gottfridsson, 2014; Verleye, 2015). In addition, economic and pragmatic benefits may result from co-creation activities, such as economic gains (Moeller et al., 2013) and better fit with consumer needs (Hoyer et al., 2010).

In order to design services tailored to the needs of the people affected by these services, leveraging co-creation efforts to purposefully integrate their lived experience in the design process is a critical prerequisite (Vink & Oertzen, 2018). This is especially the case for health care, which often includes vulnerable people and continues to be affected by an unbalanced division of power between patients and healthcare professionals, which can lead to serious service failings (Berry, 2019; Farrington, 2016; Lukersmith et al., 2016). To give people more agency in the health system, the World Health Organization (2017) advocates the transition toward people-centered health services, which requires reconceptualizing people as active participants in the design, development, and delivery of health services (Tsekleves & Cooper, 2017). As the role of patients is changing from being passive recipients of care to actively contributing personal resources and engaging in diverse activities within healthcare systems, there is a growing demand for co-creative practices that transcend mere dialogue to genuine partnership between patients, healthcare professionals, and other affected people (Lukersmith et al., 2016; McColl-Kennedy et al., 2017a).

Research suggests that co-creative practices between patients, family caregivers, and healthcare professionals during the management of health positively affect individuals' well-being and quality of life, while simultaneously holding the potential to decrease the burden on the healthcare system (McColl-Kennedy et al., 2012; McColl-Kennedy et al., 2017b). Besides contributing to the delivery of healthcare services, there is growing awareness of the importance of involving patients and family caregivers during healthcare innovation (McColl-Kennedy et al. 2017a). Patients and family caregivers have situated and unique understandings of their own health contexts, and prior studies have demonstrated their interest and potential to contribute effective ideas in service innovation (McColl-Kennedy et al., 2017a; Tian et al., 2014). Participating in healthcare innovation gives patients, their families, and healthcare staff opportunities to reflect on and shape their healthcare experience and provide input into the redesign of the overall system (Donetto et al., 2015).

There is strong alignment between people-centered care and service design including: seeing the patient as an expert; recognizing that a person's life is more than their healthcare interactions; attending to the shift in power between actors; focusing on people's needs; and, importantly, acknowledging that health is co-created (Malmberg et al., 2019). Service design can aid in catalyzing the shift from the biomedical model pervasive in healthcare systems today toward person-centered care by co-creating services. Working towards the aim of people-centered care, the co-creation of healthcare services through service design can manifest itself in various forms along the different phases of the service process, including co-ideation, co-valuation, co-design, co-testing, co-launching, co-production, and co-consumption (Oertzen et al., 2018, see Fig. 24.1). This involves the meaningful engagement of both patients, or people with lived experience, as well as healthcare professionals in the service design process. The

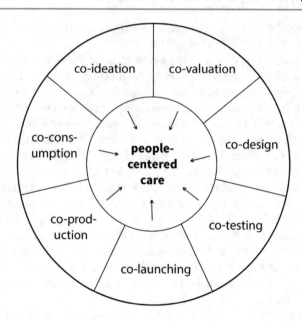

Fig. 24.1 Various forms of co-creation through service design contributing to people-centered care. *Source* Author's own illustration with content adapted from Oertzen et al. (2018)

Fig. 24.2 Photographs of participation in the service design including co-ideation, co-valuation, co-design, and co-testing. *Source* Experio Lab

following case offers an example of such co-creation efforts through service design in health care.

24.5 A Case of Co-creation Through Service Design: Experio Lab

Experio Lab leverages service design to facilitate a cultural shift toward people-centered care in eight regional healthcare systems across Sweden. It brings together designers, healthcare professionals, administrators, community stakeholders, patients, and families in a process of co-creation to support ongoing adaptation and innovation in health services. Experio Lab's project called "First Line" exemplifies the dynamics of co-creation throughout the service design process. The First Line project spanned over two years working with a newly opened clinic for children and youth mental health in Karlstad, Sweden. The aim was to develop new services that could help meet youth, who were digital natives, on their own terms and build the capabilities of the clinical staff to more actively work with children and youth in the development of their services (Szücs Johansson et al., 2017). In what follows, we describe some of the dynamics of co-creation in this project, based on insights from interviews of the designers and the clinical staff involved.

To support the process of co-creation, a multidisciplinary design team was established including two staff from the clinic and two designers from Experio Lab. The project started with a course in design for the staff involved to build their knowledge on the service design process. Youth were engaged throughout the process including through field research, interviews, workshops, and later one was hired as a formal advisor. The design research using cultural probes and ethnography was done by designers and staff together, to connect with and better understand the needs of the youth that were intended to benefit from the service. Attempting to meet youth where they were at, the team went into schools to do interviews, observations, and workshops with youth. Reflecting on this process, one of the clinical staff members said:

> When we went to the schools, I think it was important that we came to their area and asked them for advice. I think it would have been different if they came to us. Then they would have been visitors. Now it was there arena.

In the early part of the process, a number of workshops were held with youth to build knowledge of their needs and context. Describing these early engagements, one designer recalled:

> They were both those that had been previously to this care unit and also random kids. So we started working with them. Just as more to understand what it is like to be young today, ... what do you do on your weekday? ... how do you think, what do you think about.

Insights were analyzed by the design team and feedback workshops were held with youth to validated the findings. Gradually the process moved from understanding needs and context toward developing ideas together. As part of this process, a co-creation workshop was held with youth, clinical staff, teachers, family members, politicians, and other community stakeholders. Here ideas were developed between people by passing ideas between people and building on each others' ideas. In addition, a process of "trendstorming" was used where patterns in current changes were identified and discussed and desirable aspects used to inspire new ideas.

This co-creation process also involved stakeholders prototyping together. One clinical staff involved highlighted:

> Prototyping was new for me. All the ideas, I for sure wouldn't have come up with all the creative ways to put it out. I would have never come up with that. For me when they put lego on the table to do the prototype it was, uhhh? But the youngsters just vft, vft [speedy sound]. For me it was new. I am used to whiteboards and power points, but not the free creative.

While it was a new process for the staff and involved different ways of working, the staff also talked about how working with youth in this way helped them to see the resourcefulness of youth and catalyzed a shift in power dynamics in how they interacted with youth. One staff person said (Szücs Johansson et al., 2017),

> It was very rewarding to meet young people who didn't seek your help. Now you could change your position – you are the experts and I am here to learn. It was very fun. Usually young people come to us with a problem and we need to be the experts. Now it was the opposite. We were the listeners. That is always very fun and educational. That is empowering for the young people. We are not here to educate them, they are educating us.

In this process, the staff were able to inquire and understand things about youth that were well outside of the scope of their treatment. The ideas that were developed were also evaluated and prioritized by youth as the process moved forward. One of the designers on the project said:

> We actually had the kids in the network prioritize. Like what issues do you think is important for us to work with? And then we did the same with all staff. And then we had a discussion so ... how are you thinking differently?

This helped to see how youth and staff may have different ideas about how to move forward and interrogate why that might be. Another designer reflected on this:

> if you look at the operational plan of the care unit, you see that they actually have a preventive scope in there. But then we have different ideas of what that is. In their sense it is going out and talking to schools. So it's a matter of making them see that it could also be something else completely.

The ideas brought forward and prioritized by youth helped the staff see how their service could evolve beyond what they had imagined and gave them ideas about different service offerings, including simple things like a mental health day.

The feedback process on the prototypes was iterative, involving larger groups at, for example a local youth center, and also one on one feedback sessions. Recounting one of these interactions a designer shared:

> On Tuesday, we met one girl and did a prototype and she has been involved since day 1 of the project and she's also former visitor at (the clinic). So she's really good. So first we had small prototyping with her where we presented our ideas and we had a lot of questions. And she gave us a lot of feedback on that.

Talking about the process of getting feedback, another designer shared the kind of discussion they had with youth about the prototype of the app:

> So this idea is about how you can see if something is wrong and you should get some help or not. And it's like a website or it can be an app as well. And maybe you can get to know about it in school but you don't have to do it in school. You can do it at home or whatever. And you just log in…yeah that is a question if you should log in or leave it open.

The perspectives that youth shared were fundamental in the ongoing redesign of the service. For example, one designer shared how the youth changed the direction of the digital service by highlighting the need for exploring multiple, coexisting emotions:

> I can't say I'll have just one feeling, maybe I'll have more feelings. And then this started developing into something…and there was another idea that we've seen is some way of sort of tracking your mood over time. And they started working with this. Ok maybe look one day I would feel both happy, sad and confused and I would like to see if that changes over time.

Along with the process of engaging youth, the clinical staff continued to be involved in shaping the direction of the service. Engaged in this process, one of the designers stated:

> So after today we have a meeting with (the clinic) to start looking at ok how will these solutions fit into their work schedule.

Through this iterative approach, one of the concepts got funding to beta test A firm, Oceans Observations, was bought in to support this development with youth and clinical staff involvement throughout the development process. Through this process, a new Web service was launched called hurmårdu.nu (howareyou.now in English). The goal was to help young people understand their feelings and comfortably chat with clinical staff. Based on learnings from the ongoing prototyping, the service uses emojis and chat to create a low threshold for taking contact and seeking help with emerging mental health issues.

The process of co-creation changed how the service was delivered, shifting power dynamics between the youth and clinical staff. One clinical staff member reflects on their approach saying:

> When I finish the session here, I ask 'Have we talked about the right things? Have I asked too much? Have I asked too little?

The Experio Lab case above highlights integrating co-creation between different actors (in this context youth and clinical team) through service design in the development and consumption of health services, by leveraging their expertise and co-directing the focus of the service. Hereby, co-creation efforts spanned from co-ideation, co-valuation, co-design, and co-testing, all the way to co-production of the health service (Fig. 24.2).

24.6 Overcoming the Challenges of Co-creation in Health Care

While co-creation is a necessity and has immense value, there can be challenges in taking such a participatory, collaborative approach in health care. For example, it can be difficult to combine different knowledge bases, such as the expertise of clinicians and the lived experiences of patients (Carr et al., 2009; Sellen, 2017). Some stakeholders of the service also have additional barriers to engagement that make active co-creation challenging (Tobiasson et al., 2015). In the Experio Lab case shared above, there was a challenge engaging all ages that were being served by the clinic. One staff member stated:

> Here we take young people from six years, but I don't think we can expect the younger segment to answer these kind of questions. But the older ones can related to being 11 or 12 no that long time ago.

In addition, there can be issues engaging those that are not already being served within such co-creation processes. One designer said:

> We did interviews with people who have been at the care unit is that they were extremely satisfied with the service... They were like just very grateful that they existed. So I think we realized quite soon that the people we want to address are the people that are not going there. That don't find the place or that wait too long, when things have gone too bad for them to actually seek help.

Furthermore, having people with lived experience engaged in lengthy service design initiatives is difficult, often relying on self-selecting groups that are not necessarily representative (Farrington, 2016). Furthermore, many stakeholders may not want to or be able to engage in a co-creation process for a variety of reasons. Continuity of engagement of those involved is also a common issue.

At times, there is also an issue with timing as active co-creation takes a major investment of time for all actors involved. Participating people confessed:

> One thing that has been a struggle all along is getting (the clinical team) to take the time or finding the time to work with us. That has been hard. (Designer)

> A lot of us felt a lot of stress. It took a lot of time and we didn't know what would come out of it... Every minute we put in this project, our visitors have to stand back. (Clinical staff)

This highlights the important trade off that clinical staff experience in relation to investing their time in co-creation within the service design process or simply focusing on delivery. The staff also highlighted how having different youth involved throughout rather than continuity took more time was a challenge in the process:

> Once we have a prototype, we should have the same group. It took so long to get them on the same track. Hard to get the right feedback.

Critically, the issue of power dynamics is fundamental in co-creation. Without addressing power asymmetries head on, co-creation can simply become a participation facade (Farrington, 2016). This creates a risk of reproducing oppressive practices through the engagement of stakeholders in the co-creation of healthcare services (Donetto et al., 2015). This reproduction of oppressive practices can happen by conducting activities aimed at empathy but that ultimately result in actors projecting their assumptions on to the experiences of others (Cipolla & Bartholo, 2014; Vink & Oertzen, 2018). It is important to note the difference between empathy, which tends to promote placing oneself in the shoes of others (Kouprie & Sleeswijk Visser, 2009), and the integration of lived experiences—the direct first-hand experience of a particular condition or identity (Vink & Oertzen, 2018). The case above shows the value of working actively with clinical staff to reflect on their power positions within the service context and integrate insights from co-creation in a way that helps to change their way of interacting with youth.

24.7 Conclusions

Service design is playing an increasingly prominent role in supporting change and innovation within the health sector, particularly in relation to catalyzing co-creation. By presenting some of the key benefits and challenges of co-creation supported by service design in health care, we hope to draw attention to the nuanced approaches required to support meaningful engagement and reduce potential harms in the process. The types of co-creation presented in Fig. 24.1 can aid practitioners in thinking about how actors can be meaningfully engaged in all aspects of creating service experiences. The Experio Lab case offers concrete examples of how these different engagements might transpire and potential challenges that often need to be faced along the way, although many of these dynamics are extremely context-dependent. Practitioners should be aware of these challenges and think proactively about strategies they might employ to support meaningful co-creation processes that avoid a participation facade. Co-creation offers powerful transformative potential within health services, and there is great value in thoughtfully and strategically leveraging service design to support this process.

References

Aghdam, A. R., Watson, J., Cliff, C., & Miah, S. J. (2020). Improving the theoretical understanding toward patient-driven health care innovation through online value cocreation: systematic review. *Journal of medical Internet research, 22*(4), e16324. https://doi.org/10. 2196/16324. PMID: 32329736 PMCID: 7210492.

Berry, L. L. (2019). Service innovation is urgent in healthcare. *AMS Review, 9*(1/2), 1–15. https:// doi.org/10.1007/s13162-019-00135-x

Carr, V., Sangiorgi, D., Büscher, M., Cooper, R., & Junginger, S. (2009). Clinicians as service designers? reflections on current transformation in the UK health services. In *Presented at the 1st Nordic Conference on Service Design and Service Innovation in Oslo*, Norway, Accessed 24–26 November 2009.

Chen, Y.-H., Wu, J.-J., & Chien, S.-H. (2016). Impact of initial trust, involvement, and mood on trusting belief: Evidence from the financial industry in Taiwan. *Journal of Service Theory and Practice, 26*(1), 91–108. https://doi.org/10.1108/JSTP-11-2014-0252

Cipolla, C., & Bartholo, R. (2014). Empathy or inclusion: A dialogical approach to socially responsible design. *International Journal of Design*(2), 87–100.

Collmann, N. (2017). Redesigning the rules for healthcare innovation. In Mager (Ed.), *Service design impact report health sector* (pp. 16–22). Service Design Network.

Dabholkar, P. A., & Sheng, X. (2012). Consumer participation in using online recommendation agents: Effects on satisfaction, trust, and purchase intentions. *The Service Industries Journal, 32*(9), 1433–1449. https://doi.org/10.1080/02642069.2011.624596

Donetto, S., Pierri, P., Tsianakas, V., & Robert, G. (2015). Experience-based co-design and healthcare improvement: Realizing participatory design in the public sector. *The Design Journal, 18*(2), 227–248. https://doi.org/10.2752/175630615X14212498964312

Engström, J., & Elg, M. (2015). A self-determination theory perspective on customer participation in service development. *Journal of Services Marketing, 29*(6/7), 511–521. https://doi.org/10. 1108/JSM-01-2015-0053

Farrington, C. J. (2016). Co-designing healthcare systems: Between transformation and tokenism. *Journal of the Royal Society of Medicine, 109*(10), 368–371. https://doi.org/10.1177/ 0141076816658789

Freire, K., & Sangiorgi, D. (2012). Service design and healthcare innovation: From consumption to co-production to co-creation. In *Paper presented at the Exchanging Knowledge Conference Proceedings of the 2nd Service Design and Service Innovation Conference in Linköping*, Sweden. Accessed 1–3 December 2010.

Gottfridsson, P. (2014). Different actors' roles in small companies service innovation. *Journal of Services Marketing, 28*(7), 547–557. https://doi.org/10.1108/JSM-04-2013-0082

Hoyer, W. D., Chandy, R., Dorotic, M., Krafft, M., & Singh, S. S. (2010). Consumer cocreation in new product development. *Journal of Service Research, 13*(3), 283–296. https://doi.org/10. 1177/1094670510375604

Kouprie, M., & Sleeswijk Visser, F. (2009). A framework for empathy in design: Stepping into and out of the user's life. *Journal of Engineering Design, 20*(5), 437–448. https://doi.org/10. 1080/09544820902875033

Lukersmith, S., Schneider, C. H., Salvador-Carulla, L., Sturmberg, J., Wilson, A., & Gillespie, J. (2016). *What is the state of the art in person-centred care? An expert commentary brokered by the Sax Institute for the Australian commission on safety and quality in health care*. Ultimo, Australia: Sax Institute.

Mager, B. (2017). *Service design impact report: Health sector*. Service Design Network. Accessed 22 Feb 2018, from https://www.service-design-network.org/books-and-reports/impact-report-health-sector.

Malmberg, L., Rodrigues, V., Lännerström, L., Wetter-Edman, K., Vink, J., & Holmlid, S. (2019). Service design as a transformational driver towards person-centered care in healthcare. In M. A. Pfannstiel & C. Rasche (Eds.), *Service design and service thinking in healthcare and hospital management* (pp. 1–18). Theory, Concepts and Practice, Springer International Publishing AG.

McColl-Kennedy, J. R., Vargo, S. L., Dagger, T. S., Sweeney, J. C., & Van Kasteren, Y. (2012). Health care customer value cocreation practice styles. *Journal of Service Research, 15*(4), 370–389. https://doi.org/10.1177/1094670512442806

McColl-Kennedy, J. R., Snyder, H., Elg, M., Witell, L., Helkkula, A., Hogan, S. J., & Anderson, L. (2017a). The changing role of the health care customer: Review, synthesis and research agenda. *Journal of Service Management, 28*(1), 2–33. https://doi.org/10.1108/JOSM-01-2016-0018

McColl-Kennedy, J. R., Hogan, S. J., Witell, L., & Snyder, H. (2017b). Cocreative customer practices: Effects of health care customer value cocreation practices on well-being. *Journal of Business Research, 70*(C), 55–66. https://doi.org/10.1016/j.jbusres.2016.07.006.

Moeller, S., Ciuchita, R., Mahr, D., Odekerken-Schröder, G., & Fassnacht, M. (2013). Uncovering collaborative value creation patterns and establishing corresponding customer roles. *Journal of Service Research, 16*(4), 471–487. https://doi.org/10.1177/1094670513480851

Nisbett, A. (2017). Redesigning breast cancer diagnostics. In *The Service Design Award Annual* (pp. 148–151 and 138–141). Service Design Network, Köln.

Oertzen, A.-S., Odekerken-Schröder, G., Brax, S. A., & Mager, B. (2018). Co-creating services—Conceptual clarification, forms and outcomes. *Journal of Service Management, 29*(4), 641–679. https://doi.org/10.1108/JOSM-03-2017-0067doi:10.1108/JOSM-03-2017-0067

Russo-Spena, T., & Mele, C. (2012). "Five Co-s" in innovating: A practice-based view. *Journal of Service Management, 23*(4), 527–553. https://doi.org/10.1108/09564231211260404

Sanders, E. B. N., & Stappers, P. J. (2012). *Convivial toolbox*. BIS Publishers.

Sellen, K. (2017). Problem based learning: Developing competency in knowledge integration in health design. In *Presented at the International Conference on Engineering and Product Design Education in Oslo*, Norway.

Sheng, X., & Zolfagharian, M. (2014). Consumer participation in online product recommendation services: Augmenting the technology acceptance model. *Journal of Services Marketing, 28*(6), 460–470. https://doi.org/10.1108/JSM-04-2013-0098

Simon, H. A. (1969). *The science of the artificial*. MIT Press.

Szücs Johansson, L., Vink, J., & Wetter-Edman, K. (2017). A Trojan horse approach to changing mental health care for young people through service design. *Design for Health, 1*(2), 245–255. https://doi.org/10.1080/24735132.2017.1387408

Tian, K., Sautter, P., Fisher, D., Fischbach, S., Luna-Nevarez, C., Boberg, K., Kroger, J., & Vann, R. (2014). Transforming health care: Empowering therapeutic communities through technology-enhanced narratives. *Journal of Consumer Research, 41*(2), 237–260. https://doi.org/10.1086/676311

Tobiasson, H., Sundblad, Y., Walldius, Å., & Hedman, A. (2015). Designing for active life: Moving and being moved together with dementia patients. *International Journal of Design, 9* (3), 47–62.

Tsekleves, E., & Cooper, R. (2017). Emerging trends and the way forward in design in healthcare: An expert's perspective. *The Design Journal, 20*(sup1), S2258–S2272. https://doi.org/10.1080/14606925.2017.1352742

Vahdat, S., Hamzehgardeshi, L., Hessam, S., & Hamzehgardeshi, Z. (2014). Patient involvement in health care decision making: a review. *Iranian Red Crescent Medical Journal, 16*(1), 1–7. PMID: 24719703. https://doi.org/10.5812/ircmj.12454. PMC3964421.

Verleye, K. (2015). The co-creation experience from the customer perspective: Its measurement and determinants. *Journal of Service Management, 26*(2), 321–342. https://doi.org/10.1108/JOSM-09-2014-0254

Verrinder, J. (2012). E.ON and 100% open launch crowdsourcing project. Accessed 1 July 2021, from https://www.research-live.com/article/news/eon-and-100open-launch-crowdsourcing-project/id/4006939.

Vink, J., & Oertzen, A.-S. (2018). Integrating empathy and lived experience through co-creation in service design. In *Paper presented at the 6th Service Design and Innovation Conference on Proof of Concept in Milano* (No. 150, pp. 471–483), Italy. Linköping University Electronic Press.

Weisser, T., Jonas, W., Mager, B. (2018). Successfully implementing service design projects. *Touchpoint, 10*(1), 34–40.

World Health Organization (2017). What are integrated people-centred health services?. Accessed 1 July 2021, from https://www.who.int/servicedeliverysafety/areas/people-centred-care/ipchs-what/en/.

Birgit Mager is Co-Founder and President of the International Service Design Network, publisher of Touchpoint, the international Journal of Service Design. Since 1995 Birgit Mager holds the first European professorship on "Service Design" at the University of Applied Sciences Cologne, Germany and since then has developed the field of Service Design constantly in theory, methodology and in practice. Her numerous lectures, her publications and her projects have strongly supported the implementation of a new understanding of the economical, ecological and social function of design in the domain of services.

Anna-Sophie Oertzen is a co-creation adept, exploring innovative ways to design and deliver human-centric and profitable applications and solutions, with a coined interest for the healthcare sector. Anna-Sophie holds a PhD in Service Design and Innovation, is an accredited Service Design Trainer with the global Service Design Network Academy, and a Marie Curie Alumni of the Service Design for Innovation Network, funded by the European Union.

Josina Vink is an Associate Professor of Service Design at the Oslo School of Architecture and Design (AHO) and Design Lead within the Center for Connected Care (C3) in Norway. Josina has over 10 years of experience as a service designer working in international healthcare contexts, including in Canada, the United States, and Sweden. They have developed new services, supported policy change, facilitated shifts in practices across sectors, and led social lab processes. Josina's research aims to contribute to building more systemic service design theories and approaches, as well as understanding health systems transformation.

Story-Centered Co-creative Methods: A Means for Relational Service Design and Healthcare Innovation

Rike Neuhoff, Nanna Dam Johansen, and Luca Simeone

Abstract

Building on empirical evidence gathered from a case study with dementia family caregivers in the Danish healthcare system, the chapter looks at how story-centered co-creative methods, i.e., an iterative practice of gathering and (co)producing stories, can ignite and sustain relational service design and how this can contribute to healthcare innovation. These story-centered co-creative methods can work particularly well not only to build relationships with and among participants but also to foster greater levels of trust, sensitivity, and empathy in service design projects. While facing the challenges of supporting their loved ones suffering from dementia, family caregivers have to interact with multiple and different actors, including an array of different physicians, specialists, nurses, and other professional caregivers. Story-centered co-creative methods can support the engagement of these diverse actors and invite them to embrace each other's perspectives while reflecting, thinking, and acting on how healthcare services can be improved and innovated. When involved in a design process that builds safe, informal, and authentic spaces for self-expression, these actors truly benefit from the transformative power of the service design process itself. The chapter provides theoretical reflections on this

R. Neuhoff · L. Simeone
A. C. Meyers Vænge 15, 2450 København, Denmark
e-mail: rne@create.aau.dk

L. Simeone
e-mail: lsi@create.aau.dk

N. D. Johansen (✉)
Ny Kongensgade 6, 1472 København, Denmark
e-mail: ndj@rfintervention.dk

M. A. Pfannstiel et al. (eds.), *Service Design Practices for Healthcare Innovation*,
https://doi.org/10.1007/978-3-030-87273-1_25

process-based view of service design and offers practical advice that can both inform the practice of service design professionals and ignite innovation within healthcare organizations.

25.1 Introduction: A Critical View on Healthcare Innovation

Like every system, the healthcare system is an interconnected set of elements that is coherently organized in a way that achieves a purpose (Meadows, 2008). Elements in a healthcare system are, among others, the hospitals, the healthcare practitioners, the patients, the doctors' equipment, and the technologies employed. Its interconnections are the relationships that play out among relevant actors in various socio-technical contexts of interaction and that are affected by components such as organizational affiliations and cultures, hierarchical structures and power dynamics, the rules of the game and the communication patterns between the actors (Vink et al., 2019). Innovating healthcare systems entails engaging with these interconnections by taking into consideration the potentially different needs and wants of a multitude of actors—from professionals, to policy-makers, researchers and not least also patients and their families (Janssen, 2016).

Innovation within healthcare is usually equated with progress in technology for the purpose of improving efficiencies, costs, and patient-, user-, or customer-experiences and treatment (Jones, 2013) to ultimately create competitive advantages (Vetterli & Scherrer, 2019). This view is limited for various reasons. First, this view tends to embody inaccurate mental models that limit the understanding of people entering the health system to patients, customers, or users (Jones, 2013). As Jones (2013) argues, a medical view of wellness and sickness, i.e., a view in which a person enters the health system as a patient, might be relevant in some circumstances, but this identity is not persistent across the ongoing experience of health seeking. Neither is health the result of a service transaction but rather of a context of care, which can draw on professional, familial, community, and personal resources. Thus, the market-based perspective that equates health seekers with customers is inaccurate, too. Naming a health seeker as a user of a service ignores that services are co-created (e.g., Jones, 2013; Vargo & Lusch, 2008). Moreover, such a perspective focuses solely on treating people when they are sick, whereas preventive services are radically underutilized, contributing to healthcare systems worldwide being severely overburdened and the health of populations being worse than necessary (Levine, 2019). The recognition of these rather limiting roles of health seekers has led healthcare systems aiming to innovate their care models to become more dignified, compassionate, and enabling toward health seekers (Health Foundation, 2014).

Second, though technological innovation certainly has the potential to make existing healthcare procedures more convenient for the users, innovation within healthcare tends to benefit healthcare providers more than health seekers as the actual purpose is usually to reduce costs and improve efficiency instead of improving care (Jones, 2013). This is a classic dilemma within healthcare and related to the fact that individuals who have a health need are the ones whom the health system is obliged to serve, however they are not the ones paying, which limits their influence and power (ibid.) and offers little incentives for healthcare institutions to support other kind of innovation activities (Vårdanalys, 2017).

Third, a perspective that mainly focuses on technological change as a means to create value and reduce costs tends to disregard these other types of innovation that can potentially create bigger value for health seekers and reduce costs (Jones, 2013). An example for such other kinds of healthcare innovation is the work conducted by the RED team of the Design Council, which pioneered a radical new, participatory healthcare model that completely reinvents the relationship between health provider and seeker, i.e., as a partnership, which pursues to ultimately enable people to take care of their own health, and thus making them service co-creators (Cottam & Leadbeater, 2004). Along the same lines, Experio Lab in Sweden aims to innovate the Swedish healthcare system by employing inclusive service design approaches that alter institutions and thus contribute to cultural transformation within healthcare (Vink et al., 2019). An example that reinvents the purpose of healthcare from treatment to prevention is the Accountable Care Organization's model of care, which focuses on drawing attention to the life of health seekers, as a way to avoid and reduce (re)admittances (Winblad et al., 2017). As Meadows (2008) emphasizes, altering the purpose of, or the relationships within a system, can bring about deep systemic change.

This background reveals an opportunity for service designers to rethink conventional practices and explore alternative methods and approaches that can support them in altering the existing relationships into preferable ones. With this study, we attempt to address this opportunity space. We draw on two indicators about how relationships may be meaningfully altered. First, in service design, in particular collaborative processes are used to meaningfully influence the relationships embedded within a system (Vink, 2019). Second, scholars from several domains have identified the power of story-centered methods for relationship building (Cottam, 2011; Kieboom et al., 2015; Killick & Boffey, 2012). As such, our research explores the combination of both. For the purpose of this chapter, we conceptualize service design as a service in itself and examine how story-centered co-creative methods—i.e., an iterative practice of gathering and (co)producing stories—can ignite and sustain more relational service design. We then reflect on how such an approach, in turn, can contribute to innovation within healthcare.

The chapter is organized as follows. Section 25.2 provides some background on theory related to service design, the value of the service design process, and story-centered co-creative methods. In Sect. 25.3, we show how these story-centered co-creative methods were applied in the context of a project with dementia family caregivers. In Sect. 25.4, we present the findings, in particular how the approach contributed to a more relational service design practice. Section 25.5 concludes with a discussion of the contributions and implications for service design and healthcare innovation.

25.2 Literature Review

This section reviews literature, on the one hand, to more closely look into the prevailing understanding of service design, and the (often overlooked) transformative power of the processual aspects of service design. On the other hand, it examines how story-centered co-creative methods can potentially reinforce more relational service design.

25.2.1 Relational Service Design for Healthcare Innovation

As competition between healthcare organizations rises, there has been a growing recognition for service design to drive forth innovation that can lead to efficient and effective service delivery, and improve service quality and user satisfaction (Pfannstiel & Rasche, 2019). Within this context, service designers have explored various directions. For example, Jørgensen et al. (2011) stage co-creative service design interventions to reinforce the understanding of the important role of textiles in hospital interior to create environments that are experienced as healing environments, rather than as environments designed solely for efficiency and hygiene. Kushniruk and Nøhr (2016) promote participatory design approaches to improve the design and evaluation of information systems in healthcare, so to support successful adoption and user satisfaction, and Boyd et al. (2012) describe how service design methods, such as co-creative workshops, contribute to understanding and improving patient experiences and services within healthcare organizations. These examples illustrate how, in particular, the collaborative dimension of service design is expected to lead to successful outcomes.

Interestingly, when critically reflecting on the ways service designers have engaged in healthcare projects, it becomes evident that, to date, service design is mostly emphasized as a means to an end, whereas the extent to which service design creates value in the actual process of designing remains rather unexplored. However, for example, Vink (2019) pays attention to not only the effect of method choices on design outcomes, but also to how the methods affect the actors involved in service activities, and indicates benefits and reflections on value released through the active participation of actors in service design processes. She reports how clinic personnel started seeing youth with mental health issues as more capable and resourceful after working with them in a co-design workshop, and how this in turn positively influenced their relation toward them. Contributions like this suggest that the participation of actors in service design activities is a distinct form of socially significant activity (Dilnot, 1982) that can contain a transformative power for those involved (Akama and Prendiville, 2016; Kurtmollaiev et al., 2017). It is stressed that it is a way of thinking, communicating, and giving that encourages actors' awareness and reflexivity in regard to the context under consideration and its constraints, which is seen as the cornerstone of realizing meaningful change (Dilnot, 1982; Steen et al., 2011; Vink, 2019). Within this novel understanding, service design and its associated methodologies are no longer considered as just a means to innovate services or as a phase in the service development process. Instead, it is also recognized that the co-creative design process, regardless of the output, is valuable as it has the potential to contribute to meaningful transformation for the actors involved (Kurtmollaiev et al., 2017; Wetter-Edman et al., 2014).

Given the recognition of an embedded value co-creation process, i.e., that value is also co-created in-context when designing (Wetter-Edman et al., 2014), and inspired by the broad idea that "service" is a process of integrating unique knowledge and skills for the benefit of other actors (Vargo & Lusch, 2008), research exploring service design has begun to understand its collaborative dimension as a service in itself (Manzini, 2015; Vink et al., 2016). This understanding implies co-creative service design being in itself something that can be designed, so that it supports the actors participating in its process in the best possible way.

This collaborative dimension of design is deeply based on interpersonal interactions and challenges the standard way of conceiving and offering services—characteristics which are, according to Cipolla and Manzini (2009), associated with relational services. Thus, the practice also inevitably depends on the relational qualities taking place during its operation (Cipolla & Manzini, 2009), i.e., the way in which people feel or behave toward each other. Cottam (2011) emphasizes the importance of relational approaches for public sector innovation, such as within healthcare—approaches that focus on relationship building and on supporting people to advance their inherited capabilities (Cottam, 2011). This understanding values services that are collaborative and social and which contribute to fostering social capital. As such, considering service design as relational, the practice is able to bring forth conditions that can be characterized as collective, shared, caring, creative, and relational and to transform the relations within the system (Cottam, 2011).

25.2.2   Story-Centered Co-creative Methods as a Lever to Foster Relational Service Design

In examining research and practices aimed to bring forth more relational services, the mention of story-centered methods is particularly striking. For example, Cottam emphasizes how the "ability to tell a story - of where you have come from and where you hope to go - is a significant indicator of progress and of resilience" (2011, p. 143). As a method in design projects related to health, storytelling can work for identifying who is at health risk, for measuring personal development, as well as (active participation in) progress. According to Cottam (2011), stories work as indicators of developmental change and lie at the heart of relational practices (ibid.). Also, Kieboom et al. (2015) highlight the powerful role of stories for realizing relational services. They argue that building a relation and realizing change starts with people's stories, i.e., stories about hopes, fears and aspirations, about the past, the present, and the future. According to them, stories are a means to produce knowledge, and to highlight and reflect the contextual experiences, ideas and knowledge of people, which form a starting point for a new, more relational story. Furthermore, they emphasize that reading your own or another person's story encourages a reflective process that challenges assumptions and perceptions, and which can reveal new possibilities. Killick and Boffey (2012, p. iv), who explore stories and storytelling in the context of foster carers and the children who are looked after, highlight them as "one of the most powerful tools you can imagine" in regard to relationship building. According to them, they are a means to support reflection and the development of empathy, and social and emotional literacy. Baskerville (2011) examines the impact of storytelling as a culturally inclusive approach to teaching and learning. Her reportings suggest that privileging students' voices through storytelling not only advances their understanding of themselves, others and cultural perspectives, but also fosters compassion, tolerance, and respect for differences. She highlights that the approach aids in establishing caring and supportive educational environments and in enhancing the students' connectedness and relationships (Baskerville, 2011).

Within the service design field, the impact of story-centered co-creative methods remains rather unexplored. However, given the above analysis, the authors assume that a story-centered co-creative approach can reinforce relational service design. Applying this approach within the healthcare system is seen as particularly valuable as it can potentially contribute to alter the relations between health providers and seekers and thus drive forth impactful innovation that can lead to meaningful systemic change within healthcare. Given this background, the authors of this chapter found it worthwhile to explore the following research question: Can story-centered co-creative methods, i.e., an iterative practice of gathering and (co) producing stories, ignite and sustain relational service design within healthcare?

To reinforce the notion to shift the focus away from final output, the designers' aim was not to transition through the process phases associated with service design (e.g., Design Council, 2019) as to craft a new service (experience), but to intentionally linger in the research phase in order to unfold and explore the potential it may embed.

25.3 Case Study

This research conducted an in-depth analysis of a single case study (Eisenhardt, 1989; Eisenhardt & Graebner, 2007; Yin, 2009), which was concerned with the lives of dementia family caregivers in the context of the Danish healthcare system (Dam Johansen & Neuhoff, 2020). Dementia is a growing challenge to nations worldwide, including Denmark. The Danish Dementia Research Centre estimates the annual direct health and social costs associated with dementia to be approximately DKK 8 billion (Jørgensen, 2021), not including the loss of earnings and informal care of the approximately 400,000 Danish dementia family caregivers (Nationalt Videnscenter for Demens, n.d.).

Caregivers of people with dementia, hereinafter referred to as "caregivers", have a significant high risk and level of suffering from a variety of physical and psychological health issues (Brodaty & Donkin, 2009; McCabe et al., 2016) and are often considered as "the invisible second patients" (Brodaty & Donkin, 2009, p. 1). The research conducted in this project has shown that in most cases the caregivers' well-being is inevitably dependent on the well-being of their relative with dementia, which emphasizes health as familial, and inherently and intimately social (Jones, 2013). Generally, being a caregiver is not just temporal, based on need, but an enduring and authentic characteristic (ibid.). Caregivers have their own individual journey of health seeking related to their role. Yet, due to their patient-centered orientation, health systems do not do justice to this continuous process of seeking health from people who are not (yet) patients. However, as the informal care provided by caregivers is an indispensable part of healthcare systems worldwide (Yghemonos, 2016), supporting them in their role (e.g., by enabling them to take care of their own health) is important.

In this project, the service designers' role was not to "intervene and solve problems", but to "listen, challenge and support a process of discovery and transformation" (Cottam, 2011, p. 140). The ultimate goal was to emphasize service design as a relational and co-creative service and to create the conditions for something shared, collective, and relational to grow (ibid.).

25.3.1   Employing Story-Centered Co-creative Methods in a Case Study with Dementia Family Caregivers

In order to explore their impact on relational service design, the designers experimented with story-centered co-creative methods, i.e., an iterative practice of gathering and (co)producing stories, that cannot necessarily be found in the traditional service design toolbox (e.g., Penin, 2018; Polaine et al., 2013).

However, a critical first step for designers who plan to stage a co-creative design project is to build an initial foundation of knowledge about the people and the context under consideration (Jørgensen et al., 2011). Therefore, the designers conducted initial preparatory activities, which included desk research and a semi-structured in-depth interview (Kvale, 1996) with a consultant from the Danish Alzheimer Association. The aim was to learn about dementia, the challenges of caregivers, and which actors and healthcare organizations operate in the context of dementia in Denmark. Through the research and the expert interview, the designers learned more about the various challenges that caregivers face and how they relate to the stages of a dementia disease.

The next step of the design process was to collect stories of caregivers, or in other words, to give them a room to tell about their life, role, and situation. In order to collect those stories, the designers conducted conversations (Kieboom et al., 2015) as a more relational methodological counterpart to traditional interviews, which are a common tool to generate qualitative research data. Though only rarely mentioned as an explicit research method within design, some practitioners point out the advantages of conversations over interviews. According to them, interviews have "a structured formality that places limits on the discussion, they're also guided by someone who doesn't have a close personal relationship with the subject. The interviewee may seem like they're answering questions honestly, but what they're usually doing is filtering their answers based on assumptions about what the interviewer expects to hear. They may worry about being judged for their responses, or they may simply not feel comfortable giving an honest answer" (Motivate Design, 2019). Opposed to interviews, conversations are rather "organic, chaotic even. There's less of a fear of being judged or concern that answers might be held against anyone. They can probe into personal information that wouldn't be appropriate for an interviewer to ask. While the results are unfiltered, messy, and sometimes inconsistent, it's a more honest representation of what a person thinks and feels" (ibid.).

In this project, five in-depth conversations were conducted. The aim of the designers was to establish a genuinely interested and trustful relationship with the caregivers, as to make the person feel comfortable, so she can be an authentic version of herself. Therefore, the aim was to make the atmosphere informal and as such authentic toward their lived experiences (Pierri, 2017). When possible, the designers would meet the caregivers in the comfort of their homes, as to help them convey their memories, feelings, and experiences in a more detailed way (Stickdorn & Schneider, 2012). To create an atmosphere characterized by informality, various decisions were taken. For example, the designers did consciously not bring a laptop but captured important information in a conversation template and journey map, which contained a catalogue of relevant questions. Instead of following the questions one by one, the aim was to have a curious, naturally flowing conversation, which thus sometimes got off-course, but which therefore revealed great insights into the dementia caregivers' actual feelings and thoughts.

After each conversation, the designers crafted a narrating story about the experiences that the respective caregiver had shared. To transform the knowledge generation into an inclusive activity that challenges common power structures— e.g., that the designer is the expert and the "interviewee" only a research subject (Sanders & Stappers, 2008)—and that reinforces relational qualities, the story was then handed over to the caregiver to let them check and suggest changes that were more in line with their perceived reality, whereupon the designers rewrote it. It was an iterative process of co-writing a story, which perceived the caregivers as the experts of their own experiences (Sanders & Stappers, 2008). The stories were later on used as a means to communicate the caregivers' experiences to other caregivers involved in the design process and to create empathy and understanding for their situation.

When all stories were collected and co-written, a collective evaluation was organized, where all caregivers participated (Kieboom et al., 2015). This collective evaluation can be considered as a more relational counterpart to co-creative workshops, which are a conventional way in service design to leverage the know-how of a group (Stickdorn et al., 2018a). Usually, in service design, the primary aim of workshops is the joint production of a concrete output, for example personas, system maps, or similar (ibid.). However, while the collaborative nature of workshops and their contribution to evoking a feeling of shared ownership over what is designed is recognized, their particular implication and role for meaningful relationship building remain rather unexplored (Aguirre-Ulloa & Paulsen, 2017). In this project, the designers' main aim was to explore to what extent a more informal setting, i.e., a collective story evaluation, opposed to a workshop, can help to establish and shape the intangible relationships between the participants. In this respect, the design of the workshop experience in itself played a particularly important role. As some researchers point out that the design process is particularly valuable and transformative when informal (Kieboom et al., 2015) and authentic to the lived experiences of people (Pierri, 2017), the designers organized and facilitated the collective evaluation in the framework of a joint dinner. The designers made sure to provide a suitable and informal venue that offered an intimate atmosphere, as well as providing sufficient time for getting to know each other. The caregivers' stories were read out loud and served as a means to learn about each other's experiences, challenges, and highlights. Thereupon, food was served and the caregivers had time to have an informal conversation. Afterward, the designers presented the initial research findings and facilitated their joint evaluation.

25.4 Analytical Description of the Story-Centered Co-creative Methods Applied in the Case Study

In this section, we present the findings. In particular, we show how the preparations, the story collection through conversations, the story co-writing, and the collective evaluation contributed to a more relational service design practice.

25.4.1 Preparations

The preliminary knowledge generation turned out to be an invaluable requirement when following a relational approach. Learning about the contextual realities of caregivers and staging compassionate invitations proved to be crucial to make the caregivers recognize the good intentions and feel trust in the project, which sparked their interest to participate, and laid the foundation for a relationship and sustainable collaboration in the first place. When the project was initialized, the preparatory research about dementia made the designers feel empathy for the caregivers, which in turn ensured a high level of respect, understanding and dignity toward them.

25.4.2 Story Collection Through Conversations

With regard to the caregivers, the value of conversations became particularly clear. One caregiver pointed out that she had never before been asked about how she felt with their relatives' dementia disease, and others expressed gratitude for taking the time to listen to their experiences. Another caregiver, who had never received support in her role, actively started asking for help from the healthcare system after the conversation, which, according to her, made her become aware of the various actors and offers that could support her. Here, the preparatory activities on the sides of the designers again proved to be valuable. The conversations were also helpful for the designers in many ways. The caregivers' level of openness and honesty, from the designers' point of view, grew in the course of the conversation, and seemed in total significantly higher than in traditional interviews. As the conversations did not have a structured formality and pre-set time limit, there was enough time for the conversation to get off-course. These moments, in which the caregivers may share seemingly irrelevant information, were often particularly insightful and unfiltered in relation to their lived realities and, as such, enabled the designers to generate profound knowledge.

However, the method also posed various challenges. While in an interview the roles are clearly distributed, i.e., there is an interviewer who asks questions and an interviewer who answers the questions, a conversation is characterized in particular by the fact that the actors are at eye level and that the conversation is naturally flowing, informal, and organic (Motivate Design, 2019). As such, to actually manage to have a conversation instead of an interview, the designers had to share information about themselves as well. For example, both designers had themselves experienced Alzheimer's in their circle of friends or family and thus shared their own personal feelings about it as well. The question that arises is of a personal nature and relates to whether you as a designer are willing to give so much insight into your private life, even though the interaction actually takes place in a professional work context. In a way, this background also poses a methodological dilemma. On the one hand, this mutual exchange is what constitutes the difference between an interview and a conversation, of which the latter ultimately helped to foster a trustful relationship between designers and caregivers. On the other hand, it is certainly critical to look at the extent to which the designers thereby biased the caregivers and the information shared. Here however, it might be naive to expect a relational approach to be unbiased, as personality, values and beliefs are inevitably involved in relations. The extent to which this is justifiable is beyond the scope of this chapter but would have to be discussed in another occasion.

25.4.3 Story Co-writing

The iterative story co-writing was a novel, powerful, and reflective approach to collaboratively engage with research data. For the designers, it was a way to deeply internalize the information and to ensure their correct interpretation. The method

enabled the typical knowledge generation process to be more inclusive, emphasizing the caregivers' role as experts of their experiences, by giving them agency
and ownership over the research (Kieboom et al., 2015; Sanders & Stappers, 2008).
Furthermore, the method deepened the exchange of knowledge and interpretation as
exemplified by the following quote, given by one of the participants after reading
her own story: "Sorry to give you all these remarks, I truly loved your story of our
story, but I find some things need to be corrected (i.e. titles etc.), and I have to make
sure that you really understand the reality of our living and everyday life and the
background for my choices for my husband and me".

For the caregivers the method was valuable in various ways. One caregiver for
example expressed that the process and the story was an eye opener to her, as it led
her to see her experiences in a new light. According to her, she would always feel
like not doing enough justice to her relative with dementia, which made her feel
guilty. However, when reading her own story, she realized how much love, time,
and effort she had spent on her relative and that, objectively speaking, there was no
reason to feel bad at all. She expressed that the story method made her take over
another perspective, which helped her to let go of some distressing feelings.
Another caregiver even used the final story (see Fig. 25.1) to communicate her
reality toward her family. According to her, the story contributed to evoke a greater
level of empathy and awareness of her situation in them. As such, the method seems
to be suitable to tackle the general challenge of caregivers, i.e., that family, friends,

Fig. 25.1 Exemplary excerpt of a co-written story. *Source* Author's own illustration (2021)

and also society often lack knowledge, awareness, understanding, and empathy for the disease in general but especially how it is to be in the role of a caregiver (Blankman et al., 2012). However, it must be acknowledged that writing a compelling story is neither easy and straight-forward, nor something designers are necessarily trained to do. What helped the designers in this project is to take turns writing, building on each other's formulations and thereby iteratively writing a first draft, before sending it out to the caregivers.

25.4.4 Collective Evaluation

The stories' usefulness as a communication means (Kieboom et al., 2015) was again proved during their collective evaluation. The collective evaluation can be seen as a more collaborative, caring, and relational counterpart to the in service design often conducted workshop. The use of the stories in the collective evaluation led to compassionate conversations within the group, where the caregivers would relate to each other's experiences, give advice, and discuss the healthcare system. The sequence of the event, in particular the allocation of time to get to know each other in the beginning of the evening, seemed valuable, as, as a result, the collective evaluation had an informal atmosphere in which the caregivers were open and confident to share their opinions and seemed to feel comfortable to be themselves. Furthermore, one caregiver for instance expressed gratitude for enabling her to connect with others who can relate to her situation. According to her, it gave her invaluable information and motivation to approach key healthcare actors for their support. Another caregiver emphasized that she had been a part of many projects tackling issues related to dementia, however never before she had been involved in one that was conducted with so much warmth and which gave great weight to her opinions and experiences. She expressed a wish for higher levels of co-creation and creativity in public sector projects as well. The participants expressed the wish to connect and stay in touch, whereupon a shared Facebook group was created.

25.5 Discussion

Many agree that healthcare systems should rely on relational innovation, i.e., innovation that supports impactful interconnections rather than focusing on (re) designing the elements of the system, such as technology, as this is usually of least impact for meaningful change (Aguirre-Ulloa & Paulsen, 2017; Meadows, 2008). However, to date, there is not yet an exhaustive understanding of what constitutes beneficial relationships, nor how we design for relational services (Aguirre-Ulloa & Paulsen, 2017). This chapter aimed to expand this understanding, by conceptualizing service design as a service in itself, i.e., one that is "deeply based on interpersonal interactions" (Cipolla & Manzini, 2009, p. 4), and which can hence be designed. As a means to drive forth-relational practices and services, story-centered and co-creative methods have been mentioned in various works (e.g., Cottam, 2011; Kieboom et al., 2015). Therefore, the authors of this chapter found it worthwhile to explore the impact of such methods in the context of service design, in particular, to see whether they can ignite and sustain a more relational practice. The study with dementia family caregivers showed that these story-centered co-creative methods contribute to building relations that are characterized by trust, sensitivity, and empathy. These relationships led to safe, informal, and authentic design environments, which not only ensured a sustainable engagement from the caregivers, but also greater levels of honesty, while making them more open toward the transformative potential and active power of the service design process. In this study, the transformative power relates to how the active participation of the caregivers led to valuable awareness, reflections, interactions, and advanced inherited capabilities that improved their lived reality. These findings emphasize the importance of acknowledging the embedded value co-creation process as part of the overall service design process, which when properly leveraged can greatly expand the value released through service design. This embedded value co-creation process is very much focused on the actors participating and on how to generate the highest possible value for them in the actual moment of designing. It sees these actors as the experts of their own realities and adapts the role of the designer from a problem solver to someone who supports a process of individual reflection and transformation.

In many respects, however, this approach was not an easy choice but brought with it challenges of which one should be aware in advance. Firstly, while taking on the role of a supporter is a very fulfilling experience, it also demands more than just design capabilities but a lot of emotive resources. For example, this project required to support participants in emotionally difficult situations, which as a designer one is not necessarily trained in. Secondly, the designers had to be very flexible in the planning and execution of the individual activities, on the one hand, because of the emotional strain on the caregivers, and on the other hand, because of the unpredictability of the events that can occur in relation to dementia. Thirdly, this approach requires significantly more time than an ordinary, e.g., human-centered, approach. However, we want to argue that this time is meaningfully invested, considering that the value of the service design process was significantly leveraged.

The authors of this chapter suggest that employing this approach in the context of healthcare projects, which not only engage health seekers but also health professionals, may significantly contribute to meaningful healthcare innovation. First, such an approach could be a means to reinforce the advancing person-centered movement within healthcare (Eaton et al., 2015; Health Foundation, 2014; Tsekleves & Cooper, 2017; Van Royen et al., 2010), as it helps to eliminate the inaccurate mental models that limit the understanding of people to patients, customers, or users. As the approach engages with none of these roles in particular, but rather considers people as co-creators and as the experts of their lives, which relates in part but not exclusively to these roles, it can potentially reinvent the relationship between health professionals and health seekers. Second, it could also be a contribution to clinical preventive services, as the approach, to some extent, enabled people, who are at significant high risk to suffer from a variety of physical and psychological health issues (Brodaty & Donkin, 2009), to take care of their own health and improve their well-being, including for example through awareness, change of perspective, reflections, networking, and the feeling of being noticed and taken seriously. Third, we assume by making the relations emerging from health-care projects employing this approach enter the real-life contexts (Björgvinsson et al., 2010), the chances of transforming ordinary healthcare services into relational services that are more emotionally supportive, humane, and caring (Aguirre-Ulloa & Paulsen, 2017) increase. For example, healthcare practitioners participating in a project that employs such an approach may alter the way they see and support health seekers in their individual journey of health seeking (Cottam, 2011; Vink et al., 2019). Unfortunately, it was not possible to engage healthcare professionals in this specific case study due to the outbreak of COVID-19 in 2020. We therefore see a great potential in exploring what impact it may have to use the story-centered co-creative methods to foster relationships and empathy across actors of the healthcare sector. This would be an interesting and important area for future research.

In this project, the impact of relational co-creative service design has been explored through a single case study with dementia family caregivers. Service design is increasingly applied to tackle the complex problems of today's societies, with healthcare being only one of many examples (Polaine et al., 2013). We suggest that the approach may prove valuable in all those contexts where success is or ought not to be measured only in terms of competitive advantages, profit, or efficiency, but rather in terms of the level of value it provides to individual actors and society, or in other words, in terms of the level of social innovation. These contexts could for example be within healthcare, welfare, or education (Polaine et al., 2013).

Given this background, we suggest future research to experiment with the approach and to explore its impact across a variety of contexts. It would also be interesting to pay special attention to the aforementioned challenges that a designer may meet when applying the approach, and to find out to what extent they can be reduced. This could for instance be an investigation and discussion of the extent to which research employing a relational co-creative approach becomes biased. In this project, the designers' personality, values, and beliefs cannot be considered as external but found their way into the relationships established. Whether this is defensible and of integrity would be worth discussing.

25.6 Conclusion

By conceptualizing service design as a service in itself, this research explored how story-centered co-creative methods, i.e., an iterative practice of gathering and (co) producing stories, can ignite and sustain relational service design. Through a case study with dementia family caregivers in the context of the Danish healthcare system, we have highlighted how story-centered co-creative methods aid service designers in fostering greater levels of trust, sensitivity, and empathy in the relations with and among the participants of a service design project, and in establishing safe, informal, and authentic design environments. By demonstrating how relational service design supports actors in advancing their inherited capabilities, this chapter further expands the understanding of the transformative power of the service design process and offers insights for service designers and healthcare practitioners interested in employing a relational approach for healthcare innovation.

References

Aguirre-Ulloa, M., & Paulsen, A. (2017). Co-designing with relationships in mind. *FormAkademisk - Forskningstidsskrift for Design Og Designdidaktikk, 10*(1). https://doi.org/10.7577/formakademisk.1608.

Akama, Y., & Prendiville, A. (2016). Embodying, enacting and entangling design: A phenomenological view to co-designing services. *Swedish Design Research Journal, 9*(1), 29–40. https://doi.org/10.3384/svid.2000-964X.13129.

Baskerville, D. (2011). Developing cohesion and building positive relationships through storytelling in a culturally diverse New Zealand classroom. *Teaching and Teacher Education, 27*(1), 107–115. https://doi.org/10.1016/j.tate.2010.07.007.

Björgvinsson, E., Ehn, P., & Hillgren, P.-A. (2010). Participatory design and "democratizing innovation." In *Proceedings of the 11th Biennial Participatory Design Conference on - PDC '10* (p. 41). https://doi.org/10.1145/1900441.1900448.

Blankman, K., Ellenbogen, M., Graham, N., Hogg, L., Mittler, P., Piot, P., Splaine, M., Vernooij-Dassen, M., & Watt, A. (2012). *World Alzheimer report 2012: Overcoming the stigma of dementia—Executive summary* (p. 18).

Boyd, H., McKernon, S., Mullin, B., & Old, A. (2012). Improving healthcare through the use of co-design. *New Zealand Medial Journal, 125*(1357), 76–87.

Brodaty, H., & Donkin, M. (2009). Family caregivers of people with dementia. *Dialogues in Clinical Neuroscience, 11*(2), 217–228.

Cipolla, C., & Manzini, E. (2009). Relational services. *Knowledge, Technology & Policy, 22*(1), 45–50. https://doi.org/10.1007/s12130-009-9066-z.

Cottam, H. (2011). Relational welfare. *Soundings, 48*(48), 134–144. https://doi.org/10.3898/136266211797146855 .

Cottam, H., & Leadbeater, C. (2004). *RED PAPER 01 HEALTH: Co-creating Services*. Design Council.

Dam Johansen, N., & Neuhoff, R. (2020). *The impact of relational co-creative research in service design practice. A co-creative case study with dementia family caregivers in the Danish welfare system*. Copenhagen: Aalborg University (Ed.).

Design Council. (2019). *What is the framework for innovation? Design Council's evolved Double Diamond*. Design Council. Accessed 21 May 2021. https://www.designcouncil.org.uk/news-opinion/what-framework-innovation-design-councils-evolved-double-diamond.

Dilnot, C. (1982). Design as a socially significant activity: An introduction. *Design Studies, 3*(3), 139–146. https://doi.org/10.1016/0142-694X(82)90006-0.

Eaton, S., Roberts, S., & Turner, B. (2015). Delivering person centred care in long term conditions. *BMJ, 350*(h181).

Eisenhardt, K. M. (1989). Building theories from case study research. *The Academy of Management Review, 14*(4), 532–550. https://doi.org/10.2307/258557.

Eisenhardt, K. M., & Graebner, M. E. (2007). Theory building from cases: opportunities and challenges. *Academy of Management Journal, 50*(1), 25–32. https://doi.org/10.5465/amj.2007. 24160888.

Health Foundation. (2014). *Person-centred care made simple: What everyone should know about person-centred care.* London: Health Foundation (Ed.).

Janssen, M. (2016). *Situated novelty: A study on healthcare innovation and its governance.* Rotterdam: Erasmus University Rotterdam (Ed.). https://repub.eur.nl/pub/93264/.

Jones, P. (2013). *Design for care: Innovating healthcare experience* (ast ed.). New York: Rosenfeld Media.

Jørgensen, K. (2021). *Demens koster mindst 8 mia. Kr. Årligt.* Nationalt Videnscenter for Demens (Ed.). Accessed 21 May 2021. https://videnscenterfordemens.dk/da/nyhed/demens-koster-mindst-8-mia-kr-aarligt.

Jørgensen, U., Lindegaard, H., & Rosenqvist, T. (2011). Engaging actors in co-designing heterogeneous innovations. In *Proceedings of the 18th International Conference on Engineering Design: Impacting Society through Engineering Design* (pp. 453–464).

Kieboom, M., Sigaloff, C., van Exel, T., & Vrouwe, W. (2015). *Lab practice: Creating spaces for social change.* Kennisland (Ed.). Accessed 21 May 2021. https://www.kl.nl/en/publications/lab-practice-creating-spaces-for-social-change/.

Killick, S., & Boffey, M. (2012). *Building relationships through storytelling a foster carer's guide to attachment and stories.* London: Fostering Network.

Kurtmollaiev, S., Fjuk, A., Pedersen, P. E., Clatworthy, S., & Kvale, K. (2017). Organizational transformation through service design: The institutional logics perspective. *Journal of Service Research, 21*(1), 59–74. https://doi.org/10.1177/1094670517738371.

Kushniruk, A., & Nøhr, C. (2016). Participatory design, user involvement and health IT evaluation. In E. Ammenwerth & M. Rigby (Eds.), *Evidence-based health informatics: Promoting safety and efficiency through scientific methods and ethical policy* (pp. 139–151). Amsterdam: IOS Press.

Kvale, S. (1996). *Interviews: An introduction to qualitative research interviewing.* Thousand Oaks: SAGE Publications Inc.

Levine, S. (2019). Health care industry insights: Why the use of preventive services is still low. *Preventing Chronic Disease, 16*(E30), 1–6. https://doi.org/10.5888/pcd16.180625.

Manzini, E. (2015). Design, when everybody designs: An introduction to design for social innovation (R. Coad, Trans.). Boston: The MIT Press.

McCabe, M., You, E., & Tatangelo, G. (2016). Hearing their voice: A systematic review of dementia family caregivers' needs. *The Gerontologist, 56*(5), e70–e88. https://doi.org/10.1093/geront/gnw078.

Meadows, D. (2008). *Thinking in systems.* In D. Wright (Ed.). White River Junction, Vermont: Chelsea Green Publishing.

Motivate Design. (2019). What is the difference between interviews & conversations? Motivate Design (Ed.). Accessed 21 May 2021. https://www.motivatedesign.com/what-is-the-difference-between-interviews-conversations/.

Nationalt Videnscenter for Demens. (n.d.). *Pårørende til mennesker med demens.* Nationalt Videnscenter for Demens. Accessed 7 May 2021. from https://videnscenterfordemens.dk/da/paaroerende-til-mennesker-med-demens.

Penin, L. (2018). *An introduction to service design: Designing the invisible.* London: Bloomsbury Visual Arts.

Pfannstiel, M. A., & Rasche, C. (Eds.). (2019). *Service design and service thinking in healthcare and hospital management: Theory, concepts, practice.* Cham: Springer International Publishing. https://doi.org/10.1007/978-3-030-00749-2.

Pierri, P. (2017). Decentralising design. Raising the question of agency in emerging design practice. *The Design Journal, 20*(sup1), S2951–S2959. https://doi.org/10.1080/14606925. 2017.1352805.

Polaine, A., Løvlie, L., & Reason, B. (2013). *Service design: From insight to implementation* (1st ed.). New York: Rosenfeld Media.

Sanders, E. B.-N., & Stappers, P. J. (2008). Co-creation and the new landscapes of design. *CoDesign, 4*(1), 5–18. https://doi.org/10.1080/15710880701875068.

Steen, M., Manschot, M., & Koning, N. D. (2011). Benefits of co-design in service design projects. *International Journal of Design, 5*(2), Xy–Yy.

Stickdorn, M., & Schneider, J. (2012). *This is service design thinking: Basics, tools, cases.* Amsterdam: BIS Publishers.

Stickdorn, M., Hormess, M. E., Lawrence, A., & Schneider, J. (2018a). *This is service design methods: A companion to this is service design doing.* Sebastopol: O'Reilly Media, Inc.

Tsekleves, E., & Cooper, R. (2017). Emerging trends and the way forward in design in healthcare: An expert's perspective. *The Design Journal, 20*(*sup1*), S2258–S2272. https://doi.org/10.1080/14606925.2017.1352742.

Van Royen, P., Beyer, M., Chevallier, P., Eilat-Tsanani, S., Lionis, C., Peremans, L., Petek, D., Rurik, I., Soler, J. K., Stoffers, H. E. J. H., Topsever, P., Ungan, M., & Hummers-Pradier, E. (2010). The research agenda for general practice/family medicine and primary health care in Europe. Part 3. Results: Person centred care, comprehensive and holistic approach. *The European Journal of General Practice, 16*(2), 113–119. https://doi.org/10.3109/13814788.2010.481018.

Vårdanalys. (2017). *Lag utan genomslag [Act without impact].* Vårdanalys (Ed.). Accessed 21 May 2021. https://www.vardanalys.se/in-english/reports/act-without-impact.

Vargo, S. L., & Lusch, R. F. (2008). Service-dominant logic: Continuing the evolution. *Journal of the Academy of Marketing Science, 36*(1), 1–10.

Vetterli, C., & Scherrer, C. (2019). Service innovation by patient-centric innovation processes. In M. A. Pfannstiel & C. Rasche (Eds.), *Service design and service thinking in healthcare and hospital management: Theory, concepts, practice* (pp. 55–67). Cham: Springer International Publishing. https://doi.org/10.1007/978-3-030-00749-2_4.

Vink, J. (2019). *In/visible—Conceptualizing service ecosystem design.* Karlstad University studies. Accessed 21 May 2021. http://urn.kb.se/resolve?urn=urn:nbn:se:kau:diva-71967.

Vink, J., Wetter-Edman, K., Edvardsson, B., & Tronvoll, B. (2016). Understanding the influence of the co-design process on well-being. In *Service Design Geographies. Proceedings of the ServDes.2016 Conference* (pp. 390–402).

Vink, J., Joly, M. P., Wetter-Edman, K., Tronvoll, B., & Edvardsson, B. (2019). Changing the rules of the game in healthcare through service design. In M. A. Pfannstiel & C. Rasche (Eds.), *Service design and service thinking in healthcare and hospital management: Theory, concepts, practice* (pp. 19–37). Cham: Springer International Publishing. https://doi.org/10.1007/978-3-030-00749-2_2.

Wetter-Edman, K., Sangiorgi, D., Edvardsson, B., Holmlid, S., Grönroos, C., & Mattelmäki, T. (2014). Design for value co-creation: exploring synergies between design for service and service logic. *Service Science, 6*(2), 106–121. https://doi.org/10.1287/serv.2014.0068.

Winblad, U., Mor, V., McHugh, J. P., & Rahman, M. (2017). ACO-affiliated hospitals reduced rehospitalizations from skilled nursing facilities faster than other hospitals. *Health Affairs (Project Hope), 36*(1), 67–73. https://doi.org/10.1377/hlthaff.2016.0759.

Yghemonos, S. (2016). The importance of informal carers for primary health care. *Primary Health Care Research & Development, 17*(6), 531–533. https://doi.org/10.1017/S1463423616000360.

Yin, R. K. (2009). *Case study research: Design and methods.* Thousand Oaks: SAGE.

Rike Neuhoff is a PhD student at the Department of Architecture, Design and Media Technology at Aalborg University in Denmark. Her current research explores how design-driven foresight can support participatory transformation processes. A particular focus is on the potential of scenario building as a means to enable actors to collaboratively envision and enact sustainable urban futures. Rike holds a Master of Science in Service Systems Design from Aalborg University in Denmark. As a service designer, she has worked on projects in Germany, Denmark, and Norway.

Nanna Dam Johansen is a service designer in the Intervention Unit at the Rockwool Foundation. She is passionate about the cross section between service design and social innovation, and how design can be used to explore complex, systemic challenges. Her core interests focus on inclusive design processes that set the lived experiences of the users in the center and build relationships across various actors. She has worked on several innovation projects within the healthcare and welfare context, both in the public sector and within non-profit. Nanna holds a Master of Science in Service Systems Design from Aalborg University Copenhagen.

Luca Simeone is Associate Professor at Aalborg University in Denmark. His main interest is in how strategic thinking can support design-based innovation and management processes. Luca has conducted research and teaching activities in various international centres (Harvard, MIT, Polytechnic University of Milan, Malmö University, and University of the Arts London), (co) authoring four books and other publications for venues including CoDesign, Journal of Business Research, Journal of Knowledge Management, Technovation, the Design Journal and R&D Management Journal.

Digital Storytelling to Share Service Experiences and Find Insights into Health Care

26

Mira Alhonsuo, Melanie Sarantou, and Satu Miettinen

Abstract

This chapter explores the value of including digital storytelling in service design for improving the quality, safety and convenience of health-related services. The aim of the chapter is to explore how stories of healthcare experiences can be shared through digital tools to garner critical insights into creating innovative healthcare services and improving the quality of treatment. The data were collected through the personal stories of the authors regarding health treatment and care processes; these were shared as digital diaries within a closed network through the digital tool and communication platform WhatsApp. The stories were autobiographical reflections on service journeys that mirrored, for example, the rehabilitation process of a child from a mother's point of view and the self-narrated treatment of spinal injury and rehabilitation from an adult's point of view. WhatsApp enabled multiple methods of communication: written text, voice recordings, pictures, videos, emojis and graphics interchange format (GIF). The tool enabled documentation of and reflections on service moments or feelings that were encountered in health-related environments. The platform also provided freedom of expression in a safe and trusted environment, as the diary authors were able to control access to the content. The digital data were transferred from WhatsApp into an online whiteboard tool and were explored by the authors in-depth through collective autoethnography. The outcomes of this

M. Alhonsuo (✉) · M. Sarantou · S. Miettinen
Faculty of Art and Design, University of Lapland, Yliopistonkatu 8, 96300 Rovaniemi, Finland
e-mail: mira.alhonsuo@ulapland.fi

M. Sarantou
e-mail: melanie.sarantou@ulapland.fi

S. Miettinen
e-mail: satu.miettinen@ulapland.fi

study offer insights into how digital tools can be used to better scope and collect the experiences of healthcare users and explore the role of storytelling in developing meaningful and innovative healthcare services and treatment quality.

26.1   Introduction

The field of health care is well-known for its siloed, complex and multilayered processes that include people both with a variety of expertise and from different backgrounds. Health care is a universally used service that impacts both economies and quality of life (Bowen et al., 2013). Health-related services are a "routine part of our lives, but it is often anything but routine for the people receiving it" (Goodwin, 2020, p. 37). Healthcare services are often used unintentionally, without knowledge about how long they will be used or at what cost. Indeed, users often have to rely on different experts who practise in different silos. Although different design disciplines have strongly emphasised the value of the user experience in improving health care (e.g. Bate & Robert, 2007), this patient-oriented approach, as a method in service design, still lacks documentation in the literature (Simonse et al., 2019).

The journey of the patient can be long, and patients' experiences can vary depending on their cases and treatment. Patients might encounter different experiences, such as fear, frustration, trauma and happiness, during clinical care. Family members are often similarly involved, as they follow the patient's the journey closely. Their role can either be passive, in which they simply hope for the best, or more active, in which they are involved with rehabilitation or home-based care. Regardless, the experiences of family members are equally important. Still, healthcare services often seem unspecified, complex and impersonal, and they cannot be mapped in the same way as service journeys in, for example, online shops or grocery stores. Therefore, the meaning of more personalised service journeys, as well as the experiences and touchpoints (e.g. artefacts) in time and space, must be better understood (Kimbell, 2009).

In this study, the authors shared their personal health-related cases by using the communication platform WhatsApp. The service journeys experienced and collected via autoethnography for this research included the rehabilitation process of a child from a mother's point of view, the self-narrated treatment of and rehabilitation from spinal injury from an adult's point of view, and a case of low iron levels found during an occupational health check. After the autoethnographies were shared, the data were collected in an online whiteboard platform. The authors engaged in a two-hour workshop during which they used a storytelling approach to share their experiences and further develop the identified challenges.

Written and oral narratives, or storytelling, play a crucial role in sharing and understanding experiences (Bate & Robert, 2007). Therefore, this study aimed to understand how using digital tools helps better scope and collect the experiences of healthcare services, as well as what role storytelling has in developing meaningful and innovative healthcare services and treatment quality. The study presented the findings of the online storytelling work session and collective autoethnography (CAE) work session in a whiteboard platform.

26.2 Overview of the Theory

The scope of the project was to explore the role of digital storytelling as a way to share health-related service experiences. The next section introduces the overview of the theory, interconnecting the fields of service design, tools for communication and digital storytelling for sharing service experiences.

26.2.1 Service Design

Service design is a human-centred, multidisciplinary practice that uses visual, performative and embodied tools and design methods (Polaine, 2013). Collaborative thinking and acting stimulate knowledge-sharing and learning, which are important especially during collaborations between complex multilevel services in which different groups and individuals act (Alhonsuo et al., 2020). Service designers are usually facilitators in the co-design sessions (Manzini, 2015; Meroni & Sangiorgi, 2011), and these facilitators must have the emotional skills necessary to work with different communities (Soto, 2021). Soto (ibid.) identified these emotional skills as embodied knowledge, emotional awareness and collective spirit.

Healthcare services are complex and challenging to develop, as they rely on interactions between various stakeholders (Bowen et al., 2013). Thus, many healthcare organisations invest in service design (Freire & Sangiorgi, 2010; Mager & Alonso, 2017), in which the essential element is understanding peoples' experiences when they use a service (Mager, 2010). Different tools for mapping these experiences help simplify the complexities of developing healthcare services and provide unique insights. The general methods of service design stem from ethnographic research (e.g. Segelström & Holmlid, 2015) that aims to gather a holistic picture of the researched topic, engage the relevant stakeholders and understand their experiences by interviewing and observing them (Creswell, 2014). In this research, visualisation plays a crucial role to understand the relationship between digital storytelling and data analysis in digital environments, so service designers utilise a variety of visualisation and concretisation tools and methods (Koh et al., 2011; Shneiderman et al., 2013).

The service design handbooks have introduced many different tools for observing, understanding and defining the experiences of others, and one of the most-used tools is a *service journey* (e.g. Stickdorn & Schneider, 2011). The service journey is a visualised process that provides a holistic picture of the service across a timeline from the end-user's point of view. When zooming into the service journey, different service moments can be observed during which, for example, interactions happen through different touchpoints. These touchpoints are tangible or intangible contact points between the end-users and the service providers (Stickdorn & Schneider, 2011). In a holistic journey, touchpoints are crucial elements for creating a successful service. Therefore, the meaning of more personalised service journeys, as well as personal experiences and touchpoints in time and space (Kimbell, 2009), must be understood. Such touchpoints can mean different things to people, and each brings different values to the service as a whole.

26.2.2 Tools for Communication

Different visualisation tools are typically used in service design. Visualisation is used for multiple reasons. First, it helps perceive complex services, such as resources and ecosystems of health care (Miettinen & Alhonsuo, 2019), and second, it supports communication. Furthermore, as Segelström (2010) stated, visualisation helps service designers define insights from the users' data, as well as articulate identified insights and preserve empathy of the users throughout the visualisation.

Aguirre et al. (2016) defined three tools for facilitation: generic tools (e.g. post-its, whiteboards, markers), templated tools (e.g. predefined formats, canvases or templates) and contextual tools (e.g. those designed specifically for a certain context or activity). These definitions show that communication can occur through different means. For example, Kronqvist et al. (2013) created a patient journey as a game board for sarcoma-type cancer patients and used tangible props to assist the interviews, thereby helping patients remember and discuss their lived experiences. The authors of the present study shared an interest in the self-documentation tools that enabled them to share their experiences instantly while capturing their narrative data to analyse the different healthcare journeys they experienced.

26.2.3 Digital Storytelling for Sharing Service Experiences

Storytelling is a method used in co-design and service design that highlights the users' needs (Kankainen et al., 2012) and can therefore be a way to develop services. Although Layton et al. (1998) stressed that healthcare service experiences are best observed through face-to-face communication with patients, the value of documenting personal, health-related experiences during the real service cannot be denied. Furthermore, designers in the healthcare context are increasingly utilising patient journey approaches, which as a method still lack careful analysis and documentation in the literature (Simonse et al., 2019).

Experiences are not that simple to study, measure or map, but they are truly important to consider when developing healthcare services. Storytelling, or narration, plays a crucial role in helping understand how people experience something (Bate & Robert, 2007). According to Hurwitz et al. (2004), "Storytelling invokes words uttered and heard or written and read, images depicted and deciphered, or gestures enacted and understood" (p. 1). These words "are the vessels or messengers of meaning and experience, capable of transporting an unanalysable past into an analysable present in the form of stories and anecdotes" (Bate & Robert, 2007, p. 39).

The importance of understanding people's experiences, especially with health-related services, is meaningful for many reasons. First, the experiences vary; it is often impossible to define the service journey in advance. People often end up using healthcare services unintentionally, not knowing how much those services will cost or what will happen. Second, the service users in health care come from different backgrounds, so considering different needs helps improve the services (e.g. their accessibility). Third, healthcare service users include not only the patients receiving care but also the family members, who similarly need information and participate in care, for example, from home. Based on the holistic service experience point of view, the service journey must be perceived as a bigger picture with touchpoints as supporting details, and how the experience affects these levels from service journey to touchpoints must be determined.

This paper discusses the meaning of documenting experiences while using healthcare services and how these experiences can be translated into game-board-type service journeys. Furthermore, it suggests solutions for the identified challenges to create new service innovations.

26.3 Storytelling Phases

In this study, collective autoethnography was adopted as research strategy, while the communication platform WhatsApp was employed in the collection of data. The insights into shared experiences were discussed and analysed collaboratively during an online workshop between the authors of this chapter. This section introduces these analytical approaches, activities and methods during the workshop and discuss them in more detail.

26.3.1 Collective Autoethnography

CAE, a qualitative research method, was adopted as the methodological approach for this research. In addition, CAE is collaborative and autoethnographic (Chang et al., 2016). The data collection methods included digital diaries, online workshops with group discussions and note-taking in an online whiteboard platform. The interdependencies in this research, which resulted from teamwork and knowledge-sharing, presented an opportunity to use CAE to understand the roles of the team members, their interactions and these roles' contribution to the development of the research and the design outcomes.

CAE is a subjective approach that draws on insider knowledge and personal experience (Ellis & Adams, 2014). The collective and reflexive nature of CAE means that it is non-exploitative and accessible, which characteristics make those who are subjects of research more at ease with the research process. CAE entails a focus on self-interrogation and is also a pragmatic and iterative approach to inquiry due to its joint elements of data collection and analysis (Chang et al., 2016). Lapadat (2017) described CAE as a multivocal approach whereby several researchers collaborate through sharing and reflecting upon personal experiences, discussion, knowledge-sharing and data interpretation. Thus, CAE entails a shift from personal to group agency, as the roles of the researcher and the research participants are vested in one person, which increases personal engagement (Lapadat, 2017).

CAE enabled the author-researchers to use their three individual storylines of health-related experiences and collectively reflect and analyse these storylines to identify key forthcoming themes during an online workshop. The limitation of this study was the small number of research participants; however, the autoethnographic methodology focused on in-depth understanding and development of something novel.

26.3.2 Digital Diaries

This study utilised the communication platform WhatsApp as a way for the authors to share personal health-related service journeys. WhatsApp enabled multiple ways to communicate experiences through written text, voice recordings, pictures, videos, emojis and graphics interchange format (GIF). Instead of limiting the usage of these features, the authors observed the best ways to share their personal health-related experiences. The WhatsApp communication platform was selected because the authors were familiar with its features due to daily use. The authors also had previous experience utilising WhatsApp as a platform for documenting narratives for research purposes, and this experience enabled easy utilisation of this platform for the present study.

The authors started to record their shared narratives in closed WhatsApp groups after planning the research. During the planning phase, the authors briefly shared their experiences and agreed upon the best digital tools to capture their stories and enable the other members in the group to participate, ask questions and leave comments. Two of the authors were able to define their cases right away, while the third author, who had no personal health story to share when the research diaries commenced, shared her health experience later during the process. All authors started their online diaries by sketching a short background for their experiences, and all authors participated in the diaries through comments, emojis, questions, support and empathy with one another's experiences and learnings. The selected platform provided many opportunities regarding when and how many comments could be given. For example, at some points, an author only read what others had commented, while at other times, that author would write something.

26.3.3 Online Workshop for Collective Data Analysis and Sharing Experiences

The online workshop, which followed the collection of diary entries in WhatsApp, was held in May 2021. The online workshop aimed to analyse the data from the WhatsApp diaries to offer insights into using digital tools to better scope and collect the experiences of healthcare users and explore the role of storytelling in developing meaningful and innovative healthcare services and treatment quality. The participants were the three authors of this paper.

One of the authors prepared the workshop in Miro, an online whiteboard for visual communication. The data from WhatsApp was visualised in the format of a service journey, in which the WhatsApp messages formulated a timeline (see Fig. 26.1). Furthermore, the following exercises for data analysis and service ideation were visualised. The authors received a reminder the day before the workshop asking them to read through the messages before the workshop and prepare themselves on the topic. The two-hour online workshop consisted of four different activities, which are described below in detail.

This chapter provides an example of how to apply practise-based design research (Muratovski, 2015) when developing healthcare services. This design science-related approach fits well when developing ideas for practical design solutions, as service design methods play a role not only in collecting data but also in analysing data.

26.3.3.1 Activity 1: Identifying Feelings and Needs for Service Experiences

The first activity related to the visualised service journey (see Fig. 26.1). The authors read their own stories and identified two main topics: (1) adjectives, keywords or feelings that described the critical health-related "moments" that defined the authors' experiences of their different journeys and (2) a need, idea or wish that could have helped in the moment. The aim of this activity was to identify and define some of the important experiences or moments of the journeys more in depth. After this activity, the authors identified a phase (moment/experience) that they believed was the most crucial to develop.

26.3.3.2 Activity 2: Highlighting the Most Critical Moment

The selected phase of the authors' personal stories was copy-pasted into the next task (see Fig. 26.2), during which time everyone was given time to share it through storytelling while the others were listening and simultaneously note-taking and identifying critical insights from a quality, safety and convenience point of view. These insights were written down on sticky notes. Afterwards, the sticky notes were discussed together.

Fig. 26.1 Visualised service journey of the WhatsApp data. *Source* Author's own illustration (2021)

Fig. 26.2 Second activity of the workshop. *Source* Author's own illustration (2021)

26.3.3.3 Activity 3: Ideation Based on the Story

The third exercise focused on creating new health-related service solutions. Four different areas were chosen to drive the innovation: (1) minimum viable service, which has zero resources; (2) service, which works as a take-away; (3) online service; and (4) dream service with endless resources (see Fig. 26.3). The service ideas that did not belong to these categories were written outside of the marked areas in the Miro environment (e.g. the orange frame seen in Fig. 26.2). Ideation lasted for approximately 8–10 min and was followed by a short debriefing session. During this session, the person whose story it was discussed the ideas and applied them to his/her experiences.

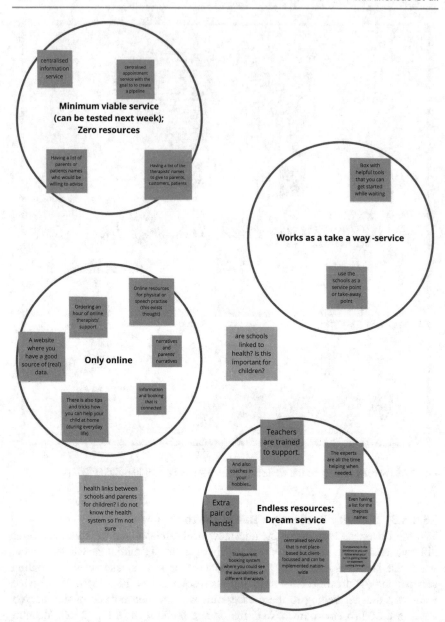

Fig. 26.3 Idea circles. *Source* Author's own illustration (2021)

26.3.3.4   Activity 4: Analysis

The last activity focused on analysing both the usage of digital tools to better scope and collect experiences and the role of storytelling in developing meaningful and innovative healthcare services (see Fig. 26.4).

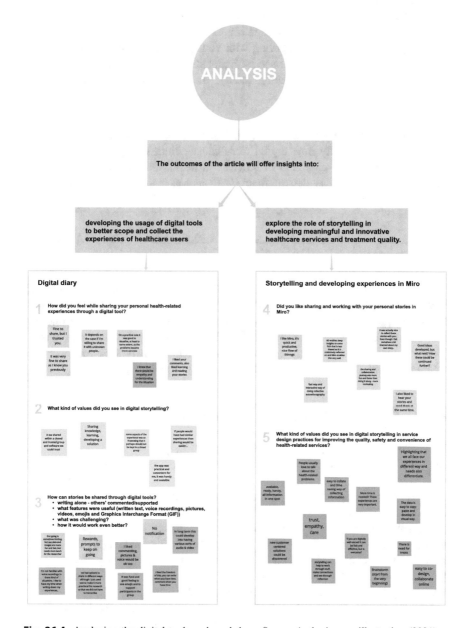

Fig. 26.4 Analysing the digital tools and workshop. *Source* Author's own illustration (2021)

During the final phase of the workshop, the collaborative data collected in the Miro environment were analysed using previously identified questions, as follows:

- "How did you feel while sharing your personal health-related experiences through a digital tool?"
- "What kind of values did you see in digital storytelling?"
- "How can stories be shared through digital tools?"
- "Did you like sharing and working with your personal stories in Miro?"
- "What kind of values did you see in digital storytelling in service design practices for improving the quality, safety and convenience of health-related services?"

Responses to these questions were noted in Miro. These notes were further analysed and discussed to identify how digital tools can facilitate engagement and collect data to support the development of services in health-related fields. The authors used thematic analysis as part of their CAE approach to identify main themes, which are discussed below.

26.4 Findings

The CAE approach enabled the authors to collaboratively and critically discuss and identify key forthcoming themes from their personal experiences. Due to the collaborative approach, more balanced and critical perspectives emerged; the findings were less biased as they were independent from the findings of only one person. Thus, the findings revealed the qualities that participants may seek for their user experiences and data captured through storytelling on online platforms.

26.4.1 Sharing Within Circles of Trust

The meaning of sharing stories was discussed with people the authors' trusted. Generally, sharing personal information about health-related journeys seemed easier when it did not involve sharing with strangers. The following reflections confirmed this finding: "It was very fine to share as I knew you previously", and "It depends on the case if I'm willing to share it with unknown people". However, one participant noted in Miro that the problem with sharing stories only with closed and trusted groups is that the information may not reach wider audiences. The authors noted, "Some aspects of the experience were so frustrating that it perhaps should not be kept in a closed group". Furthermore, sharing stories with someone outside of close circles could even create an opportunity for healing.

Moreover, peer support during diary-sharing in WhatsApp, which was predominantly experienced as positive and empathic, was highlighted during the CAE analysis. Comments from the authors included, for example, "If people would have had similar experiences then sharing would be easier". Peer-support enables not only receiving empathy from people who have had similar experiences but also the sharing of advice and knowledge.

26.4.2   Sharing via Trusted Software that is Used Everyday

The usage of digital software was also discussed. It was obvious that the platform for sharing had to be easy to use and in everyday use. Furthermore, the channel must be trusted when discussing personal health-related topics. One author emphasised, "The app was practical and convenient for me, it was handy and available whenever I needed it and had a free moment to reflect on my experiences, or when I was using public transport and had a moment to document my thoughts".

Using popular platforms may be a practical method for capturing data from health users, but due to a wide variety of software, mobile devices, operating systems and communication applications, choosing one platform that will answer to the needs of all users may be difficult. Some users may have different perspectives regarding what they consider trusted software. Additionally, trust, availability and usability of software may only be appropriate in particular cultures or regions. Thus, ethical considerations and rules may be needed to provide guidelines for using specific software or platforms.

26.4.3   Empathy Through Commenting

Although the experiences were shared between people who already knew each other, the importance of empathy cannot be overemphasised. One comment defined the three key qualities of commenting as "trust, empathy, care". Another observation related to commenting on WhatsApp messages and learning: "I liked your comments, also liked learning [from your experiences] and reading your stories". Although the topics were dealing with sometimes stressful and challenging health-related cases, the way to communicate was considered "fun and [it was a] good feeling to use emojis and to support participants in the group". Cognitive empathy, or the ability to understand another's intentions, and affective empathy, the attempt to experience a situation from another's point of view (Bloom, 2017; Brink et al., 2011), were both experienced. Saarikivi (2018) and Brink et al. (2011) stated that empathy is the only skill through which humans can understand the emotions of others, and therefore, empathy supports humans' collective intelligence. Furthermore, storytelling stimulates empathy (Brink et al., 2011; Saarikivi, 2018).

26.4.4   Value of Sharing Knowledge and Learning

The value of sharing knowledge was seen throughout the digital diaries and workshop. The visualisation helped others perceive the story and made it more concrete. As one of the authors commented in Miro, "On a practical note it was good to visualise [the stories and the health-related journeys in Miro], at least to some extent, as the problems became more concrete". The author found that the visual aspects of the workshop, such as the timelines of the journeys and how the different discussions were grouped and visually clustered, assisted their analysis, as they were able to see similarities and differences between the data more prominently. Collaborative work with Miro-enhanced peer-to-peer learning (Kuure & Miettinen, 2013) often occurred during the service design workshop, and this was essential for ideating suitable solutions and concepts for healthcare services.

26.4.5   Motivation for Sharing

One of the challenges discussed was motivating people to continue sharing or reminding them to share their stories. The authors discussed how they could provide "rewards, prompts to keep on going". However, the freedom to share was also seen as a value: "I liked the freedom of this [approach to use WhatsApp to share and document our personal stories in digital diaries], you can write when you have time, comment when you have time". Additionally, knowing that the data from the digital journeys would be utilised later during the workshop motivated the authors to share their experiences.

Still, the interest to continue sharing stories via the personal WhatsApp groups waned during the data collection period. The authors had to remind each other about their aim to continue to share updates. When the third author experienced unforeseen health issues, the interest in sharing returned. Therefore, significant events can stimulate continued interest in the online diary method, provided that trustful relationships continue.

26.4.6   Developing Experiences Through Collaborative Methods in an Online Platform

The storytelling workshop was seen as a beneficial way to share the journeys. One of the authors emphasised that "the sharing and collaborative journey was more fun and faster than doing it alone, [it was] more motivating". The online whiteboard platform (Miro) was a good platform for sharing and collectively reflecting on the stories, as the following comments highlighted: "I like Miro, it's quick and productive [and it offers a] nice flow of things", and "Collective autoethnography enables deep insights that are less biased as we collectively reflected on [our experiences while] Miro enabled this very well".

The visuality of the platform and the online four-step workshop journey, which were based on service design methods that utilise customer journeys, enabled the author-researchers to identify possible ideas for improving health-related services. Furthermore, the collaborative methods facilitated commitment and feelings of being heard and understood. These qualities are essential when steps are taken to implementation of new service journeys.

26.5   Conclusion

Digital diaries were seen as a valuable method for documenting health-related service journeys, and the Miro digital environment enabled the transfer and mapping of stories into a visual and user-friendly format that the researchers found engaging. The format resulted in a productive workshop; the analysis was completed in a short timespan (two hours) due to the way the workshop and "raw" data were organised. Additionally, the format of the workshop was designed to include focus-group or collaborative discussion, storytelling and collaborative note-taking, which enhanced the CAE approach.

Collaborative work enabled the authors to envision some quick takeaway solutions that could be realised immediately, such as sharing peer-to-peer or expert contact information or providing patients with info packages. Additionally, it enabled work on some concept ideas for solutions, such as online or mobile services needed to meet challenges caused by more remote locations. The workshop helped in wording the service needs in a more concrete format to address these needs.

The Miro whiteboard was a suitable tool for mapping the service journey in a timeline that clearly indicated key service moments. The authors created their service journeys mainly through written format. Documentation of the touchpoints did not occur in the way that WhatsApp could have made possible as many of the functions available in WhatsApp were not used apart from emojis and texts. Only a few pictures were taken, and the written narrative clearly played a bigger role. As Simonse et al. (2019) stressed, patient journey approaches still lack documentation; thus, this digital diary could be one way to create easy access and collect the experiences of healthcare users through their stories and recollections. Digitalisation also makes applying and using the data easier (e.g. those data collected during workshops).

The digital diary, which is an ideal autoethnographic method, supported documenting the personal service journeys, personal experiences and meaningful touchpoints that were encountered. In combination, the digital Miro environment collected and visualised the digital story data in time and space (Kimbell, 2009). As a tool, digital diaries support capturing and later memorising personal journeys to better recall, reflect on and discuss the details of these journeys. The data from the digital diaries can be utilised in a game-board style, as Kronqvist et al., (2013) did in their study with sarcoma-type cancer patients. Both in their study (Kronqvist et al., 2013) and the authors' research, the lived experiences were easier to discuss when assisting props or visualisation around the topic were created. Visualising a service journey that is more personalised provides value not only for service development but also for increasing the meaningfulness of personal stories.

The value of the digital storytelling approach used in this case example (in this case, referring to the use of closed groups and digital platforms that the participants trusted and were familiar with) stimulated, as reported, "trust, empathy, care". One author noted in the Miro environment that "people usually love to talk about health-related problems, especially when they are older", but this does not mean that they will opt for less trusted online applications. Therefore, working within trusted groups and with trustworthy applications and devices will stimulate service users' participation in this kind of data collection.

Additionally, the availability and ease of use of devices and software can stimulate participation, but researchers should remember that kind prompts may be needed; service users can lose interest in their personal diaries. Thus, engaging methods that stimulate users' interest are a service consideration for this kind of data collection. The value of the digital storytelling approach, as summarised by one of the authors, lies in the assurance that "new customer-centred solutions could be discovered".

26.6 Discussion

This chapter explored digital storytelling and the online workshop as methods in CAE approaches to improve health-related services. The outcomes offered insights into how digital tools can be used to collect and scope the experiences of healthcare users. Furthermore, the role of storytelling in developing meaningful and innovative healthcare services and treatment quality was explored.

The digital diary, storytelling and collaborative analysis methods could be successfully used in health-related contexts to collect and analyse data through the use of trusted digital tools and in collaboration with users. This data collection may result in deeper and qualitative insights into user experiences. As a diary can only reveal a certain amount of data, layering methods (digital diary and storytelling) and incorporating collaborative analysis can enable deeper insights for researchers working in hospital service environments. Qualitative insights from the data may also flow from expressing services and experiences verbally. Such performative approaches may yield different results to providing feedback through, for example, questionnaires or surveys.

Designers should design pleasant user journeys in data collection and research processes while stimulating service users and research participants to implement future research methods that explore what can or ought to be. While the limitations of the digital diary approach have been addressed in the findings of this chapter, the digital diary, storytelling and online workshops can serve as the early stages of health-related development, such as brainstorming, needs mapping and identification of personal insights.

References

Aguirre, M., Agudelo, N., & Romm, J. (2016). Facilitating generative emergence within large-scale networks: Unpacking six dimensions of design practice. In Jones, P. (Ed.), *Proceedings of Relating Systems Thinking and Design (RSD5), October 13–15, 2016 Symposium*, Peter Jones, OCAD University, Toronto, Canada.

Alhonsuo, M., Sarantou, M., Hookway, S., Miettinen, S., & Motus, M. (2020). Participation of healthcare representatives in health-related design sprints [Conference session]. In *The 6th International Conference on Design Creativity (ICDC 2020), 26–28 August, 2020*. Oulu, Finland: University of Oulu.

Bate, P., & Robert, G. (2007). Bringing user experience to healthcare improvement: The concepts, methods and practices of experience-based design. Abingdon, UK: Radcliffe Publishing.

Bloom, P. (2017). Against empathy: The case for rational compassion. New York City, United States: Random House.

Bowen, S., McSeveny, K., Lockley, E., Wolstenholme, D., Cobb, M., & Dearden, A. (2013). How was it for you? Experiences of participatory design in the UK health service. *CoDesign, 9*(4), 230–246. https://doi.org/10.1080/15710882.2013.846384.

Brink, T. T., Urton, K., Held, D., Kirilina, E., Hofmann, M., Klann-Delius, G., Jacobs, M. A., & Kuchinke, L. (2011). The role of orbitofrontal cortex in processing empathy stories in 4- to 8-year-old children. *Frontiers in Psychology, 2*(80), 1–16. https://doi.org/10.3389/fpsyg.2011. 00080.

Chang, H., Ngunjiri, F., & Hernandez, K. A. C. (2016). *Collaborative autoethnography*. New York, United States: Routledge.

Creswell, J. W. (2014). *Research design: Qualitative, quantitative, and mixed methods approaches* (4th ed.). Thousand Oaks, CA: Sage.

Ellis, C., & Adams, T. E. (2014). The purposes, practices, and principles of autoethnographic research. In P. Leavy (Ed.), *The Oxford handbook of qualitative research* (pp. 254–276). Oxford, Oxford University Press.

Freire, K., & Sangiorgi, D. (2010). Service design and healthcare innovation: From consumption to co-production to co-creation. In S. Clatworthy, J. V. Nisula, & S. Holmlid (Eds.), *ServDes Conference Proceedings* (pp. 39–50). Sweden: Linkoping.

Goodwin, S. (2020). *Meaningful healthcare experience design: Improving care for all generations* (1st ed.). New York, United States: Productivity Press.

Hurwitz, B., Greenhalgh, T., Skultans, V. (2004). Introduction. In B. Hurwitz, T. Greenhalgh, & V. Skultans (Eds.), *Narrative research in health and illness* (pp. 1–20). London. https://doi. org/10.1002/9780470755167.ch1.

Kankainen, A., Vaajakallio, K., Kantola, V., & Mattelmäki, T. (2012). Storytelling group: A co-design method for service design. *Behaviour & Information Technology, 31*(3), 221–230. https://doi.org/10.1080/0144929X.2011.563794.

Kimbell, L. (2009). The turn to service design. In G. Julier & L. Moor (Eds.), *Design and creativity: Policy, management and practice* (pp. 157–173). Oxford: Berg.

Koh, L. C., Slingsby, A., Dykes, J., & Kam, T. S. (2011). Developing and Applying a user-centered model for the design and implementation of information visualization tools. In *2011 15th International Conference on Information Visualisation* (pp. 90–95). https://doi.org/ 10.1109/IV.2011.32.

Kronqvist, J., Järvinen, M., & Leinonen, T. (2013). Games as design medium: Utilizing game boards for design enquiry with cancer patients. In *ServDes. 2012 Conference Proceedings Co-Creating Services: The 3rd Service Design and Service Innovation Conference, 8–10 February*, Espoo, Finland (pp. 121–132). Linköping: Linköping University Electronic Press.

Kuure, E., & Miettinen, S. (2013). Learning through action: Introducing the innovative simulation and learning environment service innovation corner (SINCO). In T. Bastiaens & G. Marks (Eds.), *Proceedings of World Conference on E-Learning in Corporate, Government, Healthcare, and Higher Education 2013*, October 21, 2013 in Las Vegas, NV, USA.

(pp. 1536–1545). San Diego: Association for the Advancement of Computing in Education (AACE).

Lapadat, J. C. (2017). Ethics in autoethnography and collaborative autoethnography. *Qualitative Inquiry, 23*(8), 589–603. https://doi.org/10.1177/1077800417704462.

Layton, A., Moss, F., & Morgan, G. (1998). Mapping out the patient's journey: Experiences of developing pathways of care. *Quality in Health Care: QHC,* 7 Suppl, S30–S36. PMID: 10339033.

Mager, B. (2010). Service design: An emerging field. In S. Miettinen & M. Koivisto (Eds.), *Designing services with innovative methods* (pp. 28–43). Helsinki and Kuopio: University of Art and Design (Ed.).

Mager, B., & Alonso, A. (2017). *The service design impact report: Health sector.* Köln: Service Design Network (Ed.).

Manzini, E. (2015). Design in a changing, connected world. *Strategic Design Research Journal, 7* (2), 95–99. https://doi.org/10.4013/sdrj.2014.72.06.

Meroni, A., & Sangiorgi, D. (2011) *Design for services* (1st ed.), Edited by R. Cooper. Surrey: Gower Publishing: London.

Miettinen, S., & Alhonsuo, M. (2019). Service designing a new hospital for Lapland Hospital District. In M. A. Pfannstiel & C. Rasche (Eds.), *Service design and service thinking in healthcare and hospital management: Theory, concepts, practice* (pp. 481–497). Cham: Springer Nature. https://doi.org/10.1145/3340764.33.44898.

Muratovski, G. (2015). *Research for designers: A guide to methods and practice.* London: Sage.

Polaine, A. (2013). Play, interactivity and service design: Towards a unified design language. In S. Miettinen & A. Valtonen (Eds.), *Service design with theory: Discussions on change, value and methods* (2nd ed., pp. 159–168). Rovaniemi: LUP Lapland University Press.

Saarikivi, K. (2018). *Empathy, emotion, technologies and human experience* [Video]. The Evolving Role of Service Design, HKISDNC18. Accessed June 1, 2021, from https://www.bing.com/videos/search?q=Saarikivi+Katri+2017+youtube+empathy&view=detail&mid=2CAA151A10E26A4ABBFB2CAA151A10E26A4ABBFB&FORM=VIRE.

Segelström, F. (2010). *Visualisations in service design.* Dissertation, Linköping University (Ed.), Linköping, Sweden.

Segelström, F., & Holmlid, S. (2015). Ethnography by design: On goals and mediating artefacts. *Arts and Humanities in Higher Education, 14*(2), 134–149. https://doi.org/10.1177/1474022214560159.

Shneiderman, B., Plaisant, C., & Hesse, B. W. (2013). Improving healthcare with interactive visualization. *Computer, 46*(5), 58–66. https://doi.org/10.1109/MC.2013.38.

Simonse, L., Albayrak, A., & Starre, S. (2019). Patient journey method for integrated service design. *Design for Health, 3*(1), 82–97. https://doi.org/10.1080/24735132.2019.1582741.

Soto, M. (2021). *Emotional skills for service designer in co-creation practices.* Acta electronica Universitatis Lapponiensis 300. Rovaniemi: Lapland University Press.

Stickdorn, M., & Schneider, J. (2011). *This is service design thinking: Basics, tools, cases.* (7th ed.). Amsterdam: BIS Publishers.

Mira Alhonsuo (Master of Arts) is a researcher and service designer for multiple service design projects at the University of Lapland. Currently, she is finalising her PhD research and focusing on health-related service development especially in the early phase of development process. She has examined research cases in digital services, healthcare services as well as with different companies and organisations. Her research interests include service design methods, empathy, narratives, process visualisation, and public service development, especially in the healthcare sector.

Dr. Melanie Sarantou is a senior researcher at the University of Lapland, Finland, investigating how arts and narrative practices impact on marginalised women in communities in Namibia, Lapland, Russia and Australia. Her PhD holistically mapped Namibian craft and design through a postcolonial lense. Her current research focuses on the role of arts in societies that exist on the margin of Europe in the European Commission-funded Horizon 2020 project titled "Action on the Margin: Arts as Social Sculpture".

Dr. Satu Miettinen is professor of Service Design at the University of Lapland, Finland, with research interests spanning the themes of design methods in engaging with the Arctic region, service design methods for inclusion, the participatory development of services, as well as socially responsible art and design methods.

Printed in the United States
by Baker & Taylor Publisher Services